Interpreting Educational Research

An Introduction for Consumers of Research

Daniel R. Hittleman
The City University of New York/Queens College

Alan J. Simon
Metis Associates, Inc., New York

MERRILL
an imprint of Prentice Hall

Upper Saddle River, New Jersey   Columbus, Ohio

Library of Congress Cataloging-in-Publication Data

Hittleman, Daniel R.
    Interpreting educational research : an introduction for consumers
of research / Daniel R. Hittleman, Alan J. Simon. — 2nd ed.
        p.   cm.
    Includes bibliographical references and index.
    ISBN 0-13-242553-X
    1. Education—Research. 2. Research—Methodology. 3. Education—
Research—Evaluation.   I. Simon, Alan J.   II. Title.
LB1028.H537 1997
370'.78-dc20   96–14642
                                                                                    CIP

Cover photo: P. Buddle/H. Armstrong Roberts
Editor: Kevin M. Davis
Production Editor: Linda Hillis Bayma
Production Coordination: WordCrafters Editorial Services, Inc.
Design Coordinator: Julia Zonneveld Van Hook
Cover Designer: Rod Harris
Production Manager: Laura Messerly
Illustrations: Carlisle Communications, Ltd.

This book was set in Meridien by Carlisle Communications, Ltd. and was printed and bound
by R. R. Donnelley & Sons Company. The cover was printed by Phoenix Color Corp.

 © 1997 by Prentice-Hall, Inc.
Simon & Schuster/A Viacom Company
Upper Saddle River, New Jersey 07458

Earlier edition © 1992 by Macmillan Publishing Company, a division of Macmillan, Inc.

Printed in the United States of America

Excerpt (p. 156) from INFORMAL READING-THINKING INVENTORY by Anthony V. Manzo,
Ula Casale Manzo, and Michael C. McKenna, copyright © 1995 by Harcourt Brace & Company,
reprinted by permission of the publisher.

10   9   8   7   6   5

ISBN 0-13-242553-X

Prentice-Hall International (UK) Limited, *London*
Prentice-Hall of Australia Pty. Limited, *Sydney*
Prentice-Hall Canada Inc., *Toronto*
Prentice-Hall Hispanoamericana, S. A., *Mexico*
Prentice-Hall of India Private Limited, *New Delhi*
Prentice-Hall of Japan, Inc., *Tokyo*
Simon & Schuster Asia Pte. Ltd., *Singapore*
Editora Prentice-Hall do Brasil, Ltda., *Rio de Janeiro*

To Carol and Carole,
with our continued love

Preface

We intend the second edition of *Interpreting Educational Research: An Introduction for Consumers of Research* to be used in introductory research courses in which elementary and early childhood education teachers, reading specialists, special education teachers, and content area teachers at the middle and secondary school levels are prepared as consumers rather than as producers of educational research. We provide preservice and in-service teachers with basic knowledge and skills for reading, interpreting, and evaluating both quantitative and qualitative educational research, so that they can make instructional decisions based upon those research results. This knowledge base is useful for teachers who collaborate in research projects with college and university faculty. In addition, we provide a guide for composing teacher-as-researcher action research projects and reviews of research.

Through directed learning activities, which are based on current integrated language arts principles and practices for reading and writing content area discourse, we guide readers to independence in the use of techniques for reading, interpreting, evaluating, and writing about education research. The evaluation of educational research is approached by us in such a way that teachers will become research consumers by understanding the underlying methodological and procedural assumptions used by educators who are research producers. In essence, teachers are guided in research literacy learning to think as research producers.

NATURE OF THE REVISION

Our revisions consist of updating most examples of research methodology and replacing the five complete research reports in Appendix B. The examples are current curriculum-based quantitative and qualitative research reports representing the fields of elementary, middle, and secondary school general and content area education, reading education, and special education. We have updated and expanded the coverage of qualitative research. And we have added information and strategies for locating research reports in electronic databases.

ORGANIZATION

The text is organized into eleven chapters and three appendices. In Chapters 1, 2, and 3, we lead the reader to an understanding of research designs, the general procedures of research producers, and a plan for reading research reports. In Chapters 4 through 9, we present extended discussions of the aspects of research design and methodology and illustrations of the manner in which research producers present them in research reports. In Chapters 10 and 11, we provide information about reading and writing reviews of research and about sources for locating research reports. In the appendices are a glossary of key terms, five complete research reports for additional study and analysis, and ethical standards for conducting educational research.

We begin each chapter with a graphic overview of the content and focus questions so readers can attend to the key ideas of the chapter and the interrelationships portrayed in the structured overview. In the main body of the chapters we have techniques for reading, interpreting, and writing about specific sections of research reports. In the activities section at the end of each chapter we present ways for the reader to gain greater understanding of the key concepts and proficiency in applying the evaluative techniques. For each of these activities, we provide the reader with feedback in which we give samples of how we might respond to our own students' work.

Special features of the text are the following:

- The text is intended for teachers with a range of backgrounds: generalists, reading specialists, special educators, and middle and secondary school teachers.
- The examples used throughout the text are drawn from current curriculum-based research literature which these teachers will find relevant to their specific instructional situations. All forms of research are illustrated.
- The material is conceptualized for consumers of educational research.
- The text is intended to teach preservice and in-service teachers, in a nonthreatening, supportive manner, to read and write about educational research. A step-by-step process leads teachers to understand and use research reports.
- Information about strategies for reading both quantitative and qualitative (ethnographic or naturalistic) research is included.
- The chapters begin with a structured overview of the content.
- Specific strategies that have proven effective for the reading of typical content area texts and the writing of content-area-related expository prose are applied to the reading of research reports and the writing of research reviews.
- Ample practice is provided for developing the reader's skills in evaluating educational research.
- The text provides the reader with an understanding of integrative reviews and meta-analyses and gives guidance in the preparation of action integrative reviews.
- A glossary contains the definitions of all key terms presented in the text.
- The appendices contain complete research reports for additional practice in evaluating research or for use in class assignments.
- The text is intended to provide teachers with the knowledge and skills to act as teacher-researchers and to create classroom-based action research projects and reviews of research.

Acknowledgments

No book is done without the support, input, and assistance of others, and we are indebted for the help and assistance of many people. We are grateful for the encouragement and support of our colleagues at CUNY/Queens College, who have used the first edition and have provided us with invaluable insights for the revision. We are appreciative of the comments and critiques of our students and have incorporated several of their ideas in the revision. We express thanks to colleagues at Metis Associates, Inc., New York, for their support.

We are appreciative of the critical comments and reviews of Maurice R. Berube, Old Dominion University; J. Kent Davis, Purdue University; Thomas D. Dertinger, University of Richmond; and Karen Ford, Ball State University. We have given extensive consideration to their concerns and questions, and we have incorporated many of them in the revision; however, we ultimately take responsibility for the interpretations and perspectives about research presented in the text. We also are extremely grateful for the help and assistance by Kevin Davis and Linda Bayma of the editorial staff at Merrill, an imprint of Prentice Hall, and the thoughtful guidance of the editing process by Linda Zuk at WordCrafters Editorial Services, Inc.

Brief Contents

Contents

CHAPTER 8   READING AND INTERPRETING RESULTS SECTIONS   221

CHAPTER 9   READING AND EVALUATING DISCUSSION SECTIONS   279

CHAPTER 10   READING AND INTERPRETING REVIEWS OF RESEARCH   295

Figures and Tables

CHAPTER 1

The Research Process

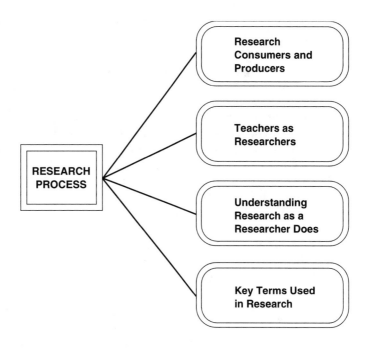

FOCUS QUESTIONS

1. Why do educators conduct research?
2. What is the distinction between research consumers and research producers?
3. What does it mean to understand research as a research producer does?
4. What are some key terms used in research?

Teachers at all levels continually make decisions about instructional activities such as curriculum, teaching techniques, classroom management, and student learning. They base these decisions on their experiences, other teachers' experiences, and their understanding of accumulated knowledge about education. Much of the knowledge about teaching and learning comes from educational researchers who seek answers to educational questions or try to clarify some existing educational issue. One sign of a productive profession such as education is the systematic attempt by its researchers and practitioners to examine the knowledge base upon which the profession functions. For the purposes of this book, the systematic attempt to examine a knowledge base is called research.

Research is the systematic attempt to (a) collect information about an identified problem or question, (b) analyze that information, and (c) apply the evidence thus derived to confirm or refute some prior prediction or statement about that problem. Educational research is not unique within the total research community; it is the application of some generally accepted systematic procedures to examining the knowledge base of education. Akin to educational research is educational evaluation, the use of research techniques to judge the effectiveness of existing, in-place programs of instruction. For the general purposes of this book, educational evaluation is considered a subarea of educational research.

Five characteristics seem indicative of a profession whose members research its knowledge base (Berliner, 1987). First, professionals work at verifying ideas and practices believed to be effective. Often teachers read about a "new" teaching technique in a professional journal and say, "We've known that all along!" As professionals, however, teachers cannot rely entirely on a common sense approach; intuition needs to be supported and substantiated through research.

Second, professionals work at discovering new ideas and practices. The need for new ideas and practices is almost self-evident but is exemplified by an idea that has been extensively researched, was once new, and is now common in schools: the application of reciprocal teaching, which features guided practice in applying learning strategies (Rosenshine & Meister, 1994).

Third, professionals clarify ideas that are designed to simplify teaching. This is illustrated by research results about cooperative learning procedures when they are applied to problem solving in various subject areas (Qin, Johnson, & Johnson, 1995).

Fourth, although professional educators try to simplify teaching, they often express ideas that may complicate everyone's teaching. An example of this effect is the body of research findings indicating how the learning of many students with disabling conditions is improved in mainstream classes as opposed to self-contained classes (Leinhardt & Pallay, 1982; Madden & Slavin, 1983).

Fifth, professionals discover ideas and practices that are counter-intuitive. For example, many educators assume that grouping in self-contained classes according to students' ability permits students to work more effectively with peers and to have instruction adapted to their performance level. Regarding mastery learning, however, research evidence does not seem to support this contention. Instead, it shows that students may achieve more when they are in classes of mixed ability for most of the day. Cross-grade assignments also may increase students' achievement. Limited grouping of students at the same level seems effective only when it is done for specific skill instruction (Slavin, 1987a, b).

RESEARCH CONSUMERS AND PRODUCERS

This book is intended for research consumers—the people who read, interpret, and apply the information systematically collected and examined (researched) by others. Like research producers, research consumers are interested in answering educationally related questions; however, they do so by reading and applying research producers' results, rather than by conducting research.

Research consumers need to read research with a mindset similar to that of research producers—similar, but not the same. Research producers need certain skills to put different phases of educational research into operation. They need technical competence in applying research strategies. Research consumers, on the other hand, need to understand decisions facing research producers, possible alternatives they may consider at those decision points, and implications of researchers' results and conclusions. Also, they need a means of judging the adequacy of research producers' work.

We believe a research consumer can more fully understand educational research by reading research as a research producer does. The research consumer reads research by reconstructing the researcher's message and constructing a meaning from the information on the page—much as students reconstruct a message during a class lecture and then construct its meaning for themselves. The reader may create meanings different from those intended by the writer (as may a listener in response to a speaker). Research consumers reach understanding by reconstructing the ideas of research producers as well as by constructing meanings of their own. A consumer's understanding is constructed from that person's prior knowledge and prior experiences, combined with that person's maturity and his or her proficiency in manipulating research ideas.

Research consumers need to understand the ethical standards by which research producers should be guided in their activities. The American Educational Research Association (AERA) has adopted a set of ethical standards for conducting educational research. Although research producers' compliance with these standards is voluntary, researcher consumers should be aware of their existence and contents. The standards are found in Appendix C.

TEACHERS AS RESEARCHERS

Although the concept of teachers as researchers is not new, our understanding of how important it is for classroom teachers to collaborate with research producers and to produce research themselves has been increasing (Burton, 1991; Erickson, 1986; Johnson, 1993; McFarland & Stansell, 1993; Olson, 1990; Santa, 1988; VandDeWeghe, 1992). This text is not intended to create research producers. Even so, the mindset of "understanding research as a researcher does" presented here and the ideas about research methods and research evaluation presented in subsequent chapters will provide teachers with the background knowledge and understanding they need to participate in such research projects.

Teachers need to assume the responsibility of examining their own practices (Erickson, 1986; Patterson & Shannon, 1993). Since teachers are increasingly being held responsible for what and how they teach, they need to take leadership in determining what insights about learning and teaching should be systematically applied in classrooms. It is especially important that classroom teachers collaborate with researchers when changes in curriculum and instructional procedures are being reevaluated. Curriculum and instructional leadership should not be expected to come solely from university research centers and state and federal agencies; instead, teachers are being called upon to participate in research that will significantly affect what happens in the classroom. Collaborating in this research

> (1) reduces the gap between research findings and classroom practice, (2) creates a problem solving mindset that helps teachers when they consider other classroom dilemmas, (3) improves teachers' instructional decision making processes, (4) increases the professional status of teachers, (5) helps empower teachers to influence their own profession at classroom, district, state, and national levels, and (6) offers the overriding and ultimate advantage of providing the potential for improving the educational process for children. (Olson, 1990, pp. 17–18)

The research procedures that are often associated with the idea of teachers as researchers are those of qualitative and action research (see the subsection "Action Research" in Chapters 7 and 8) and the subsection "Preparing Action Reviews of Research" in Chapter 10. Teacher-researcher studies are attempts to explain the experience of teachers and students as they are enacted in actual classrooms. Inquiry, reflection, and action characterize what is done by teacher-researchers (Burton, 1991; Patterson & Shannon, 1993). Inquiry is purposeful observation of all aspects of classroom life. Reflection is the systematic attempt to understand the multiple layers of meaning of what happens in classrooms. Action is the altering of classroom practice as a result of the new understanding. These activities might even be considered a "re-searching" experience (Burton, 1991, p. 230) in that they are not trying to create educational laws but to reexamine the often hidden dynamics of teaching and learning, look at them in a new light, and take an instructional stance based on what is seen.

UNDERSTANDING RESEARCH FROM THE PERSPECTIVE OF A RESEARCHER

Research producers present the results of their research in reports. (The specific form of those reports is discussed in Chapter 3.) To comprehend a research report fully, the research consumer must understand research producers' processes in conceptualizing, developing, implementing, and reporting research. To illustrate the process, the way one research team might develop a project is described below. Although the process is presented linearly for illustrative purposes, research consumers should realize that the process actually may not unfold in such a clear sequence. The researchers may start and stop several times, reject questions and possible solutions, and encounter many pitfalls.

The researchers select a problem area and specify research questions.

From personal experience, professional readings, or discussions with colleagues, our hypothetical research team selects a problem area for study. For example, thoughts arise about the writing performance of middle school students who are learning disabled. (The differing and often confusing definitions of learning disability will be disregarded here.) These thoughts flow from an array of concerns, a few of which follow.

First, many students with learning disabilities are mainstreamed for particular academic classes. Second, writing skill has increasingly become an issue in the teaching and learning of content areas other than language or communication arts. Third, different writing skills may be needed in different content areas (e.g., science, social studies, mathematics, or technology).

The researchers are concerned about the use to which the answers of these questions might be put. These concerns lead to other questions. Are the answers to be applicable only to the students in one specific school, grade level, or class? Are the answers to be used for the students in an entire district, state, region, or nation? Should the writing of students with learning disabilities be compared with that of students who do not have such disabilities?

The next set of concerns deals with the teaching and learning of writing. The researchers wish to know: What is the writing performance of students with learning disabilities and how does it compare with that of students without disabilities? What can be done to help the students with disabilities write effectively in the content areas? Of equal importance to the researchers is: Are these questions interrelated or can any one of them be answered without answering the others?

(The question "Why do students with learning disabilities write the way they do?" is also of concern. However, seeking answers to it moves the researcher away from a primary concern with instruction.)

The researchers examine and search databases to review existing research results and define terms.

At this point, the researchers try to find out what other researchers have done to answer these or similar questions. By consulting books, educational encyclopedias, professional journals, and electronic databases, the researchers gain insights about what others have done and what conclusions were drawn from their research. The researchers know their work is based on certain assumptions, one of which is that it will add to the body of educational knowledge. Their aim is to help other researchers and practitioners reach some agreement about the controversy surrounding the teaching of writing to students with learning disabilities.

After reviewing the material from these sources, the researchers conclude that the meaning of certain terms requires clarification. For example, they realize that several terms are defined differently by different researchers: *learning disability, language arts, communication arts, content area classes, writing, composing, mainstreaming,* and *regular education*. The researchers select an accepted definition or create a new one to enhance communication with other researchers and users of the research.

The researchers formulate researchable questions.

Now they return to the questions about the teaching and learning of writing. A decision must be made about answering one or more of them. They decide to answer three questions and must now determine whether those questions need to be answered in a specific order. The answer is yes, because the answer to the question "What can be done to help students with learning disabilities write effectively in the content areas?" presupposes answers to the others. So, the researchers decide to first answer the questions "What is the writing performance of students with learning disabilities?" and "How does that performance compare with the performance of students without learning disabilities?" (a question of major concern since the researchers wish to examine the writing of students with learning disabilities in mainstream classes).

The researchers select research designs.

The researchers now have three possible studies. (It is possible for the researchers to conduct these three studies as one, but this is not done here so that the three different research plans can be highlighted.) For each, they need a different research plan, or design. **Research designs** are methods for answering questions. Just as skilled craftspeople and artisans have several methods for manipulating their raw material, so do researchers. Some research designs are more appropriate or effective for answering certain questions. Also, more than one plan may be appropriate or effective for answering a particular question.

In the first study, the researchers want to describe the writing performance of students with learning disabilities. The description is to be in statistical and in non-statistical form (see **quantitative research, qualitative research,** and **statistics** in Glossary). They decide on several activities. They decide to describe the students' processes for beginning a writing task, their topics and organization of ideas, the maturity of their vocabulary and sentence structure, the grammatical form of their works, and the physical aspects of their writing.

To compare the writing of students with learning disabilities to that of students who do not have such disabilities in a second study, the researchers will collect the same data from both groups. They plan a statistical and nonstatistical comparison of the two types of students.

For the third study, "What can be done to help students with learning disabilities write effectively in the content areas?", the researchers will set up one or more instructional programs and look at them singly and in combination to see which has the greatest effect (or any effect) on the writing performance of these students.

The researchers determine the research method.

The three plans have both common and unique aspects. The common aspects include efforts the researchers must make to determine (a) where and when the research is to occur, (b) with whom specifically the research will be done, (c) with what device students' characteristics and their writing will be assessed, and (d) how they will analyze the information (see **data** in Glossary) they collected.

In selecting a location, the researchers think about conducting the studies in a special site such as a college educational clinic or a middle school classroom. Both have advantages and disadvantages. An educational clinic allows the researchers better control of the data collection environment and the opportunity to make unobtrusive observations and recordings. However, the setting is not educationally natural, since the students need to be brought to it under special circumstances. A classroom lets the researchers observe and collect data in the setting where the students usually learn and work. However, a classroom has distractions that might influence the data collection and the students' performances in ways the researchers may not recognize. After weighing the pros and cons, the researchers decide to conduct all three studies in middle school classrooms, fully aware that they must make some effort to reduce or eliminate the possible influence of certain distractions.

The researchers describe and select the students to be used in the study.

The researchers are interested in doing the study with middle school students. The specific group of students for the study is selected with consideration for the ability of the researchers to pass on the results to others in similar urban centers. They select a middle school affiliated with their college because its total student population reflects the range of ability and performance test scores and demographic characteristics of the county as a whole. All students classified as learning disabled in grades five through eight, in both mainstreamed and self-contained classes, are included.

The researchers must describe the students for others, so they collect relevant data normally found in students' permanent records—information such as age, sex, grade level, educational history, and attendance.

The researchers select tests to score the students' writing.

The researchers also begin to document the students' writing performance. To do this, samples of the students' writing in content area classes are obtained and scored or analyzed by some accepted system. The researchers have the option of using one or more achievement tests or a scoring system known as holistic scoring. Or, they may analyze the students' composings by nonnumerical analysis.

The researchers conduct the study.

The researchers now have enough information to answer the first question, "What is the writing performance of students with learning disabilities?" To answer the second question, "How does that performance compare with the performance of students without learning disabilities?" the researchers collect the same data about students who do not have learning disabilities. Because it is impractical to collect data about all such students in the middle school, the researchers decide to randomly select a portion of the students without learning disabilities at each grade level.

As the researchers proceed, another question arises. The researchers want to know, "Are teachers using any instructional strategies and techniques that seem to enhance the learning of students who are learning disabled?" To answer this question, they set up a series of classroom observations and teacher interviews. They wish to determine possible answers to this question by collecting information about what occurs in classrooms while teaching and learning are happening. As they collect this information, they sort it and seek out patterns of teacher-learner interactions.

To answer their last question, "What can be done to help students with learning disabilities write effectively in the content areas?" the researchers select and prepare instructional activities and collect additional data. Using the information gleaned from other research, from professional sources, and from their classroom observations and teacher interviews, the researchers create or select three instructional programs that have shown promise for teaching students who are learning disabled. The researchers' question now becomes "Which of these instructional programs help the students who are learning disabled write effectively in content area classes?" or "Which of the programs cause the students to write effectively?"

The researchers decide how long (for how many days, weeks, or months) the instructional program will last and who will do the actual teaching. They plan to have all content area teachers in the middle school participate in a special eight-week after-school workshop about implementing one of the instructional programs. The teachers are to use the techniques for the 12 weeks following the workshop.

Additional data about students' writing performance are collected during and after the instructional programs. The researchers now conduct the studies.

The researchers analyze the data and determine implications of the research.

After conducting the study and collecting the data, the researchers analyze the data using appropriate statistical (quantitative) and nonstatistical (qualitative) methods. Then, they determine what implications the results have for other researchers and teachers.

The researchers publish their results.

After conducting its research, the team produces a written report. For example, after beginning activities to answer their third question, the researchers describe (a) their reason for conducting the study; (b) the conclusions they and others have made about previous research; (c) the steps they took to select the students, the writing scoring procedure, and the instructional activities; (d) the in-service workshop, the instructional programs, and the way they were used in the content area classes; and (e) the statistical and nonstatistical results.

KEY TERMS USED IN RESEARCH

Most key research terms are defined as they occur in this book. A few, however, are introduced now because they underpin most of the discussions. Additional information about these and other key terms is given elsewhere. The Glossary contains all key terms discussed in this book.

variable   In the broadest sense, a variable is anything in a research situation that varies and can be measured. It can be a human characteristic (of students or teachers) or it can be a characteristic of classrooms, groups, schools and school districts, instructional materials, and so on. These characteristics are called variables, and they can be measured. Educationally relevant traits of humans, among many, include age, intelligence, reading scores, learning style, level of motivation, sensitivity to noise, and ethnicity. Educationally relevant nonhuman characteristics include, among many, the size of print in textbooks, the number of times an event occurs, the location of schools, the economic status of families, and students' attendance records.

research design   The research design is the plan used to study an educational problem or question. Two basic research designs based on the way information, or data, is collected and analyzed are **quantitative research** (statistical data analysis) and **qualitative research** (nonstatistical data analysis). In the example of the research team used in this chapter, a combination of these two types was used. The team also used three subcategories of quantitative research: descriptive, comparative, and causative. **Descriptive research** provides information about one or more variables. **Comparative research** provides an explanation about the extent of a relationship between two or more variables. **Experimental,** or causative, **research** provides information about how one or more variables influence another variable.

hypothesis   A hypothesis is a tentative statement about how two or more variables are related.

In current practice, many researchers convey the relationship as a prediction, a statement of purpose, or a question. For the causative design used by the research team in our example, the researchers' question "Which of the instructional programs help students with learning disabilities write effectively in content area classes?" could be approached in these forms:

Directional hypothesis: There will be an improvement in the way middle school students with learning disabilities write after receiving effective writing instruction in content area classes.

Prediction: Instructional program A will produce a greater improvement in the way middle school students with learning disabilities write in content area classes than will instructional program B.

Statement of purpose: The purpose of the study is to determine whether either of two instructional programs helps middle school students with learning disabilities to improve their writing.

Question: Which of the two instructional programs causes middle school students with learning disabilities to write more effectively?

subjects   The subjects are the particular individuals used in the research. One group of subjects in the example in this chapter consisted of all students classified as learning disabled in grades five through eight in mainstreamed and self-contained classes in an urban middle school. In the comparative and causative designs, the researchers also used as subjects a small group of students who were not learning disabled. They randomly selected a portion of the students without learning disabilities at each grade level. This selected group is a sample of all the students without learning disabilities in the school. The **population** is the larger group with which the researchers think their results can be used. They are interested in being able to pass on the results about students with and without learning disabilities in middle school to other educators in other urban centers.

generalizability   When research producers' results can be extended to other groups (for example, to other students with and without learning disabilities in urban centers), these results are said to have generalizability. That means, a research consumer in a different urban center can have confidence in applying the producers' research results because they are applicable to middle school students with and without learning disabilities in urban centers.

Table 1.1
Overview of the Research Process

The Research Team's Activity	Phase of Research and Location of Information within this Text
Selecting a problem area; specifiying research questions and defining terms	Reading and Evaluating Introductory Sections, Chapter 4
Searching databases	Locating Information about Research Reports, Chapter 11
Selecting research designs	Research Designs, Chapter 2
Describing and selecting subjects	Reading and Evaluating Subject Sections, Chapter 5
Selecting data collection devices	Reading and Evaluating Instrument Sections, Chapter 6
Conducting the study	Reading and Evaluating Procedure Sections, Chapter 7
Analyzing the data	Reading and Interpreting Results Sections, Chapter 8
Determining implications of the research	Reading and Evaluating Discussion Sections, Chapter 9
Reporting the results	Reading and Evaluating Research Reports, Chapter 3; Reading and Interpreting Reviews of Research, Chapter 10

OVERVIEW

The ideas in this book are organized to reflect the phases of research as research producers would go through them. In Table 1.1, the phases of research undertaken by the research team in the example are linked to the information in later chapters.

ACTIVITIES

Each chapter has an activities section in which the book's readers are asked to apply the chapter's content. Two sources of feedback are available to the reader. The first consists of the authors' ideas immediately following the activities. The second consists of the course instructor's feedback.

Activity 1. Write a summary of the key ideas found in the chapter. The focus questions at the chapter beginning should be used as a guide to structure your summary.

Activity 2. Using Table 1.1 as a guide, read the research report "Results of an Early Intervention Program For First Grade Children At Risk for Reading Disability" below. As you read the report, locate the particular sections in which information is given. Do not be concerned with fully understanding the report.

McCarthy, P., Newby, R. F., & Recht, D. R. (1995). Results of an early intervention program for first grade children at risk for reading disability. *Reading Research and Instruction, 34*(4), 273–294. Reprinted by permission of The College Reading Association.

Results of an Early Intervention Program for First Grade Children At Risk for Reading Disability

Patricia McCarthy

Wauwatosa School District
Cardinal Stritch College

Robert F. Newby

Medical College of Wisconsin

Donna R. Recht

University School of Milwaukee

ABSTRACT

(1) Thirty-eight first grade children with low emergent literacy skills who were at risk for difficulty in learning to read were tutored for a median of 58 half-hour sessions in addition to their regular classroom instruction. The tutoring (Early Intervention Program, EIP) focused on word recognition, phonetic application and comprehension in context. The EIP children's word recognition in isolation and in context, reading speed, and comprehension were superior to well-matched controls at completion of tutoring, at the end of first grade, and at third trade. At grade three, the EIP group was equivalent to a group of average-reading classmates on word recognition in context, acceptable accuracy and answering comprehension questions, but not on word recognition in isolation or on reading speed.

(2) The past decade has seen a blossoming of interest in intensive intervention programs for kindergarten and first grade children who are at risk for reading failure. Since transition rooms and retention in grade have not been effective in resolving early achievement delays (Holmes & Matthews, 1984), educators have sought alternative approaches to help children with weak early literacy skills. Several major research studies have shown significant benefits from individual tutorial programs with first grade children. These programs emphasize one-to-one child-specific tutoring in addition to routine classroom instruction. The goal is for children to develop reading and writing strategies so they can learn successfully within a regular classroom. While the present context does not allow a comprehensive review of this previous work, several highlights deserve mention.

(3) The basic theory behind this type of intervention emphasizes the need to interrupt a "causal chain of escalating negative side effects" (Stanovich, 1986, p. 364) that slow-to-develop readers often experience. In an interactive model of reading, the reader constructs meaning from the print. In learning to read, the reader uses background knowledge, recognizes words holistically, and can utilize phonetic strategies within a contextual setting. Children who experience early difficulty learning to read typically come to school with less exposure to print and developmental readiness to devote attention to print (Stanovich, 1986). Alternatively, they are personally impulsive,

have difficulty with sustained attention, or are reluctant to take risks in learning activities, which leads to behaviors that are not conducive to learning to read (Clay, 1993a). Their initial reading problems can compound as they receive less text exposure than good readers during the acquisition phase, instruction with reading materials that are too difficult for them, and fewer opportunities to practice their emerging reading skills (Stanovich, 1986). This in turn delays their development of reading automaticity, syntactic mastery, vocabulary knowledge, and conceptual skills (Ball and Blachman, 1991). As Slavin (1993, p. 11) argues, "success in the early grades does not guarantee success throughout the school years and beyond, but failure in the early grades does virtually guarantee failure in later schooling."

④ The results of previously studied intervention programs have been impressive. Bradley and Bryant's (1985) landmark study demonstrated significant gains in reading and spelling skills with a tutorial program that emphasized manipulation and categorization of sounds with children aged five and one half years to seven years. This study compared two different intervention variations with both nontreated children and children who received the same amount of one-to-one training in semantic rather than phonological categorization. The treatment effects for the two phonologically trained groups remained robust at a third-grade follow-up. Specifically, children receiving forty treatment sessions involving a combination of sound categorization and practice in manipulating word families with plastic letters were almost one year better than the nonspecific effects control group in reading word recognition, and almost one and one half years better in spelling. Ball and Blachman (1991) reported similar initial treatment gains by small groups of kindergarten students who received a combination of phoneme awareness instruction with letters on plastic tiles, sound categorization tasks like Bryant and Bradley's intervention (1985), and training in letter names and letter-sound associations. Training in letter names and letter-sound associations alone did not yield comparable gains. Generalization of Ball and Blachman's (1991) results was limited

by their use of a general kindergarten sample rather than an at-risk sample, and they have only reported immediate posttreatment testing rather than long-term follow-up results.

⑤ Several research monographs on the Reading Recovery program have been published by the program's directors at the Ohio State University (e.g. Pinnell, DeFord & Lyons, 1988; Pinnell, Lyons, DeFord, Bryk & Seltzer, 1991). Originally developed by Marie Clay (1985) in New Zealand, Reading Recovery tutoring focuses on the individual child as he/she reads and writes connected text. Each one-to-one lesson includes reading familiar easy books which the child has read before, the child writing his/her own stories cooperatively with the teacher, and reading new books. The teacher takes a "Running Record," a form of miscue analysis, on a book each day to provide immediate information regarding the child's reading development. Instruction is thus individualized to each child's needs and focuses on developing good reading strategies, including directional movement, one-to-one matching, self-monitoring, using multiple cue sources, and self-correction. Phonological analysis and decoding skills are emphasized in context and are addressed in writing and included in reading new materials. Children reading in the lowest 20% of their classes who received up to 60 sessions of Reading Recovery instruction have risen to average reading levels by the end of their first grade year, in contrast with children receiving small-group Chapter 1 instruction. Children receiving individual tutoring with the Reading Recovery methods have maintained treatment gains in follow-up testing during the school year after intervention occurred, but a small-group adaptation of the Reading Recovery methods and two alternative individual tutoring models did not yield such gains. Treatment results have been stronger for the approximately three quarters of treatment sample who have been judged to be strong enough readers to be "successfully discontinued" from the program than for the remaining one quarter of the sample who completed the full 60 sessions of intervention without meeting criteria for discontinuation; the latter group has remained below average in long-term follow-up studies.

⑥   Wasik and Slavin (1993) reviewed outcome studies on several prominent programs, particularly Reading Recovery and Success for All (Slavin, Madden, Karweit, Dolan & Wasik, 1992). In general, the programs showed substantial treatment gains over the course of the first grade year in contrast with relevant control groups. Programs that included comprehensive models of reading, provided multifaceted instructional interventions, and used certified teachers rather than paraprofessionals tended to achieve stronger results. Follow-up studies have shown that treatment gains persist at least through 3rd grade, and some programs have shown a reduction in retentions or special education referrals over time. Wasik and Slavin (1993) compared different studies by computing treatment effect sizes (differences between treatment group versus control group on mean posttest or follow-up scores, divided by the posttest or follow-up standard deviation of the control group). In this method, effect sizes that approach or exceed 1.0 are felt to represent substantial treatment gain or maintenance. Some of these studies show decreasing effect sizes from posttest immediately following treatment to follow-up testing several years later, but this modulation in effect size is generally attributable to increasing variability in the outcome measures over time rather than an erosion of the initial mean treatment differences. Wasik and Slavin (1993) ⑦ interpreted the paradoxically reducing effect sizes in the Reading Recovery studies as a diminishment in the importance of the treatment gains even though the absolute magnitude of the treatment gains were maintained, and they pointed out that the relatively more stable sizes over time in Success for All represented an absolute widening of the differences between treatment groups and control groups over time, probably in response to the continued intervention available to the treatment groups beyond first grade.

   While the general value of these programs has been illustrated well in previous research, various important details of the instructional approaches have not been adequately investigated. For example, Iverson and Tumner (1993) added a phonological training element to the standard Reading Recovery program, which shortened the number of sessions that were felt to be necessary before discontinuing students from the program but did not yield incremental gains on most outcome measures in comparison to a standard Reading Recovery comparison group. Outcome measures included a battery of early reading and writing skills (Clay, 1985, 1993b; see also Method for Initial Treatment Study below), the Dolch word list (Dolch, 1939), and a number of phonological processing tests. Because discontinuation criteria were not objectively operationalized or judged by raters blind to treatment condition, and because long-term follow-up data are not yet available, the advantages of the phonological addition in this study remain unclear, beyond the immediate cost-savings of the reduced number of sessions used. None of the previous studies has thoroughly examined the complex interplay among different aspects of the reading process in long-term follow-up, including different types of reading accuracy (i.e. decoding of word lists in isolation, reading accuracy in context, acceptable accuracy without changing test meaning), reading fluency or automaticity (i.e. reading rate), or different types of reading comprehension (i.e. free recall or answering of questions). Early interventions may improve some but not all of these aspects of reading, and the implications of such differential improvement may be important.

   The present research program differs from ⑧ the previous studies in several ways. First, we emphasize integrated reading skills in tutoring. This refers to the child's ability to appropriately combine semantic, syntactic and graphophonic cues automatically while reading. This is similar to the Reading Recovery research but contrasts with the Bradley and Bryant (1985) and Ball and Blachman (1991) studies, which focused more narrowly on teaching children to manipulate sounds. Sound manipulation is an important precursor to phonics, hence to success with fluent word identification, but neither study taught reading per se. Second, we examine the reading process in detail at follow-up. The long-term follow-up measures in Reading Recovery (Pinnell et al., 1988) and Success for All (Slavin et al., 1992) focused on unidimensional measures of text reading level and/or standardized achievement tests, with success measured by student reading achievement within the average range. Third, we use carefully matched cohorts of children from equivalent schools for comparison controls. The Reading Recovery research has generally used comparison groups with initial random placement into the Reading Recovery tutoring versus an alternative type of compensatory help, or a random sample of children from the discontinued Reading Recovery treatment group versus a random sample of children from the same grade level. Fourth, teacher training in the present program uses the instructional structure of the Clay (1985, 1993b) model, combined with systematic videotaping and feedback by a support team composed of multiple professionals working in the context of their normal school calendar and school assignments. Reading Recovery trains teachers over a year at a central site. The present program trains teachers to provide feedback to each other as they work with children in their own schools. Training is viewed as staff development that involves increased knowledge about the reading process, increased awareness of child behaviors, and interactive reflection with peers on effective teaching. The Reading Recovery training is beyond the economic and pragmatic constraints of many school systems.

(9) The study presented here demonstrates the effects of the Early Intervention Program (EIP) in the School District of Wauwatosa. This district is located in a middle-class to upper-middle-class suburb of Milwaukee, Wisconsin, and cultural diversity is enhanced by a metropolitan desegregation program. The district has collaborated with a reading/language arts department at a local college and a neuropsychology department at a medical school for research design and consultation. Prior to implementation of the EIP, first grade children in this school district had little exposure to additional reading help. Concern about children's initial reading difficulty combined with information in the professional literature about the success of Marie Clay's early intervention led to the formulation of the EIP. The EIP was elaborated from the work of Marie Clay (1985, 1991,

1993b) and from available outcome information on Reading Recovery. Pilot research on the EIP started during the 1989-90 school year. Since that time, there have been four yearly cohorts. The present report focuses only on the 1990-91 and 1991-92 cohorts, which have had the longest and most comprehensive follow-up evaluation thus far. For clarity, the present report separates the data into two studies, the initial first grade treatment results and the third grade follow-up results.

(10) In the initial treatment study, we predicted that children receiving EIP in addition to their regular classroom instruction would show greater gain than control children with the same level of reading problems who received only regular classroom placement, in six key areas of early reading development: concepts about print, emerging sight vocabulary (indicated by child-generated written vocabulary), understanding of sound/symbol relationships (indicated by writing to dictation), oral reading accuracy, acceptable reading accuracy that maintained essential meaning in context, and reading comprehension. These predictions were constructed to test the basic notion that specialized intensive intervention should yield positive results at the time of treatment. We did not predict a treatment effect in the reading readiness skill of alphabet recognition, because the regular first grade curriculum was felt to be as likely as the EIP to develop this area.

(11) We also predicted that the initial treatment gains in the six key areas would continue through third grade, and that the EIP children would perform at similar levels as average readers at their schools. These predictions were constructed to reflect the main goal and hope of all specialized intensive early intervention programs since Bryant and Bradley's (1985) classic study, i.e. that children at risk can be helped to "catch up" and stay caught up within the broad range of abilities within their classrooms. Measures of reading rate were added at this point in the program because informal observations as the program developed over time suggested that the previously at-risk children might be lagging in reading automaticity in spite of their gains in other important reading skills. It was expected

that treatment effect sizes would modulate over time, as in previous similar studies of intensive intervention programs for children at risk (Wasik & Slavin, 1993).

METHOD FOR INITIAL FIRST GRADE TREATMENT STUDY

Subjects

The subjects were 38 first grade children with low emergent reading skills, 19 from each of two elementary schools in the same suburban school district. Children were drawn from a total of 5 classrooms. These children were identified by their former kindergarten teachers and current first grade teachers as being in the lowest third of their classes in reading skills during the first semester of first grade. The groups from the two different schools were matched as pairs on age, receptive vocabulary skill, Marie Clay's (1985, 1993a) measures of early reading abilities (see Outcome Measures, below), and a global five-point Likert rating of emergent reading skills by their teachers. Two students from each school spoke English as a second language. No students were enrolled in special education or Chapter 1 services at the time of the study.

Experimental Design

Children from one school participated in the EIP program in addition to their regular first grade classroom instruction, and children from the other school received no extra intervention outside their regular first grade classroom placements. Pragmatic concerns regarding teacher assignment to schools, resources for teacher training, and scheduling prevented random assignment of children to treatment groups, so the groups were carefully matched on all outcome measures at pretest. The two schools were located in adjacent neighborhoods in the same school district, and were equivalent in socioeconomic makeup, size, physical facilities, and general curriculum. The communication arts curriculum in this district supports the use of literature for reading instruction. Basals are used as a source of additional stories. Phonics is taught through whole group instruction, conferencing, and developmental writing. The EIP children received a median of 58 (mean 49, range 18 to 82) 30-minute daily one-to-one tutoring sessions during either the fall or spring semesters of first grade.

Intervention

The EIP program was based on the assumption that all children can learn to their own ability within a supportive school environment, and that reading is a learned behavior for which some children require an active, intensive instructional program for success. Its purpose was to help these targeted readers who needed extra time, individualization and attention to achieve parity with their classmates in reading. Tutoring sessions for the program were scheduled at different times from the children's routine language-arts curriculum involvement within their first grade classrooms, so the intervention represented an "add on" rather than a "pull out" from standard instruction time.

Each EIP lesson involved three ten-minute segments. In the first segment, children reread books that they had covered in previous lessons. Four books of increasing difficulty were utilized on a rotating basis. The goal of this segment was to promote reading fluency and use of the good reader strategies that form the focus of the Reading Recovery Program (Clay, 1993b). In the second segment, children wrote a message of their own composition in standard spelling, with explicit instruction from the tutor in sound segmentation and relations with the alphabetic code. The phonological training involved two strategies: In the Elkonin boxes strategy (Clay, 1985), the child slowly articulated the sounds in a word sequentially while at the same time manipulating corresponding counters. In the "stretch it out" strategy (Clay, 1993; Griffith & Olson, 1992), the child slowly articulated sounds in a word while choosing the appropriate alphabetic symbols to represent sounds. In the third segment, tutors presented new reading material using the guided reading format (Clay, 1991; Ministry of Education, 1985). The basic philosophy of guided reading requires the child to apply good reader strategies to the text independently, with support from the tutor.

(16) The senior author served as program coordinator and provided tutoring to six of the EIP subjects. She trained three additional tutors for the project. Three of the tutors were certified reading specialists, and the fourth had a masters degree in reading with over 20 years experience as a first grade classroom teacher. Throughout the two years of the present study the four tutors met weekly for a two hour training session, which was structured using the cognitive coaching method (Costa & Garmston, 1985). Initially, the team watched videotaped lessons of the coordinator, who modeled instruction with the children. As time went on, each tutor was responsible for presenting a videotaped lesson on a rotating weekly schedule. The videotaped segment addressed theoretical elements of emergent reading and writing, as well as serving as a vehicle for interaction and coaching within the team (Joyce & Showers, 1982). Adherence to the EIP program was monitored by monthly direct observation by the program coordinator, and by examination of the daily running records and lesson plans (Clay, 1985, 1993a) detailing students' performance in the ongoing training sessions.

(17) Students received a maximum of 82 treatment sessions. All but two children were discontinued before the targeted maximum number of 75 sessions was completed, at the point when they were judged by the team of tutors to exhibit strategies of good readers independently in lessons and in the classroom, and when they were judged by their classroom teachers to be reading at or above the average level in their classes. All children were incorporated in the analyses presented below, including the two who simply ended tutoring after 75 or 82 sessions; the latter received a few extra sessions in an attempt to solidify her gains and increase independence.

Outcome Measures

(18) These measures included Marie Clay's (1985, 1993a) Observation Survey, a list of 25 primer level words constructed specifically for the present study, and three story selections from the Wright Company series (Cowley, 1983, 1987a, 1987b). Each child received one story at the preprimer level ("Night-time" for the first year cohort, or "The Seed" for the second year cohort) and one story at the first grade level ("Just This Once" for both cohorts). None of the children had previous exposure to these stories at home or at school. All measures were given at pretest and at posttest (when the EIP member of each pair ended the instruction program), except the first grade level story was given at posttest only because it was too difficult for all children at pretest. Both pretesting and posttesting were completed by one of the EIP teachers or by the reading resource teacher at the control school. The specific variables measured were as follows:

1. Letter Identification (Clay, 1985, 1993a). (19) The child reads randomly placed upper and lower case letters of the alphabet, with two letters written in different script forms. Credit is given if the letter name, sound or a word beginning with that letter is given. Score is the number correct out of a maximum of 54.

2. Concepts About Print (Clay, 1985, 1993a). The child demonstrates his/her understanding of the conventions of our printed language by responding to questions asked by the teacher as the teacher reads text which includes special features such as upside down print and misspelled words. Examples of concepts evaluated by this text include distinguishing elements in reading, such as letter, word, top, bottom, front, back, punctuation and one-to-one matching. Score is the number correct out of a maximum of 24.

3. Writing Vocabulary (Clay, 1985, 1993a). The child is asked to write all the words he/she knows within a ten-minute time limit. The teacher can prompt words that the teacher feels the child might know. This measure is an indicator of emerging sight vocabulary. Score is the number of real words spelled correctly, including proper nouns.

4. Hearing and Recording Sounds in Words-Dictation Task (Clay, 1985, 1993a). The child is asked to write a standard sentence that is dictated by the examiner. Correct sounds

(phonemes) and letters (graphemes) are credited. This measure is an indicator of phonological analysis skills. Score is the number correct out of a maximum of 37.

5. Primer Level Word List (see Appendix A). The child reads aloud a list of 25 basic words commonly appearing in emergent literature and on high-frequency word lists. The child is provided with a marker to aid visual focus. Two scores are computed: percent of words read correctly within one second, and percent of words read correctly without time limit.

6. Oral Reading Speed in Context. The child orally reads two stories, and the examiner records time to completion. Score is words per minute.

7. Oral Reading Accuracy in Context. The child orally reads two stories, and the examiner notes all miscues (omissions, substitutions, insertions; self-corrections are counted as miscues). Score is the percent of words read correctly.

8. Acceptable Reading Accuracy in Context. On the same stories as in (6), the examiner subtracts from the record of total miscues those miscues that do not change the meaning of the passage and that are syntactically correct. Therefore, self-corrections are not counted as miscues for this computation. Score is the percent of words read acceptably under these criteria.

9. Free Recall Reading Comprehension. On the same stories as in (6), the examiner

asks the child to retell the story in his/her own words. Teachers record the child's recollections. One point is given per proposition recalled or inference made. Score is the percent of propositions and inferences from the story that are included in the retelling, in any sequence.

10. Reading Comprehension Questions. On the same stories as in (6), the examiner asks the child six open-ended questions, three of which are explicit and three implicit. A list of correct answers was compiled by the EIP teachers prior to administration. Any answers that varied from this list were judged by the team as a group. Score is the percent of questions answered correctly.

RESULTS OF INITIAL FIRST GRADE TREATMENT STUDY

The two groups were not significantly different   on age or baseline test scores at pretest (see Table 1). This result was expected, due to the careful pairwise matching of subjects on the measures. Both groups showed average receptive vocabulary Peabody Picture Vocabulary Test—Revised standard score 98). The present suburban clinical sample was average to low-average in comparison to available urban non-clinical reference groups of first graders in Ohio and six year olds in New Zealand who have been given Clay's measures (third to fifth stanines; Clay, 1993a).

Table 1   Mean (Standard Deviation) Age and Baseline Test Scores on EIP versus Control Groups

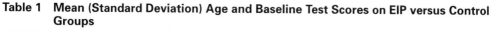

Variable	EIP (n=19)	Control (n=19)	t
Age (years)	6.6 (0.3)	6.6 (0.3)	0.00
Peabody Picture Vocabulary Test-Revised (standard score)	99.7 (12.0)	98.7 (11.7)	0.27
Letter Identification (maximum 54)	49.6 (4.9)	49.0 (5.9)	0.33
Concepts About Print (maximum 24)	15.6 (2.9)	16.0 (3.1)	−0.43
Writing Vocabulary (number of words)	18.7 (14.3)	20.4 (16.1)	−0.35
Dictation Task (maximum 37)	20.0 (12.7)	20.3 (13.2)	−0.06
Word List Reading (maximum 25)	13.3 (10.0)	12.0 (9.1)	0.42
Teacher Rating (maximum 5)	2.2 (0.8)	1.8 (1.2)	0.95

Table 2   Mean Pretest and Posttest Scores for EIP and Control Groups

Variable (form, maximum value)		EIP (n=19) Pre	EIP (n=19) Post	Control (n=19) Pre	Control (n=19) Post	F^a	Effect Size^b
Reading Readiness							
Letter Identification	M	49.6	53.6	49.0	53.1	0.03	−0.01
(raw, maximum 54)	SD	4.9	1.0	5.9	1.1		
Concepts About Print	M	15.6	20.8	16.0	18.9	15.79***	0.95
(raw, maximum 24)	SD	2.9	1.4	3.1	2.0		
Writing Measures							
Writing Vocabulary	M	18.7	48.9	20.4	38.3	16.98***	0.65
(raw, no maximum)	SD	14.3	11.4	16.1	16.2		
Dictation Task	M	20.0	34.5	20.2	31.2	5.97*	0.50
(raw, maximum 37)	SD	12.7	2.5	13.0	6.6		
Word List							
Flash Presentation	M	50.6	87.7	43.2	74.1	13.54***	0.79
(percent correct)	SD	39.9	11.4	33.5	17.3		
Untimed Presentation	M	53.2	93.1	48.0	80.9	11.41**	0.73
(percent correct)	SD	39.9	9.5	36.3	16.8		
PrePrimer Story							
Oral Reading Speed	M	16.3	52.1	15.6	21.8	11.20**	2.55
(words per minute)	SD	14.0	23.8	5.6	11.9		
Oral Reading Accuracy	M	56.4	94.8	49.3	76.0	10.05**	0.69
(percent correct)	SD	35.5	4.3	39.9	27.2		
Acceptable Accuracy	M	57.9	96.9	51.9	78.3	9.87**	0.67
(percent correct)	SD	36.4	3.0	41.8	27.8		
Free Recall	M	17.4	41.6	22.7	31.7	3.16	0.35
(percent of idea units)	SD	19.0	25.2	25.8	27.9		
Comprehension Questions	M	65.6	93.8	68.5	80.6	9.14**	0.71
(percent correct)	SD	21.1	10.0	25.3	18.6		
First Grade Story							
Oral Reading Speed	M	—	40.6	—	44.1	0.114	−0.17
(words per minute)	SD	—	16.3	—	21.0		
Oral Reading Accuracy	M	—	91.3	—	63.5	17.76***	0.87
(percent correct)	SD	—	8.3	—	31.9		
Acceptable Accuracy	M	—	94.1	—	66.4	17.10***	0.83
(percent correct)	SD	—	7.7	—	33.2		
Free Recall	M	—	13.0	—	8.1	4.87*	0.96
(percent of idea units)	SD	—	5.3	—	5.2		
Comprehension Questions	M	—	88.9	—	50.4	29.43***	1.16
(percent correct)	SD	—	12.1	—	33.1		

[a]   F values compare EIP to Control groups on posttest scores, with pretest score on the same variable as the covariate. No variable was significantly different between groups at pretest.

[b]   Effect size = (EIP Posttest Mean - Control Posttest Mean)/Control Standard Deviation.

* $p<.05$,

** $p<.01$,

*** $p<.001$

(21) Treatment effects were determined with analysis of covariance on the EIP versus control posttest scores, with pretest scores on the same measures as covariates (see Table 2). To assist in comparing the present results with other recent research, Wasik and Slavin's (1993) method was used to compute treatment effect sizes. In this method, the difference between the mean posttest scores is divided by the posttest standard deviation of the control group.

(22) Virtually all hypotheses on treatment outcome were confirmed. The EIP group improved significantly more than the control group on concepts about print (p < .001), with an effect size approaching one standard deviation (.95). The EIP group also showed significantly greater gains than the control group on both writing vocabulary and writing to dictation (p < .05 to .001). The effect sizes for these writing measures were moderate (.50 to .65), approximately one half standard deviation.

(23) The EIP group improved significantly more than the control group on all measures of word reading skill, including both flash and untimed presentation of the word list, oral reading accuracy in context, and acceptable reading accuracy in context, with both the preprimer and first grade level stories (p < .01 to .001). The effect sizes for the reading accuracy measures were substantial (.67 to .87), approaching one standard deviation.

(24) The EIP group made significantly more gains than the control group in answering comprehension questions for both the preprimer and first grade level stories (p < .01 to .001), and in free recall comprehension for the first grade story (p < .05). The effect sizes for these comprehension measures were substantial (.71 to 1.16), approaching or exceeding one standard deviation.

(25) The EIP group was significantly better than the control group for reading speed on the preprimer story (p < .01), but not on the first grade level story (p > .50). The effect sizes for the reading speed measures varied widely (−.17 to 2.55). Both groups showed modest progress on letter identification, but this progress was not different between groups (p > .50), probably because of a ceiling effect on this measure.

METHOD FOR THIRD GRADE FOLLOW-UP STUDY

Subjects

The subjects consisted of 34 of the 38 children **(26)** who completed the initial study. Two subjects had moved out of the area and were unavailable for follow-up testing; their matched pairs were also removed from the analyses. Two other subjects had moved to different schools within the area, so follow-up data were obtained by visiting the new schools. Of the 34 children in the follow-up sample, two had been placed in learning disabilities programs, one in a program for emotionally disturbed students, and one in home-schooling.

An average comparison sample of 17 subjects **(27)** was constructed retrospectively from students at the EIP school. The group of average third graders was selected using two criteria. First, their third grade teachers nominated them as average in reading skills, compared to their classmates. Second, their Total Reading Scores from the Iowa Tests of Basic Skills administered in fall of second grade ranged between normal curve equivalents of 46 and 76.

Procedure

Children were tested individually in middle of **(28)** their third grade year, 19 to 24 months after the EIP member of each matched pair ended treatment. One follow-up measure, the 4th grade level story, was administered at the end of the third grade year, 24 to 29 months after treatment ended; children enrolled in the second cohort have not yet received the fourth grade level story at the time this report is being prepared for publication. All follow-up testing was done by the senior author.

Follow-up Measures

Follow-up measures were drawn from the **(29)** Qualitative Reading Inventory (Leslie & Caldwell, 1990).

1. Graded Word Lists. The child reads a series of graded 20-word lists progressing from the primer level up to the point where fewer than 50% of the words are read correctly.

Two scores are computed at each grade level: percent of words [read] correctly within one second, and percent of words read correctly without time limit. Only the third grade and fourth grade lists are presented in the present analyses, because of floor or ceiling effects for many subjects on the other lists.

2. Oral Reading Speed in Context. The child orally reads two several-paragraph narrative stories on topics that are familiar to most mid-elementary children. One story is at the third grade level (A Trip to the Zoo) and one at the fourth grade level (Johnny Appleseed). Scoring is the same as in the initial treatment outcome study.

3. Oral Reading Accuracy in Context, using the same stories as in (2). Scoring is the same as in the initial treatment outcome study.

4. Acceptable Reading Accuracy in Context, using the same stories as in (2). Scoring is the same as in the initial treatment outcome study.

5. Free Recall Reading Comprehension, using the same stories as in (2). Scoring is the same as in the initial treatment outcome study.

6. Reading Comprehension Questions, using the same stories as in (2). Scoring is the same as in the initial treatment outcome study, except that eight questions are provided and the scoring criteria from the QRI manual are used.

RESULTS OF THIRD GRADE FOLLOW-UP STUDY

(30) Follow-up differences were determined with one-way analysis of variance on the scores obtained from the EIP, control, and average groups during third grade (see Table 3). More sophisticated data treatment with analysis of covariance or repeated measures analysis of variance was not deemed appropriate in this situation, because the two year developmental and learning period since the initial study necessitated completely different, more advanced content on both the word lists and stories.

(31) The follow-up results were more complex than the results of the initial study. Some measures confirmed the follow-up hypotheses completely, i.e. the EIP groups both remained superior to the control group and was equivalent to the average comparison group (noted by asterisks in Table 3). Some hypotheses were confirmed partially (noted by pound signs in Table 3), and some not at all (noted by plus signs or nonsignificant results in Table 3).

(32) The hypotheses were confirmed completely for several measures of contextual reading skill, including oral reading accuracy at the fourth grade level, acceptable reading accuracy at both levels, and answering reading comprehension questions at the third grade level (p < .05 to .01). The EIP group showed a trend (p < .08) toward better answering of reading comprehension questions than both of the other groups at the fourth grade level. The effect sizes for these contextual reading differences be-tween the EIP and control groups were substantial, approaching or exceeding one standard deviation (.67 to 1.07).

(33) The hypotheses were partially confirmed for all measures of word-reading skill that had not been confirmed completely, including flash presentation of both the third grade and fourth grade word lists, untimed presentation of the fourth grade word list, and oral reading accuracy of the third grade story (p < .01). On these measures, the EIP group remained superior to the control group but was not equivalent to the average group. The effect sizes for these measures were moderate to substantial, from one half standard deviation to almost one standard deviation (.56 to .91).

(34) The hypotheses for reading speed and for free recall comprehension were not confirmed. The average comparison group was better than both the EIP and control groups on all measures of reading fluency (p < .01), and the EIP and control groups were not significantly better than each other on these measures (p > .10). The three groups were not different on free recall comprehension (p > .10).

DISCUSSION

(35) The present study demonstrated positive benefits from an Early Intervention Program (EIP) for students at risk for reading disability. Children who received a median of 58 one-to-one tutoring sessions during first grade showed better concepts about print, emerging sight vocabulary, understanding of sound-symbol

Table 3   Mean Third Grade Follow-up Scores for EIP Group, Control Group, and Average Comparison Group

Variable		EIP	Control	Average	F	Effect Size[a]
Third Grade Word List	n	16	14	17		
Flash Presentation	M	76.0	65.0	89.1	8.59##	0.58
(percent correct)	SD	19.4	19.0	8.5		
Untimed Presentation	M	80.6	70.0	94.1	11.53++	0.56
(percent correct)	SD	15.4	18.8	5.6		
Fourth Grade Word List	n	14	10	17		
Flash Presentation	M	60.0	42.0	75.9	14.40##	0.91
(percent correct)	SD	14.6	19.8	14.6		
Untimed Presentation	M	70.4	53.4	83.6	11.03##	0.82
(percent correct)	SD	16.5	20.6	11.7		
Third Grade Story	n	17	17	17		
Oral Reading Speed	M	84.8	69.8	119.5	15.62++	0.79
(words per minute)	SD	23.4	18.9	27.0		
Oral Reading Accuracy	M	94.1	89.7	96.9	15.93##	0.80
(percent correct)	SD	3.0	5.5	1.6		
Acceptable Accuracy	M	97.2	93.9	98.4	11.13**	0.75
(percent correct)	SD	2.1	4.4	1.1		
Free Recall	M	36.1	32.3	43.2	2.18	0.32
(percent of idea units)	SD	14.6	11.7	19.2		
Comprehension Questions	M	84.6	71.5	84.7	3.25*	0.65
(percent correct)	SD	16.9	20.1	15.0		
Fourth Grade Story	n	9	9	9		
Oral Reading Speed	M	69.4	65.8	101.2	6.23++	0.15
(words per minute)	SD	19.1	24.3	22.3		
Oral Reading Accuracy	M	94.1	87.4	95.9	5.50*	0.74
(percent correct)	SD	2.8	9.1	2.3		
Acceptable Accuracy	M	96.4	90.2	97.7	4.56*	0.67
(percent correct)	SD	2.7	9.2	1.6		
Free Recall	M	26.7	27.9	28.3	0.04	−0.07
(percent of idea units)	SD	7.9	16.6	12.0		
Comprehension Questions	M	71.1	48.2	53.1	3.10	1.07
(percent correct)	SD	12.5	21.4	25.4		

[a]   Effect size = (EIP Mean - Control Mean)/Control Standard Deviation.
*   p<.05, with Average = EIP > Control at p <.05 in paired comparisons
**   p<.01, with Average = EIP > Control at p <.05 in paired comparisons
p<.01, with Average > EIP > Control at p <.05 in paired comparisons
++   p<.01, with Average > EIP = Control at p <.05 in paired comparisons

relationships, word recognition skill in isolation and in context, reading speed, and reading comprehension following the tutoring period at the end of first grade than matched children who received only routine classroom placement. As predicted, both the treatment and regular classroom groups achieved reasonable proficiency in alphabet recognition by the end of first grade. Two years later, the treated children still showed better word recognition skill in context and better reading comprehension than untreated children. At the two-year follow-up, the treated children were equivalent to a comparison group of average-achieving classmates in word recognition in context and in reading comprehension, but not in word recognition in isolation or in reading rate. Treatment gains and maintenance by the EIP group were clinically substantial as well as statistically significant, approaching or exceeding effect sizes of one standard deviation of the control group. The present findings are very similar to treatment gains that have been reported by other intensive interventions for children at risk for reading disability (reviewed by Wasik and Slavin, 1993), and are based on all children who were enrolled in the program, not just those who were successfully discontinued because they reached acceptable, average reading skills before the maximum number of treatment sessions provided.

(36) Several factors probably contributed to the success of the EIP. First, experienced teachers provided instruction, which has tended to produce more positive results than paraprofessionals or briefly trained volunteers (Wasik & Slavin, 1993). Second, instruction was individually shaped by the teacher in the role of the expert evaluator (Johnston & Allington, 1989). Third, informal observation of treated children through running records and daily journals suggested that they became more reflective, increased their self-monitoring and self-correcting, and built strategies to actively construct meaning and patterns in their reading, all of which have been found to characterize successful learners in contrast with less successful learners (Brown, 1980; Johnson & Winograd, 1985; Torgesen, 1982; Vellutino, 1987). Finally, the EIP lessons were provided in noncompetitive task-involving contexts that encouraged children to solve problems themselves but to seek help when necessary, reduced feelings of failure, increased cooperation, and engaged children in reading and writing rather than leading to avoidance.

(37) Given the individualized tutoring inherent in the EIP treatment, it was not surprising that the reading word recognition and comprehension performance skills of the children in the EIP group were superior to the classroom-only children in first grade. The critical question was whether the achievement attributed to the 58 individual tutoring sessions would continue past first grade. The two-year follow-up study examined two EIP cohorts (in consecutive years) as third graders compared with their matched controls and compared with average readers, as rated by their teachers and on standardized testing. The EIP readers continued to significantly outperform their matched controls. However, would these EIP readers have the same type of performance as average readers two years after tutoring? The results suggested that the EIP readers achieved like the average readers in their word identification skill in context, in their acceptable word recognition accuracy in context, and in their ability to answer comprehension questions. They were less accurate than average readers in their ability to read isolated words on word lists, and they read more slowly than average readers.

The EIP children have made substantive (38) gains. Although their word recognition in mid-elementary school was not as accurate or rapid as the average group, the EIP children's ability to monitor words for meaning in a story setting was average. Transfer of these behaviors to classroom settings was encouraged by an emphasis on meaning, interaction with stories, writing opportunities, and assessment measures in classroom instruction. One probable cause of student success at follow-up is this continuity between the individual and classroom approaches in this district. The goal of reading instruction is to help children recognize words in meaningful contexts and to understand what they read. The EIP children appeared to be aware of making reading errors in context, and they knew how to use their reading strategies to self-correct. This extra reading work may have contributed to the EIP children's slower reading speed. In addition, they may continue to be slower in processing words until the words are overlearned through repeated readings in text. The goal of reading is not rapid reading of isolated word lists. The results suggest that the tutoring aids comprehension through the monitoring of words read in context rather than speed or automaticity of word recognition. It is likely that children with low early literacy skills need increased classroom time for processing and/or differentiated instruction as compared to average children. It is important that teachers look beyond word recognition speed as they set expectations for these children.

In the absence of well established quantitative methods for analyzing changes in chil- (39)

dren's strategic reading behaviors, qualitative observations of EIP children's progress over the course of intervention can be made. Before intervention, children tended to either overuse meaning (usually the pictures) without regard to visual match, or to overuse graph-phonic cues and not make sense. In either condition, the children often were not concerned with one-to-one correspondence as their production contained either more or less words than the printed text. As tutoring progressed, the children became more aware of the importance of making sense. They became more aware of the use of grapho-phonics to cross check the words they were reading. They also self-monitored, stopping when their word either did not make sense or did not match visually. They began rereading to pick up more cues as well as to maintain one-to-one correspondence between the spoken and written word. The understanding and use of sound segmentation was also observed in their writing. At this point, they began to transfer this ability to decode unfamiliar words when necessary in their reading at the grapho-phonic level. Towards the end of tutoring, children have integrated the semantic, syntactic and grapho-phonic cue systems so that they can use them in coordination to decode unfamiliar words and to self-correct immediately and more efficiently. They appear to use word analysis strategies much as average readers do but seem to need to apply these strategies more frequently.

(40) One outcome measure did not demonstrate treatment change at posttest or at follow-up, i.e. reading comprehension as measured by free recall. Free recall was included in the study in addition to comprehension questions for the following reasons. Free recall is often demanded in the classroom setting. It is also a more qualitatively comprehensive response to what has been read, as questions can limit child generation. In addition, the process of retelling can enhance children's processing of text information, and this benefit can transfer to the reading of subsequent text (Gambrell, Pfeiffer & Wilson, 1985). However, children in early elementary school need prompts based on the story structure in order to successfully retell stories (Morrow, 1985), and even later

elementary school children appear to require practice in order to become proficient in retelling (Gambrell et al., 1985). The EIP in the present study did not specifically train retelling, and the outcome measure in this area did not provide structured prompts, so it is not surprising that no treatment effects were observed in this area. The examiner judgement that is inherent in the free recall measure may render it psychometrically less reliable than other more objective outcome measures, thus less likely to be adequately sensitive to treatment effects.

(41) The results suggest that at risk first grade children profit from individualized one-to-one instruction that emphasizes word recognition and phonetic training in a context-rich environment. The delivery of this instruction can be done by experienced teachers who spend ongoing, cooperative time on site in peer review of their interactions and lessons with children. Results of this study indicate that the intensive weekly teacher interaction and critique provides a less expensive alternative to the yearlong intensive Reading Recovery training.

(42) The calculation of effect sizes in the present study, using the method recommended by Wasik and Slavin (1993), both highlights the clinical significance of the EIP findings and allows quantitative comparisons with previous similar research. A recent major review of meta-analysis research on the efficacy of psychological, educational and behavioral treatment (Lipsey & Wilson, 1993) proposed that effect sizes of as little as .20 (i.e. one fifth of a standard deviation difference between a treatment group and a control group) can not be dismissed as practically insignificant. Both the initial and follow-up effect sizes in the present study were substantially higher than .20, ranging from one half standard deviation to over one standard deviation on all measures that showed statistically reliable findings using traditional parametric tests. The effect sizes immediately after treatment in the present study were comparable to the modal initial effect sizes in the most impactful interventions reviewed by Wasik and Slavin (1993), i.e. Reading Recovery and Success for All. Furthermore, the follow-up effect sizes in both

the present study and a number of cohorts in the Success for All program have been comparable to the initial effect sizes, whereas the Reading Recovery follow-ups reviewed by Wasik and Slavin (1993) showed a significant decrement in effect sizes by third grade. The robust maintenance of treatment effects over time in the present study may have been attributable to the integration of the EIP approaches into the ongoing school curriculum, despite the discontinuation of the direct supplemental intervention by the end of first grade. For instance, second and third grade teachers used running records on all children in their classes, and the senior author informally assessed EIP children throughout second and third grades to monitor progress and report on these assessments to classroom teachers.

(43) Several limitations of the present study must be acknowledged. First, the control group did not receive any intervention besides routine classroom placement, so the role of nonspecific effects such as time spent in one-to-one tutoring can not be separated from the role of treatment-specific effects such as the particular curriculum that was used in the EIP. Second, subjects were not randomly assigned to treatment conditions, so a number of extraneous variables may have influenced both initial treatment outcome and long-term maintenance of treatment gains. While each participating school's teaching staff and/or demographic characteristics of the student bodies could have particular potential for such extraneous influence, this district's well-coordinated, unified elementary reading program makes it unlikely that there were extraneous curricular differences between the two schools. Third, standardized individually administered normative outcome measures were not employed, so it is difficult to quantify treatment effects in reference to students outside the school district in which the study took place. On the other hand, the present results are similar enough to the results of the other intervention programs to accept the present findings as robust.

(44) In conclusion, the EIP exemplifies an educational initiative funded by and centered in a public school system. Affiliation with collaborating research centers helped establish an experimental design so that the program's successes could be documented, a necessity in the present climate of pressure on public school budgets. The strong results discussed in this paper have ensured the continued support of this program in the school system. At the same time, it has become ethically inadvisable to continue forming control groups of students with emergent literacy problems who receive no extra intervention in the school district, so current EIP cohorts are being compared to randomly, prospectively selected samples of average classmates based on assessments at the end of kindergarten. The cohorts reported here will also be followed on a longer term basis to substantiate their continued reading success.

APPENDIX A (45)

Word List for Initial Treatment Pretest and Posttest.

and	a	I	to	said
you	he	it	in	was
on	is	go	can	one
look	no	see	down	love
boy	school	mother	like	want

AUTHOR NOTES

This project was supported by a grant from the (46) Wauwatosa School District. We gratefully acknowledge the encouragement of the Wauwatosa School Board and the former Superintendent George Goens; the consultation and collegial support of Robin Gleason, chairperson of the District's Reading Department; the collaboration of Tom Engel, principal of Wilson School, and Mary Weinfurter, reading specialist at Washington School; the tireless teaching by Carolyn Rauen and Kristin Fewel, who were the original tutors for the project, along with the senior author and Robin Gleason; the painstaking organization of materials and data by Kathy Eilbes; and the enthusiastic participation of the children and parents of the District. Correspondence should be sent to Patricia McCarthy, Wilson School, 1060 Glenview Avenue, Wauwatosa, Wisconsin, 53213.

REFERENCES

(47)

Ball, E. & Blachman, B. A. (1991). Does phoneme segmentation training in kindergarten make a difference in early word recognition and developmental spelling? *Reading Research Quarterly, 24,* 49–66.

Bradley, L., & Bryant, P. (1985). *Rhyme and reason in reading and spelling.* Ann Arbor: University of Michigan Press.

Brown, A. L. (1980). Metacognitive development and reading. In R. Spiro, B. Bruce, & W. F. Brewer (Eds.), *Theoretical issues in reading comprehension* (pp. 453–481). Hillsdale, NJ: Erlbaum.

Clay, M. M. (1985). *The early detection of reading difficulties.* Exeter, NH: Heinemann.

Clay, M. M. (1991). Introducing a new storybook to young readers. *The Reading Teacher, 45,* 264–272.

Clay, M. M. (1993a). *An observation survey of early literacy achievement.* Portsmouth, NH: Heinemann.

Clay, M. M. (1993b). *Reading recovery: A guidebook for teachers in training.* Portsmouth, NH: Heinemann.

Costa, A. & Garmston, R. (1985). Supervision for intelligent teaching. *Educational Leadership, 42,* 70–80.

Cowley, J. (1983). *Night-Time.* San Diego: Wright Group.

Cowley, J. (1987a). *Just this once.* San Diego: Wright Group.

Cowley, J. (1987b). *The seed.* San Diego: Wright Group.

Dolch, E. W. (1939). *A manual for remedial reading.* Urbana, IL: Geranol.

Gambrell, L. B., Pfeiffer, W. R. & Wilson, R. M. (1985). The effects of retelling upon reading comprehension and recall of text information. *Journal of Educational Research, 78,* 216–220.

Griffith, P. L., & Olson, M. W. (1992). Phonemic awareness helps beginning readers break the code. *The Reading Teacher, 45,* 516–523.

Holmes, C. T., & Matthews, K. M. (1984). The effects of non-promotion on elementary and junior high school pupils: A meta-analysis. *Review of Educational Research, 54,* 225–236.

Iverson, S., & Tunmer, W. E. (1993). Phonological processing skills and the Reading Recovery Program. *Journal of Educational Psychology, 85,* 112–126.

Johnston, P. H. & Allington, R. L. (1989). Coordination, collaboration, and consistency: The redesign of compensatory and special education interventions. In R. Slavin, N. Madden, & N. Karweit (Eds.), *Preventing school failure: Effective programs for students at risk* (pp. 320–354). Boston: Allyn-Bacon.

Johnston, P. H., & Winograd, P. N. (1985). Passive failure in reading. *Journal of Reading Behavior, 17,* 279–301.

Joyce, B. & Showers, B. (1988). *Student achievement through staff development.* White Plains, NY: Longman.

Leslie, L., & Caldwell, J. (1990). *Qualitative Reading Inventory.* Glenview, IL: Scott, Foresman.

Lipsey, M. W., & Wilson, D. B. (1993). The efficacy of psychological, educational, and behavioral treatment: Confirmation from meta-analysis. *American Psychologist, 48,* 181–1209.

Ministry of Education. (1985). *Reading in the junior classes.* Wellington, New Zealand: Department of Education.

Morrow, L. M. (1985). Retelling stories: A strategy for improving young children's comprehension, concept of story structure, and oral language complexity. *The Elementary School Journal, 85,* 647–661.

Pinnell, G. S., DeFord, D. E., & Lyons, C. A. (1988). *Reading Recovery: Early intervention for at-risk first graders.* Arlington, VA: Educational Research Service.

Pinnell, G. S., Lyons, C. A., DeFord, D. E., Bryk, A. S., & Seltzer, M. (1991). *Studying the effectiveness of early intervention approached for first grade children having difficulty in reading.* Columbus: Ohio State University, Martha L. King Language and Literacy Center.

Slavin, R. E. (1993). School and classroom organization in beginning reading: Class size, aides and instructional grouping. In R. E. Slavin, N. L. Kaarweit, B. A. Wasik (Eds.), *Preventing early school failure; Research, policy, and practice.* Boston: Allyn & Bacon.

Slavin, R. E., Madden, N. A., Karweit, N. L., Dolan, L., & Wasik, B. A. (1992). *Success for All: A relentless approach to prevention and early intervention in elementary schools.* Arlington, VA: Educational Research Service.

Stanovich, K. E. (1986). Matthew effects in reading: Some consequences of individual differences in the acquisition of literacy. *Reading Research Quarterly, 21,* 360–407.

Torgesen, J. K. (1982). The learning disabled child as an inactive learner. *Topics in Learning and Learning Disabilities, 2,* 45–52.

Vellutino, F. R. (1987). Dyslexia. *Scientific American, 256,* 34–41.

Wasik, B. A., & Slavin, R. E. (1993). Preventing early reading failure with one-to-one tutoring: A review of five programs. *Reading Research Quarterly, 28,* 179–200.

FEEDBACK

Activity 1

Why do educators conduct research?

Educators produce research to verify the effectiveness of teaching and learning ideas and practices already in use, to discover new ideas and practices, to develop practices that simplify people's lives, to introduce practices that complicate people's lives, and to discover counter-intuitive practices.

What is the distinction between research consumers and research producers?

Research producers need technical competence in applying research strategies—the procedures for conceptualizing, developing, implementing, and reporting research. Research consumers need skills in understanding how researchers undertake research and in reading, interpreting, and applying others' research results.

What does it mean to understand research as a research producer does?

To understand research as a research producer does means understanding research with the mindset of a research producer. To do that, research consumers need to understand (a) the research process and the decisions facing research producers, (b) the possible alternatives research producers consider at those decision points, and (c) the implications of the research producers' results and conclusions.

What are some key terms used in research?

Key research terms are (a) *variable*—anything in a research situation that can vary; (b) *design*—the plan or type of research; research can be quantitative (statistical), qualitative (nonstatistical), or a combination; (c) *hypothesis*—a tentative statement about two or more variables; (d) *subjects*—the people used in the study; and (e) *generalizability*—the ability of the results from one study to be applied to subjects not used in the study.

Activity 2

Paragraph 1: The abstract, a summary of the entire research report.

Paragraphs 2–9: Background information and what others have found in answering related questions about the topic, and why the authors are doing the research.

Paragraphs 10–11: Statements (predictions) about the researchers' purpose and the results they expect to get in the two studies (first grade and third grade).

Paragraph 12: A description of the children used in the first grade study.

Paragraph 13: The research design of the first grade study.

Paragraphs 14–17: A description of the research procedure (intervention) used in the first grade study.

Paragraphs 18–19 (items 1–10): The tests used to measure the first-grade children's reading performance. (See also, Paragraph 45.)

Paragraphs 20–25: An explanation of the results of the first grade study. The statistical data are found in Tables 1 and 2 of the study.

Paragraphs 26–27: A description of the children used in the third grade study.

Paragraph 28: A description of the research procedures used in the third grade study.

Paragraph 29 (items 1–6): The tests used to measure the third-grade children's reading performance.

Paragraphs 30–34: An explanation of the results of the third grade study. The statistical data are found in Table 3 of the study.

Paragraphs 35–39: A summary of the purpose and results of the study with ideas about what might have caused the results.

Paragraphs 40–43: The researchers' ideas about how the results can be used for instructional purposes and other research.

Paragraph 46: The reference section, containing all the other research the authors referred to in their report.

CHAPTER 2
Research Designs

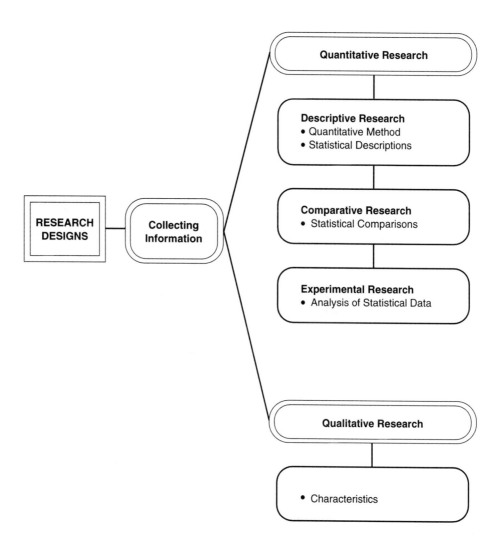

FOCUS QUESTIONS

1. What are the major designs used to conduct educational research?
2. What are quantitative descriptive, comparative, and experimental research?
3. What distinguishes the three types of quantitative research designs from each other?

4. What are the instruments used to collect quantitative data?
5. How are data analyzed in each of the three types of quantitative research designs?
6. What are central tendency and variability, and how are they measured?
7. What are the major purposes for conducting qualitative research?
8. What are the major features of qualitative research?

When researchers pose questions about educational problems, there are simultaneous concerns with one or more plans for obtaining answers. The plans, or **research designs,** structure researchers' methods for answering their questions and conducting studies. In current thought about research designs, research is categorized according to the way researchers collect and analyze information and their research purposes. Two basic research designs based on the way information, or data, is collected and analyzed are **quantitative research** and **qualitative research.** Although there are overlapping characteristics in quantitative and qualitative research, they result from different theoretical perspectives about the overall purpose of research. Despite those differences, the two types can be considered as complementary, and they may be combined in a single research project (Lancy, 1993; Slavin, 1992). The two research perspectives share at least four procedural aspects (Hillocks, 1992). Quantitative and qualitative researchers share concerns "in problem finding, in explaining the relationships of data to claims, in theory building, and in explaining particular cases in light of established knowledge and theory" (p. 59). However,

> they can and do focus on different kinds of problems. For example, quantitative methods cannot deal directly with historical problems of cause and effect or the interpretation of unique social phenomena. On the other hand, qualitative researchers find it difficult, if not impossible, to represent the responses of large numbers of individuals to different kinds of stimuli, e.g., different methods of teaching or attitudes toward social conditions or political events. In the sense that the two sets of methods allow researchers to deal with problems of different dimensions in different context, they are complementary. (Hillocks, 1992, p. 59).

COLLECTING INFORMATION

Information, or data, for quantitative and qualitative research is collected from direct observation, tests, and survey questionnaires and interviews. Researchers refer to these data collection devices and procedures as **instruments.** (The criteria for determining whether particular instruments accurately collect information are discussed in Chapter 6, Reading and Evaluating Instrument Sections. The use of instruments in qualitative research is also discussed in Chapter 7.)

Researchers usually record direct observation with an observation form, which may consist of questions about the subject's actions or categories of actions. For example, the observer may collect information in response to set questions—

"With which children did the target subject play during free-play?" or "Which child started the play?" Or, the observer might tally the subject's actions during a time period according to some predetermined categories: "Subject started play with others," "Other play with subject," "Self-initiated lone play," "Fringe observer to others' play." In qualitative research, observations are recorded in field notes, which are explained in Chapter 7.

Test information includes scores from **standardized norm-referenced tests** such as the *California Achievement Tests,* the *Gates-MacGinitie Reading Tests, 3rd edition,* the *Iowa Tests of Basic Skills,* and the *Metropolitan Achievement Tests.* The scores also may be from standardized **criterion-referenced tests** such as the *PRI/Reading Systems* or the *Life Skills Tests of Functional Competencies in Reading and Mathematics.* Competency tests also might be created by a researcher or teacher for determining learning style, reading interest, or outcomes of instruction. Some tests are given individually, others are administered to groups.

Questionnaires require the respondent either to write answers to questions about a topic or to answer orally. The answer form may be structured, in that there are fixed choices, or the form may be open, in that the respondent can use his or her own words. When the respondent answers orally and the researcher records the answers, researchers consider the instrument an **interview.** In interviews, the researcher may obtain responses to structured or open-ended questions. Interviews differ from questionnaires in that the researcher can modify the data collection situation to fit the respondent's replies. For example, additional information can be solicited or a question can be rephrased. In addition, researchers use surveys to collect information from files such as subjects' permanent school records.

QUANTITATIVE RESEARCH

Quantitative research is characterized by the use of statistical analysis. Three basic quantitative research purposes are to describe, to compare, and to attribute causality. Each of these purposes is fulfilled through the assignment of numerical values to variables and the mathematical analysis of those values. Quantitative research is predicated on the belief that variables should be mathematically measured, and adherents to this approach stress that data should be repeatedly verified. Generally, the quantitative research approach is considered to be objective, that is, "the scientific method."

In **quantitative descriptive research,** the researchers' purpose is to answer questions about a variable's status by creating numerical descriptions of the frequency with which one or more variables occurs. In **comparative research,** the researchers' purpose is to examine numerical descriptions of two or more variables and make decisions about their differences or relationships. In research to attribute causality, or **experimental research,** the researchers' purpose is to draw conclusions about the influence of one or more variables on another variable. They seek to answer "if . . . then" questions: If they do something, then what change will occur in a particular variable?

From the results of experimental research, researchers establish the influence, or **effect,** of one variable on another. Quantitative descriptive and comparative research may show status, patterns, and associations among variables, but studies of that type cannot be used to say that one variable or combination of variables probably does cause a change in, or influence, another variable. Only when researchers follow the plan for attributing causality can they establish that a particular variable may be the reason for a change in another. Causation research, or experimental research, is different from descriptive and comparative research, and that distinction cannot be over-stressed (Borg, Gall, & Gall, 1993).

Descriptive Research

Descriptive research is used when researchers want to answer the question "What exists?"

Quantitative Descriptive Method.   The quantitative descriptive research method is a procedure involving the assignment of numerical values to variables. For example, Figure 2.1 contains partial results from a questionnaire used in a descriptive study

> to determine the extent to which teachers use content area instructional practices and activities that are consistent with current views of reading and learning from text. (Gillis, Olson, & Logan, 1993)

These researchers collected data by asking teachers to circle one of five choices to indicate the percentage of instructional time they used various types of student groupings and instructional materials.

Another research team might wish to know, "What is the average intelligence of students in gifted programs in a particular county or state?" They collect and

Proportion of Teachers Reporting Percentage of Time They Use Practices and Activities in Content Area Instruction

		Practices and Activities			
	Never	1–25%	26–50%	51–75%	76–100%
Instructional context:					
Ability groups	34.9	39.4	6.1	10.6	9.1
Cooperative groups	2.9	33.8	30.9	26.5	5.9
Whole class	4.4	10.3	22.1	29.4	33.8
Textbooks	4.6	15.1	21.2	45.5	33.8
Prereading:					
Activate prior knowledge	—	28.4	13.4	14.9	43.3
Set purpose	—	28.4	13.4	13.4	44.8
Predict/preview	1.5	37.9	15.2	21.2	24.2
During reading:					
Students read silently	9.2	35.4	30.8	18.5	6.2
Students read orally	4.5	23.9	31.3	23.9	16.4
Postreading:					
Computer support	34.9	36.4	18.2	7.6	3.0
Workbooks/skills center	7.6	45.5	33.3	9.1	4.6

Figure 2.1
Partial Results from a Questionnaire (Adapted from Gillis, Olson, & Logan, 1993, p. 118.)

tabulate data and find that the average intelligence score of gifted program students is 129. Still another team affiliated with a county library system might wish to know, "What is the average reading achievement test score of a sample of beginning sixth-grade students using the public libraries in three local communities?" They collect and tabulate the data and find that the average achievement test grade equivalent score is 6.2.

However, having these two bits of information (average intelligence and average reading achievement score) does not allow the separate teams of researchers to create accurate pictures of the subjects. Average scores may give a limited picture because we know that not all gifted students had an intelligence score of 129, and not all sixth-grade students in each community had scores of 6.2. Also, anyone who observes gifted students and sixth-grade students sees that they differ in many ways other than intelligence or reading performance: personality, preferences and interests, and learning style, to name a few.

Two premises, then, underlie quantitative researchers' collection of descriptive information. First, they should collect and average information for several relevant variables. For the sixth-grade students, other variables relevant to library usage might be age, sex, intelligence, ethnicity, reading interest and preference, proximity of home to the library, and frequency of library usage. Second, after determining the average score for each variable, researchers should determine the extent to which the subjects' scores for each variable cluster near to or spread away from the average score. Two patterns of clustering are common: (a) a clustering of scores around the mean and (b) a clustering of scores either above or below the mean. The reporting of this clustering or spreading gives a picture of the subjects' similarity or dissimilarity.

Statistical Descriptions of Data.   After researchers collect data, they tally them. Figure 2.1 shows the response categories for each answer and the percentage of the total group they represent. From these data, it is possible to get a sense of how most teachers responded and whether there was uniform agreement among them.

However, most researchers following quantitative procedures use other descriptive measures of data, which are **central tendency** and **variability.** Although two common measures of central tendency researchers use in research reports are the mean and the median, the mean is the measure of central tendency they most often use. The measure of variability most often used and the one associated with the mean is the standard deviation. The following discussion is only an introduction to these measures. Chapter 8, Reading and Interpreting Results Sections, contains additional information about statistics and criteria for determining whether researchers' use of the mean, median, standard deviation, and other statistics is appropriate. Understanding the concepts of central tendency and variability is essential to understanding quantitative research designs.

Both the mean and median give researchers—producers and consumers—a sense of the middle or average score for a variable. The **mean** is an arithmetical average—one adds up individual scores and divides by the number of scores. The **median** is the middle score of a group of scores arranged in ascending order. The mean and median may not be the same for a particular group of scores. For example, the mean (middle) (median) score of the following groups is the same

(25), but the means of the two groups are different—the first is 33.57 and the second is 40.85:

$$10, 15, 20, 25, 40, 50, 75$$
$$4, 17, 24, 25, 26, 91, 99$$

The **standard deviation (SD)** is used with the mean to show how the other scores are distributed around the mean. The use of the SD lets research producers and consumers see how homogeneous (alike) or heterogeneous (varied) a group is. For example, the children entering the kindergarten classes in one school might have a mean age of 64 months (5 years, 4 months) and an SD of 4 months. In this group of kindergarteners, most children (approximately two-thirds) would be between 60 and 68 months in age. For another group of children entering kindergarten in another school with the same mean age (64 months) but an SD of 7 months, two-thirds of the children would be between 57 and 71 months in age. The first group of kindergarten children would be more homogeneous in their ages than would be the second group.

Table 2.1 shows an example of mean and standard deviation reporting. The table reports information from an investigation of the effect of reading placement on reading achievement of at-risk sixth-grade students with reading problems

Table 2.1

Example of Mean and Standard Deviation Reporting: Means and Standard Deviations of CTBS Test Scores by Group

| | | Testing | | | |
| | | Pre | | Post | |
Group	n	M	SD	M	SD
		Vocabulary Test			
Disabled Reader:					
Instructional Level	84	636.56	25.40	660.77	25.61
Frustration 1	88	633.60	27.98	660.02	25.95
Frustration 2	25	630.80	26.80	644.48	35.05
Slow Learner:					
Instructional Level	42	622.76	33.95	641.12	45.55
Frustration 1	51	615.78	39.76	642.27	32.43
Frustration 2	14	604.79	35.31	617.21	48.32
		Comprehension Test			
Disabled Reader:					
Instructional Level	84	637.90	50.77	692.33	41.40
Frustration 1	88	645.75	48.92	692.99	41.76
Frustration 2	25	622.90	61.08	662.40	60.47
Slow Learner:					
Instructional Level	42	603.02	50.06	651.40	49.81
Frustration 1	51	609.65	41.39	652.58	66.38
Frustration 2	14	593.79	45.61	643.64	55.56

Source: Homan, Hines, & Kromrey (1993).

(Homan, Hines, & Kromrey, 1993). The two groups of readers were "disabled reader" and "slow learner." They were tested with two instruments: a vocabulary test and a comprehension test. The table gives the number of subjects (*n*), the mean scores (M), and the standard deviations (SD) for both pre- and posttesting and for groups at three levels of reading performance: Instructional Level, Frustration 1, and Frustration 2. The table shows that on the vocabulary test, a group of 84 disabled readers had an average pretesting score of 636.56. The standard deviation was 25.40, resulting in the scores of about two-thirds of the students being clustered between 661.96 and 611.16. The same group of students had a posttesting average of 660.77, and about two-thirds of them had scores between 686.38 and 635.16.

Comparative Research

Comparative research lets researchers examine relationships including similarities or differences among several variables. These variables might represent characteristics of the same group of subjects or those of separate groups. That is, researchers might compare the writing performance and self-concept of members of a single group of subjects, or they might compare the writing performance and self-concept of two groups. Comparative research is more common than is pure descriptive research, but comparative research depends on knowledge generated from descriptive research. All researchers use descriptive data. Quantitative researchers apply statistical procedures to answer questions about similarities, differences, and relationships among variables, whereas qualitative researchers apply verbal analyses to answer similar questions.

Also, researchers can use the statistical comparative data to make predictions. When researchers find two variables that are strongly statistically related, they can use one variable to predict the occurrence of the other. They cannot, however, use relationship information to show that one variable is the cause of a change in another.

For example, a group of researchers conducted a comparative study of Israeli preschool, remedial, and elementary school teachers' teaching performance. They found consistent differences among the three groups of teachers in affective variables but not in direct, actual teaching behavior. The preschool teachers were seen to be the most flexible, democratic, and expressive in warmth (Babad, Bernieri, & Rosenthal, 1987). The essential aspect to this comparative research is that researchers made no attempt to determine causality. In fact, the researchers state "the results provide no hint as to what might have caused the observed pattern" (p. 414).

Statistical Comparisons of Data. After researchers following a quantitative procedure collect data, they calculate measures of central tendency (the mean) and variability (the standard deviation) as they do in descriptive research. These measures by themselves, however, do not provide evidence of difference or relationship. One or more statistical procedures can be used to determine whether differences exist between or among groups. Any of the statistical procedures used in comparative research are similar to those used in experimental research. Research consumers must realize that statistical procedures are tools for answering research questions; they are not the research. They help researchers determine whether an apparent difference or relationship is large enough to be considered real. They also help researchers determine the extent to which they can be confident about their research conclusions. (Chapter 8, Reading and Interpreting Results Sections, contains an extended discussion about the research reality, or significance, of differences and relationships.)

One statistical procedure used in descriptive research is the **Chi square.** Table 2.2 contains an example of a Chi square analysis. The information is from a study that examined how teachers responded when students made miscues (deviant oral reading responses) (Lass, 1984). Two types of miscues ([a] attempted pronunciation of word even when wrong and [b] refused or hesitated response) were compared to two types of teacher responses ([a] supplied word and [b] all other kinds of responses). The analysis showed that teachers who dealt with unattempted miscues supplied words more often than they used all other responses combined.

A statistical procedure used extensively in comparative research is **correlation.** Correlations show whether two or more variables have a systematic relationship of occurrence. That is, they help researchers answer questions about the scores: Do high scores for one variable occur with high scores for another (a positive relationship)? or Do high scores for one variable occur with low scores for the other variable (a negative relationship)? The occurrence of low scores for one variable with low scores for another is also an example of a positive relationship.

Table 2.3 shows an example of correlation reporting. The table contains information from a study about the relationships between topic-specific background knowledge and measures of total writing quality (Langer, 1984). It shows the obtained relationships among four ways of evaluating students' writing: (a) teachers' marks, (b) a measure of coherence, (c) counting the words and clauses, and (d) a holistic scoring method. The relationship between the holistic scoring method and the teachers' marks is positive and significant—high coherence scores

---

Table 2.2

Example of Chi Square Reporting: Attempted Miscues vs. Refusals/Hesitations and Teacher Response

	Miscues				
	Attempts		Refusals/ Hesitations		
	EO[a]	AO[a]	EO	AO	Raw Total
Teacher response:					
Supplied word	105.5	93	13.5	26	119
All other	237.5	250	30.5	18	268
Total		343		44	387

[a]EO = Expected occurrences; AO = Actual occurrences.

$\chi^2 = 19.83$ with 1 degree of freedom ($p < .001$).

Source: Adapted from Lass (1984).

Table 2.3

Example of Correlation Reporting: Relationships among Writing Measures

	Correlations (*n* papers)		
	Teacher's Mark	Coherence	Words/Clause
Holistic score	.44[a] (57)	.06 (99)	.25 (96)
Teacher's mark		.27 (22)	−.15 (20)
Coherence			−.10 (96)

[a]p < .01

Source: Adapted from Langer (1984).

were given to the work of the same students who received high teacher marks. On the other hand, the relationship between coherence and the number of words and clauses, which is negative, was not significant. Therefore, the relationship between these two scoring methods can be said to be unrelated (or nonsignificant). (A detailed explanation of significance is in Chapter 8, Reading and Interpreting Results Sections.)

Researchers also use correlations in comparative studies to make predictions. Researchers can predict the existence or occurrence of one variable when a strong relationship has been established between that variable and another. For example, the high positive correlation shown in Table 2.3 between the holistic scoring method and teachers' marks of students' papers might be used to make this prediction: Students' writing that receives high scores through holistic scoring procedures most likely will receive high marks from teachers. Holistic scoring is not the cause of students receiving high marks from teachers. Whatever characteristics make students' writing receive high scores in one scoring method probably are responsible for high scores in the other, but the research data reported in Table 2.3 give no inkling what that third, causative variable is. Thus, researchers' use of one variable as a predictor of another variable or event is not justification for considering the first variable as a causative factor.

Experimental Research

In experimental research, researchers set out to answer questions about causation. They wish to attribute the change in one variable to the effect of one or more other variables. For example, one group of researchers (Team A) may be concerned with finding answers to questions such as "Will students who receive one type of reading aid (text with focusing questions interspersed every three paragraphs) have better comprehension than students who have a second reading aid (text with key ideas underlined)?" Another research team (Team B) may want to know "Will students who are taught to use calculators for solving mathematical problems do better on final tests than students who do not receive that instruction?""

The influencing variable—the one to which researchers wish to attribute causation—is called the **independent variable.** Independent variables are measurable human and nonhuman characteristics. For example, age (years or months), intelligence (average, above average, superior), sensitivity to noise (high or low), intensity of light (high or low), frequency of an occurrence (never, sometimes, often), and teaching style (democratic, autonomous), to name a few, can be independent variables. Sometimes the independent variable is called the *experimental variable.* When the independent variable is an activity of the researcher, it is called a *treatment variable.* Researchers manipulate or subcategorize all independent variables; they can study the effects of two or more aspects of the variable by subcategorizing it. In the questions of Team A and Team B above, the treatment, or activity, in Team A's research is type of reading aid (focus questions or underlining). Team B's treatment is type of mathematics instruction (with calculator or without calculator). When nontreatment characteristics such as age or intelligence are used as independent variables, researchers can also subcategorize them (for example, 6-year-olds, 8-year-olds; average, above-average intelligence).

The acted-upon variable—the one being studied for possible change—is called the **dependent variable.** Not all human characteristics can be used as dependent variables. Reading ability is something that researchers might wish to change, as is degree of self-concept or teachers' comprehension-questioning behavior. Something such as age, obviously, cannot be a dependent variable, because individuals' ages are not subject to modification—people will mature according to their biological clocks. The dependent variable for Team A is comprehension performance and for Team B is problem-solving performance on tests.

An example of the attribution of causality is found in the research of a team that studied special education students. They wanted to find out the effect of implementing a process for readying students to transition successfully from special education resource rooms to regular classrooms for mathematics instruction (Fuchs, Fuchs, & Fernstrom, 1993). They found that special students who received instruction that involved the use of curriculum-based measurement and transitional programing had substantially reduced time spent in special education math classes and significantly greater math achievement on posttests. In this study, the transitional programing (identifying needs through curriculum-based measurement and teaching needed skills) was the independent variable; math progress was the dependent variable.

The following is an example of the attribution of causality in a study without a treatment. A team of researchers studied how parent configuration (two-parent, mother-extended, or solo-mother) and number of siblings affect first graders' conformity to a model of student role as measured by their absences, latenesses, and conduct marks (Thompson, Entwisle, Alexander, & Sundius, 1992). Here, differences in first graders' roles as students (dependent variable) were examined to see if it changed as a result of their family structure (independent variable). However, the researchers did not engage in an activity, or treatment.

Researchers can study the individual or combined effect of several independent variables on a dependent variable, or of one independent variable on two or more dependent variables. An example of experimental research in which two independent variables were examined had the purpose of testing the effects on students' comprehension of providing them with relevant background knowledge and two versions of content area text (McKeown, Beck, Sinatra, & Loxterman,

1992). In the study, the two independent variables were (a) provision of background knowledge and (b) coherence of the text. The dependent variable was comprehension of the text.

A study in which one independent variable was examined for its effect on several dependent variables set out to determine whether

> text explicitness would enhance children's *silent reading rates, their ratings of story interest, their abilities to recall stories and answer questions about them,* and *ratings of their overall understanding of stories* [italics added to identify the dependent variables]. (Sundbye, 1987, p. 86)

The researcher can conclude that something (text explicitness) caused a change in something else (students' reaction to stories). Researchers can make causative conclusions because they make decisions about the control of variables that are not of concern in descriptive or comparative research. **Control** is use of procedures by the researchers to limit or account for the possible influence of variables not being studied. They use these controls before the research is done (a priori). The control of these **extraneous variables** can be done in one or more ways. Two ways to develop control in experimental studies are presented below. (Extended discussions of these and other ways to control extraneous variables are found in Chapter 5, Reading and Evaluating Subject Sections, and Chapter 7, Reading and Evaluating Procedure Sections.)

In the study about the use of relevant background knowledge and two versions of content area text (McKeown, Beck, Sinatra, & Loxterman, 1992), a variable that might possibly affect students' reading comprehension is reading ability. The researchers controlled for the possible effect of students' reading ability by dividing them equally into two groups based on the results of a standardized reading test. This way, the researchers had two groups of comparable readers, and the results could be determined to be the result of factors other than reading ability.

However, other variables might account for researchers' results. To control for the possible effect of such things as students' interest, learning style, and general learning ability and possible researcher bias in selecting the subjects, researchers can use randomization to group the subjects in the treatment groups (those to whom the independent variables were applied). **Randomization** is an unbiased, systematic selection or assignment of subjects. When they use randomization, researchers assume that most human characteristics are evenly distributed among the groups.

In the above illustrations, researchers had the opportunity to manipulate the independent variable before doing the research. Sometimes, however, researchers want answers to questions but cannot manipulate the independent variable for practical or ethical reasons. They realize a condition exists and are unsure about what might have been its cause. For example, researchers might be interested in why some children develop autistic tendencies after birth. They question whether prenatal conditions might account for the development of the autistic tendencies. In such a case, it would be unethical to create an experimental study in which researchers manipulate the prenatal environment. But by starting with the effect (children with autistic tendencies) and identifying possible causes (nutrition, mother's age, ingestion of abusive substances, illness), researchers can try to establish a cause-effect relationship. This ex post facto (after-the-fact) research is called **causal-comparative research.**

The name causal-comparative research can be confusing when discussing experimental research. This type of research is comparative because researchers compare possible independent variables to see which variable, if any, has a strong relationship with the already known outcome. It is more than comparative research because the data analysis procedures do more than compare or correlate; the researchers analyze data with the purpose of establishing causality. Since researchers cannot establish a cause-effect relationship experimentally, they do so rationally. They take already intact groups—mothers whose children show autistic tendencies and mothers whose children do not—and compare them statistically under controlled conditions. The groups already differ on the independent and dependent variables. The researchers do not induce differences; they seek to identify one or more preexisting conditions (independent variables) in one group that exist to a lesser degree in the other. When researchers identify one or more conditions, they can attribute causality; however, this attribution may be less strong than in an experimental design where the researchers can control all of the variables.

An illustration of causal-comparative research in education is given in a study about reading comprehension and creativity in the use of English by blacks (DeLain, Pearson, & Anderson, 1985). The research team

> explored the hypothesis that the rich and varied experience of black youth with figurative language outside school would enhance their understanding of figurative language in school texts. Results confirmed that for black students, "sounding" skill, as well as general verbal ability, has a direct influence on figurative language comprehension. Black language ability influences figurative language comprehension indirectly through its effect on sounding skill. For white students, only general verbal ability affects figurative language comprehension. (p. 155)

In this exploratory study, the independent variables, "sounding" or "playing the dozens" and general verbal ability, already existed within and varied between black and white students. The researchers could not manipulate the variables, nor could they teach the ritual-insult verbal play in a school setting. Also, differences in the dependent variable, understanding figurative language, existed. The researchers, in an ex post facto study, examined the possible causative linkage. They used causal-comparative research to draw conclusions about the positive influence of black youths' ability to "sound" and their ability to understand school-based figurative language.

A limitation of causal-comparative research is that researchers cannot have the same assurance that they do in experimental research about the cause-effect linkage. Often, and whenever possible, causal-comparative results need to be confirmed by experimental research. Causal-comparative research also lacks other controls used by researchers in experimental research. Randomization of subjects among treatments or the creation of closely comparable groups is usually not possible. Also, researchers cannot control the quality of students' previous experiences that relate to the independent variable. And, the people selected for the study may differ on some other variable that the researchers did not consider.

These limitations show up in causal-comparative research as an estimate of unaccounted-for influence. When there is a large unaccounted-for influence, researchers must seek and test other independent variables for the possible cause of a recognized result.

Analysis of Experimental Statistical Data. After data are collected in experimental studies, measures of central tendency (means) and variability (standard deviations) are created. This descriptive information forms the basis of other statistical procedures. When researchers conduct simple one-variable studies, they use a common statistical procedure known as the *t*-test. The **t-test** is used to determine whether the difference between the means of two groups on a dependent variable is significant; that is, whether the examined results could have happened by chance or whether the researchers can reliably attribute the difference to the influence of the independent variable.

But, as discussed previously, single-variable studies provide limited insight about educational questions. Multiple-variable research requires the calculation of many *t*-tests, which is awkward, possibly misleading, and limiting since the interaction among multiple variables cannot be shown by *t*-tests. To overcome this limitation, researchers use the **analysis of variance (ANOVA).** Results of an ANOVA are reported in **F-ratios.** ANOVAs are used to determine whether differences can be attributed to one or a combination of independent variables.

Table 2.4 contains a common form for reporting ANOVA results. The information is taken from a study about the effect of reading placement (instructional

Table 2.4
Reporting of ANOVA Results: Summary Tables for a Two-Way Analysis of Variance

Analysis of Variance of Vocabulary Achievement Scores
by Potential and Placement Level

Source	df	MS	F
Potential (A)	1	9236.14	10.45**
Placement (P)	2	4107.70	4.65*
Potential X Placement (AP)	2	167.09	0.19
Error (S/AP)	298	884.12	
Total	303		

$* p < .05$ $** p < .01$

Analysis of Variance of Comprehension Test Scores
by Potential and Placement Level

Source	df	MS	F
Potential (A)	1	38070.15	17.11**
Placement (P)	2	4083.84	1.84
Potential X Placement (AP)	2	1434.62	0.67
Error (S/AP)	298	2224.74	
Total	303		

$** p < .01$

Source: Homan, Hines, & Kromrey, 1993.

level vs. above instructional level) and reading potential (disabled reader vs. slow learner) on reading achievement of at-risk sixth-grade students with reading problems (Homan, Hines, & Kromery, 1993). The results show that there were significant differences for vocabulary achievement based on Potential and Placement. There was no difference shown in vocabulary achievement when Potential and Placement were considered together (Potential x Placement). On comprehension tests, only Potential showed significant differences. (Chapter 8 contains a more detailed discussion of the concepts of significance and ANOVA.)

QUALITATIVE RESEARCH

Qualitative research is a term used for a broad range of research strategies that has roots in the research of the social sciences, especially the field research of anthropology and sociology (Bogdan & Biklen, 1992; Eisner, 1991; Firestone, 1987, 1993; Guthrie & Hall, 1984; Jacob, 1987, 1988; LeCompte, Millory, & Preissle, 1992; Lincoln & Guba, 1985; Marshall & Rossman, 1995; Smith, 1987; Smith & Heshusius, 1986; Van Maanen, Dabbs, & Faulkner, 1982; and Wilson, 1977). Terms closely associated with qualitative research are **ethnographic** and ethnologic **research** and interpretive research. Some researchers distinguish between ethnography and ethnology as types of qualitative research methods. For the purposes of this text, the terms ethnography and ethnology are used solely for the type of research undertaken by anthropologists studying whole cultures. They are not used for the work of researchers from education, psychology, and social science who borrow the terms but not the underlying theoretical framework of anthropological ethnography (Jacob, 1989). Some researchers prefer the term "interpretive research" to avoid the connotation of defining research as "nonquantitative" since some sort of quantification can be used (Erickson, 1986).

Characteristics

Qualitative research is characterized not by the use of numerical values but by the use of text—written words—to document variables and the inductive analysis of the collected information. Qualitative researchers are not concerned with numerical (statistical) analysis of the frequency of when or how things happen. They look to inductively answer research questions by examining students and others who influence them in natural contexts, in interaction with other people and objects in their surroundings (Hatch, 1995). Although that approach is often considered as subjective, it is based on broad and comprehensive theoretical positions.

Qualitative research can be subcategorized by the expected outcomes of a study (Eisner, 1991; Marshall & Rossman, 1995; Peshkin, 1993). The basic qualitative research purposes are to describe, to interpret, to verify, and to evaluate. In *descriptive analysis,* the researcher gives an account of a place or process. The purpose is to visualize a situation as a means for understanding what is happening. In *interpretive analysis*, the researcher explains or creates generalizations. The purpose is to develop new concepts or elaborate on existing ones. The researcher provides insights that might lead to teachers changing their behavior, refining their knowledge, or identifying problems. Interpretive analysis also can be used to develop new theories. In *verification analysis*, the researcher verifies assumptions, theories, and generalizations. In *evaluative analysis*, the researcher provides judgments about policies, practices, and innovative instructional practices. The researcher tries to answer questions such as "Has an instructional procedure been implemented? With what impact? What has the process of implementation been like? How has it worked? For whom has it worked? Are there any exceptions?"

Qualitative research has several distinct features (Bogdan & Biklen, 1992; Eisner, 1991; Firestone, 1987; Guthrie & Hall, 1984; Jacob, 1987, 1988; Lancy, 1993; Lincoln & Guba, 1985; Smith, 1987; Smith & Heshusius, 1986; Van Maanen, Dabbs, & Faulkner, 1982; Wilson, 1977). First, the issue of context is central to qualitative research. Researchers collect data within the natural setting of the information they seek, and the key data collection instruments are the researchers themselves. This means that researchers wishing to study educational questions must collect relevant information at the data source through direct observation and personal interviews. Contexts (that is, schoolwide situations as well as individual classrooms) do not mean just people and their actions. Contexts are not static, they shape and are shaped by the people involved (teachers and students) as well as the intentions of instruction, the resources available, and the particular time the events are happening (Graue & Walsch, 1995).

The methods for data collection are participant observing, interviewing, reading diaries, scanning records and files, using checklists, and conducting case studies. The basic premise for these methods is that people do not act in isolation. Their behavior and actions occur in specific social contexts or situations, and, therefore, these behaviors and actions must be studied in their natural settings. Researchers must become part of the natural setting and function as participant observers: In educational environments, students and teachers must accept qualitative researchers as regular members of the classroom and not just as observers.

It is on the point of **participant observer** that some researchers distinguish between qualitative and ethnographic research. If researchers do not collect data in natural settings as total group members, the research may be considered by some researchers as qualitative but not ethnographic. Ethnographic research to them requires researchers to be fully integrated members of the educational environment. This distinction has been called the *insider and outsider perspective* (Lancy, 1993; Van Maanen, Dabbs, & Faulkner, 1982). The insider becomes part of the group and tries to detail what the members of the group know and how this knowledge guides their behavior. The outsider remains separate and tries to describe aspects of the social situation about which the groups' members may be unaware. Rarely, however, do participant observers function as pure outsiders or insiders.

The second major feature of qualitative research is that the data are verbal, not numerical. Although qualitative researchers may use checklists to count the frequency of occurrences of educational events, behaviors, and activities, these quantifications are for noting trends and not for presenting pictures of averages.

Third, qualitative researchers are concerned with the process of an activity rather than only the outcomes of that activity. In educational settings, qualitative researchers look at instructional activities within the total context of classrooms and schools. They want to describe the ongoing interactions occurring during instruction rather than to note only whether the students have increased their test scores.

Fourth, qualitative researchers analyze the data rationally rather than statistically. The outcomes of much qualitative research are the generation of research questions and conjectures, not the verification of predicted mathematical relationships or outcomes. This is an additional key feature of qualitative research. Because some qualitative research is descriptive, many of its data collection procedures are similar to those found in quantitative descriptive research. A distinguishing feature between the two is the use in qualitative research of the search for logical patterns within and among aspects of the research setting. To some researchers, especially those who hold to a strong belief in quantitative analysis, qualitative analysis may seem to lack objectivity. Nevertheless, the contributions of qualitative researchers are their ability to identify and interpret patterns of human responses as a result of their knowledge, experiences, and theoretical orientations to education. (Chapters 7 and 8 contain additional discussions about the role of subjectivity in qualitative research.)

An illustrative qualitative research study involved a field investigation of classroom management from the perspective of high school students (Allen, 1986). The study was based on the assumption "that classroom contexts interact with students' agenda and result in variations in students' perspectives of the management of the classroom" (p. 438). Data were gathered (a) from the students' perspective, (b) from different classroom management situations, (c) by uncovering the students' agendas, and (d) by analyzing the underlying theoretical constructs. To become part of the groups, the researcher enrolled in a ninth grade schedule so that he could learn about the students' perspective by taking the role of a student. He wished to gain the students' confidence, so he asked the teachers to treat him as any other student. After the classes began, he avoided contact with the teachers. The researcher attended four morning classes each day and did not volunteer information about himself to the students until they questioned him. Then, he emphasized his student role, deemphasized that of being a researcher, and participated in classwork, activities, tests, and homework assignments. During class he took observational notes under the guise of taking class notes.

In sum, qualitative research views "classroom behavior in the larger context of cultural standards and patterns of behavior, goals of participants, behavior settings, and social influences beyond the classroom. The implications are significant for our understanding of education" (Jacob, 1987, p. 38).

Figure 2.2 contains a summary comparison of quantitative and qualitative research.

	Quantitative Research	Qualitative Research
Words used to describe	experimental hard data empirical postivist statistical objective	ethnographic fieldwork naturalistic descriptive participant observation soft data subjective
Key concepts	variables operationalize reliability validity statistical significance replication prediction	contextualization process field notes triangulation insider/outsider perspective meaning is of chief concern making judgments
Design	structured predetermined	evolves over time flexible developing hypotheses
Data	statistical operationalized variables	descriptive field notes documents interviews
Sample	randomized control for extraneous variables size is important	nonrepresentative can be small
Techniques	experiments standardized instruments structured interview structured observation	observation open-ended interview review of documents participant observation researcher as instrument
Data analysis	deductive statistical	ongoing inductive
Problems with approach	control of extraneous variables validity	time consuming data reduction is difficult reliability generalizability nonstandardized procedures

Figure 2.2
Comparison of Qualitative and Quantitative Research

SUMMARY

What are the major designs used to conduct educational research?

Two basic research designs based on the way information, or data, is collected and analyzed are quantitative research and qualitative research.

What are quantitative descriptive, comparative, and experimental research?

Descriptive research is done to answer questions about a variable's status. Comparative research is done to make decisions about two or more variables' differences or relationships. Experimental research is done to draw conclusions about the cause-effect relationship between two or more variables.

What distinguishes the three types of quantitative research designs from each other?

Descriptive and comparative research may reveal status, patterns, and associations among variables, but only experimental research can be used to attribute causality.

What are the instruments used to collect quantitative data?

Data are collected with instruments, which are direct observation forms, tests, and surveys (questionnaires and interviews).

How are data analyzed in each of the three types of quantitative research designs?

In descriptive research, information most often is described with means and standard deviations. In comparative research, in addition to the descriptive measures of data, two common statistical procedures are correlation and the Chi square. In experimental research, common statistical procedures are the *t*-test and analysis of variance or ANOVA.

What are central tendency and variability, and how are they measured?

Central tendency is the average or middle score in a group of scores. The middle score is called the median; the arithmetic average score is called the mean. Variability is the extent to which other scores in the group cluster about or spread from the mean. The variability is usually reported as the standard deviation.

What are the major purposes for conducting qualitative research?

The basic qualitative research purposes are to describe, to interpret, to evaluate, and to verify.

What are the major features of qualitative research?

The major features of qualitative research are that (a) data is collected within natural educational settings and the major data collection instrument is the researcher observer; (b) data is verbal, not numerical; (c) researchers are concerned with process rather than outcomes alone; and (d) data are analyzed rationally, not statistically.

ACTIVITIES

Effective learning can be gained from the following activities when they are done with another class student. This peer interacting can follow a simple format:

a. Each student reads and does an activity.

b. Each student explains to the other what the response is and why that response is chosen.

c. The students' responses are compared to the authors' feedback.

d. If there are differences between peer responses or between peer responses and the authors' feedback, students should refer to the text or the course instructor for verification.

Activity 1

For each of the research purposes, questions, and hypotheses listed below, indicate (a) the type of research design (descriptive, comparative, experimental, causal-comparative, qualitative) and (b) the research variables. For experimental or causal-comparative designs, differentiate between the independent and dependent variables. **Note**: Some of the studies have more than one research purpose.

1. The researchers interviewed elementary teachers about their teaching theories and classroom practices. (Hughes & Wedman, 1992)

2. [The researchers] compared the lesson on addition and subtraction of signed whole numbers in three seventh-grade Japanese mathematics textbooks with the corresponding lesson in four U.S. mathematics textbooks. (Mayer, Sims, & Tajika, 1995).

3. The researchers investigated the effects of type of narrative text (story vs. play) and mode of reading (group oral vs. silent) on reading comprehension performance of high-, average-, and low-ability junior high school pupils. (Mullikin, Henk, & Fortner, 1992)

4. The hypotheses of the study were that, regarding one wage earner from each household in a small town (a) higher levels of education will be associated with higher volumes of certain (but not all) content of reading than lower levels of education; and, (b) occupational category will be associated with different volumes of certain (but not all) content for reading. (Guthrie, Seifert, & Kirsch, 1986).

5. [The researchers purpose] was to identify variables meaningfully associated with mainstreaming success in science classes. . . . Evidence gathered included using observational field notes, student and teacher products, videotaped records, curriculum marterials, and interviews with students, teachers, and administrators (Scruggs & Mastropieri, 1994)

Activity 2

Using a research report of your own choosing or one from Appendix B, (a) locate the research hypothesis, purpose, or question, (b) indicate the research design, and (c) identify the research variables. For experimental or causal-comparative research, indicate the independent and dependent variables.

FEEDBACK

Activity 1

1. (a) This was descriptive research. (b) The research variables were the teachers' theories and practices. Data were collected that described the theories and classroom practices of the teachers. No causality was presumed.

2. (a) The study was comparative. (b) The research variable was the mathematics lessons. The researchers compared how lessons were presented in the mathematics textbooks of two countries. Again, no causality was presumed.

3. (a) The study was experimental. (b) The two independent (experimental) variables were "type of narrative text" and "mode of reading." The dependent variable was "reading comprehension." Causality *was* presumed—the experimental variables would cause a change in the pupils' comprehension.

4. (a) The study was causal-comparative because both the independent variables, "higher levels of education" (hypothesis a) and "occupational category" (hypothesis b) were in existence prior to the study. The dependent variable in both parts of the study was "content of reading. (b) Causality *was* presumed—level of education and occupational category would cause differences in reading content.

5. (a) The study was qualitative descriptive. Although it is not entirely possible to identify it as qualitative research, one signal that the researchers were conducting a qualitative study is the use of "field notes" for data collection. (b) The researchers wish to identify variables that deal with success in mainstreaming students in science classes.

CHAPTER 3

Reading and Evaluating Research Reports

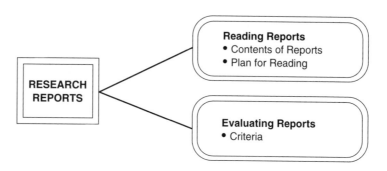

FOCUS QUESTIONS

1. What are the major sections of research reports?
2. What is an effective strategy for reading research reports?
3. What are the criteria for evaluating the quality and appropriateness of research reports?

Research consumers read research reports to increase their general knowledge about educational practice, to acquire knowledge that they can apply in professional practices, and to gain insights about effective instructional procedures that they can use in classrooms.

A **research report** is not research. Research is conducted by systematically collecting information about an identified problem or question, analyzing the data, and, on the basis of the evidence, confirming or disconfirming a prior prediction or statement. A research report is a summary of researchers' activities and results. Research consumers can judge the effectiveness of research producers and the appropriateness of their results only by reading and evaluating research reports.

Research reports are pictures of research: They are representations of what researchers have done and how they wish to present their research procedures to the public. Four pictures of research are possible: (a) good research methodology, well reported; (b) good research methodology, poorly reported; (c) poor research methodology, well reported; and (d) poor research methodology, poorly reported.

Research consumers' ability will be tested in identifying the second and third pictures. In situation (b), researchers might have conducted appropriate research and reported it inappropriately; in situation (c), they might have conducted inappropriate research and dressed it in the garb of an appropriate research report.

This chapter explains the contents of research reports, presents models of well-written research reports, demonstrates effective report-reading procedures for research consumers, and lists questions for evaluating the quality of research reports. These evaluative questions form the bases for discussions in succeeding chapters about reading and analyzing research methods.

READING RESEARCH REPORTS

Contents of Research Reports

Research reports contain information related to research producers' questions and their research activities. This information is organized to show researchers' efforts in

Selecting a problem area

Specifying research questions

Describing subjects

Describing instruments

Explaining procedures and treatments (if appropriate)

Presenting results based on data analyses

Discussing implications

The information is generally organized into sections with headings such as Background or Literature Review; Purpose, Questions, or Hypotheses; Method, including Subjects, Instruments, and Procedure; Results; Conclusions; and References.

The **background section** contains (a) an explanation of the researchers' problem area, (b) its educational importance, (c) summaries of other researchers' results that are related to the problem (called a literature review), and (d) strengths from the related research that were used and weaknesses or limitations that were changed. The background section is often preceded by an **abstract**, a summary of the report. Researchers usually omit the literature review from the abstract.

The **purpose section** contains the specific goal or goals of the research project. These can be expressed as a statement of purpose, as questions, or as a hypothesis. The following is an example from a research report in which both a purpose and specific questions are expressed.

> The overall focus of this study, then, was to examine the role that varying levels of context and dictionary definitions play in college students' acquisition of new words, assessed under four different testing formats. The following two questions were posed:
>
> 1. Are there significant differences in subjects' abilities to learn and remember new vocabulary words depending on strength of context and adequacy of dictionary definitions?

2. Can significant differences in subjects' abilities to learn and remember new vocabulary words as a function of context and dictionary definitions be replicated across four levels of word knowledge? (Nist & Olejnik, 1995, p. 179)

From reading the purpose section, research consumers can identify and classify the type of research and the research variables (independent and dependent when appropriate). In the above example, the words *role*, *play*, and *acquisition* indicate that something is making something else change. They are clues to the type of research method—in this case, experimental research. In questions Q1 and Q2, the independent variables were "strength of context" and "adequacy of dictionary definitions." In Q2, a third independent variable, "levels of word knowledge," was included. In Q1 and Q2, the dependent variables were "ability to learn" and "ability to remember new vocabulary words."

Sometimes, researchers (for example, Nist & Olejnik, 1995) do not place their purpose, questions, or hypotheses in a section with a separate heading. In such cases, they include this information in the background section, most often in the section's last paragraph.

The following is an example in which hypotheses are stated in a subheaded section. Notice how the researcher predicted the expected results.

Research Hypotheses

The following hypotheses were made:

(a) The on-set/rime analogy explanation is a more viable explanation than the phoneme blending explanation for how young children learn to recode unfamiliar graphophonological print phonologically;

(b) the more print words children recognize, the better they are able to make analogies between letter strings representing onsets and rimes in known and unknown words to recode unknown ones phonologically; and

(c) young children's ability to recode unfamiliar print phonologically is constrained when they have difficulty reversing their perceptions of parts and wholes in print. (Moustafa, 1995, p. 468)

The **method section** of research reports usually contains several subsections. These are: subjects, instruments, and procedure.

The **subjects section** contains a description of the individuals included in the study, giving general information about such factors as age, sex, grade level, intellectual and academic abilities, and socioeconomic level. It also contains the number of subjects and an account of how the subjects were selected and assigned to groups. The subjects section is sometimes labeled "Sample" or "Participants." The following is a typical subjects section:

The sample included 118 students from Grades 3 and 6 in three middle-class elementary schools in an urban area of inland southern California. All three schools were ethnically diverse, with approximately 60% White, 30% Hispanic (predominately Mexican-American), 5% Black, and 5% Asian-American students each. Three hundred fifteen students who were asked to participate in the study had, according to school records and teachers' reports, at least average proficiency in English. None was classified as being gifted, having learning or emotional problems, or being involved in special education. One hundred twenty-nine students returned parental consent forms and were included in the original sample. Data from 11 of the students—that is, 6 third graders and 5 sixth graders—were not usable because of problems with tape recording, student absence, and faulty procedure. The numbers and ages of the students who remained in the sample were: 18 boys, 41 girls (mean age = 9.0 years, SD = 0.3) at Grade 3 and 29 boys, 30 girls (mean age = 12.1 years, SD = 0.4) at Grade 6. This sample represented 11 third-grade classrooms (3 to 9 students, median = 5, from each classroom) and 10 sixth-grade classrooms (2 to 9 students, median = 7, from each). (Newman & Schwager, 1995, p. 357)

The **instruments section** contains a description of the data collection instruments: observation forms, standardized and researcher-made tests, and surveys. When instruments are standardized tests, researchers usually assume the readers' familiarity with them and do little more than name them. (In Chapter 6, Reading and Evaluating Instrument Sections, is an explanation of how readers can obtain information about unfamiliar standardized tests.) When instruments are less well known, researchers describe or give examples of them and give evidence of their effectiveness. If tests other than standardized tests were administered, researchers explain the testing circumstances and the qualifications or training of the test givers and provide information about the test and how it was constructed. If observations or surveys were used, researchers relate how they were done and how the observers or interviewers were trained.

The following is a typical instruments section, which explains in detail how the researchers developed one instrument, an attitude inventory, and which refers to another, unexplained test, a cloze test.

INSTRUMENTS

The Student Attitude Inventory (SAI) was used as a pre- and post-test measure. Constructed by the researchers, the SAI contains 33 questions related to five areas: listening (7 items), speaking (7 items), reading (8 items), writing (6 items), and self-perceptions as learners (5 items). The items contained in the SAI were generated from a compilation of statements made by elementary students over a period of four years, who were responding to learning activities presented by preservice teachers during language arts practicum assignments. The practicum assignments included integrated language arts activities and elementary students would spontaneously comment about how much they enjoyed or disliked specific kinds (i.e., listening, reading, speaking, or writing) of activities. Preservice teachers reported students' comments to the university instructors, who sorted the comments according to the area represented. The researchers (i.e., course instructors) pulled from the item groupings the most frequently occurring statements and edited them for content and clarity.

The SAI may be administered individually or in a group setting, with respondents marking the face illustration that best represents their feelings. Five face illustrations are shown at the end of each question, ranging from a big smile to a big frown. Respondents are told that the face illustrations represent the following feelings: very happy, happy, neither happy nor sad, sad, and very sad. The SAI includes questions, such as *Listening:* How do you feel when someone reads a story to you? How do you feel when your teacher tells you the steps to follow in an activity rather than having you read the steps? *Speaking:* How do you feel when someone asks you to tell about something that has happened to you or something that you have done? How do you feel when you are given the chance to tell someone about a story that you have read? *Reading:* How do you feel when you are asked to read written directions and the teacher does not explain them? How do you feel when you have the opportunity to read magazines? *Writing:* How do you feel when you are writing a note to a friend or parent and you do not know how to spell a word? How do you feel when your teacher asks you to write a story? *Self- perceptions as Learners:* How do you feel when you are asked to complete an assignment alone? How to you feel when you are asked to be the leader of a group activity?

A Likert scale, ranging from 5 to 1, is used to score the SAI with 5 representing "very happy" and 1 representing "very sad." Area scores on the SAI are obtained by summing the item responses in each of the five areas. The possible scores for Listening, Speaking, Reading, Writing, and Self-Perceptions as Learners are 35, 35, 40, 30, and 25, respectively. Summing the area scores produces a possible total score of 165. The researchers examined the internal consistency of the SAI and found that alpha coefficients for the area scores were as follows: .74 (Listening), .74 (Speaking), .82 (Reading), .77 (Writing), and .74 (Self-Perceptions as Learners), with .93 being the alpha coefficient for the overall (total) score. The validity of the SAI was examined by correlating the total scores obtained by a sample of 47 elementary students on the SAI with their total scores on the Elementary Reading Attitude Survey (ERAS); the obtained Pearson Product Moment correlation coefficient was .44 ($p < .002$), which the authors considered to be adequate for research purposes.

An oral cloze test was administered at the beginning of the study to determine whether differences existed initially between the treatment and comparison groups in their abilities to meaningfully process oral language. The cloze test contained 9 sentences with deletions representing 3 categories: final, initial, and medial positions (i.e., 3 sentences per deletion category). (Thames & Reeves, 1994, pp. 296–298)

The **procedure section**, a subsection of the method section, contains a detailed explanation of how researchers conducted their study. In descriptive and comparative studies, researchers explain how data were collected and analyzed. In experimental studies, researchers also describe the treatments and how they were administered. If special instructional materials were prepared for the study, they are described and often sample portions are included.

The following example is a typical procedure section. It is taken from an experimental study about the effects of literacy-enriched play settings and adult mediation of the children's play on the children's literacy-related play.

PROCEDURES

Baseline period. Prior to the intervention phase of the study, children's play behaviors during their 1-hour indoor free play time were observed in each classroom over a 2-day period. Following an observational procedure developed by Smith and Connolly (1980), a research assistant first identified a particular child, then recorded (using a small portable tape recorder) the general activity and the specific behavior exhibited by the child for a period of 40 seconds. Ten seconds were used to rest and then to identify the next child for observation. In this manner, children's play behavior in each classroom was observed by two trained research assistants over a 17-minute period, followed by two additional rounds. Because activity spans for this age group generally occur every 10 minutes, this procedure allowed us to observe each child engaged in a variety of play behaviors. Three rounds were recorded each day, for a total of six samples per child over the 2 days.

Research assistants were asked not to interpret behavior, but to record only the children's actual behaviors in play. These behaviors were then categorized into demonstrations of handling (focusing on the physical exploration of a literacy object), reading (attributing meaning to environmental and functional print), and writing (attempting to use printed marks as a form of communication) to provide a detailed analysis of children's literacy-based play activities.

Intervention. Guided by principles established in our previous research (Neuman & Roskos, 1990b; 1992), we redesigned a play area into a literacy-enriched office setting in the six intervention classrooms. Specifically, these changes were defined by: (a) the principle of definition (clearly demarcating play settings from one another); (b) the principle of adaptation (reworking typical play settings to resemble real-life literacy contexts); and (c) the principle of familiarity (inserting a network of prototypical literacy objects into known settings). Thus, through the strategic placement of semifixed structures, like shelves and classroom furniture, we adapted an existing play area (an art table) into an office play setting and included such signs, labels, and common objects as a telephone, calendar, in/out trays, and paper and pencils to encourage literacy interactions through play. In this respect, we interpreted the concept of "office" broadly as any location where daily human affairs may be handled using literacy.

In each setting, we inserted seven alphabetic labels or signs (e.g., OFFICE EXIT). As shown in Figure 1 [not reprinted here], a large "office" sign designated the play setting in each room. Signs in their typical logos were displayed prominently throughout the play space. For example, the word "EXIT" was located above the doorway in each "office"; the "COME IN, we're OPEN" sign was placed in front of the play setting when it was available for play and replaced by "Sorry, We're CLOSED," at the end of each play session. A "time in/time out" sign was displayed on the bulletin board at all times. Each setting also included "Hello, my name is . . ." labels for children as they entered the play area and play money for all "cash" transactions. Our goal, in strategically locating these signs and labels in functional settings, was to simulate a context that might encourage children to read print as if it were in their real-life environment.

In addition, each setting included 10 common functional print items (e.g., telephone book, calendar) that one might see in any typical office, like a gas station or a clinic. Designed to be used by the children, these items were easily available and clustered together in the office setting to enhance sustained literacy interactions. For example, a telephone, telephone book, and message pad were organized together in one area, whereas materials for mailing letters—stationery, envelopes, stamps, and mail box—were placed in an adjacent area. Clustering these items allowed for at least four to six children to play in the office setting at one time.

Following these design changes, parent-teachers and teachers met with researchers and two research assistants to discuss the general procedures of the project. Although we asked that the structural features of the setting and signs and labels remain consistent throughout the study, parent-teachers were encouraged to take responsibility for the office play setting in their respective classrooms, to keep it well-stocked with materials from our storeroom, and to "invent" new projects or scenarios over the course of the project to encourage children to make use of the play setting. Further, because it was important to monitor children's play, parent-teachers were asked to remain around the office area during free play time and not to be drawn into other classroom tasks or activities. Classroom teachers and aides were encouraged to observe and interact with children in areas other than the office play setting.

Parent-teachers from the two intervention groups met separately with the research team. Those assigned to intervene in the office play setting (Group 1) were asked to actively assist young children in their literacy-related play. Didactic teaching of letters or numbers was discouraged; rather, we suggested that what young children seemed to need most were conversations with adults in ways that might serve to integrate their knowledge of the world. For example, adults might contribute to extending a play scene by "taking an order" or helping the child to "write a prescription" or modeling a relevant literacy behavior, like "making a list"—behaviors that were contingent on children's efforts and interests. These examples were designed to give parent-teachers general guidelines for interactions, rather than specific strategies, with the understanding that they themselves might be our most knowledgeable informers.

Those assigned to monitor the office play setting (Group 2) were encouraged to observe children's play, to take notes on the quality of the play behavior, to describe children's favorite activities, to step in when necessary to end a dispute, but not to directly "play" with the children. Basically, they were asked to establish "rapport" behaviors (Wood, McMahon, & Cranstoun, 1980), giving gentle reminders to children that an adult was available if necessary, but with subtle encouragement to interact among themselves.

The office play setting was "open" to children for 3 days a week over a 5-month period. This schedule allowed teachers flexibility in arranging field trips and other special projects on the other 2 days. During the 3 days, the parent-teacher would announce that the office was "open" by displaying the sign, "COME IN, We're OPEN," and encouraging the children to play there during their free time. However, no children were ever assigned to the office play setting; instead, they were allowed to move freely about all areas in the classroom.

During the free play time, the "interactive" parent-teachers, Wanda, Michelle, and Lolita (Group 1), were active participants in children's spontaneous free play in the office. In this group, they were likely to sit at one of the desks with the children by their side and assist in their play activities by using the literacy objects for functional purposes, like "ordering a pizza" or "taking a telephone message." On the other hand, the "monitoring" parent-teacher (Group 2) would first focus on setting the stage in play and then would observe children's ongoing activities. James, for example, would situate himself in a rocking chair outside of the play space and record interesting vignettes to share with us, while the other parent-teachers, Tracy and Nancy, would monitor from inside the office, often cleaning and straightening children's papers. Although children might ask them occasional questions, they would rarely become involved in the play other than to find some materials or to settle a dispute. In neither case, however, were parent-teachers aware of our interest in children's learning of environmental or functional print. Rather, the goal of the project was to encourage children to simply enjoy playing with print.

A research assistant was assigned to each intervention group and visited classrooms twice weekly. The purpose of these visits was to ensure fidelity to the specific intervention treatment, to informally chat with parent-teachers regarding the children's play activities, and to give them positive feedback for their efforts.

Children in the nonintervention classroom continued to engage in their typical free play activities over the 5-month period. In these classrooms, parent volunteers generally provided support for teacher activities, like chaperoning on field-trips or custodial duties, but provided no direct intervention in children's classroom activities.

During the intervention. To examine the nature of children's literacy interactions, with and without adult assistance, videotaped samples of children's spontaneous free play in classrooms were collected weekly, after the play setting was in place for 1 month. Using a camcorder and a microphone system, a graduate student in language acquisition recorded 15 minutes of play activity in the office play setting in four classrooms per week, for a total of 10 observations per class. These samples yielded a total of 450 minutes, or 7.5 hours of videotaped observation for each intervention group. Rather than focus on individual children, the goal of the videotaping was to obtain samples of children's play themes and literacy interactions with others in the setting throughout the study period.

To examine the influence of the play setting on individual children's play activity, research assistants observed each child's spontaneous play after 8 weeks had elapsed, using the same procedures as in the baseline period.

Following the intervention. During the final 2 weeks of the study, each child's spontaneous play activity was systematically observed once again by research assistants. After observations were completed, two environmental print measures were administered individually to children in the intervention and nonintervention groups: (a) an environmental word reading task and (b) a functional print task.

The environmental word reading task assessed children's ability to read words from the seven labels and signs placed in the office play setting. Each sign was taken from its context in the setting, and was shown to the child in its customary logo form. In cases where there were several words on the sign, we drew the child's attention to a target word by underlining it from left to right and saying, "What does this say?" Target words were: *office, exit, out, closed, open, hello,* and *dollars.*

The functional print tasks, adapted from Lomax and McGee (1987), measured children's knowledge of the functions and uses of written language associated with the specific types of functional print in the office setting. The child was shown, one at a time, 10 functional items: a page of a telephone book, a calendar, a typed business letter, a message pad, a stamp, a catalogue, a brochure, a calculator, and a "speed-letter" (interoffice memo). He or she was asked to identify the item (e.g., What is this?) first and then asked to identify its function (e.g., What do you use it for?). Answers to the environmental word reading and the functional print tasks were recorded verbatim.

One hundred thirty-eight children comprised the final sample size of the study, representing a loss of 22% of the sample due to long-term absences and family relocations. (Neuman & Roskos, 1993, pp. 100–105, Copyright 1993 by the American Educational Research Association. Reprinted by permission of the publisher.)

The **results section** contains the outcomes of the researchers' data analyses. This section contains not only the numerical results (often presented in tables and charts) but an explanation of the significance of those results. To many research consumers, results sections are confusing because of the statistical information. (The next subsection of this chapter, A Plan for Reading Reports, explains how these sections can be read. In Chapter 8, Reading and Interpreting Results Sections, are discussions about how to judge researchers' presentations of both qualitative and quantitative data analyses.)

The following example is a typical results section. It is from an experimental study about the effects of focused Chapter 1 instruction on first-grade students' literacy. Notice that the results of the statistical analysis were reported as part of the commentary and in tables. The results are presented in relation to three perspectives (see the first paragraph of the extract). The results indicated that (a) students who began the year with few literacy proficiencies made substantial progress, (b) the students in the restructured program made greater progress than students in the regular program, and (c) the Chapter 1 students were performing at the same level as the average students in their classes on reading and writing tasks.

RESULTS

The performances of students in the restructured Chapter 1 program are discussed in relation to three perspectives: (1) absolute performances, (2) comparison to Chapter 1 students in the regular program, and (3) comparison to classmates.

Absolute Performances

For parents, teachers, administrators, and, eventually, children themselves, the critical question is, "Can children read grade-level text?" Chapter 1 teachers and administrators also asked the question, "Based on standardized test performances, which children will be eligible for Chapter 1 services next year?" These questions are answered by examining children's absolute levels of performance on reading text and, for Chapter 1 requirements, the standardized test. Table 1 presents the distribution of performances on reading text, and Table 2 presents CTBS–Reading.

In the fall, none of the children in the restructured Chapter 1 program had been able to read even a handful of words independently. In the spring, 77% of the children were able to read at a primer level (which comprises the third quarter of first grade in basal reading programs) or higher, and 55% were reading the first-grade text or higher fluently. Twenty-three percent of the group (10 children) were reading below the primer level, with 3 at the preprimer level, 4 at the predictable book level, and 3 unable to read the predictable book fluently. This group of 10 children had been asked to read the primer text, and their performances were examined on this task. Their average level of fluency was 70%.

Absolute levels were also computed to determine how many children would be designated for Chapter 1 in Grade 2, if the district used a level of 33 NCE as the cut-off. Using that criterion, 56% of the students would no longer be eligible for Chapter 1. If the level for exiting Chapter 1 was lowered to 25 NCE, as had been the case during the year of the project, only 20% of the sample would have remained in Chapter 1.

Table 1 **Percentage of Students in Restructured and Regular Chapter 1 Programs Attaining Fluency at Various Levels on Text-Level Reading Task[a]**

Level of text	Restructured Chapter 1	Regular Chapter 1
Third grade	13%	—
Second grade	18%	—
First grade	24%	6%
Primer	22%	12%
Preprimer	7%	18%
Predictable book	9%	18%
Below predictable book	7%	47%

[a]Totals may be slightly less or more than 100 due to rounding of percentages for individual categories.

Table 2 **Percentage of Students in Restructured and Regular Chapter 1 Programs at Particular NCE Levels on CTBS-Reading[a]**

Level	Restructured Chapter 1	Regular Chapter 1
75–	—	—
50–74	18%	—
33–49[b]	38%	—
25–32	24%	22%
1–24	20%	79%

[a]Totals may be slightly less or more than 100 due to rounding of percentages for individual categories.
[b]The second quartile is divided in this manner because 33 NCE had been set as the cut-off for Chapter 1 placement in this district.

Against a standard of conventional reading as measured by ability to read words, none of the children had been able to read at the beginning of the year. At the end of the year, the majority were reading the texts that are designated for the second half of grade one. However, questions remain about the comparability of this growth to students who were in the regular Chapter 1 and classroom programs.

Comparison With Regular Chapter 1 Students

Students in both the restructured and regular Chapter 1 programs scored well below the 33 NCE level on the readiness measure at the beginning of the year, as is evident in the means for the two groups (restructured: $X = 16.42$, $SD = 7.10$; regular: $X = 12.85$, $SD = 6.35$). Since the t of 2.35 for the test of differences between these two groups was significant at $p < .02$, the multivariate analysis of the six dependent variables (reading text, reading words, writing text, writing words, CTBS–Reading, and CTBS– Language Arts) included the readiness scores as a covariate.

The multivariate within-cell effect was significant (Wilks's lambda = .654, $F = 6.27$, $df = 6,71$, $p < .001$), indicating that the readiness performances accounted for a significant proportion of the variance in students' end-of-year performances. The univariate F ratios, which appear in Table 3, indicate a significant difference on all six measures. For most of the measures, the amount of variance accounted for by the readiness measure was in the range of 11 to 14% (CTBS–Language Arts, 11%; writing words, 12%; writing text, 13%; reading text, 14%). The readiness measure accounted for somewhat more of the variance on reading words (23%) and the most on CTBS–Reading (31%). The test for the interaction between readiness and program was insignificant (Wilks's lambda = .90, $F = 1.34$, $df = 6,70$, $p < .252$), indicating that the pooled covariance across groups adequately summarized the effect of the readiness measure and a separate analysis of the effect of the covariate within each group was not needed.

Even when the effect of readiness is controlled, the program effect persists, as is evident in the significant multivariate effect for program (Wilks's lambda = .567, $F = 9.02$, $df = 6,71$, $p < .001$). The presentation of univariate F ratios for program in Table 3 shows that differences between students' performances in the restructured and regular programs were significant at the $p < .001$ level for all six measures.

Absolute levels of performance for the students in the regular Chapter 1 program were also considered and are included in Tables 1 and 2. Approximately 18% of the children in the regular Chapter 1 program had reached a fluency level of primer text or higher, as compared to 77% of the group in the restructured Chapter 1 program. Eighty-three percent of the regular Chapter 1 group read below a primer level (averaging 37% fluency on the primer text). Using the criterion of 33 NCE as a cut-off, all of the Chapter 1 comparison students would return to Chapter 1 in Grade 2. If the cutoff is moved down to 25 NCE, 22% would no longer be eligible for Chapter 1.

Comparison With Classmates

This comparison considered the performances of the students in the restructured Chapter 1 program with those of classmates. Performances of Quintile 5/Chapter 1 students at the end of the year on text-level reading and writing and word-level reading and writing were compared to those of classmates ranging from high (Quintile 1) to medium-low (Quintile 4).

Prior to conducting these comparisons, an analysis was needed to establish that the quintile groups began the year with significantly different levels of readiness. First, spring performances on reading text, reading words, writing text, and writing words were compared for students who had taken the GM in the fall and those who had not. This analysis indicated no significant differences between these two groups ($F = 1.94$,

Table 3 Means and Standard Deviations for Students in Restructured and Regular Chapter 1 Programs at End of Year

Measure		Total possible	Restructured Ch. 1[a]	Regular Ch. 1[b]	Univariate F for within-cells regression[c]	Univariate F for program[c]
Reading	X		1.15[d]	.35	12.19**	25.19**
text	SD	3	.84[e]	.32		
Reading	X		27.29	11.38	22.49**	34.28**
words	SD	60	13.44	8.19		
Writing	X		4.36	3.55	11.54**	10.95**
text	SD	6	1.03	1.04		
Writing	X		16.41	6.95	10.59*	29.81**
words	SD	60	8.62	5.11		
CTBS–	X		33.78	19.08	33.73**	43.81**
Reading	SD	99	11.36	5.77		
CTBS–	X		38.25	22.78	9.55*	29.11**
Lang. Arts	SD	99	13.58	9.84		

[a]$n = 45$.   [b]$n = 34$.   [c]$df = 1,76$.
[d]Means adjusted for covariate.
[e]Standard deviations based on residuals.
*$p < .01$.   **$p < .001$.

$df = 4,44$, $p < .12$). The group by quintile interaction was nonsignificant ($F = .56$, $df = 12,117$, $p < .86$), indicating that the pattern of no differences between the tested and nontested groups was consistent across the quintiles. These analyses mean that available GM scores can be considered as indicators of a quintile's entry level.

Next, the entry level of Quintile 5/Chapter 1 was compared to those of the other 4 quintiles to determine whether differences existed between groups in fall readiness. The analysis of variance using the reading readiness scores presented in Table 4 showed a significant effect, $F = 47.92$, $df = 4, 71$, $p < .001$. Planned comparisons between Quintile 5/Chapter 1 and each of the other quintiles indicated a significant difference at $p < .01$: Quintile 1, $t = 11.92$; Quintile 2, $t = 7.72$; Quintile 3, $t = 6.06$; and Quintile 4, $t = 2.75$. Quintile 5/Chapter 1 students had a significantly lower entry readiness level than all of the other four groups in the fall.

The next analysis considered whether the performances of the Quintile 5/Chapter 1 students differed from those of any of the other groups at the end of the year. Of particular interest was the question, "Did Quintile 5/Chapter 1 students who began the year with significantly lower reading readiness scores than peers in Quintiles 3 and 4 have comparable performances to these two groups by the end of the year?" It was expected that differences between Quintile 5/Chapter 1 and Quintiles 1 and 2 would still exist since these latter two groups had had substantially higher readiness scores at the beginning of the year.

Analysis of variance indicated that differences across the quintiles existed at the end of the year for reading text ($F = 10.75$, $df = 4,95$, $p < .001$), writing text ($F = 5.28$, $df = 4,95$, $p < .001$), reading words ($F = 9.76$, $df = 4,95$, $p < .001$), and writing words ($F = 3.98$, $df = 4,95$, $p < .01$). The pattern of these differences had changed from the beginning to the end of the year. Except for one planned comparison where Quintile 2 performed significantly better than Quintile 5/Chapter 1, the scores of Quintile 5/Chapter 1 could not be distinguished statistically from those of students in either Quintiles 2 or 3. Quintile 5/Chapter 1 differed significantly from Quintile 4 on reading text ($t = 2.90$, $p < .01$), and the comparison for writing text was marginally significant ($t = 2.06$, $p < .058$). Unlike the beginning of the year, however, Quintile 5/Chapter 1

Table 4   Means and Standard Deviations for Students in Restructured Chapter 1 Programs and Classmates

	Total possible		Quintile 1[a]	Quintile 2[b]	Quintile 3[c]	Quintile 4[d]	Quintile 5 (Chapter 1)[c]
Gates-MacGinitie		X	60.38	46.88	41.14	31.13	16.42
(fall)	99	SD	15.54	10.38	18.06	6.49	7.10
Reading text		X	2.61	1.75	1.14	.60	1.22[f]
(spring)	3	SD	.83	.84	.96	.54	.92
Reading words		X	50.79	38.86	28.21	21.28	28.93
(spring)	60	SD	11.22	11.02	14.99	13.53	15.24
Writing text		X	5.29	4.92	4.00	3.53	4.47
(spring)	6	SD	.73	.92	1.10	1.33	1.08
Writing words		X	26.93	19.64	18.43	14.61	17.13
(spring)	60	SD	8.92	9.86	8.65	8.54	8.99

[a]$n = 14$.   [b]$n = 14$.   [c]$n = 14$.
[d]$n = 13$.   [c]$n = 45$.   [f]Observed means.

students had higher scores than students in Quintile 4. Only Quintile 1 had significantly higher scores than Quintile 5/Chapter 1 on all measures (reading text, $t = 5.34$, $p < .001$; reading words, $t = 5.81$, $p < .001$; writing words, $t = 3.58$, $p < .01$; writing text, $t = 3.25$, $p < .01$).

At the end of the year, Quintile 5/Chapter 1 students had performances that were indistinguishable from those of students who had begun the year substantially ahead of them in Quintiles 2 and 3, and they were ahead of peers in Quintile 4. The only group that had maintained its significant lead over Quintile 5/Chapter 1 consisted of the students who had begun the year as the highest group. (Hiebert, Colt, Catto, & Gury, 1992, pp. 559–564. Copyright 1992 by the American Educational Research Association. Reprinted by permission of the publisher.)

The **discussion** or **conclusions section** contains the researchers' ideas about the educational implications of the research results: how the results can be used in school settings or what additional research may be called for. Often this explanation is prefaced with a brief summary of the research results. When researchers obtain unusual or unexpected results, they discuss possible reasons for these results.

The following example is a typical discussion section. It is from a qualitative descriptive study about school-based management. The study was done in two parts: (a) an analysis of documents and (b) a case study.

DISCUSSION

Owing to the exploratory nature of the study, the discussion that follows is necessarily speculative. Overall, the study's findings are consistent with the conceptual framework drawn from institutional theory. This, of course, raises the possibility that the findings were merely the product of conceptual foreshadowing: We saw what the framework led us to see. However, the evidence is quite compelling and reveals that school-based management was, indeed, institutionalized and that, in this instance at least, the institutional environment in which school organizations operate was quite organized.

Conclusions

Institutionalizing school-based management. Institutional theory, it will be recalled, explains that entrepreneurs work to institutionalize structural elements, which organizations may adopt to gain social legitimacy rather than to enhance technical efficiency. Entrepreneurs typically are agents of the nation-state or the professions and promote structural elements that serve their interests.

The findings of this study, taken together, suggest that school-based management was institutionalized policy and teachers' union actors waged an explicit and coordinated campaign to shape and promote school-based management as a means to effect educational reform. Academic actors assisted by disseminating information. In the void left by the Reagan administration, these actors wove threads of past and existing reform initiatives—including a long history of school-based management programs, the effective schools movement, and concern over the school-business relationship—into the cloth of educational reform that was draped at state and local levels.

These efforts were not neutral. The actors, while falling into three fairly distinct groups, seemed to represent the interests of the education profession. The actors shared two overarching goals: (a) improve the effectiveness of public schools and (b) enhance the professional status of teachers. These goals emphasize the importance of public education, which recently has been compared unfavorably with private education by proponents of school choice, and seek to shift greater control into the hands of teachers. An important caveat must be registered, however. The data on actors' interests may represent retrospective reconstructions and justifications. This may explain why actors tended to invoke broad, societal interests and ignore more parochial or personal goals. This, in fact, is consistent with institutional theory, which explains that entrepreneurs promote their preferred structural elements by linking them to widely shared cultural beliefs, or institutions.

An organized environment. Institutional theory depicts the environments of organizations as being organized. Institutional actors tend to be organizations, because organizations rather than individuals possess the resources that are needed to support a campaign of institutionalization. In addition, these actors are often linked by networks, which facilitate coordination and regulation of members.

This study revealed, in fact, that the actors who institutionalized school-based management were organized on both levels. Most of the central actors were organizations: a foundation, a national political organization, a teachers' union, and a policy research center. Although individuals, indeed, were important, their efforts were fueled by the resources of the organizations that employed them. Further, the actors—both the organizations and individuals—were linked by a network. In fact, many of the actors had relationships that dated back to their mutual involvement in the NIE in the 1970s and to graduate school. The network enabled actors to coordinate their efforts to shape and promote school-based management.

Implications

These conclusions raise several issues. Here, we focus on the implications of three: (a) the existence of an unofficial policy environment, (b) the existence of a network linking institutional actors, and (c) the role of academic actors.

An unofficial policy environment. Studies of policy development and adoption generally examine official policy-making bodies, including Congress, state legislatures, state school boards, and local boards of education. This study reveals the existence of an unofficial policy environment, one in which entrepreneurs shape and advance policy initiatives, such as school- based management, that promote the entrepreneurs' interests.

The existence of an unofficial policy environment raises at least two crucial questions. First, what is the relationship between this unofficial environment and official policy arenas? In the case of school-based management, the absence of an active federal presence may have left a policy vacuum, one that institutional entrepreneurs filled with their efforts to shape and promote their preferences. There is also evidence that the institutionalization of school-based management preceded, if not precipitated, the adoption of school-based management policies by state legislatures and local school boards, supporting the contention that institutions limit the options available to formal policymakers (March & Olsen, 1989). Finally, there remains the possibility that policies adopted in formal arenas constrain the efforts of entrepreneurs in the unofficial environment.

A second question raised by the presence of an unofficial policy environment concerns the conceptualization of that environment. Concepts drawn from political science naturally direct most research on activity in official policy arenas. However, other conceptual perspectives may be more instructive for examining unofficial policy environments. The analogy of "entrepreneur" was revealing when applied to the actors who shaped and promoted school-based management. Thus, it might be useful to conceptualize the unofficial policy environment as a market, where policy actors, who are not constrained by many of the factors that regulate the formal policy-making process, produce and promote policy initiatives in competition with actors serving other interests.

A network structure. This study revealed that the actors who institutionalized school-based management were linked by a network. The network, it seems, enabled actors to communicate and coordinate efforts efficiently. This may account for the relatively small number of actors identified by this study; a few actors accomplished a great deal because of the relative efficiencies provided by the network. However, although networks serve to define who is included, they also define who is not. Because network members enjoy an apparent advantage in the unofficial policy environment, access to networks may be an important factor in determining who will succeed as institutional entrepreneurs. This issue takes on added importance in light of the finding that some members of the network had ties dating back to their mutual involvement in a federal agency or graduate school in the 1970s, suggesting that networks are relatively stable over time.

Role of academic actors. We raise a third issue because it hits so close to home. It concerns the role that academic actors, played in institutionalizing school-based management. Academic actors, as reported earlier, were not the chief institutional entrepreneurs. They did, however, disseminate information about school-based management through various publications to different audiences. This appeared to provide social legitimacy for school-based management despite the lack of evidence of its efficacy, thus contributing to its institutionalization. As one interview respondent observed, the words of professors carry weight because they are backed by academic credentials.

The relationship of educational scholarship to educational policy and practice has often been a point of concern and not a little contention between academics on the one side, and policymakers and practitioners on the other. Both sides, however, seem to agree that scholarship should have a substantive relationship to policy and practice. In the present instance, scholarship did not drive policy and practice, as some academics believe it should. Nor was it irrelevant, as many policymakers and practitioners believe it to be. Instead, it served the largely symbolic function of legitimating what institutional entrepreneurs had shaped, which may strike at the legitimacy of educational research. (Ogawa, 1994, pp. 544–547. Copyright 1994 by the American Educational Research Association. Reprinted by permission of the publisher.)

The **reference section** contains an alphabetical listing of the books, journal articles, other research reports, instructional materials, and instruments cited in the report. Sometimes, researchers follow the reference section with appendices that contain examples of instruments or special materials.

A Plan for Reading Reports

In most research reports, researchers use common terms and organize their ideas similarly. Research consumers, therefore, can read most reports using a basic plan, which has three phases: prereading, reading, and postreading. In the first phase, research consumers determine what they know about the topic before reading and set purposes for reading the report. In the second phase, consumers systematically read parts of the report according their own purposes. In the last phase, they confirm whether their purposes have been met and learning has occurred.

The reading plan is illustrated with two model research reports. For the first report, a comparative study using both qualitative and quantitative data collection and analysis (Dahl & Freppon, 1995), the reading plan is fully explained with reference to the report's labeled sections. For the second report of experimental research (King, 1994), the sections are labeled, but the reading plan is only outlined.

Guided Reading

First Phase: Previewing and Predicting the Research Report.   The aim of this phase is to determine why you will read the report and what kinds of knowledge or information it presents. It is like a reconnaissance mission to find out what you know about the topic and to predict whether the report meets your intended purpose. It also is a time to determine whether the report is written as a standard research report.

1. Using the research report "A Comparison of Innercity Children's Interpretations of Reading and Writing Instruction in the Early Grades in Skills-Based and Whole Language Classrooms" (pp. 64–93), answer the question "Why am I reading this report—to gain knowledge, to apply the knowledge, or to implement an instructional practice?" For this demonstration, we will assume that you desire additional information about how young children are taught in whole-language and skills-based classrooms.

2. Read the report title #1 and the first sentence of the abstract #3.

3. Answer the question "Will reading this report meet my purpose?"
   The answer is yes, because the study looks at how young children in skills-based and whole-language classrooms interpret their reading and writing instruction.

4. Answer the question "What do I know about the topic?"
   On a sheet of paper or in the margin next to the report, list what you already know about factors related to whole-language and skills instruction. Start with those listed in the title and abstract's first sentence: cross-curricular, skills-based, whole-language, innercity classrooms, kindergarten, reading, writing.

5. Read each of the major headings. Answer the question "Is the report organized using typical section headings?"

(text continues on p. 94)

Dahl, K. L., & Freppon, P. A. (1995). A comparison of innercity children's interpretations of reading and writing instruction in the early grades in skills-based and whole language classrooms. *Reading Research Quarterly, 30*(1), 50–74.

① A Comparison of Innercity Children's Interpretations of Reading and Writing Instruction in the Early Grades in Skills-Based and Whole Language Classrooms

② Karin L. Dahl

The Ohio State University, Columbus, USA

Penny A. Freppon

University of Cincinnati, Ohio, USA

③ This cross-curricular comparison focused on learner interpretations of beginning reading and writing instruction in skills-based and whole language innercity classrooms across kindergarten and first grade. Low-SES focal learners in each curriculum were observed during literacy instruction twice weekly for 2 years. Data included field notes, transcripts of reading and writing episodes, student papers, and pre/post written language measures. Qualitative findings indicated similarity in learner concern about accuracy. Cross-curricular differences centered on applications of phonics knowledge, responses to literature, coping strategies of learners experiencing difficulty, and learner perceptions of themselves as readers and writers. Quantitative findings indicated a significant difference on written narrative register favoring whole language learners.

④ **This cross-curricular comparison was initiated to shed light on two issues: first, how innercity children in the United States make sense of and interpret their beginning reading and writing instruction in the early grades of school, and second, how learners' interpretations may differ when they experience skills-based or whole language classroom programs. The comparison, therefore, addresses the consequences of differing literacy curricula as they are evident in children's interpretations.** We have chosen skills-based and whole language curricula because they are widely used and draw on sharply contrasting notions of teaching and learning. Our focus on innercity children grows from the concern that these children are often particularly vulnerable to the vicissitudes of instruction. We find the research documenting the pervasive failure of this group in literacy learning particularly troubling and see the need for research that explores the effects of curricula as documented from the learner's perspective.

Previous research on innercity children has addressed sociological issues (Ogbu, 1985), family contexts (Taylor & Dorsey-Gaines, 1988), and the influence of instructional factors such as materials, grouping arrangements, and social contexts (Au, 1991; Bloome & Green, 1984). More recent studies have addressed children's sense making within specific curricula (Dahl, 1992; Dahl, Freppon, & McIntyre, 1993; Freppon, 1991, 1993; Oldfather & Dahl, 1994; Purcell-Gates & Dahl, 1991), but have not made extended comparisons across curricula.

While patterns of failure among American innercity children in learning to read and write in the early grades have been well documented (McGill-Franzen & Allington, 1991; Smith-Burke, 1989), few studies have sought children's interpretations of their initial school experiences in reading and writing. Child-centered interpretations of learning to read and write are particularly important in the context of current debates about differing instructional approaches. In order to provide productive instructional contexts for beginning readers and writers in innercity schools, educators must know how these children experience skills-based and whole language programs and what consequences may arise.

This cross-curricular comparison was a two-step process; each curriculum was investigated separately, and then the overall comparison was conducted. The two studies involved were an investigation of sense making in skills-based classrooms (Dahl, Purcell-Gates, & McIntyre, 1989) and a study of learner interpretations in whole language classrooms (Dahl & Freppon, 1992).Both studies were designed as ethnographies so that emergent designs and multiple data sources could be used to generate detailed and layered descriptions of children's learning. **We wanted to examine the knowledge being acquired by learners (their hypotheses) and to investigate how children's opportunities, interactions, and processes of learning led to the construction of particular models of sense making.** The cross-curricular comparison was an ethnology, a comparative analysis of multiple entities (Goetz & LeCompte, 1984). It was conducted by tracing a group of students through a series of comparable data in the skills-based and whole language settings (See Griffin, Cole, & Newman, 1982, for a discussion of "tracer units.") The thick description, original contexts, and interpretations of each study were preserved in the comparative analysis (Brown, 1990). The focus was on similarities and differences of innercity children's experiences and knowledge, their sense making, across these contrasting literacy curricula.

(5) *Theoretical Perspectives*

Within each study, children's learning was viewed as transactive. Descriptions of learning events accounted for ways that learner knowledge and patterns of action, social and cultural contexts, and programs of instruction were shaped and transformed in relation to each other. Viewing language learning through a transactional lens meant accounting for the learner's actions and behaviors during instruction as well as accounting for the ways each learner's linguistic-experiential reservoir, background, and stance influenced those actions (Rosenblatt, 1989).

Within this transactive frame, we utilized two main theoretical perspectives. The first of these was the view that classroom reading and writing contexts are sociopsycholinguistic. Learning about reading and writing and engaging in both processes occur in dynamic contexts (Bloome & Green, 1984; Dyson, 1991). The sense learners make depends on social and cultural classroom contexts (Green & Meyer, 1991) and the children's own evolving understandings of written language (Dahl, 1993; Meyers, 1992). Meanings are shaped by transactions among these and other factors (Rosenblatt, 1985). Class room milieu, the child's individual stance toward literacy (Bussis, Chittenden, Amarel, & Klausner, 1985; Purcell-Gates & Dahl, 1991), development in literacy learning (Clay, 1975; Sulzby, 1985), and the dynamics within specific learning events shape and influence knowledge construction and motivation (Dahl & Freppon, 1991).

The second strand centered on the theoretical differences between the instructional approaches involved in this comparison. The skills-based curriculum is based on the idea that written language is learned through teacher-directed lessons and practiced as discrete skills that are taught sequentially. It uses specific reading and writing tasks as vehicles for skill acquisition and emphasizes a standard of accuracy and neatness as children engage in reading and writing (Knapp & Shields, 1990). Materials, usually in the form of basal readers, worksheets, and writing workbooks, are viewed as instruments for learning specific skills, and the curriculum is centered on the development of reading and writing proficiency (DeFord, 1984). In the skills-based classroom, the role of the student is to learn and integrate specific skills, participate in instruction, and engage in assigned skill practice. The teacher is responsible for structuring learner activities, providing instruction, and monitoring learner progress.

In contrast, the whole language perspective is based on the idea that written language is learned primarily in meaning-centered and functional ways, and reading and writing are learned from whole to part by engagement in the processes themselves (Edelsky, 1991; Goodman, 1986). Whole language classrooms include a variety of printed materials (trade books, catalogs, student- authored works, etc.) and students regularly write about self-selected topics in sustained writing periods. Through daily choices of reading materials and writing topics the student plays a significant role in shaping his or her own learning. The teacher "leads from behind" (Newman, 1985), demonstrating reading and writing behaviors, instructing directly, and supporting children's efforts to learn. Thus, the curriculum is primarily learner centered and driven by a view of children as active language learners (Halliday, 1978; Holdaway, 1979; Wells, 1986).

(6) *Review of Related Research*

Research in three general areas informed this comparison. The first was a group of studies adopting the situated/sociocultural perspective in the study of children's literacy learning. A second included both emergent literacy explanations of reading and writing development and documentation of sociocultural influences on the success or failure of low socioeconomic status (SES) children in school. The final area of related literature was research exploring instructional dimensions that influence children's literacy learning.

Situated/sociocultural perspective. In their British study Edwards and Mercer (1987) investigated ways that knowledge is transmitted and received in elementary classrooms. Their research was based on the premise that human thought, understandings, and knowledge construction are intrinsically social and cultural. In *Common Knowledge* (1987), these researchers describe how the process of education, investigated primarily through the analysis of classroom discourse, imparts different kinds of knowledge. Much of what children learn in classrooms is not the intended aim of instruction but rather other, "hidden agenda" knowledge rooted in the philosophy of instruction itself. Thus, most instruction aimed at transmitting general or decontextualized knowledge inevitably also imparts common knowledge that is embedded in the talk and actions of everyday classroom life.

In the United States, researchers have used ethnographic perspectives to explore routine classroom events that influence young children's sense making (Cochran-Smith, 1984; Dyson,

1989, 1991; Rowe, 1989). Cochran-Smith (1984) documented how contextualized story reading events helped children learn unique language strategies needed to interpret stories. These language strategies were conveyed through teacher/ student social interactions during read-alouds. In her investigation of children's writing, Dyson (1991) described how the child's interest, ordinary classroom interactions, and the larger social world influenced writing. Similarly, research analyzing preschool children's social interactions at the writing table (Rowe, 1989) documented the social dimensions of learning and their influence as children posed, tested, and revised their hypotheses about literacy. Children learned the roles of author and audience as they interacted with each other and with their teachers. These investigations demonstrate the importance of understanding the social and cultural milieu of classrooms as contexts shaping literacy development.

In the 1990s, ethnographic investigations continued to explore additional dimensions of children's literacy learning in instructional settings. For example, Kantor, Miller, and Fernie (1992) adopted a situated perspective which acknowledged the importance of classroom social and cultural life. These researchers studied the ways literacy was integral in various classroom contexts. For example, at the art table children focused on merging media and print, while in the block area literacy served to facilitate play and friendship in structuring "rights" and "rules." Results indicated that varying classroom contexts shaped the nature of literacy events and outcomes. A related study by Neuman and Roskos (1992) revealed the influence of classroom environment and documented the effects of literacy objects in the classroom. The presence of books and writing materials merged with and shaped the talk and actions related to literacy in preschoolers' play. The study showed that inclusion of literacy objects in classroom environments increased the quantity and quality of children's literacy activity during play. These studies, in general, underscore the influence of social contexts and classroom structures on early literacy development in schools.

Emergent literacy explanations. Research addressing emergent literacy has documented that young learners are aware of written language in their environment and begin their journeys as readers and writers by participating in home literacy events (Holdaway, 1979). The amount and nature of these early experiences affects later success in learning to read and write (Harste, Burke, & Woodward, 1981; Teale, 1986). Events that help children learn that print helps "get things done" (Teale & Sulzby, 1986, p. 28) and early storybook routines shape children's interpretations of literate activity (Gibson, 1989; Harste, Burke, & Woodward, 1983; Heath, 1983; Taylor, 1983; Teale, 1984; Wells, 1986).

Sociocultural mores about literacy permeate these emergent literacy experiences (Ferriero & Teberosky, 1982; Heath, 1982; Schieffelin & Cochran-Smith, 1984). Societal orientations inform children about the ways oral and written language are used in their community and shape interpretations of school-based literacy instruction (Delpit, 1986, 1988). When the expectations of schooling are in conflict with these sociocultural mores, learners experience difficulty and often reject or fail to identify with school-based concepts (Taylor & Dorsey-Gaines, 1988). The literature on at-risk populations indicates that cultural conflicts affect school success (Donmoyer & Kos, 1993; Jordan, Tharp, & Baird-Vogt, 1992; Mitchell, 1992). Intervention programs and attempts to balance schools racially have not reversed the overall pattern that low-SES children often fail to achieve satisfactory progress in reading and writing (Ogbu, 1985; Pelligrini, 1991; Trueba, 1988). Recurring analyses of Chapter 1 programs and special remedial reading efforts often document the failure of such programs to close the gap between these learners and their grade-level counterparts (McGill-Franzen & Allington, 1991). Thus, while this body of research has enriched our understanding of early literacy development, there remains a need to investigate low-SES children's interpretations of beginning reading and writing in school.

Instructional dimensions. Classic studies of reading instruction have contributed to our understanding of the influence of different kinds of instruction on literacy learning (Bond & Dykstra, 1967; DeLawter, 1970; MacKinnon,

1959). These investigations have focused primarily on the outcomes of reading skills under specific instructional conditions. For example, MacKinnon's (1959) work investigated reading improvement when children read with a tutor and with peers. More recent studies have examined cultural factors and literacy acquisition (Au, 1991) and children's sense making under differing classroom conditions (Freppon, 1991). Freppon's comparative study focused on children's interpretations in skills-based and whole language classrooms but was limited to average readers and their concepts about the purpose and nature of reading. While these studies have described instructional differences and specific outcomes, we have yet to document children's interpretations of instruction in depth and over time in order to more fully understand what learners experience in contrasting curricula.

The current investigation, as a cross-curricular comparison, extends this body of research in a number of ways; it documents learner activity and interpretations of reading and writing across 2 years of schooling in classes with the same curriculum (skills-based or whole language), and it provides a basis for comparison of literacy learning across these years. Thus, this study extends knowledge gained from in-depth classroom studies. It provides a comprehensive account of the learner's perspective, documents and compares learner hypotheses across skills-based and whole language curricula, and draws conclusions about innercity children's success and failure in learning to read and write in these contrasting settings. The focus is on the consequences of each curriculum as seen from the perspective of the children and on the similarities and differences in children's experiences across these two instructional environments.

METHOD

Sites

The cross-study comparison involved eight classrooms in two midwest cities. The schools were matched across studies using three socioeconomic indicators. Each school contained a majority of children from urban families with low income levels, most families received public assistance, and the schools' mobility rates were high. Of the three schools involved in the skills-based study (Dahl, Purcell-Gates, & McIntyre, 1989) only two could be matched with comparable whole language sites. Thus, the comparison did not include one skills-based site included in the report of the original study (Purcell-Gates & Dahl, 1991). The elementary school populations in the cross-study comparison were representative of the racial and cultural mix typical of urban low-income populations in the midwest; that is, they included African American and White Appalachian students. At both the kindergarten and first-grade levels there were two skills-based classrooms and two whole language classrooms.

A critical aspect of the cross-study comparison was whether the skills-based and whole language classrooms selected for the study were reasonable exemplars. Three indicators were used to validate the classroom sites: teacher interviews, classroom observations, and teacher self-report data using the Theoretical Orientations to Reading Profile (DeFord, 1985). Within each study the specific classroom instructional programs were described in terms of their materials, activities, teaching routines, and learner roles.

Skills-based instruction. The skills-based kindergartens included traditional reading readiness programs with extensive emphasis on letter-sound relations; the first-grade programs used a newly adopted traditional basal program with ancillary workbooks and Dittos provided by the central administration. First-grade teachers carried out instruction in small-group sessions, while the remaining students completed seatwork assignments. Learners copied and filled in missing words for sentences written on the chalkboard, and they occasionally wrote in journals and writing workbooks. In first grade, children took part in whole-group choral reading and skill recitation lessons with the teacher. They also participated in small-group round robin reading on a daily basis and had the opportunity to select trade books from a small classroom selection when their work was complete. Teachers followed the skill sequence in the basal program and met deadlines for unit completion established by the district. Storybook reading by the teachers was separate from reading instruction and was often followed by discussion primarily aimed at recall of specific story events or characters.

Whole language instruction. The whole language classrooms utilized extended periods of self-selected independent reading and writing, and teachers worked with individual learners or small groups. The reading materials included a wide variety of children's literature and extensive classroom libraries. Instruction in first grade was carried out with whole-group sessions using extended storybook reading and included teacher demonstrations of reading strategies and skills. The writing program embraced writing workshop routines and used children's literature to suggest story themes and evoke topics. Teachers demonstrated and discussed composing processes and conducted conferences about writing skills with children. Learners engaged in daily writing about self-selected topics and also wrote in journals and shared their writing in whole-class sessions. Most first graders wrote stories that were published within the classroom. Student-authored books and whole-class collaborations were part of the classroom reading materials. Writing and reading share sessions with the whole class were included in the daily schedule.

Informants

In each study a gender-balanced sample of 12 learners in each school site was randomly selected from the classroom pool of kindergarten children who qualified for the federally funded free or reduced lunch program. Since there were two skills-based sites and two whole language sites, this pool provided 24 learners from each study. These 48 children were assessed initially for their knowledge of written language. From this initial sample of learners, the focal learners for each site were randomly selected. Since mobility rates for the schools were relatively high, the initial sample served as a reserve of learners that could be substituted if focal learners moved away early in the study.

Across both studies the focal learners represented similar numbers of urban children who were African American or White Appalachian. Of the 8 focal learners in the skills-based study, 4 were African-American children and 3 were White Appalachian. One White Appalachian learner moved away midstudy. Mobility rates were projected to be particularly high for the whole language study; thus 6 focal learners were selected in each of the two sites. There were 6 African-American children and 6 White Appalachian children. All of these focal learners remained to the end of first grade.

⑪ *Procedures*

The process for conducting this investigation involved first executing each study separately and then carrying out the cross-curricular comparison. Step One focused on students' sense making or interpretations within each curriculum and documented their opportunities and processes of learning. Step Two involved data analysis procedures for the cross-case comparison. This comparative analysis entailed tracing the focal learners through their actions and activities over time in order to examine what students learned and how instructional opportunities and patterns influenced this learning. Procedures for this comparative analysis are described in the data analysis section.

Qualitative and quantitative data collection processes in Step One were implemented in similar ways in each investigation to ensure comparability. In each study, one researcher was assigned to each school and engaged in data collection for the 2-year period. The initial task was to gain familiarity with students and classroom routines and then begin initial assessment of written language knowledge for the full sample of eligible learners. After the assessment was complete, the focal learners were closely observed across the 2-year period and, along with the children in the initial sample, assessed for written language knowledge at the end of first grade. Thus, the weekly observation of focal learners was bounded by pre- and posttests administered at the beginning and end of the study.

Qualitative procedures for documenting learner activity. In each study the researchers generated field notes in twice-weekly classroom vis-

its across the span of 2 years. One focal learner was followed closely in each observation. That learner wore a remote microphone interfaced with an audiotape recorder so that spontaneous utterances could be captured as the 2-hour observation period progressed. Particular attention was paid to learner statements and actions that indicated evolving hypotheses about reading and writing. The emphasis within these research efforts was documentation of the learner's experience as it could be substantiated in talk, reading/writing behaviors, and overt actions. The researchers shadowed focal learners and, where appropriate, probed by asking routine questions such as "What are you doing now?" or, "Tell me about that." The researcher also kept a record of instruction, learner behaviors, and the contexts in which each event occurred. Original field notes were elaborated and typed along with partial transcripts produced from audiotape recordings. Thus, the outcome of each observation was an extended set of field notes in which transcripts of learner talk, oral reading samples, and learner actions were integrated. Copies of all learner papers (writing samples, ditto sheets) were also included. These elaborated accounts and artifacts were subsequently coded by the research team for learner behaviors and strategies, then analyzed for sense-making patterns.

In both studies, the researchers functioned as participant observers but kept to the observer end of the continuum as nearly as possible, rather than intervening in learning events. The point of these observations was to determine what happens without greatly altering the classroom settings or taking a teaching role during instructional events.

Quantitative assessment of written language knowledge. In each curriculum, learners from the sample of eligible low-SES children (24 in each study) completed an array of six tasks assessing various aspects of written language knowledge. These tasks were administered at the beginning of kindergarten and the end of first grade. Both normed measures and measures unique to this study were used. Our underlying notion was that written language exists as a whole and is composed of various domains that may be

Table 1 Summary of Written Language Knowledge Assessments

Task	Description	Procedures
Intentionality	Accesses schema for written language as a system with accessible meaning	• Present printed sentence and ask child if there is anything on the paper. Probe to capture child's responses.
Concepts about print	Standardized test (Clay, 1979), taps major book reading and print concepts	• Follow established procedures using the Stones form.
Alphabetic principle	Accesses knowledge of letter-sound relations and alphabetic principle	• Present familiar environmental print in contextualized and decontextualized events. • Ask child to write 10 dictated spelling words. • Ask child to write anything s/he can and to tell about the writing.
Story structure	Accesses schema for the macrostructure of written narratives	• Read a story to the child. Take a short break to prevent rehearsal effects. Ask child to retell story. • Engage the child in puppet play. Prompt the child to "tell me a story" during the course of play.
Written narrative register	Accesses knowledge of syntactic and lexical features found in storybooks using the difference score between an oral language sample and a written language sample	• Ask the child to tell about an event such as a birthday party or family outing. • Familiarize the child with a wordless picture book. Ask the child to pretend to read the story to a doll. Encourage the child to make it "sound like a real book story."
Concepts of writing	Accesses the child's concepts about writing as a system using the written artifact generated under the "Alphabetic principle" procedure	• Ask child to tell about his/her writing.

examined at different levels. The domains selected were identified as ones related to success in learning to read and write in school (Dahl, Purcell-Gates, & McIntyre, 1989); they formed a picture of each learner's schemata about written language. These assessments included measures of intentionality, alphabetic principle, story structure, concepts about print, written narrative register, and concepts of writing. Table 1 provides a description of each task and describes procedures for task administration.

The six tasks were administered in three sessions spaced over a 3-week period. The intentionality task was first for all learners, and subsequent task order was counterbalanced across learners.

Data Analysis

⑫

A variety of data analysis procedures were utilized in the two ethnographies and the cross-curricular comparison. Table 2 presents an overview of the two-step process and outlines both qualitative and quantitative data analysis procedures for each major task.

As shown in Table 2, Step One focused on both qualitative and quantitative procedures to determine learner interpretations of reading and writing. Step Two procedures focused on comparisons of data by tracing a group of students through a series of comparable events in the skills-based and whole language settings (Griffin, Cole, & Newman, 1982). In order to understand

Table 2   Summary of Data Analysis Procedures

Step	Task	Data Collected	Analyses Conducted
Step One: Analysis of data for each study conducted separately	Task #1 (Qualitative): Document evolving learner hypotheses and interpretations of reading/writing in each study.	• Field notes across kindergarten and first grade for each study • Transcripts of learner talk • Written artifacts	• Code data (codes emerge from each data set). • Determine patterns for each focal learner. • Summarize data patterns for half-year periods. • Reduce data narratives to grids for each learner. • Aggregate learner patterns across sites. • Determine major patterns for each study.
	Task #2 (Quantitative): Document change in written language knowledge for focal learners in each study through pre/post comparison.	Pre- and postdata for each focal learner in each study on the following six measures: • Intentionality • Concepts about print • Alphabetic principle • Story structure • Written narrative register • Concepts of writing	• Score pre/post measures and analyze with ANOVA with repeated measures across focal learners within each study.
Step Two: Comparison of data across studies	Task #3 (Qualitative): Compare learner interpretations of reading/writing across skills-based and whole language settings.	• Field notes/transcript accounts of focal learner actions and utterances • Data narratives and grids	• Write global hypotheses and substantiation. • Compare across data sets using tracer units.
	Task #4 (Quantitative): Compare change in written language knowledge scores across skills-based and whole language settings.	• Six tasks measuring pre and post knowledge of written language for learners in each study	• Analyze between-group scores with a 2(Group) × 2(Time) mixed measure ANOVA with repeated measures.
	Task #5 (Combined): Compare reading processes of representative focal learners across studies.	• Reading samples from the midpoint of first grade in two contexts, self-selected trade books and teacher-selected texts	• Compare miscue and strategy patterns across contexts and across studies by proficiency levels.
	Task #6 (Combined): Compare writing events across studies and describe kind of writing produced.	• Kindergarten and first-grade writing data for two time samples (Nov. and Feb.) in both studies—includes all writing samples and related field notes	• Identify kind of writing, amount, and task. Compare across studies.

how children's sense making might differ by instructional contexts, it was necessary to examine the knowledge acquired within each approach. The similarities and differences in measures of written language knowledge for learners in the two curricula were analyzed. Further comparisons were made of learners' reading processes and writing experiences. In these analyses teachers and their actions were not under investigation. Rather, the focus was on comparing children's interpretations of reading and writing as they evolved in the skills-based and whole language classrooms.

Pattern generation across qualitative sources. In each study, coding systems were established that captured categories emerging from field note data. These codes represented both learner behaviors and the context in which they occurred. Coded data were then aggregated to determine patterns of learner behavior and evolving learner hypotheses about reading and writing within each study. Data narratives written for each focal learner further documented learner hypotheses, and grids that summarized learner sense-making patterns were generated to facilitate comparison across learners. The Appendix displays a sample grid prepared for a focal learner in first grade.

When comparisons were made across curricular settings, the grids for each focal learner from each of the sites for each half year were aligned, and successive reviews were made for patterns of behavior across several learners. Specific tracer units were used for comparison: talk and action during reading and writing, interactions during instruction, and patterns of activity during independent work. Researchers' hypotheses about similarities and differences across learners in skills-based and whole language classrooms were written by each member of the research team. Subsequently, the researchers read and reread all of the team members' hypotheses and generated a list of tentative findings for the cross-study comparison. The team reviewed substantiating data in field notes for disputed areas and compiled further documentation when clarification was needed. The tentative findings representing similarities and differences in children's reading and writing patterns were also critiqued by outside consultants

in a 2-day project review. Attention was paid in this audit to the soundness of research claims and protection against bias.

Analysis of written language knowledge assessments. Scoring procedures for the six written language tasks were drawn from the body of research supporting each task and from the range of children's responses within this study. Table 3 summarizes the scoring procedures and indicates the specific point levels within each task.

As indicated in Table 3, differential weightings were assigned to some items within specific tasks.

In the intentionality task, the salient dimension was the extent of children's understanding of print as meaningful and functional (Harste, Burke, & Woodward, 1983). Thus, the scoring range represented how close each learner came to stating that written language carries meaning. The scale was developed from children's responses in this study as they were questioned about a sentence printed on a piece of paper.

In the story structure task, weighted scores were assigned for various components of the macrostructure of story according to their relative significance among specific story elements (Stein, 1979, 1982; Stein & Glenn, 1975, 1979; Whaley, 1981). *Setting* (character, place, time) and *reaction* (the response of the character to the problem) were assigned 2 points and *beginning, attempt, outcome,* and *ending* were each assigned 1.

The alphabetic principle and concepts of writing scoring represented increments of knowledge and sophistication indicated in children's responses. On the basis of current research, conventional spellings demonstrating visual, phonetic, and nasal sound strategies were scored higher on the scale than use of one letter to represent a word (Gentry, 1982, 1987; Read, 1971). Stories or groups of related sentences were scored higher on the scale than single words or phrases (Clay, 1975, Dyson, 1991; Harste, Burke, & Woodward, 1983; Sulzby, 1992).

Two tasks, written narrative register and concepts about print, were scored according to their prescribed procedures (Clay, 1979; Purcell-Gates, 1988).

Once scoring was complete for all tasks, pre- and posttest results for each study were ana-

Table 3 Analysis and Scoring Procedures of Written Language Knowledge Assessments

Task	Scoring Process	Scoring Rubric
Intentionality	Range of scores 1–5	1=No evidence of the concept of intentionality 2=Response limited to view related to school factors 3=Child sees purpose of writing as labeling or naming 4=Child identifies writing as something serving broader purpose 5=Strong evidence of concept that written language carries meaning
Concepts about print	Scored using Clay's (1979) protocol for Stones	N/A
Alphabetic principle	Scoring scale applied to all three measures with the most frequently occurring level used, range of scores 1–8 points	1=No evidence of letter-sound knowledge (scribbles, pictures) 2=Single letter represents word (*P* for "pink," semiphonetic) 3=Two letters represents a word (*PK* for "pink," semiphonetic) 4=Maps all sounds heard (*DA* for "day," phonetic) 5=Maps letter-sounds based on articulation, no nasal articulation (*SG* for "song," phonetic) 6=Maps letter-sounds based on articulation, includes vowels (*PLEY* for "play," phonetic) 7=Conventional spelling demonstrated; shows visual, phonetic, and nasal sound strategies 8=Majority of words spelled conventionally
Story structure	Range of scores 0–8 points, all elements scored	2 pts.=Setting 2 pts.=Reaction involving response of character(s) to formation of a goal 1 pt.=Beginning or precipitating event of an episode 1 pt.=Response of the character to the problem 1 pt.=Outcome or stated success or failure of the attempt 1 pt.=Ending—providing a consequence
Written narrative register	Scored using Purcell-Gates (1988) protocol	N/A
Concepts of writing	Range of scores 1–7, each artifact scored	1=Drawing: line borders, picturelike marks 2=Scribbles: writinglike marks, scribbles, shapes 3=Letter/number forms: scribbles with letters, letterlike, numberlike forms 4=Letters mixed: pictures with embedded print, letters with numbers 5=Letters: Ungrouped letters, letter strings 6=Words: Pseudowords, words 7=Words/sentences: Extensive word writing, sentences, or stories

lyzed for within-group and between-group findings. While the number of students tested in each curriculum was the same at the beginning of kindergarten, patterns of student mobility within these innercity sites reduced the numbers of students tested at the end of first grade. In the skills-based curriculum the initial sample of 24 changed to 15, and in the whole language sample the change was from 24 to 21.

The statistical procedure for cross-curricular comparison was a two-factor hierarchical arrangement augmented by a within-group variable. This one-between/one-within-groups design with provision for unequal Ns (Kennedy & Bush, 1985, pp. 521–531) used a repeated measures analysis. The between-groups variable was the skills-based or whole language treatment, and the within-groups variable was the array of six pre- and posttests (intentionality, story structure, alphabetic principle, concepts about print, written narrative register, and concepts of writing). For each measure, a group (skills-based vs. whole language) $\times$ time (pretest, posttest) mixed model analysis of variance (ANOVA) with repeated measures was computed using a $p < .05$ alpha level. Subjects with missing data (due to task refusal) were eliminated from the specific dependent variable only.

This design was chosen because it provided for two specific characteristics of the cross-curricular comparison. First, there was no random assignment of learners to treatments; instead, learners came from intact skills-based or whole language classrooms. Second, teachers differed in spite of careful selection procedures. While teachers were chosen as excellent exemplars of their particular curriculum and had comparable time periods in which to carry out their instruction, there was some variation across teachers. The design we used was appropriate for intact classrooms when they comprised levels of the nested variable (Kennedy & Bush, 1985, p. 522), and it made provision for teacher variation by nesting teachers within the treatment variable.

Analysis of reading processes and writing events. As part of the cross-curricular comparison, analyses were conducted to examine and compare reading processes and writing events across studies. After both studies were concluded, a subsample of six first-grade focal learners, three skills based and three whole language, were selected for a direct comparison of actions during the reading process. These children represented a range of reading experience and ability. The group included a proficient reader, an average reader, and a less-experienced reader from the skills-based and whole language classrooms. Criteria for learner selection were based on triangulated data from field notes, miscue analysis of actual reading samples, and teacher judgment. The sampling of learner reading behaviors was carried out with reading samples from the midpoint of first grade to the end of that year. The classrooms from which these six children were selected included opportunities both to read self-selected trade books and to participate in small-group reading lessons with the teacher. Thus, two contexts, independent reading of self-selected trade books and teacher-directed reading of texts selected by the teacher, were compared across skills-based and whole language first grades. Analysis of reading processes entailed identifying patterns from miscue and strategy data in reading samples across contexts and comparing these patterns across studies by levels of proficiency.

Comparative analysis of writing events that focal learners experienced was also conducted at the conclusion of both studies. The kindergarten and first-grade writing artifacts from November and February, time samples that captured representative periods of instruction and learner activity, were reviewed. The purpose was to describe the writing tasks and generally the kind of writing that focal learners produced during these periods. Field note descriptions of learner behaviors during writing events also were collected for each of the focal learners during these periods. Analysis of writing events entailed tabulating types of writing artifacts for focal learners within the sampled time periods and determining patterns in learner actions and responses to writing activities.

RESULTS

The findings from this cross-curricular comparison spanned three general areas: patterns of learner sense making, written language knowledge measures, and contrasts among reading processes and writing events.

Qualitative Findings: Patterns of Learner Sense Making

The qualitative findings focused on interpretations that learners made of their instructional experiences. In the skills-based and whole language investigations, patterns of behavior were taken as indicators of learner hypotheses about reading and writing. Thus, common patterns across the data grids of the majority of focal learners were taken as learner interpretations of a particular curriculum. Comparison across the two studies revealed five areas in which there were prominent patterns.

Pattern 1: Interest in accuracy. In both studies most focal learners were concerned about accuracy. Comparisons of children's talk and actions across the two groups revealed an interest in "getting it right." In kindergarten, children erased repeatedly when learning to form letters and spell words. They asked each other about letter forms, erased, worked on writing that did not measure up to their standards, and tried again. In first grade they tried to accurately map letters and speech sounds and searched for correctly spelled words by looking through books or using available environmental print. These accuracy-focused behaviors sometimes occurred in whole language groups in spite of the teacher's advice to "get your ideas down" or the direction to spell words as they sounded. In both studies these behaviors were evident in learners with various levels of expertise in reading and writing. It appeared that learners began school with some focus on accuracy and sustained that interest in both curricula.

The concern of focal learners in both studies with accuracy was of particular interest because these two instructional settings differed greatly in their demand for production of correct written language responses. One of the main tenets of the whole language philosophy is acceptance of errors as potentially productive in the learning process. In contrast, the skills-based curriculum is aimed at mastery of specific skills or subskills through practice, and correct responses were highly valued in the skills-based curriculum.

Pattern 2: Phonics growth. While a general progression toward understanding of letter-sound relations occurred among children in both studies, cross-curricular analysis of reading and writing behaviors for January, February, and March of first grade indicated differing strategies for using letter-sound knowledge. Table 4 presents the range of phonics strategies in reading and writing that were recorded in field notes about focal learners during these months. Examples are provided in parentheses to clarify specific strategies. Use of specific strategies is indicated with an x under each focal learner's number. As would be expected, some learners used more than one strategy during this period.

The patterns of strategy use in phonics indicate some areas of similarity. During this period both skills-based and whole language learners used strategies that showed they were gaining awareness of phonics and experimenting with letter-sound relations. The differences were evident in the cluster of whole language learners (8 of the 12 focal learners) using strategies that demonstrated application of their letter-sound knowledge. One skills-based focal learner demonstrated application of letter-sound relations through her conventional reading and use of transitional spellings.

These differences in application of phonics knowledge seemed to reflect the writing experiences in each curriculum and the contexts for phonics practice. Children in whole language classrooms experimented with letter-sound relations during daily writing experiences. These writing periods included individual teacher conferences and frequent peer interactions where coaching on letter-sound relations took place. There also were teacher demonstrations of writing processes in which letter-sound mapping was explained (Freppon & Dahl, 1991).

The letter-sound practice in skills-based classrooms was conducted for the most part as seatwork. There were teacher demonstrations of sounding out with the whole group but rarely were these episodes connected to the reading or writing of connected text. Instead, they were part of separate skill instruction. Learners dependent on the curriculum and learners who were inclined to be more passive approached phonics skill lessons as part of their daily paperwork. Their perspective appeared to be that it needed to be completed to please the teacher. Often these children did not put their phonics skills to use when reading.

Table 4 Comparison of Phonics Strategies in Mid First Grade

	Strategy	Whole Language Learners												Skills-Based Learners						
		1	2	3	4	5	6	7	8	9	10	11	12	13	14	15	16	17	18	19
Gaining awareness of letter-sound relations	Copies words to complete writing tasks																X	X		X
	Makes series of guesses to identify unknown word in reading (*BL-, BLO, BLAY, BLOK, PLAY, PLOK* for "plate")																	X		X
	Writes single letter for salient sound in a word, context: teacher support (*D* for "these;" *ICP* for "I saw pigs")	X				X	X			X										
	Represents some phonemes with appropriate letter (*GT* for "cheetah")							X		X	X									
Experimentation with letter-sound relations	Sounds out words in reading by exaggerating sounds (*FA LA GUH* for "flag")														X		X			
	Represents some phonemes in word with appropriate letters (*CLSRME* for "classroom;" *WI* for "why")			X					X								X			X
	Produces a nonsense word in reading by using graphophonic cues									X									X	X	X
	Miscues with matching for the word's beginning sound (*RED* for "rose", *ME* for "many")							X					X		X	X	X			
Application of letter-sound relations	Uses letter-sound relations to self-correct in reading (*SHIVER* corrected to "shouted")	X						X	X			X								
	Produces transitional spelling for unknown words (*HED UNDR THE HAYSAK* for "hid under the haystack")	X						X			X	X	X	X						
	Produces conventional spelling				X															
	Reads conventionally using well-organized graphophonemic knowledge				X				X		X	X		X					X	

Note: Whole language learners: 1=Addie, 2=Ann, 3=Carlie, 4=Charlie, 5=Douglas, 6=Eustice, 7=Isaac, 8=Jason, 9=Maury, 10=Shemeka, 11=Tara, 12=Willie; Skills-based learners: 13=Audrey, 14=Ellen, 15=Eric, 16=Janice, 17=Mary Ann, 18=Maya, 19=Rodney.

Pattern 3: Response to literature. Learners in both studies demonstrated enjoyment of literature. Almost all focal learners were attentive during storytime and listened with rapt attention as stories were read. Storybooks clearly were a source of pleasure and interest within each curriculum.

The cross-study analysis of children's responses to literature, however, revealed considerable differences in the hypotheses children held about trade books. These differences were related to two areas: (a) the nature and amount of experience that children had with trade books, and (b) the insights that children demonstrated about books.

The role that children's literature played in the skills-based sites was relatively small. Learners in these classrooms listened to storybooks read by their teacher and occasionally explored some trade books after completing their work. For the most part, basal readers and skill worksheets served as the primary reading materials in these classrooms. Even when trade books were available, focal learners tended to stay with their basal materials.

The participation structures during storybook reading were restricted in skills-based classrooms. Teachers preferred that children listen to stories quietly and save their comments until the story's end. Teachers asked children comprehension questions about each story, and children commented about favorite events during story discussions.

A representative storybook lesson occurred when the teacher read *What Mary Jo Shared* (Udry, 1966) while the children listened. This story involved a little girl's quest for something unique to take to school to share. As the story unfolded the little girl considered various animals, such as grasshoppers and even an imaginary pet elephant. At the end of the story the teacher asked if anyone could really have an elephant for a pet. There were several opinions, but Eric was adamant and began vigorously shaking his head yes. He announced, "I keep it outside." The teacher asked, "What would you feed it?" and Eric turned to the page in the book that told what elephants ate. This exchange formed the pattern for successive questions about what children would do and what the book said. Learners, including Eric, were adept at finding information that the book offered and adding their opinions.

The role that children's literature played in the whole language classrooms was somewhat different. Trade books were a central vehicle for literacy instruction. Each day children listened and interacted as several books were read by their teacher. Further, learner-chosen trade books were read by children independently each day in first grade, and many books were incorporated into daily writing experiences. Isaac, for example, was a learner who used familiar books to prompt writing topics. He wrote personal versions of many storybooks, changing the plot or adding a personal twist to the language.

Participation structures during storybook reading with the teacher varied across the two whole language sites, but generally learners in these classrooms were encouraged to participate actively during storybook sessions. Children made predictions, commented on illustrations, asked questions about the story, stated opinions, responded to wordings and letter-sound relations, and acted out story events.

A typical storybook session occurred, for example, when the teacher read a predictable book entitled *Oh No* (Faulkner, 1991). The plot involved a series of mishaps, each resulting in a spot appearing somewhere. The recurring phrase *Oh no* was part of each episode. Children listened and looked at the words and pictures. Midway through the story their comments were particularly revealing.

Teacher: [reading and pointing to the words]
There's a spot on my skirt. There's a spot on my pants, cause I fell in the dirt.
Chris: It looks like mud.
Teacher: Would it make sense if it says mud?
Children: Yes.
Isaac: It's D . . . dirt.
Terry: If you don't know what the words say, you can look at the pictures and see if the pictures tell.
Teacher: Look at the words and the pictures. [nods]
That's good, Here's another one.
There's a spot on my sweater.

Chris: It doesn't look like a sweater. [pause] It doesn't look like a spot.

Teacher: Does it look like a shirt?

Children: [all at once] Yes. Well maybe. No

Teacher: So we have to look at the words to figure it out.

Kira: But sweater and shirt start with the same.

Teacher: Same letter.

Cindy: They should put tee shirt because that's what it looks like.

Teacher: So you don't think this makes sense. But it says—

Terry: But down there they put sweater.

Teacher: Shirts starts with *SH*, shhhhh.

Maury: Just like *The Shrinking Shirt.*

Willie: And *Jump Frog Jump* [when the protagonist says "shh."]

Teacher: *There's a spot on my tie. There's a spot on my chin from this blueberry pie. Oh no!*

Willie: On that page it's just one word, and on the other one it tells where it came from.

Teacher: That's right. It doesn't tell where the spot on the tie came from.

LaWanda: It could say, "from the hot dog he ate."

Teacher: [doubling back] *There's a spot on my chin from this blueberry pie.*

Kira: Every time I see that it makes me want to eat.

Teacher: *There's a spot on my shorts* [children all reading along]. *There's a spot on my knee.*

Doug: That don't look like knee.

Kira: It sounds like a *E* for knee.

Teacher: There are *E*s in it.

Sandy: Two *E*s.

Teacher: *There's a spot on my dress everybody can see. Oh no!*

Isaac: Look, it's kind of a pattern with the pattern [Oh no] and the letters too. First it says *S* then *D* then *S*.

Shemeka: [exasperated] It would make sense if they said where the spot came from and then on the next page tell where it came, before—and then said "Oh no."

Teacher: So you want "Oh no" on every page? [Shemeka nods in agreement.]

Teacher: *There's a spot on my spoon—*

Terry: Probably from not washing good.

Charlie: From somebody eating with it.

Teacher: *There's a spot on my bowl. There's a spot on my cup and it looks like a hole. Oh no.*

Sara: [commenting about the illustration] You know what they should do; they should make water coming out.

Isaac: It looks like a clock. Turn it [the page] back.

[The teacher turns back so the illustration can be scrutinized, then resumes reading.]

Teacher: *There's a spot on my hand. There's a spot on my face . . .*

Chris: Oh! Oh! I know, I know.

Willie: I know what that's gonna be.

Maury: She's got chicken pops.

Teacher: [reviewing] *There's a spot on my face.*

Tara: "Oh no" on the next page.

Willie: That's gonna be spots everywhere 'cause she got the spots off her plate.

Isaac: Turn it back to the spoon. It looks like a spot.

Maury: I got the chicken pops right now!

In this segment of storybook interaction, it was clear that learners were engaged in figuring out how the story worked. They attended to pattern and thought about story language, sound-symbol relations, and illustrations. They critiqued the story and related their own experiences to its events. The teacher stopped the story as requested, supported children's efforts to clarify, and listened to volunteered ideas.

When the two representative vignettes about storybook read-alouds were compared, differences in learner opportunities were evident. In the skills-based example, *What Mary Jo Shared,* the learners' responses were elicited at the end of the story only and guided by the teacher's questions. Children participated by using story information to support their opinions. In the whole language example, the discussion took place throughout the story reading event. It was based on learner observations and included teacher responses and questions. The opportunity to construct meaning was present throughout the whole language read-aloud lesson.

Interacting with storybooks in these ways clearly contributed to what these children knew about stories and how they responded to trade books. Data analyses revealed that children in whole language classrooms demonstrated a range of insights from their experiences. These patterns were not evident among learners in skills-based classrooms. Three categories of interpretation were evident: learning storybook language, gathering intertextual knowledge, and adopting a critical stance.

Learning storybook language was evident in children's writing. Their written stories included dedication pages, illustrations, dots to indicate continuing events, and formulaic endings. Patterns of action indicated children were learning about written language from reading and listening to trade books. The following story written in October of first grade by Isaac demonstrated this influence.

The Scary Hairy Spider

When me and Ricky was playing outside, we
   saw a spider and Ricky picked up the spider.
I said, "Ooo gross!"
And I said, "Ricky put that spider down or you
   will get bit and . . .
if you get bit, don't come to me!"
And . . . if you come I will not help you.
And if you ask me twice, I still won't help you.

The End

The story was written in book form, with each line on a separate page. It included illustrations and a title page and was typical of many stories written about daily experiences but shaped by structures and language patterns found in books.

Gathering intertextual knowledge was demonstrated by whole language children in first grade as they spontaneously talked about characters, events, and plot arrangements across stories. Children appeared to be building a story world that included a repertoire of story elements. The following comments were characteristic of this learner pattern:

"Oh that reminds me of the butcher, the baker, and the candlestick maker."
"You have to look for the cat. It's like *Each Peach Pear Plum*" [Ahlberg & Ahlberg, 1985].
"That looks like a Eric Carle book."

Learners appeared to have a memory for books and used their intertextual knowledge as they participated in story events. In contrast, no pattern of intertextual insights was present in the skills-based study. Learners' attention was directed toward other matters when stories were read by the teacher, and their spontaneous utterances did not include these connections.

Adopting a critical stance was shown as children in whole language classrooms made suggestions about how professional authors could improve their stories. Children criticized story endings and talked about what would improve the illustrations. In skills-based classrooms children talked about story events and answered comprehension questions. There were few critical comments about stories.

Pattern 4: Coping strategies of learners experiencing difficulty. In both skills-based and whole language classrooms the least proficient readers and writers developed various ways of dealing with teacher expectations and instructional demands. While the patterns of behavior and strategies for coping were similar in some ways for children in the two studies, the cross-study contrasts were significant.

The similarities in behavior patterns were most evident in teacher/student conferences at the individual level. When skills-based teachers gave one-on-one help to learners experiencing difficulty, the children could focus on the lesson and increase their learning efforts. Outcomes of one-on-one interactions in skills-based classrooms often resulted in children getting the correct answer or showing they understood. Similarly, in whole language classrooms, one-on-one teacher/student interactions were productive for learners experiencing difficulty. In this context, learners responded positively and increased their efforts to accomplish the expected task.

The greatest difference in coping behaviors across studies occurred when these same learners worked on their own. Interestingly, passivity appeared to be the most pervasive coping strategy for learners experiencing difficulty in skills-based classrooms. Their strategies also included bluffing their way through reading lessons by reading paralinguistically and copying from others without efforts to produce meaning on their own. Field observations showed that learners sat and stared for periods of time, marked randomly on worksheets just to finish them, and waited for or asked for help.

Their behaviors indicated they weren't making sense of what they were doing. One learner acted out somewhat aggressively, but in general the coping behaviors of children experiencing difficulty in the skills-based study seemed aimed at just getting through the assigned reading or writing activity. Rather than "taking on the task" of reading, they tended to avoid it and found ways to get by in the classroom (Purcell-Gates & Dahl, 1991).

One exception to this pattern was a skills-based learner who coped by creating opportunities for individual instruction. Creating a "school for one" (Dahl, Purcell-Gates, & McIntyre, 1989) entailed one of two strategies, either acting out sufficiently to be required to stay after school or interrupting small-group instruction by holding up the workbook, looking baffled, and asking, "What I pose a do?" in a loud voice. Both strategies produced private sessions with the teacher in which personal instruction was given and the learner's questions answered.

The coping behaviors of comparable children from whole language classrooms were shaped by the social contexts in their classrooms. Learners often interacted with their peers when they didn't know what to do. Within the periods of extended independent reading or writing, they tended to tag along with other learners. In doing so they seemed to establish their own support systems. For example, in group reading situations they actively listened to other children and picked up phrases and sentences, saying them along with others. When a struggling learner copied from children's papers during writing, there also was an attempt to write independently by simply adding letters, drawing, or talking about words or letters that could be added. These peer interactions indicated some attempt to carry on the activity meaningfully.

In writing, the least proficient learners in the whole language first grades developed some avoidance behaviors. These children sometimes moved around the room and interacted socially with peers. They also set up elaborate clerical duties such as getting word cards for others, becoming the illustrator in collaborative book writing, sharpening pencils, setting up supplies (paper, pencils, and crayons), and helping or organizing other helpers in writing tasks. They stalled and avoided the act of writing, often altering their behavior only in one-on-one sessions with the teacher.

Pattern 5: Sense of self as reader/writer and persistence. Among the patterns reflecting the learners' interpretations, two trends were particularly prominent in whole language classrooms. Whole language learners demonstrated in nearly every classroom observation a perception of themselves as readers and writers. Further, these learners sustained their attention in literacy episodes and persisted when engaged in reading/writing tasks.

Focal learners in whole language classrooms, particularly in the first-grade year, frequently made impromptu statements about themselves as readers and writers. Rather than focusing primarily on the acts of reading and writing, these children were interested in themselves and their progress. They frequently talked about what they knew how to do, what they were going to do next, and what they saw as a challenge or difficult task. These statements occurred spontaneously within the context of independent reading or writing time. Many remarks about self were made to no one in particular; others were part of the talk among learners as children engaged in reading and writing. The following statements are representative:

"I can read the whole book."
"I got that book at home, I already know it."
"Me and him wrote four books."
"I can read . . . just not out loud."
"I can spell that without even looking."
"When I was in kindergarten, I couldn't write or spell a thing."
"I'm a gonna write, I'm a gonna draw, I'm a gonna do one more page."
"I'll read it all by myself, I don't need any help."

Within the whole language classrooms this pattern was evident in children who read proficiently as well as in those who struggled with reading and writing, though less proficient readers and writers made more statements about what they were "gonna do" than about what they knew.

Analysis of field notes in whole language classrooms indicated that these statements were often connected with a second pattern of behavior, *persistence*. Consistently, whole language learners moved from reading one book to reading another, sustaining the act of reading across the independent reading period. Learners also read books collaboratively, talking about the pictures, commenting about the story, and reading in turns. These learners appeared to be engrossed in their reading and usually sustained their attention and effort. Sometimes learners kept reading during teachers' signals to put books away, and a few continued reading as the rest of the class began a new activity or lined up for lunch.

The pattern of persistence was evident in writing as some learners worked on the same story day after day or initiated an elaborate writing project and worked on it continuously with the support of friends throughout a given writing period. For example, Eustice, one of the least proficient writers in first grade, began a six-part book about his family. Each separate section addressed a different family member, and the project, spanning three consecutive writing periods with extensive teacher support, was characterized by Eustice excitedly arranging the book's sections in piles on his writing desk, wrestling with what to write about each person, and asking excitedly "Can I publish it?" over and over.

The skills-based classrooms also contained these patterns of sense of self and persistence, but the patterns were restricted to the most proficient readers and writers. Maya, for example, commented "I'm writing without even looking at the board." The pattern was evident in writing events also. For example, Audrey, being assigned to copy a group of sentences from the board and add an illustration, generated an original story. As she added speech bubbles for the characters she elaborated, "There's a red light and there's a stop sign and there's how fast you should be going. And the rain started raining and it came down splash and she said, 'Ha Jan and Pam.'" Audrey persisted with this story well past the lesson. The remote mike picked up Audrey talking through the story again later in the day, this time discussing Jan and Pam with another child (Dahl, Freppon, & McIntyre, 1994).

The frequency of these remarks and episodes differed across studies. Even for the most proficient readers and writers there were only a few scattered utterances captured in the first grade year in skills-based sites, whereas such utterances were frequent in whole language classrooms, occurring in nearly every classroom visit in the first-grade year. In the skills-based sites the less proficient readers and writers sometimes made spontaneous statements during their work, but the statements were focused on task rather than self.

"Dag, I wrote this on the wrong one."
"I [know] what I pose to do, but what I pose to do first?"
"I'm pasting my fox next to the *b*, where are you pasting yours?"
(Purcell-Gates & Dahl, 1991)

Learners in skills-based classrooms, for the most part, were engaged in teacher-directed or teacher-assigned tasks and tended to complete them diligently. Their independent reading tended to be brief, and the prevailing pattern was to abandon books after reading a page or two. The most proficient learners, however, did reread basal stories on their own and tended to sustain that activity.

Quantitative Findings: Written Language Knowledge Assessments ⑮

The pretest results in both studies showed that these randomly selected children held a very restricted view of written language (Dahl & Freppon, 1991; Purcell-Gates, 1989). When the skills-based pretest results were compared to those of the whole language study, it was clear that children in the two whole language kindergartens scored slightly lower on every measure but one. Learners in both studies tended to view written language as something for school and were generally unfamiliar with print as a way to convey meaning. Learner grasp of print conventions, the alphabetic principle, and concepts of writing indicated little familiarity with written language. Pretest data on story structure and written narrative register showed that learners were unfamiliar with the language of storybooks and the macrostructure of written stories. At the end of the first-grade year learners in both investigations demonstrated considerable improvement.

Of particular interest in this cross-curricular comparison was whether there were significant differences in the quantitative measures when the skills-based and whole language posttest data were compared. A 2 (Group) × 2 (Time) mixed measures ANOVA with repeated measures was carried out on all six of the written language measures. Tables 5 and 6 present these data.

A significant Group × Time interaction was obtained for written narrative register only [F $(1,2)=27.95$, $p <.05$] with the whole language group scoring higher on the posttest than the skills-based group. The effect size was .07 (Hedges, 1982). Significance was not obtained on any of the other five outcome measures.

Contrasts in Reading Processes and Writing Events across Studies (16)

The analysis of reading processes involved a proficient reader, an average reader, and a less experienced reader from each curriculum. Each was selected as representative of the given proficiency level within the curriculum. Three findings were evident from the comparison of reading samples for the selected learners at each level of proficiency.

Table 5   Means and Standard Deviations Obtained on Outcome Measures

	Skills-Based		Whole Language	
	Pretest	Posttest	Pretest	Posttest
Intentionality (1–5)	2.71 (1.68)	4.43 (1.22)	2.29 (1.35)	4.86 (0.65)
Concepts about print (0–24)	7.27 (4.30)	16.60 (4.69)	6.43 (3.88)	18.52 (2.77)
Alphabetic principle (1–8)	1.13 (0.35)	4.60 (1.45)	1.05 (0.22)	4.48 (1.63)
Story structure (1–8)	3.29 (1.59)	4.57 (1.83)	3.62 (1.75)	5.43 (1.33)
Written narrative register* (0–102)	23.92 (18.52)	43.00 (16.95)	19.58 (13.43)	63.42 (18.20)
Concepts of writing (1–7)	3.71 (1.92)	5.93 (1.21)	3.49 (1.88)	6.43 (0.51)

Note: The scores under each measure are the possible range, except for written narrative register, which is the actual range. Standard deviations are in parentheses.

* Significant Group × Time interaction ($p<.05$) was obtained.

Table 6   ANOVA Table for Written Narrative Register

Source	DF	SS	MS	F
Between				
A Group	1	956.47	956.47	3.91
B/A Teachers within Group	2	489.04	244.52	
Within				
C Time	1	15297.07	15297.07	171.93
AC Group × Time	1	2486.88	2486.88	27.95*
BC/A	2	177.94	88.97	

*$p<.05$

First, the reading behaviors of the selected skills-based learners differed across teacher-directed and independent reading contexts. The skills-based learners used strategies independently that they did not use with the teacher. A finer grained analysis of these patterns is included in McIntyre (1992). In contrast, the selected whole language learners read in similar ways in both contexts.

A second finding was that the whole language learners at each proficiency level demonstrated greater breadth strategically in both teacher-directed and independent contexts. Generally, the strategies of the skills-based learners were to identify known sight words, try to use letter-sound relations, and wait to be told an unknown word. The whole language learners generally used picture clues, skipped unknown words, reread and self-corrected, used letter-sound relations, asked for help, and commented about the story.

Third, the levels of engagement, as shown by patterns of learner persistence, effort, and interest in reading, were different across studies among learners who were average or less experienced readers. In the skills-based study, these two clusters of children did not demonstrate involvement by staying with reading tasks independently. Their whole language counterparts, in contrast, were persistent in their reading and highly active as they read independently.

Descriptions from these comparisons at each proficiency level are presented in the sections that follow. The contrasts include miscue data and evidence of reading strategies from reading samples during the mid and latter part of first grade as documented in teacher-directed and independent contexts.

Proficient readers: Audrey and Charlie. Audrey was the most proficient reader in her skills-based (SB) classroom. She read accurately and fluently in a word-calling manner in teacher-directed contexts, often waiting to be told an unknown word and sometimes sounding words out. Audrey's independent reading involved more strategies. Sometimes she read parts of a story conventionally, then switched to a focus on letter-sound cues. She seemed to experiment or play with the text when reading alone. Consis-

tently, she was actively engaged in reading and performed as a persistent reader in both teacher-directed and independent contexts.

Charlie, in a whole language (WL) classroom, alternated between oral and silent reading. His oral reading substitutions in both teacher-directed and independent contexts indicated that he used all three cuing systems as well as picture clues. Charlie commented while reading and discussed the story line with himself. He worked on unknown words and said occasionally, "I don't know this one." He used letter-sound cues and rereading to figure out words.

Average readers: Mary Jane and Jason. In teacher-directed lessons Mary Jane (SB) simply stopped reading when she came to an unknown word. She read only the words she knew and relied on the teacher to supply unknown words. Teacher encouragement led to the inclusion of some letter-sound cues, though these were rarely employed in independent reading. Working alone, Mary Jane did not tend to remain engaged in reading.

Jason (WL) used a wide range of strategies such as skipping, rereading, and picture clues across contexts. Miscue data indicated that he used story meaning and sentence structure to identify unfamiliar words and that sometimes his substitutions showed an overreliance on phonics. Jason stayed with a story when it was difficult and sometimes commented about what he was reading.

Less experienced readers: Rodney and Ann. Rodney (SB) demonstrated a limited range of skills when reading with the teacher. He guessed at words using his repertoire of sight words (*was? it? is?*) and used picture clues, though often without success. His independent reading often consisted of talking about the story and using picture prompts. By the end of first grade his independent reading had declined, and Rodney tended to avoid reading in any context.

Ann (WL) used several strategies to get unknown words across contexts: rereading, letter-sound mapping, and using picture cues. Miscue analysis indicated an overreliance on phonics using the beginning sound only. Ann often talked about the story, and her independent reading behaviors indicated an active and engaged stance.

Analysis of writing tasks and products indicated that focal learners in skills-based classrooms, for the most part, produced written answers on assigned worksheets as their writing activity in kindergarten. Of these, most tasks involved circling letters that corresponded to beginning sounds of pictured items (e.g., *t* for *tub*) and identifying whole words that corresponded to pictures or color names.

In the whole language kindergartens, writing involved exploration. Learners produced letter strings, usually with accompanying drawings and sometimes with meaning assigned after the work was complete. Children copied environmental print, often adding illustrations, and some writing artifacts included invented spelling.

The contrasts between curricula were more pronounced in first grade. In skills-based classrooms, writing was primarily for sight word and specific skill practice. Children copied sight words from the board, either lists or sentences, and participated in workbook activities that called for copying the correct word or sentence or circling a sight word and its matching picture. Learners worked on making their writing neat and on spelling each word correctly.

While learners routinely completed this writing as "paperwork," there also was some interest in composing. A writing event from the November samples captured this phenomenon. The writing task was to use words written on the board (*rowboat, motorboat,* and *sailboat*) to write a sentence in the *Think and Write* workbook. The workbook page provided places for children to draw and write. The teacher's directions were, "Write a sentence about a boat. You could name the boat. If you need help spelling, raise your hand."

Jamie, a first grader in the skills-based study, began by drawing. After his rowboat picture was complete, he wrote *CAN BOAT* on the lines provided under the picture square. Next, he said "Go" and wrote *GO*. Looking determined, Jamie read his sentence so far under his breath, wrote *TWO* and then reread the sentence again, this time pointing to each word. Continuing the effort, Jamie frowned for a moment, then said "the" and wrote it. He looked at the sentence, sort of scanning it and added an *S* to the word *boat*. His text read *CAN BOATS GO TWO THE*. Jamie then paused thoughtfully and raised his hand to request the word *river*. The episode ended as Jamie said the word he needed over and over.

Writing in this instance was focused at the sentence level, and the assigned topic was related to a basal story. Jamie was engaged in writing his intended meaning and carefully monitored his work.

A comparable writing event in whole language classrooms occurred in the same time period involving Willie, also a first grader. During the writing workshop period, Willie wrote a spinoff story for the book *The Chocolate Cake*, which he had read earlier. He copied the title and used the book's format. Looking at the book, Willie wrote:

DTA SAID M-M-M-M-M. [Dad]
GRONDMA SAID M-M-M-M. [Grandma]
MYAAT SAID M-M-M-M. [my aunt]
BODY SAID M-M-M-M-M. [baby]

As he slowly said each person's name, Willie looked to the side and listened to the sounds, then he wrote the letters. Next, he copied the repeated phrase from the first page of the book. He arranged one sentence to a page, placing the sentences at the bottom as if illustrations would follow. Willie reread his four pages, then smiled and added the last *WILLIE SAID M-M-M-M.*

In this event there was an effort to map letters and sounds and a supporting text to structure the project. There was no revision after rereading.

In general, when writing tasks and products were compared, the differences reflected the function that writing served in each curriculum. In the skills-based classrooms, the learners completed teacher-assigned writing tasks designed to provide practice in skills. In the whole language classrooms, the writing periods were centered on learner-generated topics and learner exploration of written language. Children often received help from their peers and from the teacher.

The kinds of writing produced differed markedly across curricula. In first grade the children in whole language classrooms primarily produced work at the sentence, paragraph, and story levels. First graders in skills-based classrooms also produced some stories, but for the most part they worked on completing workbook assignments or on text written by the teacher on the board. Many writing tasks included sentence completion, fill in the blanks, and sentence or sight word copying with choices that learners could make among words.

(18) *Comparison of Learning Opportunities*

While the focus in this cross-curricular comparison was on learner interpretations of beginning reading and writing instruction, contrasts in learning opportunities were evident. In the sections on phonics growth, response to literature, and writing tasks, we described learner patterns of behavior which related to each curriculum. In Table 7 we summarize the learning opportunities in these three areas.

While we recognize that a comprehensive account of differing learning opportunities across curricula is beyond the scope of this article, some distinctions can be drawn from our field note accounts. The two vignettes that follow are representative of reading instruction in skills-based and whole language first-grade classrooms and serve to illustrate differences in learning opportunities during teacher-directed lessons.

Table 7   Learning opportunities across curricula

Aspect of Literacy	Curriculum	Learning Opportunities
Phonics growth	Skills-based	Letter-sound relations were addressed in skill lessons. Teachers showed how to sound out words, and learners sounded out words as they read aloud. Worksheets about phonics were required as seatwork. Boardwork asked learners to copy words grouped by letter-sound patterns.
	Whole language	Teachers demonstrated sounding out during whole-group instruction with big books. In reading lessons letter-sound relations were one of the cuing systems that learners used to figure out words. Writing workshops included help for individual learners grappling with what letters to write for their intended meaning. Peers provided letter-sound information during daily writing.
Response to literature	Skills-based	Children listened to stories read aloud and responded to the teacher's questions. Children read trade books of their choice when their seatwork was completed or during morning lunch-count routines.
	Whole language	Tradebooks were the primary reading material, and learners read books of their choice independently. Read-alouds with the teacher included children's talk during the story. Information was provided about authors, illustrations, genre, and connections across literary works.
Writing tasks and products	Skills-based	Writing tasks were assigned and generally addressed specific skills in the basal program. Learners copied sentences using basal sight words. During boardwork they completed sentences by choosing from word choices that were generated by class members. They worked on specific writing lessons in the *Think and Write* workbook. There were some periods where writing journals were used.
	Whole language	Daily writing workshop periods included sustained writing about self-selected topics. Teachers provided individual conferences during writing workshops. They also demonstrated using letter-sound knowledge to spell words. Learners used trade books to prompt topics and word choices. They copied from books. Peers suggested ideas to one another and worked together on spelling. Learners wrote stories and read them to others.

Reading vignette—Skills-based. In one skills-based classroom, the teacher introduced the basal story "The Yellow Monster," which told about a yellow bulldozer that some children had discovered. She talked briefly to the small group about the author, explained what the word *author* meant, and then read an abstract of the story. She added, "So during the story you should be thinking about . . . what IS the monster." The children then began to read the story aloud one by one as others followed along, some pointing to the words as they listened. The teacher urged children to focus carefully on words. "Look at the word . . . what's the word?" she said repeatedly. The children not reading aloud said the word to themselves when the teacher stopped a reader. For example, Shirika read some words incorrectly during her turn. The teacher intervened, "Look at the word, that is not what it says. Put your finger under the sentence *it likes to dig.* The next word is *follow.*" Shirika repeated *follow.* During their turns, each of the five children in the group read three or four story sentences. Maya took her turn:

Maya: *"Here is the monster," said Nina.*
"Don't go too near it."
"Oh, I know what that is," said Linda.
*"This monster is big and yellow. It's a helping
     monster," said Tom.*
Teacher: Said who?
Maya: Tim.
Teacher: O.K.

The story continued with the next reader and the next until it ended with teacher talk about reading carefully rather than rushing and saying the wrong word. "When you come across a word that you don't know, I want you to take the time to figure out what it is. Sound out the word or ask someone," she urged. Learners were then instructed to reread the story, practice the words and think about them on their own.

Reading vignette—Whole language. The whole language teacher and a small group of children looked through their copies of a new paperback, and they talked about what they liked from their initial scanning. They discussed what the story was going to be about after looking at the pic-

tures and noting some of the words. Then one child simply began to read aloud, and others joined in. The teacher moved in and out of the children's parallel oral reading (reading so the children's voices predominated). When children faltered, the teacher asked questions, prompted with the sound that matched the beginning of the word, or asked about the picture. She also asked children to talk about the story, make predictions, and clarify what they thought. The teacher asked, "How do you know?" and "Why do you think that?" as children told their ideas. Midway through the story the teacher asked learners to "read with my finger" and pointed to one particular sentence, encouraging children to reread it with her. Children read the sentence but stumbled on the word *gate.* They talked about how they figured out the word (the various cuing systems they used). The teacher asked children to discuss the developing story in light of its beginning and then invited them to finish on their own. She said, "I'll let you find out what other trouble they get into." After children finished reading on their own, some were asked to do rechecks (rereadings) to clear up parts where they had trouble.

Reflection. In these two vignettes the learning opportunities differed markedly. Learners in the skills-based lesson had the opportunity to focus sharply on words, take their reading turn, listen to others, and practice reading the story on their own. Their attention was directed to the point of the lesson, and they received consistent coaching from their teacher as they read. In contrast, the whole language lesson was more diverse. Learners received various kinds of assistance, they were encouraged to use multiple cuing systems, and each reader read nearly all of the story. There was an opportunity to think about how to read and construct a sense of the story.

When data from Table 7 reporting learning opportunities in phonics, response to literature, and writing tasks are considered along with the reading instructional patterns illustrated in the vignettes, several contrasts are evident. The skills-based curriculum placed children, for the most part, in teacher-directed contexts where they engaged in reading or writing practice and interpreted or made sense of concepts from the instructional program. There was a focus on specific skills and practice opportunities assigned by the teacher. In contrast, the whole language curriculum engaged learners in sustained periods of reading and writing. Planned lessons took place in teacher-directed contexts, there was direct skill instruction focused on strategies, and learner choice was pervasive. Further, individual conferences provided contexts for instruction and support for independent reading and writing efforts.

(19) CONCLUSIONS AND DISCUSSION

This cross-curricular comparison had two goals: It sought to capture learners' interpretations of beginning reading and writing instruction across the first 2 years of schooling in skills-based and whole language classrooms, and it structured a comparison across these two contrasting literacy curricula. The point was to make visible the similarities and differences across curricula in the children's interpretations of reading and writing and to extend our understanding of these curricula for innercity children.

The results presented a somewhat paradoxical picture. On the one hand, some findings, particularly those from quantitative measures, indicated a number of similarities in learning outcomes as measured by the tasks assessing written language knowledge. The cross-curricular comparison also documented that children made progress in both approaches. Given the controversy about direct or indirect instruction, especially for minority children (Delpit, 1986, 1988), and the "great debate" about phonics, these findings were of particular interest.

On the other hand, many of the findings demonstrated that learners made different senses of reading and writing in light of their experiences. The significant difference in written narrative register was taken to reflect curricular differences. Whole language learners generated significantly more syntactic and lexical features of story language, and they experienced extended exposure to and interaction with storybooks. In contrast, skills-based classrooms offered less emphasis on literature experiences.

The findings about letter-sound relations suggested that we have been asking the wrong questions. The important issue was not how children were taught in school-based settings, but rather what sense they could make. Unquestionably, phonics learning varied among focal learners in both studies. The essential difference was in the application learners made of their letter-sound knowledge and whether it was meaningful to them in terms of their understanding of written language knowledge. Children in one-on-one conferences with the teacher in both curricula seemed able to focus on letter-sound relations with teacher support. In independent writing contexts in the whole language classrooms children also learned to look twice at letters and sounds tended to apply letter-sound relations more often during reading and writing episodes.

Finally, the cross-curricular comparison indicated distinctive differences in the affective domain (Turner, 1991). Learners in whole language classrooms expressed extensive interest in themselves as literacy learners. Moreover, their talk and actions revealed an understanding of their strengths and weaknesses as readers and writer. The linked patterns of sense of self as reader/writer and persistence indicated the establishment of a "disposition for learning" and provided evidence of learner ownership and a positive attitude toward literacy. In the skills-based study these two patterns were evident only among the most proficient readers and writers. This learner pattern was considered important in light of the vexing problem of patterns of failure that often characterize innercity learners in public schooling.

The paradox of differing findings from qualitative and quantitative data merits some explanation. In this comparison qualitative and quantitative data sources were considered as multiple perspectives revealing various kinds of information. The qualitative data tapped learner utterances and patterns of action over time and thus yielded data that revealed learner interpretations of reading and writing. The quantitative measures, in contrast, served as pre/post samples and indicated students' written language knowledge in specific domains. Because the sampling and focus differed in some areas across qualitative and quantitative data, the respective findings also differed. For example, data about attitudes toward reading and writing were prominent in the qualitative data but not sampled in the specific quantitative tasks. Similarly, data about accuracy in reading and writing events, responses to literature, and coping strategies of learners were evident in qualitative data, but not assessed in quantitative tasks.

There were three areas where qualitative and quantitative data converged in focus. First, in the area of written narrative register (knowledge of the language of storybooks), the qualitative and quantitative findings were in agreement and favored whole language. Second, in phonics knowledge, the qualitative and quantitative findings were at odds. Qualitative data indicated more application of letter-sound knowledge in daily writing events in whole language classrooms, but this difference was not supported in the quantitative alphabetic principle findings. Third, in writing production there was a difference in qualitative and quantitative findings. The former indicated greater sustained writing experiences for whole language learners, yet the quantitative task assessing writing showed no significant difference in the kinds of writing learners produced.

The disagreement in alphabetic principle findings suggests that, as assessed in these tasks, the two curricula may not differ widely in the phonics knowledge that learners gain. The difference was in what learners in differing curricula did with their phonics knowledge. Finally, in the area of writing production, the differences between qualitative and quantitative findings reflected learner interpretations of the writing task. Whole language learners responded to the writing task as a prompt for knowledge display. They produced lists of words or lists of sentences instead of their usual stories. The testing context and the task prompt appeared to shape learner interpretations about what the task required.

On a more general level, this cross-curricular comparison indicated differences in children's fundamental understandings about what literacy was for. The distinction between literacy skills and literate behaviors is central to understanding the contrasting outcomes documented in this comparison. Literacy skills are the concepts and behaviors that learners use as they read and write. They are elements of proficient reading and writing that are taught and practiced in most school-based settings. Literate behaviors are somewhat broader; they include learners reflecting on their own literate activity and using oral language to interact with written language by reacting to a story, explaining a piece of writing, or describing a favorite book to another person (Heath & Hoffman, 1986). Literate behaviors also include taking on the tasks of reading and writing, valuing one's own experience and personal language and connecting them with written language, and communicating about written language experiences. When learners see their own experience as valid knowledge and use reading and writing for their own purposes, the journey toward literate behaviors is soundly under way.

Children as sense makers in these two studies seemed to exemplify the distinction between literacy skills and literate behaviors. Some of the children in skills-based classrooms did not weave together the "cloth of literacy" (Purcell-Gates & Dahl, 1991, p. 21) nor move beyond their role as answer makers. Generally, they participated in reading and writing events, completed their work and learned literacy skills, but did not get involved personally nor see reading and writing as going beyond something for school. The children in whole language classrooms also learned skills and engaged in literate behaviors. Importantly, some degree of literate behavior was demonstrated by children of all levels of proficiency in these classrooms.

Learners who demonstrated the disposition for learning took on the task of reading and writing for their own purposes. The majority of children in whole language classrooms and the most proficient readers in the skills-based sites demonstrated this pattern of engagement and ownership. Thus, the greatest difference appeared to be not what was being taught, but what children were learning—about themselves, about reading and writing, about school.

The comparison of these two studies was restricted to urban, low-SES children learning to read and write in skills-based and whole language kindergarten and first-grade settings. No standardized measure of phonemic awareness was used in the array of quantitative measures that were part of the pre/post comparison. Thus, claims about phonics growth are limited to patterns that were documented in field notes of classroom observations. Comparative studies are generally limited by the extent to which the data being compared are parallel. This current study compared the outcomes of 4 years of research in eight classrooms in two very different instructional settings. Thus, it is important to clarify some potentially troubling issues that arise in any comparative study and particularly in one of this duration and complexity.

The current research project was guided by some overarching principles. First, children's knowledge construction was identified through patterns of learner talk and action. Researchers focused on the learners' perspectives, and codes and categories emerged from the actual learner behaviors in all eight classrooms. What these learners said and did in consistent ways over time formed the basis of sense-making categories. Second, the instructional contexts of the skills-based and whole language classrooms clearly acted to shape children's behaviors in various ways. Students' talk and actions can only be made manifest within the bounds of behavior considered acceptable in any classroom. The theoretical differences between the skills-based and whole language curricula, subsequent teacher and student reading and writing behaviors, and classroom rules of conduct determined to a large extent the written language interactions that could be observed in these studies. Third, we combined this understanding with careful and rigorous analysis of children's observable actions across both instructional contexts. The reported similarities and differences between skills-based and whole language groups were grounded in what these children, from highly similar low-SES populations and cultural groups, did to make sense of written language in these contrasting curricula.

The contrasts in learner sense making across studies reinforced the notion that we must consider the learner's perspective and individual differences in reading and writing development in order to understand children's reading and writing behaviors. Beyond documenting classroom curricula and their consequences, we need to know what children believe, what events and contexts shape their thinking, and how instruction can better fit children's evolving knowledge and skills.

In the final analysis, acquiring the disposition for learning may be the most critical occurrence in the early grades. The innercity learners in our study have many years of schooling ahead of them. The prognosis for children who are engrossed in books at the first-grade level and who think of themselves as readers and writers and are mindful of their strengths and weaknesses appears hopeful. It suggests at least the possibility that these children may continue to choose to read in the grades ahead and that they might sustain their roles as writers. In contrast, those who in first grade have already disengaged from literacy instruction appear to have begun the pattern of turning away from school (Dahl, 1992). The contrasts in this cross-curricular comparison tell us that learners making sense of themselves in terms of their experiences in the early grades and that these early learner perceptions may establish patterns with far-reaching consequences.

Directions for Future Research ㉒

Future studies that compare across curricula might focus on some of the issues raised in this investigation. The area of phonemic awareness could be investigated across curricula in terms of instructional interactions and learner interpretations. The contrasting learning opportunities in skills-based and whole language classrooms should be investigated in detail. Finally, cross-curricular comparisons need to extend to the upper grades, where investigations of sustained instruction across 2 or more years in whole language and/or traditional basal programs have rarely been conducted with primary focus on learner interpretations.

REFERENCES

Ahlberg, J., & Ahlberg, A. (1985). *Each peach pear plum.* New York: Scholastic.

AU, K. (1991). *Cultural responsiveness and the literacy development of minority students.* Paper presented at the annual meeting of the National Reading Conference, Palm Springs, CA.

Bloome, D., & Green, J. (1984). Directions in the sociolinguistic study of reading. In P.D. Pearson (Ed.), *Handbook of reading research* (Vol. 1, pp. 395–422). New York: Longman.

Bond, G.L., & Dykstra, R. (1967). The cooperative research program in first-grade reading instruction. *Reading Research Quarterly, 2,* 5–142.

Brown, M.J.M. (1990). *An ethnology of innovative educational projects in Georgia.* Paper presented at the annual meeting of the American Evaluation Association, Washington, DC.

Bussis, A.M., Chittenden, E.A., Amarel, M., & Klausner, E. (1985). *Inquiry into meaning.* Hillsdale, NJ: Erlbaum.

Clay, M.M. (1975). *What did I write?* Portsmouth, NH: Heinemann.

Clay, M.M. (1979). *Stones: The concepts about print test.* Portsmouth, NH: Heinemann.

Cochran-Smith, M. (1984). *The making of a reader.* Norwood, NJ: Ablex.

Dahl, K. (1992). Ellen, a deferring learner. In R. Donmoyer & R. Kos (Eds.) *At-risk learners: Policies, programs, and practices* (pp. 89–102). Albany, NY: State University of New York Press.

Dahl, K. (1993). Children's spontaneous utterances during reading and writing instruction in whole language first grade classrooms. *Journal of Reading Behavior: A Journal of Literacy, 25*(3), 279–294.

Dahl, K.L., & Freppon, P.A. (1991). Literacy learning in whole language classrooms: An analysis of low socioeconomic urban children learning to read and write in kindergarten. In J. Zutell & S. McCormick (Eds.), *Learner factors/teacher factors: Issues in literacy research and instruction* (40th Yearbook of the National Reading Conference, pp. 149–158). Chicago: National Reading Conference.

Dahl, K., & Freppon, P. (1992). *Literacy learning: An analysis of low-SES urban learners in kindergarten and first grade.* (Grant No. R117E00134). Washington DC: Office of Educational Research and Improvement, U.S. Department of Education.

Dahl, K.L., Freppon, P.A., & McIntyre, E. (1994). *Composing experiences of low-SES emergent writers in skills-based and whole language urban classrooms.* Manuscript submitted for publication.

Dahl, K.L., Purcell-Gates, V., & McIntyre, E. (1989). *Ways that inner-city children make sense of traditional reading and writing instruction in the early grades.* (Grant No. G008720229). Washington, DC: Office of Educational Research and Improvement, U.S. Department of Education.

DeFord, D.E. (1984). Classroom contexts for literacy learning. In T. Raphael (Ed.), *The contexts of school-based literacy* (pp. 161–180). New York: Random House.

DeFord, D.E. (1985). Validating the construct of theoretical orientation in reading instruction. *Reading Research Quarterly, 20,* 351–367.

DeLawter, J.A. (1970). *Oral reading errors of second grade children exposed to two different reading approaches.* Unpublished doctoral dissertation, Columbia University, New York.

Delpit, L.D. (1986). Skills and other dilemmas of a progressive black educator. *Harvard Educational Review, 56,* 379–385.

Delpit, L.D. (1988). The silenced dialogue: Power and pedagogy in educating other people's children. *Harvard Educational Review, 58,* 280–298.

Donmoyer, R., & Kos, R. (1993). At-risk students: Insights from/about research. In R. Donmoyer & R. Kos (Eds.), *At-risk students: Portraits, policies, programs, and practices* (pp. 7–36). Albany, NY: SUNY Press.

Dyson, A.H. (1989). *Multiple worlds of child writers: Friends learning to write.* New York: Teachers College Press.

Dyson, A.H. (1991, February). Viewpoints: The word and the world—reconceptualizing written language development or do rainbows mean a lot to little girls? *Research in the Teaching of English, 25*(1), 97–123.

23

Edelsky, C. (1991). *With literacy and justice for all: Rethinking the social in language and education.* New York: Falmer Press.

Edwards, E., & Mercer, N. (1987). *Common knowledge.* New York: Methuen.

Faulkner, K. (1991). *Oh no.* New York: S & S Trade.

Ferriero, E., & Teberosky, A. (1982). *Literacy before schooling.* Exeter, NH: Heinemann.

Freppon, P.A. (1991). Children's concepts of the nature and purpose of reading and writing in different instructional settings. *Journal of Reading Behavior: A Journal of Literacy, 23,* 139–163.

Freppon, P.A. (1993). *Making sense of reading and writing in urban classrooms: Understanding at-risk children's knowledge construction in different curricula* (Grant No. R117E1026191). Washington, DC: Office of Educational Research and Improvement, U.S. Department of Education.

Freppon, P.A., & Dahl, K.L. (1991). Learning about phonics in a whole language classroom. *Language Arts, 69,* 192–200.

Gentry, J.R. (1982). An analysis of developmental spelling in GYNS AT WRK. *The Reading Teacher, 36,* 192–200.

Gentry, J.R. (1987). *Spel is a four-letter word.* Portsmouth, NH: Heinemann.

Gibson, L. (1989). *Literacy learning in the early years through children's eyes.* New York: Teachers College Press.

Goetz, J.P., & LeCompte, M.D. (1984). *Ethnography and qualitative design in educational research.* New York: Academic Press.

Goodman, K. (1986). *What's whole in whole language?* Portsmouth, NH: Heinemann.

Green, J., & Meyer, L. (1991). The embeddedness of reading in classroom life: Reading as a situated process. In C. Baker & A. Luke (Eds.), *The critical sociology of reading pedagogy* (pp. 141–160). The Netherlands: John Benjamins.

Griffin, P., Cole, M., & Newman, D. (1982). Locating tasks in psychology and education. *Discourse Processes, 5,* 111–125.

Halliday, M.A.K. (1978). *Language as a social semiotic: The social interpretation of language and meaning.* Baltimore, MD: University Park Press.

Harste, J., Burke, C., & Woodward, V.A. (1981). *Children, their language and their world: Initial encounters with print* (Grant No. NIE-G-790132). Washington, DC: National Institute of Education.

Harste, J., Burke, C., & Woodward, V.A. (1983). *The young child as writer-reader, and informant* (Grant No. NIE-G-80-0121). Washington, DC: National Institute of Education.

Heath, S.B. (1982). What no bedtime story means: Narrative skills at home and school. *Language in Society, 11,* 49–76.

Heath, S.B. (1983). *Ways with words: Language, life, and work in communities and classrooms.* New York: Cambridge University Press.

Heath, S.B., & Hoffman, D.M. (1986). *Inside learners: Interactive reading in the elementary classroom* [Videotape]. Palo Alto, CA: Stanford University.

Hedges, L.V. (1982). Estimation of effect size from a series of independent experiments. *Psychological Bulletin, 92*(2), 490–499.

Holdaway, D. (1979). *The foundations of literacy.* Portsmouth, NH: Heinemann.

Jordan, C., Tharp, R.G., & Baird-Vogt, L. (1992). Just open the door: Cultural compatibility. In M. Sarvia-Shore & S.F. Arvizu (Eds.), *Cross-cultural literacy* (pp. 3–18). New York: Garland.

Kantor, R., Miller, S.M., & Fernie, D.E. (1992). Diverse paths to literacy in a preschool classroom: A sociocultural perspective. *Reading Research Quarterly, 27,* 185–201.

Kennedy, J., & Bush, A.J. (1985). *An introduction to the design and analysis of experiments in behavioral research* (pp. 521–531). Lanham, MD: University Press of America.

Knapp, M.S., & Shields, P.M. (1990). Reconceiving academic instruction for children of poverty. *Phi Delta Kappan, 71,* 752–758.

MacKinnon, A.R. (1959). *How do children learn to read?* Toronto: Coop Clark.

McGill-Franzen, A., & Allington, R.L. (1991, May/June). The gridlock of low reading achievement: Perspectives on practice and policy. *Remedial and Special Education, 12*(3), 20–30.

McIntyre, E. (1992). Young children's reading behaviors in various classroom contexts.

Journal of Reading Behavior: A Journal of Literacy, 24(3), 339–391.

Meyers, J. (1992). The social contexts of school and personal literacy. *Reading Research Quarterly, 27*, 297–333.

Mitchell, V. (1992). African-American students in exemplary urban high schools: The interaction of school practices and student actions. In M. Saravia-Shore & S.F. Arvizu (Eds.), *Cross-cultural literacy* (pp. 19–36). New York: Garland.

Neuman, S.B., & Roskos, K. (1992). Literacy objects as cultural tools: Effects on children's literacy behaviors in play. *Reading Research Quarterly, 27*, 203–225.

Newman, J. (1985). Insights from recent reading and writing research and their implications for developing whole language curriculum. In J. Newman (Ed.), *Whole language: Theory in use* (pp. 7–36). Portsmouth, NH: Heinemann.

Ogbu, J.H. (1985, October). *Opportunity structure, cultural boundaries, and literacy.* Paper presented at the Language, Literacy, and Culture: Issues of Society and Schooling seminar, Stanford University, Palo Alto, CA.

Oldfather, P., & Dahl, K. (1994). Toward a social constructivist reconceptualization of intrinsic motivation for literacy learning. *Journal of Reading Behavior: A Journal of Literacy, 26*(2), 139–158.

Pellegrini, A. (1991). A critique of the concept of at risk as applied to emergent literacy. *Language Arts, 68*, 380–385.

Purcell-Gates, V. (1988). Lexical and syntactic knowledge of written narrative held by well-read-to kindergartners and second graders. *Research in the Teaching of English, 22*, 128–160.

Purcell-Gates, V. (1989). Written language knowledge held by low-SES, inner-city children entering kindergarten. In S. McCormick & J. Zutell (Eds.), *Cognitive and social perspectives for literacy research and instruction* (39th Yearbook of the National Reading Conference, pp. 95–105). Chicago: National Reading Conference.

Purcell-Gates, V., & Dahl, K. (1991). Low-SES children's success and failure at early literacy in skills-based classrooms. *Journal of Reading Behavior: A Journal of Literacy, 23*(1), 1–34.

Read, C. (1971). Pre-school children's knowledge of English phonology. *Harvard Educational Review, 41*, 1–34.

Rosenblatt, L. (1985). Viewpoints: Transaction versus interaction—A terminological rescue operation. *Research in the Teaching of English, 19*, 96–106.

Rosenblatt, L. (1989). Writing and reading: The transactional theory. In J. Mason (Ed.), *Reading and writing connections* (pp. 153–176). Needham Heights, MA: Allyn & Bacon.

Rowe, D.W. (1989). Author/audience interaction in the preschool: The role of social interaction in literacy lessons. *Journal of Reading Behavior: A Journal of Literacy, 21*, 311–349.

Schieffelin, B.B., & Cochran-Smith, M. (1984). Learning to read culturally. In H. Goelman, A. Oberg, & F. Smith (Eds.) *Awakening to literacy* (pp. 3–23). London: Heinemann.

Smith-Burke, M.T. (1989). Political and economic dimensions of literacy: Challenges for the 1990's. In S. McCormick & J. Zutell (Eds.), *Cognitive and social perspectives for literacy research and instruction* (39th Yearbook of the National Reading Conference, pp. 19–34). Chicago: National Reading Conference.

Stein, N.L. (1979). *The concept of story: A developmental psycholinguistic analysis.* Paper presented at the annual meeting of the American Educational Research Association. San Francisco, CA.

Stein, N. (1982). The definition of a story. *Journal of Pragmatics, 6*, 487–507.

Stein, N.L., & Glenn, C.G. (1975). *A developmental study of children's recall of story material.* Paper presented at the meeting of the Society for Research in Child Development, Denver, CO.

Stein, N.L., & Glenn, C.G. (1979). An analysis of story comprehension in elementary school children. In R.O. Freedle (Ed.), *Discourse processing: Advances in research and theory* (Vol. 2, pp. 53–120). Norwood, NJ: Ablex.

Sulzby, E. (1985). Children's emergent reading of favorite storybooks: A developmental study. *Reading Research Quarterly, 20*, 458–481.

Sulzby, E. (1992). Transitions from emergent to conventional writing. *Language Arts, 69,* 290–297.

Taylor, D. (1983). *Family literacy: Young children's learning to read and write.* Portsmouth, NH: Heinemann.

Taylor, D., & Dorsey-Gaines, C. (1988). *Growing up literate: Learning from inner-city families.* Portsmouth, NH: Heinemann.

Teale, W.H. (1984). Reading to young children: Its significance for literacy development. In H. Goelman, A. Oberg, & F. Smith (Eds.), *Awakening to literacy* (pp. 110–121). London: Heinemann.

Teale, W.H. (1986). Home background and young children's literacy development. In W.H. Teale & E. Sulzby (Eds.), *Emergent literacy: Writing and reading.* Norwood, NJ: Ablex.

Teale, W.H., & Sulzby, E. (1986). Introduction: Emergent literacy as a perspective for examining how young children become writers and readers. In W.H. Teale & E. Sulzby (Eds.), *Emergent literacy: Writing and reading.* Norwood, NJ: Ablex.

Trueba, H. (1988). Culturally-based explanations of minority students' academic achievement. *Anthropology and Education Quarterly, 19,* 270–287.

Turner, J. (1991). *First graders' intrinsic motivation for literacy in basal instruction and whole language classrooms.* Paper presented at the annual meeting of the National Reading Conference, Palm Springs, CA.

Udry, J.M. (1966). *What Mary Jo shared.* Chicago: Albert Whitman.

Wells, G. (1986). *The meaning makers.* Portsmouth, NH: Heinemann.

Whaley, J. (1981). Story grammars and reading instruction. *The Reading Teacher, 34,* 762–771.

Received June 30, 1992
Final revision received January 27, 1994
Accepted February 10, 1994

APPENDIX (24)

Sample Grid of Learner Patterns

Grids summarize learner patterns of activity in reading and writing as documented in field notes. They include notations about activity during instructional periods, information about stance, and dates of important vignettes.

Name: Willie
Time interval: Jan.–May of first grade
Curriculum: Whole language

Reading activity:

Reads whole books with teacher, discusses gist. Frequent near-conventional reading. Miscues show balance of cuing systems, many strategies. Close monitoring of own reading. Self-corrects. Begins to vary strategies in independent reading—sometimes telling a story for pages with extensive text, then reading conventionally pages with a small number of sentences. Often reads collaboratively with friend, alternating pages.

Writing activity:

Writes books with partner, suggests words, writes some sentences, talks about what could come next in story. Sustained writing every period from February on. Writes about personal experience. Composing behavior includes saying words and phrases as he writes them, rereading, asking for spelling, completing the written piece.

Instruction periods (whole group):

Reads along with the teacher. Continually interrupts story reading with comments about patterns or statements connecting prior knowledge with story.

Stance:

Active, interested in reading and writing. Sustains independent work, often deeply engrossed.

Vignettes:

January 16 Sustained reading with teacher, whole book.
March 6 Revision conference with teacher, adds quotation marks.

The answer is yes: background #4, Method, #8, Results #13, Conclusions and discussion #19, References #23, and Appendix #24. The researchers have used additional headings and subheadings. They are also important, especially in the Results section because they help you identify the qualitative and quantitative results.

Second Phase: Reading the Research Report.   The aim of this phase is to find information suggested by your purpose for reading and to confirm or modify your list of known information. Your purpose determines whether you read the entire report or only select sections.

6. As you read the report, keep alert to two things: (a) Your purpose is to obtain information about children's interpretations of their reading and writing, and (b) Some factors will add to your list and some will modify or contradict items on your list of factors related to young children's reading and writing. As you read, note that key information regarding the purpose has been printed in boldface type.

7. Read the research report sections in the following order (note that several sections have been intentionally omitted from the list):

> Abstract (3)
> Introduction (4), first paragraph
> Theoretical perspectives (5)
> Purpose (7)
> Sites (9)
> Informants (10)
> Conclusions and discussion (19), (20), (21), (22)

You will not read the remaining sections now because the information to meet your reading purpose can be obtained in the previously listed sections.

Third Phase: Confirming Predictions and Knowledge.   The goals of this phase are to verify that the your purpose has been met and to immediately recall key information. You should now decide which information supports the proposed research consumer purpose and adds to your knowledge base.

8. Refer to the list you made during the first phase, step 4, and revise it by adding new information and deleting inappropriate information. Answer the question "Were the classroom settings (sites) and subjects (informants) similar to those in my own school situation so that the insights drawn from the results can be applied there?"

9. Write a short (two- to three-sentence) statement that applies to the proposed purpose for reading the report and contains the report's key points. (The statement should contain information from the boldface text in the report.)

Independent Reading.   Using the report of experimental research "Guiding Knowledge Construction in the Classroom: Effects of Teaching Children How to Question and How to Explain" (King, 1994), on pages 95–115, apply the reading plan procedures.

(text continues on p. 116)

① # Guiding Knowledge Construction in the Classroom: Effects of Teaching Children How to Question and How to Explain

Alison King

California State University San Marcos

② Following teacher-presented science lessons, pairs of fourth and fifth graders studied the material by asking and answering each others' self-generated questions. In one condition students' discussion was guided by questions designed to promote connections among ideas within a lesson. In a second condition discussion was guided by similar lesson-based questions as well as ones intended to access prior knowledge/experience and promote connections between the lesson and that knowledge. All students were trained to generate explanations (one manifestation of complex knowledge construction). Analysis of post-lesson knowledge maps and verbal interaction during study showed that students trained to ask both kinds of questions engaged in more complex knowledge construction than those trained in lesson-based questioning only and controls. These findings, together with performance on comprehension tests for material studied, support the conclusion that, although both kinds of questions induce complex knowledge construction, questions designed to access prior knowledge/experience are more effective in enhancing learning.

③ Contemporary constructivist theories of learning maintain that when individuals encounter new information they use their own prior knowledge and personal experience to help them make sense of that new material (Resnick, 1987). During this meaning-making process, individuals may draw inferences about the new information, take a new perspective on some aspect of their existing knowledge, elaborate the new material by adding details, and generate relationships between the new material and information already in memory. Each of these procedures helps individuals reformulate the new information or restructure their existing knowledge and thereby achieve deeper understanding (Brown & Campione, 1986; Brown, Bransford, Ferrara, & Campione, 1983). According to Wittrock's model of generative learning (e.g., Wittrock, 1974, 1990), understanding and memory of material are enhanced when individuals actively construct knowledge and integrate it in these ways, rather than simply memorize information as presented. Those self-generated inferences, elaborations, and relationships are personally meaningful and anchored in that individual's own experience. These views of learning are consistent with contemporary connectionist theories as well as network models of memory (e.g., Anderson, 1976; Baddeley, 1976: Rumelhart & McClelland, 1986; Schank, 1975), which claim that the structure of memory is associative. During the process of reformulating information or constructing knowledge, new associations are formed and old ones altered within the individual's knowledge networks or structures. These links connect the new ideas together and integrate them into that individual's existing cognitive representations of the world. Adding more and better links results in a more elaborated and richly integrated cognitive structure that facilitates memory and recall.

Because knowledge construction is an internal cognitive process, researchers studying this area must look for external indications that knowledge construction is taking place. Although written tests and other learner-developed products can reveal evidence that new knowledge has been constructed or existing knowledge reformulated, overt indications of on-line knowledge construction require an analysis of process data; for example, learners' think aloud when they work alone during learning or their verbal interaction when they work in pairs or groups. Verbal indicators of knowledge construction may include simple restatements of information and paraphrasing of material; however, more complex knowledge construction is indicated by explanations, inferences, justifications, hypotheses, speculations, and the like (Chan, Burtis, Scardamalia, & Bereiter, 1992; King & Rosenshine, 1993). Chan et al. (1992) have shown that the level of such knowledge-construction activity exerts a corresponding direct effect on learning. And two lines of research (e.g., Chi, Hutchinson, & Robin, 1989; Webb, 1989) have consistently shown that when students provide self-explanations during study, their performance on learning tasks is enhanced.

Several recent studies have demonstrated that knowledge construction can be made intentional through instructional interventions. For example, generative summarizing has been used to reformulate material read, thus enhancing text comprehension (e.g., Armbruster, Anderson, & Ostertag, 1987; Wittrock, 1974, 1990; Wittrock & Alesandrini, 1990). Elaboration strategies have been used to facilitate integration of new facts with prior knowledge (e.g., Pressley & Levin, 1986; Pressley, McDaniel, Turnure, Wood, & Ahmad, 1987; Pressley, Wood, Woloshyn, Martin, King, & Menke, 1992). Idea-prompting statements have been used to improve creative writing (e.g., Scardamalia, Bereiter, & Steinbach, 1984); and various questioning procedures have been used to stimulate inferencing and explanation (e.g., Graesser, 1992; Graesser & Franklin, 1990; King, 1989, 1990, 1992; King & Rosenshine, 1993; Martin & Pressley, 1991; Pressley et al., 1992). In each of these studies learners

were prompted to think about new material in such a way that they transformed that material in some manner, thus constructing new knowledge.

Guided Questioning and Knowledge Construction

One of those instructional interventions is based on a cognitive strategy known as *guided cooperative questioning.* In guided cooperative questioning students use a set of thought-provoking question stems such as "What are the strengths and weaknesses of . . . ?" "What would happen if . . . ?" and "Why is . . . important?" go generate their own specific questions on the material being studied. Then in small groups or pairs they pose their questions to each other and answer each other's questions. In a series of studies in small-group discussion contexts conducted by the present author, students used this strategy for learning material presented in teacher-led lessons and lectures. Results of those studies showed that students using guided cooperative questioning performed better on comprehension of the material than did comparison students who simply discussed the material (King, 1989), used unguided cooperative questioning (King, 1990), used cooperative questioning with less-elaborated stems (King & Rosenshine, 1993), or used similar questions generated by other students (King, in press). Furthermore, the guiding questions consistently elicited elaborated explanations, inferences, justifications, speculations, and other outward signs of complex knowledge construction (King, 1989, 1990; King & Rosenshine, 1993). Therefore, it was concluded that such overt constructive activity enhances learning.

Findings also indicated that the effectiveness of the guided questioning strategy can be attributed to the format of the guiding questions. Specifically, the format of those questions helped the learners to generate specific kinds of questions that prompted them to think about and discuss the material in specific ways such as comparing and contrasting, inferring cause and effect, noting strengths and weaknesses, evaluating ideas, explaining, and justifying. As a result, during discussion the learners tended to make those same kinds of connections among ideas. Presumably the mental representations they constructed reflected those same precise and explicit links between and among the ideas in that material. Such highly elaborated and richly integrated mental representations would provide more cues for recall and would be more stable and durable over time; and this could account for strategy users' improved comprehension of the material and for their enhanced ability to remember it later on (King & Rosenshine, 1993).

Results such as these led to the speculation that the use of different types of guiding questions might promote the building of qualitatively different knowledge structures. For example, particular question stems might prompt individuals to construct new representations of the presented material in long-term memory; in effect, they would be constructing new knowledge of the material presented in the lesson per se. In contrast, other types of questions might promote connecting the new material to existing knowledge structures. These questions would, in effect, go beyond the lesson by linking it to prior knowledge relevant to the lesson topic, and resulting in the construction of more complex mental representations (cf. internal and external connections, Mayer, 1980, 1984). To illustrate, generic questions that are simply "comprehension" oriented such as "What does . . . mean?" and "Describe . . . in your own words" might help students to define central concepts and recall the main ideas from the lesson; whereas questions that are more integrative in nature such as "How are . . . and . . . similar?" and "How does . . . affect . . . ?" might induce learners to connect and integrate several of the newly presented ideas. The mental representations of individuals using these two different types of questions would presumably differ somewhat, the former being less complex and the latter more complex; however, they would *both* be lesson based, that is, representations of the newly presented material. On the other hand, in contrast to those lesson-based questions, certain other question stems might prompt students to go beyond the lesson content to access their prior knowledge and personal experience and connect the new material to existing knowledge structures, thus embellishing those existing mental representations and thereby constructing more complex knowledge. For example, such "experience-based" questions as "How does . . . tie in with . . . that we learned before?" might prompt learners to "mindfully" (see Pressley et al., 1992; Perkins & Salomon, 1989) access their relevant prior knowledge and link the new material to their existing knowledge structures. Other experience-based questions might encourage an even broader view of the lesson material and how it relates to the leaner's everyday experience and knowledge of the world. To illustrate, experience-based questions such as "How could . . . be used to . . . ?" and "What would happen if . . . ?" call for creative thinking. They require learners to access a wider range of material from their own experience to be able to make the needed links. To establish, for example, how a lesson concept could be used to explain an everyday occurrence or solve an everyday problem, students have to think further. Presumably, the different mental representations resulting from the lesson-based and experience-based constructive activity would affect memory and recall for the material differently (cf. the distinction that Kintsch in 1986, makes in learning from text between mental representations that are text-based models and ones that are situation models).

In addition to training students to generate thoughtful questions to induce constructive activity in each other, we speculated that knowledge construction might be further promoted if students were also trained in how to generate explanations and other verbal manifestations of knowledge construction. In particular, if children could be provided with guidance in how to explain, the effects of using the guided questioning strategy combined with this explanation training might be even more pronounced (cf. Chi et al., 1989; Webb, 1989). Furthermore, training students in how to explain would reduce effects resulting from individual differences in ability to generate explanations.

(4) *The Present Study*

In the present study, two different guided questioning strategies and unguided questioning were compared. In one questioning condition, students' discussion was guided by the use of lesson-based questions intended to induce construction of knowledge of the lesson itself by facilitating connections among the ideas within the lesson. In a second condition, students' discussion was guided by both lesson-based and experience-based questions. The experience-based questions went beyond the material being studied and were specifically intended to access prior knowledge and experience. In the third condition, which served as a control, questioning was not guided. Students in all three conditions received training in how to explain.

The purposes of the present study were (a) to compare the effects of the two guided questioning-explaining strategies and the explanation-only control group on immediate comprehension of presented material and retention of that material over time, (b) to assess the quantity and quality of overt knowledge construction activity of students in the three conditions as evidenced by analysis of the content of their tape-recorded discussions of lesson content, (c) to assess students' cognitive representations of lesson material as evidenced by the knowledge maps they constructed, and (d) to determine the effects of explanation training within the control group by comparing both pre- and posttreatment lesson comprehension scores and knowledge maps.

METHOD

(5) *Sample and Design*

Twenty-eight fourth graders and 30 fifth graders in one suburban elementary school in southern California were combined into one class to participate in the study. These particular students were selected because they constituted the classes of two teachers who had expressed interest in learning new cognitive strategies for use in the classroom. Students in both classes were normally distributed in terms of ability and ethnicity. Ten of the students did not ob-

tain parental permission to have their discussions tape-recorded or were main-streamed special education students. Those 10 students were paired nonrandomly with each other so as to include them with their classmates in all of the learning activities; however, their verbal interaction was not taped and data from their tests were not used in any of the analyses.

The remaining 48 students were randomly assigned to one of the three conditions separately by grade: guided questioning-explaining in which students' discussions were guided by the use of questions designed to promote connections within the lesson material (lesson-based questioning with explanation); guided questioning-explaining in which students' discussions were guided by the use of both lesson-based and experience-based questions (experience-based questioning with explanation); and a control group untrained in questioning but directed to engage in questioning (unguided questioning with explanation). Within conditions and grade level students were randomly assigned to dyads. This process resulted in the following configuration within conditions: lesson-based questioning with explanation, $n = 16$, four dyads of fourth graders and four dyads of fifth graders; experience-based questioning with explanation, $n = 18$, four dyads of fourth graders and five dyads of fifth graders; unguided questioning with explanation, $n = 14$, three dyads of fourth graders and four dyads of fifth graders. Assignment to conditions and dyads was made without regard to gender or ethnicity. Consequently, although most dyads were heterogeneous on ethnicity, some of the dyads were same-sex and some were mixed-sex.

Overview of Procedures. (6)

All instruction, training, practice, and testing connected with this study was designed as part of the regular science curriculum for these students. All of these activities were carried out in the students' classroom environment with their regular teachers under supervision of the investigator. The two teachers whose classes participated worked as a team to conduct all activities over a period of 3 weeks. The teachers received extensive training from the investigator in how to teach the explanation procedure and the question-generation strategies to their students.

The instructional materials consisted of a series of lessons constituting a unit titled "Systems of the Body." To determine prior knowledge of the unit topic, each student constructed a knowledge map of systems and parts of the body. Immediately following an initial lesson, a test of comprehension of that lesson was administered. The following day students (as a group) received training and practice in how to formulate explanations. In the next session, students in the two questioning conditions were pulled out separately by condition and trained in their respective questioning strategies. They were provided with strategy prompt cards on which their guiding questions were listed. In each of the next two sessions a lesson was presented to the whole class, and then students got into their dyads to practice using their questioning and explaining strategies in discussing the material presented. During the next session (posttest session) a lesson was presented, students discussed it in their pairs (this time their discussions were tape-recorded); then they completed the written posttest and constructed knowledge maps representing the lesson content. The next session (transfer session) consisted of presentation of a new lesson, discussion in pairs but without the prompt cards (again taped), followed by testing and knowledge mapping. The final session (retention session) consisted only of the administration of a 7-day retention test on the material presented in the posttest lesson followed by construction of a knowledge map on the entire unit "Systems of the Body."

(7) *Materials*

Instructional materials. The unit on systems of the body was developed from school district curriculum materials. The unit consisted of five lessons, each covering one system of the body: circulatory, digestive, respiratory, brain and nervous, and skeletal-muscular. The five lesson plans were developed collaboratively by the investigator and the two teachers.

Strategy prompt cards. Three sets of individual hand-held strategy prompt cards were developed for the corresponding three conditions. These cards were used by the students during the practice and subsequent lesson-discussion sessions to prompt their discussion. The cards for each condition, shown in Figure 1, were the same color; however, their content differed according to condition. The cards for the lesson-based questioning condition contained three *comprehension questions* and seven *connection questions,* as did the experience-based questioning cards. However the last three connection questions on the experience-based questioners' cards explicitly guided students to access prior knowledge (e.g., "How does . . . tie in with . . . that we learned before?"). Although four of the connection questions were the same for these two groups, the students were trained to use them differently, as described in a following section. The control students' prompt cards contained only instructions to discuss the lesson by asking questions and giving explanations, but their cards provided no guiding questions.

Teacher Training (8)

The two teachers met with the investigator for two sessions (of 1 hour and 3 hours) prior to the beginning of the study for training in how to teach skills of explanation and question-generation as well as use of the lesson materials to present the five lessons. The same materials and procedures were used in training the teachers as the teachers were expected to use with the students. These materials included the explicit lesson plans, color overheads, and strategy prompt cards; and the procedures included explicit instruction, use of examples, and cognitive modeling followed by scaffolded practice with corrective feedback. These materials and procedures are described more fully in following sections.

Strategy Training, Practice, and Treatment (9)

All training, practice, and testing occurred in conjunction with lesson content from the unit; that is, these activities were situated within specific learning contexts (Brown, Collins & Duguid, 1989).

Explanation training. The teachers used a procedure developed by the author (King, in

Comprehension questions
Describe . . . in your own words.
What does . . . mean?
Why is . . . important?

Connection questions
Explain why . . .
Explain how . . .
How are . . . and . . . similar?
What is the difference between . . . and . . ?
How does . . . affect . . .?
What are the strengths and weaknesses of . . .?

Prompt card given to students in the lesson-based questioning condition

Comprehension questions
Describe . . . in your own words.
What does . . . mean?
Why is . . . important?

Connection questions
Explain why . . .
Explain how . . .
How are . . . and . . . similar?
What is the difference between . . . and . . ?
How could . . . be used to . . .?
What would happen if . . .?
How does . . . tie in with . . . that we learned before?

Prompt card given to students in the experience-based questioning condition

DIRECTIONS:

Discuss the lesson with each other.

Ask each other questions.
Answer each other's questions by giving explanations.

Prompt card given to students in the unguided questioning condition

Figure 1 Prompt Cards

preparation) for teaching the skill of explanation. Briefly, the teachers first explained to the students the differences between describing something (telling the "what" about it) and explaining it (telling the "why" and "how" of it). In doing so they used examples of description and explanation from students' previous (pretreatment) lesson on the circulatory system. Then the teachers demonstrated how to develop an explanation using concepts and processes from that same lesson. The proceeded to scaffold the students in acquisition of the skill of explaining while they continually emphasized the importance of (a) telling how and why, (b) using students' own words to do so, and (c) connecting the idea being explained to something already known. The appendix shows the procedure and one example the teachers used for teaching how to explain.

Questioning training. The two trained-questioning groups received their training and instructions in question generation separately. Students in both groups used material from the lesson on the circulatory system for training and practice in question generation.

In both conditions, the teacher first taught students to differentiate between "memory" questions (those requiring them to simply remember and repeat what they had heard and memorized from the lesson) and "thinking" questions (those that require them to not only remember information from the lesson but also think about that information in some way). She provided examples of memory questions (e.g., "What are the main parts of the circulatory system?") and thinking questions (e.g., "Describe in your own words how the circulatory system works."). The teacher pointed out that every memory question could be converted to a thinking type of question. She demonstrated this from the overhead on which memory and thinking questions were paired. Then she used modeling and scaffolding to assist students to generate additional examples of both, first as a group and then individually. Thinking questions were further classified into comprehension questions and connection questions. She stated that comprehension questions "check how well you understand the lesson" and "ask you for a definition in your own words or ask you to tell about something you learned about—but in your own words, not the teacher's words," e.g., "Describe in your own words how the circulatory system works." Connection questions were defined as linking two ideas from the lesson together (e.g., "What is the difference between arteries and veins?" and "Explain how what happens in the heart affects what happens in the arteries."). Several examples of both kinds of questions were provided on the overhead, and the students were then given their question prompt cards. Using the question stems provided on the prompt cards, the same modeling and scaffolding procedures were followed to provide for student practice in generating examples of both comprehension questions and connection questions.

Students in both groups were told that asking and answering their own (and others') comprehension and connection questions would help them to understand and remember the material presented in the lessons. Students were then assigned to dyads, where they practiced asking each other questions on the lesson they had on the circulatory system. Partners used their newly acquired skills of explanation to answer the questions posed by their partners.

Scripted materials were used to ensure that the same procedures for teaching about questioning and training in question generation were followed for both the lesson-based questioning group and the experience-based questioning group. However, experience-based questioners were trained to use their connection questions to generate experience-based questions as well as lesson-based ones. Experience-based questions explicitly related the lesson material to students' prior knowledge and experience, that is, material learned in a previous lesson or their general knowledge of the world. Students were told that "some thinking connection questions link ideas from the lesson to ideas outside of the lesson, that is, things you already knew about." Examples of such questions were given: "Explain how the circulatory system is similar to a tree," "What do you think would happen if our hearts were smaller?" and "How is the circulatory system related to the digestive system?"

Students in the explanation only (control) group did not receive any training in questioning but did receive the same explanation training as the questioners did. During the sessions when the treatment students received questioning training, control students practiced discussing the same lesson content. Instead of a question prompt card, these students received a prompt card with instructions to discuss the lessons fully with their partners by asking and answering each others' questions (see Figure 1). The control students were also told that asking and answering each others' questions on the material would help them to understand and remember it better.

Practice. Following each of the next two lessons of the unit (the digestive system and the respiratory system), which were presented to the class as a whole, the students in all conditions got into their dyads. They practiced their respective questioning and explaining strategies by discussing the lesson using the prompt cards appropriate to their condition. The teachers and two experimenters monitored the dyads to ensure that students were following directions and using their questioning and explaining strategies correctly. Additional modeling and scaffolding were used as needed. Following all training and practice sessions, the prompt cards were collected to avoid the potential problem of students sharing the questions with their peers in other conditions.

Treatment. The lesson for the treatment (posttest) session was on the brain and nervous system. It was conducted 6 days after the last practice session. This session was carried out in the same manner as the practice sessions with the exception that the dyads' discussions were tape-recorded. By way of explanation, the teachers told the students "We want to tape your discussion because we want to be sure you are all participating, and we can't listen to all dyads at the same time." Because of lack of access to a sufficient number of tape recorders, taping was carried out in two sessions. For the first session, half of the dyads from each of the three conditions (randomly selected prior to the session) discussed the lesson and were taped. They then took a written posttest and constructed a knowledge map of the brain and nervous system while the second session of discussion taping was taking place with the remaining dyads, who then completed their written tests and knowledge maps. Discussion-taping time was 10 minutes for each session. Students had not been told that they would be tested.

A transfer session was conducted 3 days later to determine whether students would maintain the use of their strategy unprompted and with a new lesson. In this session the teachers presented a lesson on the skeletal-muscular system. The students discussed the lesson content as before but were not given their prompt cards for guidance, nor were they reminded to ask questions or explain. Students who asked for their cards were told "You can discuss the lesson without the cards." Discussion time was again 10 minutes. Students' discussion was again taped in the same manner as mentioned previously, and they completed a written comprehension test and a knowledge map on the lesson content.

(10) *Tests*

Measure of both cognitive and metacognitive performance were administered. Tests of lesson comprehension were administered to all students individually at pretreatment, posttreatment, transfer, and retention to assess their literal comprehension of the material presented as well as their ability to make inferences and connections beyond that material. At the conclusion of the posttest and transfer sessions, students constructed knowledge maps of the presented lesson content. They also constructed knowledge maps of the unit topic prior to the study and at completion. In addition, verbal protocols were taken during the students' discussion following the posttest and transfer. These protocols were to be examined for evidence of strategy maintenance/transfer as well as instances of explanation and other verbal behaviors that might indicate knowledge-construction activity. Metacognitive measures were completed by students during strategy training, practice, and each of the sessions in which they discussed lessons.

Lesson comprehension tests. The four lesson comprehension tests were developed by the author based on the lesson plans used and materials provided in the instructional unit.

Each test addressed only material covered in its related lesson. The pretreatment test of lesson comprehension, administered following the first lesson and prior to the beginning of training and treatment, was used to determine students' pretreatment ability to understand material presented in a teacher-led lesson. Two tests were constructed based on the posttest lesson, one for administration at the end of the posttest session and the other seven days later to assess retention of that lesson material. A test was also administered at the transfer session to assess comprehension of the transfer lesson. Students completed all comprehension tests individually. The difficulty level of all tests was set high to avoid ceiling effects. Each test contained 10 items in multiple-choice format that assessed students' literal comprehension of points emphasized in the lesson and five questions in open-ended written format that assessed their ability to make inferences, provide explanations, integrate concepts within the lesson, or go beyond what was presented in the lesson. An example of multiple-choice items used is, "The muscles are controlled by the: (a) cerebellum, (b) spinal cord, (c) cerebral cortex." Multiple-choice items were scored at one point each for correct answers for a total of 10 points possible for the literal understanding part of the test. Examples of the open-ended questions are, "Why would a human be totally unable to function without a cerebrum?" and "How is the autonomic nervous system related to the respiratory system?" Answers to these questions were not explicitly stated in the lesson and required inferencing and/or explanation based on material that was explicitly provided. Students could receive up to two partial points for each open-ended question for a total of 10 points possible for the inferential/integrative part of the test. Responses to the open-ended questions were evaluated independently by two raters who were blind to condition. Interrater reliabilities ranged from .88 to .92 for the inferential/integrative parts of the four tests. Any differences were reconciled through discussion to determine the data to be used in analyses. Internal consistency for the four comprehension tests ranged from .56 to .78 for the literal (multiple-choice format) parts of the tests and .52 to .61 for the inferential/integrative (written-response format) parts. These reliabilities are understandably low given the small number of items on each part of the tests. Perhaps using more than 10 items on the literal part of the tests and 5 on the inferential/integrative parts would bolster the reliabilities.

Knowledge mapping. Knowledge mapping was used as a means of assessing the accuracy and complexity of children's constructed knowledge for each lesson and for the unit as a whole. A knowledge map of a given topic was considered to be a reflection of the child's mental representation of knowledge about that topic and therefore a valid indication of that child's current state of understanding. Such maps, often called semantic maps, are graphic representations of information and consist of nodes that represent concepts, parts, or attributes and links to represent relationships among the nodes. Semantic maps are commonly used as a way of representing declarative knowledge about a particular topic (e.g., Jones, Pierce, & Hunter, 1988–9; McKeown & Beck, 1990). Knowledge mapping of this sort had been used for assessment purposes in a previous study (King & Rosenshine, 1993) as well as by several other researchers (e.g., Leinhardt & Smith, 1985; Leinhardt, 1987; Naveh-Benjamin, McKeachie, Lin, & Tucker, 1986; Novak & Gowan, 1984). According to their teachers, students in the present study had previously learned to construct semantic maps of this sort and had used the procedure often over the preceding few months.

The investigator used lesson plans and videotapes of the lessons to construct model knowledge maps for each of the posttest and transfer lessons and for the unit as a whole. These maps showed component parts and various characteristics and functions of the systems; and they depicted hierarchical ordering and other relationships among parts. Using these models as a standard, students' knowledge maps were analyzed to assess their accuracy and completeness and for evidence of attempts to construct more complex knowledge in the form of connections among concepts within the unit and connections to their prior knowledge and other world knowledge not specifically covered in the lessons. The knowledge maps were evaluated holistically and rated on a scale of 1 to 5 by two independent raters blind to condition. Interrater reliabilities ranged from .90 to .92 for the four knowledge maps. Discrepancies in ratings were resolved through averaging and those averages were used in the analyses.

Metacognitive self-monitoring. As mentioned previously, after each lesson's discussion session students rated how well they understood the materials as well as their use of specific aspects of the explaining and questioning procedures. In the two guided questioning conditions students answered the questions "How well did I do in making up comprehension questions?" "How well did I do in making up connection questions?" and "How well did I explain to others?" In the control condition students answered "How well did I discuss today's lesson?" In all three conditions students also answered "How well do I think I understand today's lesson?" Each item was rated on a 5-point scale. These scales clearly have face validity, but because they rely on students' self assessments of their verbal behavior, they may not be highly reliable. However, the repeated use of these metacognitive measures was expected to help students to monitor their application of the strategies, thus enhancing strategy use, as they have been found to do in studies by Davey and McBride (1986) and others (e.g., Brown, 1987).

Strategy use. Following the retention tests at the end of the study all students rated their perceptions of the strategy's helpfulness in learning. On a 7-point scale students responded to: "How helpful was this questioning strategy in helping you learn and remember the information in this unit on the parts and systems of the body?" Students' perceptions of the helpfulness of a strategy have been found to influence their continued use of that strategy (Pressley, Levin, & Ghatala, 1988).

Student verbal interaction. The two sets of verbal protocols were analyzed to identify examples of knowledge constructive activity. The coding scheme used was the same as one used previously by the author (King & Rosenshine,

Table 1   Coding Scheme for Question Generation and Knowledge Construction

Questions	Knowledge-Construction Statements
Integration question Goes beyond what was explicitly stated in the lesson, connects two ideas together, or asks for an explanation, inference, justification, etc.	**Knowledge integration** Makes new connections or goes beyond what was provided in the lesson—explanations, inferences, relationships between ideas, justifications, statements linking lesson content to material from outside the lesson (prior knowledge and personal experience)
Comprehension question Asks for a process or term to be described or defined	**Knowledge assimilation** Definitions, descriptions, and other material paraphrased in students' own words
Factual question Asks for recall of facts or other information explicitly covered in the lesson	**Knowledge restating** Simple statements of fact or information gleaned directly from the lesson or prior knowledge.

1993) with one exception described later. The coding scheme, summarized in Table 1, consists of three levels of questions and three corresponding levels of knowledge construction.

As in a previous study (King & Rosenshine, 1993), questions were coded according to what they asked for. Thus, factual questions simply asked for recall of facts or other information explicitly covered in the lesson; that is, they simply called upon memory for presented material (e.g., "How many bones are in the body?" and "Name two kinds of neurons.").

Comprehension questions were ones that asked for a process or term to be described or defined. These questions were at the comprehension level. Additionally, although they too called on memory in the sense that they asked for recall of material presented and could be answered by restating definitions verbatim as presented by the teacher, they also provided opportunities for students to paraphrase definitions and procedures in their own words and thus could induce a more complex level of knowledge building on the part of the responder. The generic comprehension questions on students' prompt cards, shown in Figure 1, were designed to prompt children to generate specific comprehension-type questions. Examples of comprehension questions students asked are "What does autonomic mean?" and "Describe in your own words what a neuron is."

Integration questions (King & Rosenshine, 1993), which were labeled connection questions on the children's prompt cards, were thought-provoking questions that required students to go beyond what was explicitly stated in the lesson by linking two ideas together in some way (e.g., "How is the cerebellum different from the medulla?" and "How is the spinal cord like this overhead projector cord?"), or asking for an explanation, or requiring some sort of inference, justification, or speculation (e.g., "What do you think would happen if we had no bones?"). Questions following the format of any of the connection questions in Figure 1 were coded as integration questions; however, not all integration questions followed the structure of the provided connection questions.

Three levels of knowledge-construction statements were identified, ranging from low to high in complexity, and roughly corresponding to the three kinds of questions. Simple statements of information or facts gleaned directly from the lesson or from prior knowledge or experience were coded as knowledge restating (King & Rosenshine, 1993), the lowest level of knowledge construction. For example, in response to the question "What is the muscle attached to the bone with?" a knowledge restatement was "It is attached by ligaments."

In a previous study on knowledge construction (King & Rosenshine, 1993) all of the indicators of complex knowledge construction were grouped into one category labeled "explanations." In contrast, in the present study these indicators of knowledge construction were separated into two categories: knowledge assimilation (roughly corresponding to the declarative form of the "assimilation" level in the constructive activity scale developed by Chan et al., 1992), and knowledge integration. Knowledge assimilation statements were statements that demonstrated understanding of the material by paraphrasing definitions or processes presented in the lesson; that is, the definition was not restated verbatim, but was translated into a student's own words and often elaborated upon. For example, in response to the integration question "How are bones and muscles similar?" the statement "They attach to each other and help each other do their work" shows understanding of the interdependence of the two subsystems and is stated in the students' own words; and therefore was coded as a knowledge assimilation statement. Similarly, the following statement on the importance of the nervous system appears to be in the student's own words and shows knowledge assimilation: "It is important because if we didn't have it we wouldn't be able to feel and breathe and move—and think. The brain sends messages to the nervous system—to all parts of the body and the nerves send messages back to the brain. They send messages on what to do and the reason it is important is because we wouldn't be able to do anything."

Statements that integrated aspects of the new material in some manner or in some way went beyond the material presented in the lesson were evidence of more complex constructed meaning. Therefore, explanations, inferences, interpretations, relationships between ideas, justifications, speculations, and statements linking the lesson content to material from outside the lesson (prior knowledge) were coded as knowledge integration. For example, one student's description of the nervous system, "It is like the school office phone. The office phone has different lines—there are a lot—they can all be used at once without interfering with each other—to send messages back and forth," shows knowledge integration because it explains a concept by linking the new information about

the nervous system to the student's prior knowledge about telephone systems. When one student asked "What is the most important part of your body?" her partner demonstrated knowledge integration by making the inference "It is the brain and the brain stem." This response was coded an inference rather than knowledge restating because this information had not been stated explicitly in the lesson.

It was expected that, during discussion, integration questions would induce construction of complex knowledge (knowledge integration), whereas comprehension questions would induce knowledge assimilation. Similarly, factual questions could be expected to elicit restatement of factual knowledge (see Table 1). However, any type of question could (presumably) elicit any type of response and therefore be said to induce any level of knowledge construction.

It should be noted that the act of generating questions, particularly comprehension and integration questions, is also knowledge-constructing activity because it requires some reconceptualization to generate such questions. However, in the present study the question-generation type of knowledge construction was instructed for and prompted during treatment and was therefore not classified as exclusively knowledge construction.

Students' verbal interaction was coded by a rater blind to treatment condition and purpose of the experiment. To establish reliability, 10 protocols were randomly selected for coding by a second rater also blind to condition and experimental treatment. Interrater reliability on the six verbal interaction categories ranged from .92 to .99. Both raters examined the lesson plans or viewed the videotape of the lesson prior to rating to facilitate accuracy in coding of children's statements as having been restated verbatim or paraphrased, and covered in the lesson or not covered. The number of student questions and statements during the 10-minute discussion session were totaled for each dyad in each of the six verbal interaction categories. Thus, for both the posttest and transfer sessions, the data used in the analysis for each category represents the sum of two children's verbalization over a period of 10 minutes.

RESULTS

The unit of analysis used in all subsequent analyses for lesson comprehension and verbal interaction was the dyad. This unit of analysis was used because the process of knowledge building during dyadic interaction was viewed as being interdependent; that is, the responses (and often the questions) of one partner are, to a great extent, elicited or stimulated by the questions and statements of the other partner. Therefore, all student verbal interaction data (questions and knowledge-building statements) were collapsed within each dyad for the posttest discussion session as well as for the transfer discussion session. Similarly, although the comprehension tests and knowledge maps were completed by students independently, partners' scores on these measures would have been affected by the joint knowledge-building activity within their dyad. Therefore, total scores on these measures were combined for each dyad. Means and standard deviations for these data, as well as significant post hoc comparisons, are presented in Table 2.

Separate 3 (Strategy) × 2 (Grade Level) analyses of variance (ANOVAs) on the pretreatment tests of lesson comprehension and the pretest knowledge map of the content of the science unit showed no significant differences among the three conditions and no significant Grade × Strategy interactions. On the literal part of the lesson comprehension test, analyses revealed $F(2, 18) = 1.89$, $p = .19$ for grade and $Fs = (2, 18) < 1$ for both strategy and interaction effects; and for the inferential/integrative part, $Fs < 1$ for strategy and grade and $F(2, 18) = 1.26$, $p = .31$ for the Grade × Strategy interaction. On knowledge mapping, results were $F(2, 18) = 3.39$, $p = .08$ for grade, $F(2, 18) < 1$ for strategy, and $F(2, 18) = 1.29$, $p = .30$ for the Grade × Strategy interaction. Therefore, it was concluded that, prior to treatment, the three groups did not differ on their knowledge of the content to be covered in the unit, nor on their ability to learn from teacher-presented lessons. Neither did the fifth graders differ from the fourth graders in these respects.

Lesson Comprehension

Strategy × Grade Level ANOVAs revealed no significant differences between fourth and fifth graders on comprehension of the posttest lesson, $F(2, 18) < 1$, or retention, $F(2, 18) < 1$, and no significant interactions. Therefore, scores on these lesson comprehension tests were collapsed across the two grades for the following analyses.

ANOVAs were used to determine effects of the three strategies on comprehension of the posttest lesson, on retention of that material 7 days later, and transfer. In each case when these ANOVAs were significant, Fisher's Protected LSD post hoc procedure was used to examine pairwise comparisons among the three group means (see Seaman, Levin, & Serlin, 1991, for a discussion of the appropriateness of the Fisher test when no more than three means are compared).

Posttest. Analyses revealed that, for the literal part of the posttest, $F(2, 21) = 3.56$, $p < .05$, and for the inferential/integrative part, $F(2, 21) = 4.17$, $p < .05$. As Table 2 shows, the post hoc comparisons among the means for the three conditions on the posttest revealed that both the experience-based questioners and the lesson-based questioners performed significantly better than controls on literal comprehension as well as on inference/integration. These findings indicate that the guiding questions, whether lesson-based or experience-based in content, foster both literal comprehension as well as inference/integration.

Retention. At retention, significant effects were also found for the literal part of the retention test, $F(2, 21) = 16.34$, $p < .001$, and for the inferential/integrative part, $F(2, 21) = 11.99$, $p < .001$. Fisher post hoc tests revealed that experience-based questioners outperformed lesson-based questioners who in turn outperformed controls on both the literal and inferential/integrative parts of the retention test. These results suggest that experience-based questions are superior to lesson-based ones in promoting retention of learned material over time.

Transfer. The ANOVAs on the comprehension test for the transfer lesson were nonsignificant for both literal comprehension, $F(2, 21) = 2.18$, $p = .15$, and inference/integration, $F(2, 21) < 1$, indicating no differences among groups on comprehension at transfer.

To determine how interaction within dyads might have contributed to these learning outcomes, student verbal interaction during the posttest study session and the transfer study session was analyzed for quantity and quality of questions asked and knowledge-construction statements made. First, to determine whether there were any grade level differences on these variables, Strategy × Grade Level ANOVAs were conducted on the six verbal interaction variables for the posttest study session and the transfer study session. There were no significant grade effects for any of the variables at posttest. For fact questions, integration questions, total questions, knowledge restatement, knowledge assimilation, and knowledge integration, all Fs $(2, 18) < 1$. And for comprehension questions, $F (1, 18) = 4.1$, $p = .06$ (means $= 4.45$ & 2.92 for fourth and fifth grade, respectively). There were no significant Grade × Strategy interactions. Nor were any differences found at transfer. For fact questions, integration questions, total questions, knowledge restatement, all Fs $(2, 18) < 1$; and for knowledge assimilation, $F (2, 18) = 1.52$, $p = .26$, and for knowledge integration, $F (2, 18) = 3.54$, $p = .08$ (means $= 1.00$ & $.08$ for fourth and fifth grade, respectively). There were no significant Strategy × Grade interactions. These results indicate no grade differences; therefore, scores on the questioning and constructive activity variables were collapsed across the two grades for the subsequent analyses.

Questioning and knowledge-construction statements at posttest. Inspection of Table 2 shows that, although there were no differences among the three conditions on total number of questions asked during the posttest discussion session, $F (2, 21) < 1$, students in the three conditions tended to ask different kinds of questions. ANOVAs on the data for questioning showed no differences among conditions for assimilation questions, $F (2, 21) = 2.01$, $p < 15$, but revealed differences for factual questioning, $F (2, 21) = 6.16$, $p < .01$, and integration questioning, $F (2, 21) = 19.35$, $p < .001$. These latter analyses were followed up with Fisher post hoc comparisons. Students in the control group asked significantly more factual questions than students in the experience-based condition. Students in both the experience-based questioning condition and the lesson-based questioning condition asked more integration questions than the controls. This latter finding is not surprising because this is the type of question students in the two questioning conditions had been trained to ask and were prompted to ask.

A somewhat similar pattern of performance was demonstrated on the three levels of knowledge construction statements. Separate ANOVAs revealed significant differences among conditions on knowledge restating, $F (2, 21) = 6.73$, $p < .01$, knowledge assimilation, $F (2, 21) = 6.08$, $p × .01$, and knowledge integration, $F (2, 21) = 8.00$, $p < .01$. Fisher post hoc comparisons revealed that the controls made significantly more factual statements than did both the experience-based questioners and the lesson-based questioners. Also, students trained in experience-based questioning and those trained in lesson-based questioning demonstrated significantly more knowledge assimilation than did the control group. And, in terms of the highest level of knowledge construction, the experience-based questioners made significantly more knowledge integration statements than did the controls and the lesson-based questioners, who made somewhat more (but not significantly more) integration statements than the controls, $p = .10$.

These findings lend some support to the notion of a correspondence between level of questioning and level of knowledge-construction activity, suggesting that level of questioning used may induce level of knowledge construction taking place. For example, not only did the control group operate at the lowest level of questioning, asking mostly factual questions (65% of their questions were factual), but also their statements were primarily at the lowest level of knowledge construction, with 88% of their statements being knowledge restatement. In contrast, experience-based questioners operated mostly at the highest level of questioning and knowledge construction. A full 51% of their questions were at the integration level with another 28% at the comprehension level; whereas 21% of their statements were knowledge integration ones, the highest level of constructive activity, and another 40% were knowledge assimilation. These findings suggest that when students ask integration and comprehension questions they are more likely to engage in complex levels of knowledge construction, and when they ask factual questions they are more likely to engage in knowledge restating, the lowest form of knowledge construction.

Students' integration statements during the posttest discussion were examined further to identify those integration statements that were experience-based, statements that clearly referred to that student's existing knowledge or personal experience, and those that were lesson-based, ones referring to material within the lesson. An ANOVA on these data revealed significant differences among conditions for experience-based integration statements, $F (2, 21) = 5.41$, $p < .05$. Post hoc comparisons revealed that experienced-based questioners made significantly more experienced-based integration statements than did the lesson-based questioners, $p < .05$, who made more than controls, $p < .05$ (means = 1.67, 1.25, and .29, respectively). This finding suggests that the experience-based questioners actually did make some of the sorts of experiential connections and linkages to their prior knowledge that they had been trained to make. Furthermore, these findings show that accessing prior knowledge occurs infrequently in a naturally occurring spontaneous discussion, the control condition. The ANOVA for lesson-based integration statements was also significant, $F (2, 21) = 3.91$, $p < .05$. Post hocs revealed that experienced-based questioners made significantly more lesson-based integration statements than did lesson-based questioners, $p \times .05$, and controls, $p \times .05$ (means = .89, .13, & .14, respectively).

Questioning and knowledge-construction statements at transfer. In the transfer discussion session, during which students did not use their prompt cards, the pattern of questioning and knowledge construction activity was not as clear cut. Again, there were no differences among conditions on total questions asked, $F (2, 21) < 1$. Nor were there any differences for factual questions, $F (2, 21) < 1$. However, there were differences among conditions on comprehension questions, $F (2, 21) = 8.91$, $p < .01$, and post hoc comparisons revealed that students trained in lesson-based questioning asked significantly more comprehension questions than did the experience-based questioners and the controls. Although the analysis for integration questions was only marginally significant, $F (2, 21) = 3.03$, $p = .07$, and therefore the post hoc test was not performed, the means in Table 2 clearly show that both experience-based and lesson-based questioners asked substantially more integration questions at transfer than did controls.

The ANOVAs on the knowledge construction data from the transfer session showed no significant differences among conditions for knowledge restating, $F (2, 21) = 1.16$, $p > .30$, knowledge assimilation, $F (2, 21) = 3.16$, $p > .05$, and knowledge integration, $F (2, 21) = 1.05$, $p > .35$. However, inspection of the means in Table 2 shows that both the experience-based questioners and the lesson-based questioners demonstrated somewhat more knowledge assimilation than the control group and they showed some indication of knowledge integration. Here, too, integration statements were examined more closely to identify ones that were experience-based and those that were lesson-based. Although the ANOVA for experience-based integration statements was non-significant, $F (2, 21) = 2.44$, $p = .11$, experience-based questioners made somewhat more experience-based statements than did the lesson-based questioners and controls (means = .78, .25, .00, respectively). The ANOVA on lesson-based integration statements was nonsignificant, $F (2, 21) = 1.00$.

Knowledge Mapping

The knowledge maps were constructed by the children as measures of their knowledge representation. In general, most of the children's knowledge maps depicted parts of a particular system of the body and facts about that system, but did not arrange them in hierarchical fashion nor show other relationships among them; that is, most of the maps were simple one-level ones that appeared unintegrated and were without evidence of clustering beyond that first level. All of the knowledge maps appeared to be lesson bound, or unit bound in the case of the pre- and postlesson knowledge maps of the unit topic, and they did not indicate connections to prior knowledge and other world knowledge not specifically covered in the lessons. Unfortunately it became clear that the students had not after all, prior to the beginning of the study, learned how to construct knowledge maps other than the simple component-parts sort with nodes linked to the central concept only. When asked about this, the teachers acknowledged that the students had not learned how to develop and depict hierarchical relationships among component parts. Because of their lack of prior skill in constructing sufficiently complex maps, the children undoubtedly were unable to graphically represent certain aspects of their knowledge structures, such as nodes representing prior knowledge and interrelationships (links) between and among various nodes. Therefore, the children's knowledge maps could not have accurately reflected the total complexity of their mental representations. Consequently, the maps were a valid measure of only the accuracy and completeness of the children's knowledge and not of its complexity. Therefore, the maps were evaluated only for accuracy and completeness.

An ANOVA on the knowledge maps for the posttest lesson was marginally significant, $F (2, 21) = 2.59$, $p = .09$, and inspection of the means in Table 2 shows that the experience-based questioners and the lesson-based questioners constructed somewhat more accurate and complete maps than did the controls. The analysis on the maps from the transfer lesson (muscles and bones) was significant, $F (2, 21) = 4.97$, $p < .05$, and post hocs revealed that the experience-based questioners produced better maps than did either the lesson-based questioners or the controls. The ANOVA for the posttreatment knowledge maps of the systems of the body unit was also significant, $F (2, 21) = 4.34$, $p < .05$, and post hocs showed that both of the trained questioning groups outperformed the controls.

Explanation-Only Control Group Analyses

To determine whether the explanation-only control group students improved in their abil-

ity to comprehend lessons, at both literal and inferential levels, separate repeated measures ANOVAs were conducted on dyads' scores for the literal portion and the inferential/integrative portion of the comprehension test on the pretest lesson (the circulatory system lesson) and the posttest lesson (the brain and nervous system lesson). Results indicated that over the span of this study the explanation-only control group students improved their skill in literal comprehension of teacher-led lessons, $F (1, 13) = 12.24$, $p < .05$ (means = 7.14, & 11.71 from pre to post) and they also improved in their ability to make inferences, explain, and integrate material from that lesson, $F (1, 13) = 7.91$, $p < .05$ (means = 1.36 & 3.14 from pre to post). These control students also increased their knowledge of the systems of the body over the duration of the study as indicated by a repeated measures ANOVA conducted on their scores for the pretest and posttest knowledge maps of the systems of the body unit, $F (1, 13) = 10.50$, $p < .05$ (means = 4.43 & 5.43 from pre to post). These results may suggest that simply learning how to explain can promote learning; however, there are no pre-post comparisons for knowledge integration or knowledge assimilation activity to support such a conclusion.

Student Ratings of Their Lesson Comprehension

A 3 (Strategy) × 3 (Time) repeated measures ANOVA was conducted on the individual students' ratings of how well they understood the lessons at practice sessions 1 and 2 and at posttest. The means for the three groups on the three lessons ranged from 4.28 to 4.78 on a 5-point scale. This analysis revealed no significant effect for strategy, or time, and no significant interaction. These results suggest that all three groups believed they understood the lesson material equally well regardless of which strategy was used, and their impression of their understanding did not improve or decrease over the period of the study.

Student Ratings of Their Ability to Generate Questions and Explanations

Three separate 2 (Strategy) × 4 (Time) repeated measures analyses were conducted on the experience-based questioners' and lesson-based questioners' ratings of how well they made up comprehension questions and connection questions and how well they explained things to their partner during the questioning sessions. For generating comprehension questions there was no significant effect for strategy, $F (1, 96) = 1.73, p > .05$. However, the effect for time was significant, $F (3, 96) = 13.16, p < .001$ (means = 3.73, 4.05, 4.59, 4.31 from early to later sessions), indicating that students in both of the questioning conditions believed that they improved in their ability to generate comprehension questions over time. There was no Strategy × Time interaction. A similar pattern emerged for connection questions, with no significant effect for strategy, $F (1, 96) = < 1$, and a significant effect for time, $F (3, 96) = 6.65, p < .001$ (means = 4.14, 3.71, 4,51, 4.34 from first to last session). Again, apparently students believed that they improved with practice in generating connection questions.

The repeated measures analysis for generating explanations revealed no significant effect for strategy and the effect for time only neared significance, $F (3, 96) = 2.37, p = .07$. The means for the four sessions were 4.00, 4.35, 4.48, and 4.46, indicating little change over time in students' ratings of their ability to explain. This may suggest that, according to students' perceptions, they learned well how to explain from their initial training session in explanation.

A one-way repeated measures analysis was conducted on the control group students' ratings of how well they discussed lesson material. The effect for time was significant, $F (3, 55) = 10.71, p < .001$ (means = 3.36, 4,36, 4.96, & 4.50 over the four sessions), indicating students' sense of improvement with practice.

Student Ratings of Strategy Helpfulness

An ANOVA was used to examine students' end-of-study ratings of how useful they found their strategy to be for helping them learn the material in their science unit. On a 7-point scale, means were 4.64, 5.72, and 4.89 for the control, lesson-based questioning, and experience-based questioning groups respectively. There were no significant differences among conditions, $F (2, 45) = 2.51, p > .09$.

DISCUSSION ⑬

Results of this study indicate that when children use questions that guide them to connect ideas within a lesson together or connect the lesson to their prior knowledge, they engage in complex knowledge construction which, in turn, enhances learning; and these learning effects are stronger for questions that connect to prior knowledge. These results are consistent with Wittrock's (1990) model of generative learning that indicates that material generated in relation to prior knowledge is more memorable. This study also shows that elementary age children can be trained to generate these kinds of questions for themselves, and they can also be taught how to formulate explanations, one manifestation of complex knowledge construction.

Knowledge Construction ⑭

Using guided questioning to stimulate discussion not only elicited verbal indicators of knowledge construction, but also enhanced comprehension and retention of presented material as well as knowledge mapping of that material. Although the children in both of the guided questioning strategy conditions outperformed their peers in the control group on lesson comprehension; as predicted, the experience-based questioners retained even more of the material over time than did the lesson-based questioners. This may suggest that connecting new material to existing knowledge structures, as the experience-based questioners were trained to do, facilitates retention more than does connecting concepts within the new material, as the lesson-based questioners were trained to do. Such a conclusion is consistent with the distinction that Kintsch (1986) makes between learning *about* text and learning *from* text. Kintsch points out that when a reader constructs a mental representation that is based only on the material read, that is, the mental representation is a text-based model of the material, that material can be remembered well; however, constructing a broader *situation* model facilitates inferencing as well. Similarly, in the present study, constructing a lesson-based model may have been less likely to promote memory and inferencing at retention than was integrating the material into existing knowledge in the continuous process of building more extensive mental representations of the world. The findings for knowledge integration lend support to this view. Not only did the experience-based questioners make more knowledge integration statements during the posttest discussion than did the lesson-based questioners, but also significantly more of their integration statements were experience-based ones as compared to those of the lesson-based questioners.

The finding that the experience-based questioners engaged in more integration-level knowledge construction suggests that their knowledge structures were more *integrated* than those of the other groups, and the fact that they retained the material better over time suggests that those knowledge structures were also more *stable*. Furthermore, the finding that more of the experience-based questioners' integration statements were experienced-based than were those of the lesson-based questioners and controls suggests that their knowledge representations were also more global, more richly integrated with their existing knowledge and personal experience, than those of their peers. These findings together suggest that such stable, integrated, and global knowledge structures were a result of the use of experience-based questions. It may be that experience-based questions are more beneficial to learning than lesson-based questions or unguided questioning because they prompt students to access and use their prior knowledge and experience during knowledge construction, and, as a result, help them to construct more complex knowledge.

If it had been possible to assess students' posttreatment knowledge structures by evaluation of their knowledge maps as originally planned, there might have been additional specific evidence to support the conclusions regarding the complexity of the children's posttreatment knowledge structures. In any case, the posttest maps of the experience-based questioners were more accurate and complete than those of the lesson-based questioners and controls, suggesting greater complexity of their mental representations. But why would the mental representations of the experience-based questioners be more accurate and complete than those of the lesson-based questioners when those maps only showed material from the lesson per se and did not go beyond the lesson to show connections to prior knowledge? The superiority of the experience-based questioners' maps over those of the lesson-based questioners can presumably be accounted for by the fact that during that posttest discussion session experience-based questioners made more integration statements, more of which were experience-based connections, than did the lesson- based questioners. Perhaps the quantity and type of their knowledge integration statements at posttest resulted in such strong links to prior knowledge that the new material became sufficiently anchored in their mental representations as to be well reflected in their knowledge maps. The fact that they retained more of the posttest material after 7 days than did the lesson-based questioners suggests that their mental representations actually were more stable as well as more complete and accurate.

It should be pointed out that these effects on knowledge construction (i.e., lesson comprehension and retention, knowledge-construction statements, and knowledge mapping) cannot be explained by a metacognitive mediator, that is, students' perception that they were highly capable in using their strategy. For the metacognitive measures, there were no differences among conditions on students' ratings of their ability in lesson comprehension, questioning, and explaining, nor on their perception of the helpfulness of their strategy. Although these results suggest that self-monitoring and sense of strategy competence alone cannot account for differences among groups on knowledge construction, as pointed out previously, such self-ratings are not particularly reliable indicators of metacognition.

Role of Questioning in Knowledge Construction ⑮

Findings from this study suggest a correspondence between level of questioning and level of knowledge-construction statements, with integration questions (the highest level of questioning) inducing knowledge integration (the highest level of knowledge construction) and factual questions (the lowest level of questioning) inducing knowledge restatement (the lowest level of knowledge construction). At posttest the two groups trained in questioning asked more integration questions that did the controls. Furthermore, the experience-based questioners operated at the highest level of knowledge construction as indicated by the quantity of integration statements they made. Conversely, the controls operated at the lowest level of knowledge construction as evidenced by their asking more factual questions and making more knowledge restatements. Apparently when students ask integration and comprehension questions they are more likely to engage in higher levels of knowledge construction; and when they ask factual questions they are more likely to engage in knowledge restating, the lowest form of knowledge construction. Some additional support for this conclusion was found in students' behavior during the transfer session. In the transfer lesson discussion the experience-based questioners and the lesson-based questioners did not have their question cards to prompt them to ask their integration and comprehension types of questions and they asked somewhat more factual questions and made somewhat more restatements of knowledge than they had in the posttest session.

(16) *Transfer*

In the transfer lesson discussion, both the experience-based questioners and lesson-based questioners did ask more integration questions than the controls, indicating that both of the trained questioning strategies were maintained at least to some extent in an unprompted context with new lesson material. Thus, these questioning strategies appear to be easily learned and used in an elementary classroom context even without prompting. However, despite the fact that those students rated highly both their ability to ask comprehension and connection questions and their ability to explain things, they did not maintain the same level of questioning or constructive activity in the transfer context, when they no longer

had the question cards to prompt them, as they had in the posttest session. One explanation for these results may be that students needed more practice in generating questions and may have needed the support of the question prompts for a longer period of time to internalize the stems. Other researchers (e.g., Davey & McBride, 1986; Graesser, 1992; Palincsar & Brown, 1989; Pressley et al., 1992) have pointed out the need for considerable training in question generation before that skill is acquired, let alone maintained. Or perhaps students were reluctant to use their questioning strategies on their own and may have needed more practice in applying them in other contexts before transfer effects could be expected.

Strategy effects on comprehension at transfer were disappointing. It seems reasonable to expect that questions that deliberately establish links to the world outside the lesson (i.e., experience-based questions) would facilitate transfer to other non-lesson-based contexts to a greater extent than would lesson-based questions. However, there were no differences among conditions on lesson comprehension at transfer, and the experience-based questioners asked no more integration questions and made no more knowledge-integration statements than the lesson-based questioners did. However, their knowledge maps were more complex than those of the other two groups. By way of possible explanation, it should be recalled that, in contrast to their peers, a greater proportion of the experience-based questioners' integration statements at transfer were linkages to prior knowledge, that is, experience-based ones versus lesson-based ones; and this may have resulted in more richly integrated knowledge representations. If the experience-based questioners did achieve such richly integrated knowledge representations, that might explain the greater complexity of their knowledge maps, which in effect were an external reflection of those mental representations. Again, it is possible that the experience-based questions would have had an effect at transfer with more practice in question generation and more extended use of the question prompt cards.

This study provides evidence that questioning strategies can be used to facilitate the knowledge construction process, which in turn enhances learning. Moreover, it lends support to the Chan et al. (1992) finding that knowledge-constructive activity has a direct effect on learning.

(17)

APPENDIX

Procedure and Example Used for Teaching How to Explain

- Explanations don't just tell what something is or describe it—they tell the *how* and *why* about it
- Explanations should be in our own words—not just repeating an explanation we have heard and memorized
- When we explain something we often use information we already have to make what we are explaining clearer (like comparing the new information to something we already know about)
- Explanations often connect two things or ideas or link a procedure and an idea together

Description	*Explanation*

Definition:

Describing something or telling what happened (telling the "what")

Explaining something or explaining what happened (telling the "why" and "how" of it)

Example:

Description of the circulatory system

The circulatory system is made up of the heart, veins, arteries, and blood. Some of the arteries and veins are small, and some are large. The heart pumps blood through the arteries and veins.

Explanation of the circulatory system

We need a circulatory system in our bodies to move the blood around to all parts of the body because the blood carries oxygen, which is food for the cells of the body. All parts of the body need the oxygen to grow and function. The circulatory system is just a way of getting that oxygen moved around. The tubes the blood moves in are the arteries and veins. The arteries and veins are all connected, like highways and roads, so they can transport blood to any place in the body. Near the heart the arteries and veins are large because they have a lot of blood to carry, and as they get closer to one part of the body or to a cell they become much smaller (like freeways, highways, streets, roads, and dirt paths). They can also be seen as being like branches of a tree that get smaller as they get closer to the leaves because they don't have so much to carry to only one leaf. The heart is a pump and it pumps the blood so that it keeps moving around in the network of arteries and veins. The heart pumps by squeezing in and then releasing over and over and over (like making a fist and relaxing it).

REFERENCES

Anderson, J. R. (1976). *Language, memory and thought.* Hillsdale: Erlbaum.

Armbruster, B. B., Anderson, T. H., & Ostertag, J. (1987). Does text structures/summarization instruction facilitate learning from expository text? *Reading Research Quarterly, 22,* 331–346.

Baddeley, A. D. (1976). *The psychology of memory.* New York: Harper & Row.

Brown, A. L. (1987). Metacognition, executive control, self-regulation and other more mysterious mechanisms. In F. E. Weinert & R. H. Kluwe (Eds.), *Metacognition, motivation, and understanding* (pp. 65–116). Hillsdale, NJ: Erlbaum.

Brown, A. L., Bransford, J. D., Ferrara, R. A., & Campione, J. C. (1983). Learning, remembering and understanding. In J. H. Flavell & E. M. Markman (Eds.), *Handbook of child psychology, Vol. III: Cognitive development* (pp. 77–166). New York: Wiley.

Brown, A. L., & Campione, J. C. (1986). Psychological theory and the study of learning disabilities. *American Psychologist, 41,* 1059–1068.

Brown, J. S., Collins, A., & Duguid, P. (1989). Situated cognition and the culture of learning. *Educational Researcher, 18,* 32–42.

Chan, C. K. K., Burtis, P. J., Scardamalia, M., & Bereiter, C. (1992). Constructive activity in learning from text. *American Educational Research Journal, 29,* 97–118.

Chi, M. T. H., Hutchinson, J. E., & Robin, A. F. (1989). How inferences about novel domain-related concepts can be constrained by structural knowledge. *Merrill-Palmer Quarterly, 35,* 27–62.

Davey, B., & McBride, S. (1986). Effects of question-generation training on reading comprehension. *Journal of Educational Psychology, 78,* 256–262.

Graesser, A. C. (1992). Questioning mechanisms during complex learning. (Technical report). Arlington, VA: Cognitive Science Program, Office of Naval Research.

Graesser, A. C., & Franklin, S. P. (1990). QUEST: A cognitive model of question answering. *Discourse Processes, 13,* 279–303.

Jones, B. F., Pierce, J., & Hunter, B. (1988–9) Teaching students to construct graphic representations. *Educational Leadership, 46*(4), 20–25.

King, A. (1989). Effects of self-questioning training on college students' comprehension of lectures. *Contemporary Educational Psychology, 14,* 366–381.

King, A. (1990). Enhancing peer interaction and learning in the classroom through reciprocal peer questioning. *American Educational Research Journal, 27*(4), 664–687.

King, A. (1992). Comparison of self-questioning, summarizing, and notetaking-review as strategies for learning from lectures. *American Educational Research Journal, 29*(2), 303–323.

King, A. (1993). Making a transition from "sage on the stage" to "guide on the side." *College Teaching, 41*(1), 30–35.

King, A. (in press). Autonomy and question asking: The role of personal control in guided cooperative questioning. *Learning and Individual Differences.*

King, A., & Rosenshine, B. (1993). Effects of guided cooperative questioning on children's knowledge construction. *Journal of Experimental Education, 61,* 127–148.

Kintsch, W. (1986). Learning from text. *Cognition and Instruction, 3*(2), 87–108.

Leinhardt, G. (1987). Development of an expert explanation: An analysis of a sequence of subtraction lessons. *Cognition and Instruction, 4,* 225–282.

Leinhardt, G., & Smith, D. A. (1985). Expertise in mathematics instruction: Subject matter knowledge. *Journal of Educational Psychology, 77,* 247–271.

Martin, V. L., & Pressley, M. (1991). Elaborative interrogation effects depend on the nature of the question. *Journal of Educational Psychology, 83,* 113–119.

Mayer, R. E. (1980). Elaboration techniques that increase the meaningfulness of technical text; An experimental test of the learning strategy hypothesis. *Journal of Educational Psychology,* 770–784.

Mayer, R. E. (1984). Aids to prose comprehension. *Educational Psychologist, 19,* 30–42.

McKeown, M. G., & Beck, I. L. (1990). The assessment and characterization of young learners' knowledge of a topic in history. *American Educational Research Journal, 27,* 688–726.

Naveh-Benjamin, M., McKeachie, W. J., Lin, Y., & Tucker, D. G. (1986). Inferring students' cognitive structures and their development using the "ordered tree technique." *Journal of Educational Psychology, 78,* 130–140.

Novak, J. D., & Gowan, D. B. (1984). *Learning how to learn.* Cambridge University Press.

Palincsar, A. S., & Brown, A. L. (1989). Instruction for self-regulated reading. In L. B. Resnick & L. E. Klopfer (Eds.), *Toward the thinking curriculum: Current cognitive research* (pp. 19–39) Alexandria, VA: Association for Supervision and Curriculum Development.

Perkins, D. N., & Salomon, G. (1989). Are cognitive skills context-bound? *Educational Researcher, 18,* 16–25.

Pressley, M., & Levin, J. R. (1986). Elaborative learning strategies for the inefficient learner. In S. J. Ceci (Ed.), *Handbook of cognitive, social, and neuropsychological aspects of learning disabilities* (pp. 175–212) Hillsdale, NJ: Lawrence Erlbaum.

Pressley, M., Levin, J. R., & Ghatala, E. S. (1988). Strategy comparison opportunities promote long-term strategy use. *Contemporary Educational Psychology, 13,* 157–168.

Pressley, M., McDaniel, M. A., Turnure, J. E., Wood, E., & Ahmad, M. (1987). Generation and precision of elaboration: Effects on intentional and incidental learning. *Journal of Experimental Psychology: Learning, Memory, and Cognition, 13,* 291–300.

Pressley, M., Symons, S., McDaniel, M. A., Snyder, B. L., & Turnure, J. E. (1988). Elaborative interrogation facilitates acquisition of confusing facts. *Journal of Educational Psychology, 80*(3), 268–278.

Pressley, M., Wood., E., Woloshyn, V. E., Martin, V., King, A., & Menke, D. (1992). Encouraging mindful use of prior knowledge: Attempting to construct explanatory answers facilitates learning. *Educational Psychologist, 27,* 91–109.

Resnick, L., (1987). *Education and learning to think.* Washington, DC: National Academy Press.

Rumelhart, D. E., & McClelland, J. L. (1986). *Parallel distributed processing: Explorations in the microstructure of cognition.* Cambridge: MIT Press.

Scardamalia, M., Bereiter, C., & Steinbach, R. (1984). Teachability of reflective processes in written composition. *Cognitive Science, 8,* 173–190.

Schank, R. C. (1975). *Conceptual information processing.* North Holland: Amsterdam.

Seaman, M. A., Levin, J. R., & Serlin, R. C. (1991). New developments in pairwise multiple comparisons: Some powerful and practicable procedures. *Psychological Bulletin, 110,* 577–586.

Webb, N. M. (1989). Peer interaction and learning in small groups. *International Journal of Educational Research, 21*–39.

Wittrock, M. C. (1974). Learning as a generative process. *Educational Psychologist, 11,* 87–95.

Wittrock, M. C. (1990). Generative processes of comprehension. *Educational Psychologist, 24,* 345–376.

Wittrock, M. C., & Alesandrini, K. (1990). Generation of summaries and analogies and analytic and holistic abilities. *American Educational Research Journal, 27,* 489–502.

Manuscript received May 6, 1993
Revision received September 30, 1993
Accepted November 3, 1993

First Phase: Previewing and Predicting the Research Report.   Set your purpose and identify known information about the topic. Determine which sections are to be read.

Suggested purpose: Reading to identify a possible effective instructional practice.

Suggested main headings to be read: one (title), two (abstract), four (purpose), five (sample), six (procedures), eleven (question scheme), thirteen through sixteen (discussion and conclusion).

Second Phase: Reading the Research Report.   Read the report sections and identify key information. Note the researcher's use of italicized subheadings as organizational signals.

Third Phase: Confirming Predictions and Knowledge.   Verify that your purpose has been met and recall key information. If the purpose has not been met or if additional information needs to be identified, select sections to be read or reread.

Suggested sections as sources of additional key information: nine (all subsections and Figure 1), ten (all subsections), seventeen (Appendix).

Suggested sections to be read additionally (if needed): twelve (all subsections).

EVALUATING RESEARCH REPORTS

Informed consumers effectively compare and shop in a store for products by using a set of criteria. Research consumers can "shop" among research reports to identify well-written reports of appropriate methodology. You have already taken the first step in being a research consumer: learning to read research reports like a research producer. The second step is using the questions in Figure 3.1 to evaluate research reports.

The questions are about each of the major aspects of research reports. At this point in your learning, you should not be expected to answer all the questions appropriately. Because the content and length of research reports are often determined by the editors of the journals or books in which the reports appear, our determinations as research consumers about the appropriateness and adequacy of the information in a report will necessarily be subjective. Remember that these subjective decisions change as you gain increased understanding of research methods and research reporting and as you gain more experience in reading and evaluating research reports and writing about them. Your work with this text is a beginning step in acquiring understanding and experience.

The questions presented in Figure 3.1 provide an overview of the discussions in later chapters. The major headings within Figure 3.1 represent common, major headings found in research reports published in professional journals. As you can see reviewing the previously cited reports, researchers modify these major headings to fit their purposes and to highlight particular information. Research reports in other sources—books, encyclopedias, newspapers, and popular magazines—may have different organizations and formats. Some of these variations are discussed in later chapters.

ABSTRACT

Organization. Is information about the major aspects of the research—purpose, subjects, instruments, procedures/treatment, results—included?
Style. Is the abstract brief and clearly written?

INTRODUCTORY SECTION

Problem Area. Are the problem area and its educational importance explained? Are the researchers' assumptions and theoretical perspectives about the topic explained?

Related literature. Are research studies related to the problem area presented? Has the related research been evaluated and critiqued? Does the intended research logically extend the understandings from the related research?

Hypothesis(es), Purpose(s), Question(s) in Quantitative Research. Is there a purpose that can be studied in an unbiased manner? Are the research variables (independent and dependent, when appropriate) easily identified from the hypothesis, question, or purpose statement? Are key terms or variables operationally defined?

Purpose(s), Question(s) in Qualitative Research. Is the relationship between the study and previous studies explicit? Is there a clear rationale for the use of qualitative procedures? Are researchers' assumptions and biases expressed?

METHOD SECTION

Subjects. Are target populations and subjects, sampling and selection procedures, and group sizes clearly described? Are these appropriate for the research design?

Standardized and Other Instruments. What instruments are used in the study? Are they appropriate for the design of the study? Are the instruments valid for collecting data on the variables in the study and are reliability estimates given for each instrument? Are researcher-made instruments included (or at least samples of the instrument items)? Are the instruments appropriate for use with the target population and the research subjects? In the case of authentic, or performance-based, assessments, what evidence is presented that the devices reflect realistic samples of students' learning?

Design and Procedure in Quantitative Research. Are the research design and data collection procedures clearly described? Is the research design appropriate to the researchers' purpose? Can the study be replicated from the information provided? In experimental designs, are treatments fully explained? Are examples of special materials included?

Design and Procedure in Qualitative Research. Are research questions stated and additional questions generated? Is the method explained in detail? Has researchers' presence influenced the behavior of the subjects? Is there abundant evidence from multiple sources?

RESULTS SECTION

Data Analysis in Quantitative Research. Are the statistical procedures for data analysis clearly described, and are they appropriate for the type of quantitative research design?

Research Validity in Quantitative Research. Are the procedures free from the influence of extraneous variables? Does the study have any threats to its internal and external validity?

Significance in Quantitative Research. Are statistical significance levels indicated? Does the research have practical significance?

Data Analysis in Qualitative Research. Are the processes for organizing data, identifying patterns, and synthesizing key ideas as hypotheses and research questions clearly described?

Research Validity in Qualitative Research. Are there multiple procedures for corroborating research evidence and researchers' judgments?

DISCUSSION SECTION

Discussion (Conclusions, Recommendations). Are conclusions related to answering the research question(s), and are they appropriate to the results? Is the report free from inappropriate generalizations and implications? If inappropriate, are suggestions for additional research provided?

Figure 3.1
Questions for Evaluating Research Reports

ACTIVITY

Select a research report from Appendix B or from a professional journal. With a partner, another student in the class, read the research report. Use the peer-interacting procedure discussed in the Activities section of Chapter 2 and the Research Report Reading Plan discussed in this chapter. You and your partner should take turns explaining the reason for selecting sections to be read and the location of key information. Discuss differences you may have about these choices.

CHAPTER 4

Reading and Evaluating Introductory Sections: Abstract, Background, and Purpose

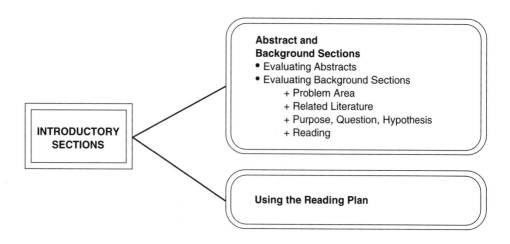

FOCUS QUESTIONS

1. What information should research consumers get from the abstract and background sections of a research report?
2. What criteria are used to evaluate abstracts?
3. What criteria are used to evaluate background sections?
4. What is the plan for reading abstracts and background sections?

In the background section, a researcher introduces readers to the problem area and its educational importance. Researchers also provide brief summaries of other researchers' results that are related to the problem area. The part with these summaries is called the **literature review**, and in it researchers indicate strengths from the related research that were used in their study and weaknesses or limitations that were changed. In many professional journals, the background section is preceded by an abstract, a summary of the report. Most often, researchers omit the literature review from an abstract.

THE ABSTRACT AND BACKGROUND SECTIONS

In the plan for reading research reports discussed in Chapter 3, the abstract and background sections are read first. From these sections, research consumers should be able to answer:

What are the researchers' issues and concerns?

What have other researchers found out about these issues?

What question(s) did the researchers try to answer?

What kind of research was conducted by the researchers, and what were the independent and dependent variables, if any?

Are the researchers' issues and concerns relevant to me as a professional or to my teaching situation?

The questions for evaluating abstract and background sections (taken from Figure 3.1, p. 117) are the following:

Evaluating Abstract and Background Sections

ABSTRACT

Organization. Is information about the major aspects of the research—purpose, subjects, instruments, procedures/treatment, results—included?
Style. Is the abstract brief and clearly written?

INTRODUCTORY SECTION

Problem Area. Are the problem area and its educational importance explained? Are the researchers' assumptions and theoretical perspectives about the topic explained?
Related Literature. Are research studies related to the problem area presented? Has the related research been evaluated and critiqued? Does the intended research logically extend the understandings from the related research?
Hypothesis(es), Purpose(s), Question(s) in Quantitative Research. Is there a purpose that can be studied in an unbiased manner? Are the research variables (independent and dependent, when appropriate) easily identified from the hypothesis, question, or purpose statement? Are key terms or variables operationally defined?
Purpose(s), Question(s) in Qualitative Research. Is the relationship between the study and previous studies explicit? Is there a clear rationale for the use of qualitative procedures? Are researchers' assumptions and biases expressed?

Evaluating Abstracts

Most abstracts are written in a particular style and manner that facilitates readers' attempts to ascertain whether the research is appropriate for their purposes as consumers. Abstracts contain information about purpose, subjects, instruments, procedure (and treatment when applicable), findings, and conclusions.

Abstracts are usually short, containing 100 to 200 words, and are set in special type or indented to distinguish them from the main body of the research report. Some journals do not require abstracts; the decision is set by the journal editors and advisory boards. Some publications, such as *Psychological Abstracts* and *Current Index to Journals in Education* (CIJE), contain short abstracts that do not have the style and content of journal abstracts. Other publications, such as *Dissertation Abstracts International*, have abstracts 600 to 800 words long that contain more information than journal abstracts. A discussion of these publications and samples of their abstract forms are found in Chapter 11, Locating Information About Research Reports.

The following abstract from a report entitled "Differences in Teaching between Six Primary and Five Intermediate Teachers in One School" illustrates the normal style. The types of information are annotated in the margin. For this demonstration, you should read the abstract for the purpose of finding out whether there is a difference between the two groups of teachers in their communications with their students.

[Purpose]

[Subjects]
[Procedure]

[Data analysis]

[Results]

This study examined differences between primary and intermediate teachers concerning teacher behaviors, teacher communications, grouping control, and materials. 6 primary classrooms (grades 1 and 2) and 5 intermediate classrooms (grades 4 and 5) were each observed for 4 45-minute periods. In addition, observers, teachers, and 5 students from each classroom responded to 2 vignettes depicting classroom situations and 1 vignette asking respondents to describe a lesson on nutrition. Responses were coded for teacher behaviors, goals, and instructional methods. Analyses of observational data showed that in comparison with teachers in intermediate grades, primary teachers used significantly more sanctions, procedural communications, and total teacher communications. Primary teachers also used a greater proportion of small-group instruction and manipulative materials than did intermediate teachers. Analysis of subjects' responses to vignettes clarified these findings and added further detail. (Van Scoy, 1994, p. 347)

Evaluative question: Is information about the major aspects of the research—purpose, subjects, instruments, procedures/treatment, results—included?

As shown by the margin annotations, the abstract contains information about the major aspects of research. What is not included is the statistical procedure used to code the subjects' responses.

Evaluative question: Is the abstract brief and clearly written?

In the example, the researcher has used only terms that any knowledgable research consumer would be expected to know. The only technical term used in the abstract (which is explained in this text) is *significantly*, which is a clue that the researcher used quantitative data analysis procedures. The abstract presents the information about the research aspects without unnecessary information.

Researchers sometimes omit specific information and merely refer to the type of information included in the full research report. Such a tactic does not provide report readers with a complete summary and might hinder their understanding of the research because the specific details of the research report are omitted. In the above abstract, the last statement illustrates this weakness. Other statements in abstracts that indicate incomplete information are "The study examined various instructional techniques," "The results are presented," and "The implications of the results are given."

Evaluating Background Sections

Background sections contain three major kinds of information. The first is the problem area and its educational importance. The second is related literature. The third is the research purpose, questions, or hypotheses.

The Problem Area.   In Chapter 1, five characteristics of a profession and its members were enumerated. Briefly, professionals (a) verify existing ideas and practices, (b) discover new ideas and practices, (c) clarify and expand information about ideas and practices, (d) express ideas that complicate educational practice, and (e) discover ideas and practices that are counter-intuitive. Researchers try to justify the importance of their research in light of these aspects of professional activity. For example, in a causal-comparative study to determine if gifted and average-ability junior high students differed in learning and study strategies, the researcher indicated that

> In general, we know that gifted students are able to achieve more in school than average-ability students (Scruggs & Cohn, 1983; Scruggs & Mastropieri, 1988). However, we also know that not all gifted children do well in school, and not all are able to achieve to their predicted level. Further research is needed to examine learning and study strategies of gifted children as they compare to less able learners. More information is also needed to determine whether the study strategies of gifted learners are adequate. Therefore, two studies were undertaken to explore these issues. These studies were designed to determine if high-ability junior high students differed from their average-ability peers on learning and study strategies. (Tallent-Runnels, et al., 1994, p. 145)

Related Literature.   Researchers also need to examine what others have found to be important. By reviewing relevant research, researchers gain insights about the problem area that should then influence their research questions and methods. During this phase of research, research producers act as consumers. They critically analyze research using questions similar to those in Table 3.1, p. 117. As a result of their evaluation, they can

1. Extend knowledge about a problem area. This can be done because the researchers see a next step in answering questions about the problem. For example, after reviewing research about parents who read aloud to their children, one group of researchers realized that no one had described the views of those parents, so their research was concerned with identifying what parents thought about reading to their children (Manning, Manning, & Cody, 1988).

2. Change or revise knowledge about a problem area. This can be done because the researchers see weaknesses or limitations in other researchers' attempts to answer questions about the problem area. For example, after reviewing research about oral reading cue strategies of better and poor readers, a researcher identified several limitations with those studies and made modifications in materials that were used, the reading task assigned to the students, and the number and type of errors evaluated (Fleisher, 1988).

3. Replicate the study. Sometimes researchers wish to redo the research of others. **Replication** means repeating an investigation of a previous study's purpose, question, or hypothesis.

Researchers can replicate research in several ways. First, they can use the same method with different subjects. In this case, the researchers keep the original purpose, method, and data analysis procedure. The subjects have the same characteristics as the original subjects, but they are different people. For example, one team of researchers replicated a study looking at the effect on learning-disabled and slowly developing readers of two instructional programs designed to teach the students how to detect their own errors (Pascarella, Pflaum, Bryan, & Pearl, 1983). In the original study, conducted by two members of the same research team, the subjects were individual students. In the replication, data were analyzed for both individual students and groups because the researchers felt that working with individuals overlooked the "potential interdependencies among individual [student] observations within the same reading group" (p. 270).

Second, in a procedure known as **cross-validation**, the researchers use the same purpose, method, and data analysis procedure to investigate subjects from a different population. For example, if the subjects in an original study were second and third graders, a different target population might be high school students.

Third, in a procedure known as **validity generalization**, the researchers use the same purpose, method, and data analysis procedure, but they use subjects from a unique population. For example, if the subjects in an original study were suburban students with hearing impairment, a different population might be rural students with vision impairment.

Fourth, researchers can reanalyze other researchers' data. In this case, no new study is undertaken. For example, after reviewing research about students' silent reading, a team of researchers indicated that the results of one study in particular did not warrant certain conclusions, so they reanalyzed the data presented by the original researchers (Wilkinson, Wardrop, & Anderson, 1988).

Purpose, Question, Hypothesis.   Most examples so far in this text have shown researchers stating their research aims as purposes or questions. This has been done because current practice in research journals is to use this form. Journal editors as well as authorities on effective reading practice feel that readers of research get a better mindset from purposes and questions than they do from hypotheses. Nevertheless, research reports are often written with traditional hypotheses.

A **hypothesis** is a conjectural statement of the relationship between the research variables. It is created after researchers have examined the related literature but before they undertake the study. It is considered a tentative explanation for particular behaviors, phenomena, or events that have happened or will happen. A hypothesis is a statement of researchers' expectations concerning the relationship between the variables in the research problem (Gay, 1992).

One way to state a hypothesis is as a **nondirectional** (or *two-tailed*) **hypothesis**, which is a statement of the specific relationship or influence among variables. Researchers use this form when they have strong evidence from examining previous research that a relationship or influence exists but the evidence does not provide them with indications about the nature or direction (positive or negative) of the relationship or influence. The following, taken from a study about the connection between computer technology and reading comprehension, are examples of nondirectional research hypotheses stated to show that differences will exist between variables. Note that the researchers do not state how—positively or negatively—using a computer to mediate manipulations of the text (the independent variable) will influence reading comprehension (the dependent variable).

1. The comprehension of intermediate-grade readers reading expository texts will be affected by using a computer to mediate manipulations of the text.

2. Comprehension of expository text will be affected by varying control of textual manipulations from the reader to the computer program. (Reinking & Schreiner, 1985, p. 540)

If the researchers' evidence supports a statement of the specific way one variable will affect another, then the research hypothesis is stated as a **directional** (or *one-tailed*) **hypothesis.** The following example contains two directional research hypotheses from a study about the effects of teacher expectations and student behavior.

The first hypothesis under investigation was that adults who are deliberate and more reserved would be more likely to adopt a task-oriented approach than would adults who are impulsive and highly sociable. Thus the reserved, deliberate adults would make more attempts to structure the task for the child, would more often redirect the child's attention to the task, and would make fewer task irrelevant comments to the child than would the sociable, impulsive adult. In addition [the second hypothesis], compared with inexperienced teachers, experienced teachers are more likely to be task oriented. (Osborne, 1985, p. 80)

In this example, the researcher predicted that teachers' temperament factors (the independent variable) would have a direct effect on how they structure children's tasks (the dependent variable). Not only was *an effect* predicted, but the *specific* effect was predicted. The research predicted that teachers with reserved, deliberate temperaments would be *more directive* and offer *fewer irrelevant comments*. The second prediction was that teachers' experience (the independent variable) would affect task orientation (the dependent variable) and that experienced teachers *would more likely* be task oriented.

Another form of hypothesis is the null hypothesis. In contrast to the research hypothesis (directional and nondirectional), the null hypothesis is used exclusively as an aid to statistical analysis and is rarely used in research reports.

Reading Background Sections.   The following, a typical background section, is taken from a report entitled "The Effect of Instruction in Question-Answer Relationships and Metacognition on Social Studies Comprehension". Key information in this background section is annotated.

[Background]   Teachers expect students to be critical readers, comprehending most of the material read in the classroom; but Durkin's (1978–1979) classroom observation studies suggest that while comprehension is expected, it is never taught. Teachers do not 'teach' comprehension during social studies instruction; they merely assess it.

Questions are an integral part of school life. They are used routinely by teachers as a means of gauging student understanding of text. Teachers ask questions, but rarely do they do anything with the student responses—except acknowledge their correctness (Durkin, 1978–1979).

Early comprehension taxonomies first classified questions by type. Pearson and Johnson's (1978) more recent comprehension taxonomy, however, labels questions based upon the demands they make on the reader. In other words, the Pearson-Johnson taxonomy categorizes questions according to the relationship between the question and the answer generated. The Pearson-Johnson comprehension taxonomy recognizes three categories of questions: textually explicit, textually implicit and scriptally implicit.

[Related literature]

Recent research in metacognition has recognized that some children appear to be more capable of processing information efficiently when taught to monitor their own comprehension and to use reading strategies that take into account the variety of reading tasks assigned in school (Brown, 1981, p. 504). Raphael (1982) used the Pearson-Johnson comprehension taxonomy to develop a Question-Answer Relationship (QAR) model which could be used to teach students to successfully respond to four types of questions typically found in content area textbooks. The QAR model categorizes questions based upon the location of the answer generated by a query. The Question-Answer Relationship model considers the demands that questions make upon readers as they strive to arrive at correct responses.

[Purpose]

This research study was designed to teach students the QAR model and to provide additional metacognitive instruction in conjunction with the adopted social studies textbook. The social studies instruction provided was used in place of the basal reading instructional program typically employed for reading instruction. Three research questions were posed: Would students, as a result of the QAR and metacognitive instruction, complete the social studies textbook questioning tasks more successfully? How would students perform on the different types of QARs in the social studies text following the treatment? Would student scores on a global reading comprehension measure increase as a result of the social studies QAR-metacognitive instruction? (Benito, Foley, Lewis, & Prescott, 1993)

Evaluative question: Are the problem area and its educational importance explained?

In the example, the researchers succinctly presented the importance of the problem area. Although the first paragraph is short, the researchers indicate the importance of questioning in the teaching of comprehension and substantiate this with references.

Evaluative questions: Are research studies related to the problem area presented? Has the related research been evaluated and critiqued? Does the intended research logically extend the understandings from the related research?

In the third and fourth paragraphs, the researchers provide a summary of relevant research results. In the fifth paragraph, the researchers indicate their two major purposes. What research consumers need to determine is: Do the purposes provide the means for extending the results of the previous research? This question can be answered in relation to the next evaluative question.

Evaluative questions: Is there a purpose that can be studied in an unbiased manner? Are the research variables (independent and dependent) easily identified from the hypothesis, question, or purpose statement? Are key terms or variables operationally defined?

The first research purpose in the example was to determine if students, as a result of the QAR and metacognitive instruction, complete the social studies textbook questioning tasks more successfully. For this purpose, the researchers collected data to examine their claim that these strategies are more effective. The second purpose was to determine how students would perform on different types of QARs in the social studies text following the treatment. It was possible to conduct this comparative and experimental study without bias; the only way research consumers can be confident that no bias was introduced would be to evaluate the method section (this is discussed in the next four chapters). No terms needed special definition.

USING THE RESEARCH READING PLAN WITH ABSTRACT AND BACKGROUND SECTIONS

By using the research reading plan presented in Chapter 3 (see p. 63) for the initial reading of abstracts and background sections, research consumers can efficiently seek out information in a particular order. The abstract and background sections of the report "Learning Science in a Cooperative Setting: Academic Achievement and Affective Outcomes" by Lazarowitz, Hertz-Lazarowitz, and Baird (1994) on the following pages contain annotations to illustrate the suggested order of reading. For this demonstration, you should read the report for the purpose of gaining knowledge about how children can use cooperative group strategies in learning science.

Read the abstract and background sections using the following steps:

1. The title is read to gain a broad overview of the research topic.

2. In this report, the first paragraph of the background section is the abstract. The first sentence of that paragraph is read to gain a general understanding of the researchers' concern.

3. The paragraph containing the researchers' research purposes, questions, or hypotheses is read to gain a specific understanding of the research. This information is usually found at the end of the background section.

4. From reading 1, 2, and 3, research consumers can determine that the purpose (gaining knowledge) will be met by reading the report. In the margin of this text or on a piece of paper, note what you already know about the topic.

5. The remainder of the abstract (the first paragraph) is read to gain a sense of the subjects, research methodology, and findings.

6. The remainder of the background section is read to gain an understanding of cooperative learning and science educators' thoughts about science education, and the related literature subsection is read to understand what other researchers know about cooperative learning in science classrooms.

Learning Science in a Cooperative Setting: Academic Achievement and Affective Outcomes

Reuven Lazarowitz

Department of Education in Technology and Science, IIT Technion, Haifa 32000 Israel

Rachel Hertz-Lazarowitz

School of Education, Haifa University, Haifa 31999 Israel

J. Hugh Baird

Department of Secondary Education, Brigham Young University, Provo, Utah 84602

ABSTRACT

A learning unit in earth science was taught to high school students, using a jigsaw-group mastery learning approach. The sample consisted of 73 students in the experimental group and 47 students who learned the topic in an individualized mastery learning approach. The study lasted 5 weeks. Pretests and posttests on academic achievement and affective outcomes were administered. Data were treated with an analysis of covariance. The results show that students of the experimental group achieved significantly higher on academic outcomes, both normative and objective scores. On the creative essay test, the differences in number of ideas and total essay score were not significant between the groups, although the mean scores for number of words were higher for the individualized mastery learning group. On the affective domain, jigsaw-group mastery learning students scored significantly higher on self-esteem, number of friends, and involvement in the classroom. No differences were found in cohesiveness, cooperation, competition, and attitudes toward the subject learned. The results are discussed through the evaluation and comparison of the two methods of instruction used in this study.

The cooperative learning movement began in junior high schools as part of the desegregation process, aiming at facilitating positive ethnic relations and increasing academic achievement and social skills among diverse students (Aronson, Stephan, Sikes, Blaney, & Snapp, 1978; Sharan & Hertz-Lazarowitz, 1980; Slavin, 1980). However, elementary teachers quickly recognized the potential of cooperative methods, and such methods were adopted freely in elementary schools before becoming widespread on the junior and senior high level. It has only been during the past few years that application of cooperative learning has been studied extensively with these older students.

Cooperative learning methods generally involve heterogenous groups working together on tasks that are deliberately structured to provide specific assignments and individual contributions from each group member. Cognitive as well as social benefits are expected, as students clarify their own understanding and share their insights and ideas with each other as they interact within the group (Deutsch, 1949).

Experiments in the science laboratory have always required students to work in groups of two to four, due to the constraints of experimental processes and limited equipment and supplies. Thus, science courses are a natural curriculum area for examining cooperative learning practices. Now that cooperative methods are being refined to develop particular capabilities in the students, science teachers need to examine ways of structuring specific tasks to achieve the academic, affective, and socialization goals for their students. Although most of the studies of cooperative learning in the high school science classroom have centered around the cognitive outcomes of achievement testing and process skills, affective and social outcomes are also significant with students of this age. But few studies in science classes have attempted to assess such aspects of students' progress.

As part of a previous revision, the science faculty at the high school where this study was conducted developed an exemplary individualized mastery learning (IML) program for teaching science. This program seemed to alleviate the severe motivational problems and the extreme individual differences among the students in this rural/blue-collar community. Students learned to work independently on their science studies. They had almost no lectures and few large group activities. As they worked through their assignments, however, they were free to interact with other students. Looking in on a typical class, one would see several clusters of two or three students working together, sometimes tutoring each other, sometimes just talking through an assignment. Yet at least half of the class members would be working all alone. The importance of the overall social setting in the classroom as it relates to learning (Bruner, 1986, p. 86) and the central function of social interaction as learning occurs (Vygotsky, 1978, p. 106) seemed to have been ignored. Therefore, group mastery learning (GML), a cooperative learning technique, was suggested as an antithesis to IML for teaching science over short periods. The cooperative mode of instruction considers learning as a cognitive as well as a social process, where students interact with each other as well as the teacher.

To bring the social dimension back to science classrooms, the researchers chose to implement GML in Grades 11 and 12. The goal of the study was to investigate the GML's impact of the method on the individual student's academic achievement, creativity, self-esteem, and number of friends and on the overall learning environment of the classrooms. The researchers were also concerned with the students' attitudes toward earth science, the course being taught at the time of the experiment. Both cognitive and affective outcomes for students who participated in the cooperative GML approach were compared with outcomes for students who studied the same topic in an IML approach.

The study addressed a number of questions (3) related to academic and nonacademic outcomes of the two methods of study. First, it sought to determine whether academic achievement of the students taught in the cooperative GML mode would be different from the achievement of students who learned in an individualized method. Second, it sought to determine whether gains or losses would be seen in nonacademic outcomes, such as classroom learning environment, social relations, and students' self-esteem experienced by the students. The results of this study may support more use of cooperative learning in high school science.

LITERATURE SURVEY

The literature concerning cooperative learning (6) methods in science classrooms has shown positive outcomes on many but not all academic subject areas and cognitive skills. Academic achievement has been revealed as significantly higher in studies on earth science (Humphreys, Johnson, & Johnson, 1982); chemistry, biology, and physics (Okebukola, 1985; Okebukola & Ogunniyi, 1984); biology (Lazarowitz, Baird, Hertz-Lazarowitz, & Jenkins, 1985; Lazarowitz & Karsenty, 1990; Lazarowitz, 1991; Watson, 1991); and physics (Scott & Heller, 1991). Group work in junior high school biology classrooms and laboratories enhanced students' learning and research skills. Under cooperative methods of learning, these students developed stronger reporting skills, and at the same time showed greater understanding and enjoyment of the subject matter (Walters, 1988).

In contrast, other studies comparing cooperative and individualized learning have not revealed significant differences in students' academic progress or cognitive development. For example, Sherman (1988) found that teaching ecology in a cooperative mode did not make a difference in students' learning. Tingle and Good (1990) attempted to apply cooperative methods specifically to problem-solving skills in chemistry; they found comparable skills were developed whether students worked individually or in groups.

Although results have not consistently shown the advantage of cooperative learning over more traditional teaching methods for promoting strictly academic achievement in science, studies have consistently shown greater effectiveness on nonacademic aspects of science study. Tingle and Good (1990) also found that cooperative methods resulted in a more supportive climate for learning and in increased student ability to organize projects, divide and assign the work, and take responsibility for completing it. Although these abilities are not necessarily manifest in achievement scoring, all of them are significant in the study of science. The capacity of students to remain on-task while working on science projects is one of those significant related capabilities. Studies have consistently reported that on-task behavior is higher when students learn through cooperative methods as opposed to individualized learning modes (Lazarowitz, Hertz-Lazarowitz, Baird, & Bowlden, 1988; Rogg & Kahle, 1992). Additional learning factors that have been demonstrated to be strengthened by group processes include inquiry skills and self-esteem (Lazarowitz & Karsenty, 1990). The factor of individual differences in preferred learning style was included in cooperative learning research by Okebukola (1988), who reported that students who preferred to learn in the cooperative mode made more progress than they did when they were instructed in a competitive mode.

From this review of existing studies, one may conclude that when science students are given tasks that demand high levels of cognitive skills and/or personal characteristics such as perseverance and positive attitudes toward science, cooperative learning has the potential to contribute significantly to cognitive and affective development.

SUMMARY

The background section contains an introduction to the researchers' problem area and the educational importance they place on their study. Researchers also provide a brief literature review of other researchers' results that are related to their problem area. Researchers usually indicate strengths from the related research that were used in their study and weaknesses or limitations that were changed. Based upon an examination of the related literature, a researcher determines whether to develop a new study or replicate or repeat a study. It is common to find the researchers' purposes at the end of this section. Some research reports contain traditional hypotheses, which often are stated as directional or nondirectional research hypotheses. Nondirectional hypotheses are statements that a possible influence exists but the researcher does not indicate whether it is a positive or negative influence. Directional hypotheses contain statements of the specific way one variable will affect another. In many professional journals, the background section is preceded by an abstract, a summary of the report.

ACTIVITY

Use the research reading plan and the evaluation criteria on page 126 to read and evaluate the abstract and background sections of two reports on pages 130–131 and 132–133.

Douglas, S., & Willatts, P. (1994). The relationship between musical ability and literacy skills. *Journal of Research in Reading, 17,* 99–107.

The Relationship Between Musical Ability and Literacy Skills

Sheila Douglas and Peter Willatts

Auchterderran Staff Development and Resources Centre and University of Dundee

ABSTRACT

Research has shown that a relationship exists between phonological awareness and literary skills. It has been suggested that a structured programme of musical activities can be used to help children develop a multi-sensory awareness and response to sounds. The relationship between musical ability and literacy skills was examined in a study that showed an association between rhythmic ability and reading. A further pilot intervention study showed that training in musical skills is a valuable additional strategy for assisting children with reading difficulties.

INTRODUCTION

The Relationship between Aural Skills and Reading

Children's awareness of speech sounds, or 'phonological awareness' as it is often called, appears to play an important role in learning to read (Bryant et al., 1990; Treiman, 1985). Bryant and Bradley (1985) have shown that backward readers have difficulty in breaking up words into their component sounds. They argue that there exists a continuum stretching from children who are particularly insensitive to such phonological segmentation through to those who find no difficulty. Moreover, they claim that their research shows that backward readers can be moved up this continuum.

Bradley and Bryant (1983) conducted a study involving four- and five-year-olds to measure phonemic awareness (awareness of individual sounds) in children who had not begun formal reading instruction. For this study they chose the 'oddity task' in which children were asked to identify which word was different in a set of three or four spoken words. In each set the first, middle, or final sound in one of the words was different from the rest (e.g. pig, *hit,* pin; or give, *pat,* girl, get).

Reading ability was assessed three years later and a highly significant relationship was found with the children's earlier achievement in the oddity task. Children who were better at identifying the sound which was the odd one out had higher reading scores.

Bradley and Bryant pointed out that this relation did not establish that differences in phonemic awareness caused the differences in reading achievement. Because some other factor may have influenced the scores both in the oddity task and reading assessments, they carried out a subsequent instruction study in an attempt to show that phonemic awareness leads to improved reading skills.

They selected 65 of the children who had been most unsuccessful on the oddity task and divided them into four groups, giving each group 40 individual tutoring sessions. The children in the first two groups were shown how to compare the first, middle and final sounds of words. In addition, the children in the second group were taught how these sounds corresponded to alphabetic letters. The children in the third group were shown how to arrange words in semantic categories (e.g. hen and pig are farm animals). The fourth group had no special training.

When the children were tested after the training period, the first group, who had only been taught phonemic awareness, scored better on a reading assessment than either the group trained in semantic categories or the group with no training, although the differences were not statistically significant. In contrast, the reading scores of the group trained in phonemic awareness and letter/sound correspondences were considerably higher than all the other groups. Bradley and Bryant's experiment suggests that the ability to link letter knowledge and phonemic awareness is likely to be important in reading.

In an earlier study, Bradley (1981) attempted to show that a multi-sensory approach to teaching poor readers about written words was more successful than other methods. The method used by Bradley was similar to one which was pioneered by Gillingham and Stillman (1956), known as 'Simultaneous Oral Spelling'.

The children taking part in the study were taught by three different methods to read twelve words. The first method was Bradley's (1981) version of 'Simultaneous Oral Spelling' which involved three major elements—seeing the word, spelling out the letters and writing movements. The second method did not include spelling out the letters, and the third method omitted the writing element.

After four weeks the backward readers were considerably more successful at spelling the words taught by 'Simultaneous Oral Spelling' than by the other two methods. Bryant and Bradley (1985) believed that this multi-sensory approach was successful because it encouraged poor readers to make connections between reading and spelling.

Bryant and Bradley's assertion that ability to differentiate sounds is a crucial factor in learning to read successfully is supported by Wisbey (1980) who has suggested that working with sounds through music may also be related to success in reading. Wisbey proposed that many intelligent children fail to become literate because of undetected hearing problems during infancy or early childhood.

According to Wisbey, many children with early hearing problems either outgrow the symptoms or have them treated, so that when tested at a later date, no hearing defect is apparent. As a result, the consequences of the early hearing problems are left untreated.

Whereas Bradley (1981) found that a programme involving a multi-sensory approach to reading and spelling was beneficial in helping backward readers to improve their literacy skills, Wisbey (1980) proposed that reading difficulties could be prevented by using musical activities to help children develop a multi-sensory awareness and response to sounds.

A study by MacLean et al. (1987) goes some way towards reinforcing Wisbey's (1980) suggestion that an early involvement in musical activities can prove beneficial in preventing problems with later literacy skills. MacLean et al. found that knowledge of nursery rhymes was strongly related to phonological skills.

The present study was undertaken to explore this possible link between musical ability and literacy skills, but before proceeding further, two questions must be answered—what is musical ability and how can it be measured?

Some researchers (e.g. Mursell and Glenn, 1966) believe that musical ability can be defined as a single, if somewhat complex, ability, whereas Seashore (1938) prefers the notion that musical ability can be broken up into separate abilities such as pitch discrimination, rhythm, timbre, etc. As Lowery (1952, p. 18) says, 'Music . . . is a subjective phenomenon, depending on the activity of the listener's mind . . . it only begins when the heard sounds are recognised as possessing a meaningful relation to each other.'

Sounds have a 'meaningful relation' to each other in terms of pitch and rhythm. Timbre and dynamics may enhance the performance, but a melody can be recognised however loudly it is played (Bentley, 1966). Consequently, for the purpose of this study, it was decided to concentrate on pitch and rhythm as indicators of musical ability.

Miles and Miles (1990) draw attention to the research concerned with dyslexia and music. Evidence from a variety of sources has been compiled in a booklet by Smith (1988) listing some of the difficulties encountered by dyslexics when dealing with music. It is interesting to note that the list includes 'remembering a melodic or rhythmic phrase and singing or clapping it back' (Miles and Miles, 1990, p. 49). This suggests a link between poor rhythm and pitch perception and reading problems.

The Music Department of Fife Region produced an aural awareness test for Primary Four children (i.e. in their eighth and ninth year of age) based on a text devised by Bentley (1966), but shorter and less complicated. This test was chosen for the study because it was already available on tape and was designed for the age group of subjects who were to take part in the study.

Hoover-Dempsey, K. V., Bassler, O. C., & Burow, R. (1995). Parents' reported involvement in students' homework: Strategies and practices. *The Elementary School Journal, 95*, 435–450.

Parents' Reported Involvement in Students' Homework: Strategies and Practices

Kathleen V. Hoover-Dempsey, Otto C. Bassler, Rebecca Burow

Vanderbilt University

ABSTRACT

In this study we examined homework, the most common point of intersection among parent, child, and school activities related to formal learning, in interviews with 69 parents of first- through fifth-grade students. Analyses revealed rich information about parents' thinking, strategies, and actions related to homework. Their ideas generally clustered around 5 major themes: concern for children's unique characteristics as balanced with school demands, questions about appropriate levels of independent work by children, efforts to structure homework activities, direct involvement in homework tasks, and reflections on the personal meanings of perceived success and failure in helping children with homework. Findings suggested that students' homework represented a complex and multidimensional set of tasks for parents, for which they often felt ill-prepared, by both limitations in knowledge and competing demands for their time and energy. Strategies for involving parents more effectively in students' homework are suggested, based on the general finding that parents want to be involved more effectively in their children's school learning.

Popular and professional attention to homework abounds. Writers have produced a plethora of newspaper columns (e.g., Kutner, 1992) and books of advice on helping children with homework (e.g., Maeroff, 1989; Rosemond, 1990); educators have developed numerous programs intended to ensure the productive accomplishment of homework (e.g., Anesko, Schoiock, Ramirez, & Levine, 1987; Clary, 1986; Cooper, 1989a). Scholarly studies and literature reviews of homework's contribution to school achievement have produced somewhat mixed results—many have supported its usefulness (e.g., Cooper, 1989a, 1989b; Fehrman, Keith, & Reimers, 1987; Keith & Page, 1985; Keith, Reimers, Fehrman, Pottebaum, & Aubey, 1986; Leone & Richards, 1989; Paschal, Weinstein, & Walberg, 1984; Reynolds, 1991; Shanahan & Walberg, 1985; Staver & Walberg, 1986), but other have failed to find consistent linkages (e.g., Chen & Stevenson, 1989; Cool & Keith, 1991; Cooper, 1989a, 1989b; Lee, 1985; Smith, 1990).

The variability in scholarly findings for homework may be due to shortcomings in the studies. Homework has seldom been defined fully; investigators either have assumed that its components and demands were obvious or have employed simple descriptors (e.g., time spent on assignments); both approaches have denied the variability of tasks often implicit in the generic concept. Some investigators have suggested the potential importance of parents in the home-work process (e.g., Baker & Stevenson, 1986; Chen, & Stevenson, 1989; Stevenson, Chen, & Uttal, 1990), but rarely has homework been conceptualized as a complex set of requirements involving a variety of assumptions about specific activities on the part of parents *and* children. A few notable exceptions identified patterns that may characterize many families' interactions around homework (Delgado-Gaitan, 1992; Lareau, 1989; McDermott, Goldman, & Varenne, 1984), but the dimensions of such patterns have yet to be examined systematically in a broader population. Further, the majority of studies have focused on adolescents' homework. Much less attention has been given to the highly significant precursor elementary years, arguably the years when significant patterns of parental involvement—and child attitudes and activities related to homework—are developed in ways that may influence later student attention to and performance on homework tasks.

We argue that homework is a complex and multifaceted activity that begins for most students during the early elementary years, when parents have a significant role to play in forming the attitudes—as well as patterns of strategy and accomplishment—that underlie success in homework and in school. There is an abundant literature on linkages between homework performance and academic achievement, but the critical role played by parents' assumptions and activities has largely been ignored. This inattention is detrimental to educators' understanding of parental factors that influence most children's school success.

In the study reported here we focused on describing the interactions parents reported as they assisted their children with school-related work at home. Specifically, we wanted to know what elementary school parents think about their roles and activities in relation to children's school assignments and homework success, how parents conceptualize their roles in relation to homework performance, and how—by their own reports—parents help their children complete homework.

FEEDBACK

Douglas & Willatts (1994)

Abstract. The abstract contains limited information about major aspects of the research. It contains the general purpose of the study, some general information about related literature, and a reference to the general nature of the treatments. It does not, however, contain hypotheses, specific subject characteristics (although some general characteristics are noted), information about what instruments were used for collecting data, nor how the data were analyzed or the specific results.

Background. The background section identifies the problem area and indicates the support from other researchers for the relationship between aural skills and reading. The purpose of the study is referred to in the middle of the section, not at the end where it is often found. However, there is no specific statement of purpose, question, or hypothesis.

Hoover-Dempsey, Bassler, & Burow (1995)

Abstract. Information about the major aspects of the research is presented. In comparison to the previous abstract, this one contains extensive information especially about the results (findings). From the use of the statement "ideas generally clustered around 5 major themes," the research consumer can surmise that this is a qualitative research report.

Background. The problem area and the importance of the topic to educators are stated. Related literature is reviewed, and the researchers indicate what they believe are shortcomings in those studies. In the next-to-last paragraph, they indicate their perspective of the nature of homework. Their statement of purpose, stated in the last paragraph of the section, is clear, and the type of research design (descriptive) is apparent.

CHAPTER 5

Reading and Evaluating Subject Sections

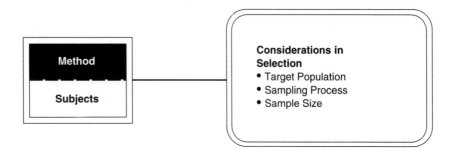

FOCUS QUESTIONS

1. What are populations and target populations?
2. What are subjects and samples?
3. What criteria should be used to evaluate subject sections?
4. What considerations do researchers give to subject selection?
5. What considerations do researchers give to sample size?

In the subject section, which is a subsection within the larger section called the method section, researchers describe the individuals, objects, or events used in their studies. In most cases, researchers wish to apply the answers to research questions to others in addition to their subjects. The hypothetical research team discussed in Chapter 1 were concerned about the extent to which their results could be applied. They were concerned about questions such as: Are the answers applicable only to the students in one specific school, grade level, or class? Can the answers be used for the students in an entire district, state, region, or nation?

Of course, subjects can be others besides students: Subjects can be teachers, principals, parents, nonschool-age individuals (preschoolers or adults), entire groups (e.g., classes, schools, or teams), and so on.

Subjects can also be nonhuman. For example, subjects can be groups of textbooks or groups of classrooms (the physical aspects of the rooms without consideration for the people in them). In such cases, researchers may be interested in studying the physical characteristics of the books or rooms. In this text, the discussion focuses on human subjects; nevertheless, the same principles of subject selection apply equally to human and nonhuman subjects. Research consumers can use the same criteria for judging the appropriateness of nonhuman subjects as they use for judging the appropriateness of human subjects.

The larger group of subjects to whom researchers wish to apply their results constitutes the **population,** which is a group of individuals or objects having at least one characteristic that distinguishes them from other groups. Populations can be any size and can include subjects from any place in the world. For example, a population of human subjects could be "students with learning disabilities," or "fourth-grade students," or "beginning teachers." In these cases, the populations are large and include people with many additional characteristics, or variables. The existence of these other variables makes it unlikely that the population will be fully homogeneous and that the research answers are equally applicable to all. "Seventh-grade social studies textbooks" is an example of a nonhuman subject population. Researchers, therefore, narrow the range of the population by including several distinguishing variables. This results in the defining of a **target population,** which is the specific group to which the researchers would like to apply their findings. It is from the target population that researchers select the **sample,** which become the subjects of their study.

Subject sections contain relevant information about the sample and how it was selected. Subject information might include age, gender, ethnicity (e.g., black, Hispanic, native American), ability level (e.g., mental maturity or intelligence), academic performance (e.g., test scores), learning characteristics, affect (e.g., emotional stability, attitudes, interests, or self-concept), and geographic location (e.g., New York State, Chicago, rural/suburban, Australia). Subject selection information should include the number of subjects, procedures for identifying subjects, methods of actual subject selection, and, in the case of experimental research, steps for assigning subjects to groups or treatments. From a subject section, research consumers should be able to answer:

What was the intended target population?

Who were the subjects?

How were the subjects selected, and did the researchers show bias in their sampling procedures?

Were the subjects truly representative of the target population?

How were the subjects assigned to groups or treatments in experimental research?

Will the research results be applicable to my teaching situation and the students I teach? (Am I part of the target population? Are my students part of the target population?)

Subject sections should be evaluated using the following questions, which are from Figure 3.1, page 117:

Evaluating Subject Sections

Subjects. Are target populations and subjects, sampling and selection procedures, and group sizes clearly described? Are these appropriate for the research design?

CONSIDERATIONS IN SUBJECT SELECTION

In subject sections, researchers should provide information about (a) the target population, (b) the sampling process, and (c) the sample size.

Target Population

Answers to researchers' questions should be applicable to individuals other than those included in the study. The group to which they wish to apply their results is the target population. When researchers can apply their results to the target population, the results are considered to be **generalizable**. An example of how a researcher identified the target population within the larger population is found in a comparative study entitled "Concepts of Reading and Writing Among Low-Literate Adults" (Fagan, 1988). The researcher's purpose was to provide information about the perceptions of reading and writing held by low-functioning adults (the population). The subjects were selected from the target populations. In the following portion of the subject section, the number of subjects is indicated along with descriptions of the target populations. (Specific information about sampling procedures has been omitted from this example.)

A possible purpose for reading the study would be to gain information to help in planning an adult literacy program.

[Subjects]

[Target populations]

Two groups of each of 26 adults who were functioning below a grade 9 reading achievement level were selected—one designated as prison inmates and the other as living in mainstream society. Prison inmates were defined as sentenced prisoners in a medium-minimum correctional institution housing approximately 300 prisoners. Adults living in mainstream society were defined as noninstitutionalized adults, that is not living in prisons, mental, or old age institutions. They were considered "ordinary" people who had freedom of movement, and who could use such city facilities as transportation, recreation, and social interaction. (Fagan, 1988, p. 48)

Because of practical considerations, researchers may not always have equal access to all members of the target population. For example, researchers might wish their target population to be urban, primary-grade students in cities of at least 500,000 people having 20 percent or more Spanish-speaking students. An examination of the U.S. Department of Education census shows that there are at least ten such cities, including Los Angeles, Houston, Miami, and New York. The researchers might be able to use the entire target population as their subjects, or they might choose to select some subjects to represent the target population. More realistically, researchers work with **accessible populations,** which are groups that are convenient but are representative of the target population. Practical considerations that lead to the use of an accessible population include time, money, and physical accessibility.

Researchers should fully describe their accessible populations and their specific subjects so that research consumers can determine the generalizability of the findings. It is the research producers' responsibility to provide the necessary descriptive information about target populations and subjects. It is the research consumers' responsibility to make the judgments about the appropriateness of the subjects to their local situation. In evaluating subject sections, research consumers can be critical of the researchers only if they have not provided complete subject information.

The Sampling Process

If researchers' results are to be generalizable to target populations, the subjects must be **representative** of the population. A representative group of subjects, called the **sample**, is a miniature target population. Ideally, the sample would have the same distribution of relevant variables as found in the target population. It is those relevant variables that researchers describe in subject sections. For example, one researcher (Swanson, 1985) felt it important to keep the same ratio of gender and ethnicity in the sample as found in the target population. She investigated whether socioeconomic status, reading ability, and student self-report reading attitude scores were differentiated by teacher judgments or reading enthusiasm.

> The sample consisted of 117 first-grade students from seven classrooms in a school system located in northeastern Georgia. The rural county has a population of approximately 8,000, of which 37.3 percent is nonwhite. The racial and gender composition of the sample maintained a representative balance. Students repeating first grade, absent during initial testing, and/or not present during reading achievement assessment were deleted from the study. (Swanson, 1985, p. 42)

The most common procedure researchers use to ensure that samples are miniature target populations is **random sampling**. Random sampling works on the principle of **randomization,** whereby all members of the target population should have an equal chance of being selected for the sample (Borg, Gall, & Gall, 1993; Gay, 1992; Kerlinger, 1973). And, the subjects finally selected should reflect the distribution of relevant variables found in the target population. Any discrepancy between the sample and the target population is referred to as **sampling error**.

The following does *not* illustrate a random sample because it is not known whether all classes had an equal chance of being selected and whether the students in selected classes represented all the students in the grade level. The classes may have been heterogeneous, but it was not indicated whether they were equal. Although the school principals may have tried to be objective, there may have been an unconscious bias.

> One self-contained, heterogeneous classroom of third-grade students ($N = 22$) and one self-contained, heterogeneous classroom of fifth-grade students ($N = 23$) from a rural school district in the midwestern U.S. participated in the study. The third-grade classroom was one of three in a K–4 building, while the fifth-grade classroom was one of two in a 5–8 building. The participating classrooms were selected by the building principals. (Duffelmeyer & Adamson, 1986, p. 194)

The following is an example of random sampling because each subject had an equal chance of selection from among the students at each grade level.

Thirty-two children were tested at each grade level; second, third, fourth, and sixth. An equal number was randomly chosen from each of three different elementary schools in a Midwestern city of 50,000. The city is a predominantly white, middle class community. Subjects were replaced by other randomly selected students if they failed a vocabulary reading test. (Richgels, 1986, p. 205)

Random sampling is conceptually, or theoretically, accomplished by assigning a number to each member of the target population and then picking the subjects by chance. One way researchers used to do this was by placing everyone's name in a hat and drawing out as many as needed (Popham & Sirotnik, 1967). A simpler way and one that is more commonly used in current research studies is to assign numbers to each possible subject and then use a list of subjects' numbers randomly created by a computer program. The specific way researchers randomize is not important. The important consideration for research consumers is that a randomized sample has a better chance of being representative of the target population than does a nonrandomized one, and therefore, the researchers' results are more likely to be generalizable to the target population.

In addition to randomly selecting subjects, it is common in experimental studies for researchers to randomly assign the subjects to treatments. The following subject section, from a study about the occurrence of behaviors that reflect social competence components and informational-processing components of problem solving, illustrates this double randomization procedure.

[Random selection]   Subjects for the study were 48 children from a middle-class, midwestern school system who were participants in a larger Logo project. From a pool of all children who returned a parental permission form (more than 80% return rate), 24 first graders (10 girls, 14 boys; mean age 6 years, 6 months), and 24 third graders (13 girls, 11 boys; mean age, 8 years, 8 months) were randomly selected. Children were randomly as-
[Random assignment]   signed to either Logo or drill and practice treatment groups, so that 12 in each treatment group were from first grade and 12 were from third grade. (Clements & Nastasi, 1988, p. 93)

An extension of random sampling involves stratification. In a **stratified random sample,** the subjects are randomly selected by relevant variables in the same proportion as those variables appear in the target population. One example of nonrandomized stratified sampling is shown in the earlier extract with subjects from Georgia (Swanson, 1985). Although the sample was stratified, the researchers did not indicate whether the subjects were randomly selected.

The National Assessment of Educational Progress (NAEP), which is financially supported by the U.S. Department of Education and conducted by the Education Commission of the States, uses a complex form of stratified random sampling.

As with all NAEP national assessments, the results for the national samples were based on a stratified, three-stage sampling plan. The first stage included defining geographic primary sampling units (PSUs), which are typically groups of contiguous counties, but sometimes a single county; classifying the PSUs into strata defined by region and community type; and randomly selecting schools, both public and private, within each PSU selected at the first stage. The third stage involved randomly selecting students within a school for participation. Some students who were selected (about 7 to 8 percent) were excluded because of limited English proficiency or severe disability. (Langer, et al., 1995, p. 172)

As indicated previously, subjects may be intact groups, for example, classes to which students have been preassigned. When intact groups are selected, the procedure is called **cluster sampling.** Intact groups are selected because of convenience or accessibility. This procedure is especially common in causal-comparative research. If a number of intact groups from a target population exist, researchers should randomly select entire groups as they would individuals.

The following subject description, which illustrates cluster sampling, is from a study that examined the instructional organization of classrooms and tried to explain why students achieved in some classes but not in others. Note that the researchers do not indicate whether their "preselected" classes were chosen through random procedures.

This study was conducted during the math instruction of eight sixth-grade classes in four elementary schools in a school district in southwest Germany. These classrooms had been preselected out of total population of 113 sixth-grade classes in this school district. . . . Altogether, 194 students and their 8 math teachers participated. (Schneider & Treiber, 1984, p. 200)

Regardless of the nature of researchers' sampling procedures, an important concern in all designs is the use of **volunteer subjects**. Volunteers by nature are different from nonvolunteers because of some inherent motivational factor. Results from the use of volunteer subjects might not be directly generalizable to target populations containing seemingly similar, but nonvolunteer, individuals or groups. For example, researchers using volunteers to study the effect of a particular study-skill instruction on social studies achievement might be able to generalize their results only to students who are motivated to learn and use such a procedure in school. Nonvolunteers might need a different kind of instruction to be successful in that subject. Researchers, then, are faced with a seemingly unanswerable question: Can results from research with volunteer subjects be generalized to nonvolunteer subjects?

The issue has wide implications, especially when human subjects are used in experimental research. It has become uniform practice within the educational research community to require the prior permission of subjects. In cases where the subjects are minors (under the age of 18 years), permissions from parents or guardians are necessary. Granting of permission is a form of volunteering. Permission for including human subjects is not a problem in descriptive or correlational research because (a) confidentiality is maintained through the use of grouped rather than individual data collection procedures and (b) such research does not involve intrusive activities. For example, an ethical and legal concern might be raised by subjects when they are assigned to what becomes a less effective treatment. They may say their educational progress was hindered rather than enhanced by the instructional activity.

Sample Size

The size of samples is important to researchers for statistical and practical reasons. There are several practical issues researchers need to consider. In collecting data, researchers must consider factors such as the availability of research personnel, the cost involved in paying personnel and securing instruments and materials, the time available for collecting and analyzing data, and the accessibility of subjects.

More important, researchers who want to generalize from the sample (the smaller group) to the target population (the larger group) should do this with as little statistical error as possible. Statistically, the size of the sample influences the likelihood that the sample's characteristics are truly representative of those of the target population (Borg, Gall, & Gall, 1993; Gay, 1992; Kerlinger, 1973). That is, the distribution of relevant variables found in the sample should not be significantly different from that of the target population. Any mismatch between the sample and the target population caused by an inadequate sample size will also contribute to sampling error.

ACTIVITIES

Activity 1

Using the focus questions at the beginning of this chapter as a guide, summarize the chapter's key ideas.

Activity 2

Read each of the following subject sections extracted from research reports. The researchers' research purposes have been included for your information. Using the questions and criteria on page 136, evaluate the studies. For each, list questions and concerns you may have about

a. Characteristics of the subjects

b. The sampling procedures

c. The representativeness of the subjects in relation to the target populations

d. The appropriateness of the subjects for the researchers' purposes

> **Extract A.** The study (a) examined the effectiveness of three methods of teaching social studies concepts to fourth-grade students, (b) tested the effects and interaction of gender and reading ability on the treatments, and (c) tested propositions concerning concept teaching: Is there a need for definitions, examples and nonexamples, and question/practice?
>
> **SAMPLE**
>
> The sample consisted of 85 subjects drawn from 10 sections of fourth-grade classes at an elementary school located in the suburbs of a small- to medium-sized southern city. Subjects were randomly assigned to one of three treatment groups. Only those subjects

who returned parental permission forms were included in the random assignment. Three experienced classroom teachers, all of whom were females, administered the treatment. (McKinney, Larkins, Ford, & Davis, 1983, p. 664)

Extract B.   The purposes of the study were (a) to describe children's out-of-school activities, with a special focus on reading, and (b) to examine the relationship of out-of-school activities to reading achievement.

SUBJECTS

The subjects were 155 fifth-grade students, 52 from two classrooms in a village school and 103 from five classrooms in a school in a middle-class area of a small city. Both communities are in east central Illinois. There were 85 boys and 70 girls in the total sample. Although there were some blue collar, low-income, and minority children in the sample, these groups were underrepresented in terms of their proportions in the nation as a whole. On the Metropolitan Achievement test, the sample was above the national average (mean percentile rank = 62.9), but showed a typical spreading in ability (SD = 25.6). Although the sample included a number of poor readers, no child was identified by teachers as a nonreader. (Anderson, Wilson, & Fielding, 1988, p. 287)

FEEDBACK

Activity 1

What are populations and target populations?

The larger group of people or objects to whom researchers wish to apply their results constitutes the population, which is a group having at least one characteristic that distinguishes it from other groups. A target population is the specific group to which the researchers would like to apply their findings.

What are subjects and samples?

Subjects are the individuals or groups included in the study. A representative group of potential subjects, called the sample, is a miniature target population. Ideally, the sample would have the same distribution of relevant variables as found in the target population.

What criteria should be used to evaluate subject sections?

From reading the subject sections, research consumers should be able to answer

What was the intended target population?

Who were the subjects?

How were the subjects selected, and did the researchers show bias in their sampling procedures?

Were the subjects truly representative of the target population?

How were the subjects assigned to groups or treatments in experimental research?

Will the research results be applicable to my teaching situation and the students I teach? (Am I part of the target population? Are my students part of the target population?)

What considerations do researchers give to subject selection?

Subjects should be representative of the large population so results can be generalized from the subjects to the target population. Random sampling, or randomization, works on the principle that all members of the target population have an equal chance of being selected for the sample. The subjects finally selected should reflect the distribution of relevant variables found in the target population.

What considerations do researchers give to sample size?

Research producers and consumers should be sensitive to any mismatch between the sample and the target population caused by an inadequate sample size. The mismatch is a source of error, called sampling error. The probability of making an error relative to sample size is unique to each data analysis procedure.

Activity 2

Extract A.   The subjects were volunteer (by parental permission) fourth-grade students from one elementary school in a suburban medium-sized southern city. No information was provided about specific demographic characteristics (e.g., age, gender, ethnicity, learning abilities, or the percentage of the total student body volunteered by their parents). Since all volunteers in the convenience sample were used, the researchers randomly assigned them so that subject variables were equally distributed across the three treatments. There is no specific way to judge from the given information whether the subjects were representative of the target population or whether the results can be generalized to other fourth-grade students. As for the researchers' purposes, the sample seems appropriate.

Questions and concerns might be raised about the characteristics of (a) the subjects in relation to the target population and (b) the volunteered students in relation to the nonvolunteered students. As a consumer, you might ask: Would the results about these instructional programs be appropriate for the students I teach?

Extract B.   The subjects were fifth-grade students from one rural village and one small city in east-central Illinois. The demographic characteristics of the subjects in relation to a potential national target population were explained. The actual target population, then, would be middle-class fifth graders from the Midwest who scored above average as readers on a standardized achievement test.

Questions and concerns might be raised about (a) whether the sample is representative of villages and small cities in the Midwest (or even Illinois) and (b) the generalizability of these results beyond the target population. As a consumer, you might ask: What applicability would these results have to my teaching situation?

CHAPTER 6

Reading and Evaluating Instrument Sections

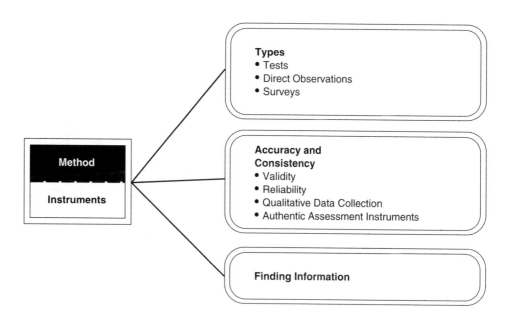

FOCUS QUESTIONS

1. What are the different types of instruments used in research projects?
2. How is information from different instruments reported?
3. What are instrument validity and reliability, and how are they determined?
4. What criteria should be used to determine whether instruments are appropriate for the research?
5. Where can information about instruments be found?
6. How should research report instrument sections be read and evaluated?

Researchers use instruments to collect data within all types of research designs. The term **instruments** is used to denote a broad range of specific devices and procedures for collecting, sorting, and categorizing information about subjects and research questions. Research consumers need to understand (a) what instruments are available to educational researchers, how instruments categorize information, and how data from different instruments are reported; (b) what criteria should be used to determine whether instruments accurately present information; and (c) how instrument sections in research reports should be read and interpreted.

From an instrument section, research consumers should be able to answer:

What types of instruments were used?

Were the standardized instruments valid and reliable for the research project?

Were the instruments appropriate for use with the target population and the research subjects?

Will the research results be applicable to my teaching situation and the students I teach because the instruments are appropriate for use with the students I teach?

Instrument sections describing standardized instruments should be evaluated using the following questions, which are from Figure 3.1, page 117:

Evaluating Instrument Sections

Standardized and Other Instruments. What instruments are used in the study? Are they appropriate for the design of the study? Are the instruments valid for collecting data on the variables in the study and are reliability estimates given for each instrument? Are researcher-made instruments included (or at least samples of the instrument items)? Are the instruments appropriate for use with the target population and the research subjects? In the case of authentic, or performance-based, assessments, what evidence is presented that the devices reflect realistic samples of students' learning?

TYPES OF INSTRUMENTS

Researchers collect data with tests, direct observation (including observation of student work products, known as authentic assessments), and surveys. These instruments provide data about subjects' characteristics (as reported in subject sections) and about subjects' responses in various situations (as reported in procedure sections) in reports of all three kinds of research. Information about instruments discussed in any section of a research report is usually given in the instrument section.

Tests

Test information includes scores from individual or group standardized norm-referenced tests, standardized criterion-referenced tests, competency tests, and researcher-made tests.

A **standardized test** is one for which the tasks and procedures of administering, recording, scoring, and interpreting are specified so other testers can make comparable measurements in different locations (Harris & Hodges, 1995). The test constructors use accepted procedures and research the test's (a) content, (b) procedures for administering, (c) system for recording and scoring answers, and (d) method of turning the results into a usable form. Everything about the test has been made uniform (standardized) so that if all its directions are correctly followed, the results can be interpreted in the same manner, regardless of where the test was administered.

Standardized tests are of two main types: norm-referenced and criterion-referenced. Norm-referenced tests compare individuals' scores to a standardization, or norming, group. A **norming group** consists of individuals used in researching the standardization of the test's administration and scoring. The section in this chapter called Accuracy and Consistency of Instruments contains a discussion about how to determine the appropriateness of a relationship between a norm group and a target population.

The scores from norm-referenced tests are reported as standard scores (e.g., SS = 53), grade equivalents (e.g., GE = 4.6), percentiles (e.g., 67th percentile, or percentile rank = 67), stanines (e.g., 5th stanine, or stanine = 5), or normal curve equivalents (e.g., NCE = 72). Each of these scores can be used to describe subjects' characteristics or subjects' relative performance. Additional information about the different types of scores is in Chapter 8, Reading and Interpreting Results Sections.

In the following example, from a subject section, percentile scores are used to describe the subjects.

Purpose of the study: To determine if subject matter text could be rewritten such that students' comprehension of unfamiliar topic words could be enhanced.

[Sample]

[Percentiles]

Subjects were 55 eighth grade students enrolled in two state history classes at a university laboratory school. They first were stratified by reading ability according to their reading percentile scores on a standardized achievement test (Stanford Achievement Test, 1981), and then grouped by high and average ability levels. The high ability group, with 28 subjects, had scores ranging from 75–99, with a mean score of 89.28 (SD = 7.14). The average ability group, with 27 subjects, had scores ranging from 12–68, with a mean score of 47.80 (SD = 12.59). (Konopak, 1988, p. 4)

On **criterion-referenced tests,** or measurements, students' performance is tested in terms of the expected learner behaviors or to specified expected levels of performance (Harris & Hodges, 1995). Scores on these tests show students' abilities and performances in relation to sets of goals or to what a student is able to do. They do not show subjects' rankings compared to others, as norm-referenced tests do. A standardized criterion-referenced test is one for which the administration and scoring procedures are uniform but the scoring is in relation to the established goals, not to a norm group.

The assessment of students' work and the products of their learning, commonly referred to as *authentic assessment,* has increasingly replaced or supplemented other test data in research. This form of data, similar to criterion-referenced tests, is used to compare students' performance and products (e.g., oral reading, writing samples, art or other creative output, and curriculum-related projects) to specified levels of performance. In authentic assessment, researchers use materials and instruction that are true representations of "the actual learning and activities of the classroom and out-of-school worlds" of the children (Hiebert, Valencia, & Afflerback, 1994, p. 11).

Through using authentic assessment, teachers are expected to provide students with meaningful educational experiences that facilitate learning and skill development as well as greater understanding of what is needed for good performance (Messick, 1994). Specifically,

> authentic assessments aim to capture a richer array of student knowledge and skill than is possible with multiple-choice tests; to depict the processes and strategies by which students produce their work; to align the assessment more directly with the ultimate goals of schooling; and to provide realistic contexts for the production of student work by having the tasks and processes, as well as the time and resources, parallel those in the real world. (pp. 17–18)

Direct Observation

When collecting data from **direct observation,** researchers take extensive field notes or use observation forms to record the information. They categorize information on forms in response to questions about subjects' actions or categories of actions. Or, researchers tally subjects' actions within some predetermined categories during a specified time period. Field notes consist of written narrative describing subjects' behavior or performance during an instructional activity. These notes are then analyzed, and the information is categorized for reporting. The analysis can start with predetermined categories, and information from the notes is recorded accordingly. Or, the analysis can be open-ended in that the researchers cluster similar information and then create a label for each cluster.

The following description of an observational assessment and the information in Figure 6.1 are from a naturalistic investigation (Clements & Nastasi, 1988). Notice how the researchers explain their instrument and provide examples of the behaviors to be categorized.

Purpose of the study: To study the occurrence of first- and third-grade students' behaviors that reflect social competence components and information-processing components of problem solving while using computers in school.

INSTRUMENTS

Observational Assessment of Social Behaviors.

The observation scheme was adapted from a more comprehensive instrument (covering six components of social competence) developed by the second author to assess social behaviors (Nastasi & Clements, 1985). Behavioral indicators of social problem solving included cooperative work, conflict, and resolution of conflict. Indicators of effective motivation included self-directed work, persistence, rule determination, and showing pleasure at discovery. [Figure 6.1, top] lists the behaviors observed and provides an operational definition of each. Reliability of the instrument was assessed in previous research; interrater agreement, established through simultaneous coding of behaviors by two observers, was 98% (Nastasi & Clements).

Observational assessment of information-processing components.

As stated, initial analysis of the data on social behaviors revealed that (a) one of the most striking differences between the experimental (Logo) and control (drill and

Observation Scheme for Social Behaviors

Behavior	Definition
Social problem solving	
Cooperative work	Child works with another child on an academic task (i.e., jointly engages in computer activity) without conflict (as opposed to cooperative play—engagement in nonacademic activities or conversation not related to the task at hand).
Conflict	Child engages in verbal or physical conflict with another child.
Resolution of conflict	Child reaches successful resolution of conflict, without adult intervention.
Effectance motivation	
Self-directed work	Child initiates or engages in an independent work activity without teacher's coaxing or direction: including constructive solitary or parallel work.
Persistence	Child persists on a task after encountering difficulty or failure without teacher's coaxing or encouragement.
Rule determination	Child engages in self-determination of rules, for example, making plans or establishing parameters of a problem situation. Includes use of verbal heuristic for solving problems.
Showing pleasure	Child shows signs of pleasure at solving a problem or at discovery of new information (e.g., child cheers after reaching a solution).

Observation Scheme for Information-Processing Components

Component	Definition	Examples
Metacomponents		
Deciding on nature of the problem	Determining what the task is and what it requires	"What do we make here?" "We gotta go over here, then put lines around it like our drawing."
Selecting performance components	Determining how to solve the problem: choosing lower order components	"Read the list [of directions] again, but change all the LEFTs to RIGHTs for this side." "How are we gonna make this thing go over this way? We did RIGHT 20. What's 90 − 70 . . . 20, right? We need not RIGHT 90, but 70!" "We got to add these three numbers."
Combining performance components	Sequencing the components selected	"First you have to get it over that way a little . . . LEFT 45, then FORWARD 30." "We'll make the turtle go up this way about 10, then RIGHT 90 and 10 down, then FORWARD halfway—5—and we're done."
Selecting a mental representation	Choosing an effective form or organization for representing relevant information	No verbalizations recorded
Allocating resources	Deciding how much time to spend on various components	"That's enough time talking. We should draw it." "We got it." Let's think and make sure."
Monitoring solution processes	Keeping track of progress and recognizing need to change strategy	"Put 70." "70? We already did 50 . . . type FORWARD 20." "You're gonna go off the screen, I'm telling you."
Being sensitive to external feedback	Understanding and acting upon feedback	"I know—if it's wrong it goes 'blub, blub, blub' and sinks down."
Performance components	Executing the task; includes encoding and responding	"5 times 7 is 35." "Type R-I-G-H-T-4-5." "It says, 'What is 305 − 78?' "
Other	Miscellaneous; includes off-task and uninterpretable verbalizations	"They're recording us, you know." "I'm tired of this; can we do another game?"

Figure 6.1

Sample Information from an Observational Assessment. (Clements & Nastasi, 1988. Adapted by permission of the publisher.)

practice) groups was in determining rules and (b) as defined, the construct of rule determination was too general. The rule-determination category involved planning, establishing parameters for problem solving, and use of verbal heuristics. A more detailed framework was needed to differentiate among such metacognitive behaviors.
Therefore, a scheme for categorizing information-processing components of problem
solving was constructed based on the componential theory of Sternberg (1985). The
following metacomponents were delineated in the present study: deciding on the nature of the problems; selecting performance components relevant for the solution of
the problem; selecting a strategy for combining performance components; selecting a
mental representation; allocating resources for problem solution; monitoring solution
processes; and being sensitive to external feedback. Frequencies of behaviors indicative of each metacomponent were recorded. Performance components, used in the actual execution of a task, included such behaviors as encoding, applying, and reporting.
These behaviors were relevant to problem solution, but not reflective of metacognitive
processing. Because the investigation focused on metacomponential processes, behaviors were not defined more specifically than the "performance" category level. A final
category of "other" included off-task behaviors. [Figure 6.1, bottom] presents the definitions and examples of behaviors for each category. Interrater agreement was 87%.
(Clements & Nastasi, 1988, p. 95. Copyright 1988 by the American Educational
Research Association. Reprinted by permission of the publisher.

In the above extract, the researchers indicate that the material shown in
Figure 6.1 provides an operational definition of each behavior. For example, for
the behavior *Social problem solving, cooperative work*, they specify the particular subjects' activities that would be counted as an instance of the behavior. An **operational definition** is a definition of a variable that gives the precise way an occurrence of that variable can be seen. In the Clements and Nastasi study, the
operational definitions were verbal. Operational definitions can also be test scores.
In the Konopak (1988) study dicussed earlier, high- and average-ability students
were operationally defined by percentile ranges on the Stanford Achievement
Test. (To aid research consumers in understanding technical vocabulary and determining the appropriateness of operational definitions, there are specialized professional dictionaries. Chapter 11, Locating Information About Research Reports,
contains information about locating and using these dictionaries.)

Surveys

Surveys include questionnaires, interviews including focus groups, scales, inventories, and checklists.
    Questionnaires require the respondent to either write or orally provide
answers to questions about a topic. The answer form may be *structured* in that
there are fixed choices, or the form may be *open-ended* in that respondents can use
their own words. Fixed-choice questionnaires may be called **inventories**. They
may require subjects to simply respond to statements, questions, or category labels
with a "yes" or "no," or they may ask subjects to check off appropriate information within a category.
    Questionnaires also are used to collect information from files such as subjects'
permanent school records. When the respondent answers orally and the researcher

---

1. Approximate number of students in your department:
   undergraduate _____ graduate _____

2. What is your department's emphasis?
   ( ) categorical   ( ) cross-categorical

3. Does your department offer a course on *working with parents of exceptional students?*
   ( ) yes   ( ) no

   a. Is *working with parents of exceptional students* included as a component of another course?
      ( ) yes   ( ) no

   b. Is working with parents of exceptional students offered by another department?
      ( ) yes   ( ) no

   c. Is the course required by your department?
      ( ) yes   ( ) no
      At what level? (mark each that applies)
      ( ) graduate   ( ) undergraduate

   d. Is the course required for certification by your state's Department of Education?
      ( ) yes   ( ) no

Figure 6.2

Sample Information from a Questionnaire. (From Hughes, Ruhl, & Gorman 1987.)

records the answers, the instrument is considered an **interview.** Interviews are used to obtain structured or open-ended responses. They differ from questionnaires in that the researcher can modify the data collection situation to fit the respondent's responses. For example, additional information can be solicited, or a question can be rephrased.

The following explanation of a fixed-response questionnaire is from a descriptive study, and sample questions from that questionnaire are presented in Figure 6.2.

Purpose of the study: To determine the nature, extent, and impact of preservice training for special educators working with parents.

INSTRUMENT

Survey I questionnaire is displayed as [Figure 6.2]. Questions on the survey form included demographic information and series of questions designed to ascertain whether content on working with parents was offered [in college courses preparing special education teachers] and, if so, to what extent. Respondents whose departments [of special education] offered a course on this topic were asked to provide a course syllabus, which became permanent product data. (Hughes, Ruhl, & Gorman, 1987, p. 82. Copyright 1987 by Teacher Education and Special Education)

The following explanation of an inventory is from a study to develop a way to measure student achievement in terms of a school's local curriculum. Sample items from the inventory are presented in Figure 6.3. Notice that although the instrument was labeled an inventory, its items could easily be restructured as questions.

Purpose of the study: To describe a model for a schoolwide curriculum-based system of identifying and programing for students with learning disabilities.

The final measure used in the [Curriculum-Based Assessment and Instructional Design] (C-BAID) process is the environmental inventory. Its purpose is to assist teachers in identifying factors that may facilitate or impede instruction in the classroom. It is used to provide information once a particular student is determined to be significantly discrepant from peers either academically, in work habits, or both. The checklist used in C-BAID is an adaptation of ones previously developed [by other researchers]. The inventory is based on the ABC model of instruction and thus focuses on the Antecedents, or events taking place prior to or during instruction; the Behavior, or how learners perform; and the Consequences, or events taking place after learners have performed. Many of the variables selected for inclusion in the environmental inventory have been shown to be positively correlated with academic achievement [by other researchers]. The environmental inventory can be conducted by the school psychologist or principal. Classroom teachers may also complete the inventory after a lesson has ended. A portion of the inventory is shown in [Figure 6.3]. (Bursuck & Lesson, 1987, pp. 23, 26)

Consequences   Teacher, target learner, and peer responses to learner behavior (c)

C1   Teacher response to correct answer:

meaningful immediate reinforcement _____
meaningful delayed reinforcement _____
no reinforcement _____

C2   Target learner response to success:

positive _____   negative _____   no response _____

C3   Peer response to target learner's correct answer:

positive _____   negative _____   no response _____

C4   Teacher response to incorrect answer:

immediate feedback _____ delayed feedback _____
modeled correct responses _____
required learner to imitate correct response _____
no corrective feedback _____
punishment or sarcasm _____

C5   Target learner response to incorrect response or failure:

guessed _____
corrected self _____
gave up and said "I don't know" _____
made another response _____   (please describe)_____
sat and said nothing _____
became negative and refused to work _____
became hostile (i.e., engaged in verbally and/or physically aggressive behavior) _____

C6   Peer responses to target learner's incorrect answer:

positive _____   negative _____   no response _____

Figure 6.3
Sample Information from an Inventory. (Bursuck & Lesson, 1987, 17–29)

Perceptions of Current Working Conditions		Preferred Working Conditions	
Condition	Percent	Condition	Percent
Average current wages		*Preferred wages*	
No pay	41%	No pay	5%
Less than $1/hour	23%	Less than now	.4%
$1.01 to $2.50/hour	10%	Same as now	49%
$2.51 to $3.34/hour	.3%	More than now	25%
Above $3.35/hour	3%	Much more	12%
Don't know	21%	Not sure	9%
Current interaction with nonhandicapped		*Preferred interactions*	
Never	7%	Less than now	2%
Rarely	13%	Somewhat less	4%
Sometimes	22%	Same as now	54%
Frequently	46%	Somewhat more	30%
Don't know	11%	Much more	10%
Current responsibility and advancement opportunities		*Preferred responsibility and advancement opportunities*	
Never	36%	Less than now	0%
Rarely	13%	Somewhat less	.4%
Sometimes	28%	Same as now	59%
Frequently	25%	Somewhat more	28%
Don't know	17%	Much more	12%
Current level of work without supervision		*Preferred level of work without supervision*	
Never	17%	Less than now	0%
Rarely	13%	Somewhat less	2%
Sometimes	28%	Same as now	52%
Frequently	25%	Somewhat more	29%
Don't know	17%	Much more	17%
Requirements to exhibit "normal" behavior during work		*Preferred level of requirement to exhibit "normal" behavior during work*	
Never	14%	Less than now	3%
Rarely	7%	Somewhat less	5%
Sometimes	16%	Same as now	66%
Frequently	25%	Somewhat more	20%
Don't know	38%	Much more	7%
Current performance of same tasks as nonhandicapped workers		*Preferred level of performance of same tasks as nonhandicapped workers*	
Never	19%	Less than now	9%
Rarely	14%	Somewhat less	3%
Sometimes	19%	Same as now	61%
Frequently	21%	Somewhat more	28%
Don't know	26%	Much more	7%

Vocational Placement

Current Placement		Preferred placement	
Institution	10.4%	Institution	5.6%
Home (no program)	17.2%	Home	4.0%
Activities center	23.3%	Activities center	25.6%
Sheltered workshop	43.7%	Sheltered workshop	52.0%
Competitive employment	5%	Competitive employment	12.8%

Attitudes Toward Work

Work should be a normal part of life for my son or daughter.

Strongly Disagree	Mildly Disagree	Not Sure	Mildly Agree	Strongly Agree
4%	2%	18%	16%	60%

Figure 6.4

Sample Information from a Likert-Type Scale. (Hill, Seyfarth, Banks, Wehman, & Orelove, 1987, 9–23. Reprinted with permission.)

Scales commonly measure variables related to attitudes, interests, and personality and social adjustment. Usually, data are quantified in predetermined categories representing subdivisions of the variable. Subjects respond to a series of statements or questions showing the degree or intensity of their responses. Unlike data from tests, which are measured in continuous measurements (e.g., stanines 1 through 9, or percentiles 1 through 99), data from scales are discrete measurements, forcing respondents to indicate their level of reaction; common forced choices are "Always," "Sometimes," or "Never." This type of data quantification is called a **Likert-type scale**. Each response is assigned a value; a value of 1 represents the least positive response.

The following explanation of a scale is from a study to assess parent attitudes toward employment and services for their mentally retarded adult offspring. Although the report does not include sample items from the survey, the presentation of the results, as shown in Figure 6.4, clearly states that a Likert-type scale was used in the original form.

Purpose of the study: To assess parent/guardian attitudes toward employment opportunities and adult services for their own mentally retarded, adult sons or daughters who are currently receiving services from adult community mental retardation systems.

The format of the survey for the attitude section was a Likert-type scale. In this section [of the survey], parents were asked to indicate the degree to which they perceived that their sons or daughters were currently exposed to the six qualitative conditions already listed and their opinions regarding the optimal amount of exposure to each practice. Therefore, attitude questions were presented in pairs. The first of the pairs asked for the parents' attitude toward the current situation as they perceived it and the second of the pair asked the parents for the preferred situation on each issue. The first item of the pairs permitted responding on a four-point Likert scale ranging from "never" (1) to "frequently" (4); a "don't know" response was (5). The responses on the second of the paired items regarding preferences employed a five-point continuum, which ranged from "much less than now" (1) to "much more than now" (5) [see Figure 6.4]. (Hill, Seyfarth, Banks, Wehman, & Orelove, 1987, p. 12)

ACCURACY AND CONSISTENCY OF INSTRUMENTS

Researchers are concerned that data they collect with various instruments are accurate and consistent. They wish to be sure they have positive answers to questions such as "Do the data represent real aspects of the variable being measured?" and "Will the data be similar if the instrument is administered a second or third time?" These questions refer to an instrument's validity and reliability. **Validity** refers to the extent to which an instrument measures what it is intended to measure. **Reliability** refers to the extent to which an instrument measures a variable consistently.

Additional information about the validity and reliability of instruments, including that concerning observations, is found in Chapter 7, Reading and Evaluating Procedure Sections.

Validity of Instruments

Instruments have validity when they are appropriate for a specific purpose and a particular population. To use an instrument with confidence, researchers must be able to answer yes to, "Does the instrument measure what it is intended to measure at the time it is being used?" and "Are the results generalizable to the intended target population?" These questions imply that instruments are not universally valid. Instruments are considered valid only for clearly identified situations and populations.

The creators of instruments (tests, observation procedures, and surveys) are responsible for establishing the validity of their instruments. When researchers use others' instruments, they must present evidence that the instrument is valid for the research project. When researchers create new instruments for their projects, they must detail how they established the instrument's validity. Research consumers want to know, "Does the instrument provide a real picture?"

An instrument's validity is investigated using one or more of several generally accepted procedures. Even though each procedure can be used to determine an instrument's validity, research consumers need assurance that the particular way an instrument was validated makes it appropriate for a particular research project.

One validation procedure establishes that an instrument has been developed according to a supportable educational, sociological, or psychological theory. The theory can relate to any human characteristic or to any aspect of society. A theory is based on supportable research and tries to explain the nature of human behavior (such as intelligence or learning) and action (such as teaching). A theory's usefulness depends on how clearly it explains those behaviors and actions. A theory should not be considered as complete; it should be considered adequate only for describing a particular set of conditions, but not all conditions. Any theory must be modified or even discarded as new evidence is encountered, and every theory should (a) explain a complex phenomenon (such as reading ability, the nature of learning disabilities, mathematics aptitude, or the social interaction within a classroom), (b) describe how the phenomenon operates, and (c) provide a basis for predicting changes that will occur in one aspect of the phenomenon when changes are made in other aspects. When an instrument's creator demonstrates the instrument as representing a supportable theory, it is said to have **construct validity.** Research consumers should expect every instrument to have construct validity. It is the researcher producers' responsibility to select an instrument with a construct validity appropriate for the research question, purpose, or hypothesis.

In the example that follows, the developers of a reading test, the "Information Reading-Thinking Inventory" (IR–TI), explain their theoretical frame of reference.

> Three principal facts encourage us to believe that a new kind of Informal Reading Inventory [IRI] can address a number of [the technical measurement problems of existing IRIs] and other emerging assessment issues and, more importantly, can result in better decisions in planning instruction. First, the IR–TI was constructed from the start to address some of the technical psychometric issues that have plagued IRIs for five decades. For example, you will see later how we were able to solve the problem of intermixing passage dependent and independent questions rather easily with a design modification that essentially separates the

two question types. A second related point is that the IR–TI attempts to be responsive to the new issues that have arisen from recent theories of comprehension and from philosophies of instruction. Chief among these new concerns is the distinction between *reconstructing* an author's intended meaning (the usual view of comprehension) and the "constructivist" concept of *constructing* a reasonable interpretation of what one reads. The IR–TI is designed to assess both of these dimensions of comprehension in a manner that grounds it in current theory by acknowledging the "constructivist" ideal of promoting higher-order literacy or literate responses. Third, the movement toward alternative forms of assessment entails reduced emphasis on product measures, such as standardized tests, and greater focus on "process" measures, or performance-based and diagnostic evaluation of the student's thinking, reflection, and strategy choices. Instead of teachers continuing the practice of not assessing at all what cannot be assessed easily and definitively, we urge teachers to use the IR–TI to become more expert in continuing to informally assess critical/creative reading and thinking in a variety of settings and classroom situations. This, again, is the basis of "performance-based" assessment. (Excerpt from INFORMAL READING-THINKING INVENTORY by Anthony V. Manzo, Via Casale Manzo, & Michael C. McKenna, copyright © 1995 by Harcourt Brace & Company, reprinted by permission of the publisher.)

A second validation procedure establishes that the instrument is measuring a specific body of information. This is an important consideration, especially when the instrument is an achievement or performance test. An instrument that is intended to measure science achievement should contain test items about the specific information the users (subjects or students) had the opportunity to learn in science classes. For example, achievement tests appropriate for use at the elementary level should contain items that test facts, concepts, and generalizations normally found in typical elementary school science curricula. When an instrument's creators demonstrate that the specific items or questions represent an accurate sampling of specific bodies of knowledge (i.e., curricula or courses of study), it is said to have **content validity.** Instruments' creators establish content validity by submitting the instruments' items to groups of authorities in the content areas. It is their expert opinions that determine whether the instruments have content validity. Before research consumers can generalize research results, it must be determined that any instruments' content is appropriate (valid) for their educational situation and student population.

In the following example, from a study to assess the perceptions and opinions of students who completed teacher education programs, the researchers explain the source of their questionnaire's content. (The "Dean's Grant" to which they refer was a federally funded grant competition for the development and implementation of preservice teacher preparation models that would prepare regular and special education teachers for the mainstreaming of special education students.)

Purpose of the study: To assess the perceptions and opinions of students who completed the teacher education program at a large midwestern university.

A questionnaire comprising four parts was used to survey students. In part 1, respondents rated 34 competency statements related to mainstreaming of handicapped students on two scales. On the first scale, the Coverage Scale, respondents rated the extent to which they thought mainstream content had been covered in their teacher education program. On the second scale, the Knowledge Scale, they rated their knowledge of the mainstream curriculum content. The 34 statements were adapted from competency statements developed during the early years of the Dean's Grant that were still being used as guidelines for infusing mainstream curriculum throughout the undergraduate program. (Aksamit & Alcorn, 1988, p. 54)

A first-level aspect of content validity is face validity. **Face validity** refers only to the extent to which an instrument *appears* to measure a specific body of information. In other words, "Does the instrument look as if it would measure what it intends to measure?" "Does a mathematics test look like actual mathematical tasks? Instruments' users, or other subject-area experts, usually establish face validity by examining the test without comparing it to a course of study (curriculum).

A third validation procedure establishes the extent to which an instrument measures something to the same degree as does another instrument. The second instrument must previously have had its validity established by one or more accepted procedures. To establish validity for a new instrument, the instrument's creator administers both instruments to the same group of individuals. The extent to which the results show that the individuals correlated, or scored similarly on both instruments, is an indication of **concurrent validity.** This is a common procedure for establishing a new instrument's validity, but research producers and consumers must interpret the new instrument's results with some caution. They must be sure of the older instrument's construct and content validity. If the older instrument has questionable construct or content validity, the new instrument may not be appropriate even though there is high concurrent validity with that older instrument. Research consumers should expect evidence about the comparison instrument's validity. Research producers should indicate the instrument used to establish concurrent validity and data about the level of correlation.

Information about an instrument's concurrent validity is usually found in studies whose purpose is to develop or assess an instrument. The following example is taken from such a study. It should be noted that the reported negative correlations were a desired result since the two instruments are meant to measure students' behavior in inverse ways.

Purpose of the study: To revise and standardize a checklist of adaptive functioning designed for school use at the kindergarten level.

CONCURRENT VALIDITY WITH WALKER PROBLEM BEHAVIOR IDENTIFICATION CHECKLIST

[Twenty] students from grade levels kindergarten, 2, 4, and 6 . . . were also used to examine the concurrent validity of the revised [Classroom Adaptive Behavior Checklist].

The teachers of these selected students were asked to complete both the revised checklist and the Walker Problem Behavior Identification Checklist (Walker, 1976), with a return rate of 70%.

The overall Pearson correlation between the total scores on the revised checklist (where higher scores indicate more adaptive behavior) and on the Walker (where higher scores indicate more problem behavior) was $-.78$ (df = 54, $p < .001$). The correlation for kindergarten, grades 2, 4, and 6 were, respectively, $-.77$, $-.84$, $-.86$, and $-.95$. (Hunsucker, Nelson, & Clark, 1986, p. 70)

A fourth validation procedure establishes the extent to which an instrument can predict a target population's performance after some future situation. This **predictive validity** is determined by comparing a sample's results on the instrument to their results after some other activity. An example of predictive validity is the ability of college admissions officers to predict college students' first-year grade point average from their scores on the Scholastic Aptitude Test (SAT).

Reliability of Instruments

Instruments are said to have **reliability** when they are consistent in producing their results. To use an instrument with confidence, researchers must be able to answer yes to "Does the instrument measure what it is intended to measure in a consistent manner?" and "Are the results going to be similar each time the instrument is used?" The implication of these questions for research producers and consumers has to do with dependability and the degree to which the results can be trusted. Reliability is not an either-or phenomenon; reliability is a statistical estimate of the extent to which the results can be considered dependable.

The creators of instruments (tests, observation procedures, and surveys) are responsible for establishing the reliability of their instruments. When researchers use others' instruments, they must present evidence of the instruments' reliability. When researchers create new instruments for their projects, they must detail how they established the instruments' reliability. Research consumers want to know, "Does the instrument give a dependable picture of data?"

Evidence of an instrument's reliability is demonstrated with one or more of several generally accepted procedures. Even though each procedure gives only an estimate of an instrument's reliability, research consumers need assurance that the particular way an instrument's reliability was determined deems it appropriate for a particular research project. Whatever procedure is used, the reliability of an instrument is given in a numerical form called the **reliability coefficient.** The coefficient is expressed in decimal form, ranging from .00 to 1.00. The higher the coefficient, the higher the instrument's reliability.

The common procedures for establishing an instrument's reliability are (a) test-retest reliability, (b) equivalent forms reliability, (c) internal consistency reliability, and (d) scorer or rater reliability.

Test-retest reliability, also referred to as *test stability,* is determined by administering the same instrument again to the same subjects after a time period has elapsed. When subjects' results are statistically compared, researchers gain evidence of the instrument's reliability over time, or its stability.

Equivalent forms reliability (sometimes called *parallel forms reliability*) is determined by creating two forms of an instrument, differing only in the specific nature of the items; the same subjects are given both forms, and their results are statistically compared.

Internal consistency reliability, which is sometimes called *rationale equivalence reliability,* is determined by statistically comparing the subjects' scores on individual items to their scores on each of the other items and to their scores on the instrument as a whole. **Split-half reliability,** a commonly used form of internal consistency, is determined by dividing the instrument in half and statistically comparing the subjects' results on both parts. The most common way to split a test is into odd- and even-numbered items.

Scorer or rater reliability, which is sometimes called *interrater* or *interjudge reliability,* is determined by comparing the results of two or more scorers, raters, or judges. Sometimes scorer reliability is presented as a percentage of agreement and not as a coefficient.

In the following example, which is taken from a previously cited study about the standardization of a behavior checklist (Hunsucker, Nelson, & Clark, 1986), two methods of establishing the instrument's reliability are used. Both methods, test-retest and interteacher (or interrater), involve the use of the Pearson correlation formula, which is explained on p. 228.

Purpose of the study: To revise and standardize a checklist of adaptive functioning designed for school use at the kindergarten level.

TEST-RETEST RELIABILITY

Subgroups of 20 subjects from grades kindergarten, 2, 4, and 6 were randomly selected from the normative group to examine the test-retest reliability of the revised checklist. The teachers of these students were asked to complete the checklist twice over a 4-week period (x elapsed days = 31.3), with a return rate of 66.2%.

Using the Pearson correlation coefficient on total checklist scores, test-retest reliability was .72 for kindergarten ($n = 11$), .95 for grade 2 ($n = 11$), .89 for grade 4 ($n = 15$), and .67 for grade 6 ($n = 26$). Using the exact agreement method for specific checklist items (agreements on both occurrence and nonoccurrence divided by total number of items), test-retest reliability was .90 for kindergarten, .92 for grade 2, .90 for grade 4, and .89 for grade 6.

INTERTEACHER AGREEMENT

Subgroups of 15 subjects from grade levels 1, 3, and 5 who were in team-taught classrooms were selected from the normative group to examine interteacher agreement for the revised checklist. Both teachers in the teaching team completed checklists for 68.8% of these selected students.

Using the Pearson correlation coefficient on total checklist scores, interteacher agreement was .92 for grade 1 ($n = 11$), .86 for grade 3 ($n = 10$), and .89 for grade 5 ($n = 10$). Using the exact agreement method for specific checklist items, interteacher agreement was .92 for grade 1, .93 for grade 3, and .86 for grade 5. (Hunsucker, Nelson, & Clark, 1986, p. 70)

In the following example, from a study involving the use of various phonemic awareness tests, the researcher uses an internal consistency reliability procedure. Note that although the type of reliability procedure is not indicated, the researcher reports a commonly used statistical formula used—the Cronbach alpha. Another commonly used formula for establishing internal consistency reliability is the Kuder-Richardson formula 20.

Purpose of the study: To determine the reliability and validity of tests that have been used to operationalize the concept of phonemic awareness.

The reliability of each test was determined using Cronbach's alpha. Seven of the tests had high internal consistency, with alpha = .83. The Roswell-Chall (1959) phoneme blending test showed the greatest reliability (alpha = .96) followed closely by the Yopp-Singer phoneme segmentation test (alpha = .95). Two tests showed moderate to high reliability: Rosner's (1975) phoneme deletion test (alpha = .78) and the Yopp rhyme test (alpha = .76). The Yopp modification of Wallach's (1976) word-to-word matching test had the lowest reliability (alpha = .58) for this sample. (Yopp, 1988, p. 168)

Other Concerns about Instruments

A common concern about instruments deals with how and by whom instruments are administered. An instrument may have validity and reliability, but the person using it must be competent and must use it in appropriate settings. For example, certain standardized tests must be administered by fully trained and qualified examiners. Standardized tests requiring special training and certified personnel include the Wechsler Intelligence Scale for Children—Revised and the Stanford-Binet Intelligence Scale, 4th edition. All instruments, whether they are tests, observations, or surveys, should be administered by appropriately trained personnel.

The following three passages illustrate how researchers indicate instrument users' proficiencies.

Purpose of the study: To investigate differences in parent-provided written language experiences of intellectually superior nonreaders and accelerated readers.

Test Administration. All 125 potentially gifted children were administered the *Stanford-Binet Intelligence Test* and Letter-Word Identification subtest from the *Woodcock-Johnson Psycho-Educational Battery* by certified examiners. (Burns & Collins, 1987, p. 243)

Purpose of the study: To compare students' instructional placements as predicted by a standardized test and an informal reading inventory.

All of the tests were administered over a period of about six weeks (three per grade) by a research assistant trained in the use of both the [Degrees of Reading Power] and the [informal reading inventory]. (Duffelmeyer & Adamson, 1986, p. 195)

Purpose of the study: To determine the effects of education, occupation, and setting on reading practices.

Procedures. A guided interview was constructed based on a review of previous research in measuring reading practice (Guthrie & Seifert, 1984). Two enumerators were recruited who were paid for their services. They had considerable experience in conducting surveys but were not experienced with reading activity inventories. In a 4-hour training session, they were informed about the purpose of the survey, taken step by step through the inventory, and given a demonstration of its administration. The enumerators individually interviewed an adult wage earner in each designated household. (Guthrie, Siefert, & Kirsch, 1986, p. 152)

A factor that may be important in test administration is the familiarity of the examiner to the subjects. Research evidence seems to show that some subjects' scores increase when they are tested by familiar examiners (Fuchs & Fuchs, 1986,

1989). Since researchers cannot always establish examiner-subject familiarity (because of time constraints or expense), research consumers need to be aware of the possible effect on results of subjects' unfamiliarity with examiners.

A second concern is when, in descriptive research, surveys or questionnaires are mailed to potential respondents. A major concern to researchers is the representativeness of the returned surveys or questionnaires. Usually, a return rate of about 70% is considered adequate to ensure that the obtained responses represent those of the entire target population (Gay, 1992). When the percentage of returns is lower, researchers should conduct follow-up activities to get additional questionnaires. Also, when the return rate is the minimum acceptable, research consumers should be concerned whether there is a difference in traits between individuals who respond to the questionnaires and those who do not.

Validity and Reliability of Qualitative Data Collection

In many qualitative research studies, the data-gathering instrument is often a participant observer. The question can be raised about the validity and reliability of the data collected by these individuals. In Chapters 7 and 8, there are extensive discussions about understanding the procedures and results of qualitative research. In those discussions, the issues of data collection validity and reliability are addressed.

Validity and Reliability of Authentic Assessment Instruments

Authentic, or performance-based, assessment systems are often criticized for not having rigorous measures of validity and reliability. The major criticisms of authentic assessment deal with issues of the nature of the standards against which student performance is judged (validity) and the ability of educators at different times to apply those standards uniformly (reliability). For example, some educators advocate the use of portfolio assessment, one form of authentic assessment. However, there is no consensus, at this time, as to what constitutes an appropriate portfolio: What should a portfolio contain as samples of a student's work? Who should determine what student work is placed in the portfolio? At what point in the instructional process and how frequently should materials be placed in a portfolio? and, What criteria should be used to determine the quality of a student's work?

Extensive research is being undertaken to answer these and related questions about authentic, or performance-based, assessment (Linn, 1994; Swanson, Norman, & Linn, 1995; Messick, 1994). For there to be validity and reliability in the authentic measurements, these researchers postulate that authentic assessment must be used with the following considerations:

1. Student performances or products used in an assessment should be based on the purposes of the testing, the nature of the subject area being tested, and the instructional theories about the skills and knowledge being tested.

2. Educators should indicate whether the focus of the assessment is the students' products or performances or the knowledge and skills needed to create the products or performances.

3. The selection of tasks to be assessed and the ways they are tested should reflect as much as possible actual school and life situations of the students. That is, the knowledge and performance tasks should be selected from the context of students' learning and should be given in situations that simulate real-life situations.

4. There should be clarity about the outcomes of the assessments in regard to generalizability: Is the assessment being used to generalize to the performance of individuals or large groups? Care should be taken that generalizations are related to, and do not exceed, the intended purpose of the assessment (see item No.1 above).

5. The method of scoring students' knowledge, products, and performances should be clear, and there should be criteria for determining appropriate outcomes and consistency in the application of those criteria.

FINDING VALIDITY AND RELIABILITY INFORMATION

Researchers do not always report the available information about instruments' validity and reliability. One reason for omitting validity and reliability information is the extensive reporting of it elsewhere. In such a case, researchers refer readers to the appropriate research report.

In the two examples that follow, the researchers use instruments whose validity information is reported elsewhere. Note that in both examples, the researchers report reliability data established in their research.

Purpose of the study: To improve understanding of the relationships between types of inservice training activities and changes in teaching behavior.

The Stallings Secondary Observation Instrument (SSOI) was used to measure teaching behavior. The validity measures obtained with this instrument in relation to student achievement and attitude has been established in previous studies (e.g., Stallings, Needels, & Stayrook, 1979). High interrater reliability (85% agreement or better) was established for the observers in this study. (Sparks, 1986, p. 218)

Purpose of the study: To investigate the planning and debugging strategies and group processes that predicted learning of computer programing in small groups with students aged 11 to 14.

Six aptitude and cognitive style measures were administered at the beginning of the workshop. These were a test of mathematical computation and reasoning; a test of verbal inference; a short form of the Raven's Progressive matrices (Raven, 1958) to measure nonverbal reasoning ability; and three tests from the Educational Testing Service (ETS) kit of cognitive factor reference tests (French, Ekstrom, & Price, 1963): Surface Development (spatial ability), Gestalt Completion (holistic vs. analytic processing), and Hidden Figures (field independence). Internal consistency alpha for these tests ranged from .64 to .92 in this sample. (Webb, Ender, & Lewis, 1986, p. 246)

Another reason for not including validity and reliability information is the instrument's extensive use in educational and psychological projects. It is assumed that its validity and reliability information is known by most of the research report's readers. This is especially true when researchers use standardized tests such as the Wechsler Intelligence Scale for Children—Revised, the Metropolitan Achievement Tests, or the Woodcock Reading Mastery Tests.

Research consumers can refer to several readily available sources to locate information about instruments' validity and reliability. When the instrument is a standardized test, research consumers can refer to the administration and technical information manuals provided by an instrument's publisher.

Research consumers may find it helpful to rely on reviews of standardized instruments. These reviews can be found in special yearbooks and handbooks, professional journals, and professional textbooks. Chapter 11, Locating Information about Research Reports, contains information about how to locate and obtain authoritative reviews about instruments' validity, reliability, and appropriateness for target populations.

SUMMARY

What are the different types of instruments used in research projects? How is information from different instruments reported?

Instruments are used to denote a broad range of specific devices and procedures for collecting, sorting, and categorizing information about subjects and research questions. Three types of instruments are used in research: tests, observations, and surveys. A standardized test is one for which the tasks and procedures of administering, recording, scoring, and interpreting are specified so that other testers can make comparable measurements in different locations. Standardized tests are of two main types: norm-referenced and criterion-referenced. Norm-referenced tests compare individuals' scores to a standardization, or norming, group. Criterion-referenced tests and various forms of authentic assessment compare students' responses to specified expected learner behaviors or to specified expected levels of performance. Test information includes scores from individual or group standardized norm-referenced tests, standardized criterion-referenced tests, competency tests, and researcher- or teacher-made tests. When collecting data from direct observation, researchers take extensive field notes or use an observation form to categorize the information. They record information on forms in response to questions about subjects' actions or categories of actions. Surveys include a broad range of devices for data collecting, such as questionnaires, individual interviews and focus groups, scales, inventories, and checklists.

What are instrument validity and reliability and how are they determined?

Validity refers to the extent that an instrument measures what it is intended to measure. Reliability refers to the extent that an instrument measures a variable consistently. When an instrument's creator demonstrates the instrument as representing a supportable educational theory, it is said to have construct validity. When an instrument's creator demonstrates the instrument as representing an accurate sampling of a specific body of knowledge, it is said to have content validity. An instrument's creator establishes content validity by submitting the instrument's items to a group of authorities in the content area. It is their expert opinions that determine whether the instrument has content validity. When the subjects' results on one instrument correlate, or result in a similar rank order of scores, with those on another instrument, the new instrument is said to have concurrent validity. A fourth validation procedure establishes the extent to which an instrument can predict a target population's performance after some future situation. This is predictive validity.

The common procedures for establishing an instrument's reliability are (a) test-retest reliability, a measure of the test's stability, (b) equivalent forms reliability, (c) internal consistency reliability, and (d) scorer or rater reliability. Test-retest reliability is determined by administering the same instrument again to the same subjects after a time period has elapsed. When the subjects' results are compared, researchers gain evidence of the instrument's reliability over time, or its stability. Equivalent forms reliability is determined by creating two forms of an instrument. The instrument should be the same in every aspect except for the specific content of the items. The same subjects are given both forms, and their results are compared. Internal consistency reliability, which is sometimes called rationale equivalence reliability, is determined by comparing the subjects' scores on individual items to their scores on each of the other items and to their scores on the instrument as a whole. Split-half reliability, a common type of internal consistency reliability, is determined by dividing the instrument in half and comparing the subjects' results on both parts. The most common way to split a test is into odd- and even-numbered items. Scorer or rater reliability, which is sometimes called interrater or interjudge reliability, is determined by comparing the results from two or more scorers, raters, or judges. Sometimes scorer reliability is presented as a percentage of agreement and not as a coefficient.

What criteria should be used to determine whether instruments are appropriate for the research?

Research consumers should answer: What instruments are used in the study? Are they appropriate for the design of the study? Are the instruments valid for collecting data on the variables in the study? Are reliability estimates given for each instrument? Are researcher-made instruments included (or at least samples of the instrument items)? Are the instruments appropriate for use with the target population and the research subjects?

ACTIVITY

Read each of the following instrument sections of research reports. The researchers' purposes have been included for your information. Using the questions and criteria on page 125, evaluate the researchers' instrumentation. For each, list questions and concerns you may have about

a. The validity of the instruments

b. The reliability of the instruments

c. The appropriateness of the instruments for the target population and research subjects

d. The appropriateness of the instruments for the reseacher's purposes

Extract A: The Cognitive Behavior Modification Study

Purpose of the study: To determine the effect of 8 hours of training based on cognitive behavior modification theory in regular grade 1 and 3 classrooms with children who had histories of mild classroom behavior problems.

Pretreatment Measures. Classroom teachers completed the teacher rating scale of the Brown-Hammill Behavior Rating Profile Scale (BRP) (1983) for each subject. This tapped teachers' perception of the children's classroom behavior. A list of 30 descriptive words and phrases was rated by the teacher as one of the following: very much like the student, like the student, not much like the student, or not at all like the student. Examples of items are as follows: Is verbally aggressive to teachers or peers, Is disrespectful of others' property rights, and Can't seem to concentrate in class. The numerical range for this measure is a raw score of 0 to 90 and a standard score of 1 to 20.

Baseline observations were made to ascertain whether children were on or off task, with these evaluations made for 10-second intervals over a period of 30 minutes, with the final measure of time on task for a subject expressed as a percentage (number of 10 sec intervals on task/total number of 10 sec intervals sample [180]). It proved possible for two raters to achieve very high interrater agreement (97%) for these ratings. On-task behavior was defined as eyes toward seatwork material, chalkboard, or other learning display centers; gathering materials immediately followed by other on-task descriptors; writing/drawing in conjunction with eyes on materials; reading assigned materials. Off-task behavior was delineated as being out of classroom; manipulating pencils, rulers, or paper; scribbling or doodling; being out of seat; talking with neighbors; whispering to someone else; motioning; making vocal noises (unrelated to work); making body movements (i.e., head on desk, head cupped in book, arms over head); not having eyes directed toward seatwork; leaning out of desk; manipulating objects on floor; being turned around in desk (Blount, 1985, p. 63). Each rater had participants' names, along with corresponding teachers' names, room numbers, and daily schedules. They used this information to plan the most efficient means of collecting baseline data (i.e., when subjects would be in their classrooms receiving direct instruction or completing independent seatwork while the teacher worked with small groups). (Manning, 1988, pp. 194–195. Copyright 1988 by the American Educational Research Association. Reprinted by permission of the publisher)

Extract B: The Voluntary Reading Study

Purpose of the study: To determine the attitudes of teachers, principals, and parents of the importance of the development of voluntary reading in the school curriculum. Also to determine the factors that contributed to those attitudes and the decisions that ensued from them regarding classroom practice.

MATERIALS

The questionnaire was designed to follow a strategy similar to the "policy capturing approach" described by Shavelson and Stern (1981) in an attempt to capture the judgment and decision-making processes of the individuals in the sample. It opened with a vignette suggesting that the school district with which each individual was affiliated was giving that teacher, principal, or parent authority to design and select materials, methods, and priorities for reading instruction. Four areas of reading instruction were named from which individuals had to make their decisions and define their priorities for the reading program: comprehension, word recognition skills, study skills, and development of voluntary reading.

Other questions sought to discover factors that affected those decisions about program and priority. Participants were asked both to rank and to rate the importance of the four areas of instruction in reading—that is, to assign a different number (1 for "the most important areas" through 4 for "the least important") to each of the four areas, then to rate each of the four on a scale of 1 to 5, 1 representing "most important," and 5 representing "least important." Thus, it was possible for an individual to assign the same rating to two or more areas, but not the same ranking. Similar Likert-type ratings were elicited concerning beliefs about conceptions of voluntary reading, institutional constraints, and personal interests that might determine personal attitudes and decisions. Subjects were told that the purpose of the investigation was to determine their attitudes towards the importance of different skills areas in the reading instructional program.

PROCEDURE

The questionnaires were delivered to teachers and principals by student teachers in the respective schools, then collected one week later. Questionnaires were mailed to parents, with a self-addressed, stamped return envelope enclosed with each questionnaire; follow-up telephone calls helped retrieve late or missing questionnaires.

The same student teachers observed and recorded by checklist the characteristics of classroom library corners, if any, that were maintained and used by teachers who participated in the study. One week after completion of the initial questionnaire, those teachers were asked to complete a checklist of their own indicating what kind of and how often literary activities were included in their own classroom instruction. It was the information from these observations and checklists that was compared with responses to the initial teacher questionnaires to determine relationships, if any, between teachers' attitudes and their classroom practices. (Morrow, 1985, p. 119)

FEEDBACK

Extract A: The Cognitive Behavior Modification Study

The BRP is a standardized instrument, and the researcher seems to be assuming that readers have access to various sources containing this information. However, the researcher described the instrument and provided sample items. Operational definitions for on- and off-task student behaviors were provided as was reliability information established during the study. The instrument seemed appropriate for the researcher's purpose.

In regard to the instrument's construct validity, however, some researchers may feel that the definitions of on- and off-task behaviors might not be appropriate for elementary students, and especially for the target population. The implications of the stated definitions seem to be that students are not learning unless their eyes are fixed to a page, and that some student interaction is an indication of not being "on task." This last point seems to be counter to the ideas expressed by some researchers investigating collaborative learning among students.

Extract B: The Voluntary Reading Study

Although a reference for the questionnaire's construct validity is provided, validity and reliability information and samples of the questions are lacking. No information about the original and follow-up return rates is provided. Also, since observations were made of classrooms, there should be an indication of observer training or reliability. Research consumers, therefore, should be wary of generalizing from the study's results.

CHAPTER 7

Reading and Evaluating Procedure Sections

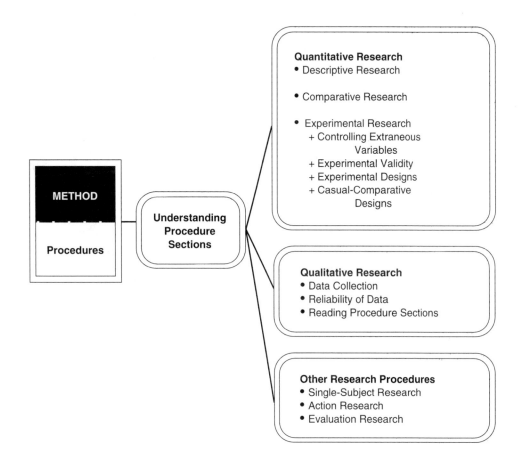

FOCUS QUESTONS

1. What concerns should research consumers have about research procedures that are common to all research designs?

2. What concerns should research consumers have about research procedures that are specific to quantitative descriptive research designs?

3. What concerns should research consumers have about research procedures that are specific to quantitative comparative research designs?

4. What concerns should research consumers have about research procedures that are specific to experimental research designs?

5. How are extraneous variables controlled in experimental research?

6. What distinguishes simple and complex experimental research designs?

7. What concerns should research consumers have about research procedures that are specific to causal-comparative research designs?

8. What concerns should research consumers have about research procedures that are specific to qualitative research designs?

9. What concerns should research consumers have about research procedures that are specific to single-subject, action, and evaluation research designs?

10. What questions should be used to evaluate procedure sections?

Researchers explain the specific way they conducted their research in procedure sections, which are subsections of method sections in research reports. If the researchers detail their procedures completely, other researchers can replicate the study. From a clear explanation of research procedures, research consumers can evaluate whether the study is free from bias and the influence of extraneous variables. Research consumers need to understand (a) how different types of research designs are implemented as studies (see Chapter 2), (b) what information should be included in procedure sections for the different types of research, and (c) what questions are used for determining whether procedure sections are complete.

From reading a procedure section, research consumers should be able to answer:

What research design was used in the study?

What special procedures were used to collect data or conduct treatments?

What special materials were used?

Was the research free from researcher bias?

Can the study be replicated from the given information?

Procedure sections should be evaluated using the following questions, which are from Figure 3.1, page 117:

Evaluating Procedure Sections

Design and Procedure in Quantitative Research. Are the research design and data collection procedures clearly described? Is the research design appropriate to the researchers' purpose? Can the study be replicated from the information provided? In experimental designs, are treatments fully explained? Are examples of special materials included?

Design and Procedure in Qualitative Research. Are research questions stated and additional questions generated? Is the method explained in detail? Has researchers' presence influenced the behavior of the subjects? Is there abundant evidence from multiple sources?

UNDERSTANDING PROCEDURE SECTIONS

Besides understanding principles of subject selection (Chapter 5) and instrumentation (Chapter 6), research consumers need to understand steps taken by research producers to collect data, devise special materials, and implement treatments. Although there are unique procedures for some types of research, several procedures are common to all types of educational research.

First, research reports should have clear and complete explanations about every step of the research so that other researchers can replicate the study. In all types of studies, there should be clear explanations about the settings from which information is collected or in which treatments were given. Research producers should indicate not only what was done but where and when data collection or treatment procedures were carried out. Research consumers can identify vague procedure sections when there is inadequate information for answering the questions given above.

Another procedure deals with the use of instructional materials. Researchers often study how subjects react to specific materials such as textbooks, stories, maps, graphs, and charts. These may be commercially produced or specially devised by researchers for the study. Research consumers need to be able to judge the appropriateness of the materials for the research situation and for use with the target population. Therefore, researchers should provide citations of published materials and samples of unpublished, specially devised materials.

A third common procedure deals with trying out the research procedures in a pilot study. A **pilot study** is a limited research project with a few subjects that follows the original research plan in every respect. By analyzing the results, research producers can identify potential problems. In descriptive, comparative, and experimental studies, researchers can see whether the data collection instruments (questionnaires, interviews, observations) pose any problems to the researchers or subjects. Researchers also have the opportunity to examine the need for modifying specially devised materials. Researchers should indicate that pilot studies were conducted and include information about modifications to instruments, materials, procedures, and treatments that resulted from analyses of the pilot study results.

PROCEDURES IN QUANTITATIVE RESEARCH

Descriptive Research

Quantitative **descriptive research** designs deal with statistically explaining the status or condition of one or more variables or events. Research consumers should be concerned that information is valid, objective, and reliable and that variables or events are portrayed accurately.

In observational research, researchers need to be concerned about factors that might affect the replicability of their studies (LeCompte & Goetz, 1982). They need to be sure that the data represent a true picture of what occurred and can be generalized to other situations. This refers to the **validity** of the research. Researchers also need to be sure that they are consistent in identifying aspects of a behavior or event so that others working in the same or similar situations could get similar results. This aspect pertains to the **reliability** of the research.

Several questions can help research consumers determine whether the results from quantitative observational studies are valid.

Could the researchers actually have seen what they reported observing?

Do the researchers' instruments limit or bias the type and extent of data that is collected? Were the data collection instruments used unobtrusively?

Are their conclusions applicable to other situations and groups?

Could the observers' presence possibly have influenced the collected data (that is, influenced the way subjects responded or events occurred)?

Could the observers have collected only unique or exotic information (data not representative of usual responses or events)?

Was there a major change in the make-up of the group being observed during the research period?

What status did the researchers seem to have in the group being studied?

Did the researchers seem to select informed subjects from whom to obtain information?

Were multiple observers used and was interrater reliability established?

The following method section is from a quantitative descriptive study.

Purpose of the study: To conduct individualized interviews with middle- and high-school students to better understand their perceptions of teachers' adaptations to meet the special learning needs of students in general education classrooms.

METHOD

Subjects

Subjects were 47 middle-school students (14 seventh graders and 33 eighth graders; 89% Hispanic, 8% Black, and 3% White non-Hispanic) and 48 high-school students (28 eleventh graders and 20 twelfth graders; 82% Hispanic, 1% Black, 16% White non-Hispanic, and 1% Asian-American or East Indian). The two schools attended by these students are located in a large city in the Southeastern United States and include a predominantly Hispanic Population. The median percentile score on the most recent administration of the *Stanford Achievement Test* reading comprehension subtest (Garner, Rudman, Karlsen, & Merwin, 1982) was 34 for the middle school and 45 for the high school.

Subject Selection.

An initial subject pool of 164 included all students in target science classes who had returned parent permission slips to participate in the study. We selected a stratified sample that represented low-achieving (LA), average-achieving (AA), high-achieving (HA), students with LD, and students who spoke English as a second language (ESOL). Our goal was to obtain 10 students from each group; however, we were successful in obtaining only 7 LA from the middle school and 8 LA from the high school. In cases with more than 10 students in a stratified group, students were randomly selected from that group to participate in the interviews.

All participating students with LD met school district criteria for classification as LD: significant discrepancy between IQ and achievement test scores, evidence of a processing deficit, and exclusionary criteria to ensure the learning disability was not due to other conditions (e.g., second language learning, physical disability). ESOL students were all classified as "Independent," no longer requiring self-contained ESOL services.

Table 1 Sex, Ethnicity, Mean Reading and Math Stanine Scores for LD, ESOL, LA, AA, and HA Students by Grade Grouping

	Sex		Ethnicity				Reading	Math	
	Female	Male	White	Hispanic	Black	Asian	Comprehension	Comp.	Appl.
	n	n	n	n	n	n	M	M	M
LD									
Middle	5	5	0	9	1	0	1.7	1.7	3.0
High	4	6	1	9	0	0	3.1	3.5	2.9
ESOL									
Middle	5	5	0	10	0	0	4.3	5.1	4.3
High	5	5	0	9	0	1	5.8	6.6	6.7
LA									
Middle	6	1	1	4	2	0	3.0	3.7	3.6
High	4	4	1	7	0	0	2.6	3.6	3.8
AA									
Middle	6	4	0	7	3	0	4.9	5.3	5.0
High	5	5	1	9	0	0	5.4	6.2	6.7
HA									
Middle	5	5	2	8	0	0	7.6	6.7	6.4
High	8	2	2	7	0	0	7.8	7.2	6.9

Note. LD = Learning Disabled; ESOL = English as a Second Language; LA = Low Achieving; AA = Average Achieving; HA = High Achieving.

For the purpose of this study, LA students were identified as those students who achieved at stanine levels of 1, 2, or 3 in reading comprehension on the most recent school district administration of the *Stanford Achievement Test.* Students in the AA group were those scoring at stanine levels of 4, 5, or 6, while students in the HA group scored at stanine levels of 7, 8, or 9.

To ensure that students did not represent more than one subgroup, students who had at some point in their school careers been in self-contained ESOL classes or in programs for LD were omitted from the LA, AA, and HA subgroups. Table 1 provides information on sex, ethnicity, and achievement for all of the subgroups.

Instrument

The instrument used in this study, *The Students' Perceptions of Textbook Adaptations Interview (SPTAI),* is an adaptation of two previously developed and evaluated instruments, *The Students' Perceptions of Teachers* (Vaughn, Schumm, Niarhos, & Daugherty, 1993) and *The Student Textbook Adaptation Evaluation Instrument* (Schumm et al., 1992).

The SPTAI consists of 11 structured questions, designed to elicit specific information, and follow-up open-ended probes, intended to encourage students to talk freely and to provide a rationale when appropriate (Bogdan & Biklen, 1992). The questions solicit students' opinions about activities, such as experiments or projects that supplement or replace textbooks; prereading activities, such as setting a purpose for reading; activities to be completed during reading, such as study guides or outlines; postreading activities, such as answering questions or writing summaries; activities that promote independent reading skills, such as teaching strategies to aid comprehension; and instructional grouping practices.

Three additional questions were included (a) to elicit information from students regarding their perceptions of the extent to which they think adaptations made for LA students who learn more slowly affected the learning of students who learn quickly; and (b) to determine if there are any other adaptations made by teachers to help students understand difficult material that they like or dislike.

Questions one through eight on the SPTAI are worded to offer students a choice between two hypothetical types of teachers, one who makes a specific adaptation and one who does not. For example, "Some teachers group students by ability levels (for example, putting kids who learn quickly together in one group, and kids who learn more slowly in another group). Some teachers group students so that ability levels are mixed. Which teacher would you prefer? Why?"

Procedures

After the SPTAI was field tested with 10 middle- and high-school students and reviewed by secondary teachers and an outside expert, the instrument was individually administered by trained interviewers. Interviews were tape-recorded, and tapes were audiochecked to ensure that responses had been accurately transcribed.

Coding Procedures

To establish codes for the interview data, two researchers independently read 20 randomly selected interviews (10 high school, 10 middle school). For each question, they searched the responses for common ideas and themes (Strauss & Corbin, 1990), which they used to develop an initial list of categories. The researchers then met to negotiate a mutual set of categories, with examples, for each question.

The two researchers used the categories to independently code the 20 previously selected interviews and then met to compare responses and revise and finalize the categories. The final coding scheme was reviewed by two independent researchers who were experienced in developing coding systems. It allowed the researchers to code each student's preference for the adaptations and his or her rationale.

Using the coding scheme, the two original researchers independently coded the transcribed responses to all the questions. Intercoder agreement was defined as the number of hits (i.e., both researchers coded the student's response in the same category) over the total number of responses. Intercoder agreement was .90. The two researchers conferred to resolve differences in coding. (Vaughn, Schumm, Klingner, & Saumell, 1995.)

Comparative Research

In quantitative comparative research, researchers examine the descriptions of two or more variables so they can make decisions about their differences or relationships. Research consumers should use the questions listed for procedures in descriptive research to determine whether the results from comparative research are valid and reliable.

The following method section, which includes the subject and procedure subsections, is from a quantitative comparative study of the different perspectives parents, teachers, and children have about the children's reading difficulties.

Purpose of the study: To examine children's reading difficulties from the perspectives of the children, their parents, and their teachers.

METHOD

Participants

Forty children, their parents, and the children's teachers participated in the study. The children attended a university reading clinic at one of two sites: a midwestern university clinic, operated collaboratively with a regional children's health care facility, (Clinic #1), N=24; and a southeastern university clinic (Clinic #2), N=16. The children, grades 1–6 (grade 1: N=5; grade 2: N=13; grade 3: N=8; grade 4: N=9; grade 5: N=3: grade 6: N=2), lived in communities near the clinics. Children were referred to the clinic because of parental and teacher concerns regarding their reading progress. Only those children whose parents and teachers both returned the clinic questionnaire were included in the study. At clinic #1, the children attended either the Fall, 1987, Winter, 1988 or the Fall, 1988 clinic session. There were 16 males and 8 females. Five of the children were African-Americans, seven had repeated at least one grade, and one was receiving special education services. Their average age score on the reading subtest of the *Woodcock Johnson Psychoeducational Reading Test* (Woodcock & Johnson, 1977) was at the 21st percentile. At clinic #2, the children attended the clinic during the Fall, 1988 session. There were 7 males and 9 females. Four of the children were African-Americans, five had repeated a grade, and three received special education services. Discrepancy scores were formed by subtracting the subject's grade placement score on standardized testing (obtained from school folders) from his/her grade level. The average discrepancy was 1.7 years/months.

University students at both clinics conducted the sessions with the children as part of a course in literacy assessment and remediation. Graduate students enrolled in the Master's of Elementary Education program provided the services at clinic #2, while clinic #1 used undergraduate students in their senior year. The university students worked one-on-one with an assigned child.

Materials

Student Interview. We developed an individually administered interview adapted from one by Wixson, Bosky, Yochum, and Alvermann (1984). The interview focused on the child's perceptions of difficulties encountered while reading. After several warm-up questions about reading habits and interests (What hobbies or interests do you have that you like to read about? How often do you read in school? How often do you read at home?), the child was asked to describe any difficulties/problems that he/she had when reading (Why do you think you're here? What difficulties do you have while reading?). If a child gave general answers such as "I need to learn how to read better", or "Reading is hard," the child was asked to elaborate ("I have trouble sounding out words" or I could read better if I could understand my science book"). The clinicians were instructed that the interview was not to be an interrogation, but rather to follow a discussion format and that probes, such as "Show me what you mean", "Tell me more about that," "Can you give me an example" were to be used to clarify responses.

Parent and Teacher Questionnaires. The first part of the parent and teacher questionnaires included open-ended questions that paralleled those which were listed on the student's. The parent and teacher were asked to list the difficulties or problems the child had when reading (What are your child's/the student's reading difficulties? Why do you feel your child needs special help with reading? What concerns, if any do you have about this student's classroom reading performance?).

The second part of the questionnaire was designed to assess perceptions of specific reading competencies by examining perceptions of the child's performance across two task conditions—listening to a story and reading independently. These tasks were chosen because they were reading activities that might occur both within the home as well as in a school setting. Twenty-one Likert-scaled items were used. Each item had a six point rating scale, ranging from 1 (hardly ever) to 6 (almost always) as well as an "I don't know" response.

The Likert items focused on comprehension, attitude toward reading and word identification. The comprehension items rated children's text-based and inferential comprehension when listening and when reading independently. Text-based comprehension included 3 items for each task condition (When listening/reading independently, the child can: Remember the story events, identify the central problem in a story, and answer questions when the answer is stated in the story). Inferential comprehension also included 3 items for each task condition (When listening/reading independently, the child can: Identify the main idea of a story, relate story events to real life experiences, and answer questions when the answer is not directly stated in the story). Attitude was evaluated with 1 item for each task condition (the child enjoys listening to a story, and the child enjoys reading).

Word identification included: (a) 2 items that evaluated letter knowledge (knows letter sounds, and can blend letter sounds together), (b) 3 items that evaluated word based strategies (uses letter sounds to identify an unknown word, tries to sound out words, and uses familiar chunks of an unknown word to figure it out), and (c) 2 items that evaluated meaning based strategies (will self-correct errors made when reading aloud, and uses the meaning of the story to figure out unknown words).

Data Collection and Analysis. The university students, who were trained in appropriate procedures as part of their course work, interviewed each child individually during the first clinic session. The interview took approximately 10-20 minutes. Statements were transcribed verbatim from the interview. Parents completed the questionnaire prior to their child receiving remedial services. Parents were also given a similar questionnaire for their child's teacher to complete and return.

Open-Ended Responses. The open-ended questions focused on the types of difficulties students experienced while reading. They were coded according to broad categories that emerged after several readings of the student, parent, and teacher responses. The following categories were identified: (a) Word identification—difficulties related to phonics, word identification, fluency and reading aloud, (b) comprehension—difficulties related to word meaning, understanding and remembering information, (c) attitude/behavior towards reading—difficulties related to a dislike or avoidance of reading and/or behavioral problems related to school reading tasks, (d) other (e.g., mention of visual or speech problems), and (e) don't know. Agreement between the two authors was greater than 90% with disagreements resolved through discussion. Children stated fewer problems than did their parents and teachers, and their responses had less elaboration. Responses to the open-ended questions were analyzed using descriptive statistics due to the small number of responses in some cells and because the categories were not discrete as some respondents mentioned more than one problem. The names of the children used in this article are fictitious.

Closed-Ended Responses. Parents' and teachers' responses to the Likert-scaled items were used to examine the children's comprehension and attitude when listening and when reading independently, as well as word identification strategies. Within the comprehension and word recognition categories, a single value was obtained by averaging across each item's scores. Thus we compared individual scores based on the average rating for all items within the category. (Yochum & Miller, 1993)

Experimental Research

In experimental research, researchers set out to answer questions about causation (Borg, Gall, & Gall, 1993; Gay, 1992; Kerlinger, 1973). They wish to attribute any change in one variable to the effect or influence of one or more other variables. The influencing variable—the one that researchers expect to cause change in subjects' responses—is called the **independent variable.** The variable researchers try to change is called the **dependent variable.** Research consumers should be concerned about whether variables other than the independent variables influenced the observed changes in the dependent variable. To have confidence in a study's results, research consumers need to understand (a) how researchers control possible influences of variables other than those under systematic study, and (b) how research producers design studies to ensure the validity of their results.

Controlling Extraneous Variables.   Variables that might have an unwanted influence on, or might change, dependent variables are called **extraneous variables.** Researchers can restrict the influence of extraneous variables by controlling subject variables and situational variables. **Subject variables** are variables on which humans are naturally different and which might influence their responses in regard to the dependent variable. **Situational variables** are variables related to the experimental condition (that is, variables outside the subjects) that might cause changes in their responses relating to the dependent variable.

For example, in a study investigating how the learning of syntactic context clues affects students' vocabulary acquisition in science, variables that might influence the results are students' general learning ability (IQ), their reading abilities, and their prior knowledge of the science topic. In this example, researchers can control the possible influence of subject and situational variables by selecting subjects of the same general learning ability and reading ability and by selecting a science topic and materials unfamiliar to all subjects. Another way researchers can account for the influence of these variables is by including them as independent variables. They can do this (a) by selecting students of different general learning and reading abilities and measuring the difference between and among the ability levels, or (b) by testing subjects' knowledge of the topic before the treatment and adjusting the after-treatment results to account for their prior knowledge. Obviously, researchers can only use as independent variables those variables that (a) they are aware of and (b) they think might influence the dependent variable.

Probably, randomization is the best way to control subject variables because it accounts for all subject variables, even those not known or suspected by the researchers to influence the dependent variable. Chapter 5 contains a detailed explanation and specific examples of randomization.

Other attempts at controlling extraneous subject variables include creating groups that are homogeneous on one or more variables and the matching of subjects on several variables. These procedures, however, do not ensure that other (and possibly influencing) variables have an equally distributed effect on all groups. When subjects cannot be randomly selected or assigned to groups, researchers can equate them statistically. The procedure known as analysis of covariance (AN-COVA) is used to equate subjects on selected variables when known differences exist. The differences, as measured by pretests, must be related to the dependent variables. (ANCOVA is explained further in Chapter 8, Reading and Interpreting Results Sections.) In the example above, differences in subjects' prior knowledge of a science topic could be used to adjust posttest outcomes statistically.

Experimental Validity.   Extraneous variables can invalidate the results of experimental studies in two ways. The first occurs when researchers and consumers cannot attribute their results exclusively to the independent variable(s). The second source of invalidity occurs when the results cannot be used with other subjects and in other educational settings.

When researchers lack assurance that changes to dependent variables can be attributed to independent variables, we say the research lacks **internal validity.** Several factors can affect the internal validity of research. These include the following:

Current Events.   Current events include any historical occurrence during the experimental period. For example, a joint U.S. and Russian spacelab project during a study about changing students' attitudes toward science careers might influence the study's outcome. Research consumers may not be aware of the coincidence of such an event during the study, but research producers should strive to be, and they should report it.

Subject Growth and Development.   Subject growth and development includes the physical, emotional, and cognitive maturational changes occurring in subjects and the periodic fluctuations that occur in human responses because of fatigue, boredom, hunger, illness, or excitement. For example, in a study about the influence of daily periods of silent reading on subjects' overall reading performance, changes in reading performance might occur because the subjects matured even without the special reading periods.

Subject Selection.   Subject selection refers to the influence that improper or biased subject selection has on results. This phenomenon is discussed above and in Chapter 5.

Attrition.   Attrition refers to the loss of subjects during experimental research. The reason for subject loss may be important and may unduly influence the results. For example, in a study about the effects on subjects with differing ethnic backgrounds of using calculators for learning of arithmetic number concepts, a major loss of subjects from any group might influence the results. A loss, say, from an ethnic group with a school dropout rate known to be high may result in a small sample with low achievement scores and an erroneous conclusion that individuals from that group do not benefit from using calculators. When attrition occurs, researchers need to determine why the loss occurred.

Testing.   In this context, testing refers to the possible positive and negative influences of pretests on results. For example, subjects' final test scores might be improved because they learned something from taking a pretest. Or, an initial interview might give subjects an inkling about what researchers are studying, thereby influencing their performance on subsequent tasks.

Instrumentation.   In this context, instrumentation refers to the influence of unreliable instruments on results. This phenomenon is discussed extensively in Chapter 6.

Statistical Regression.   **Statistical regression** refers to the tendency of extreme high and low standardized test scores to regress, or move, toward the group mean. That is, very high and very low subjects' scores on pretests seem to come closer to middle scores on posttests—higher scores become lower and lower scores become higher. Research consumers need to understand that this phenomenon may occur "when, in fact, no real change has taken place in the dependent variable" (Kerlinger, 1973, p. 320).

Interaction.   Interaction refers to the effect of several factors on each other. For example, attrition might result because of testing (subjects become threatened by the information they are asked on a pretest), or current events may influence certain subjects because of selection bias (subjects have an advantage because they experienced some event).

When researchers lack assurance that results can be generalized to other persons and other educational settings, we say the research lacks **external validity.** Several factors can affect the external validity of research. These include the following:

Subject-Treatment Interaction.   Subject-treatment interaction occurs when subjects do not represent a target population and selection procedures produce a sample that is either positively or negatively biased toward a treatment. For example, when researchers use paid subjects, these individuals may undertake the activities solely for the money involved. Volunteer subjects, on the other hand, may have certain personal characteristics (which influence them to be volunteers) that are not present in the target population.

Reactive Effects.   Reactive effects refer to special situations that make subjects in a treatment group feel special. One reactive effect occurs when they know they are part of an experiment, or they sense that something special is happening to them. This phenomenon is called the Hawthorne Effect. Another reactive effect occurs when subjects in a comparison or control group know or sense they are in competition with the treatment group, and they produce results above their normal behavior. This phenomenon is called the John Henry Effect, after the legendary railroad builder.

Multiple-Treatment Interaction.   This phenomenon might occur when researchers include more than one treatment in a study. For example, in a study to determine which study skills program might be more effective, subjects are given three content area study strategies: the SQRRR, ReQuest, and Overview methods. If each subject receives instruction about all three, the learning of one might help or hinder the learning of the others. In this case, the order in which subjects learned the strategies might influence the results.

Researcher Effects.   Research or experimenter effects refer to the influences imposed on treatments by researchers themselves. For example, when researchers use an experimental instructional program that they developed, they may exert undue (although not conscious) influence on the subjects to use the program successfully. Also, instructional techniques may be complex, and only those with the researchers' knowledge and dedication could effectively implement them.

Research producers cannot control for the effect of all possible extraneous variables. If they were to do this, much research would be difficult, if not impossible, to undertake. So, researchers do two things. They limit or manipulate pertinent factors affecting their studies' validity, and they identify as possible influences other factors that were not controllable or could not be manipulated. Research consumers need to judge whether researchers have missed or underestimated factors that might affect research validity. To do this, research consumers need to understand the experimental designs researchers use to reduce possible effects of extraneous variables.

Experimental Designs.   Experimental designs are the blueprints that researchers use in making decisions about the causative effect of one or more variables on other variables. The plans provide researchers with structures for studying one or more independent variables with one or more groups of subjects. Researchers select designs that best fit their purposes, answer questions about causation, *and* efficiently control extraneous variables.

In studying educational and psychological research, some authorities divide experimental designs into several groups, such as "true experimental," "quasiexperimental," "preexperimental," and "action" research (Borg, Gall, & Gall, 1993; Campbell & Stanley, 1963; Gay, 1992; Wiersma, 1995). The criterion for inclusion, or exclusion, from a group is the strictness with which a design controls for the effect of extraneous variables. The continuum goes from "true experimental," representing the strictest control, to "action," representing the least strict control. Other authorities consider all designs used to answer questions of causation as experimental (Kamil, Langer, & Shanahan, 1985). These researchers do not identify designs by the above criteria but by other factors. The factors are: (a) the number of independent or treatment variables and (b) the extent to which results can be generalized from the immediate subjects to a larger target population.

In the discussion here, experimental designs will be presented as a continuum from simple to complex plans. Simple experimental plans deal with a single independent variable, and complex experimental plans deal with multiple independent variables. In reading and evaluating both sets of plans, research consumers are concerned with the question "How generalizable are the results from the research subjects to other individuals and groups?"

Simple experimental designs deal with one independent variable or have subject selection procedures that limit the generalizability of their results. In Chapter 2, single-variable studies were shown to provide limited insight about educational questions. In Chapter 5, subject selection techniques that produced samples unrepresentative of target populations were discussed. Simple designs are presented here so research consumers can recognize them and understand their limitations.

In some simple experimental designs, two or more groups of subjects are studied with a single independent variable. Subjects are randomly selected and randomly assigned to a group, but each group differs in the experimental condition. An experimental condition refers to how the independent variable is manipulated, varied, or subcategorized. When treatments are involved, one or more groups are randomly designated as treatments or **experimental groups** and the other(s) as **control** (or comparison) **group(s).** In educational and psychological research, a control group

Randomized group 1 (experimental group)		
Pretest	Treatment	Posttest
Randomized group 2 (control or comparison groups)		
Pretest	Alternate treatment(s)	Posttest
Randomized group *n* (other control or comparison groups)		
Pretest	Alternate treatment(s)	Posttest

Figure 7.1
Pretest-Posttest Control Group Design

is one that has received alternative activities, not the one(s) under study. All groups are given the same pretest and posttest (survey, observation, or test). This simple experimental design is called the **pretest-posttest control group design.**

This simple experimental design is shown diagramatically in Figure 7.1.

The following method section from a research report includes the subject (sample) and procedure subsections. It is taken from a pretest-posttest control group design that has a single independent variable. The independent variable is an instructional method (IML), so it is called the treatment. Note that there are three dependent variables, but the researchers are trying to determine whether the change in each is attributable to the single independent variable.

Purpose of the study: To assess the effects of learning strategies instruction on the completion of job applications by students identified as learning disabled.

METHOD

Subjects

Thirty-three students (20 boys and 13 girls) with LD served as participants in the study. All were receiving special education services in a public high school in a city in the Northwest (population 180,000) and were classified as learning disabled by a school district multidisciplinary evaluation team. Criteria for special education classification include deficits in oral expression (as measured by the Northwestern Syntax Screening Test), listening comprehension (as measured by the Carrow Test for Auditory Comprehension of Language), and/or written expression (as measured by the Comprehensive Tests of Basic Skills). Criteria also included a significant discrepancy (at least 2 years below grade placement) between the student's estimated ability and academic performance.

Students were generally from low-SES families (qualified for free and reduced lunch). Table 1 provides additional descriptions of the participants' sex, age, race, grade level, years in special education, percentage of each school day spent in special education, IQ, and achievement.

Setting

All participants were enrolled in a pre-vocational education class for students with learning disabilities. The class was taught by a certificated special education teacher

Table 1   Subject Description

	Learning Strategy Instruction ($n = 16$)	Traditional Instruction ($n = 17$)
Gender		
Male	10	10
Female	6	7
Age		
Mean	15.9	16.3
Range	14.5–17.3	14.3–17.5
Race		
White	15	17
African American	1	0
Grade level		
12th	2	3
11th	6	7
10th	6	5
9th	2	2
Years in special education		
Mean	5.9	5.3
Range	4–8	4–9
Percentage of day in special education		
Mode	.50	.50
Range	33–83	33–83
Intelligence[a]		
Mean	98.5	96.2
Range	88–106	84–105
Reading comprehension[b]		
Mean T	35.1	33.4
Range	22–43	25–41

[a]Stanford-Binet Intelligence Scale. [b]Iowa Test of Basic Skills.

with 6 years of teaching experience at the high school level. The classroom aide was a high school graduate with 8 years of classroom assistance experience. The teacher conducted the experimental sessions during two 60-minute instructional periods. The classroom was approximately 10 m by 15 m and had 25 individual desks at which the participating students sat during the experimental sessions.

Dependent Measures

Student Performance Measures. Three mutually exclusive measures were employed to assess the effects of the learning strategy instruction on the completion of job applications by students: information omissions, information location errors, and a holistic rating of overall neatness of the job application. An omission was scored when a required item was not completed. A location error was scored when the correct information was entered in the wrong location (e.g., writing the information on the line directly below where the information was to be placed). A 5-point Likert-type scale (1 = *very messy* to 5 = *very neat*) was used to obtain a holistic rating of the overall neatness of the job application.

Interscorer agreement for omissions and location errors was determined by having two scorers independently score all of the job applications. The scorers' records were compared item by item. For omissions, agreement was noted when both scorers had marked a response as not present. Similarly, an agreement was noted when both the scorers marked the location of the information as correct or if both scorers had marked the location of the information as incorrect. Percentage of agreement for each measure was computed by dividing the number of agreements by the number of agreements plus disagreements. The percentage of agreement was 100% in both cases.

Interscorer agreement was computed for the holistic rating by having two raters independently rate all of the job applications. A Pearson product moment correlation was then calculated to estimate the reliability of the ratings. The correlation was .78, $p < .05$.

Social Validity Measure. To assess the social validity of the effects of the training, the supervisor of classified personnel at a local university employing approximately 1,200 classified staff was asked the following: "Based on this job application, if you had a position open, would you invite this person in for an interview?" The rating was completed on a 5-point Likert-type scale (1 = *very unlikely,* 3 = *undecided,* 5 = *very likely*). The supervisor rated each application and was unaware of whether it was completed under the learning strategy or traditional instruction condition.

Design

A pretest-posttest control group design was employed. Students were randomly assigned by age and gender to one of two experimental conditions: learning strategy instruction or traditional instruction. This resulted in 16 students (10 boys and 6 girls) being assigned under the learning strategy instruction condition and 17 students (10 boys and 7 girls) under the traditional instruction condition. The results of a preliminary analysis revealed that there were statistically nonsignificant differences in characteristics (i.e., intelligence, achievement, age, years in special education, and percentage of each school day spent in special education) between the two groups.

Procedure

Job Applications. Job applications for entry-level jobs were obtained from eight local businesses. Two of these job applications were selected for the pretest and posttest; two additional applications were used to conduct the training sessions (demonstration and independent practice). Although these job applications were designed to elicit the same general information, the format (e.g., sequence of information and location cues) differed. The same pretest, posttest, and training job applications were used under the learning strategy instruction and traditional instruction conditions.

Preskill Instructional Module. Students under both conditions (described below) received a prepared instructional module designed to provide the relevant prerequisite vocabulary knowledge necessary to complete a job application. This instruction was conducted, and job application information collected (discussed below), prior to pretesting. The teacher presented the prerequisite vocabulary knowledge module, using a written script, to students under both conditions. The prerequisite information included definitions for the following job application vocabulary words: (a) *birth place,* (b) *nationality,* (c) *previous work experience,* (d) *references,* (e) *maiden name,* (f) *marital status,* (g) *citizenship,* (h) *salary,* and (i) *wage.* Instruction continued until all of the students earned 100% correct on a paper-and-pencil test in which the words were matched with their respective definitions.

Students under both experimental conditions also compiled the information necessary for them to complete a job application, including (a) birth date, (b) social security number, (c) complete address, (d) telephone number, (e) educational experience, (f) previous work experience, (g) references, and (h) felony convictions (if applicable). Students then constructed a job application information card containing this information.

Students under both experimental conditions then completed the pretest job application. The teacher asked them to complete the job application as if they were applying for an actual job. She also explained that typically no one is available to help people complete job applications, and they were to use their job information card for the task. Students were provided as much time as they needed to complete the application. The teacher did not provide the students any assistance during this time. The pretest session was conducted 1 day prior to the training and posttest sessions.

Learning Strategy Instruction Condition. The job application learning strategy taught in this investigation was designed after analyzing the nature of items included on standard job applications for entry-level jobs obtained from a number of local businesses, and after completing a task analysis of the steps involved in completing a job application. The strategy was also designed in accordance with the needs and skill levels of the students. The principle steps were then sequenced and a first-letter mnemonic device was developed to facilitate students' recall of the strategy steps. This resulted in a six-step strategy called "SELECT."

Students first *S*urvey the entire job application and look for the *E*mphasized words that indicate the type of information requested (e.g., previous experience) and think to themselves, "What information do I have to have to complete the job application?" and "Do I have all of the necessary information to complete the application (check job application information card)?" If not, "What additional information do I need to get?" The students then look closely at the items on the job application for *L*ocation cues that indicate where the requested information is to be entered (e.g., line immediately below the request for information) and think to themselves, "Where does the information go?" Next, they think to themselves, "How much space do I need for the information— How big should I print the information?" and then carefully *E*nter the information requested in the appropriate location. After completing the application, the students then *C*heck to see if the information is accurate (compare with job information card) and that the job application is completed, and think to themselves, "Did I put the right information in the right locations?" If not, "I need to complete another job application." Then, Did I complete the job application?" If not, "Complete the job application." Finally, the students *T*urn the completed job application into the appropriate individual.

The special education teacher used a five-step procedure to teach the students the job application strategy during an approximately 1-hour instructional session. First, the teacher discussed the goal of the job application strategy instruction procedure (i.e., to help students accurately complete a job application) and why it is important to know how to accurately complete a job application. She also explained how they would be able to use the strategy whenever they applied for a job.

Second, an overhead transparency was used to introduce and discuss the six-step job application strategy. The teacher and students discussed the use of the strategy until it was clear that the students fully understood the steps. This was accomplished through choral responding by the students and informal checks by the teacher.

Third, using an overhead transparency, the teacher modeled the job application strategy by completing a standard job application while "thinking out loud." To actively engage the students, the teacher used prompts to encourage an interactive dialogue with the students throughout the demonstration, for example, "What is it I have to do? I need to . . ." and "How am I doing?" The students were encouraged to help the teacher. After modeling, the teacher and students discussed the importance of using self-questioning statements while completing a job application.

Fourth, students were required to verbally practice the job application strategy steps, including the self-questioning statements, until they were memorized. All of the students were able to do this correctly within a 15- to 20-minute rehearsal period. They were then required to write down the steps and associated self-questioning statements as they worked through a job application. Students were provided only one practice attempt. They were allowed to ask any questions at this time and the teacher provided corrective feedback only upon demand by the students throughout the training session.

Finally, students independently completed the posttest job application. As under the pretest condition, the teacher asked the students to complete the job application as if they were applying for an actual job. She also explained to the students that because there typically is no one there to help them complete job applications, they were to use only their job information card to complete the job application, and that they had as much time as they needed to complete the application. The teacher did not provide the students any assistance during this time. After they completed the posttest job application, the students were asked to independently describe the steps they had used, in an attempt to check whether they had employed the learning strategy. All of the students verbally stated, in sequence, the steps and associated self-questioning statements included in the learning strategy.

Traditional Instruction Condition. The same job application forms used under the learning strategy condition were used for the traditional instruction condition. During an approximately 1-hour instructional session, the special education teacher (same teacher) first discussed the goal of the job application instruction (i.e., to help students accurately complete a job application) and why it is important to know how to accurately complete a job application. She also explained how they would be able to use the things they learned whenever they applied for a job.

Next, the teacher used an overhead transparency to model how to complete a standard job application. Throughout the demonstration, the teacher explained why it was important to accurately complete job applications and instructed the students to be careful to complete all of the information and to be sure that they put the information in the correct place. To actively engage the students, the teacher used prompts throughout the demonstration, such as "What is it I have to do? I need to . . ." and "How am I doing?" The students were encouraged to help the teacher complete the job application. Students were then required to practice completing a job application. They were allowed only one practice attempt, and they were allowed to ask any questions during this time. The teacher provided corrective feedback only upon request throughout the session.

Finally, the students independently completed the posttest job application. The teacher did not provide the students any assistance during this time. Once again, these conditions (job application, instructions, and amount of time) were the same as those employed under the pretest and learning strategy instruction conditions.

Fidelity of Implementation. Fidelity of implementation was assessed under both experimental conditions by observing the teacher on the day of instruction to ensure that she followed the teaching steps associated with each of the experimental conditions. The primary researcher used a checklist to track whether the teacher fully completed the teaching functions described above under each condition. (Nelson, Smith, and Dodd, 1994). Copyright 1994 by Pro-Ed, Inc. Reprinted by permission.)

There are some other less-used simple experimental designs. One is the **posttest-only control group design,** in which the experimental and control groups are not pretested. An example of this design is an instance in which researchers have two or more randomized groups engaged in alternative activities, but they do not give a pretest. The groups are assumed to be similar because of randomization, but the differences in group results are determined only by the posttest. This procedure's weakness is that there is no assurance that the groups were equal at the start on the dependent measure (such as a reading test). Also, researchers cannot account for the effect of any subject attrition in each group.

A second simple design is the **nonequivalent control group design.** In it, the groups are not randomly selected or assigned and no effort is made to equate them statistically. Obviously, when comparison groups are known to be unequal, the research results can occur from many possible causes. A third simple design is the **matched groups** design. In it, the experimental and control subjects are selected or assigned to groups on the basis of a single-subject variable such as reading ability, grade level, ethnicity, or special disabling condition. A major limitation of this design is the possibility that one or more variables, unknown to and unaccounted for by the researchers, might influence the dependent variable.

For all simple experimental designs, extraneous variables affect the internal and external validity of the research. Research consumers should be wary of generalizing the results of simple design research to other educational settings and populations.

More complex experimental designs deal with multiple experimental and subject variables. Some complex designs are built on the pretest-posttest control group design and are expansions of it. In these complex designs, researchers not only study the effect of one variable on one or more other variables, they study the interaction of these variables on the dependent variable. Above, *subject-treatment interaction* and *multiple-treatment interaction* were noted as threats to research validity. Nevertheless, researchers can use complex designs to account for the effect of these interactions.

Not all complex designs use random selection or assignment of subjects. When randomization is not used, statistical procedures are used to account for the possible influence of the differences between and among subjects. Chapter 8 contains a discussion of these statistical procedures.

Two important threats to research validity are *subject growth and development* and *testing*. They can be accounted for in a design called the **Solomon four-group design.** Using random selection and random assignment, four groups are formed. All four groups are posttested. However, only two groups are pretested. One pretested group and one nonpretested group are then given the experimental condition.

The Solomon four-group experimental design is shown diagramatically in Figure 7.2.

Randomized group 1 Pretest	Experimental condition	Posttest
Randomized group 2 Pretest	Alternate condition	Posttest
Randomized group 3	Experimental condition	Posttest
Randomized group 4	Alternate condition	Posttest

Figure 7.2
Solomon Four-Group Experimental Design

In addition to the effect of the experimental variable, the possible effects of pretesting can be measured by comparing the posttest results of groups 1 and 3 to groups 2 and 4. If the posttest had an effect, the results of groups 1 and 2 would be higher respectively than those of groups 3 and 4. The possible effect of subjects' growth and development and current events has been controlled because both would have an equal effect on all groups.

The Solomon four-group experimental design is not often used in educational and psychological research, however, because of several limitations. The first limitation is that a large number of subjects is required. In a study employing one independent variable with no factors, approximately 100 subjects (four groups of 25 subjects) would be needed. Each additional independent variable requires another 100 subjects. Therefore, researchers use other experimental designs to control for the effect of pretesting and subjects' growth and development.

Another complex design built on the pretest-posttest control group design is called the **counterbalanced design.** In counterbalanced designs, two or more groups get the same treatments; however, the order of the treatments for each group is different and is usually randomly determined. For this type of design to work, the number of treatments and groups must match. Although the groups may be randomly selected and assigned, researchers often use this design with already existing groups of subjects—for example, when they use all classes in a grade level. A major problem with this design is the possibility of multiple-treatment interaction. Research consumers need to determine that the individual treatments are unique and that one treatment could not directly increase or decrease the effectiveness of another. Figure 7.3 shows the counterbalanced design for a three-treatment, three-group design.

Educational and psychological researchers are often concerned about questions involving multiple variables. Although the Solomon four-group design accounts for the possible influence of some extraneous variables, its use does not allow researchers to easily study two or more independent variables. In the example diagram in Figure 7.2, one independent variable is used with two subcategories: experimental condition and alternate condition. This could represent an experimental science program versus the previously used science program. Many questions are left unanswered in this design. For example, "Does the experimental science program or the existing

Group 1	Group 2	Group 3
	(randomized or unrandomized)	
	Pretest (all groups)	
Treatment C	Treatment B	Treatment A
	Interim Test 1 (all groups)	
Treatment B	Treatment A	Treatment C
	Interim Test 2 (all groups)	
Treatment A	Treatment C	Treatment B
	Posttest (all groups)	

Figure 7.3
Counterbalanced Experimental Design

program produce greater learning with girls?" "With students with learning dis-abilities?" or "Does the experimental science program lead to greater learning after shorter periods of instruction?" These are questions of interaction. Questions about the interaction of human variables and instructional and environmental situations are important to educators. Teaching and learning involve the interplay of many variables, and they do not occur in isolation.

Questions of interaction are examined in complex experimental designs called **factorial designs,** in which there are multiple variables and each is subcatego-rized into two or more levels, or factors. The simplest factorial design involves two independent variables, each of which has two factors. This is called a 2 × 2 facto-rial design. Factorial designs can have any combination of variables and factors. The practical consideration for research producers is having an adequate number of subjects in each subdivision. Generally, 15 subjects per group is considered the minimum, although group size in factorial designs can be as small as 5 subjects.

Figure 7.4 contains examples of three common factorial designs. Notice how the number of groups increases as independent variables and factors increase. Although multivariable designs can provide educators with valuable insights about teaching and learning, research consumers should be wary of research stud-ies containing what seem to be unnecessary factors. When there are too many pos-sible interactions (because there are many groups), the meaning of the interac-tions could become confusing. Research consumers need to consider whether the number of variables and factors is appropriate. As a general rule, factorial designs in experimental research larger than 2 × 2 × 2 become unwieldy.

The following method section includes subsections of subjects, materials, and procedure. The study is an example of a 2 × 4 × 2 factorial design. The indepen-dent variables and their factors are: gender (male or female), grade level (3–6), and treatment (experimental or control).

Purpose of the study: To determine the effects of a flexibly paced math program on student achievement.

METHOD

Subjects

The participants were 306 students who completed at least one year of a flexibly paced mathematics course at the Johns Hopkins Center for Talented Youth (CTY) between 1985 and 1990. Slightly more than two-thirds of the students were male ($n = 203$). Their grade levels ranged from third to sixth, with the majority from fourth (30%) and fifth (33%) grades. Students qualified for programs through a two-tiered screening process.

The Flexibility Paced Mathematics Course

The major goal of the course was to teach specific mathematics content (arithmetic, prealgebra, and beginning algebra topics) at a level matched to students' academic abil-ities and prior knowledge. Students attended 3-hour classes on the weekend for 7 months while concurrently enrolled in their schools. Not only were in-class require-ments demanding, an additional 2 to 3 hours a week were required for homework assignments. Class time included a variety of formats: individual work, small-group work, and small-group and whole-class lectures and explanations.

**2 X 2 Factorial Design
  (four groups)**

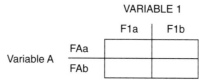

Example variables:

Variable 1: Student learning ability   Variable A: Science program
  F1a = Has learning disability   FAa = Experimental program
  F1b = Has no learning disability   FAb = Previous program

One example condition: F1a, FAa = Students with learning disabilities using the experimental science program.

**2 X 3 Factorial Design
  (six groups)**

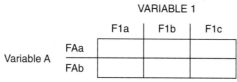

Example variables:

Variable 1: Content area study technique   Variable A: Gender
  F1a = Summary writing   FAa = Male
  F1b = Questions placed in text   FAb = Female
  F1c = Advance organizer

One example condition: F1a, FAa = Males using the summary writing content area study technique.

**2 X 2 X 2 Factorial Design
  (eight groups)**

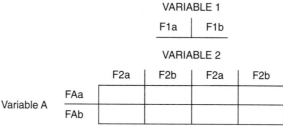

Example variables:

Variable 1: School grade   Variable 2: Textbook style   Variable A: Reading ability
  F1a = Third grade   F2a = Original textbook   FAa = Above average
  F1b = Sixth grade   F2b = Revised readability textbook   FAb = Below average

One example condition: F1a, F2a, FAa = Above-average reading-ability third-grade subjects using the original textbook.

Figure 7.4
Common Factorial Designs

Instructors coordinated the introduction of new material to individual students or small groups and encouraged them to explore a variety of problem-solving strategies (Cauley, 1991; Kamii & Joseph, 1988; Ross, 1989). Small-group collaborations provided an opportunity for students to conceptualize and communicate their ideas. Instructors and their assistants were available for guidance, modeling new skills when appropriate. With artful questioning about facts and strategies, instructors facilitated students' acquisition of new concepts and skills. The instructional approaches and settings used in the course were completely consistent with the Professional Standards advocated by the National Council of Teachers of Mathematics (see CTY, 1992a; NCTM, 1989).

Although the course was unique in many ways, content was not a distinguishing characteristic. The arithmetic curriculum included whole numbers, basic operations, fractions, decimals, percents, ratios, proportion, and measurement. The prealgebra curriculum included geometrical topics, statistics, probability, exponents, integers, variables, and simple linear equations and graphs. The algebra curriculum included beginning algebra topics, such as linear equations, inequalities, polynomials. factoring, and quadratic equations. The commercially available texts used for the course were supplemented by an in-house volume of math exercises, problem-solving activities, and other resources (for a full discussion of the course content, instructional methods, and typical classroom activities, see CTY, 1992a). Again, the character of this course is not a function of any unique content, but rather of the underlying philosophy of flexibility and individualization.

Four characteristics do distinguish the course. First, the curriculum is presented in a linear progression. Students study a topic thoroughly, demonstrate mastery, and then move on. This is in direct contrast with most elementary school mathematics programs that require students to revisit topics year after year. Second, the curriculum is flexibly paced. Instructional pacing is dependent on a student's performance in class and on a variety of standardized and teacher-made assessments. Third, no age or grade-level restrictions are imposed on a student's placement. Instructional placement is determined by the student's entering achievement level. Finally, no arbitrary restrictions are placed on the rate or the range of student progress (e.g., a fourth grader might complete all of the arithmetic sequence and move into the prealgebra curriculum within the 7-month period of the course).

Procedure

At the beginning of the math course, students were given an above-level form of the mathematics subtest from the Sequential Tests of Educational Progress (STEP), a nationally normed and standardized achievement test battery developed by the Educational Testing Service (1971). The intermediate level of the STEP, normed on sixth- through ninth-grade students, was given to students in the third through fifth grades. The advanced level, designed for ninth- through twelfth-grade students, was given to students in the sixth grade. An alternative form of the STEP was administered as a posttest either at the end of the academic year or when a student completed the arithmetic and prealgebra curriculum. (With flexible pacing, completion of a particular math sequence could take from 1 to 7 or more months, depending on a student's initial placement and subsequent pace of learning.) Results from the above-level form of the STEP, using corresponding above-level norms, were used for all pre- and postcomparisons reported in this paper.

In addition to their use for documenting the achievement growth reported in this paper, results from the STEP pretest were also used to help determine a student's initial placement in the class and to establish individualized instructional goals. Through the use of STEP scores and an analysis of a student's errors on the test, instructors were able to identify concepts and skills that a student had already learned and determine topics to be taught. This diagnostic-testing–prescriptive-instruction (DT-PI) approach has been found to be useful in matching students' needs to instruction and thus avoiding unnecessary repetition of already learned material (Durden, Mills, & Barnett, 1990; Lupkowski, Assouline, & Stanley, 1990; Stanley, 1978).

After initial placement, subsequent instruction was based on each student's performance in class and on homework, quizzes, and chapter and cumulative tests. Although students were allowed to move at a flexible, individually appropriate pace with no arbitrary restrictions on how much material they could cover, they were not permitted to move on to beginning algebra until they could demonstrate mastery of the arithmetic/prealgebra topics. "Content mastery" was operationally defined as 90% correct on all teacher-made instruments and chapter tests, as well as a score at or above the 90th percentile on the above-level STEP achievement test, using norms three grade levels above the student's current grade.

Once mastery of the arithmetic and prealgebra content was documented, a student progressed on to beginning algebra topics. Certification of mastery of beginning algebra was defined as a score at the 90th percentile using eight-grade norms on the Cooperative Mathematics Test (COOP), a nationally normed test developed and standardized by the Educational Testing Service (1964). In addition, students had to achieve a standard of 90% correct on all teacher-made assessments. (Mills, Ablard, & Gustin, 1994)

Causal-Comparative Designs.

Causal-Comparative Designs.   Causal-comparative experimental research is ex post facto, or after-the-fact, research. Researchers use it in trying to establish one or more causal effects between or among existing conditions. The researchers want answers to questions but they cannot manipulate the independent variable(s) for practical or ethical reasons. They realize a condition exists and are unsure about what might have been its cause. Causal-comparative designs are built on the posttest-only control group design.

A major concern for researchers doing causal-comparative research is that the causal effect should be one-way. The distinguishing variables must precede and be the cause of the differences. For example, Chapter 2 presents a representative causal-comparative study about the effect of black students' figurative language on their school language. The existence of out-of-school language experiences preceded their school language experiences; thus, the causal effect can be only one-way.

In using the causal-comparative design, researchers can randomly *select* subjects from target populations that differ in respect to one or more variables. Since there are no manipulated, or treated, independent variables, the subjects cannot be randomly *assigned* to groups. The subjects should be similar except for the variables being studied. For example, selection procedures can ensure that subjects are similar in such characteristics as age, socioeconomic status, or intellectual ability, so long as these are not variables that might cause the difference between groups. If it is not possible to select comparable groups, the differences between them can be equated statistically.

For research consumers to generalize the results from causal-comparative studies to other populations and educational situations, they need to be sure that any differences between groups cannot be attributed to one or more important variables that were not accounted for by the researchers. There is always the possibility that these outside variables may be the true causes of the observed differences. Also, they should be sure that researchers' description of the subjects is clear and that operational definitions are used to identify and distinguish the comparison groups. Therefore, research consumers should cautiously interpret the results of causal-comparative research, and they should expect researchers to follow up their tentative results with additional experimental research.

The following method section of a research report contains an example of a causal-comparative design. The researchers sought to determine the effect of a preexisting condition (amount of previous mathematics instruction) on mathematics achievement. It should be remembered that researchers using the causal-comparative design are trying to find causal relationships or predictions.

Purpose of the study: To examine the teaching strategies used by mothers of sons with learning disabilities and normally achieving sons.

METHOD

Subjects

The subjects were 30 boys with learning disabilities (LD), 30 boys without any reported learning problems (NLD), and their mothers. The boys were 8 to 11 years of age, and they were matched for age (LD group: $M = 9.7$ years, $SD = 11.74$ months; NLD group: $M = 9.4$ years, $SD = 7.23$ months). The mean age of the mothers was 37 years. The boys attended second through fourth grade and were drawn from schools in the province of Central Finland; all spoke Finnish as their native language. The control group consisted of boys who, according to their teacher's report, did not manifest learning problems and had not received remedial teaching. Children in both groups were individually administered the Raven Coloured Progressive Matrices (Raven, 1956) (LD group: $M = 25.83$, $SD = 4.09$; NLD group: $M = 31.60$, $SD = 3.08$) and a shortened, 30-item version of the Peabody Picture Vocabulary Test (PPVT) (Dunn & Dunn, 1981) (LD group: $M = 21.93$, $SD = 3.87$; NLD group: $M = 24.90$, $SD = 2.55$). The groups were matched for father's and mother's socioeconomic status. Parental SES was representative of the distribution in the Finnish population.

Children in the LD group had received remedial teaching in addition to regular class instruction before their referral to a clinic specializing in the neuropsychological assessment of learning disabilities (Niilo Mäki Institute, University of Jyväskylä). The goal of the assessment was to provide guidelines for more carefully focused remediation efforts. The very thorough neuropsychological assessment consisted of sensory-perceptual, motor, language, memory, and problem-solving tests (Närhi & Ahonen, 1992). Our definition of learning disability follows that presented by the National Joint Committee on Learning Disabilities (Hammill, Leigh, McNutt, & Larsen, 1981). Each subject was administered the Wechsler Intelligence Scale for Children-Revised (WISC-R) (Wechsler, 1974). Only children who had normal IQ (WISC-R total IQ above 80) and whose learning problems met the diagnostic criteria were included in the LD group.

Most of the children ($n = 27$) manifested language-based learning disabilities. Their difficulties in reading, spelling, or language were identified by teachers and confirmed by achievement testing using local norms for reading (videotaped reading of words, nonwords, and text passages at least 1.5 standard deviations below the age norms) and spelling. Language difficulties were confirmed by the following neuropsychological tests: the Token (DeRenzi & Faglioni, 1978); the PPVT; the Boston Naming Test (Kaplan, Goodglass, & Weintraub, 1983); and rapid naming tests (Denckla & Rudel, 1974; Wolf, 1986). A smaller number of children ($n = 3$) manifested primarily nonverbal learning disabilities, that is, major difficulties in arithmetic or writing. Children who were diagnosed to have primary emotional problems or who had neurological diseases or sensory impairment that may have caused the learning problems were excluded from the LD group.

Procedure

The interactions of the mother-child dyads were videotaped in a laboratory setting while the dyads worked on four structured, interactive tasks. The main focus of this article concerns the teaching task, which was designed to contain features typical of a home-work assignment. In the task, the mother and her son sat at a table next to each other. The mother was asked to teach her son a set of five pseudowords and the meanings that were attached to them. The pseudowords were phonologically acceptable letter strings in Finnish, and were easily pronounced. The mother was requested to take the teacher's role, and she was encouraged to do her best in assisting her son in memoriz-ing the new words. The experimenter reminded the pair of the similarity of the situa-tion to times when the child is at home, learning words of a foreign language as home-work. They were told that they had 10 minutes to practice the new words. The material consisted of five text cards (with the pseudoword and the object name that it corre-sponded to in Finnish), picture cards depicting the same objects, and paper and pens. The recordings took place in the video facility in the Department of Psychology, and an S-VHS camera was used, which was situated at 1.5 meters in front of the seated dyad.

Measures

Maternal Teaching. Two coders who were blind with respect to the child's group status (LD/NLD) were trained to code the data. Maternal strategies during the teaching ses-sion were coded directly from the videotapes by recording percentages of time used for each of the following mutually exclusive categories.

1. *Looking at the picture card.* Mother asked the child to compare the word and picture cards;

2. *Repetition of the words.* Mother asked the child to repeat the pseudowords and their Finnish equivalents several times;

3. *Recognition.* The mother produced the pseudoword and quizzed the child on its Finnish equivalent;

4. *Production.* The child produced the pseudoword equivalent as a response to the Finnish word presented by the mother;

5. *Writing.* Mother asked the child to write the pseudowords and their Finnish equiv-alents on paper;

6. *Drawing.* Mother asked the child to draw pictures of the pseudowords to aid in memorizing.

7. *Seeking associative connections.* Mother and child sought associations between the pseudowords and their Finnish equivalents;

8. *Narrative construction.* Mother and child constructed a narrative that bound the separate pseudowords;

9. *Word application.* Mother and child attached the pseudowords to a personally moti-vated context by giving them meanings from the child's own environment;

10. *Playing a game.* Mother and child constructed a game and played it using their own rules with the available materials.

These 10 teaching strategies used by the mothers can be divided into two main cat-egories, following an adaptation from the criteria set by Sigel (1982) for different lev-els of distancing strategies. A distinction was made between perceptually based strate-gies, which relied on information from the ongoing present, and nonperceptually based, or conceptual, strategies, which evoked mental representations of the words to be learned. The first five strategies were considered to represent low- and medium-level distancing as they referred to the present and were based mainly on rote learning. These strategies did not include negotiations between the partners. The last five strategies were considered to include higher cognitive demands. They provided associative connections and representative images for the child that helped him separate the self mentally from the ongoing present. With high-level strategies, the mothers constructed a personally motivated, meaningful context for learning the test words.

The coding consisted of recording the time that the mother used in each of the teaching strategy classes specified above. Percentages were formed by proportioning these times with the total duration of the task. Coding was done using a hand-held data collector that records data elements in terms of frequency and time duration. Total time used in the task and the amount of speech produced by the mother and child during the task were also recorded from the tapes. A measure of the child's performance on the task was reached by summing the number of the words he learned correctly.

Mother–Child Interactions. The quality of each mother-child interaction was rated on a Likert-type (5-point) scale. The following variables were used to characterize the behaviors of both mothers and children:

1. *Motivation in the task* indicated how involved both partners were in the task. Motivation was coded separately for mother and child.

2. *Emotionally* referred to the affective tone of the interchange. The atmosphere could vary from negative, nonchalant feelings, to positive, warm feelings expressed toward the partner. This variable was coded separately for mother and child.

3. *Cooperation* indicated each partner's participation in the activity. This variable was coded separately for mother and child. Extent of cooperation varied from acting alone to highest mutual involvement, in which the initiatives of the other partner were taken into consideration and the subjects appeared to strive for a mutual solution of the task.

4. *Dominance* referred to the mother's tendency to control the situation (e.g., objecting to the child's initiatives, presenting demands) and guide it toward the direction of her own wishes. This variable was coded only for mothers.

5. *Initiative* was coded only for the child and it varied from no initiatives by the child or his complete dependence on the mother's suggestions, to the child having lots of ideas and proposals for the solution of the task.

6. *Smiles* were recorded for a 5-minute sample for the mother and child separately.

Interobserver reliability was assessed on 25% of the data by having two assistants independently code the same randomly selected cases. The mean correlation between the ratings of the coders was 0.89 for low- and medium-level strategies and 0.91 for high-level strategies. The correlation for mother interaction ratings was 0.79 and for those of the children was 0.75. (Lyytinen, Rasku-Puttonen, Poikkeus, Laasko, & Ahonen, 1994. Copyright 1994 by PRO-ED, Inc. Reprinted by permission.)

PROCEDURES IN QUALITATIVE RESEARCH

In Chapter 2, the basic nature, types, and characteristics of qualitative research were presented. Chapter 6 contains a discussion of the main instrument for qualitative data collection—the researcher. The discussion here focuses on the specific activities qualitative researchers engage in to record their data. Basically, the data-gathering activities are observing people and events, interviewing people, and examining documents (Wolcott, 1992).

Data Collection

Data in qualitative studies are collected in particular contexts, that is, educational and related settings. The act of collecting contextualized data is commonly called **fieldwork.** Why a particular site was selected and how permission was obtained for researchers to access the site are important issues. Before entering the site, researchers need to answer questions relating to "What will be done at the site?" and "How will the researcher keep from disrupting the normal routine at the site?"

Researchers need to determine where on the continuum of being a participant/nonparticipant observer they will be. Sometimes this decision is determined by constraints within the fieldwork site, sometimes by the researchers themselves (Bogdan & Biklen, 1992). They need to determine whether they will act like a teacher or do what the children are doing. Their relationship to students might be influenced by factors such as gender, age, personality, and the way they are perceived by students and teachers under observation. Researchers need to be discreet while being efficient recorders of data. For example, if they openly take notes during class time, students may become curious about what is being written. In the illustrative qualitative research study given in Chapter 2, the researcher took his field notes under the guise of taking class notes.

The question of duration and frequency of observations is critical (Bogdan & Biklen, 1992; Spinder, 1992). Valuable qualitative data cannot be obtained without rapport between the subjects and researchers, so there need to be preliminary visits so all participants are comfortable. Researchers want to collect as much information as possible, and that takes time. If they are concerned about the influence of direct note-taking during observations, then they should not observe longer than their memory span. And, they must spend sufficient time at the site so they see events and relationships happening repeatedly.

While observing people and events, researchers create **field notes.** These notes are written descriptions of people, objects, places, events, activities, and conversations. These notes supplement information from official documents and interviews. An important part of these notes is the researchers' reactions, reflections, and tentative assumptions or hypotheses. Field notes can have two basic aspects, descriptive and reflective (Bogdan & Biklen, 1992). The descriptive aspect might include (a) verbal portraits of individuals, (b) reconstructions of dialogues between the researchers and others, (c) complete descriptions of physical settings, (d) accounts of particular events—who was involved, how, and what was done, (e) details about activities, and (f) the researchers' (observers') behavior. The reflective aspect of field notes might include (a) speculations about the data analysis—emerging themes and patterns, (b) comments on the research method—accomplishments, problems, and decisions, (c) records of ethical dilemmas and conflicts, (d) analysis of the researchers' frames of mind, and (e) points of clarification.

In recent years, the concept of field notes has been expanded to include the use of photographic and audio and video recording equipment. They can be used to provide records of the physical layout of the setting, artifacts, or details that would be difficult to document verbally. However, use of that equipment can be unproductive if it creates distractions among the subjects.

Field notes are not objective data in the strictest sense of the term; their form and content fully reveal that qualitative research is a subjective process. However, subjectivity should not be considered an undesirable or negative matter. Currently, there is a shift in thinking about the concept and definitions of subjectivity (Jansen & Peshkin, 1992). It no longer is thought of as distortion or bias, but as a unique, useful, personal quality of research. "When subjectivity is seen as distortion and bias, the [research] literature offers more or less prescriptive advice; when seen as an interactional quality, we learn about personal or reflexive, or political and theoretical stands" (p. 682).

Interviewing in qualitative research is used to obtain data in the subjects' own words. The purpose is to gather information from which insights on how the subjects interpret the situation being observed can be obtained (Bogdan & Biklen, 1992; Eisner, 1991). How interviews are conducted and the type of data gathered often depend upon whether the researcher is fulfilling a participant or nonparticipant role. In the latter case, the nature of the data is partly determined by the trust the subject has in the interviewer. In qualitative research, researchers generally use open-ended, informal interview techniques. They do not use fixed-response questionnaires or surveys to guide the talks. They encourage the subjects to talk about their perceptions about what is happening, what they believe about the event, and how they are feeling. Most importantly, qualitative researchers need to be good listeners. During interviews, researchers may use audio or video recorders and later transcribe the dialogues for analysis.

Another source of data is documents and artifacts (Bogdan & Biklen, 1992; Eisner, 1991). These include materials produced by the subjects (for example, samples from students' writing portfolios), students' and teachers' personal documents (diaries, letters), school records (memoranda, students' files, minutes of school board meetings, newsletters), school memorabilia (newspapers, yearbooks, scrapbooks), and documents and photographs from school and historical society archives. In certain situations, qualitative researchers may include official statistics as data. Such quantitative data can be useful for examining who collected the information and how and why it has been quantified. Quantitative data are not always objective; that is, data are often collected and quantified for social or political reasons, and, as will be explained further in the section "Data Analysis in Qualitative Research" in Chapter 8, there are inherent errors in all statistical analyses.

Reliability of Data

A concern of all researchers, quantitative and qualitative, is the representativeness of the collected data. In Chapter 6, the reliability and validity of instruments was discussed. In qualitative research, since the major instrument is the researcher, it is difficult to establish reliability of the observer. However, the reliability of researchers' data can be assured through appropriate research procedures in which researchers fully explain their procedures, verify their observations, and cross-check their sources (Bogdan & Biklen, 1992; Eisner, 1991; Hillocks, 1992; Marshall & Rossman, 1995; Pitman & Maxwell, 1992).

Qualitative researchers expect that different researchers will collect different information. In part, that results from different theoretical perspectives and beliefs about the nature and goals of qualitative research (see Chapter 2). Because qualitative researchers' backgrounds and interests may differ, they may collect different information and arrive at different interpretations. However, in all cases, the reliability of the information collected can be seen as a "fit between what they record as data and what actually occurs in the setting under study (Bogdan & Biklen, 1992, p. 48).

The issue of consistency is also related to the possible replication of a study. Even though qualitative researchers are not usually concerned with replicating a study in the strict sense of the term because of the belief that "the real world changes" (Marshall & Rossman, 1995, p. 146), there are procedures they can follow to assure the trustworthiness of their data. They can keep thorough notes and records of their activities, and they can keep their data in a well-organized and retrievable form.

Research consumers should look for the following specific evidence of data reliability (Marshall & Rossman, 1995):

1. The researchers' method is detailed so its adequacy and logic can be determined, and there is an abundance of evidence.

2. The researchers provide evidence of their qualifications as participant observers.

3. The researchers' assumptions are clear.

4. The researchers' questions are stated, and the study seeks to answer those questions and generate further questions.

5. The researchers used preliminary days of the study to generate a focus for the study.

6. The researchers were present in the research context for an adequate period of time, and the researchers observed a full range of activities over a full cycle of those activities.

7. The data were collected from multiple sources.

8. The researchers saved their data for reanalysis.

Reading Qualitative Research Procedure Sections

The following method section is from a qualitative descriptive study. Note that the subjects subsection has also been included. In the procedures section, the researcher has provided information about the classroom instructional activity and data collection and analysis procedures.

Purpose of the study: To determine how frequently, when, and for what reasons a group of second-grade writers used their peers' questions to revise their unfinished pieces.

METHOD

Subjects

The study's site was a heterogeneously grouped second-grade classroom of a cooperative teacher in Delaware who was implementing the process approach to teaching writing as described by Graves (1983). Twenty-four students participated in the study, 16 girls and eight boys.

None of the children had participated in a process-oriented writing program previous to this academic year. All had been participating in such a program for three months when this investigation began.

Procedures

[Class activity]   The writing program was implemented two days per week for approximately one hour each session. Data were collected over 25 writing sessions between January and early June, 1985.

Consistent with Graves' recommendations, each writing session began with a mini-lesson, which was followed by the writing workshop, which was followed by a sharing session. The questions raised by peers during these group conferences and the revisions made by these young writers in their texts following the sharing sessions were the focus of this investigation.

During each sharing time, the children were divided randomly into three groups. Those children who wished to share an unfinished draft brought it to the group conference. Approximately one to three children shared their drafts during each sharing session in each small group. While children who had not shared recently were encouraged to share their draft, they were never required to receive their peers' questions.

During the sharing sessions, the writers sat in the author's chair, read their pieces, and called upon their peers for questions about the content of the piece. An adult in each group recorded the peers' questions. At the conclusion of each child's reading of his/her piece and receiving the peers' questions, the adult asked the writer what he/she planned to do next and how he/she planned to do it. At the end of the sharing time, the child attached the share questions to the draft and returned both papers to his/her writing folder.

[Data collection]   Prior to the next writing session, both papers were photocopied. This photocopy of the draft provided evidence of the text as it existed prior to the insertion of any of the information identified as missing by the peers' questions.

At the conclusion of the following writing session, the previously shared draft was photocopied a second time. This second photocopy provided evidence of the state of the text after the child had one writing workshop to insert the missing information.

Once every two weeks all folders were examined for evidence of the continuation of writing on a previously shared topic. Discovered drafts were photocopied.

[Data analysis]   To determine how frequently the questions raised were used by these young writers, each question was compared against each appropriate text, by the researcher and a second rater, independently, to determine whether or not the child modified the text in the way suggested by his/her peers' questions. The two raters agreed on all but four revisions. These inconsistencies were discussed until agreement was reached.

To determine how the decision to publish a piece (Hubbard, 1985, had suggested that publishing provides children with a sense of audience and a reason for refining their work) affected the frequency of use of the peers' questions, the number of revisions made as a result of peers' questions in eventually published pieces was compared to the number of such revisions in never-published pieces.

To determine why these writers chose to use only some of the peers' questions, during May each child was questioned at the close of the writing workshop following his/her sharing to determine which peers' questions, if any, were used to revise the piece. If the child had not used all the questions, he/she was asked why he/she had decided not to use some questions. (Vukelich, 1986, pp. 300–301. Reprinted by permission of the National Reading Conference and C. Vukelich)

The next method section is from the qualitative portion of a study that combined qualitative and quantitative research procedures. The subjects section has been included. In the procedures section, the researchers have provided information about the type of data they collected and the specific fieldwork procedures they used.

Purpose of the qualitative portion of the study: To study language arts instruction as it naturally occurred and to categorize the classrooms along a continuum that was based on the teachers' emphasis given to writing extended passages.

SAMPLE

The study was conducted in a large urban school district in the Western United States, which was selected for its racial diversity and considerable variation from school to school in language arts instruction. At the time of the study, 37% of the students in the district were Mexican American; 32% were White, 29% were African American and 2% were Asian American and Native American. Only elementary schools with between 30% and 80% enrollment of Hispanic and African American students and with more than 20% of the students participating in the federal free lunch program were included in the target population. We stratified schools meeting these criteria into categories of either meaning-based or skills-based instruction on the basis of the perceptions expressed in interviews by school district administrators from divisions of instruction, special programs, and student assessment to ensure variation in instructional approach. We randomly selected six schools described by administrators as meaning based or whole language, expecting to find considerable variation among the classrooms in this category, and we selected four schools identified as skills-oriented schools.

Thirty-nine teachers of Grades 4 and 5 in selected schools participated in the study. There were 15 fourth-grade, 14 fifth-grade, and 10 fourth and fifth combined classrooms. Ten of these classrooms were designated as bilingual classrooms by the district, which meant that Spanish was the language used by the teacher to varying degrees during the day. Data were obtained from 931 students; 71% of them were of ethnic minorities (46% Mexican American, 19% African American, 4% Asian, 2% Native American). The selected classrooms ranged from 23% to 100% minority enrollment. Students participating in special programs providing additional instruction in writing were included only if the instruction was provided in the regular classroom where it could be observed.

*   *   *   *   *

Data about classroom literacy instruction in each of the 39 classrooms selected for the study were gathered from two major sources: (a) classroom observation of each teacher's reading and writing instruction and (b) interviews with teachers and principals about reading and writing instruction. In addition, we collected samples of student work to augment our observations. Following the advice of Brophy (1990, p. IX16), we used a naturalistic, narrative observational approach rather than a structured coding format, so that we could attend to the sequential flow of classroom events and the purpose and context of student activities. Each researcher received 4 hr of initial training, which consisted of discussion of the focus of observation, video training, and review of exemplary field notes from a pilot observation.

A common set of elements was attended to in all observations. These included (a) the purpose, content, and flow of activities, including the instructions from the teacher that initiated the activity, the roles of the students and the teacher during the activity, and products resulting from the activity; (b) the classroom structure and grouping; (c) the content of the direct instruction; (d) the nature of text written by students, and (e) the level of engagement. Several studies have confirmed the importance of student engagement in tasks as a precondition for learning (e.g., Brophy & Good, 1986; Fisher et al., 1981). We made periodic sweeps of the classroom at 10-min intervals, during which we recorded the number of students engaged in the task designated by the teacher and the number of students not engaged in the task.

In the fall semester of the school year, times designated for reading and writing instruction were observed twice in each classroom by a single observer. All observations took place in mid-October and in the first 3 weeks of November on days mutually agreed on by the teacher and the observer to ensure that writing instruction would occur without interruption by field trips or special programs. Observations averaged 2.24 hr per session. Twenty classrooms (those with high levels of student engagement in tasks) were observed at least twice more in the spring. A total of 285 hr were spent in observation, an average of 7.3 hr per teacher in 3.3 observations. By the close of the school year, field notes that were based on 127 observations had been collected from the 39 classrooms. This amount of time spent in observation compares favorably with other large-scale studies of classrooms (e.g., Durkin, 1979; Wendler, Samuels, & Moore, 1989).

Observers took continuous narrative field notes and in some cases audio tape-recorded the instruction. One classroom was videotaped on several occasions; the teacher and the observer agreed that the students did not behave noticeably differently when the class was videotaped. In addition, the researchers collected representative samples of children's work from the instructional periods that were observed and conducted mini-interviews with teachers, in which the observers asked the teachers about such things as deviations from the general schedule of reading and writing instruction, the activities that had preceded the observation, and the activities planned for the remainder of the week.

One-hour interviews were conducted in the spring of the school year with the teachers and their respective principals. Interview questions focused on demographic information and extensive descriptions of reading and writing instruction, including the teacher's philosophy and goals for language arts instruction, the frequency and types of writing activities assigned in and outside of class, the use of the textbook (if applicable), the integration of writing into other parts of the curriculum, and the process by which written products were produced and assessed (i.e., use of techniques such as individual conferencing, revising, and sharing with peers). Interviews were audio tape-recorded and transcribed for analysis. (Davis, Clarke, & Rhodes, 1994. Copyright © 1994 by the American Psychological Association. Reprinted with permission.)

OTHER RESEARCH PROCEDURES

Single-subject research, action research, and evaluation research are other ways researchers describe, compare, and draw causative conclusions about educational problems and questions.

Single-Subject Research

Single-subject research is any research in which there is only one subject or one group that is treated as a single entity (e.g., when an entire school is studied without regard to individual students' performances). Single-subject research may be descriptive or experimental. **Case study** is a form of single-subject research. Case studies are undertaken on the premise that someone who is typical of a target population can be located and studied. In case studies, the individual's (a) history within an educational setting can be traced, (b) growth pattern(s) over time can be shown, (c) functioning in one or more situations can be examined, and (d) response(s) to one or more treatments can be measured.

Many insights gained from single-subject and case study research have greatly influenced educational and psychological practice. Classic examples of single-subject and case study research that have produced significant hypotheses are those of Jean Piaget and Sigmund Freud. Case study research often follows qualitative research procedures, and it can often be combined with single-subject research (Bisesi & Raphael, 1995). Single-subject experimental designs are variations of pretest-posttest counterbalanced designs. The basic aim of single-subject experimental research is to "establish the effects of an intervention (that is, an independent variable) on a single individual" (McCormick, 1995, p. 1). Figure 7.5 shows three forms of single-subject experimental designs. In single-subject research, the pretest is called a **baseline measure** and can sometimes take the form of several measurements. Also, each posttest can consist of several measurements because they become the baseline for subsequent treatments. Baselines are the results to which posttest results are compared to determine the effect of each treatment.

Because of the unique relationship that can develop between researcher and subject and because of the possible effect of multiple testing and treatment, single-subject research can have its external and internal validity threatened in several ways. Single-subject research and case study research should have clear, precise descriptions of the subject. This is most important. The results of research with a single subject are not directly generalizable to a target population without replications with other individuals or without follow-up descriptive, comparative, or experimental research with larger samples. The threats to the internal validity of single-subject research include testing, instrumentation, subject-treatment interaction, reactive effects, and research effects. Research consumers should anticipate that research producers will follow the same guidelines as would be used for conducting descriptive and experimental research.

The following method section is from research done with a single subject in a pretest-posttest two-treatment design (referred to as an A–B design in Figure 7.5). The subsections have clarifying headings.

Purpose of the study: To determine the effects of a peer-tutoring procedure on the spelling behavior of a mainstreamed elementary school student with a learning disability.

METHOD

Subjects and Setting

The subject (tutee) was an 11-year-old learning disabled male student in a regular grade six classroom in a large urban school. Scores on the *Wide Range Achievement Test*

Pretest-Posttest Two-Treatment
    A–B Design
        Pretest
            Treatment A
                Posttest 1
                    Treatment B
                        Posttest 2

Pretest-Posttest Counterbalanced Two-Treatment
    A–B–A Design
        Pretest
            Treatment A
                Posttest 1
                    Treatment B
                      Posttest 2
                          Treatment A
                            Posttest 3

A–B–A–B Design
    Pretest
        Treatment A
            Posttest 1
                Treatment B
                  Posttest 2
                    Treatment A
                      Posttest 3
                        Treatment B
                          Posttest 4

Figure 7.5
Single-Subject Experimental Designs

(Jastak, Bijou, & Jastak, 1965) ranged from 2.2 to 2.4 grade equivalents for spelling and reading. The subject (S–A) demonstrated a four-year deficiency in at least two academic areas. Subject A had spent five years in and out of special education classes before he was mainstreamed at the request of his mother. Teacher reports indicated that the subject should be academically able to perform well in a lower level spelling group.

The tutor (S–B) was a male student from the same classroom as the above-mentioned subject. He was 11 years old and excelled in all academic areas. Results on the *Wide Range Achievement Test* and *Wechsler Intelligence Scale for Children—Revised* (Wechsler, 1974) indicated superior achievement and intelligence. However, the tutor did not participate in any extracurricular activities and tended to interact with few students.

The classroom was self-contained, equipped with the usual facilities, with 27 students and one certified teacher. The spelling class was divided into two groups according to achievement. Tutoring sessions occurred at a worktable in a corner of the classroom.

Response Definition

The following two dependent variables were employed in the study.

Percent Correct. Data were collected from biweekly spelling tests. The words for the spelling test were obtained from *Basic Goals in Spelling* (Kottmeyer & Claus, 1976). A response was defined as correct if it matched the spelling in the word list. The percent correct was calculated by dividing the number of correct responses by the total number of possible words for each test.

Clinical Significance. During the experimental condition the two subjects were requested to write self-reports. They were asked to indicate whether they liked the program, worked harder in it, and/or performed better than in the regular classroom lesson. In addition, the subjects rated how well they felt they were learning by marking two pluses (++) for very good, one plus (+) for satisfactory (same as in the regular class), and one minus (−) for unsatisfactory. Subjects entered their opinions in small notebooks at the end of each week.

Design Elements and Experimental Conditions

An AB design was employed to examine the effects of peer tutoring (Hersen & Barlow, 1976). A description of the experimental condition follows.

Baseline. During the baseline condition, students were given spelling tests at the middle and end of the week. The tests were corrected upon completion and feedback was communicated in the form of percent correct. This procedure was in effect for two weeks for Subject A. The same procedure was applied to Subject B in order for the experimenter to monitor whether the experimental treatment had any effect on his spelling behavior.

Peer Tutoring. In this condition, the tutee met with the peer tutor for 15 minutes each day during the regular spelling time. The peer tutor was instructed for two days using a modeling method. The experimenter presented the teaching procedure and the peer tutor was encouraged to emulate it. On the third day, the peer tutor conducted the entire session under the guidance of the experimenter. The tutor represented a good example of academic behavior, and it was anticipated that the tutee would model his behavior. The tutor presented a list of 10 words taken from *Basic Goals in Spelling (Level 5),* which coincided with the lessons of the lower spelling group. The first two word lists were taken from the lesson currently under study in the class. The third word list consisted of difficult words from the previous spelling lesson. The tutor read the words aloud, then asked the tutee to read the word list after which he orally spelled the words. Flashcards and games were used to enhance the teaching process. If the tutee experienced difficulties with a word or words, he was requested to write them out 10 times. The tutor was encouraged to offer assistance, helpful hints, and praise. On Wednesday and Friday the tutor dictated 20 words from the word lists. He checked the completed tests against his word list and tabulated the results before handing back the papers to the tutees. Difficulties and mistakes were discussed at this time. The condition was in effect for five weeks for Subject A.

Reliability

Reliability of measurement as to the percent correct on the spelling tests was assessed biweekly by having the experimenter check the tests prior to having either the peer tutor or the classroom teacher mark them. A third individual who was unaware of the experimental outcomes checked all test papers. An agreement was defined as all graders scoring a word as spelled either correctly or incorrectly. A disagreement was defined as any grader failing to score a word in the same manner as the other two. Intergrader reliability for percent correct was 96.4 percent.

Reliability of measurement as to the use of the peer-tutoring procedure was checked twice during the intervention by the principal and another classroom teacher. Reliability of measurement as to the implementation of the treatment was 100 percent. (Mandoli, Mandoli, & McLaughlin, 1982, pp. 186–187)

Action Research

Action research is quantitative or qualitative research in which results and implications are not generalized beyond the study's specific subjects and educational setting. It is the type of research that exemplifies the work done by teachers-as-researchers (see the section "Teachers as Researchers" in Chapter 1). Action researchers seek answers or solutions to specific questions or problems. Their goal is to create immediate change. Action researchers can use both quantitative and qualitative research methods and either single-subject or case study research.

For quantitative method studies, researchers use the same general plans and procedures as used in more controlled research. However, there are differences in how they select and assign subjects. Also, they do not apply strict procedures to control for the possible influence of extraneous variables. They do identify a problem area and seek out what others have done, create operational definitions, select appropriate instruments, identify possible influencing variables and factors, select appropriate designs for collecting data, and analyze data either qualitatively or quantitatively. Most often, action researchers use convenience samples. Since students are usually assigned to classes before the research begins, random selection and assignment are not possible. Experimental action research is usually done with a simple design such as a pretest-posttest control group(s) design with one or two independent and dependent variables. If the groups are known to differ on important variables, the groups can be equated statistically.

Qualitative educational action research is the collecting of information in order to understand what is happening in particular educational settings; it is an attempt to go beneath the surface to reveal the possible reasons for the situations. As with quantitative action research, qualitative action research begins with a sense that something needs attention and possible change.

Even though action research has only local generalizability, this form of research can be relevant to research consumers. If there are similarities in subject variables, educational setting, or treatment(s), research consumers may wish to replicate the study in searching for answers to their own educational questions. Therefore, research consumers should expect published action research reports to have the same specificity in detail as other research reports.

Action research, especially qualitative action research as described above, is often used in researcher/classroom teacher collaborative projects. When classroom teachers act as teacher researchers, they usually undertake action research.

The following section reports the procedures from a qualitative teacher-as-researcher case study approach. The background portion is included because procedural information is included there. Note that in keeping with the purposes of action research, the researcher focuses on the solving of local instructional problems.

Purpose of the study: To determine how the teacher could facilitate students' engagement in literature and critical thinking; and, how students' writing reflects their engagement and thinking.

After years of watching disheartened as my students' eyes glazed over in English class, I decided I needed to do something dramatic to bring classic American literature to life for them. These young adults could not easily relate to Hester Prynne and Arthur Dimmesdale's guilt in *The Scarlet Letter;* the could not identify with Edwards' methods of persuasion in "Sinners in the Hands of an Angry God"; and *The Autobiography of Benjamin Franklin* seemed to them self-serving and meaningless for today's high-tech, fast-paced world. How could I bridge the gap of time and culture? How could I help my students realize that some of the problems these writers tackle are universal and timeless? How could I help them see that literature and the history it reflects are cyclic and that the solutions to the problems we face today may be available to us in the literature of our ancestors?

At the same time I was puzzling over this problem, I discovered Atwell's *In the Middle* (1987b). Atwell's book opened up for me the idea of student ownership of exploration and learning. Her simple system of providing books, choices, time, and opportunities for response made it possible for her students to become personally involved in literature. I began to mull over how to take her ideas and combine them with the essentials of my district's American literature curriculum. Nothing came into focus for me, but I became convinced that I could not go back to directing study questions and handing down assignments. I was miserable with that approach.

Then I read Fulwiler's *The Journal Book* (1987), and something clicked. Through journals or response logs, my students could track their journeys through literature. I went to our school library to search out contemporary novels that matched by genre or theme the classics in the district's curriculum. The students could choose from among these novels and, I hoped, they would make connections between them and the assigned texts. Personal responses could be made in journals or discussions.

The next item on my agenda was to organize how I would bring students together to discuss, question, and argue about the issues raised in both the contemporary and the classic works. Again Atwell offered a suggestion. In "Building a Dining Room Table" (Atwell, 1987a), she describes how she, her husband, and a few friends gather around her dining room table to discuss books. How could I create a similar atmosphere in my classroom? How could I get students to discuss, care, and become involved?

Class discussions in the past had often been dominated by one or two people who had actually done their homework and were outgoing enough—or who felt sorry enough for me—to risk speaking up. I knew this needed to change. A colleague shared with me *Using Discussion to Promote Reading Comprehension* (Alvermann, Dillon, & O'Brien, 1987). The authors define *discussion* as differing from simple recitation in three significant ways: (1) participants in a discussion must present multiple points of view and be willing to change their minds; (2) they must interact with one another; and (3) discussions must be more substantive than the typical two- or three-word recitation. I decided to bring discussion into my classroom in the form of a "reading round table." At the outset, to keep discussion alive and interesting, I would give points for questioning, answering, defending, and extending.

I took all these elements—student choice of contemporary literature, assigned classics of American literature, response journals, and seminar-type discussion—and combined them into a program that I hoped would help students connect with literature in a personal way and would lead to an increased level of analytic thinking. Two research questions evolved: (1) How can I facilitate students' engagement in literature and their development of critical thinking? and (2) How does students' writing reflect their engagement and critical thinking?

METHODOLOGY

As my research progressed, I decided to organize my description of it around two case studies. This chapter is the result. Bissex (1990) defines *case study* as "a reflective story of the unfolding, over time, of a series of events involving particular individuals. . . . The researcher includes . . . intentions and meanings in the meaning she makes of the story and, as interpreter if not also actor, is herself a character in it" (p. 20). That is what I have tried to communicate through these case studies.

The first case study, which focuses on my first research question, describes my own interactions with 120 students in grade 11 in a large suburban high school through one unit of study during the 1989–90 school year. The data sources were my students' response journals and essays, and my evaluations of them at the close of each instructional unit. The student journals included comments from me, which I wrote regularly—sometimes daily, but most often weekly. I also kept records of my observations, particularly observations of students' participation in discussions.

The second case study attempts to address my second research question by presenting Erin's responses over the course of the year. Because I analyzed her response journals during the summer after school was over for the year, Schon (1983) would call this case study "reflection on action," a sort of reflection after the fact. In this analysis, I tried to discover the developmental changes in her levels of thinking from the beginning of the year to the end. I chose Erin because she was typical of the student who did not personally connect with literature at first. When she began to do so, she made startling progress in critical thinking.

At the beginning and end of the study, I talked with a colleague at a nearby university. Those sessions served to focus my questions and to provide a structure for this report. (Hirtle, 1993)

Evaluation Research

Educational **evaluation research** has developed to a great extent because of federal and state mandates to assess the impact (influence) of funded compensatory programs for students who are educationally disadvantaged, have limited English proficiency, or have special educational needs. It is the systematic study of existing educational programs (treatments). Evaluation researchers wish to know whether a particular instructional program or technique results in improved student performance or achievement. They can use both quantitative and qualitative research methods.

Qualitative research methods differ from quantitative methods. Qualitative analysis is inductive. Researchers use observed data to draw a conclusion. It emphasizes an examination and explanation of the processes by which the educational programs do or do not work. Qualitative analysis focuses on how instruction (teaching and learning) happens from the point of view of the students, teachers, and administrators. Quantitative research methods are deductive. They begin with predefined goals—most often the goals of the programs themselves—and focus on whether particular outcomes have been reached (Bogdan & Biklen, 1992).

Evaluation research differs from action research in several ways. These are (a) the complexity of the research designs, (b) the degree to which the possible effects of extraneous variables are controlled, and (c) the extent to which the results can be generalized to other educational settings.

Research consumers can use the following questions to help them judge the appropriateness of the evaluation researchers' statement of the problem, identification of subjects, selection of instruments, collection of data, and analysis of data.

These questions are based on standards established by a consortium of educational associations and by educational researchers (Bogdan & Biklen, 1992; Charles, 1995, Joint Committee, 1981).

1. In evaluation research using quantitative methods, could the research be useful to the school or agency conducting the study in that its results answer a clearly defined question or problem?

2. In evaluation research using qualitative methods, could the research be useful to the school or agency conducting the study in that its results provide meanings for and understandings about the processes occurring during teaching and learning?

3. In both quantitative and qualitative designs, was the evaluation research appropriate to the educational setting in that it was minimally disruptive to the subjects (administrators, teachers, students, and other school personnel)?

4. Were the rights and well-being of the participating administrators, teachers, and students protected and was information about individuals obtained and stored in such a way that confidentiality was maintained?

5. Was the evaluation research report clearly written so that the reliability and validity of the collected data and the internal and external validity of the study could be determined?

ACTIVITIES

Activity 1

Using the Focus Questions at the beginning of the chapter as a guide, summarize the chapter's key ideas.

Activity 2

Read the following sections containing research procedures for two studies. The researchers' purposes have been included for your information. Using the questions and criteria on page 170, evaluate the studies. For each, list questions and concerns you may have about

a. The appropriateness of the research design to the researchers' purposes

b. The research design and data collection procedures

c. The replicability of the study

d. The study's internal and external validity

Extract A: Successful Mainstreaming in Elementary Science Classes (pp. 208–212)

Purpose of the study: To identify variables meaningfully associated with mainstreaming success in science classes, across grade levels and across categories of disability.

METHOD

Participants

All participants were from a relatively large (about 50,000 students), middle SES school district in a western metropolitan area. This district was one of four with whom we collaborated as part of a larger project to study science and disability. We interviewed district science education administrative personnel, building level administrators, teachers, and special education personnel in that district to identify reputational cases (LeCompte & Preissle, 1993) of mainstreaming success in science (2/18/1–2/22/1; 3/7/2–3/12/2). During these periods, we also observed in identified classrooms. Three classrooms, in three different schools, were identified. During the first and second project years, we worked with these and other district teachers and specialists (along with those of the three other school districts) to develop and refine guidelines for including students with disabilities in science classes. We presented them with draft versions of our guidelines, developed from information from previous literature and previously published guidelines (e.g., Hadary & Cohen, 1978; Hofman & Ricker, 1979), and we solicited and received written feedback. We revised the guidelines based on their feedback on two separate occasions throughout the 2-year period. The final product (Mastropieri & Scruggs, 1994b) contained information on characteristics of specific disability categories, general mainstreaming strategies applied to science classes, and strategies for adapting specific science activities (e.g., electricity units) for students with disabilities. Copies were distributed to all cooperating teachers and administrators. Teachers in the three targeted classrooms were asked to refer to the guidelines when needed, but they were under no obligation to do so. Nevertheless, all teachers reported informally that they had referred to the guidelines frequently. Following is a description of each of these classrooms.

Classroom A. Classroom A was a third grade classroom of 25 students in a regular elementary school containing kindergarten through grade 6 students. The school in which Classroom A was located had enrolled 72 students with hearing impairments and contained special education teachers with specialized training in teaching students with hearing impairments, as well as specialized facilities for students with hearing impairments (e.g., fire alarms that also produced flashing lights). Classroom A included two Caucasian students with hearing impairments in science class. One was a boy with a nearly complete hearing loss, who was provided a sign language interpreter to assist in communication. The other student had a partial hearing loss, and she benefited greatly from an FM phonic ear system. In addition to the two students with hearing impairments, four students with learning disabilities, two students receiving supplementary services for low SES students (Chapter 1), and two students for whom English was a second language were also enrolled. All students who had been classified as learning disabled in these three classrooms were 2 or more years below grade level in reading. In addition, the boy with a severe hearing loss read at an early first grade level, while the girl with the partial hearing loss read at about a second grade level. The teacher, Ms. A, had about 5 years' teaching experience and held no certification in special education.

Students were seated at desks in rows, with adjacent desks touching or nearly touching one another, facing toward the teacher's desk. A wide aisle divided the class laterally into two halves, and the teacher made frequent use of this aisle in moving freely about the classroom. Desks were moved when classroom activities required it. The two students with hearing impairments were seated in the row nearest the teacher, on opposite sides of the room.

Classroom B. Classroom B was a fourth grade class located in a regular elementary school that had enrolled 17 students with visual impairments of varying severity. This school had a special education teacher who was specially trained in teaching students with visual impairments. One Caucasian girl with a nearly total visual impairment was included in this class, in addition to three students with learning disabilities. Although reading achievement is difficult to assess using traditional standardized measures with students who read braille, the girl in this classroom did read more slowly, and at a somewhat lower level, than most of her classmates. The teacher, Ms. B, had about 7 years' teaching experience and held no special education certification.

The classroom was arranged with desks in groups of four that faced one another. The visually impaired student was given additional space to accommodate a braille typewriter (brailler) and braille materials, and her desk was located in a group with two other students near the outside door, at the back of the classroom.

Classroom C. Classroom C was a fifth grade class located in a regular elementary school that had enrolled a number of students with physical disabilities and that included special education teachers who were specially trained in teaching students with physical disabilities. This school was well equipped with wheelchair ramps, adaptable classrooms, and even a playground that could accommodate students in wheelchairs. Classroom C had three Caucasian students with physical disabilities in science class. Two female students, affected by cerebral palsy, employed motorized wheelchairs to assist mobility and also exhibited significant difficulties with motor and speech activities. As a consequence, traditional academic achievement in basic skills areas was very difficult to determine. However, both students exhibited adequate listening comprehension. The third student with physical disabilities was a boy who was affected by arthritis and moved with the aid of arm braces and a motorized walker. He could accomplish, with effort, general pincer-grasp movements. His reading ability was at about grade level, but manual writing presented greater difficulties. Two students with learning disabilities also attended the science class. The teacher, Mr. C., had about 9 years' teaching experience and held no special education certification.

Classroom C was located in a small building near the other school buildings and near the special education classrooms, and it had the most unconventional interior arrangement. Teacher C had asked his students to decide the seating arrangement, and they had elected to place their desks in clusters of three or four, spread around the classroom, facing all different directions (interview, 11/14/3). Sufficient space was allocated for wheelchairs to pass throughout the classroom. One of the physically handicapped students had elected to have his desk located on the opposite side of the room from the outside door. The outside door was connected to the outside sidewalk by a wheelchair ramp, which all students used to enter and exit the classroom. The teacher's desk and teaching materials were located in a back corner of the room, and Teacher C was never observed seated at this desk during class time.

Curriculum

The cooperating district has a very positive reputation for excellence in science education, and in fact is one of a relatively small number of districts listed by the National Science Resource Center in Washington, DC as "exemplary." This district has created its own science curriculum materials, which are housed in a district distribution center. From this center, science kits for individual units are created, stored, inventoried, and delivered to teacher's classrooms throughout the district on request. Four specific units are targeted for each academic year in the elementary grades, and teachers may elect to request other age-appropriate units. According to personnel from the National Science Resource Center, such a distribution system is strongly associated with the success over time of hands-on science programs in individual school districts (Deputy Director S. G. Shuler, personal communication, 2/1/1).

The curriculum had been based originally on the Elementary Science Study (ESS) and other materials from the 1960s but had been revised on a continuous, ongoing basis, in response to teacher feedback; district needs; local cultural, geographical, and meteorological conditions; and contemporary trends in science education (interview with district science specialist, 2/18/1). The most recent revisions had included integration with other curriculum areas, such as social studies, and included reading passages of differing levels of difficulty to help accommodate diverse reading abilities. District teachers were actively involved in revising these materials on an ongoing basis. Guidelines for accommodating students with disabilities are not specifically included in these materials (they very rarely are in any science curriculum materials, e.g., Parmar & Cawley, 1993), but the materials themselves—focusing on experiential, conceptual learning and de-emphasizing textbook learning—are thought to be potentially accommodating to the needs of students with disabilities (Scruggs & Mastropieri, 1992).

The district materials have a broad, wide scope, covering areas of ecology and life sciences, earth sciences, physical sciences, and scientific method, and are distributed throughout the elementary grades. All include relevant materials for completing activities, and teacher and student editions of activity books that include brief reading passages and recording sheets for relevant activities. For example, one unit entitled "Chemistry" was developed for use in the fifth grade. During this unit, students examine and classify the physical properties of matter; manipulate and observe material changes in a clod of dirt; examine the interactions with solids and liquids in solutions, including food coloring, butyl stearate, ice, and water; measures changes in volume when alcohol and salt are combined with water; observe and measure chemical changes associated with different kinds of oxidation; combine ammonia, water, vinegar, and bromothymol blue in various solutions and record observations; combine vinegar with baking soda or salt and observe reactions; test for acids and bases with litmus paper; and study home safety with chemicals.

Another unit, entitled "Fin and Feather, Tooth and Tail," was developed for use in third grade classrooms. During this unit, students learn about and discuss adaptation; study opposable thumbs; observe and describe which teeth they use to bite and chew various foods; determine eating habits based on pictures of animal skulls; experiment with nonverbal communication and study animal warning signs; act out various types of animal locomotion and identify animals by studying their feet; simulate animal camouflage using different kinds of wallpaper, potatoes, and various art supplies; study and describe adaptation in different vertebrates; study the concept of *home range* and map out their own home ranges; study animal characteristics using jigsaw activities; and create poster presentations for an animal of their own choice.

RESEARCHER BACKGROUND, DATA COLLECTION, AND ANALYSIS

Researcher Background

We entered this project with extensive backgrounds in special education research and practice (particularly involving students with mild disabilities) but with little experience with, or knowledge of, mainstream science curriculum. If anything, the behavioral influences on the field of special education, and our knowledge of the characteristics special education students, had made us cautious of *discovery* or inquiry-based approaches, for fear that students with disabilities might be excluded or fall behind peers who pursued learning more actively and independently. Our special education methods textbook (Mastropieri & Scruggs, 1987, 1994a), based on instructional research relevant to students with special needs, recommends an approach to teaching that is more structured and teacher directed, particularly in its first edition, than the methods often proposed by science educators (e.g., Abruscato, 1992). Our previous research in science education focused on mnemonic enhancement of science facts, classifications, vocabulary, and verbal concepts with students with learning disabilities and mild mental retardation (e.g., Mastropieri & Scruggs, 1989; Scruggs, Mastropieri, Levin, & Gaffney, 1985). We have made, and have defended, several assumptions relevant to the field of special education—for example, that disabilities are conditions individuals sometimes have (although these conditions can be partly socially determined), that special education practice often can be helpful for such individuals, and that improvement in practice can be influenced by research (Scruggs, 1993; for a critique of such assumptions, see Skrtic, 1991).

During the earliest stages of this project, we first reviewed all available literature on science and students with disabilities (Mastropieri & Scruggs, 1992) and critically examined relevant science curriculum from four school districts across the nation (Mastropieri & Scruggs, 1994c). Our work in this area led us to appreciate the value of hands-on science in providing concrete and meaningful experiences to students who may experience difficulty in deriving meaning from more abstract text presentations or who may have had more limited background experience (Mastropieri & Scruggs, in press; Scruggs & Mastropieri, 1992). As we consulted literature and the expert opinion of teachers, curriculum developers, and national science organizations in developing our guidelines, we began to feel that hands-on science instruction, appropriately implemented, could be highly complementary to the special needs of students with disabilities. We had collected recommendations for adapting science curriculum for students with various disabilities. We were also aware that several other factors might be of critical importance in enhancing mainstreaming. However, we had not systematically preconceptualized all factors that might be necessary for a successful mainstream experience in science.

Data Collection

During the first and second project years, we met with district and building level administrators and collaborated with special education and regular class teachers, including the target teachers, while compiling our guidelines for facilitating mainstreaming. During the third project year, we observed and videotaped in the three science classrooms described previously over a 5-week period in the fall semester and during an additional 3-week period in the spring semester. We also interviewed students, teachers, and administrators and collected examples of student and teacher products. We made follow-up contact during the fourth project year. Overall, we collected data from a number of sources, including observational field notes, videotape and audiotape records, student and teacher products, curriculum materials, and interviews of students, classroom teachers, special education teachers, and building and district-level administrators.

Observations were made during approximately 35 class meetings during the fall semester and approximately 15 class meetings during the spring semester. Two observers were present at least twice in every classroom, so that observers would have familiarity with all settings. We videotaped at least two classes in each of the three settings and took field notes during all classes observed. Additionally, we interviewed the targeted students and peers, the three teachers and cooperating special education teachers, building principals, and district-level personnel in science education and special education. Dialogue with teachers continued throughout the investigation, as the need arose. However, all teachers were asked at least the following questions: (a) What things happen to make mainstreaming successful, and how would you define success in this context? (b) What would you say about [district name] science curriculum versus textbook-based science curriculum? (c) What specific adaptations do you make in science class for students with disabilities? And, (d) do you think administrative support, building or district level, is helpful? These interviews were recorded on audiotape. As described earlier, initial contacts with target teachers began nearly 2 years prior to our classroom observations and included follow-up contact during the year subsequent to our classroom observations.

Data Analysis

After several weeks of interviews and site visits during the third project year, we considered all sources of information collected to date. We then analyzed all data for consistencies and inconsistencies, using analytic induction and the constant comparative method (LeCompte & Preissle, 1993). Divergent cases or instances were also investigated. We then developed a preliminary list of five variables that appeared to be highly relevant to the issue of successful mainstreaming in science. This preliminary list became the basis for future analyses and was revised several times as additional information became available.

At the end of the third year of the project, the list of variables was again reconsidered with respect to all information that had been gathered throughout the project. This analysis yielded a final list of seven variables, which appeared to be consistent and robust with respect to all data sources across the three different classrooms. These variables also were supported by previous research literature, including both convergent and divergent instances. Finally, all final conclusions were re-examined to ensure that they were directly supported by evidence gathered in this investigation, a feature sometimes missing in qualitative research on learning and behavioral disorders (Scruggs & Mastropieri, in press-b).

Although it may have been less appropriate to address concerns of "reliability" and "validity," at least in the more traditional quantitative sense, in this investigation, we nevertheless wished to ensure that our data collection had been accurate and systematic and that our conclusions logically proceeded from the interactions of those data sources with our personal perspectives. We addressed these issues by obtaining multiple sources of evidence in support of each of our conclusions and by planning and implementing extended interaction with the participants. We also addressed the issue of consistency by confirming that all conclusions were supported by evidence from each classroom, considered independently. (Scruggs & Mastropieri, 1994. Copyright 1994 by the American Educational Research Association. Reprinted by permission of the publisher)

Extract B: Helping Behaviors and Math Achievement Gain of Students Using Cooperative Learning (pp. 212–216)

Purpose of the study: To examine (a) the effects of learner ability, gender, or grade level on students' performance; and (b) the nature of the cooperative group "help" on achievement gains.

METHOD

Subjects

One hundred and one students in three classes participated in the study. They were in grades 3 ($N = 36$), 4 ($N = 34$), and 5 ($N = 31$). There were 54 boys and 47 girls. There was only one class at each grade level. All students in these grades were originally included in the study. Students who moved into or out of the school during the 6 weeks of the study, or who were not able to complete pre- and posttests, were excluded in the final data analysis.

The study was conducted at a school of 290 students in northern Utah that was affiliated with a university and also with the local school district. Although approximately 70% of the population in this area is Mormon, there is a greater degree of heterogeneity at this school because it is attended by children of foreign students and ethnically diverse university faculty, as well as children from the local community.

The faculty at the school were considered exemplary teachers, selected based on their ability to model innovative educational methods. The third-, fourth-, and fifth-grade teachers in this study had taught for 18, 6, and 14 years, respectively. All held master's degrees, had positive attitudes towards math, and enjoyed teaching math.

Procedure

Achievement/Ability. Standardized math scores from the California Test of Basic Skills (CTBS) and Southwest Regional Lab (SWRL) math assessments were utilized to determine students' achievement/ability prior to the treatment. Tests were given 3 months before data collection. Girls were categorized as high-, medium-, or low-achieving students according to whether their scores were in the top quarter, the middle half, or the bottom quarter of the distribution of published standardized scores. I used the same procedure for boys. The two genders were categorized separately so there were almost equal numbers of boys and girls in each category. Teachers were consulted for confirmation of these placements. I refer to these three categories as ability levels rather than achievement levels so as not to confuse them with the primary variable of achievement gain, although I recognize that these categories may reflect achievement rather than ability.

Assignment of Students to Groups. Heterogeneity within groups, especially in terms of ability/achievement and ethnicity, has been a cornerstone of team formation in cooperative learning as advocated in teacher training and reports of research (Aronson, 1978; Johnson, Johnson, Holubec, & Roy, 1984; Kagan, 1989; Slavin, 1983). Accordingly, in this study, ability was used as basis for group assignments. High-, medium-, and low-ability boys and girls were assigned to groups of five to six students so that each team included students of both genders and the three ability levels. Ethnic variations were also distributed among teams.

Instruction on Helping Behaviors. All students received instruction on helping behaviors for 3 weeks, as Webb (1988) recommended, including the concept that only giving answers was not considered help and was discouraged. Students practiced helping behaviors and received feedback daily during the 3 weeks preceding the data collection and continued doing this during the 3 subsequent weeks of the study as well.

Methods of instruction and reinforcement of helping behaviors included: direct instruction, role play, modeling, calling attention to students and teams engaged in helping behaviors, giving points to teams engaged in helping behaviors, periodic review of what these behaviors entailed, and teacher feedback to students regarding the effectiveness of their use of helping behaviors.

Teachers elicited phrases from students describing what students did and said when giving explanations, asking for help, and receiving explanations. Students responded with statements such as "we put our heads together"; "go through step by step"; "repeat"; "say, 'please help me' "; "shrug shoulders, raise eyebrow, and point to a problem after getting a teammate's attention"; "say 'This is what you do first' "; "say 'You have to find the least common denominator first' "; "smile"; "say thanks"; "pay attention"; "be considerate"; and "don't give up." Teachers put up charts with these words to remind students of examples.

During role plays, one or two pairs of students acted out sample ways in which one student could ask for help and another could give explanations or other useful help. Occasionally, students acted out what not to do. Sometimes teachers read "script starters"; for instance, "Tom is staring at the first problem, $1/2 + 1/4 = $ ____, but he doesn't know what to do and he isn't asking for help. If Darshana says, 'It's three-fourths,' is that helping? What can she do to really help Tom?"

Direct instruction on helping behaviors, role plays, and eliciting phrases from students took only a few minutes on an average of every other day at the beginning of team work time. Modeling of helping behaviors, calling attention to appropriate examples, giving teams points for helping each other, and positive reinforcement were all behaviors in which teachers engaged as they monitored students while they worked in teams. A summary chart of ways in which teachers can help students develop helping behaviors is presented in Appendix A. Further details on these strategies are found in Nattiv (1990).

Students worked in teams daily for under an hour a day during the 3 weeks before videotaping and 3 subsequent weeks. On some days students were in teams for 40-minute periods, but on other days direct instruction lasted for portions of that time. These students and teachers had not been trained previously in cooperative learning or specifically in helping behaviors.

Cooperative Learning Instruction. The cooperative learning format used in this study was Student Teams–Achievement Divisions (STAD) (Slavin, 1986). In this strategy all students were first taught with direct instruction. Then students practiced the concepts in teams rather than doing individual seatwork. Students tutored each other. All students had the same material. Students wanted their teammates to understand the concepts because each student took a test on the concepts and students earned points for their teams. Team total points were determined by combining how much each student on the team improved over her/his average on previous math tests. The ILE Percentile Improvement Scoring System developed by Slavin was used (Kagan, 1989). Students wanted their teams to get as many points as possible. Following the test, teams learned of test results and received recognition.

The STAD format is described in detail in the handbook written by its originator (Slavin, 1986). Components that were added to STAD for this study included (1) initial teambuilding and ongoing skill building as described by Kagan (1986), (2) instruction on helping behaviors as described in the previous section, and (3) greater structure in the implementation of STAD by assigning each student on each team a specific task or role within the team. For instance, in a method labeled by Kagan (1989) as Pairs Check, students worked in pairs (or triads) within their groups. Students alternated roles of solving problems, checking, and coaching. After every few problems each pair of students confirmed solutions with the other pair(s) in the group. Numbered Heads Together and Color Coded Co-op Cards, two other methods described by Kagan (1989), were also used.

Students practiced math concepts in the same teams for 3 weeks prior to data collection. During the portion of the study in which they were tested, the third graders studied multiplication, including story problems; students in the fourth grade studied measurement of distance, area, and volume; and the fifth graders studied complex fractions. In all three grades, most of the cognitive processing involved comprehension, computation, and application. Some lessons included story problems, so problem solving was also expected. Manipulatives were an integrated aspect of the curricula in all grades. Third graders used groups of buttons, sticks, and small objects. Fourth graders measured real items. Fifth graders used paper pies and squares, cut up into eighths, sixteenths, and other fractions. In each class, the teacher used the cooperative learning structure (which included direct instruction and then team practice) for approximately 40 minutes per day, each day of the week.

Data Collection. Each class was videotaped a mean time of 80 minutes per week by one of three hired technicians. Each team was videotaped several times, with approximately 30 minutes per team over the 3 weeks, during team practice on the math content. Each team was videotaped an average of twice a week for 5 minutes each time. Only one team per classroom was videotaped at a time. Three video cameras were used, but never more than one camera per class. Microphone extensions from the video camera recorded all verbal communication, and the camera picked up nonverbal cues as well.

Each student on a team was listed on the observation instrument, and whenever one of the eight helping behaviors occurred, it was coded under the student's name. Behaviors were coded sequentially, as they occurred. Whenever a behavior went on for over 30 seconds, it was recorded again.

Three coders were trained to analyze the tapes using the following behavioral categories for each student: gives explanation, receives explanation, asks for help (and receives it), gives help other than explanation, receives help other than explanation, gives answer only, receives answer only, receives no help (after requesting it). Coders were trained initially in individual sessions with the primary investigator. All coders initially viewed the same sample footage that illustrated the eight behaviors. First they were shown examples, then they verbally compared codings with mine as they went along, and finally they recorded codings independently. The three coders practiced until they reached 85% agreement in all behavioral categories. Agreement was calculated after coding several tapes by dividing the number of behavioral events observed by the coder by the number of behavioral events observed by the primary investigator and later also by the other coders. At that point coders were given tapes to code. Two coders analyzed each tape. Interrater agreement was above 80% on each tape for all categories.

It is important to note that these eight categories are based on a five-category system Webb used in her previous studies. Her categories consisted of "gives explanation," "gives help other than explanation," "receives explanation," "receives help other than explanation," and "receives no help" (Webb, 1987).

To adapt the categories to younger students, I altered some categories. The first two categories, "gives explanation" and "receives explanation," remained the same. They refer to the more complex helping behaviors involving showing or telling how or why. Examples of student behaviors in each of the eight categories are presented in Appendix B.

Webb's categories "gives help other than explanation" and "receives help other than explanation" refer to telling or being told the correct answer. These behaviors do not contribute or could actually be detrimental to achievement because they do not equip the receiving student with any additional learning cues. Likewise a student who gives the answer without explanation is not reprocessing any of the learning. For instance, a student who asks for help with "2/3 minus 1/2" and is told "the answer is 1/6" without any hint about how to arrive at that answer may be just as confused as before. Since such behaviors are actually not helpful, I reclassified them as "gives answer only" and "receives answer only." However, in observing upper-elementary-school students, there was evidence of a middle category of behavior that was helpful but not sophisticated enough to be called an explanation. This included such comments as "look on the other side," "you got the wrong number," "try it again," "now it's your turn," as well as helpful gestures such as bringing math manipulatives to a partner to help him/her work out a solution. I therefore retained the two categories of "giving/receiving help other than an explanation" but gave them new meaning.

I added another category, "asks for help (and receives it)," after a conversation with Noreen Webb during which she made the recommendation. This category was coded when a student asked for help and received either an explanation or other meaningful help. I retained Webb's category "receives no help" and used it when a student asked for help and got no response.

Videotaping was done on a team-by-team basis. Behaviors by individuals other than the team being taped were not coded. If a non-team-member or the teacher asked or answered a question or engaged in one of the helping behaviors, it was not recorded.

Students took weekly pretests and posttests on the specific content covered during the 3 weeks. These tests were part of the published textbook material packets from Harcourt Brace Jovanovich (*Mathematics Today*, 1987).

Teacher Training. The teachers received nine 2-hour in-service training sessions on components of cooperative learning during 5 months prior to implementation. I conducted the sessions, adapting the training models of Kagan and Slavin that I learned when I became a Certified Cooperative Learning trainer in 1984 at the University of California, Riverside, where Spencer Kagan was my mentor. Topics addressed included philosophical rationale, overview of research findings, step-by-step details of several specific cooperative learning strategies (STAD, Jigsaw, Co-op Co-op Pairs Check, Color Coded Co-op Cards, Numbered Heads Together), team formation, discipline/management, improvement points, charts and record keeping, grading, ways to teach and reinforce helping behaviors, team building, specific application to math, and creative lesson planning. Most training was conducted in experiential cooperative learning groups. All of the teachers used the manual *Cooperative Learning Resources for Teachers* (Kagan, 1986).

Teachers had not received training in cooperative learning previously. One teacher had tried grouping students, but not according to any consistent framework. Similarly, cooperative learning was new to the students as well.

All of the teachers received additional follow-up assistance. Just before they started using cooperative learning instructional strategies, teachers met with me and/or other colleagues to facilitate a smoother beginning by discussing teaching strategies, lesson plans, and other elements of implementation. These meetings continued throughout the 6 weeks.

All teachers involved in this study implemented cooperative learning competently. Because I was in their classrooms about every 2 days, I was confident that I could correct minor implementation problems before major problems arose, and such was indeed the case. I gave information to teachers as needed regarding the effectiveness of implementation. Also, each teacher met individually with me at least twice to discuss extensively progress, possible problems, and successes and to provide general anecdotal information. (Nattiv, 1994. Copyright © 1994 by The University of Chicago Press)

FEEDBACK

Activity 1

What concerns should research consumers have about research procedures that are common to all research designs?

All research reports should have clear and complete explanations about every step of the research. All instruments should be valid and reliable and be administered by trained examiners. Research procedures should be tested in pilot studies.

What concerns should research consumers have about research procedures that are specific to quantitative descriptive research designs?

They need to be sure the data represent a true picture of what occurred and can be generalized to other situations. This refers to the validity of the research results. Researchers also need to be sure that they are consistent in identifying aspects of a behavior or event and that others working in the same or similar situations would get similar results. This refers to the reliability of the research results.

What concerns should research consumers have about research procedures that are specific to quantitative comparative research designs?

Research consumers should use the questions for procedures in descriptive research to determine whether the results from comparative research are valid and reliable.

What concerns should research consumers have about research procedures that are specific to experimental research designs?

Research consumers should be concerned about whether variables other than the independent variables caused the observed changes in the dependent variable. Variables that might have an unwanted influence on, or might change, dependent variables are called extraneous variables. One of the best ways to control subject variables is through randomization. When subjects cannot be randomly selected or assigned to groups, researchers can equate them statistically.

How are extraneous variables controlled in experimental research?

Variables that need to be controlled to maintain the internal validity of experimental research are current events, subject growth and development, subject selection, attrition, testing, instrumentation, statistical regression, and interaction. Variables that need to be controlled to maintain the external validity of experimental research are subject-treatment interaction, reactive effects, multiple-treatment interaction, and research effects.

What distinguishes simple and complex experimental research designs?

Simple and complex experimental research designs are distinguished by (a) the number of independent or treatment variables and (b) the extent to which results can be generalized from the immediate subjects to a larger target population. Experimental designs are a continuum from simple to complex plans. Simple experimental plans deal with single independent variables, and complex experimental plans deal with multiple independent variables. Simple experimental designs deal with one independent variable or have subject selection procedures that limit the generalizability of their results. More complex experimental designs deal with two or more experimental and subject variables.

What concerns should research consumers have about research procedures that are specific to causal-comparative research designs?

A major concern for researchers doing causal-comparative research is that the causal effects should be one-way. Since there are no manipulated, or treated, independent variables, the subjects cannot be randomly assigned to groups. For research consumers to generalize the results from causal-comparative studies to other populations and educational situations, they need to be sure that any differences between groups cannot be attributed to one or more important variables that were not accounted for by the researchers. There is always the possibility that these outside variables may be the true causes of the observed differences. Also, they should be sure that the researchers' description of the subjects is clear and that operational definitions are used to identify and distinguish the comparison groups.

What concerns should research consumers have about research procedures that are specific to qualitative research designs?

Qualitative research reports should show how the researchers' method is detailed so its adequacy and logic can be determined, and there should be an abundance of evidence. Research consumers should be sure that the researchers provide evidence of their qualifications as participant observers. They should be sure that the researchers' assumptions are clear, that the researchers' questions are stated, and that the study sought to answer those questions and generate further questions.

The research report should indicate that the researchers used preliminary days of the study to generate a focus for the study, that the researchers were present in the research context for an adequate period of time, and that the researchers' observations are of a full range of activities over a full cycle of those activities. The research consumer should ascertain that the data were collected from multiple sources. The researchers should have saved their data for reanalysis.

What concerns should research consumers have about research procedures that are specific to single-subject, action, and evaluation research designs?

Single-subject research is any research in which there is only one subject or one group that is treated as a single entity. Single-subject research may be descriptive or experimental. Action research is directed to studying existing educational practice and to producing practical, immediately applicable findings. The questions or problems studied are local in nature. Evaluation research is applying the rigors of experimental research to the judging of the worth or value of educational programs, projects, and instruction. Threats to the internal validity of single-subject research include testing, instrumentation, subject-treatment interaction, reactive effects, and researcher effects. Research consumers should expect research producers to adhere to the same guidelines as used for conducting descriptive and experimental research. Research consumers should expect published action research reports to have the same specificity in detail as other research reports. Research consumers can use several questions to help them judge the appropriateness of the evaluation researchers' statement of the problem, identification of subjects, selection of instruments, and collection and analysis of data.

What questions should be used to evaluate procedure sections?

Are the research design and data collection procedures clearly described? Is the research design appropriate to the researchers' purpose? Can the study be replicated from the information provided? To evaluate qualitative experimental research, the question is: Has the researchers' presence influenced the behavior of the subjects? In studies with treatments: Are experimental procedures fully explained? Are examples of special materials included? To determine research validity: Are the procedures free from the influence of extraneous variables? Does the study contain any threats to its internal and external validity?

Activity 2

Extract A: Successful Mainstreaming in Elementary Science Classes   This was a qualitative comparative study in which the researchers observed several classrooms and collected information about mainstreaming practices. Since their purpose was to gather information, their design was appropriate. The research project spanned three years, and during that time the researchers were active participants in the school district's plan for creating mainstreaming guidelines. The participants were identified and the characteristics of each observed classroom were detailed. The instructional program and materials used in the classrooms were also described. In keeping with the generally accepted procedures for qualitative research, the researchers described their research and educational perspectives about special education. The data were analyzed over the three years, and the researchers addressed the issue of the reliability and validity of their data. However, despite the references to trying to control for threats to reliability and validity, the specific procedures were not explicit. For example, they indicate that they "addressed the issue of consistency," yet they do not indicate that this was done by anyone other than themselves.

Extract B: Helping Behaviors and Math Achievement Gain of Students Using Cooperative Learning   Overall, the design was appropriate to the researcher's purposes. The design used was a 2 (two aspects of gender) $\times$ 3 (three ability groups) $\times$ 3 (three grade levels) factorial with a pretest-posttest. The experimental variables (no treatments) for the first purpose were these three factors. The experimental variables (treatments) for the second purpose were instruction on helping behavior and cooperative learning instruction. The dependent variable for the second purpose was mathematics performance. Although the researcher took care to balance the groups at each grade level according to gender and ability, there is no indication that the children were assigned randomly. The treatments are explained, and the location of additional information pertaining to the treatments is indicated. The way data were collected and analyzed is detailed. The researcher has included information about establishing interrater reliability. The researcher used a coding system from another researcher, which is appropriate; however, modifications were made to the coding system without any indication of whether those changes altered the validity of the coding. One question left unanswered was "What possible influence did the television cameras have on the subjects' behavior?" Another question pertains to the influence of the researcher: "Since the researcher trained the teachers in conducting cooperative learning procedures and was often present in the classrooms, did his direct involvement have an influence on the subjects?"

CHAPTER 8

Reading and Interpreting Results Sections

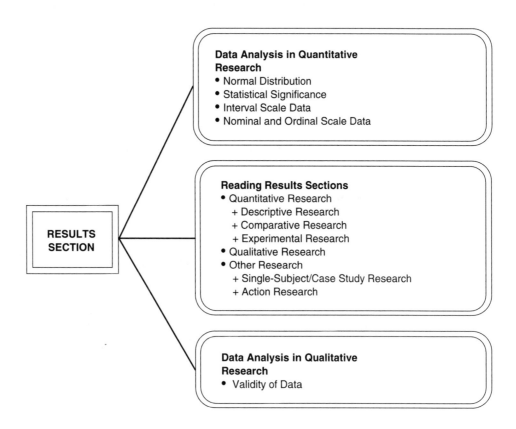

RESULTS SECTION

Data Analysis in Quantitative Research
- Normal Distribution
- Statistical Significance
- Interval Scale Data
- Nominal and Ordinal Scale Data

Reading Results Sections
- Quantitative Research
  + Descriptive Research
  + Comparative Research
  + Experimental Research
- Qualitative Research
- Other Research
  + Single-Subject/Case Study Research
  + Action Research

Data Analysis in Qualitative Research
- Validity of Data

FOCUS QUESTIONS

1. What are the different ways quantitative data are recorded?
2. What is a normal distribution curve?
3. What statistical procedures are used in educational and other behavioral science research?
4. What is statistical significance?
5. What are the ways data are analyzed in qualitative research?
6. What criteria should be used to read and evaluate results sections?

After collecting data, researchers use several methods to describe, synthesize, analyze, and interpret the information. In all types of quantitative research, statistical procedures facilitate understanding of a vast amount of numerical data. These procedures are the techniques by which researchers summarize and explain quantitative data and determine the existence of relationships and causal effects. In qualitative research, the outcomes of research are the generation of hypotheses and research questions, not the verification of predicted relationships or outcomes. Therefore, qualitative researchers use verbal rather than statistical procedures to analyze data. These inductive analytic procedures involve organizing data, identifying patterns, and synthesizing key ideas as research questions and hypotheses.

Research consumers need to understand (a) the way researchers match data analysis procedures to research designs, (b) the different statistical analyses available to educational and other behavioral and social science researchers, (c) the assumptions researchers make about those analyses to use them effectively, (d) the concept of statistical significance and the criteria generally used to set the point at which results can be considered as reliable, (e) the assumptions researchers make about qualitative data analyses, and (f) the way to read and interpret results sections in quantitative and qualitative research reports.

From reading results sections, research consumers should be able to answer:

What types of data analysis were used?

What statistical analyses did the researchers use?

Were the statistical analyses appropriate for the researchers' questions, purposes, or hypotheses and for the research design?

What were the research results?

Were the results of quantitative research statistically significant?

Were the qualitative analyses appropriate and logical?

Were the results of practical use and importance?

Will the results be applicable to other educational settings, especially the one in which I teach?

Results sections should be evaluated using the following questions, which are from Figure 3.1, page 117:

Evaluating Results Sections

Data Analysis in Quantitative Research. Are the statistical procedures for data analysis clearly described, and are they appropriate for the type of quantitative research design?

Research Validity in Quantitative Research. Are the procedures free from the influence of extraneous variables? Does the study have any threats to its internal and external validity?

Significance in Quantitative Research. Are statistical significance levels indicated? Does the research have practical significance?

Data Analysis in Qualitative Research. Are the processes for organizing data, identifying patterns, and synthesizing key ideas as hypotheses and research questions clearly described?

Research Validity in Qualitative Research. Are there multiple procedures for corroborating research evidence and researchers' judgments?

DATA ANALYSIS IN QUANTITATIVE RESEARCH

Data analyses in quantitative research involve the use of statistics. **Statistics** are numerical ways to describe, analyze, summarize, and interpret data in a manner that conserves time and space. Researchers select statistical procedures after they have determined what research designs and types of data will be appropriate for answering their research questions. For example, in answering descriptive research questions, statistics let researchers show the data's central tendencies and variability. In answering comparative and experimental research questions, other statistics allow researchers to draw inferences and make generalizations about target populations. In all three types of research, the specific statistical procedures are determined by the research design and by the type of data that are collected. And, in comparative and experimental research, statistics are tools that let researchers gain two other insights: (a) an estimate of the sampling error—the error (or difference) between the research sample and the target population, and (b) the confidence with which research producers and consumers can accept the results.

The way quantitative data are recorded depends on the instruments (measuring devices) used. Data are recorded as (a) intervals, (b) rankings, (c) categories, and (d) ratios. Each means of recording data requires the use of different statistics. **Interval scales** present data according to preset, equal spans. They are the most common form of data reporting in education and the social sciences, and they are identified by continuous measurement scales: raw scores and derived scores such as IQ scores, standard scores, and normal curve equivalents. They are the way data from most tests are recorded.

Rankings, or **ordinal scales,** show the order, from highest to lowest, for a variable. There are no indications about the value or size of differences between or among items in a list; the indications refer only to the relative order of the scores. For instance, subjects can be ranked according to their performance on a set of athletic tasks, and what will be reported is the order in which they scored (e.g., first, second, third), not their actual accumulation of points. Olympic medal winners are reported using ordinal scales. Data from surveys and observations are often recorded in this manner.

Categories separate data into two or more discrete aspects, such as male-female, red-white-blue, or always-frequently-infrequently-never. The data can be reported as numbers of items or as percentages of a total. Data recorded this way are considered **nominal scales.** Data from surveys and observations are often recorded in this way.

Ratio scales, less frequently used in educational and other behavioral and social science research than the other three, show relative relationships among scores, such as half-as-large or three-times-as-tall. In dealing with educational variables, researchers usually do not have much use for these presentations.

Normal Distribution

Chapter 2 contains an explanation of central tendency and variability. The most common forms of each of these statistics for interval scale data are the mean and the standard deviation. To reiterate, the **mean** is the arithmetical average score,

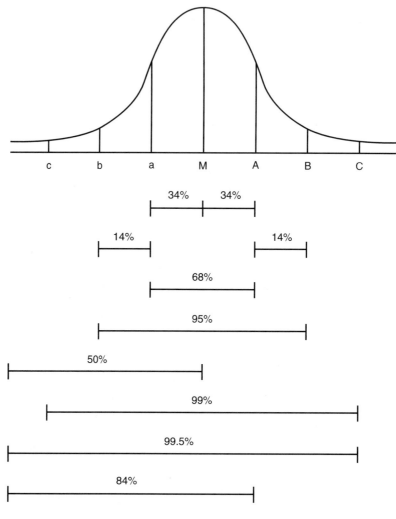

Figure 8.1
The Normal Distribution Curve

and the **standard deviation** (SD or σ) shows how far from the mean are most of the other scores. The SD is based on the concept that given a large enough set of scores, they will produce a graph in the shape of a bell. This graph is called the **normal distribution curve.** This graph, which is shown in Figure 8.1, represents a theoretical statistical picture of how most human and nonhuman variables are distributed. Using as an example a human variable such as ability to draw human figures as measured by a test, the curve would show that few people have scores indicating little of the trait (the extreme left end of the graph), that is, an inability to draw human figures, and few people have scores showing a great deal of the trait (the extreme right end of the graph), that is, a great ability to draw human figures. The center of the graph shows that most people have scores indicating some ability to draw human figures. This distribution is commonly called the **norm.**

There is a direct relationship between the SD and the normal distribution curve. Starting at the center, or mean, of the distributed variable, each SD represents a fixed, specific proportion of the population indicated in Figure 8.1 by the vertical lines. For example, the range between the mean and either extreme end of the graph (left or right) equals 50% of the population represented by the graph. The ranges between the mean and +1 SD (the area M ↔ A) and the mean and −1 SD (the area a ↔ M) each equal a little more than one-third (34%) of the distributed population. The ranges between +1 SD and +2 SDs (A ↔ B) and −1 SD and −2 SDs (b ↔ a) each equal about 14% of the population. Therefore, the range of scores included between −1 and +1 SD (a ↔A) equals about 68% of the population, and between −2 and +2 SDs (b ↔ B) equals slightly over 95%. Most statistical procedures are based on the assumption that data approximate the normal distribution curve. In reality, the graphs produced from the data of many research studies are not as symmetrical as the normal distribution curve.

Frequently, scores used in research are derived from *raw* standardized test scores (the number of items correct). **Derived,** or converted, **scores** are changed to other scores such as *grade equivalents, age equivalents, percentiles, normal curve equivalents, stanines,* or other *standard scores.* Figure 8.2 illustrates the more common of these derived scores and relates them to the normal distribution curve.

Each of these derived scores is used to describe test performance, and their relation to the normal curve allows the user to compare performance on several measures of performance. The research consumer should note the different derived scores that fall at the mean and the SD points on the normal curve illustrated on Figure 8.1.

Statistical Significance

The normal distribution curve is also called the *normal probability curve* because it is used to estimate the likelihood of an interval score or set of interval scores happening by chance. In comparative and experimental research, researchers want to be sure that the observed differences between the means of two or more groups of subjects or two or more variables are truly different. That is, they want to know if the difference is a reliable one. If these means differ, researchers need to know the extent to which the difference could have happened by chance. When the observed difference between these means is large enough to be beyond a predetermined chance level, the difference is considered as significant. **Statistical significance** occurs when the difference between the means of two sets of results exceeds a predetermined chance level. Researchers can thus know how confident they can be about the conclusions they make from their findings.

Three interrelated factors are usually considered in a statistical analysis: (a) the difference between group means, (b) the variability of the groups, and (c) the number of subjects in each group. All other things being equal, there is an increased likelihood that difference(s) between the means of two or more sets of scores is statistically significant when (a) the difference between the means becomes larger, (b) the variability of each set of scores becomes smaller, or (c) the size of the sample increases. These three relationships can be seen in Figure 8.3.

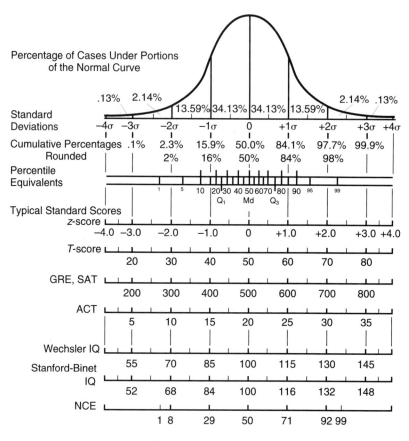

Figure 8.2
Common Derived Scores

When researchers statistically conclude if a difference or relationship exists, there is the possibility of error. Two kinds of error can occur: (1) Researchers accept the results as true when they are not, and (2) researchers do not accept the results as true when they actually are.

For example, in the first error, researchers find what appears to be a statistically significant difference in student performance over previous performance when using a new instructional program. However, because of imperfections in sampling procedures (subject selection error) and the measuring instruments (reliability estimates), there may not be a true difference in student performance after using the new program. In such a case, the researchers will have concluded that the new instructional program is better than the old one when in fact that is not true. In the second error, researchers do not find a significant difference in student learning when actually there is a difference. In this case, there is a change resulting from teachers' use of an instructional technique, but the researchers do not observe it. The second error may also result from imperfections in the sample and instrumentation.

The possibility of statistical significance increases as

differences between means		variability		sample size
↓	or	↓	or	↓
get larger		gets smaller		gets larger

Figure 8.3
Factors Affecting Statistical Significance

In educational and other behavioral and social science research, researchers try to avoid making the first type of error, but to do this they increase the possibility of making the second. Relative to the discussion of the normal probability curve, researchers have agreed to use certain probability levels. These conventional levels correspond to the extreme ends of the curve and designate a very small chance of the first type of error. It is important to realize that research producers and consumers *never* know whether either of these two error types is being made.

Researchers report the probability that the first type of error has occurred as a decimal. The probability level is shown in research reports as $p = .05$. This means that the chances of concluding that differences or relationships exist when they truly do not exist are no more than 5 chances out of 100. These are odds similar to one's likelihood of winning a state lottery. Sometimes researchers report the probability level as $p < .05$, which is read as "the probability is less than 5 chances out of 100," or as $p \leq .05$, which is read as "the probability is equal to or less than 5 chances out of 100." Of course, when researchers realize that the probability is even less than $p = .05$, they may report it as $p = .01$ or even as $p = .001$.

Research consumers need to be wary of accepting any results (even if they are statistically significant) without considering whether the results are practical or meaningful in educational settings. What is of prime importance to research consumers is the usefulness of the results in terms of improving teacher effectiveness, student learning, and efficient uses of instructional resources. To determine whether research results have **practical significance,** research consumers need to answer: How effectively can the results be used in my teaching situation?

Degrees of Freedom.   Frequently, tables reporting the results of statistical analyses include an entry which identifies the **degrees of freedom** (*df*) used in the analysis. For the purposes of this text, degrees of freedom can be best understood as the number of ways data are *free* to vary in a statistical problem (Gay, 1992; Kerlinger, 1973; Wiersma, 1995). In practice, degrees of freedom ordinarily are a function of the number of subjects and groups being analyzed. Usually, degrees of freedom are the total number of subjects or groups minus one. After the frequency of scores has been identified, then the variation remaining equals the number of subjects or groups minus one.

Interval Scale Data

Statistical procedures used with interval scales are based on certain assumptions, all of which are related to the concept of a normal distribution curve. These statistical procedures are called **parametric statistics.** In using parametric statistics, researchers are trying to draw some conclusion from the differences between the means of sample groups or sets of scores.

The assumptions for using parametric statistics are:

The variables are measured in interval scales.

The score of any subject is not influenced by those of any other subjects; that is, each is an independent phenomenon.

The subjects are selected from and represent a normally distributed population.

When the research involves two or more groups of subjects, each of which represents different populations, the variables that distinguish each population are similarly distributed among each population.

A common parametric statistic is the *t-test.* It is used when there are two sets of scores, to determine whether the difference between the means of the two sets of scores is significant. It is reported as numbers such as $t = 1.6$ or $t = 3.1$. After determining the value of t, researchers consult a statistical table to determine whether the value is a significant one. A *t*-test can be used, for example, to examine the mean scores in reading and mathematics for one group of subjects, or it can be used to examine mean scores in reading for two different groups of subjects. The *t*-test is used frequently in single-variable comparative and experimental research, and its use is limited by the same factors that limit single-variable research.

Another parametric statistic used with interval data in comparative research is the **product-moment correlation,** which refers to the quantified relationship between two sets of scores for the same group of subjects. The result of the arithmetic computation is a **correlation coefficient,** which is expressed as *r*, a decimal between -1.0 and $+1.0$. The most common interval scale correlation coefficient is the **Pearson product-moment correlation.** Correlations show whether two or more variables have a systematic relationship of occurrence—that is, whether high scores for one variable occur with high scores of another (a positive relationship) or whether they occur with low scores of that other variable (a negative relationship). The occurrence of low scores for one variable with low scores for another is also an example of a positive relationship. A correlation coefficient of zero indicates that the two variables have no relationship with each other, that is, are independent of each other.

Correlations can also be used to establish predictions. When a strong relationship has been established between two variables, a correlation can be used to predict the possible occurrence of either variable. The predictive use of correlation is important for such educational endeavors as early intervention programs for students with special needs. For example, certain tests, including tests of basic concepts and cognitive abilities, are appropriate for young children and are highly predictive of students' later school performance.

Table 2.3 (Chapter 2, p. 37) shows how correlation coefficients are reported in table format, from a study about the relationships between topic-specific background knowledge and measures of overall writing quality. When correlation coefficients are statistically significant, they indicate that the variables are probably systematically related. In other words, the two variables *go together;* significant correlations do not indicate that there are any *causal* effects of one variable on the other. In Table 2.3, the relationship between the holistic scoring method and teachers' marks is positive and significant—high coherence scores were given to the same students' work that received high teacher marks. On the other hand, the relationship between coherence and the number of words and clauses, which is negative, was not significant, and therefore the two scoring methods can be said to be unrelated. Again, no causality is implied, nor should it be assumed.

When research designs call for examining differences among the means of two or more groups of subjects or two or more variables, they frequently use the **analysis of variance** (ANOVA), which is reported in F-ratios. The advantage in using an ANOVA is that several independent variables as well as several factors can be examined. In its simplest form, ANOVA can be thought of as a multiple *t*-test. The ANOVA is appropriate for use with some comparative research designs and with experimental research designs such as the pretest-posttest with multiple control groups, the Solomon four-group design, counterbalanced designs, common factorial designs, and causal-comparative designs. The ANOVA procedure can be used when more than one independent variable is involved. Table 2.4 (Chapter 2, p. 41) shows the ANOVA results for a two-way factorial design from a study using two independent variables: the effect of two levels of reading potential (disabled reader vs. slow learner) and two levels of reading placement (at instructional level vs. above instructional level). Notice that the researchers indicated two significance levels: $p < .05$ and $p < .01$. The results show that there were differences in results (on the dependent variable: vocabulary achievement) based on the subjects' reading potential and for their reading placement. There was no difference in vocabulary achievement when potential and placement were considered (Potential x Placement). On comprehension tests, only Potential showed significant differences ($p < .01$).

An important feature of ANOVA is that it can show the **interaction effects** between and among variables. In Chapter 7, the negative consequence of treatment interaction was discussed, as well as the possibility of measuring the interaction in factorial designs. Interactions are also expressed as F-ratios within an ANOVA table, and often the interaction is illustrated in a graph. For research consumers, treatment interactions permit instructional modifications for particular groups of learners. For example, referring again to Table 2.4, there were no significant two-way interactions (Potential x Placement) for achievement in either vocabulary or comprehension. That can be interpreted as indicating that with this group of subjects, how they are placed for instruction and what their achievement potential is do not *together* influence how they will achieve in vocabulary and comprehension. In this case, there is no interaction effect.

In previous chapters, reference was made to situations in which two or more groups of subjects differ on one or more variables, thereby limiting the generalizability of the studies' findings. The differences might have occurred because preexisting groups of subjects were used instead of randomly selected and assigned groups of subjects. When research producers think these variables might influence the dependent variables under study (and the variables are not features that are used to distinguish between groups, e.g., distinguishing between male and female, or high and low mathematical performance), they use a statistical procedure to equate the groups on these independent variable factors.

One frequently used procedure is known as **analysis of covariance** (ANCOVA). Its use allows researchers to examine differences among the means of groups of subjects as if the means were equal from the start. They do this by adjusting the differences in the means to make them hypothetically equal. The procedure is similar to the use of a "handicap" in bowling or golf leagues to balance out differences among players and teams. In all other ways, ANCOVAs are interpreted like ANOVAs.

When researchers wish to examine the relationships among more than two variables, they can use a **multiple correlation** technique (also called *multiple regression* technique). The procedure is interpreted similarly to a single correlation coefficient. Multiple correlations can also be used to make predictions. Prediction scores are reported as a multiple correlation coefficient, or *R*, and have the same range as single correlations. Multiple correlation coefficients are used frequently in causal-comparative experimental research because they combine ANOVA and correlational techniques. Research consumers need to keep in mind that the causality in causal-comparative research is assumed because of a strong, highly predictive relationship. This assumed causality needs to be reconfirmed by further experimental studies.

Nominal and Ordinal Scale Data

When researchers collect data that are measured in nominal and ordinal scales, they must use different types of statistics. These statistics, called **nonparametric statistics,** work on different assumptions. Nonparametric statistics are used when:

The populations do not have the characteristics of the normal distribution curve.

Symbols or numbers are used as labels on categories (nominal scales).

An expected or rank order is apparent but the order is not necessarily equally spaced as is the case with interval data.

For each parametric statistical procedure there are corresponding nonparametric statistical procedures. In general, nonparametric statistics are less frequently used in educational and other behavioral and social science research than are parametric. Table 8.1 shows corresponding parametric and nonparametric statistics.

One popular nonparametric statistical procedure is the **Chi square test** (X^2). It is used to test the significance of group differences when data are reported as frequencies or percentages of a total or as nominal scales. Table 2.2 (Chapter 2, p. 36) shows an example of Chi square reporting from a study that examined how teachers responded when students made miscues (deviant oral reading responses). In their analysis, the researchers found that teachers who dealt with unattempted miscues supplied words more often than they used all other responses combined.

Table 8.1
Corresponding Parametric and Nonparametric Statistics

Parametric	Nonparametric
t-test	Mann-Whitney *U* Test
ANOVA	Friedman two-way analysis of variance
	Kruskal-Wallis one-way analysis of variance
Pearson product-moment correlation	Spearman rank-order correlation

Indications of statistical significance are interpreted the same for nonparametric statistics as they are for parametric statistics.

DATA ANALYSIS IN QUALITATIVE RESEARCH

In qualitative studies, researchers verbally analyze data. This involves examining and organizing notes from interviews and observations and reducing the information into smaller segments from which they can see patterns and trends. In addition, researchers interpret the meanings of these patterns and trends and create research hypotheses and questions for verification in further research. Qualitative researchers begin their analyses while still in the research setting and finish it after all data have been collected. An important point about qualitative research is that qualitative researchers often do measure and count; in other words, they quantify some data. However, they do not use statistical analyses to verify or support their results and conclusion, nor do they consider statistical probabilities.

Research consumers should expect qualitative researchers to fully explain their analysis methods so that the logic of their decisions can be followed and evaluated. In Chapter 2 there is a discussion of the features of qualitative research methods, and in Chapter 7 are questions that can be used to determine the reliability of observational research. Research consumers may wish to review those sections before continuing the discussion here, which is a synthesis of the ideas of several scholars who use qualitative research methods (Bogdan & Biklen, 1992; Firestone, 1987; Howe, 1988; Jacob, 1987; Lincoln & Guba, 1985; Marshall & Rossman, 1995; Van Maanen, Dabbs, & Faulkner, 1982; Wiersma, 1995; Wilson, 1977).

In the research setting, commonly called the field, qualitative researchers continually make decisions that narrow their study. They may start out with broad questions and begin looking at an entire educational setting, but as their study proceeds they concentrate on smaller issues and create more specific analytical questions. Data collection is an additive process. New information is looked for and collected on the basis of previous data because the qualitative researchers are interpreting as they assemble additional information. This does not mean they discard or selectively omit information. On the contrary, they maintain extensive onsite field notes. It is the influence of the events in the field and their ongoing interpretation of those events that guide qualitative researchers in their search for additional information. For example, while observing middle school science lessons to study teachers' use of graphic organizers, a qualitative researcher takes notes in one class about students' collaborative activities in examining and recording the mealworm's life cycle. What the researcher notes is a combination of formalized small-group behaviors and seemingly unstructured, random student interaction. Noting this, the researcher later seeks out information leading to a hypothesis about a possible interrelationship among teachers' teaching style, their development of student collaborations, and students' use of graphic organizers.

One procedure used by qualitative researchers to support their interpretations is **triangulation,** a procedure for cross-validating information. Triangulation is collecting information from several sources about the same event or behavior. For example, in studying parents' attitudes about their involvement in their children's homework activities, data would be collected from interviews with parents, students, siblings, and teachers and from observations of parent-student behaviors during homework activities.

After collecting data in the field, qualitative researchers organize their data by sifting through the information and clustering seemingly similar ideas. These categories of information are labeled for ease of use and cross-referencing. Qualitative researchers start with broad categories:

Settings (*where* teaching and learning occur)

Situations (*when* an activity or behavior occurs)

Activities (*what* teachers and students do)

Behaviors (*how* teachers and students act and respond)

Techniques or methods (*how* and *why* teachers and students respond to an event)

Socializations (*with whom* teachers and students regularly interact)

Depending on the nature of their data, these categories may be expanded, subdivided, eliminated, or renamed. Some notes may be cross-referenced because they contain information relevant to more than one category.

Research consumers need to know the coding categories qualitative researchers use and how the classification systems were developed and revised. Since qualitative analyses are subjective, producers of qualitative research should be explicit about their theoretical formulations and their conceptual positions regarding the topic being investigated. When these are not explicitly stated in research reports, research consumers need to be aware that these formulations and positions usually are reflected in researchers' purpose questions and classification systems.

Validity of Data

An important aspect of quantitative research is the generalizability. In qualitative research, the arguments for generalizability are not particularly strong; that is, qualitative researchers do not presume to be able to generalize from one classroom to another (Erickson, 1986; Firestone, 1993; Nielsen, 1995).

However, that does not mean that a qualitative study should not have internal validity (Spinder, 1992). Research consumers need to be able to identify the "trustworthiness" of the inferences qualitative researchers draw from their data. Nor are qualitative researchers usually concerned with the replicability of their studies or with a broad generalizability of their results.

Research consumers should not ask, "Does the research apply to all individuals within a target population?" Rather, consumers might try to determine whether other researchers have made similar or different conclusions about the instructional implications of the research topic. More importantly, research consumers should concern themselves with determining whether the researchers' conclusions and instructional implications have meaning for the students with whom they are acquainted, being fully aware that there might be more than one interpretation of the researchers' analyses.

Research consumers should understand that validity in qualitative research is relative to the researchers' purpose and the circumstances under which the data were collected. Each set of qualitative researchers analyzes data differently depending upon their theoretical perspectives, which should be stated explicitly. Research consumers should look for the following specific evidence of data validity in qualitative research reports (Biklen, 1993; Marshall & Rossman, 1995; Maxwell, 1992):

1. The researchers acknowledge, show sensitivity about, and maintain an ethical stance toward the individuals being researched.

2. The researchers' work and their analyses "in-field" are fully documented; the logic of their data categorizations are evident; and the relationships among those concepts seem accurate within an identified theory of learning and instruction.

3. The researchers' descriptions are factual, and they provide evidence of minimal distortion because of possible errors of omission and commission; they include cases or situations that might challenge their emerging hypotheses or conclusions.

4. The data were collected from more than one source (triangulation), and there is evidence confirming the accuracy of the respondents' accounts.

5. The researchers are tolerant of ambiguity; they have searched out alternative explanations through multiple sources of data and have devised ways for checking the quality of their data.

6. The researchers show evidence of formulating and reformulating their interpretations and analyses of data; there are comparisons of data and checks of hypotheses against new data.

7. The researchers are self-analytical and recognize the limits of their subjectivity; they show evidence of guarding against value judgments in their analyses.

8. The researchers' results are presented in a manner such that others might be able to use them (if deemed appropriate).

9. The study is linked to the larger educational context in which the data were collected.

10. The researchers acknowledge the limitations of their study as far as generalizing to other educational settings.

READING RESULTS SECTIONS

The results sections of research reports are usually the most difficult for research consumers to read and interpret. Often research consumers are intimidated by the statistical procedures and the presentation of numerical data in charts and tables. However, these sections can be read systematically if the reading plan outlined in Chapter 3 is followed. By the time research consumers read the results sections, they should already know the researchers' purpose, questions, and research design; major results and conclusions; target population and subject selection technique; instrumentation; and research method. What is left to understand are the specific results relative to the research questions.

Results sections are read during the third phase of the reading plan, when the research consumer is confirming predictions and knowledge (see p. 94). The goal of this phase for research consumers is to verify that their (not the research producers') purposes have been met and to decide what information supports the researchers' purpose and adds to their (the consumers') knowledge base.

In reports of quantitative research, the results of statistical procedures such as the *t*-test, correlation, and ANOVA are not always put into table format; the numerical information may be part of the general discourse of the report because of space limitations. Research consumers should expect, however, that the reports' authors give an explanation of the numerical information whether it is within the text or in tables.

You should review the questions in Evaluating Results Sections at the beginning of this chapter before reading the following portions of this chapter, in which the results sections for each of the studies whose method sections were discussed in Chapter 7 are presented.

Quantitative Research

Descriptive Research. The following results section is from a quantitative descriptive study (see Chapter 7, pp. 172–174, to review the method section of this study). Note that the researchers report their results as percentages, but they do not do any statistical analysis of the data.

Purpose of the study: To conduct individualized interviews with middle- and high-school students to better understand their perceptions of teachers' adaptations to meet the special learning needs of students in general education classrooms.

RESULTS

Table 2 summarizes students' responses by achievement level. Tables 3, 4, 5, and 6 provide students' responses by category and rationale with representative supporting comments for selected interview questions.

Table 2 Summary of Students' Responses by Achievement Group (Frequency & Percentages)

	LD		ESOL		LA		AA		HA	
Question	N	%	N	%	N	%	N	%	N	%
1. Prefers experiments	15	75	15	75	11	73	16	80	14	70
Prefers textbook	4	20	2	10	2	13	2	10	0	0
Both	1	5	3	15	2	13	2	10	6	30
2. Write summaries	15	75	13	65	13	87	13	65	16	80
No summaries	5	25	7	35	2	13	6	30	4	20
Depends	0	0	0	0	0	0	1	5	0	0
3. Study guides	14	70	18	90	12	80	19	95	16	80
No study guides	6	30	2	10	2	13	0	0	3	15
Depends	0	0	0	0	1	7	1	5	1	5
4. Tell purpose	20	100	19	95	14	93	19	95	20	100
No purpose	0	0	1	5	1	7	1	5	0	0
5. Teach strategies	20	100	20	100	15	100	20	100	20	100
No strategies	0	0	0	0	0	0	0	0	0	0
6. Homogenous groups	10	50	9	45	10	67	7	35	5	25
Heterogeneous groups	10	50	11	55	5	33	12	60	14	70
Depends	0	0	0	0	0	0	1	5	1	5
7. Stay in same groups	8	40	5	25	1	7	5	25	5	25
Change groups	12	60	12	60	14	93	12	60	15	75
No preference	0	0	3	15	0	0	3	15	0	0
8. Teacher assigns	9	45	8	40	9	60	11	55	11	55
Students choose	11	55	11	55	6	40	8	40	8	40
No preference	0	0	1	5	0	0	1	5	1	5
9. Work alone	4	20	6	30	3	20	5	30	5	25
Work in pairs	12	60	6	30	6	40	9	45	5	25
Work in groups	4	20	7	35	5	33	3	15	5	25
Depends	0	0	1	5	1	7	3	15	5	25
10. Peer tutoring	18	90	20	100	12	80	19	95	17	85
No peer tutoring	2	10	0	0	3	20	1	5	3	15
11. Same test for all	10	50	13	65	11	73	13	65	16	80
Different tests	10	50	7	35	4	27	7	35	4	20
12. Same homework	13	65	15	75	10	67	16	80	16	80
Different homework	7	35	5	25	5	33	4	20	4	20
13. Adapt lesson	18	90	18	90	15	100	20	100	15	75
Do not adapt lesson	1	5	2	10	0	0	0	0	5	25
Depends	1	5	0	0	0	0	0	0	0	0
14. Changes slow class	19	95	14	70	12	80	17	85	19	95
Do not slow class	1	5	6	30	3	20	3	15	1	5

Note. LD = Learning Disabled (*N*=20); ESOL = English as a Second Language (*N*=20); LA = Low Achieving (*N*=15); AA = Average Achieving (*N*=20); HA = High Achieving (*N*=20).

Textbook Adaptations vs. No Adaptations (Questions 1–5)

Students in both grade groupings (middle and high school) overwhelmingly agreed that textbook adaptations help them understand difficult content material (see Table 2). However, students differed somewhat on their rationales for selecting adaptations. In general, middle-school students preferred adaptations to promote **interest** whereas high-school students, in general, preferred adaptations to promote **learning.**

Of the textbook adaptations, students were most enthusiastic about learning strategies, with 100% of the sample favoring strategy instruction. Students of all groups commented that strategies make learning more effective. A middle-school student with LD said, "They help students to see, step-by-step, what the material is about." Many students reported that strategies help promote independence as in the case of a HA middle-school student, "I prefer a teacher who will provide techniques and strategies at the beginning and then let students go on their own after that"; and an AA high-school student, "Strategies help prepare students better for studying in college where they're not as likely to receive such help." Thus, a majority of students recognized that strategies can help make learning easier. An AA middle-school student commented, "You don't have to rack your brains to figure out how to do it."

Also highly favored were purpose statements (preferred by 95% of the students), because "they tell you want the point is." As expressed by one HA student, they help you "focus on salient content." Study guides or outlines (preferred by 83%) "tell you what to focus on" and "help you understand better."

Seventy-five percent of the same preferred projects and experiments to textbook reading, because "they are more interesting and fun" and because they facilitate under-standing. One LA student explained, "I prefer experiments and projects because the teacher gets more involved in the class, whereas with other assignments the teachers do not get involved." Another LA student commented, "I would love for someone to create a better way to teach chemistry or create a book which would be easier and more interesting to read. It seems every time I try to read a textbook, it's like I'm reading Chinese or something." Fourteen students (15%) advocated the combined use of text and direct experiences as in the case of the HA student who said, "Projects are fun, but the book explains it better."

Although the majority of students felt they learned by writing summaries or answering questions (74% of the total sample, and 65% of the ESOL and AA students), this was not a well-liked learning procedure. Those who favored writing summaries explained that doing so "helps you understand and remember better." However, as noted by one middle-school ESOL student, "Most kids don't like it, but if you don't do it, you won't learn anything." Students who did not like summaries thought they were too much work, and preferred other activities, such as discussions.

Heterogeneous vs. Homogeneous Ability Grouping (Question 6)

Slightly more students preferred heterogeneous to homogeneous grouping (55%). Interesting differences emerged between grade-level groups and among achievement groups regarding grouping (see Tables 2 and 3). Middle-school students tended to be more in favor of homogeneous groups (57%) and high-school students more in favor of heterogeneous groups (67%). Although we had expected to find the opposite, the majority of LA students (67%) favored homogeneous grouping, and the majority of HA students (70%) favored heterogeneous grouping. In fact, the 5 HA students who preferred homogeneous grouping were all middle-school students—100% of the high-school HA students favored mixed ability grouping.

The most common rationale for grouping by ability levels was that "slower students hold back faster students." Most students who favored ability grouping, particularly middle-school and low-achieving students, were concerned about high-achieving stu-dents, worrying that "higher students would be bored by easier work." An LA student indicated that it "slows down other students a lot; that's why we should have every-one categorized with people of their same ability." But some students who preferred homogeneous groups were concerned about slower students: "That [ability grouping] gives everyone a chance to learn. If you put someone slow with people who learn fast, he won't understand and he'll do bad in that class."

Students who favored mixed ability grouping noted that "higher kids can help lower kids." Most students who preferred mixed groups demonstrated a concern for slower students though others were also concerned about their own learning. One HA student favored mixed groups, "as long as an individual's grades would not be inhibited by some-

Table 3 **Frequency of Students' Responses with Breakdown by Rationale and Representative Supporting Comments for Question 6: "Do You Prefer Grouping by Ability Levels or Mixed Groups?"**

Categories & Comments	MS	HS
Prefers grouping by ability levels	**27**	**14**
1. Rationale: Faster students learn better	19	6
"Slower students hold back faster students."		
"Brighter students get bored with slower students."		
2. Rationale: Slower students learn better	7	7
"If you put someone slow with people who learn fast, he won't understand and he'll do bad in that class."		
"The teacher could help those who don't learn fast."		
3. Rationale: Equity	1	1
"Slower kids might copy from higher kids."		
Prefers mixed groups	**20**	**32**
1. Rationale: Benefits faster students	2	3
"You learn more when you explain to others."		
2. Rationale: Benefits slower students	14	31
"Smarter students can help slower students."		
"It pushes slower kids to do better."		
"Separate groups by ability level stigmatize the slower learners."		
3. Rationale: Equity	4	4
"Everyone should learn the same things."		

Note. MS = Middle School; HS = High School.

one else's incompetence." A few students, such as this high-school AA student, noted that "separate groups by ability level stigmatize the slower students." Some students who preferred heterogeneous groups pointed out that there are also benefits for the high-achieving students; for example, "You learn more when you explain it to others."

SAME GROUPS VS. DIFFERENT GROUPS (QUESTION 7)

Most students were in favor of sometimes changing groups (68%) (see Table 2), with LA students most strongly favoring this practice (93%). Students conveyed that by switching groups, students can "learn different things" and "get to know other people." By comparison, students who prefer not to switch groups like the familiarity that comes from working in one group and feel they "work better in a constant environment."

Teacher Assignment vs. Student Selection of Groups (Question 8)

Differences were found between the two grade groupings and among ability groups regarding group selection. Whereas most middle-school students (64%) would like to select their own groups, most high-school students (63%) preferred that the teacher assign students to groups. The majority of LD and ESOL students (55%) preferred that students choose their own groups. The majority of LA, AA, and HA students (60%, 55%, and 55%, respectively) preferred that the teacher assign students to groups. Most of the students who would like to select their own groups said that they "don't want to get stuck with kids they don't like" and that they want to work with their friends. Some students favoring student selection were of the opinion that "students know best who they can work with." Students who would rather have the teacher assign groups expressed concerns about task completion and felt they could accomplish more without their friends. Many students said something similar to this comment made by a high-school student with LD, "If I pick my friends I'll just sit and talk and the work won't be done."

Working Alone, in Pairs, in Groups (Question 9)

Forty percent of all students interviewed said they would prefer to work in pairs rather than alone or in larger groups. The preference for pairs was particularly prevalent among students with LD, with 60% selecting this option. Preferences for working alone or in larger groups were equally divided (with 24% and 25% of the students, respectively, selecting each). Middle-school students showed more inclination toward groups, high-school students toward working alone. Eleven percent of all students noted that their preference depended on the assignment. As one student explained, "I prefer to do in-class assignments in a group, but at-home assignments alone so my grade doesn't suffer from someone else's incompetence." Students who preferred to work by themselves noted that there are "fewer distractions" when working alone and that they "do not like to depend on anyone else." Students who preferred working with one other student commented that students in pairs can help one another without the chaos often present in larger groups. Students who prefer working with many students rationalized that "the work is spread out more" and "there are more people to explain things." Some students commented, "Groups are more fun."

Peer Tutoring vs. No Peer Tutoring (Question 10)

The overwhelming majority of students (91%) stated a preference for peer tutoring, with no real differences between grade levels and few differences among achievement groups. Most students supported their preference for tutoring by describing the benefits of tutoring for tutees. As expressed by one HA high-school student, "Students can often explain material better than the teacher. It's better for students to understand a smaller amount of material well [learned from a tutor] than to keep up with teacher

Table 4   Frequency of Students' Responses with Breakdown by Rationale and Representative Supporting Comments for Question 10: "Should Students Who Understand Difficult Material Tutor Students Who Do Not Understand?"

Categories & Comments	MS	HS
Prefers tutoring	**44**	**42**
1. Rationale: Tutor learns better	3	3
"Sometimes the smarter students learn more when they are teaching someone else, because they can catch their mistakes."		
2. Rationale: Tutee learns better	27	29
"Students can often explain material better than the teacher. It's better for students to understand a smaller amount of material well (learned from a tutor) than to keep up with teacher lectures through more chapters but not really learning."		
3. Rationale: More motivating	11	7
"I like to help others."		
"It's easier to relate to another student."		
4. Rationale: Helps teacher	7	6
"It helps the teacher. She can't go person to person helping each student."		
Prefers no tutoring	**3**	**6**
"Students might make mistakes and make matters worse for the student who doesn't understand."		
"It's the teacher's responsibility."		

Note. MS = Middle School; HS = High School.

lectures through more chapters but not really learning." An ESOL student revealed, "In calculus I don't know what the teacher is talking about, but if someone else explains it to me, I get it." A few students described the benefits of tutoring for tutors; for example, "Sometimes the smarter students learn more when they are teaching it to someone else because they can catch their mistakes." The few students who did not like tutoring remarked that "it was the teacher's job to get them to understand."

Same Tests and Homework vs. Different Tests and Homework (Questions 11 and 12)

The majority of students thought that all students should be administered the same tests (66%) and the same homework (74%). This result is consistent with findings from our previous research (Vaughn, Schumm, Niarhos, & Daugherty, 1993; Vaughn, Schumm, & Kouzekanani, 1993). However, more middle-school than high-school students believed that some students should receive different homework and/or tests (36% and 40% for middle-school students compared with 17% and 27% for high-school students).

Students with LD were split 50/50 regarding their preference for same vs. different tests, compared to an 80/20 split among HA students. Equity was proffered as the rationale by almost all students, both those who thought all students should receive the same tests and homework and those who felt that tests and homework should be different for some students. Many students exclaimed that it is "not fair to change a test or homework for some students." Other students pointed out that "it's more fair" to give different tests and homework because of students' different ability levels. When students who advocated giving everyone the same tests and homework were asked a follow-up question regarding whether it would be OK to give a different test to a student with LD or an ESOL student, most students said that it would be all right. Some students noted that these students with special needs should be placed in other classes.

Table 5   Frequency of Students' Responses with Breakdown by Rationale and Representative Supporting Comments for Question 13: "Should Teachers Change the Way They Are Teaching (e.g., Slow Down) When Some Students Don't Understand?"

Categories & Comments	MS	HS
Prefers teacher not to change lesson	**4**	**4**
"The teacher should continue the lesson as long as the majority of the class understands it."		
Prefers teacher to change lesson	**40**	**43**
1. Rationale: Better for learning	25	28
"I've been in this position and I found that by changing, the teacher has made the material more understandable."		
"If students are confused and the teacher keeps going, they'll just get more confused. They won't get any better."		
2. Rationale: More motivating	4	1
"Otherwise, students who learn slower say, 'Forget this, I'm never going to get this,' and they give up."		
3. Rationale: Teacher's role	5	9
"This will help struggling students and show the teacher cares about them. Teachers are here to help students learn, not to make it more difficult for them."		
"It's probably the teaching method and not the material that is responsible for the difficulty with understanding the lesson."		
4. Rationale: Equity	3	3
"Everyone has the same right to learn."		
5. Other	3	0

Note. MS = Middle School; HS = High School.

Table 6   **Frequency of Students' Responses with Representative Supporting Comments for Question 14: "Do Adaptations to Assist Students Who Are Having Difficulty Slow Down the Rest of the Class?"**

Categories & Comments	MS	HS
Does not slow down the class	8	7
"I don't think it slows down students who already understand, because practice makes perfect. They might get bored after a while, but they won't forget it."		
A little, but not too much	18	19
"Others can work on assignments during this time so it is sort of a benefit for them."		
"Not much. If anything, it gives them a better understanding of the lesson. Most students are courteous and won't complain."		
Somewhat/It depends	7	11
"It depends. If the teacher makes changes that are drastically different from what they were doing, it could unfairly slow down the students who already understand. If they make occasional changes until students catch up, however, that would be okay."		
A lot	14	10
"A lot. It is boring for those who understand."		
"You may get only half the lesson content you're supposed to get."		
Other	0	1
"The person should go to the teacher other than class time so as not to slow the class, like before or after school."		

Note. MS = Middle School; HS = High School.

Adapt Lesson vs. Do Not Adapt Lesson (Question 13)

Almost all students (91%) felt teachers should slow down or change lessons when some students did not understand the lesson content. No real differences between grade level groups were noted on this issue, but a few differences emerged among achievement groups. In contrast with LA and AA groups (100% of the students favored adaptations), 25% of the students in the HA group opposed adaptations.

As shown in Table 5, the majority of students who favored adaptations did so because changes were perceived as facilitating learning. As expressed by one high-school AA student. "I've been in this position and I found that by making changes, the teacher has made the material more understandable." Some students emphasized that it is the teacher's role to assist all students; for example, "This will help struggling students and show the teacher cares about them. Teachers are here to help students learn, not to make it more difficult for them." And one middle-school HA student pointed out, "It's probably the teaching method and not the material that is responsible for the difficulty withy understanding the lesson." A few students noted, "Everyone has the same right to learn."

How Much Do Adaptations Slow Down the Rest of the Class? (Question 14)

The majority of students (85%) expressed the opinion that adaptations to assist students who are having difficulty **do** slow down the rest of the class; however, close to half of these students (46%) felt that this is beneficial (see Table 6). Although middle- and high-school students' opinions differed little on this issue, differences were noted among achievement groups. Specifically, 95% of the students in the LD and HA groups felt that adaptations slow down lessons, compared with 70% of the students in the ESOL group.

Fifty-five percent of the total sample felt that adaptations either do not slow down the class or slow down the class a little, but not too much; for example, "I don't think it slows down students who already understand, because practice makes perfect. They might get bored after a while, but they won't forget it." Or, as another student pointed out, "Others can work on assignments during this time so it is sort of a benefit for them."

On the other hand, 44% of all students felt that adaptations inhibit some students too much; for example, "It depends. If the teacher makes changes that are drastically different from what they were doing, it could unfairly slow down the students who already understand. If they make occasional changes until students catch up, however, that would be OK." Many students were concerned that changes could slow down some students a lot, limiting content coverage and creating boredom. Several of these students recommended that slower students receive help outside of class or be placed in a different class.

Although many students expressed the view that adaptations slow down some students a great deal, these students still preferred that teachers make adaptations. However, many reported that their teachers did not typically make adaptations. One student stated it this way, "Very few of my teachers abide by these preferences (e.g., textbook adaptations). I believe that it is for this reason that I become bored of school and turn my interests toward out-of-school activities. It is not the text that makes the student, but the method teachers use. Plain and simple, teachers do not teach anymore!" (Vaughn, et al., 1995)

Comparative Research. In quantitative comparative research, researchers examine descriptions of two or more variables and make decisions about their differences or relationships. They can make predictions about one variable based on information about another. Research consumers should be concerned that only appropriate generalizations are made from comparative and predictive data. The following results are from a comparative study of the relationship among several variables (see Chapter 7, pp. 174–176, to review the method section of this study). Note that researchers have analyzed data using MANOVA, a multivariate or factor analysis of variance, which means that the researchers were analyzing data from two or more independent variables at the same time. Research consumers should interpret MANOVA results similar to ANOVA results. The researchers have not presented the results of their statistical analyses in table form. The purpose of this study is to examine children's reading difficulties from the perspective of others.

RESULTS

Reading Problems Reported by Children, Parents, and Teachers

The first analysis looked at the difficulties reported by each group by lower elementary (grades 1–3) and by upper elementary (grades 4–6) grade levels (see Table 1). Of the 40 subjects in each group, thirty-seven children, thirty-three parents, and thirty-eight teachers reported at least one reading difficulty, with four children, seventeen parents, and twenty-four teachers reporting 2 or more.

Thirty-three of the forty children in the study reported difficulties with word identification, with lower elementary children expressing more concern about this problem than older children. Few comprehension or attitude/behavior problems were mentioned, and when they occurred, the older children were more likely to report them. Parents' most frequently stated problem was word identification with the older children's parents expressing the most concern. Parents also reported

Table 1   Reading Problems Reported by Children, Parents, and Teachers

	Children		Parents		Teachers	
	Gr(1–3) n (%)	Gr(4–6) n (%)	Gr(1–3) n (%)	Gr(4–6) n (%)	Gr(1–3) n (%)	Gr(4–6) n (%)
Word ID	22 (67%)	11 (55%)	10 (29%)	11 (41%)	18 (34%)	8 (32%)
Comprehension	2 (6%)	4 (20%)	8 (23%)	7 (26%)	16 (30%)	9 (36%)
Attitude/Behavior	4 (12%)	4 (20%)	10 (29%)	8 (30%)	13 (25%)	7 (28%)
Other	3 (9%)	0 (0%)	1 (3%)	0 (0%)	5 (9%)	0(0%)
Don't Know/No Response	2 (6%)	1 (5%)	6 (17%)	1 (4%)	1 (2%)	1 (4%)

more difficulties with comprehension and attitude/behavior than did children. In addition, they also reported more concern about attitude/behavior problems than their children's comprehension. Teachers reported about the same level of concern for both word identification and comprehension difficulties, and they referred to comprehension problems more frequently than did children and parents.

In addition to the previously described problems, other miscellaneous difficulties were reported for the lower elementary children. Three children mentioned difficulties such as "No problem," "Following lines," and "Losing your place." One parent attributed her third grade child's difficult to "Poor eyesight in kindergarten." Three teachers reported difficulties with the successful completion of workbook pages and skill sheets. One teacher was concerned about the child, "Being unable to apply skills to reading," and another reported that the child's difficulties were due to, "Speech and hearing patterns."

Agreement among Child, Parent, and Teacher

Next, we examined the extent to which individual child-parent-teacher triads reported the same problem (see Table 2). At the lower elementary level, there were 26 triads with at least one member reporting a word identification problem, 22 triads with at least one member reporting a comprehension problem, and 18 triads with at least one member reporting an attitude/behavior problem. At the upper elementary level, there were 13 triads with at least one member reporting a word identification problem, 10 triads with at least one member reporting a comprehension problem, and 10 triads with at least one member reporting an attitude/behavior problem.

When child-parent-teacher triads were examined, the most frequently agreed upon problem, regardless of grade level, was word identification. Agreement for all problems appeared to increase with age with the actual percentages still being relatively low, ranging from 28% (11 triads) for word identification to 10% (three triads) for attitude/behavior. Across all problem areas, parents and teachers agreed more frequently with each other than with the children, and the pattern of agreement appeared to be different as well. In contrast to the child-parent-teacher agreement which favored word identification, parents and teacher most frequently agreed upon difficulties with attitude/behavior for lower elementary children and comprehension for upper elementary. However, the agreement level for the lower elementary parent-teacher triads was still relatively low, ranging from 33% to attitude/behavior to 23% for comprehension. The upper elementary parent-teacher triads had higher percentages of reported agreement for all three problem areas, ranging from 70% for comprehension to 46% for word identification.

Table 2 Agreement by Reading Problem and Grade Level

	Grades 1–3			Grades 4–6		
	Word ID n=26 n (%)	Comp n=22 n (%)	Att/Beh n=18 n (%)	Word ID n=13 n (%)	Comp n=10 n (%)	Att/Beh n=10 n (%)
Child-Parent-Teacher	6 (23%)	1 (5%)	1 (6%)	5 (38%)	2 (20%)	2 (20%)
Parent-Teacher	7 (27%)	5 (23%)	6 (33%)	6 (46%)	7 (70%)	5 (50%)

Parents' and Teachers' Assessment of Children's Reading

The comprehension analysis compared teacher's and parents' Likert-scaled ratings of children's text-based and inferential comprehension when listening to a story and when reading independently. A 2 task condition (listening, reading independently) X 2 respondent (parents, teachers) X 2 grade (lower elementary, upper elementary) MANOVA, using the two comprehension categories (text-based, inferential) as dependent variables, was performed. Differences were revealed by respondent (F=6.681, p=.0139), task condition (F=24.443, p=.001), and their interaction (F=13.335, p=.0008). Parents rated children's listening comprehension as 4.487 (SD=1.36) and reading comprehension as 3.59 (SD=1.37). Teachers rated children's listening comprehension as 3.66 (SD=1.34) and reading comprehension as 3.40 (SD=1.26). Differences were found between the parents' ratings (F=45.949, p=.0001) and the parents' and teachers' ratings of the children's listening comprehension (F=36.379, p=.0001). Parents rated listening higher than reading, and they also rated it higher than did teachers. No differences were found between the text-based and inferential categories or between grade levels.

The attitude analysis compared parents' and teachers' scaled ratings of children's attitude when listening to a story and when reading independently. A 2 task condition (listening, reading independently) X 2 respondent (parents, teachers) X 2 grade (lower elementary, upper elementary) MANOVA was performed. A significant two-way interaction existed between respondent and task condition (F=7.537, p=.0093). Parents rated attitude when listening as 4.81 (SD=1.15) and when reading as 3.06 (SD=1.11). Teachers rated attitude when listening as 4.5 (SD=1.12) and when reading as 3.39 (SD=1.38). Differences were found between parents' (F=94.21, p=.0001) and teachers' ratings (F=33.92, p=.0001). Both rated listening higher than reading independently. No grade level differences were found.

The word identification analysis compared parents' and teachers' ratings of three word identification categories (letter knowledge, word-based strategies, & meaning-based strategies). A 2 respondent (parents, teachers) X 2 grade (lower elementary, upper elementary) MANOVA, using the three word identification categories as the dependent variables, was performed. Differences were found between word identification categories (F=5.92, p=.0048). Letter knowledge was 3.84 (SD=1.22), word-based strategies was 2.90 (SD=1.17), and meaning-based strategies was 3.04 (SD=1.49). Differences between letter knowledge and word-based strategies (F=9.31, p=.0036), and between letter knowledge and meaning-based strategies (F=8.43, p=.0054) were significant. Both rated letter knowledge higher than either word-based or meaning-based word identification strategies. (Yochum & Miller, 1993)

Experimental Research.   Researchers use experimental designs when conducting research about the causative effect of one or more variables on other variables. The plans provide researchers with structures for studying one or more independent variables with one or more groups of subjects. Researchers select designs that best fit their purposes, answer questions about causation, and control extraneous variables.

The common experimental designs are discussed in Chapter 7 and illustrated in Figures 7.1 (p. 181), 7.2 (p. 186), 7.3 (p. 187), and 7.4 (p. 189).

The following results section is taken from a pretest-posttest control group design that has one independent variable and three dependent variables. In this section, the results of an analysis of variance (ANOVA) are presented, but they are not presented in table form since the subjects did not differ at the start on pretest measures. The table shows only the groups' means and standard deviations. (The method section of this report is in Chapter 7, pp. 181–185.)

Purpose of the study: To assess the effects of learning strategy instruction on the completion of job applications by learning disabled students.

RESULTS

Preliminary analyses indicated that there were nonsignificant differences between the groups on the pretest measures. Posttest measures were analyzed in condition (traditional, strategy) by gender (male, female) analyses of variance (ANOVAs). For every dependent measure, only a significant main effect for condition was obtained. The *F* values for these effects, along with the means and standard deviations for each of the dependent measures, are presented in Table 2.

The findings indicate that students who received instruction in the learning strategy condition made statistically significant lower numbers of information omission errors and location errors than students under the job application instruction condition. Additionally, these students received statistically significant higher holistic ratings on their job applications than their counterparts. There were statistically nonsignificant main effects for gender and nonsignificant condition by gender interactions for all of the dependent measures.

Confidence in these results is strengthened by the results of the checks for fidelity of implementation conducted under both experimental conditions. These findings

Table 2   Mean Number of Information Omissions and Location Errors, and Mean Holistic Rating of Overall Application Neatness

Dependent Measure	Group		$F(1, 31)$
	A	B	(Condition)
Omissions	5.35	0.63	15.29*
	(2.55)	(0.63)	
Location errors	1.35	0.25	5.29**
	(0.99)	(0.25)	
Neatness rating	3.37	4.46	7.25***
	(1.05)	(0.51)	

Note. Group A refers to the traditional instruction condition and Group B refers to the strategy instruction condition. Numbers in parentheses are standard deviations.
*$p<.001$, **$p<.05$, ***$p<.01$.

showed that the teacher fully completed the teaching functions described above under each condition.

The social validity measure was analyzed in a condition (traditional, strategy) by gender (male, female) ANOVA. A significant main effect for condition was obtained, $F(1,31)$ = 6.12, $p < .05$. There were statistically nonsignificant main effects for gender and condition by gender interactions for the social validity measure. The effects of the job application training on the ratings ($1 = \textit{very unlikely}$ to $5 = \textit{very likely}$) by the supervisor of classified personnel suggest that students under the learning strategy condition (mean = 4.21; SD = 0.46) would be more likely to receive invitations for job interviews after training than those under the traditional condition (mean = 2.88; SD = 1.02). (Nelson, Smith & Dodd, 1994. Copyright 1994 by PRO-ED, Inc. Reprinted by permission)

The next results section is from a 2 x 4 x 2 factorial design. The independent variables and their factors are gender (male or female), grade level (3–6), and treatment (experimental or control). (See Chapter 7, pp. 188–191, for the method section of this study.)

Purpose of the study: To determine the effects of a flexibly paced math program on student achievement.

RESULTS

The achievement gains reported are based solely on results from standardized achievement tests (the STEP and COOP). For comparability, the raw scores on the different forms (pre- and postforms) and levels of the tests were converted to standard scores. All scores and comparisons are from above-level forms (three grade levels higher than the students' school placement) of the STEP, using comparable above-level norm tables (e.g., sixth-grade norms for third graders, seventh-grade norms for fourth graders, and so on).

Achievement Pretest Scores

Although all students in the course had high scores on the quantitative reasoning test (SCAT) administered for eligibility, they varied greatly in mathematics knowledge on entering the course, as assessed by an above-level achievement test (STEP). This variation in pretest achievement scores was found at all grade levels and can be seen in Table 1 with standard scores that ranged across approximately 60 points, or about 60% of the possible range. The standard divisions reported in Table 1 are consistent with those reported for normative samples reported in the STEP manual. It is interesting to consider, however, that highly able students such as these are usually treated as a homogeneous group for instructional purposes, especially since they all scored in the top three percentiles on in-level tests. It is only through above-level testing that the actual variability in their ability and full extent of their knowledge becomes apparent.

Percentile ranks for above-level norm groups, corresponding to the mean STEP scores in Table 1, provide a context for evaluating the precourse knowledge levels of the students. As a group, the students in fourth through sixth grades came into the program with achievement levels higher than 50% of students three grade levels higher than their own. Third graders were only slightly lower at the 35th percentile rank. Because of above-level testing, it was possible to make such comparisons directly without having to use estimates based on an extrapolation of scores to higher grade-level equivalents. Given their high pretest achievement scores, most of these students would be underchallenged and misplaced in a grade-level mathematics program.

Table 1   First Year Achievement: Pre- and Posttest STEP Scores by Grade Level

| Grade Level | Standard Score | | | |
	M	Percentile Rank	Range	SD
3rd (*n* = 51)				
Pretest	427	35th	403–465	12.9
Posttest	450	81st	418–483	15.8
4th (*n* = 92)				
Pretest	438	54th	412–479	11.6
Posttest	466	87th	426–485	14.2
5th (*n* = 101)				
Pretest	448	54th	419–480	12.6
Posttest	474	87th	441–486	8.8
6th (*n* = 62)				
Pretest	461	62nd	426–482	12.1
Posttest	480	86th	437–493	9.4
Total (*n* = 306)				
Pretest	444			16.5
Posttest	469			15.5

Note. Scores are standardized and can range from 400 to 500. All standard scores and percentiles are based on above-grade level testing (students take tests designed for students who are 3 grade levels higher), as well as above-grade-level group norm comparisons (3 grade levels higher).

Posttest Scores

The mathematics achievement test (STEP) was administered as a posttest (again above-level) when a student completed the arithmetic/prealgebra sequence or at the end of the 7-month course period. Therefore, posttest scores reflect learning over a period of no more than 7 months (approximately 72 instructional hours) and, in some cases, much less time. As shown in Table 1, the range of scores shifted significantly upwards. After exposure to the flexibly paced mathematics class, these academically talented students, on average, performed better than 80% of a normative sample of students three grade levels higher than their own.

Achievement Gains

Arithmetic/Prealgebra. To assess whether or not students who began in the arithmetic/prealgebra portion of the course made significant achievement gains in the math program, their pre- and posttest STEP scores were compared. A 2 × 4 × 2 (Gender × Grade Level × Pre/Post Scores) repeated measures analysis of variance (ANOVA), with pre- and posttest STEP scores as the repeated measures, was conducted. There was no significant interaction between achievement gain and gender or grade level. In other words, both males and females, as well as all grade levels, showed equal pre- to posttest gains in achievement scores. The overall main effect for achievement gain from pretest to posttest was statistically significant ($F(1, 298) = 940.5$, $p < .001$). Effect sizes (*d*), yielding the degree of difference between means in standard deviation units, were calculated for pre/posttest scores at every grade level. Effect sizes were large (Cohen, 1977), ranging from 1.6 standard deviations for third graders to 2.4 standard deviations for fifth graders.

As can be seen from the percentile ranks in Table 1, students at each grade level moved up significantly in percentile rank with third graders displaying the greatest increase, moving from the 35th to the 81st percentile rank (according to 6th grade norms). The largest achievement gain was an increase of 56 standard scale points attained by a fifth grader, with four other students also obtaining gains of 50 points or more. These individual standard-score gains are equivalent to moving from below the fifth percentile rank to above the 90th percentile rank (in comparison to students three grade levels higher). Individually, 87% of third graders, 95% of fourth graders, 94% of fifth graders, and 87% of sixth graders exceeded normative gains as expressed in percentile rank increases. Of those students not showing percentile rank gains, the majority had pretest scores above the 90th percentile, which are subject to the unreliable nature of score distributions at this level.

To appreciate the remarkable nature of the achievement gains made by these students, it is important to consider that normative tables are constructed in such a way that "normal" learning patterns for students at all levels are reflected by maintaining the same percentile rank from the beginning of the school year to the end of the school year (i.e., "normal" pre- to posttest raw score gains are necessary for a student to stay at the same percentile rank relative to other students starting at the same achievement level). For students in this study to make such large gains in their percentile rank, they had to learn a remarkable amount of mathematics content in a short period of time (no more than a 7-month period). This kind of extraordinary gain in learning, however, is only possible when students are allowed to continue learning outside the bounds of a grade-appropriate curriculum. And the magnitude of the gains is only noticeable when above-level testing is done. These remarkable gains are a testament to what highly able students are capable of achieving when they are presented with appropriately challenging instruction and content and allowed to learn at their own pace.

To determine whether the effects of the flexibly paced mathematics program resulted in learning above and beyond that found in students of similar ability without exposure to the program, a "control group" comparison was undertaken. To make such a comparison, students in this study served as their own controls. The STEP pretest achievement scores for beginning fourth-grade students entering the program (after a year in a regular math class and no exposure to the flexibly-paced class) were compared with STEP posttest scores from ending third-grade students who had been exposed to the flexibly paced class for one year. Three independent tests showed that third, fourth, and fifth graders' posttest scores were significantly higher ($p < .001$) than pretest scores for entering students ($t(141) = 4.93$, $t(191) = 9.22$, $t(161) = 7.88$, respectively). To be sure, the extra instructional hours these students received should result in some additional increase in achievement scores. The amount of additional learning expected, however, should be judged in relation to the substantially higher percentile rank of the students who had been in the program for one year as compared to students new to the program. This comparison shows a difference of 25 to 33 percentile points.

Algebra

Many students mastered arithmetic and prealgebra material in their first year of the flexibly paced class. However, only a subset of these students returned for a second year to study algebra topics. If they returned the following year, they were pretested to assess retention of their learning. If they again demonstrated mastery of the prerequisite topics, they were placed in the algebra sequence. An examination of these students' progress in the algebra class provided confirmation of their readiness for the subject.

Thirty-seven students were placed in the algebra sequence in their second year. They included 3 fourth graders, 12 fifth graders, and 13 sixth graders, and 9 seventh graders. From this group of 37 students, 29 (78%) "mastered" the algebra material by attaining a score at or above the 90th percentile according to eighth-grade norms within the 7-month period of the class. The remaining students scored well above the median score

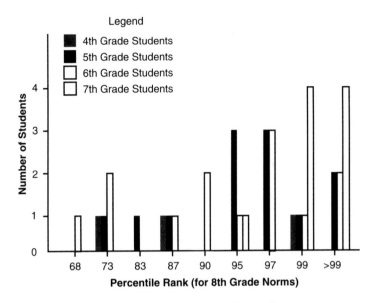

Figure 1. Second year students' algebra performance.
Note. n = 37. Grade level is for students' second year in the program.

Table 2   Retention: Mean STEP Scores and Standard Deviations by Pre- and Posttest, Grade Level, and Gender

		Retention Scores				
		Year 1 Posttest STEP			Year 2 Pretest STEP	
Grade Level	*n*	*M*	*SD*		*M*	*SD*
3rd	26	449	14.4		444	14.7
4th	29	466	11.9		462	14.2
5th	23	472	9.0		472	6.8
6th	10	472	8.6		474	8.3
Gender						
Female	36	462	13.8		458	16.1
Male	52	464	16.2		462	17.5
Total	88	463	15.2		461	16.9

Note. Scores are standardized and can range from 400 to 500.

for eighth graders on the Cooperative Mathematics Test (COOP), as can be seen in Figure 1. The lowest score (earned by a sixth-grade student) was at the 68th percentile for eighth-grade norms. What is interesting is that grade level was not highly related to percentile rank on the algebra posttest. Students from the fourth through the sixth grades had scores across the range of percentile ranks from the 73rd to the 99th percentile.

Retention

To address the issue of whether or not students who excel at such a rapid pace retain the knowledge and skills they learn, the scores of 88 students who completed one year of the math program and continued the following year were selected for further study. Retention was measured over a 5-month period by comparing the student's posttest score for the first year with his or her pretest score in the fall of the second year. Means and standard deviations for scores (post- and pretest) by grade level and gender are presented in Table 2.

A 2 × 4 × 2 (Gender × Grade Level × Pre/Post Scores) repeated measures ANOVA, with post- and pretest scores as the repeated measure, was conducted. There was no significant change in scores; scores remained relatively the same over the 5-month interval. The pretest score for the second year was 99 percent of the posttest score for the first year. In addition, there was no interaction between retention and grade level or gender; the amount of retention was the same for males and females, and across all grade levels. (Mills, Ablard, & Gustin, 1994)

Causal-comparative research is ex post facto, or after-the-fact, research, because researchers are trying to establish a causal effect between existing conditions. Researchers want answers to questions but cannot manipulate the independent variable(s) for practical or ethical reasons. They realize a condition exists and are unsure about what might have been its cause. Causal-comparative designs are built on the posttest-only control group design.

The following results section contains an example of a causal-comparative design (see Chapter 7, pp. 192–194, for the method section of this study). The researchers sought to determine the effect of a preexisting condition (amount of previous mathematics instruction) on mathematics achievement. It should be remembered that researchers using the causal-comparative design are trying to find causal relationships or predictions.

Purpose of the study: To examine the teaching strategies used by mothers of sons with learning disabilities and normally achieving sons.

RESULTS

Mothers' Teaching Strategies

Differences between the LD and NLD groups were tested by using a one-way ANOVA. The mean proportion of the low- and medium-level teaching strategies used by the mothers did not significantly differ between the groups. However, the mothers of NLD children ($M = 19.90$ vs. $M = 9.13$) used more high-level strategies, $F(1,58) = 4.06$, $p < .05$, and the total time they used in teaching ($M = 76.5$ vs. $M = 66.1$) was higher, $F(1,58) = 4.63$, $p < .05$, than that of the mothers of children with LD. No differences between the groups were found in the amount of speech produced by both mothers and children during the task.

Mother-Child Interactions

Maternal motivation in the task did not differentiate the groups. However, the mothers of children with LD showed more dominance ($p < .05$) and expressed less emotionality ($p < .01$) and cooperation ($p < .05$) while teaching their children (see Table 1). Children's lower level of motivation and initiative in the LD group may be one reason for their mothers' behavior. Children with and without LD differed significantly in motivation ($p < .001$), initiative ($p < .01$), emotionality ($p < .001$), and cooperation ($p < .001$). The inactive and noncooperative behavior of the children with LD may partly follow from their earlier experiences with learning tasks.

Table 1   Differences in the Rated Quality of Mother-Child Interaction

	LD Group		NLD Group		
Interaction Variables	*M*	*SD*	*M*	*SD*	*F*
Mother					
Motivation in the task	3.47	1.22	3.67	1.03	0.47
Dominance	3.03	1.03	2.50	1.04	3.96*
Emotionality	3.57	0.77	4.17	0.65	10.60**
Cooperation	4.10	0.76	4.57	0.73	5.91*
Child					
Motivation in the task	2.77	1.19	3.80	1.13	11.88***
Initiative	2.67	0.88	3.30	1.02	6.89**
Emotionality	3.37	0.72	4.20	0.71	20.30***
Cooperation	3.46	0.82	4.53	0.63	32.00***

Note. *df* = 1, 58. LD = learning disability; NLD = non-learning disabled.
p < .05, **p* < .01, ***p* < .001.

Table 2   Correlations Between Mother-Child Interaction Variables

		Child			
Mother	Group	Task Motivation	Initiative	Emotionality	Cooperation
Task motivation	LD	.50**	.31*	.46*	.30*
	NLD	.53***	.29	.19	.50**
Dominance	LD	−.18	−.40**	−.11	−.18
	NLD	−.23	−.21	−.42**	−.37*
Emotionality	LD	.44**	.49**	.54**	.27
	NLD	.14	−.08	.52**	.20
Cooperation	LD	.44**	.31*	.31*	.48**
	NLD	.06	−.05	.30*	.14

Note. LD = learning disability; NLD = non-learning disabled.
p < .05, **p* < .01, ***p* < .001.

Correlations indicated that interdependence between mother and child behaviors was stronger in the LD group than in the NLD group. Twelve of the 16 coefficients reached significance in the LD group, whereas only 6 coefficients reached significance in the NLD group (see Table 2). The initiative of the children with LD correlated significantly with their mothers' motivation, emotionality, and cooperation. A significant correlation was also found between cooperation of mother and child. The NLD children's initiative did not correlate with any variable describing the quality of their mothers' interaction. The nondisabled children seemed to be more independent and self-regulated in their task performance. Dominance, which was a prominent feature for mothers of the LD group only, correlated with children's low level of initiative ($p <$ .01). The corresponding correlation was not significant in the NLD group, but dominance in the mothers of nondisabled children correlated negatively with the children's emotionality ($p <$ .01) and cooperation ($p <$ .05).

Children's Task Performance

The children with LD were less successful in learning the words than were the NLD children, $F(1,58) = 37.79$, $p <$ .001, as indicated by the fewer number of words learned (LD group: $M = 2.53$, SD = 1.17; NLD group: $M = 4.13$, SD = 0.82). The mothers' motivation

Table 3   Correlations Among Variables Associated with Children's Performance

	Child's Task Performance	
Interaction Variables	LD Group	NLD Group
Mother		
Task motivation	.47**	.22
Emotionality	.53**	.09
Proportion of high-level strategies	.31*	−.03
Child		
Task motivation	.59***	.48**
Initiative	.38*	.28
Emotionality	.42**	.13
Cooperation	.42**	.32*

Note. LD = learning disability; NLD = non-learning disabled.
*$p < .05$, **$p < .01$, ***$p < .001$.

Table 4   Level of Teaching Strategies Among Mothers of Group with Learning Disabilities

	Low-and Medium-Level Strategies Group		High-Level Strategies Group		
Interaction Variables	M	SD	M	SD	F
Mother					
Task motivation	2.87	0.96	4.14	1.17	10.68**
Emotionality	3.19	0.65	4.00	0.68	11.10**
Cooperation	3.81	0.64	4.43	0.76	5.72*
Smiles	9.56	6.74	19.28	13.67	6.35*
Child					
Task performance	2.06	1.12	3.07	1.00	6.87**

Note. $df = 1, 28$.
*$p < .05$, **$p < .01$.

and emotionality were found to be highly correlated with the children's learning outcome in the LD group (see Table 3). The proportion of high-level strategies used by the mother covaried also with child's performance in the LD group. No corresponding associations between children's performance and mothers' behavior were found in the NLD group, which might partly result from the reduced variance of this group. In addition, child's initiative and emotionality was positively associated with learning of the words in the LD group, although not in the NLD group. However, children's own motivation and cooperation were significantly associated with learning outcome in both groups. Scores on the Raven and the PPVT for children in either group were not related to their performance.

Variation in Maternal Strategies Within the LD Group

Some mothers of children with LD appeared particularly sensitive to their children's skills, used positively motivating teaching strategies, and redirected their children's failing attention. These findings demonstrate the relevance of looking at within-group variation of the teaching strategies used by mothers of the LD group. Ten mothers were identified who failed to employ any high-level strategies, and six were identified who used them only randomly (under 8%). These mothers were classified to form the low- and medium-level strategies group ($n = 16$). The proportion of high-level strategies varied between 12% and 72% among the rest of mothers of children with LD. These mothers were classified as belonging to the high-level strategy group ($n = 14$). Comparison of mother-child interactions in these groups revealed that mothers using high-level distancing strategies were more involved in the task, expressed more emotionality and cooperation, and smiled more during the task (see Table 4). Children also learned significantly more test words in the high-level strategy group. (Lyytinen, et al., 1994. Copyright 1994 by PRO-ED, Inc. Reprinted by permission.)

Qualitative Research

The following results section is from a qualitative descriptive study (see Chapter 7, pp. 198–199, to review the method section of this study). Note two things about the results section. The researcher has answered specific questions that relate to her data analysis procedures. And, although some quantification was done (percentages of responses), the data were verbally, not statistically, analyzed.

Purpose of the study: To determine how frequently, when, and for what reasons a group of second-grade writers used their peers' questions to revise their unfinished pieces.

RESULTS

How frequently did the children insert the requested information into their texts?

To answer this question the percentage of changes made by each child in his/her texts as a result of the questions raised during the sharing sessions was calculated.

Six of the 24 children (25%) made no changes in their texts as a result of their peers' questions. Three of these six children chose to share only once between January and June.

Eighteen of the 24 children (75%) inserted into their texts, typically at the end, at least some of the information identified as missing by their peers' questions. Six of these 18 children incorporated responses into their texts to more than 50% of the questions they received from their peers. The range of these children's percentage of questions used was from 60 to 100%. Two of these children were nondiscriminating; every question asked was answered by inserting the missing information at the end of their pieces. For one of these two children, the change over the data collection period was from inserting the requested information in phrases (for example, in response to "Why did you have to go to the hospital?" Mathy inserted "Because my eye puffed up" at the end of her text) to inserting the requested information in sentences (for example, in response to "How sunburned did you get?" Mathy inserted "I got a little bit of sunburn."). The other 12 of these 18 children used their peers' questions sometimes, but not often, to modify their text. The range of these 12 children's percentage of changes made as a result of their peers' questions was from 14 to 40%.

Did publishing affect how frequently these writers used their peers' questions for text revisions?

To answer this question the percentage of revisions made in eventually published and in never published drafts by those fourteen children who had shared both kinds of drafts was calculated and compared.

For slightly more than half (57%) of these children, more revisions were made in eventually published than in never published drafts. For five of these children, the decision to publish had a significant effect on their decision to use their peers' questions; they made no revisions based on their peers' questions in never published pieces.

Those three children who made some revisions based on their peers' questions in both eventually published and never published drafts made from 15 to 85% more revisions in drafts which were eventually published.

Four of the 14 children (28%) used their peers' questions more frequently to revise never published pieces.

Two children (14%) revised, based on their peers' questions, equally as often in published and never published drafts. One of these children made no changes based on his peers' questions in either eventually published or never published drafts; the other child inserted information based on every question asked by her peers in eventually published and never published drafts.

What reasons did the children provide for their decisions not to use their peers' questions?

During one month (May) the children were asked to provide reasons for their decisions not to use their peers' questions. The most frequently provided reason (30%) was that the child did not know the answer to the question raised by his/her peer. Typically, these rejected questions were requests for specific information, for details, for example, "Why did Baby Anna put her hand in the garbage?" which the writer did not possess. (Roni answered, "I can't answer that! I can't read her mind!")

While the second and third most frequently provided reasons seem similar, the focus of the child's response was different. The focus of the "I didn't want to use the question" response (20%) was the quality of the piece as it existed; the writer liked it as it was. The focus of the "The question wasn't good" (15%) was the value of the question of the peer. In the writer's opinion, the question "What day did that happen?" was unimportant.

Five other reasons were provided by the children. Fifteen percent of their responses were of the "I'm not going to publish this piece" type. This response implied that since the child did not intend to publish the piece no revising to make the meaning clear for others was necessary. "I already answered that question in my piece" was suggested 8% of the time as the reason for rejecting a question. The writer contended that the question-asker had not listened carefully to the reading of the pieces. Six percent of the responses focused on the relationship between the writer and the question-asker. "I didn't like (a child's name)" was typical of the responses in this category. Since the question-asker was not liked, his/her question was not used to guide the piece's revision. Four percent of the responses were of the "I already answered that question during sharing time" type. These responses suggested that the answer to the question had been given orally during the sharing session. Finally, "My parents wouldn't want me to answer that question" was suggested once as the reason for rejecting a question. This response indicated that the answers to some questions were unacceptable.

Every child questioned provided a reason for his/her decision not to insert the requested information into the text. (Vukelich, 1986, pp. 302–303. Reprinted by permission of the National Reading Conference and C. Vukelich)

The next results section is from the qualitative portion of a study that combined qualitative and quantitative research procedures. (See Chapter 7, pp. 199–200, to review the method section of this study.) In their "Qualitative Analysis," the researchers explain the procedures used to categorize the data as well as their interpretations (results). The results of the qualitative portion of their study were used in setting up the quantitative analysis. That is, their categorizations of the "type of text," "exercises," and "extended texts" used in the observed classrooms became the factors that were later statistically analyzed.

Purpose of the qualitative portion of the study: To study language arts instruction as it naturally occurred and to categorize the classrooms along a continuum that was based on the teachers' emphasis given to writing extended passages.

Qualitative Analysis

Coding and Data Reduction. In coding our field notes, we followed procedures described by Miles and Huberman (1984). Codes were derived from the initial foci of research and from the incremental reading of the field notes and were given operational definitions. The codes addressed various aspects of reading and writing instruction: management and student engagement, type of lesson, type of activity, locus of control, and types of assessment. We used Ethnograph qualitative analysis software (Seidel, Kjolseth, & Seymour, 1988) to group episodes from field notes by code within and across classrooms. Using the computer-generated data patterns of the codes and a re-reading of the original field notes, we prepared summaries for each classroom. We used data from the interview transcripts to augment and revise the summaries.

Classification of Classrooms by Level of Engagement. It is apparent that academic learning is not likely to occur when students are not engaged in classroom activities. Nystrand and Gamoran (1991) have broken the construct of student engagement into three levels: (a) disengagement, which can be identified by students declining to undertake assigned tasks and not attending to discussion or instruction; (b) procedural engagement, which can be identified by students' accommodation to classroom regulations through paying attention and completing tasks; and (c) substantive engagement, which involves a "sustained personal commitment" (p. 262) to understanding and exploring the topic of instruction. In our analyses, we distinguished only between the first two levels, disengagement and procedural engagement. Students were coded as engaged if they were either procedurally or substantively engaged. Engagement at the procedural level is associated with achievement (Fisher et al., 1981; Nystrand & Gamoran, 1991, p. 281), and is a proxy measure of classroom management that is distinct from the content of instruction. Substantive engagement, on the other hand, is likely to be associated with a broad pattern of instructional discourse of which the choice and content of writing activities are important elements, along with peer interaction and higher level questioning (Nystrand & Gamoran, 1991, p. 270); substantive engagement is too closely linked to the nature of writing instruction to serve as a control variable.

We coded individual students as engaged or disengaged in sweeps of the classroom conducted at least once in each 10-min interval, according to whether the students were involved in activities directly related to the task designated by the teacher at the time of observation. Thus, if the teacher had designated a period of time for students to write a story, individual students who were looking outside, discussing ideas for math or science problems, or out of the room were coded as not engaged. The data supported classification of classrooms into three levels, on the basis of the average percentage of students coded as engaged across sweeps: high engagement (more than 75% of the students were engaged in the current task), moderate engagement (50% to 75%), and low engagement (fewer than 50%). To check the reliability of the classification, two researchers independently classified each classroom from coded field notes. The percentage of identical classifications across the 39 classrooms was 87%. When discrepancies were obtained, the classroom was placed in the category assigned by the researcher who actually observed in it.

Categorizing Instruction by Type of Text Written by Students. Three approaches to categorizing classrooms according to characteristics of writing instruction were initially explored: (a) attention to meaning, which we defined as a communicative purpose for writing activities; (b) attention to process, which we defined as modeling the processes used by expert writers, with steps of idea formation, drafting, revising, and editing; and (c) type of text written by students. The first two typologies were of theoretical interest but were not supported by our data. That is, we were unable to arrive at definitions of classroom types on the basis of actual data that could support reliable classification of classrooms by independent analysis on either of these dimensions. The third dimension, type of text written by students, lent itself to clear operational definitions that supported reliable classification of classrooms.

We developed typology of classrooms that was based on the type of text written by students. We were able to categorize the writing products in the 39 classrooms as either "exercise-like" or "extended text." The classification was based on the length of text produced by the student and on the amount of choice exercised by the student in the generation of text. We considered a product to be an exercise (a) if the text produced by students consisted of individual words or single sentences or (b) if student choice and initiative were absent or nearly absent. This meant for example, that stories or paragraphs, which might normally be considered whole texts were considered to be exercises if students were merely inserting sentences or words into a formulaic master. However, if students wrote the text themselves, even though prompted by teacher or textbook, the product was classified extended text.

Exercises. The most common type of exercise was the workbook or ditto exercise, and these were used to teach a wide variety of content ranging from punctuation and other text mechanics to grammar and vocabulary. These types of exercises were also used in conjunction with reading comprehension and to teach aspects of composition, such as paragraph format or story beginnings and endings. Writing assignments that were focused on grammar, spelling, and vocabulary mastery were also classified as exercises. These typically involved the students' supplying punctuation marks or other short answers, the production of sentences, and other types of focused practice of language or composition skills. Written responses to questions, either teacher-made or from the text, were coded as exercises because students' responses were typically brief and constrained by the preceding text.

Extended Texts. Extended texts were defined as texts consisting of several lines written by students in which students exercised some autonomy and initiative. This definition included paragraph-length texts in cases where the content could not be easily predicted, that is, in cases where each student was apparently able to write relatively uninhibitedly. The types of extended texts produced in classrooms reflect the broad range of writing that one would expect in society, as well as texts that are common only in classrooms. For example, students wrote letters, stories, obituaries, jokes, journals, and poems in addition to book reports, summaries of reading, and notes on mini-lectures. We were struck by the diversity of writing and the variety of tasks and interactions that occurred in conjunction with the writing.

We classified classrooms according to predominance of writing tasks for students. Two researchers (who were aware of the major hypotheses of the study but unaware of the achievement outcomes for particular classrooms) worked together to classify the classrooms into two categories: those in which writing tasks consisted most of exercises and those in which the writing of extended texts predominated. Each of these categories was further divided into two levels, thus producing four categories that were based on the relative amount of time that students spent working on the two types of tasks: (a) mostly exercises, (b) mixed, mostly exercises, (c) mixed, mostly extended text, and (d) mostly extended text. Three additional researchers, working from descriptions of the characteristics of the different categories, then classified the 39 classrooms. Seven classrooms were classified as emphasizing mostly exercises; 12 as mixed, mostly exercises; 8 as mixed, mostly extended text; and 12 as most extended text. Teachers in classrooms categorized as extended text were more likely than teachers in other classrooms to use a process approach to writing (i.e., use of revision, peer editing, etc.). However, some teachers whose students frequently wrote extended texts did not emphasize intermediate stages of writing or vary the process from task to task. There was not consistent relationship between the type of product produced by students and the nature of the process used.

In classrooms classified as mostly exercises, written products consisted primarily of short (word, phrase, or sentence) responses to questions posed by the teacher or appearing on worksheets or in workbooks. The distinguishing characteristic of texts produced by students in the other classrooms was the length of the text and the relative autonomy and initiative allowed to the students in their writing. We found enough variation in the relative production of exercises and extended texts in the two mixed categories to differentiate between ones whose products were predominantly exercises and those whose products were predominately extended texts. However, there was considerable overlap across types of classes. Differences among the classrooms, with the exception of those classified as mostly exercises, consisted of differences in the amount of time devoted to working on extended texts or exercises. One cannot assume that extended text implies a process (i.e., use of revision, peer editing, etc.) approach on the part of the teacher, although there is doubtless some relationship between the type of product and the nature of the process used. (Davis, Clarke & Rhodes, 1994. Copyright © 1994 by the American Psychological Association. Reprinted with permission).

Other Research

Single-subject research, action research, and evaluation research are other ways researchers describe, compare, and draw causative conclusions about educational problems and questions.

Single-Subject and Case Study Research.   The following results section is from research done with a single subject in an A–B design. Note that although data were collected and presented in graph form, no tests of statistical significance were performed. Therefore, the research consumer does not know whether the subject's increased spelling scores after tutoring differed significantly from those before tutoring or whether the difference might be attributed to chance or error variations. (See Chapter 7, pp. 201–204, to review the method section of this study.)

Purpose of the study: To determine the effects of a peer-tutoring procedure on the spelling behavior of a mainstreamed elementary school student with a learning disability.

RESULTS

Percent Correct

The overall results indicated that the tutee obtained a greater percent of accuracy on the spelling tests during the peer-tutoring condition than during the baseline condition. As shown in Figure 1, the student increased his mean percent correct from 61.25 percent in baseline to 77.5 percent in the peer-tutoring condition, that is, an improvement of 16.25 percent. The spelling performance of the peer tutor (S–B) did not decrease during either of the experimental conditions; it was 100 percent.

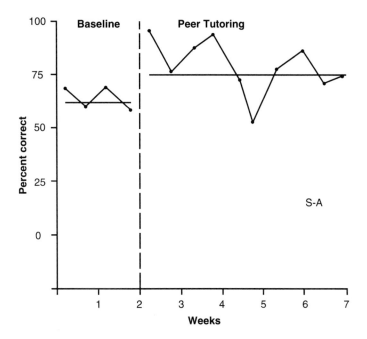

Figure 1
The percent correct on biweekly spelling tests across the duration of the study. Solid horizontal lines indicate condition means.

Table 1   Weekly Subject Ratings of the Experimental Treatment

	Rating		
Subjects	Very Good	Satisfactory	Unsatisfactory
A	2	2	1
B	3	2	

Clinical Significance: Student Self-Reports and Ratings

Both the tutee and the tutor rated the peer-tutoring procedure favorably (see Table 1). The program was rated as very good five times, satisfactory on four occasions, and unsatisfactory once. Subject A rated the program as unsatisfactory on the day when he scored 45% on his spelling test. (Mandoli, Mandoli, & McLaughlin, 1982, pp. 187–188)

Action Research.   Action research is descriptive, comparative, or experimental research in which results are not generalized beyond the study's specific subjects and educational setting. Action researchers seek answers to immediate questions or problems.

The following section reports the outcomes from a qualitative teacher-as-researcher project (see Chapter 7, pp. 204–206, for the method section of this study). Note that in this action research study no tests of statistical significance were done on the tabulated data. The researcher's purpose was the process of collaboration and its impact on solving a problem of concern to the participating teachers. Action research is useful to research consumers if there are similarities in subject variables, educational setting, or treatment(s). In such cases, research consumers may wish to replicate the study in searching for answers to their own educational questions.

Purpose of the study: To determine how the teacher could facilitate students' engagement in literature and critical thinking; and, how students' writing reflects their engagement and thinking.

WHAT CAN I DO?: CASE STUDY #1

I was eager to see how my decision to adopt new instructional methods in my classroom would affect students' response to literature. The instructional cycle, which was repeated in each unit throughout the year, included these elements: an assigned text; choice of a contemporary novel connected to the assigned text; response logs with teacher comments; book talks; seminars; critical analysis papers; and evaluation. I hoped that with these elements I would find at least part of the solution to my first research question: How can I help my students become involved in literature and think critically about what they read? The description that follows is based on what happened during one unit that year and shows what I felt was a successful outcome to my research question.

To help them connect with Nathaniel Hawthorne's classic *The Scarlet Letter,* I had my students select a related novel from a list of contemporary fiction. As they read, they were asked to write their reactions to the novel in their response logs. I gave the students what they thought were minimal and far too general instructions:

> Each time you finish reading a section, jot down your reactions. What you write will be determined by how you respond. Did you especially like or dislike a section? Why? Do you sympathize with a character? Why? Did a section confuse you or impress you? Why? What would you especially like to remember? Do you see a theme emerging? Does anything seem particularly symbolic? Note any words you don't know and look up the definitions. Write any questions you'd like answered.

I was immediately greeted with a barrage of questions: Do you want all of this for each chapter? How many vocabulary words do we have to have? How many pages does each entry have to be? Does spelling count? What about punctuation? How are you going to grade? I was concerned about words such as "do you want," "have to," and "must be," so I again explained that this was a personal process and that each individual would be in the driver's seat when it came to deciding amount, content, and number of vocabulary words. Spelling and punctuation would not count; those skills would be checked only in papers that had been edited and submitted for evaluation. Grades for the journals themselves would be based on effort. Most of my students were suspicious. Some resented the lack of specific guidelines; others were looking for a trick; a few were delighted because they thought the amount of work would be minimal. I urged them to trust me and told them that they were beginning what I hoped would be an exciting journey toward connecting to *The Scarlet Letter.*

The next day I began reading and responding to what the students were writing in their logs. I was dismayed to discover that almost no one responded in a personal or critical way. What I read were pages and pages of summaries. Instead of repeating the instructions to the whole class, I responded by writing questions in the logs. To one student's summary of the episode in which Louie Banks quits the football team in Chris Crutcher's *Running Loose,* I wrote, "Have you ever heard of anyone being intentionally injured in football? What would you do if you were in Louie's position?" That sparked a dialogue, and it opened the door for this student to write more personal comments in his journal.

Not all the students had problems becoming personally involved with their novels. Alisha found many points of connection in Richard Peck's *Close Enough to Touch.* She first related to the theme of loneliness:

> In the book *Close Enough to Touch,* the main character is very close to his girlfriend Dory. They do a lot of things together and they are in love. Then Matt is left alone because of Dory's tragic death. I have never had anybody close to me die, but I can easily relate to Matt. In grade nine I got really close to a boy and I fell in love. Then that summer he moved away. This was really hard for me because we were like best friends. I felt so alone and sad.

She then mentioned an episode from a television show that related to the guilt Matt was experiencing.

During the time Alisha was reading this book and responding to it in her log, a student at our school committed suicide. Alisha's response to this tragedy was played out in her log:

> Matt tells Linda, "Dory's beginning to fade for me. I can't remember her face. Not missing her is about as bad a feeling as missing her. I'm somewhere between grief and guilt."
>
> I can somewhat relate to Matt's guilty feeling, although my situation is much different. When Stan died I sort of felt guilty for not knowing him. I felt guilty for being so happy while he must have been so very unhappy.

Writing these sorts of journal entries about contemporary novels and personal events seemed to help Alisha have a more personal response to the *The Scarlet Letter.* She began to write descriptively about the book in her log and to give her own opinions about Puritan society:

> The people outside the door start saying Hester Prynne should be put to death. The people watch her come out of the prison with a baby. She holds the baby close to her, to hide the letter "A" sewn on her dress. I get the impression that decorations on clothing are not socially accepted. She is wearing the red "A" so that everyone will know what she has done.
>
> Hester is very beautiful and delicate, but she must feel very bad inside. She will be alienated from everyone else because of the scarlet letter. "It had the effect of a spell, taking her out of the ordinary relations with humanity, and enclosing her in a sphere by herself."
>
> Hester had to show herself and the baby to the people. "The unhappy culprit sustained herself as best a woman might under the heavy weight of unrelenting eyes, all fastened upon her and concentrated on her bosom." Hester must have felt very alone, ailienated [sic] and guilty. She might feel the way I felt when I first moved here. I had no friends and I felt like everyone was judging me. It's not the same exact thing, but maybe she felt the same way.

Alisha was able to transfer the way she responded personally to contemporary novels to her reading of a classic work without any formal lessons.

All the students had been given the same instructions to look for themes from their contemporary novels in the life of Hester Prynne. I encouraged those students who were having trouble making this connection to use a metacognitive strategy: I suggested they go back to an early entry in their log where they had summarized or made an initial comment about a book they were reading. When they found a passage that reflected guilt, alienation, or loneliness, I urged them to make a note in the margin of their response logs and think about those themes in relation to *The Scarlet Letter.*

Kristi was one of the students who complained about the lack of concrete instructions. She did not read for pleasure, but spent hours studying and practicing for the drill team. She was very goal oriented and grade oriented. Following my suggestion, she reread her responses to Ellen White's *Life without Friends,* focusing on the hunt for examples of guilt, loneliness, and alienation. A later journal entry shows her surprise at the personal connections she was able to make:

> First, Beverly shows signs of alienation when she says that everyone only took her father's side. Another example is when she asks her stepmother to leave her alone, Beverly is actually choosing to be alienated from others. Beverly's life in some ways reminds me of a friend of mine. This girl always complains that she had no friends but yet it is like she alienates herself from others by not talking and by always staying home, declining invitations to go out. I'm really enjoying this book because it is so different from any other book I've read.

Analysis of *The Scarlet Letter* was not nearly as difficult for her as it would have been had she not first read and responded to an easier-to-relate-to contemporary novel. She easily found examples of guilt and alienation in this classic, commented on Hawthorne's style, and used metaphor to relate to everyday life. She also challenged and encouraged herself as she read:

> Guilt is shown when Hester is thinking about her deed and the effect it will have on Pearl. The phrase is "She knew that her deed had been evil; she could have no faith, therefore, that its result would be for good. Day after day, she looked fearfully into the child's expanding nature; ever dreading to detect some dark and wild peculiarity, that should correspond with the guiltiness to which she owed her being." Loneliness and alienation are described in the following sentences: "Pearl was a born outcast of the infantile world. She was an example of evil and a product of sin, she had no right among christened infants." This goes back to the beginning of my journal when I described Pearl's friends.
>
> The book is really getting interesting, I love it. However, lots of the description is so confusing. I can handle it because I'm in an Honors class! One way of relating this story to school life would be if you have ever noticed when a teacher yells at a student, everyone turns and stares. This is like the emblem that alienates Hester, however this is done with language.

Seminar Discussion

The next step in my instruction was the seminar. I felt strongly that students should determine the points they wanted to discuss. Romano (1987) says that when "searching people interact in a classroom, ideas spark and learning occurs in countless ways" (p. 176). That's what I wanted our seminars to be: not a time when I talked and the students listened and parroted back my words, but a time for student-generated learning.

I set up the seminar as a graded discussion. Points would be awarded for topics raised, expanded on, answered, or extended; points would be deducted for speaking out of turn, interrupting, or insulting another student. I would participate when I felt something was being missed or neglected, but would try to keep my comments to a minimum.

Our first seminar consisted of a lively discussion. The students raised controversial questions about whether Pearl acted as she did because she was possessed or because of the environment in which she was raised; they argued about the point at which evil overcame Roger Chillingworth. Students dragged out books and journals to support the side they chose.

Discussion at first was dominated by the more extroverted students and it took several attempts for the students to rectify that situation. As a group, we finally decided that body language had a great deal to do with who was being called on. Handwavers, grunters, and people who all but fell out of their chairs seemed to command the most attention. At first I acted as moderator, but in the following days we appointed other moderators. We finally settled on appointing a student to raise the first question and call on people until each point was thoroughly discussed; then that person would call on someone else to raise the next question, and that second questioner would act as moderator for the discussion that ensued. With this method, we had several moderators and involved more students in the seminar. However, the people who used body language still seemed to gain more than their fair share of attention. It was a problem we resolved to work on.

The response to the seminars was overwhelmingly positive. I was interested in how students felt these discussions compared to traditional teacher-led discussions so I asked them to make subjective evaluations. Julia wrote as follows:

> I have gotten so much more out of the seminars because, especially with a book that is hard to understand, when everyone pulls together and puts in ideas more things and symbols are clearer. Also, I feel like more of an adult in this situation and I think more mature thinking is encouraged with this kind of an atmosphere.

Stephanie said that she liked the seminars much better than questions:

> I have found out a lot more information in this seminar than I could ever learn from a worksheet. Some of these questions would not have even entered my mind without the seminar. I like hearing other people's views on those questions.

On the negative side, students mentioned that there were so many people in the seminar group that they often did not get a chance to comment. Many times what they wanted to say was expressed by someone else before they could be called on. Overall, however, the class and I felt the seminars were a success, and we looked forward to continuing these discussions.

Analytic Papers

The next step for me was to prepare my students for writing analytic papers. I felt students should choose their own topics so they could explore issues that were meaningful to them. As a class we brainstormed for issues or questions that were of interest. Many of the points that were raised had been discussed but not fully resolved in seminars; these were issues that seemed to depend on each reader's interpretation. One of the most popular issues was the question of who had committed the greater sin—Hester and Arthur or Roger Chillingworth. Scott chose this issue for his paper. In it he argued as follows:

> The sin of Chillingworth is far worse than that of Hester or Dimmesdale. He committed not only one sin, but two. His first one was against nature. He committed the first sin the day he married Hester. He knew she didn't love him and that he wasn't the man to marry her. Chillingworth's second sin is far worse than any other one. His sin is the subordination of the heart to the mind. He becomes willing to satisfy his fellow man for his own selfish interests.

Scott chose with this paper to take some risks. He made some assumptions about moral values and degrees of right and wrong. As a reader, I responded emotionally to his sensitive, idealistic assertion that Chillingworth's "subordination of the heart to the mind" was the far greater sin. As a teacher, I was delighted with his personal involvement with this composition. He was actively involved from the beginning to the end in a book that in years past had seemed so dry, sterile, and incomprehensible to students.

Marie also displayed a great depth of understanding and feeling in her analysis of symbols in *The Scarlet Letter:*

> A common object that many people see may mean nothing to most; yet to another person, it may serve as a reminder of his or her most sinful or regretted act. The sight of a playing child brings a smile to most faces along with thoughts of younger, happier days; in Nathaniel Hawthorne's novel, Pearl serves to remind Hester of her shame. . . . Pearl's attire reminds us of Hester first emerging from prison, when the letter was described as being "surrounded with an elaborate embroidery and fantastic flourishes of gold thread."

Marie clearly demonstrates her analytic skills in this passage. This was made easier for her because of the pool of resources she had available in her response journal. The relationships between the characters in the book and real-life situations that were mentioned in other papers were also inspired by the journals. (Hirtle, 1993)

SUMMARY

What are the different ways quantitative data are recorded?

Statistics are numerical ways to describe, analyze, summarize, and interpret data in a manner that conserves time and space. Researchers select statistical procedures after they have determined what research designs and types of data will be appropriate for answering their research questions.

In answering descriptive research questions, statistics let researchers show the data's central tendencies and variability. In answering comparative and experimental research questions, other statistics allow researchers to draw inferences from samples and make generalizations about target populations. In all three types of research, the specific statistical procedures are determined by the research design and the type of data that are collected. And, in comparative and experimental research, statistics are tools that let researchers gain two other insights: (a) an estimate of the error (or difference) between the research sample and the target population, and (b) the confidence with which research producers and consumers can accept the results.

Data are recorded as (a) categories, (b) rankings, (c) intervals, and (d) ratios. Each requires the use of different statistics. Interval scales present data according to preset, equal spans. They are the most common form of data reporting in education and social science, and they are identified by continuous measurement scales: raw scores and derived scores such as IQ scores, standard scores, and normal curve equivalents. Interval scores are the form in which data from most tests are recorded. Rankings, or ordinal scales, show the order, from highest to lowest, for a variable. There are no indications as to the value or size of differences between or among items in a list; the indications refer only to the relative order of the scores. Subjects can be ranked according to their performance on a set of athletic tasks, and what will be reported is the order in which they scored (e.g., first, second, third), not their actual accumulation of points. Data from surveys and observations are often recorded in this manner. Categories separate data into two or more discrete aspects, such as male-female, red-white-blue, or always-frequently-infrequently-never. The data can be reported as numbers of items or as percentages of a total. Data recorded in this way are considered nominal scales. Data from surveys and observations are often recorded in this way. Ratio scales, less frequently used in educational and other behavioral and social science research than the other three, show relative relationships among scores, such as half-as-large or three-times-as-tall.

What is a normal distribution curve?

Parametric statistics are based on the concept that if a set of scores is large enough, the scores will be distributed systematically and predictably. They will produce a graph in the shape of a bell, which is called the normal distribution curve. There is a direct relationship between the standard deviation (SD) and the normal distribution curve. Starting at the center, or mean, of the distributed variable, each SD represents a fixed, specific proportion of the population.

What statistical procedures are used in educational and other behavioral science research?

A common parametric statistic is the t-test. It is used when the difference between two sets of scores is being tested. It is reported as numbers such as $t = 1.6$ or $t = 3.1$. Another parametric statistic used with interval data in comparative research is the product-moment correlation, which refers to the quantified relationship between two sets of scores for the same groups of subjects. The result of the arithmetic computation is a coefficient of correlation which is expressed as r, a decimal between -1.0 and $+1.0$. When research designs call for examining differences among the means of two or more groups of subjects or two or more variables, they frequently use the analysis of variance (ANOVA), which is reported in F-ratios. The advantage in using an ANOVA is that two or more variables as well as two or more factors can be examined. In its simplest form, ANOVA can be thought of as a multiple t-test. The ANOVA is appropriate for use with some comparative research designs and with experimental research designs such as the pretest-posttest with multiple control groups, the Solomon four-group design, counterbalanced designs, common factorial designs, and causal-comparative designs. Analysis of covariance (ANCOVA) allows researchers to examine differences among the means of groups of subjects as if the means were equal from the start. They do this by adjusting the differences in the means to make them hypothetically equal. In all other ways, ANCOVAs are interpreted like ANOVAs. When researchers wish to examine the relationships among more than two variables, they can use multiple or partial correlation techniques. These procedures are interpreted similarly to a single correlation coefficient.

For each parametric statistical procedure there are corresponding nonparametric procedures. In general, nonparametric statistics are less frequently used in educational and other behavioral and social science research than are parametric.

What is statistical significance?

In comparative and experimental research, researchers want to be sure that the differences between the means of two or more groups of subjects or two or more variables are truly different. If the means differ, researchers need to know whether the difference happened by chance. When the difference between the means is large enough that it cannot be attributed to chance, the difference is considered as significant and, therefore, reliable. Statistical significance occurs when results exceed a particular p, or chance, level and researchers are confident about the conclusions they make from their findings. When researchers determine whether a difference or relationship exists, there is the possibility of error. Two kinds of error can occur: (a) researchers accept the results as true when they are not, and (b) researchers do not accept the results as true when they actually are.

What are the ways data are analyzed in qualitative research?

In qualitative studies, researchers analyze data by examining and organizing notes from interviews and observations and reducing the information into smaller segments from which they can see patterns and trends. In addition, they interpret the meanings of these patterns and trends and create research hypotheses and questions for verification in further research. Qualitative researchers begin their analyses while still in the field and finish it after all data have been collected. An important point about qualitative research is that qualitative researchers often do measure and count; in other words, they quantify some data. However, they do not use statistical analyses to verify or support their results and conclusions, nor do they consider statistical probabilities. In the field, qualitative researchers continually make decisions that narrow their study. They may start out with broad questions and begin looking at an entire educational setting, but as their study proceeds they concentrate on smaller issues and create more specific analytical questions. Data collection is an additive process: New information is sought and collected on the basis of previous data, because the qualitative researchers are interpreting as they assemble additional information. One procedure used by qualitative researchers to support their interpretations is triangulation, a procedure for cross-validating information. Triangulation is collecting information from several different sources about the same event or behavior.

What criteria should be used to read and evaluate results sections?

Research consumers need to be able to answer these questions about research reports: What types of data analyses were used? What statistical analyses did the researchers use? Were the statistical analyses appropriate for the researchers' questions, purposes, or hypotheses and for the research design? What were the research results? Were the results of quantitative research statistically significant? Were the qualitative analyses appropriate and logical? Were the results of practical use and importance? Will the results be applicable to other educational settings, especially the one in which I teach?

ACTIVITY

Read the results sections in Extracts A and B. They are from the same studies as the method sections presented in the Activities portion of Chapter 7, pages 207–219. Using the questions and criteria discussed in this chapter, evaluate the studies. For each, list questions and concerns you may have about

a. The appropriateness of the statistical procedures to the researchers' purposes and designs
b. The indicated statistical significance levels
c. The practical significance of the research
d. If it is a qualitative study, the processes for organizing data, identifying patterns, and synthesizing key ideas as hypotheses and research questions

Extract A: Successful Mainstreaming in Elementary Science Classes

Purpose of the study: To identify variables meaningfully associated with mainstreaming success in science classes, across grade levels and across categories of disability.

RESULTS AND DISCUSSION

Our first consideration was: Were the three science classrooms successful in mainstreaming students with visual, physical, auditory, and learning disabilities? Our conclusion, based on all available evidence, was that these classrooms had been successful. Teachers (interviews, 2/5/3; 2/10/3) stated that mainstreaming efforts were successful and that they defined success in this context as meaningful participation, throughout the school year, in classroom science activities and classroom discussion and as completion of (possibly adapted) classroom assignments. Administrators generally concurred with these statements (e.g., 11/13/3).

Our analysis of field notes and videotapes suggested that all students did in fact participate meaningfully in science activities and class discussion and that they completed relevant classroom assignments. For example, the girl with a mild hearing impairment in Classroom A led the class in a data collection and recording activity (videotape record, 11/20/3); the student with a visual impairment in Classroom B took her regular turn in a "Simon Says" communication activity (videotape record 2/10/3), and children with physical and learning disabilities participated fully in an activity involving testing for the presence of chemical acids and bases in Classroom C (field notes, 11/16/3; 11/20/3). Teacher B reported that her student with a visual impairment completed assignments throughout the year, using the brailler and/or peer recorders, although sometimes additional prompting was needed to ensure task completion (interview, 2/10/3).

We did observe a negative instance of successful mainstreaming, using the same definition, in a school in a small village in northern Italy, in which inclusive practices were being undertaken as part of Italy's national education policy (Organisation for Economic Co-Operation and Development, 1985). In one such classroom, we observed one student with disabilities independently coloring a coloring book while all other students were participating in class discussion and relevant activities (videotape record, 3/15/4). Such practices would not be considered to be successful mainstreaming by the standards employed in this investigation, because the student was simply physically present in the classroom, without actively participating in relevant classroom activities.

Analysis of all data collected for this investigation revealed seven variables which appeared to be meaningfully associated with observed mainstreaming success, across categories of disability and grade level. These seven variables included administrative support; support from special education personnel; an accepting, positive classroom atmosphere; appropriate curriculum; effective general teaching skills; peer assistance; and disability-specific teaching skills. Each is now described in detail.

Variable 1: Administrative Support

All classrooms clearly benefited from administrative support for the mainstreaming effort, provided both at the district and the building level. Interviews with science education and special education district personnel confirmed that integration of students with disabilities had a high priority in the district and that an active, problem-solving approach was used to facilitate such mainstreaming efforts. In interviews, all building administrators also voiced strong support for mainstreaming efforts and were well informed about mainstreaming activities being undertaken in their buildings. Further, all administrators took apparent pride in mainstreaming successes at their schools. The principal of School C, for example, openly praised Teacher C for his work on developing the mainstreaming guidelines and his work with physically handicapped children (field notes, teacher meeting, School C, 11/12/3). Principals of all three schools could readily identify by name the teachers who were most facilitative in mainstreaming (interviews with principals, 2/18/1–2/20/1; 11/12/2; 11/13/2; 11/13/3). In turn, teachers in interviews in this investigation spoke positively of their administrative support and administrative arrangements and underlined the importance of this variable. Research literature has also underlined the importance of administrative support in promoting mainstreaming (e.g., Center, Ward, Parmenter, & Nash, 1985).

District and local administration had also provided excellent physical facilities for meeting the needs of students with disabilities. All buildings were single story and provided very easy access between classrooms. More specifically, School A included fire alarms with flashing lights and distributed FM systems when needed to all teachers interacting with students with hearing impairments. School B offered braillers, closed-circuit televisions, and adapted computer systems. School C had single-story construction and ramps whenever needed (e.g., to make portable buildings accessible), in addition to a wheelchair-accessible playground.

Variable 2: Support From Special Education Personnel

The direct assistance of special education teachers and staff was very much in evidence in all three classrooms. Teacher A communicated regularly with special education teachers about her students with hearing impairments and learning disabilities (Teacher A interview, 2/5/3); a licensed sign language interpreter provided a necessary communication link. Teacher B relied on the special education teacher and aide to provide braille curriculum materials and interlining (writing in between braille lines), braillers, and methods and materials for reducing stereotypic behaviors and other special problems (Teacher B interview, 2/10/3). Teacher C received regular assistance and support from special education teachers regarding the needs of his students with physical disabilities. In addition, a special education undergraduate student from a local university was employed to assist students with physical disabilities in the classroom (Teacher C interview, 2/5/3).

All teachers acknowledged the necessary assistance of special education staff in interviews, and observational records and interviews with principals supported the critical role played by special education personnel. These teachers and staff were seen to assume responsibility in several critical areas, including assisting students with disabilities to and from class, monitoring and adjusting class procedures and assignments, preparing regular education students for students with disabilities prior to mainstreaming, conferring with classroom teachers, recommending teaching strategies, and providing social support for their mainstreaming efforts. These roles follow very closely those identified in a major mainstreaming text (Wood, 1993, p. 51).

Overall, the ongoing support of special education personnel appeared to play a critical role in the continued presence of students with disabilities in regular classrooms. Teacher B, for example, commented,

[Special education teacher] is really great to work with. I know she's busy, but she's always got a moment for me when I need to talk to her about [name], or if I am having a problem, or if I am not sure of something. She is always there for me, which I think is very important. (Interview, 2/10/3)

Similarly, Teacher C commented,

[Special education teacher] came in and talked specifically about my children and my classroom. She was very supportive. She wanted to know exactly what we were doing and how we were doing it—how we were making it so this child could be mainstreamed into my classroom. I just felt like whatever I asked for they [special education staff] were going to see if it's feasible and work with me to get it that way. I feel like they trust me, too. (Interview, 2/5/3)

Investigations by others have also underlined the important role of special education personnel in supporting mainstreaming efforts. Glang, Gersten, and Morvant (in press), for example, described the critical role of special education personnel working in a consultant capacity in improving basic skills functioning of students with disabilities in the regular education classroom.

Variable 3: Accepting, Positive Classroom Atmosphere

All teachers not only accepted the idea of diverse learning needs in their classrooms but voiced opinions that all students benefited from the atmosphere created by such diversity. Teacher A remarked to her class (videotape record, 2/10/3),

We're all different in some ways. Even [name] wears glasses. And the twins, they were different, weren't they? You have to expect that kind of difference; it's sometimes fun and happy to work with someone who is a little bit different. You don't always want to work with the same kinds of people, do you? It makes life more exciting to work with different kinds of people.

Teacher B commented, "I think it is something I have set up. Everybody belongs here . . . I work very hard to make all my kids feel accepted" (interview, 2/10/3). Teacher C concurred, "I think if a teacher puts some effort into it, everything can be adapted so that [students with disabilities] can do it" (interview, 2/5/3).

Evidence for positive classroom atmosphere was also obtained in observations of all classrooms. All three teachers were seen to be very accepting of divergent answers and other unexpected responses from all students. This open environment was also perceived by students with and without disabilities as positive and accommodating, as expressed in student interviews. For example, when asked how it feels to come to science class, the boy with hearing impairments in Classroom A signed, "Fine, I like to come to Room #—" (field notes, 2/10/3).

One specific way in which this open classroom atmosphere was expressed across classrooms was in teacher responses to incorrect answers or statements. Each of the three teachers responded positively to both correct and incorrect statements, reinforcing correct answers and following incorrect statements with further questioning, and expressing approval for the student volunteering a response (field notes, all classes). For another example, all three teachers took a very personal view of the teaching process, knew all their students well, and interacted with them in a friendly, positive manner. Interviews with students suggested that students were aware of, and appreciative of, this personal approach to teaching.

In contrast, a negative or hostile atmosphere can hinder mainstreaming efforts. Centra (1990) described the accounts of several students with learning disabilities who had encountered a lack of acceptance in mainstream environments and the resulting negative effects. For instance, one female student reported,

> I was put in Mr. Sheldon's class to see if I could do the work. He found out that I was having a hard time. I was supposed to go to resource to take tests and all that. He would always say, "You can't go." You know, he was always sticking his nose up at me. He never said anything to me; he would just be failing me. . . . He was like—he wanted nothing to do with me whatsoever. It hurt really bad. I finally went down to guidance and told them I couldn't take it any more. (p. 151)

Variable 4: Appropriate Curriculum

Scruggs and Mastropieri (1992) argued that science curriculum that deemphasized textbook and vocabulary learning and emphasized active exploration of scientific phenomena would be likely to be associated with mainstreaming success. This hypothesis was partially supported by previous research—such as, that of Bay et al. (1992), MacDougall et al. (1981), Linn et al. (1979), Putnam et al. (1989), and Morocco et al. (1990)—all of which demonstrated to some extent the facilitative effects of activities-oriented curricula on mainstreaming outcomes. Further support is evidenced by an experiment by Scruggs, Mastropieri, Bakken, and Brigham (1993), who demonstrated that students with learning disabilities in self-contained classes learned and applied more science information from activities-oriented lessons than from textbook/lecture lessons. More recent research has supported the value of more inquiry-based teaching methods in promoting science learning of students with learning disabilities and mild mental retardation (Scruggs, Mastropieri, and Sullivan, 1994).

In the present investigation, students with disabilities were typically performing markedly below grade level in reading and writing skills. Further, many of them lacked experiences or prior knowledge relevant to the areas being studied. In this context, activities-oriented lessons allowed all students to experience, explore, and investigate new phenomena for themselves, without reliance on literacy skills. Finally, the nature of the curriculum allowed them to interact freely with peers, who could lend assistance or support when needed. All the teachers expressed appreciation for the facilitative effects of the science curriculum. For example, Teacher C remarked,

> Science curriculum is easily adaptable if you work with cooperative groups. . . . I am not a textbook person. I think it makes it easier if they have a hands-on experience; they can actually see what's going on. That's not just for handicapped children, but for every child. . . . Some of these kids that have come from [classrooms for students with physical disabilities] to a regular classroom have never seen things like this before [science materials]. If you explain it they have no concept, no idea, of what's going on. When you actually go ahead and show them, they're just as fascinated [as nondisabled students] and they can come up with their own ideas of "Why did it happen?" and "How did it happen?" and so forth. (Interview, 2/5/3)

Teacher A expressed a similar opinion:

> [Students are successful] because science is so hands-on, and that's exactly what our special needs children need. They need the hands-on activities to help them understand and learn. . . . There's no way that these kids can't learn something because they don't have to sit and read a book. They might not catch on to . . . one part of our activity that day, but there are so many activities. . . . I think each and every one of them learns something. (Interview, 2/5/3)

Teacher B also agreed, "The hands-on science is nice . . . the kids have a good time using it . . ." (interview, 2/10/3).

Interviews with classroom teachers revealed that all appreciated the value of concreteness and meaningfulness in teaching science to students with disabilities. These two variables have been considered extremely important in special education methods textbooks (e.g., Mastropieri & Scruggs, 1994a).

Teachers also remarked positively about the role of the district administration in making hands-on science activities easily available to teachers, thus ensuring that such activities are more likely to take place. Teacher B commented,

> Most of the [materials] are included in the kit, which makes it very nice, and very easy to use, and the kids . . . have a good time using it too, because we can do all the experiments and we don't have to worry about if we've got enough of this. They've experimented to make sure they have enough of everything. (2/10/3)

Variable 5: Effective General Teaching Skills

Teachers in all classrooms employed many, if not most, of the effective teaching skills described by—for example, Brophy and Good (1986) and Rosenshine and Stevens (1986). Mastropieri and Scruggs (1994a) summarized many of these as the *SCREAM* variables: structure, clarity, redundancy, enthusiasm, appropriate pace, and maximized student engagement. Structure and clarity were employed in shaping the purpose and focus of overall lessons, but they were not used to stifle or suppress student divergent thinking. Redundancy was applied as needed, typically in summarizing or reinforcing lesson content. Enthusiasm was expressed by all teachers toward the content of each lesson, in order to focus attention and model positive attitudes toward science. Finally, appropriate pace and maximized student engagement were employed to maintain a positive learning atmosphere (all field notes).

In addition, all teachers employed well-established and systematic behavior management programs, although the structure appeared more concrete in the lower grades and less so in the higher grades. For example, all elementary teachers posted class rules; the third grade teacher also posted possible rewards and penalties. Teacher A used a number of tangible rewards and prizes to keep her third grade class attentive and appropriately engaged; Teacher B used goldfish crackers to reinforce task engagement, but she discontinued this during the year and later relied more on direct appeals for cooperation:

> First, I would do it just on behavior. If they were working together well, then they would get the goldfish. And then I slowly progressed into looking at the outcomes . . . then I wean them off of it, because I want it to become more intrinsic, instead of extrinsic and always wanting that food reward. (Interview, 2/10/3)

Teacher C used more abstract cues, such as "E.O.M." (for "Eyes on me"), when he felt the need to refocus his fifth grade students' attention. He also used longer term rewards (e.g., class party, field notes, 11/19/3) for cooperation and task engagement. Nevertheless, all teachers effectively enlisted the cooperation and task engagement of their respective classes. Finally, all teachers were seen to use the positive, personal relations they had established with students to engage their support and cooperation with classroom activities.

These effective teaching procedures did not appear to serve as an inhibiting effect on students' efforts to construct scientific knowledge; on the contrary, these procedures appeared to create an atmosphere that was conducive to, and respectful for, scientific learning (see also Scruggs & Mastropieri, in press-a; Mastropieri, Scruggs & Bohs, 1994). In all classes, the overall structure of the lessons was maintained, while students were encouraged to express divergent thoughts regarding particular lessons. The open acceptance of different ideas appeared to be related to the open acceptance of diversity in the classrooms, described previously.

Overall, the structure and order of the classrooms, within the context of free inquiry, served to establish and maintain an overall environment that was safe, predictable, and facilitative of the needs of students with disabilities, who appeared to benefit greatly from these environments. Such environments also appeared to be facilitative of peers' appropriate interaction with students with disabilities. The present observations are further supported by one of the few teacher effectiveness studies to include mainstreamed handicapped students (Larrivee, 1985). Teacher behaviors said to be facilitative of mainstreaming included positive feedback, ensuring a positive success rate, using time efficiently, and reducing off-task behavior.

Variable 6: Peer Assistance

In all classrooms, nondisabled student peers were also employed to assist students with disabilities. For instance, Teacher A employed students to provide social and communicative support for the hearing impaired children; Teacher B employed student peers to assist the blind girl's movements through the classroom, and Teacher C employed peers to assist and encourage physically handicapped students with science activities. All teachers employed peer assistance for students with learning disabilities (field notes, videotape records, interviews with teachers).

Classroom observations and interviews suggested that nondisabled peers generally felt positively about lending assistance to students with disabilities and felt that they learned from the interactions. Questioned by Teacher A about working with "extra special" people in the room (field notes, 2/10/3), students replied, "helpful," "great," "I feel happy and fun and different," "I'm surprised at how I learned to make signs like that." One student reported that working with students with disabilities was "frustrating," a response which was also openly accepted by Teacher A.

In the present investigation, peer assistance, commonly described as an important mainstreaming strategy in the literature (e.g., Lewis & Doorlag, 1991; Wood, 1993), seemed clearly necessary. These three classrooms, while not excessive in class size, were nevertheless large enough to render it impossible for the teacher to provide all necessary individual assistance. The use of small groups for many of the classroom activities provided opportunities for classroom peers to provide necessary support for students with special needs. Typically, students enjoyed helping other students, as evidenced by interviews and observational records, and appeared to gain additional insight and focus on relevant tasks as a consequence of lending assistance. Teacher B, commented,

> The kids are real good with her . . . but I'm not sure if that's because they are just used to having blind kids on campus. [Name] has always been in their classroom, so she is just one of the persons there . . . They really try to help her. In fact, to the point they are sometimes too helpful, and I have to stop them. . . . They do too much for her. (Interview, 2/10/3)

Teacher C, referring to a student with physical disabilities, commented (interview, 2/5/3), "She's put with kids who'll work with her. They work directly with her all the time. . . ." Referring to students with learning disabilities, Teacher C commented,

> There's a lot of peer tutoring that goes on with those children. They have to be with kids who grab the concepts. [They can] explain it to them in terms they can understand. I usually put my LD children with somebody that is a higher achiever. They usually are successful that way. (Interview, 2/5/3)

These teacher observations have been supported to some extent by neo-Piagetian researchers (e.g., Perret-Clermont, 1980), who have suggested that higher functioning students can be helpful in leading lower functioning students in constructing scientific knowledge.

Interestingly, the idea of students helping other students as a normal class function appears to have been accepted by students with disabilities. One student with hearing impairments remarked, "[I'm] sort of happy [to come to the mainstream class] because I get to help other people out" (field notes, 2/10/3). This supports the results of a previous meta-analysis, which found that students with disabilities could serve as tutors and that they benefited socially and academically when they did so (Cook, Scruggs, Mastropieri, & Casto, 1985–1986).

Variable 7: Disability-Specific Teaching Skills

Although all three teachers lacked formal special education certification, all exhibited skill in adapting their instruction to the special needs of specific disability areas. These skills went beyond the general teacher effectiveness skills and were acquired through previous experience with students with similar disabilities, interaction with the special education teachers, and consultation with the guidelines for mainstreaming in science (Mastropieri & Scruggs, 1994b), which we provided to all participating teachers. As Teacher A commented, "When you work with these children, you learn that if you explain something to them and they don't understand it, you have to take another route" (interview, 2/10/3).

These diverse skills impacted directly on the disability areas of the students being mainstreamed. For example, Teacher A moved her students with hearing impairments to the front row; used a clear, direct speaking voice; did not stand in front of light sources; used pantomime when necessary; and carefully repeated important information. Periodically, she checked for understanding and comprehension (field notes and videotape records). Such procedures also appeared to be helpful for others in the class, including her nonnative English speaking students. When relevant, she openly discussed the special needs of her students. In a communication activity ("Telephone"), she allowed classroom peers to hold hands in a circle and send a tactual, rather than a vocal, message around the group (field notes, 11/12/3). At another time, she allowed classroom peers to use her own microphone to communicate with the hearing impaired girl. She then used this example to discuss diverse communication needs (field notes, 11/16/3). In a lesson on opposable thumbs of primates, she adapted an activity which involved taping students' thumbs, so that manual signing would not be inhibited (field notes, 11/9/3).

Similar to the activities of special education teachers in the Linn, Hadary, Rosenberg, and Haushalter (1979) study, Teacher A promoted the acquisition of language in her science teaching:

> Lots of visual—Any new words, we draw pictures of the new words, we put them on the board, the kids interact with those new words, act out new words, to learn vocabulary. With the kind of kids I work with, it's really the main focus, because they don't know vocabulary, they don't hear it like other kids hear it, and [vocabulary enhancement] reinforces [their learning]. (Interview, 2/10/3)

Such enhancement was also thought to be helpful for her students served by Chapter 1, nonnative English-speaking students, and students with learning disabilities—which suggests that even *disability-specific* interventions can have positive applications with other students. Teacher A also carefully monitored data recording tasks with her students with learning disabilities who appeared to exhibit literacy problems, blackboard copying problems, or other perceptual-motor problems (videotape record, 11/20/3).

Teacher B also adapted her instruction for the special needs of her visually impaired student, as shown throughout in field notes, videotape records, and interview data. She used careful, concrete descriptions, avoiding vague referents, and was careful to note when more visually oriented tasks were being employed:

> There are more concrete models I have to provide. . . . If she can feel it, she'll understand it better that way. . . . [If she doesn't understand the vocabulary] she says, "Let me see it," and that is her way of seeing it—holding it and touching it. (Interview, 2/10/3)

Teacher B trained classroom peers to offer an arm to the visually impaired girl, rather than push or pull her into position. Teacher B provided additional space and furniture for a brailler and braille reading materials. Teacher B also implemented a self-monitoring strategy to control stereotypic head movements:

> We just put a bean bag on top of her head. [Special education teacher] did it for walking back and forth to her classroom, because we have to improve her posture, because she has a gait to her walk and she has nothing physically wrong. It is just not being able to see what she is doing and get reinforcement by watching how other kids walk. . . . So I saw her walk into the classroom one day with it on, and she put it on her desk, and her head started moving around as soon as she took it off and set it down. And I said, "[name], put that bean bag back on your head." And the kids are real accepting—which really helps. And when we start something new like that—wearing a bean bag is not your ordinary, normal, everyday thing. And I could see [other students] weren't going to say anything, but . . . it is different from the rest. [So I said], "Boy, [name], this is really going to improve your posture. And, that is what models do to improve their posture." So the rest of the kids kind of think it is neat, too. (Interview, 2/10/3)

Teacher B also noted when the student's disability appeared to impact positively in classroom activities. For instance, in a "Simon Says" activity used as part of a communication unit, she told the class that the student appeared to have an advantage in not being distracted by irrelevant or contradictory visual cues (videotape record and field notes, 2/10/3).

Teacher C also used several specific techniques for accommodating students with physical disabilities. He consulted his class about their preferences for seating arrangements and, using their input, arranged his classroom in clusters of desks that left larger open spaces to facilitate the movement of wheelchairs. He used Velcro bindings to help one student keep his braces attached to his desk, yet easily disengage them manually when needed. He also arranged for this student to have a lower desk than other students and for the other two students with physical disabilities to have large desks to accommodate their wheelchairs (interview, Teacher C, 2/5/3). When engaged in lessons that involved a good deal of fine motor control—for example, mixing chemicals and solutions—peers provided necessary assistance (field notes, 11/16/3). When conducting a reaction time experiment, in which all students were to be tested individually, he adapted relevant apparatus to be engaged manually rather than with the feet for one student who was unable to use her feet for this purpose (videotape record, 2/14/3). When introducing reaction time, he used as an example his own reaction time in avoiding the path of an electrically driven wheelchair. When working in cooperative groups, students were periodically required to be the group "getter," which meant collecting/obtaining relevant materials from a centrally designated space. Students with physical disabilities also played the role of getter when it was their turn, and Teacher C signaled them when it was easiest to acquire group materials and provided assistance as needed (e.g., field notes, 2/14/3). Overall, disability-specific teaching skills appeared to play an essential role in the successful inclusion of students with disabilities in all three science classes.

In contrast, inappropriate adaptations can result in learning failures. Centra (1990), for example, cited a student's recollections of inappropriate learning adaptations: "When the rest of the class did their reading work, the teachers took me and a few others who had trouble reading and had us do puzzles in the corner. I didn't learn anything!" (p. 147). Although such an example seems extreme, Parmar and Cawley (1993) reported that many currently available science textbooks recommend "adaptations" that are not far removed from this example. (Scruggs & Mastropieri, 1994. Copyright 1994 by the American Education Research Association. Reprinted by permission of the publisher.)

Extract B: Helping Behaviors and Math Achievement Gain of Students Using Cooperative Learning

Purpose of the study: To examine (a) the effects of learner ability, gender, or grade level on students' performance; and (b) the nature of the cooperative group "help" on achievement gains.

RESULTS

The first part of the analysis was conducted to see if gender, grade, or ability was related to achievement gain. Gain scores were used in order to measure how much students learned, since pretest performance varied from 3% to 89%. A major factor in determining the method of analysis was the need to correct for the ceiling effect as much as possible. The use of the pretest as the covariate appears to have corrected for this fairly well, because the slope is close to -1 ($-.889$), so that there is almost a full unit of decrease in the gain score for every unit increase in the pretest score. The high-ability group began with higher pretest scores ($x = 67\%$), so their gain scores could not be as high as those of low-ability students, who began with lower pretest scores ($x = 22\%$). Therefore, a three-way factorial analysis of covariance (ANCOVA) (gender X grade X ability) was conducted with the pretest as the covariate. Achievement gain was the dependent variable.

The ANCOVA was conducted primarily to determine whether students in different grades (3, 4, 5), of different gender (male, female), or of varying ability levels (low, middle, high) showed different achievement gains. Table 1 shows that there were no

Table 1   ANCOVA Tests of Significance for Achievement Gains ($N = 101$)

Independent Variable	df	MS	F	Significance of F
Pretest (covariate)	1	15,624.74	139.72	.000
Ability	2	247.39	2.21	.116
Gender	1	41.06	.37	.546
Grade	2	26.25	.23	.791
Ability × gender	2	2.67	.02	.976
Ability × grade	4	18.76	.17	.954
Gender × grade	4	19.51	.17	.840
Ability × gender × grade	4	76.61	.69	.604
Within cells	80			

Table 2 Coefficients of Multiple Determination (N = 101)
Dependent Variable = Achievement Gain

Step and Variable Entered	R^2	R^2 Change	F Change	Significance of Change
1 Pretest	.7546	.7546	304.4672	.0000
2 Receives no help	.8485	.0939	60.7473	.0000
3 Gives explanation	.8874	.0388	33.4280	.0000
4 Receives explanation	.9138	.0264	29.3987	.0000
5 Receives other help	.9192	.0055	6.4138	.0000
6 Gives other help	.9231	.0039	4.7941	.0310

Table 3 Multiple Regression Table of Coefficients (N = 101)
Dependent Variable = Achievement Gain

Variable in Equation	B	SE B	Beta	T	Significance of T
Pretest	−.827	.034	−.907	−24.38	.0000
Receives no help	−7.999	1.382	−.184	−5.78	.0000
Gives explanation	1.194	.265	.184	4.51	.0000
Receives explanation	.795	.256	.125	3.11	.0025
Receives other help	.994	.388	.098	2.56	.0019
Gives other help	.749	.342	.092	2.19	.0310
Constant	70.172	2.175		32.26	.0000

statistically significant differences on any of these three independent variables, nor were there any statistically significant interactions.

The extreme significance of the pretest showed the importance of using it as a covariate. The assumption in using the pretest as the covariate in order to correct for the ceiling effect is that as the pretest score increased, the gain would decrease. Such was indeed the case. The slope was −.889 with a standard error of 0.75 and a T value of −11.82 ($p < .000$).

A stepwise multiple regression was next conducted, with the helping behaviors and the pretest as the nine independent variables and achievement gain as the dependent variable. This was done to determine the unique contribution of each behavior after accounting for the contribution of the pretest. As expected, the pretest accounted for the greatest amount of variance (75.5%). Following that, "receiving no help after requesting it" accounted for over 9.4% of the variance. The next largest unique contribution (3.9%) was made by the variable "gives explanation," followed by "receives explanation" (2.6%). These variables all made significant contributions to achievement gains ($p = .000$, $p = .000$, and $p = .003$, respectively), as did "receives other help" ($p = .02$) and "gives other help" ($p = .03$). The other three variables ("asks for help and receives it," "gives answer only," and "receives answer only") did not make significant contributions to the regression equation, although "asks for help" approaches significance ($p = .06$). Table 2 shows the results of this analysis in more detail.

Table 3 shows that "receiving no help after requesting it" related negatively to gains. The other helping behaviors in the equation related positively to the gain scores.

Table 4   ANOVA Tables of Significant Effects on Helping Behaviors (N = 101)

Variables	df	MS	F	Significance of F
Gives explanation:				
Ability	2	155.99	20.84	.000
Error	83	7.49		
Receives explanation:				
Ability	2	179.17	25.88	.000
Error	83	6.92		
Asks for help (and receives it):				
Ability	2	351.86	35.72	.000
Error	83	9.85		
Gives other help:				
Ability	2	70.66	13.73	.000
Error	83	5.15		
Receives other help:				
Ability	2	45.66	12.70	.000
Error	83	3.60		
Gives answer only:				
Ability	2	3.20	5.77	.005
Grade	2	2.52	4.54	.014
Error	83	.56		
Receives answer only:				
Ability	2	2.05	5.91	.004
Grade	2	1.16	3.34	.040
Ability × Grade	4	1.23	3.55	.010
Error	83	.35		
Receives no help (after requesting it):				
Ability	2	.85	3.71	.029
Error	83	.23		

Subsequently, a forced-entry multiple regression analysis was conducted to confirm the findings. The same variables emerged as significant contributors to achievement gains. The three nonsignificant contributors remained nonsignificant.

A final research question dealt with whether students of different ability levels, grades, or gender engaged in significantly different helping behaviors. A three-way factorial analysis of variance (all gender and ability levels) was conducted for this purpose. There were significant effects of ability on all behaviors. There were no significant gender effects on any of the behaviors, nor were there any statistically significant interactions between gender and ability regarding the behaviors. In fact, gender and gender interactions were far from approaching significance (p = .546, .976, .840, .604; see Table 1). There were two cases where grade was significant. These were for the behaviors of "gives answer only" and "receives answer only." Table 4 shows all the significant effects on all behaviors.

Since there was a violation of the assumption of homogeneity of variance underlying the ANOVA test for some of the behaviors ("receives explanation," "asks for help and receives it," "gives answer only," and "receives no help after requesting it"), a Krusal-Wallis test was also conducted to confirm the results of the factorial ANOVA. This is a nonparametric test that does not require that assumption of homoscedasticity. Table 5 shows the results of the Kruskal-Wallis test. Due to the robustness of the factorial ANOVAs it was assumed that those effects that were highly nonsignificant in the

Table 5   Kruskal-Wallis Test Showing Significant Effects of Ability and Grade on Helping Behaviors (*N* = 101)

Helping Behaviors	Chi-Squares Corrected for Ties	Significance Level
Receives explanation—Ability	45.901	.0000
Asks for help (and receives it)—Ability	52.085	.0000
Gives answer only:		
Ability	6.753	.0342
Grade	6.397	.0408
Receives no help (after requesting it)—Ability levels	9.032	.0109

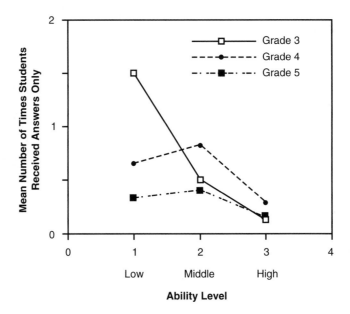

Figure 1

Interaction between grade and ability on helping behavior "receives answer only"

ANOVA would remain nonsignificant in the nonparametric test since nonparametric tests are less powerful. Table 5 shows the chi-square values and significance levels for these behaviors.

High-ability students gave far more explanations, more "other help," and more answers than low-ability students, with middle-ability students engaging in these behaviors at a frequency between the other two groups. Correspondingly, low-ability students received the most explanations, other help, and answers and also asked for help most often.

Figure 1 shows the interaction effect of ability and grade level on the behavior "receives answer only." This was the only statistically significant interaction found in the analysis. Low-ability third graders received more answers than low-ability fourth or fifth graders, or than any other low-, middle-, or high-ability students in any grades.

Table 6   Mean (and Standard Deviation) of Occurrences of Helping Behaviors That Showed Significant Effects by Ability and Grade (N = 101)

Behavior	Ability			
	Low	Medium	High	Total
Gives explanation	.720 (.936)	3.333 (2.917)	5.920 (3.108)	3.327 (3.188)
Gives other help	1.120 (1.013)	2.588 (2.539)	4.520 (2.452)	2.703 (2.524)
Receives explanation	5.800 (3.240)	4.196 (2.926)	.640 (.638)	3.713 (3.235)
Receives other help	3.400 (2.381)	2.177 (1.862)	.720 (.678)	2.118 (2.026)
Asks for help	8.040 (3.835)	6.216 (3.460)	.920 (.954)	5.356 (4.103)
Gives answer only:	.320 (.476)	.490 (.704)	1.000 (1.118)	.574 (.817)
Grade 3	.333 (.500)	.667 (.840)	1.333 (1.414)	
Grade 4	.250 (.463)	.556 (.705)	1.375 (.916)	
Grade 5	.375 (.518)	.200 (.414)	.250 (.463)	
Receives answer only:	.800 (.764)	.529 (.644)	.160 (.374)	.505 (.658)
Grade 3	1.444 (.727)	.500 (.618)	.111 (.333)	
Grade 4	.625 (.518)	.667 (.767)	.250 (.463)	
Grade 5	.250 (.463)	.400 (.507)	.125 (.354)	
Receives no help after requesting it	.400 (.646)	.216 (.461)	.000 (.000)	.208 (.476)

Table 6 presents the means and standard deviations for the number of occurrences of helping behaviors on which ability and/or grade had significant effects. The frequencies of each behavior refer to the total observational period. (Nattiv, 1994. Copyright © 1994 by The University of Chicago Press.)

FEEDBACK

Extract A: Successful Mainstreaming in Elementary Science Classes. In qualitative observational studies, researchers should identify the categories for organizing their data. Although the researchers do not identify the initial categories for sorting their data, they clearly identify the seven trends that seem to characterize successful mainstreaming. Each trend, or variable, is supported by descriptive examples. The main question research consumers need to consider is: How much of the success that was seen is due to the researchers' close involvement with establishing the curriculum and professional development of the teachers? Surely, they were more than participant observers. It is to the researchers' credit that they clearly detail their background (see Chapter 7, pp. 208–212), and it seems it was their intent to let the research consumer judge the validity and reliability of their data collection and analysis. Overall, the researchers have taken care to document their ideas and to relate them to other research results.

Extract B: Helping Behaviors and Math Achievement Gain of Students Using Cooperative Learning. The researcher used several statistical procedures to analyze the data—analysis of covariance (ANCOVA) and multiple regression analysis. The ANCOVA was used instead of analysis of variance (ANOVA) because of differences in the pretest scores of the three ability groups. Without that correction, it would not be possible to determine whether any changes in the subjects' behavior were due to the treatments or their ability. The results indicate that the subjects' mathematics achievement on posttests was significantly influenced by the pretest, their ability, and whether they received no help, gave explanations, received explanation, or received help from others. The results can be questioned for practical significance because of the strong influence of the pretest on the subjects' final mathematics achievement. It may be that the treatments had no real effect, but the taking of the pretest influences the subjects as to what to expect on the posttest.

CHAPTER 9

Reading and Evaluating Discussion Sections

FOCUS QUESTIONS

1. What information should research consumers get from discussion sections of research reports?
2. What criteria should be used to evaluate discussion sections?
3. What is the plan for reading discussion sections?

In Chapter 3, a plan for reading research reports is set out. The plan calls for the reading of the discussion section as part of the second stage of the plan. The demonstrations of the plan show that discussion sections usually contain several types of information: (a) a restatement of the researchers' purposes (or research questions or hypotheses), (b) a summary of the results, (c) a discussion or interpretation of those results, and (d) recommendations based on those results. By reading the discussion section together with the abstract, research consumers have an overview of the research project.

From reading discussion sections, research consumers should be able to answer:

What were the researchers' purposes for the study?

What were the researchers' major results?

How did the researchers interpret their results?

What recommendations did the researchers make for applying the results to instructional situations or for future research projects?

Are the researchers' issues and concerns relevant to me as a professional or to my teaching situation?

Discussion sections should be evaluated using the following questions, which are from Figure 3.1, page 117:

279

Evaluating Discussion Sections

Discussion (Conclusions, Recommendations). Are conclusions related to answering the research question(s), and are they appropriate to the results? Is the report free from inappropriate generalizations and implications? If inappropriate, are suggestions for additional research provided?

UNDERSTANDING AND EVALUATING DISCUSSION SECTIONS

Some researchers label the discussion sections as conclusions, summary, or implications, and they may subdivide the section to highlight specific information. As a research consumer, you will have determined the specific format of research producers' discussion sections during the first, or preview, phase of the reading plan.

A common procedure for research producers is to begin discussion sections with a statement of the research purpose and then to follow that with a statement of their results and, in the case of quantitative studies, whether the results were statistically significant. In the remainder of the section, they usually explain (a) whether the results answered their research questions, (b) how their results relate to related literature presented in the introduction, and (c) what implications the results have for practitioners and other researchers.

The following section, called "Conclusions" by the researchers, has all the elements of a discussion section in a quantitative research report.

Purpose of the study: To investigate a broad-based program to foster children's social development that includes supportive teacher-student relationships and opportunities for students to interact and collaborate in cooperative groups.

CONCLUSIONS

[Purpose]

[General results]

[Specific results]

The goal of the present project was to devise, implement, and assess the effectiveness of a comprehensive school-based program designed to enhance children's prosocial orientations. In this paper we have demonstrated, through quasi-experimental analyses, that the program was implemented by classroom teachers and that it had substantial positive effects on children's interpersonal behavior in the classroom (without impeding their achievement).

Children in the first-cohort classrooms participating in the program over 5 years of program implementation were observed to be more supportive, friendly, and helpful, and to display more spontaneous prosocial behavior toward one another than children in a group of comparison classrooms. A replication with a second cohort, in kindergarten and grade 1, produced similar results. Outcomes such as these have not often been investigated in classroom observational studies, despite a growing concern with problems relating to students' interpersonal behavior in classrooms and recent calls for schools to renew their emphasis on preparing students for responsible roles in our democratic society (e.g., Bastian, 1985; Honig, 1985). If social development is a legitimate goal of elementary education, then research identifying factors that can serve to promote it is essential. The project described in this paper is one such effort.

When the program developed in this project is being fully implemented, students exercise considerable autonomy and self control: they help make decisions about their classrooms, participate in rule-development and revision, discuss and help solve classroom problems, and in general develop a shared sense of membership in, and responsibility for, their community. It is our expectation, as Dewey (1916) suggested long ago and others have more recently (e.g., Wood, 1986), that engaged participation in activities such as they should help to prepare students for adult democratic responsibilities.

[Relation to
other research]
The approach to classroom organization and activity embodied in this program, particularly its attempt to minimize the use of extrinsic incentives, represents a fairly radical departure from some of the classroom management systems currently in vogue (e.g., Canter's, 1976, "assertive discipline"). It is however, quite consistent with the ideas and findings of much recent research concerning the conditions that enhance intrinsic motivation. Several researchers (see Lepper, 1983) have investigated the deleterious effect on intrinsic motivation of the use of external incentives (rewards in particular), often from an attributional perspective. Ryan, Connell, and Deci (1985), in a discussion of classroom factors that influence the development of students' self-regulation and intrinsic motivation for learning, emphasize teachers' provision of autonomy and decision-making opportunities, and the minimization of external control "in a context of adequate structure and guidance" (p. 44). The present findings suggest that these factors may also play a role in enhancing students' social orientations and behavior.

[Significance]
The two general aspects of classroom life that have been found to be related to children's social development in prior research—establishment of supportive teacher-student relationships and provision of opportunities for collaborative interstudent interaction—are incorporated in our Positive Discipline and Cooperative Activities program components, respectively. These aspects have previously been investigated separately. Our approach has been to combine these, along with other consistent elements (providing experiences in helping and understanding others; exposure to and discussion of examples of prosocial behavior, motives and attitudes) in to a general, pervasive, and coherent whole. We believe that the data reported in this paper indicate that the total program has had clear and strong effects on children's classroom behavior. We do not know whether these results could have been obtained with less than the total program (for example, with Developmental Discipline alone, or Developmental Discipline combined with Cooperative Activities). Because these elements are designed to be mutually supportive and interrelated (and are in fact intercorrelated), it is somewhat arbitrary and perhaps somewhat misleading to describe them as separate "components." We do intend, however, to conduct a series of natural variation analyses to try to assess the relative influence on student social behavior of various combinations of teacher behavior and classroom activity measures.

[Implications]
It is our hope and expectation that through participating in an environment in which certain central values of the society are both discussed and exemplified (e.g., mutual concern and respect, responsibility, helpfulness), such values and behaviors consistent with them will become more deeply ingrained in the children. While the present data, indicating substantial effects on students' behavior in the classroom, reflect only some surface aspects of the kinds of change we hope to engender, including a long-range commitment to democratic values, they do suggest that such changes may result from participating in this program. In other papers, we will be describing effects outside the classroom and on other areas of children's functioning. (Solomon, Watson, Delucchi, Schaps, & Battistich, 1988, pp. 545–546. Copyright 1988 by the American Educational Research Association. Reprinted by permission of the publisher.)

Research consumers need to evaluate research producers' interpretations of results carefully for unwarranted or over-generalized conclusions. They need to examine four aspects of research producers' conclusions: (a) predicted results (in the case of quantitative research), (b) unpredicted results, (c) statistical and practical significance, and (d) further research or replications of the studies.

Researchers should explain whether results logically answer their research purposes or questions. Also, they need to indicate whether results are consistent with results of other researchers. As stated in Chapter 4, background sections provide three major kinds of information: problem areas and their educational importance, related literature, and research purposes. Research consumers need to compare research producers' conclusions about anticipated or predicted results with the information provided in background sections. Also, research consumers need to determine whether research producers have drawn appropriate conclusions from the research designs and statistical procedures they used. For example, quantitative research producers should not conclude causality from descriptive or comparative research, and they should not generalize beyond the target population in any category of research.

Since comparative studies provide information about the existence of relationships (similarities and differences), it is not appropriate for research producers and consumers to infer a causal effect among variables. Most research producers avoid making this error, as did the researchers of a spelling program who found the existence of strong relationships but appropriately indicated that "the results support the idea of a common conceptual base for varying aspects of word knowledge" (Zutell & Rasinski, 1986, p. 111). This is not a statement of causation but of coexistence.

Nevertheless, the error of inferring causality from relationship studies is common. In the following passage, taken from a newspaper article about educational television and young children, note the italicized portions. Those statements imply causation, an inappropriate conclusion based on correlation data.

In the 25 years since "Sesame Street" was created, assorted studies have shown that it helps preschool children learn about numbers and the alphabet, and thus helps prepare them for school.

A new study, being released today, takes that conclusion two steps further. It found that preschoolers in low-income areas around Kansas City who had watched educational television programming, including "Sesame Street," not only were better prepared for school but actually performed better on verbal and math tests as late as age 7 than would have been expected otherwise.

Conversely, it found that preschoolers who had watched primarily adult programming and entertainment cartoons performed worse on those later tests than would have been expected.

"This study shows that terrific television causes kids to be more receptive to learning, more receptive to reading, more receptive in school," said Peggy Charren, founder of the now-inactive advocacy group Action for Children's Television and now a visiting scholar at Harvard University's School of Education, who has read the new study.

The study was done by a research team at the Center for Research on the Influences of Television on Children at the University of Kansas. It was unusual in both length and depth.

In all, 250 children were followed for three years, some from age 2 to 5, others from age 4 to 7. In that period, each child was assessed four times in the researchers' office and four times in the child's home. Each assessment session lasted two hours and included the child's parents. Between visits, the parents were interviewed by telephone every two months, and kept a diary of the child's activities.

The families were mostly low-income, with some moderate-income. Statistical controls were applied to family income, parents' education, preschool attendance, the child's first language, the home environment and other factors that could affect test scores and school readiness measurements.

The study also found that among these children, those who had watched children's educational programs in general and "Sesame Street" in particular spent more time reading than those who had watched more adult programming or noneducational cartoons.

"Most other studies have looked at television generally in its effect on kids and their intellectual development, but not at specific different types of television," said Dr. Aletha C. Huston, who performed the study with her husband, Dr. John C. Wright. Both are professors of human development at Kansas.

Dr. Huston also said she believed that the study was *the first to assess television's effect on children* as young as 2, "at least with this extensive a form of measurement." (Mifflin, 1995)

The researchers' statements seem inappropriate because factors other than educational television might have resulted in the children knowing "numbers and the alphabet" and spending "more time reading." The cause of watching educational television, learning about numbers and letters, and reading books might be an undisclosed factor reflecting special aspects in the children's upbringing—that is, certain family dynamics that lead to these school-linked behaviors.

In the next example, taken from a newspaper article about the relationship between television viewing and school achievement, a more appropriate statement is made. (It has been italicized for emphasis.)

A team of social scientists in California is not prepared to say that watching "B. J. and the Bear" made students do poorly in school, but the researchers do maintain that children who watched the show regularly were the students most likely to have low scores on standard achievement tests. The next most likely shows to have been viewed by low-achieving students were "The Incredible Hulk" and "Dance Fever."

New results such as these are providing fresh insight into the possible links between television viewing and classroom achievement. Several such studies from around the country were discussed publicly for the first time last week at the annual meeting of the American Educational Research Association in New York City.

It is widely believed that children who spend more time watching the popular programs on commercial television tend to be lower achievers in school, but researchers have yet to show that television causes that poor performance. (Maeroff, 1982)

Researchers sometimes need to explain results that they did not expect. For example, one research team found that one of their treatments produced an unusual outcome. The following discussion section shows how those researchers put forth a possible reason for the unexpected finding.

Purpose of the study: To examine the effects on students' comprehension of voiced versions (i.e., prose that invites reading) of more and less coherent texts.

DISCUSSION

In this study, students were presented with one of four versions of a passage, either its original form taken directly from a textbook, a version of the textbook passage with features of voice added, a more coherent version of the original textbook passage, or a version that exhibited both coherence and voice. Given that the present study worked with four versions of one base text, the study should be viewed as an initial exploration of whether text that appears to be more engaging can provide advantage for readers. There has been a long-standing assumption that more lively text language will lead to better reader outcomes, but heretofore there was no empirical evidence to back up those intuitions. Thus we felt that it was important to delve into the area of the value of "vivid language," "liveliness," and other such qualities of text that are attributed to tradebooks and tend to be lacking in textbooks. Given the findings, further research is now warranted for fleshing out the effects of these more elusive text qualities.

The results showed the strongest advantage for the passage that exhibited both coherence and voice, with the coherent passage showing advantage over the other two in performance on questions, and over the original textbook version in recall. These results pertained to students' responses on recall and questions immediately after reading. The same results were obtained on the questions after a week's delay, yet differences in recall after delay did not reach significance.

As mentioned earlier, the study unfortunately provided for a somewhat flawed test of how much text content was retained after delay. A problem apparently arose because some of the students in the study were given a tradebook to read that was about the Revolutionary War period. The book is a lively and interestingly written one, and it seemed to have left an impression on at lest some of the students. We saw this effect, particularly in recalls of students who read the textbook and voiced textbook versions, because some of their recalls included information that was accurate about the period, but had not been contained in the passages they read for this study. Additionally, some of the students in both textbook conditions improved in the quality of recall after a week's delay.

The effect of the tradebook was not noticed in the coherent and voiced coherent conditions, probably for two reasons. First, fewer students in these conditions had read the tradebook (8 vs. 12). But more importantly, it seems that these students were less in a position to benefit from additional information or another exposure to engaging text, since they had already developed higher quality representations of the events portrayed in the texts. Thus the same potential for enhancing comprehension did not exist for readers of the coherent passages as for readers of the textbook passages.

Interestingly, exposure to the tradebook did not have the same effect on question performance. Perhaps that is because, although students who had read the tradebook account were able to add some of that information to their retelling, they seemed unable to enhance their responses to the questions that required them to understand the role of certain information within the chain of events (i.e., the three issue questions). Thus, although we cannot be as definitive as we would like about the retention effects from a coherent text with features of voice, there is a suggestion that positive potential exists for lasting effects. This suggestion is based on the results of the question measure and the trend in the recall data.

The present study focused on the understanding that students can get from working independently with texts that exhibit various characteristics. Yet when texts are used in classrooms, instructional and social factors mediate the text interaction. For example, teachers may provide background, add explanations, or question students about their understanding. Additionally, other students may question or comment on the text and provide responses to teacher questions. The ways in which these influences may interact with text features is an issue for further study. The results of this study do not speak directly to that issue, but consideration of the pattern of results may provide some basis for pursuing the interaction of classroom factors with text characteristics.

The overall pattern of results in this study indicates that comprehension is promoted when text is written to exhibit some of the features of oral language, to communicate the immediacy of events and emotional reactions of agents, and to vitalize relationships among agents. The pattern of results adds to our understanding of the relationship between interesting or engaging features of text and comprehension. Previous research pointed out problems in adding isolated pieces of engaging information to text, finding that such information was well remembered, but to the detriment of central information in a text (Britton et al., 1989; Duffy et al., 1989; Garner et al., 1989; Graves et al., 1991; Hidi & Baird, 1988; Wade & Adams, 1990). The present study indicates that, when engaging features are used to enhance central information, comprehension of that central material can be improved.

The present findings also extend caveats about the role of interesting or engaging text features, however. That is, the results of this study suggest that such features may not have effect when added to a text that lacks coherence. The voiced version of the textbook passage did not enhance comprehension. This finding highlights our notion that the role of voice is to engage students in a text. Potential for engagement, however, is not productive if the content of the text is not accessible. In the case of the textbook versions, the information provided seems just too far beyond the reach for most young students to make sense of it on their own, even when the language of the text promotes engagement.

Potential for increasing comprehension through voice may be better realized under certain text circumstances. One such circumstance involves situations that are pivotal to making sense of a text. That is, students who received the voiced coherent passage were better able to recall the concepts of representation and the colonists' protests, which were central to the conflict between Britain and the colonies. On the other hand, voice features did not improve recall of Britain's reaction of removing the taxes. The role of this information was made less crucial to comprehension of the passage because another, simpler and more general, statement of resolution existed—that "things quieted down." Students were apparently able to substitute this information to satisfy the need for closure to the events, rather than using the more specified information about Britain's action. Thus students seemed to fill in the needed information in the most accessible way.

Another circumstance that may optimize the potential for the effects of voice is situations that can portray emotion and active response. These qualities characterized the segments of text that showed a difference in recall between the coherent and voiced coherent passages. However, the better remembered concepts—representation and protest—were also central to the situation portrayed in the text, so it cannot be determined whether the enhancement was due to the voicing of those specific concepts or to a general effect of voicing that interacted with their role in the text.

A more general consideration of the circumstances under which features of voice enhance understanding is the extent to which the concept of voicing texts can be implemented. One direction to explore is whether voicing is appropriate for text content other than history. Our results allow us to speculate that voicing may be more widely applicable. Consider the three voicing themes used here—orality, activity, and connectivity. Certainly, features of oral language can be brought to bear on text presentations of a wide range of phenomena and need not be restricted to sequences of human action. The theme of activity was used here in relation to human events in a causal sequence. Yet, one component of activity, the notion of immediacy of events, could apply to sequences of events in the natural world as well. Connectivity pertains to relationships both among text agents and between the text and the reader. Although the first type may be limited for some content, features of text that provide for relationship between reader and text, such as directly addressing the reader, have wide applicability.

The essential concept is that, for understanding to be developed from encounters with text, readers need to engage with the text. Engagement should be possible for an almost endless assortment of text types and topics. The key is to discover elements through which engagement can be promoted. Creating texts so that they exhibit features of voice is certainly one of those elements, and the extent of its applicability is an interesting question for further study.

In the meantime, how can insights about engaging texts be applied to classroom instruction? A ready resource of engaging material exists in tradebooks. Tradebooks on historical topics can bring the past alive for young readers, and may help to reinforce the motivations and principles that drove people to action.

In focusing on bringing engagement to encounters with text, however, one must not lose sight of other text aspects that may need to be present to promote understanding. Our results suggest that engaging features can contribute to understanding when such features coincide with a coherent presentation of ideas. Engaging text might invite a reader's participation, focus attention within a text, and place emphasis on certain ideas. But once a reader's engagement and attention are activated, the text ideas that are attended to must have adequate connection and explanation to allow the building of meaning. (Beck, McKeown, & Worthy, 1995, pp. 232–234)

For some reason, quantitative research reports published in journals all seem to have statistically significant results. Less often published are studies with non-significant results. Reports of this kind sometimes occur when one set of researchers attempts to show that particular treatments do not produce results that other researchers have previously produced. It is important that professionals examine each others' work and that researchers be able to replicate their work. In fact, many journals will ask for "responses" from researchers when publishing studies that seem to refute their position. Research consumers need to examine both sets of reports for biases, and they need to determine the practical significance of all research. For example, the July/August/September 1994 issue of *Reading Research Quarterly* contains an exchange of ideas:

McCarthy, S. J. Authors, text, and talk: The internalization of dialogue from social interaction during writing.

Bloome, D. Response to McCarthy: On the nature of language in classroom literacy research.

Rowe, D. W. Response to McCarthy: The limitations of eclecticism in research.

McCarthy, S. J. Response to Bloome: Violence, risk, and the indeterminacy of language.

McCarthy, S. J. Response to Rowe: Aligning methods to assumptions.

Consumers need to be concerned with the applicability of researchers' results to their own educational situation: "Are the results generalizable to my local educational setting and can the treatment, when there is one, be implemented with practical considerations given to time, effort, money, and personnel?"

Researchers often cite questions that their research has left unanswered. These questions can, and often do, become the research purposes in future studies by the researchers themselves or by other researchers. The questions might be about research design, research procedures, subject selection, instrumentation, data analysis, or research results. Research consumers need to examine the logic of these recommendations.

ACTIVITY

Read the following discussion sections (and a portion of the purpose section for Extract B). Using the questions and criteria discussed in this chapter, evaluate the discussion section. Using the limited information available to you, list questions and concerns you may have about:

a. the applicability of the results to your teaching situation

b. the researchers' purposes for the study

c. major results

d. recommendations for applying the results to instructional situations and future research projects

Extract A: Promoting Helping Behavior in Cooperative Small Groups in Middle School Mathematics.

DISCUSSION

Summary of Results

(1) This study compared the effects on verbal interaction and achievement of two instructional programs: cooperative learning with instruction and practice in basic communication skills and helping skills (giving and receiving elaboration; the experimental condition) and cooperative learning with instruction and practice in basic communication skills only (the comparison condition). Minority students were more likely to give and receive elaborated help, and were less likely to receive the answer without elaboration, in the experimental condition than in the comparison condition. Their posttest achievement was also higher in the experimental condition than in the comparison condition. The differences between instructional conditions in verbal interaction and achievement were larger for one teacher than for the other teacher. No significant differences between conditions, in verbal interaction or achievement, appeared for white students.

Interpretation and Unanswered Questions

(2) These results show that training and practice in communication skills and prosocial behavior, important as these activities are for preparing students for group work, will not by themselves encourage students to engage in the kinds of verbal interaction that have been shown to relate to achievement: giving elaborated responses rather than only the answer when other students need help. To encourage giving and receiving elaborated responses, training and practice activities should focus specifically on these desired behaviors.

(3)   Although the experimental cooperative learning program developed here promoted beneficial verbal interaction and higher achievement than the comparison program, at least among a subgroup of students, several questions about the results remain. First, why did differences between instructional conditions in verbal interaction emerge among Latino and African-American students but not among white students? White students were equally active, in terms of giving and receiving help, in both conditions. Minority students in the experimental condition were also active in giving and receiving help. Minority students in the comparison condition, however, were less active, at least in terms of giving elaboration and answers, and receiving elaboration when they

requested help. The experimental program, then, seemed to have increased the participation rates of Latino and African-American students.

(4)   Previous research has shown that white students tend to be more active and influential than minority students in multiracial groups in the classroom, whereas minority students tend to be less assertive, talk less, and give fewer suggestions and less information than white students (Cohen, 1982; Cohen, Lotan, & Catanzarite, 1990). Perhaps the instruction on helping behaviors in the experimental condition in the present study gave Latino and African-American students tools to use to overcome tendencies toward reticence in heterogeneous groups.

(5)   Second, why were differences between instructional conditions in verbal interaction larger for one teacher than for the other? As shown earlier, students' elaborations were more frequent and more detailed in the former teacher's classes than in the latter teacher's classes, and the difference was accentuated in the experimental condition. This result was ascribed in part to the different questioning styles of the teachers during whole-class discussion—posing general questions for students to answer versus asking for specific numerical procedures and answers—and to students in the experimental condition being especially sensitive to their teacher's instructional styles because of the focus on helping behavior in preparation for group work in this condition. These results show the potentially strong effects that teacher modeling can have on ensuing student behavior in small groups (see also Yackel, Cobb, & Wood, 1991; Palincsar, Stevens, & Gavelek, 1989).

(6)   Third, why did the experimental program have significant effects on the more complex achievement outcomes (comparing the magnitudes of fractions, solving word problems with fractions, estimating fractional areas of diagrams) but not on numerical exercises based only on procedures (adding and subtracting fractions, reducing fractions, mixed numbers)? Because previous research on cooperative learning has demonstrated positive effects on higher and lower level reasoning skills (Johnson & Johnson, 1990; Slavin, 1990), we expected similar effects for all achievement measures. Perhaps the heavy emphasis on numerical procedures in the curriculum, as well as students' previous experiences and preconceptions of their skills on these procedures (the audiotapes were sprinkled with comments such as "I hate these" and "I'm no good at these"), made them especially resistant to influences of student interaction. Students had less experience with comparing fractions, solving word problems with fractions, and estimating fractional areas of diagrams, so feedback from other students could have a greater impact on their learning. A question to be explored further, then, is whether the kind of intervention program developed here may have stronger effects for novel material than for familiar material.

Future Research

(7)   When exploring the effects of instructional programs on Latino and African-American students, future studies should use samples large enough to distinguish between different ethnic groups. Although the behavior and achievement of Latino and African-American students in the present study were similar, the number of cases in each group was too small to analyze in detail. Also, recent research suggests that these ethnic groups may sometimes differ on relevant variables, such as cooperative-competitive social orientation (Widaman & Kagan, 1987).

(8)   If future research confirms that certain types of instruction designed to teach students how to work effectively in small groups are more successful for some groups of students than for others, future studies should carefully examine the sociocultural factors that may explain the differences. The effectiveness of an instructional program may be related in part, for example, to students' entering communication skills, their

willingness to communicate with and help others, and their tendencies toward reticence or assertiveness in heterogeneous groups.

(9)   Although the instructional conditions used in the present study produced differences in students' verbal interaction and achievement, the magnitude of the differences was modest. Future studies could modify training in helping behavior to produce stronger effects on verbal interaction and learning. Although students gave more elaboration in response to students' need for help, the elaboration was not always very effective for learning. Some elaboration lacked detail or concentrated on numerical procedures rather than justifying the reasons for the procedures. But even highly elaborated responses were not always effective for learning. One reason may be that students were rarely given an opportunity to apply the elaboration to solve problems for themselves: Without that opportunity, they may not realize that they still do not understand how to solve the problem and need further help (Nelson-Le Gall, 1981; Vedder, 1985). Two recent studies showed that applying explanations to the work at hand was more strongly related to learning than was listening to the explanations without using them to try to solve problems (Webb, 1992; Webb, Troper, & Fall, 1992). Students could be trained to pose follow-up problems for other students to solve independently as a test of understanding and an opportunity to diagnose misconceptions.

(10)   The effectiveness of elaboration might be increased still further by training students to build on what other students already know and understand, to use multiple symbolic representations in their explanations (e.g., figures and pictures in addition to numbers), and to generate specific examples (see Shavelson, Webb, Stasz, McArthur, 1988).

(11)   Although there were differences between conditions in the frequency of elaboration, elaboration occurred rather infrequently. Specific techniques could be incorporated into the instructional program to encourage students to give more elaboration. For example, students could be trained to use question stems like those developed by King (1992) to ask each other questions to generate high-level discussion of mathematical problems (e.g., *Why* is the answer this, *how* do you get that? *What* would happen if you changed this? *How* is this related to that?). Or students could be required to give elaboration as in teaching the rest of the group a new type of problem (as in Jigsaw: Aronson, Blaney, Stephan, Sikes, & Snapp, 1978), alternating teaching problems to one another (Lambiotte et al., 1987), or assuming the role of elaborator as part of scripted cooperation (Hythecker, Dansereau, & Rocklin, 1988) or nonscripted cooperation (Johnson & Johnson, 1987). Students could also be required to check each other's understanding and encourage their participation using analogous roles and/or scripts (such as taking turns playing the coach in checking each others' understanding in mathematics, Kagan, 1992). This may help draw into group interaction students who do not know what questions to ask, those who may not even realize that they do not understand, and those who are not engaged in the task.

(12)   To further shape group interaction, the role of the teacher could also be changed. In this study, except when carrying out activities to prepare students for group work, the teacher assumed a monitoring role, with minimal intervention. In contrast, Yackel et al. (1991) developed a more active role for the teacher to help students construct norms for small-group behavior. In Yackel et al.'s project, the teacher used positive and negative situations that she observed during group work, as well as hypothetical scenarios, to initiate discussions with the entire class about their general obligations in group work and their responsibilities in specific cases (e.g., sharing, cooperating, achieving consensus about the answer, justifying one's own work, understanding other students' procedures). It should also be possible to train teachers to observe group work for instances of high- and low-quality elaboration and use them as the basis of whole-class discussions of appropriate helping behavior. These ongoing discussions would help clarify

what constitutes highly elaborated responses, as well as remind students of the importance of giving elaborated responses.

(13)   The present study used material from a traditional mathematics curriculum and textbook with a heavy emphasis on mathematical procedures. More recently, a higher priority is being placed on problem-solving and higher order thinking skills in mathematics instruction (e.g., California State Department of Education, 1985, 1987; Conference Board of the Mathematical Sciences, 1983; National Council of Teachers of Mathematics, 1980, 1989), and in other fields. With a richer curriculum that includes problems that focus on conceptual understanding, the instructional program developed here may have even stronger effects on verbal interaction and learning outcomes because of greater opportunities for students to reveal and discuss their different perceptions about mathematics. This possibility needs to be tested.

(14)   Finally, future studies should explore alternative designs. The present study compared two cooperative learning programs: a longer one with instruction in both communication skills and helping skills versus a shorter one with only instruction in communication skills. To separate the effects of length of the intervention and nature of instruction, future studies should manipulate these variables independently. For example, programs could be compared that differ in the nature, but not length, of instruction. It would also be useful to include a control group to show how students interact when they receive no specific preparation for group work. Finally, the present study collected data on verbal interaction on only one occasion, possibly limiting the representativeness of the interaction data. In future studies, collecting data about verbal interaction at the beginning of the study and on multiple occasions during the study would reveal important information about the stability of student behavior as well as make it easier to interpret the effects of the instructional interventions on student behavior.

Conclusion

(15)   This study shows that an instructional program focused on improving students' ability to help others in cooperative small groups can have significant positive effects on their behavior and learning outcomes. The strong results for Latino and African-American students suggest that this kind of program may be successful for improving the learning experiences and outcomes of traditionally underachieving groups in middle school mathematics. (Webb & Farivar, 1994. Copyright 1994 by the American Educational Research Association. Reprinted by permission of the publisher.)

Extract B: Capturing Preservice Teachers' Beliefs About Schooling, Life, and Childhood

PURPOSE

(1)   Our purpose in this study was to identify root beliefs that entry level education students bring with them to a teacher education program. By root beliefs, we mean beliefs that influence and shape one's actions and ideas. In the study, we discern patterns among the metaphors students use to describe their sense of schooling, life, and childhood; identify and determine patterns in the self-selected adjectives students use to describe the ideal student, teacher, administrator, and parents; describe patterns of association among the self-selected adjectives and the chosen metaphors of life and childhood; and identify relationships among the metaphors of life and childhood, ways that students describe themselves on a self-esteem inventory, and ways that they describe their school experiences, both desired and recalled.

DISCUSSION

(2) Our findings show that elementary teacher education students remember their elementary school experience as being a focused, cohesive, positive, social activity, as in being in a family or on a team. Although they similarly view their secondary school experience like this, some hold views of high school as being less positive and cohesive (i.e., prison/crowd). For both levels of schooling, students' preferred images were of a positive, social phenomenon (i.e., family and team). These results are consistent with those of an earlier study involving students in the United States and in other countries (Hardcastle et al., 1985).

(3) Some participants (nearly one third) think that life is like a tree growing. In terms of metaphors of childhood, the majority of participants indicated that being a child is like a flower blossoming. Other studies with similar populations have identified both of these metaphors in roughly comparable proportions to that in the present study (Yamamoto et al., 1990). These metaphors suggest the notion of organic development. What we presently do not know is how to interpret this notion of organic development. Is it of the kind Ashton-Warner (1973) suggests in which organic development is deep seated and fully contained within the individual, created and affected by one's life? Or, is the notion more of a natural, genetic encoding? Given either interpretation, it seems to us that the potential for conflict in some teacher preparation programs exists especially in those in which a dominant theme is that knowledge and the development of self is socially constructed.

(4) The adjectives that students generated to describe adult roles (i.e., teachers, parents, and administrators) imply that these persons should above all else be caring. Other adjectives, along with caring, suggest that these adult roles go further, to a nurturing relationship with children. A number of studies (e.g., Brookhart & Freeman, 1992) have found that elementary teachers, both preservice and inservice, describe teaching as grounded in interpersonal relationships. This study supports those findings, with one notable exception. A certain group of students are entering teaching believing that elementary teaching involves academic qualities as well as interpersonal ones.

(5) The adjectives that participants selected to describe children suggest qualities of purpose and compliance. Although other findings suggestive of the qualities of teachers exist in the literature (Brookhart & Freeman, 1992), there is a marked absence of current, similar descriptions of the qualities of children that prospective teachers expect to encounter in their pupils. More than 30 years ago, Torrance (1963), in questioning teachers using an ideal pupil checklist, found many similar characteristics. Torrance's data suggest that ideal pupils are courteous, industrious, energetic, and considerate of others. These characteristics are similar to those in this study: *motivated, cooperative, eager, interested,* and *caring*. While the students see adults as nurturing, they see children as submissive and compliant, yet happy. We are reminded of Rousseau's discussions in *Emile* of the contradictory nature of childhood as viewed by adults: Children were to be happy while adults controlled children's choices in the name of their best interests.

(6) We started with the idea that education students would separate themselves into distinct groups by root metaphors that would provide complex descriptions uniquely consistent with these particular analogical views. What we found instead was considerable overlap in the descriptions (adjectives) across the metaphor groups. This finding suggests that students may be operating from simplistic and naive views of children that cross over actual differences in the root images that these teachers-to-be hold within themselves. These findings are consistent with some of the developmental and life span/contextual models of teacher development noted by Pintrich (1990). They

also support Comeaux's (1992) finding that education students differentiate between the way they preferred to learn as students and the methods they select for use with their future pupils. As students they enjoyed learning in groups and dialoguing with their teacher, yet they designed lessons for pupils utilizing didactic methodologies.

(7)   Above all, the findings for metaphors of life and childhood suggest that these teachers-to-be see the school as an environment to nurture children. Our data show that students believe the schooling experience should be family- and/or team-like. In American culture, the concepts of family and team both rest upon caring, support, and interdependency of their members. The adjectives selected similarly describe these functions for adult roles.

(8)   Students come into teacher education programs with fairly consistent, vague views of schooling and children. Typically, faculty know little about the views students hold and thus have little if any knowledge of how these characteristics will interact with the dominant concepts incorporated within respective teacher education programs. Part of the failure of some students to learn program concepts may be a result of the clash between views within themselves and those contained in the preparation programs. This may explain some of the frustrations faculty feel when students do not adopt professed program views of schooling, teaching, and learning (e.g., a constructivist approach, which at a root level strikes a contrast to the preeminence of *organic* metaphors). Pajares (1992) points out that it may be the reason some teaching practices continue despite being ineffective and counterproductive. This clash may also explain research results showing little effect of program design on students' acquisition of the extant knowledge of learning to teach (Tabachnick & Zeichner, 1984). One way to reduce the negative consequences of such a clash and the resultant loss of student professional learning is to provide entering students feedback on their held beliefs, surfaced through techniques like that used in this study (cf. Yonemura, 1982), and discuss how these contrast with dominant program concepts and orientations. By providing students with prior information about possible points of disagreement between their ideas and those of faculty and program elements, greater congruence and accommodation may be obtained and more optimal outcomes attained.

(9)   Our findings suggest that too many faculty in teacher education programs operate with little knowledge of who their students are and the dominant beliefs they may hold upon entry into teacher preparation programs. For the faculty in teacher preparation programs to better argue their case, they must better incorporate the fundamental views of students into professional programs of study. By incorporate, we mean to acknowledge and show relationships between students' beliefs and those upon which the teacher preparation program rests. For example, given that students entering elementary education programs may believe that teaching should be based upon a caring and nurturing relationship with children, these qualities should be a starting point for selecting and orienting students to professional education programs. These characteristics should become central in the dialogue of core education courses serving to guide and reinforce the content of the professional experience. Such dialogues will enable students to better bridge their held beliefs with the core concepts and responsibilities they will assume as they enter teaching. We also recommend that faculty directly challenge student-held beliefs when they determine them to be inappropriate or dysfunctional.

(10)   Finally, we believe it is important to better understand the processes by which students' root metaphors change over time and the factors that influence them to change. In our experience, some of these views change as a result of interaction with the program design, some as a result of maturation, and some as a result of experience with children, teachers, schools, and parents. Nonetheless, our knowledge of how these views are developed, sustained, and/or changed over time required additional attention and constitutes an important path for scholarly inquiry. (Mahlios & Maxson, 1995. Copyright © 1995 by Corwin Press, Inc. Reprinted by permission of Corwin Press, Inc.)

FEEDBACK

Extract A: Promoting Helping Behavior in Cooperative Small Groups in Middle School Mathematics. The section begins with a restatement of the researchers' purposes and a summary of the research findings (paragraph 1). The use of the word *effects* indicates that this was a quantitative experimental study. The researchers begin their discussion with an interpretation of the results (paragraph 2) and then indicate questions they have about some of their findings (paragraphs 3–6). Their explanations of the possible results are discussed in relation to findings of other researchers. Their suggestions for future research (paragraphs 7–14) are made in relation to their own results and those of other researchers. Their conclusion (paragraph 15) is a restatement of their results.

Overall, Webb & Farivar's discussion can be judged as appropriate because they provide the expected information. Whether a research consumer agrees or disagrees with their interpretations depends upon that person's educational philosophy and background on the topic.

Extract B: Capturing Preservice Teachers' Beliefs About Schooling, Life, and Childhood. Although it is apparent from the Purpose (paragraph 1) that this was a descriptive study, it is not possible to determine that it was a quantitative study. The discussion begins with a statement of the researchers' results and a comparison of them with other research (paragraph 2). The researchers indicate a question they have about their findings (paragraph 3) and then compare their results to other research (paragraphs 4–5). The researchers then discuss how their results differ from those they anticipated (paragraph 6) and interpret what those results seem to indicate (paragraphs 7–8). They end with ideas about the educational implications of their results (paragraphs 9–10).

Mahlios & Maxon's discussion can be judged as generally appropriate. Moreover, they do not over-extend (generalize beyond their data) recommendations as to how the information can be used by teacher educators.

CHAPTER 10

Reading and Interpreting Reviews of Research

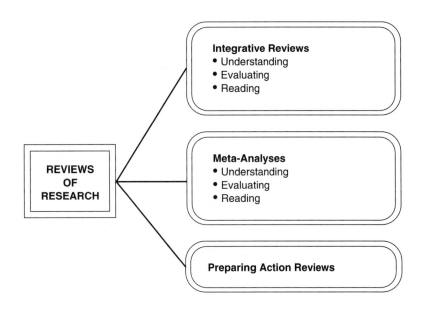

FOCUS QUESTIONS

1. What are integrative reviews of research?
2. What criteria are used to evaluate integrative reviews of research?
3. What are meta-analyses?
4. What criteria are used to evaluate meta-analyses?
5. How are action integrative reviews of research prepared?

In Chapter 4, part of the discussion about introductory sections dealt with researchers' brief summaries of other researchers' results that were related to a research problem area. In these limited reviews, called **literature reviews,** researchers indicate strengths from reviewed research that they used in their own research and weaknesses or limitations in the reviewed research that were changed. A set of questions was given in Chapter 4 so that research consumers could evaluate how critically researchers analyzed related research. These limited literature searches, however, are not intended to be comprehensive, or in-depth, reports of research related to a problem area. When researchers report comprehensive reviews of research related to problem areas, they do so in integrative reviews of research or in meta-analyses of research.

Comprehensive reviews of research are important to educators—both research producers and research consumers. First, preparers of research reviews provide overviews of the research related to a particular problem area. They explain why the problem area is important as a research concern and also report the extent to which the problem area has been researched. Second, research reviewers provide information about the types of research designs used to study the problem, and they may show methodological changes over time in how research producers approached the problem. Third, they identify and define key terms related to the problem area, and they may discover differences in the operational definitions researchers used. Fourth, research reviewers can provide insights about the appropriateness of research producers' methodology. This is important for research consumers when they wish to determine the generalizability of results from various research situations to other teaching and learning situations. Fifth, and possibly the most important reason for these reviews, reviewers join together and interpret the results from a group of research studies dealing with a research problem area. Through their interpretation of the collective results and their general commentary, research reviewers in education indicate trends in the development of concepts about learning and instruction. These ideas help research producers understand possible areas for future research and help research consumers gain insight about education-related issues.

Research consumers need to understand (a) researchers' reason(s) for preparing reviews of research, (b) the way research reviewers prepare integrative reviews of research, (c) the rationale underlying meta-analyses of research and the procedures for doing meta-analyses, and (d) the way to read and interpret integrative reviews and meta-analyses of research.

From reading an integrative review or meta-analysis of research, research consumers should be able to answer

How did the research reviewer define their problem area?

What questions did the research reviewer seek to answer and why did he or she think the answers would be important for educators to know?

How did the research reviewer locate relevant research reports?

How did the research reviewer determine what studies to include in the review?

What procedures did the research reviewer use to analyze and interpret the results of the research?

What conclusions did the research reviewer make from the research?

Research consumers should keep in mind that research related to any educational problem can be summarized, interpreted, and reported for different purposes and for different consumers (Ladas, 1980). For example, research can be reviewed to point out weaknesses or limitations in instruction and make recommendations for improvement in teaching practices. Or, it can be reviewed to establish the improvement of research practices. Or, it can be reviewed to influence broad educational policy and provide conclusions for applied use. The reviews can be directed at audiences such as researchers, those in power or influential positions, practitioners, or the public at large. Research consumers, then, need to identify the intended audience(s) of integrative and meta-analytic reviews of educational research.

INTEGRATIVE REVIEWS OF RESEARCH

An integrative review is undertaken as a research project in which the source of data is the primary research reports of other researchers. These reviews are more than summaries of research; **integrative reviews of research** are critical examinations of research producers' methods and conclusions and of the generalizability of their combined results.

Understanding Integrative Reviews of Research

Integrative reviews consist of five stages (Cooper, 1982; Jackson, 1980): (1) problem formation, (2) data collection, (3) evaluation of data quality, (4) data analysis and interpretation, and (5) presentation of results.

The stages of integrative reviews are summarized in Table 10.1. The table includes the characteristics of each stage of the review process and the issues research reviewers need to address. For each stage, these include (a) a research question that needs to be asked, (b) the activities that need to be done, (c) the sources of differences among reviewers that can cause variations in their conclusions, and (d) the possible sources of threats to the validity of the review. The discussion that follows is based on ideas expressed in several sources (Abrami, Cohen, & d'Apollonia, 1988; Cooper, 1982; Jackson, 1980).

Problem Formulation. The first stage begins with a search of existing integrative reviews for ideas about questions or hypotheses. Ideas are sought for questions about the phenomenon being researched and variations in methods that might account for variations in results. In addition, questions might be formulated from available theory and the reviewers' own insights. Research reviewers then set out operational definitions for key concepts within the problem area. These definitions may reflect those used by primary researchers or may be created for the research review. Research reviewers use the operational definitions to identify relevant primary research studies for inclusion in the integrative review. For example, the following is how one team of research reviewers operationally defined key concepts and linear and nonlinear texts. Note that the reviewers indicate the references upon which they based their operational definitions.

Purpose of the review: To examine empirical investigations that related to subject-matter information and interest and that involved connected discourse presented either in traditional written form or on computer.

Table 10.1
The Integrative Review Conceptualized as a Research Report

| | Stage of Research | | | | |
Stage Characteristics	Problem Formulation	Data Collection	Data Evaluation	Analysis and Interpretation	Public Presentation
Research Question Asked	What evidence should be included in the review?	What procedures should be used to find relevant evidence?	What retrieved evidence should be included in the review?	What procedures should be used to make inferences about the literature as a whole?	What information should be included in the review report?
Primary Function in Review	Constructing definitions that distinguish relevant from irrelevant studies.	Determining which sources of potentially relevant studies to examine.	Applying criteria to separate "valid" from "invalid" studies.	Synthesizing valid retrieved studies.	Applying editorial criteria to separate important from unimportant information.
Procedural Differences that Create Variation in Review Conclusions	1. Differences in included operational definitions. 2. Differences in operational detail.	Differences in the research contained in sources of information.	1. Differences in quality criteria. 2. Differences in the influence of nonquality criteria.	Differences in rules of inference.	Differences in guidelines for editorial judgment.
Sources of Potential Invalidity in Review Conclusions	1. Narrow concepts might make review conclusions less definitive and robust. 2. Superficial operational detail might obscure interacting variables.	1. Accessed studies might be qualitatively different from the target population of studies. 2. People shared in accessible studies might be different from target population of people.	1. Nonquality factors might cause improper weighting of study information. 2. Omissions in study reports might make conclusions unreliable.	1. Rules for distinguishing patterns from noise might be inappropriate. 2. Review-based evidence might be used to infer causality.	1. Omission of review procedures might make conclusions irreproducible. 2. Omission of review findings and study procedure might make conclusions obsolete.

Source: Cooper (1982). Copyright 1982 by the American Educational Research Association. Adapted by permission of the publisher.

We use the term *linear text* to designate connected discourse presented in written form where decisions relative to processing are left solely to the reader. Defined in this manner, linear text is text of a more traditional nature—that is, the writings students are apt to encounter in textbooks, journals, and magazines. *Nonlinear text* is also connected discourse; however, it is discourse accompanied by some type of data base management system. This system guides or prompts readers to reaccess or extend the main text through associative computer-based links to other informational screens (see Gillingham, Young, & Kulikowich, in press, for an extensive discussion of the nature of nonlinear text). One category of nonlinear texts that we will inspect in this review, for example, is hypertext. With the evolution of situated theories of learning that emphasize rich and unique learning environments (e.g., Brown, Collins, & Duguid, 1989; Greeno, 1989; Resinick, Levine, & Teasley, 1991), nonlinear texts, such as hypertext, have gained in popularity. Many of these hypertexts are part of extensive multimedia systems that include not only nonlinear texts but also supporting videos, maps, and commercial movie clips (Christense, Giamo, & Jones, 1993; Trumbull, Gay, & Mazur, 1992). Therefore, it is important to consider the impact of these more nontraditional texts on the acquisition of subject-matter knowledge (Bolter, 1991b). (Alexander, Kulikowich, & Jetton, 1994, pp. 202–203)

Data Collection.   In collecting, organizing, and summarizing data, research reviewers try to use as many information sources as possible. An important responsibility of research reviewers is to identify the target population, accessible population, and sample of primary research reports. The target population of primary research reports is the total body of research reports about which generalizations can be made. Therefore, accessible populations of research reports may be determined by the availability to researchers of library holdings and electronic databases. The sample population of research reports is the specific research reports the reviewers select for review. Practical considerations for reviewers about selection relate to the resources for locating primary research reports (see Chapter 11, Locating Information About Research Reports) and the time period(s) to be covered (e.g., only research published between 1980 and 1990). Also, research reviewers cluster research reports by research designs, since each type of research must be judged by separate criteria.

Data Evaluation.   In evaluating data quality, research reviewers set up evaluation criteria before they search the literature. As a rule, research reviewers use critical questions about research that are similar to those about primary research reports included in this text (see Figure 3.1, p. 117, and Chapters 4 to 9).

Analysis and Interpretation.   In analyzing and interpreting data, the research reviewers should explicitly state how they made inferences, and they should distinguish between inferences they made on the basis of individual studies and those they made as a result of their review of a group of studies.

Public Presentation.   In presenting their results, authors of integrative reviews try to avoid omitting details and evidence. In other words, in making an integrative review of research comprehensible, they attend to the same factors that make a primary research report understandable.

The article on pages 301–320 is taken from an integrative research review about the cognitive processes used by English-as-a-second-language learners. It includes the general background and introduction, the procedures for locating and selecting research reports, the categorization of the studies and the general findings of the primary researchers, and a summary and discussion of the combined findings. What has not been included here, for reasons of space, are the table containing brief summaries of the primary reports and the references.

Evaluating Integrative Reviews of Research

Research consumers need to determine whether research reviewers have critically analyzed and interpreted the data they present. The information in Table 10.1 under the dashed line (the lower portion of the table) and the following discussion indicate characteristics in research reviews that may lead them to be invalid. Research consumers need to identify whether research reviewers controlled variables that could threaten the internal and external validity of their reviews.

Procedural Differences that Create Variation in Review Conclusions and Sources of Potential Invalidity in Review Conclusions. In the problem formulation stage, research reviewers should identify differences that exist among their operational definitions, those of other reviewers, and those found in the sampled research. Reviewers should indicate how the specific details of the reviewed studies differ. Research consumers should be able to distinguish precisely between aspects of primary researchers' methods that research reviewers believe are relevant to their critique and those that are not.

In the data collection stage, research reviewers should identify differences that exist between the target population of available studies, their sample of studies, and studies used in other reviews. The target population of research studies consists of all published research reports related to the problem area. The studies selected for analysis constitute the review sample. Research consumers need an understanding of the target population of studies and the representativeness of the reviewers' sample of studies. Also, research reviewers determine their own criteria for including or excluding primary research reports from their reviews, so it is possible for research reviewers to select different samples of studies for analysis. (This limitation is similar to the one discussed in Chapter 5 about the need for research consumers to be sensitive to primary researchers' identification of their target populations and subject selection techniques.) Research reviewers should explain the time span covered by the research and the type of research designs used. And, research consumers need assurance that there was no selection bias. Differences in conclusions by different research reviewers can result from differences in their samples.

Also, research consumers need to understand subject sampling procedures used by primary researchers. It is possible for several primary researchers to use similar labels for their subject while actually dealing with different target populations. Research consumers should expect research reviewers to delineate the operational definitions used in primary researchers' subject selection.

In the data evaluation stage, research reviewers should indicate what differences exist between the criteria they used for evaluating the research and those

Fitzgerald, J. (1995). English-as-a-second-language learners' cognitive reading processes: A review of research in the United States. *Review of Educational Research, 65*(2), 145–190. Copyright 1995 by the American Educational Research Association. Reprinted by permission of the publisher.

English-as-a-Second-Language Learners' Cognitive Reading Processes: A Review of Research in the United States

Jill Fitzgerald

The University of North Carolina at Chapel Hill

An integrative review of United States research on English-as-a-second-language (ESL) learners' cognitive reading processes suggested that, on the whole, ESL readers recognized cognate vocabulary fairly well, monitored their comprehension and used many metacognitive strategies, used schema and prior knowledge to affect comprehension and recall, and were affected differently by different types of text structures. In the main, where United States ESL readers' processes appeared to be used differently from those of native English readers, the differences were in speed and depressed activation of selected processes. Significantly, overall, the findings from the studies suggested a relatively good fit to preexisting reading theories and views generally thought to describe native-language readers. However, the quantitative differences between processes of ESL readers and those of native English readers indicated that the preexisting theories and views might need to be revisited and elaborated to address a subset of factors special to ESL learners.

Ethnic and racial diversification in the United States is growing, particularly among school-age children. In our schools there are currently about 2.3 million students identified as having "limited English proficiency" (United States Department of Education, 1992). About 50% of all Californian students speak a language other than English as their primary, or only, language, and it is predicted that by 2030 that percentage will increase to about 70% (E. Garcia, 1992a). As non-White Hispanic and Asian/Pacific Islander presence in schools increased considerably from 1976 to 1986 (by 6% and 116%, respectively), Caucasian and non-Hispanic enrollment decreased (by 13%) (E. Garcia, 1992a). However, the educational achievement, including reading achievement, of language minorities has not kept pace with that of English-speaking Caucasians. For example, among Hispanics there is a 40% high school dropout rate, a 35% grade retention rate, and a two- to four-grade-level achievement gap (E. Garcia, 1992b).

As our population has become more diverse, educators' concerns about English-as-a-second-language (ESL) literacy have also increased. Perhaps as an outgrowth of such concerns, more and more research has been conducted on ESL reading issues over the last decade or so. Many facets of ESL reading have been studied, ranging from instructional evaluations to sociocultural issues to cognitive processes. The purpose of this article is to characterize United States research and integrate findings in one area of ESL reading, namely, *cognitive processes.*

For the purposes of this review, ESL learners in the United States were considered to be individuals living in the United States who meet the federal government's definition of "limited English proficient" (Public Law 100–297 [1988]). These individuals (a) were not born in the United States, (b) have native languages other than English, (c) come from environments where English is not dominant, or (d) are American Indians or Alaskan natives from environments where languages other than English impact their English proficiency levels. The term *ESL learner* is used as a special case of the more general term *language minority,* which refers to individuals who are living in a place where they do not speak the majority's language. *Cognitive reading processes* refers to any internal or mental aspects of reading—that is, aspects of the brain's activity during reading (q.v. Bernhardt, 1991; Just & Carpenter, 1987).

By focusing solely on cognitive reading processes, I do not in any way wish to imply that other aspects of ESL reading are unimportant. To the contrary, some other aspects, such as the social setting in which students learn to read English, the classroom instructional method, and congruence between learners' native-language culture and the target-language culture, may be as important, if not more important, than ESL readers' cognitive processes. Further, there may be interactions of cognitive processes with other aspects of ESL reading. Notably, researchers investigating cognition in ESL reading have tended not to explore such complex interrelations, highlighting instead isolated cognitive features.

Also, I do not want to imply that this article reflects an English-only position. It does not. Research suggests that many benefits may accrue from the development and maintenance of bilingualism, and some long-term benefits of bilingual education might outweigh those gained from English-only approaches (Hakuta, 1986; Hakuta & Gould, 1987; Snow, 1987; Wong Fillmore & Valadez, 1986).

There are several reasons why an in-depth integration of research findings on United States ESL learners' cognitive reading processes is needed. First, there are currently countless situations in our country where ESL programs are offered in lieu of bilingual education programs (Hakuta & Gould, 1987; U.S. Department of Education, 1991, 1992). Also, ESL reading is a significant component of bilingual education programs. Further, there are situations where ESL learners do not have the benefit of teachers trained in ESL issues. More ESL students are served by Chapter I reading programs (about 1.2 million) than by Title VII pro-grams (about 251,000), which are specially designed for ESL learners (U.S. Department of Education, 1992). It is highly likely that many Chapter I reading teachers have little back-ground in ESL issues. Equally important, many ESL learners spend the majority of their school hours in regular classroom settings with teach-ers who also often have little background in ESL issues. A better understanding of the read-ing processes used by ESL learners could bene-fit virtually all teachers—ESL, bilingual, read-ing, and regular classroom teachers alike—as well as their students.

Second, to my knowledge no prior in-depth synthesis of reading-process research done solely with ESL learners either in the United States or in general has been con-ducted. A few selective reviews (e.g., Grabe, 1991; Hatch, 1974; Swaffar, 1988) and at least one comprehensive review (Bernhardt, 1991) of research in the broad area of second-lan-guage reading have been done. Both selective and comprehensive broad-based reviews of second-language reading research can cer-tainly make significant contributions to our understanding of second-language reading processes. For example, Bernhardt used her review to begin to build a model of second-language reading.

However, it is not clear to what extent selec-tive or broad-based reviews of second-lan-guage reading research deeply inform on spe-cific issues such as cognitive processes, or to what extent conclusions drawn from such reviews apply to specific second languages and/or to specific settings in which a second language is learned. Indeed, authors of selec-tive reviews generally do not intend to reveal details about a wide array of specific issues (and sometimes about any specific issues), and authors of broad-based reviews may not intend to imply that any generalizations drawn hold for any and all specific target languages. At the very least, drawing both general and specific conclusions from selective or sweeping reviews of second-language reading research is ardu-ous. For example, after reviewing second-lan-guage data-based studies dating back to 1974, ranging from text analyses and reader factors to instruction and assessment, Bernhardt (1991) concluded that it was "extremely difficult" (p. 20) and "tantamount to impossible" (p. 68) to synthesize the information, largely due to "the wide array of subject groups studied [later referring to wide variability in language groups and language-proficiency levels], experimental tasks, and methodologies employed" (p. 20).

At least two factors might critically affect second-language reading processes (q.v. Grabe, 1991) and therefore impede generalizations about selected second-language cognitions across certain target languages and certain language-learning settings. A first factor is the target language to be learned. For example, there is some evidence that the target language may be relevant to any conclusion about the difficulty of various genres in second-language reading (Allen, Bernhardt, Berry, & Demel, 1988) and that the magnitudes of correlations between first- and second-language reading achievement may be different depending upon the languages involved (Bernhardt & Kamil, 1993; Bossers, 1991; Brisbois, 1992; Carrell, 1991).

A second factor which might potentially affect second-language learners' reading is the sociopolitical context in which the second language is learned. For example, elective bilinguals, such as students in their home cultures who are learning a foreign language, can be distinguished from circumstantial bilinguals, such as immigrants to a new country who more or less *must* learn a new language (Valdes, 1991). These groups are often quite different, not only in motivations for learning English, but also in educational background and socioeconomic status (Krashen, 1985a; Valdes, 1991). Any of these variables could impact how individual learners approach texts in the target language, how rapidly they advance, and ultimately, how well and how much they read.

Because the target language to be learned and the sociopolitical context in which second-language learning occurs may affect language minorities' learning about reading, reading development, reading achievement, and reading processes, it may be important to control for, or consider, these contexts when reviewing studies of second-language reading. One way (though not the only way) to do this is to select a particular target language in a particular type of setting and to review research done under those circumstances in order to see if an in-depth characterization would emerge for each particular group. This could be done for different languages and types of setting, and ultimately, comparisons could be made across the successive, highly detailed, particular characterizations. The comparative benefits and problems associated with such an approach as compared to sweeping reviews remain to be detailed.

The present review is a modest first step in such a programmatic approach; it scrutinizes research done on one target language group in one particular setting. Specifically, it attempts an in-depth integration of findings from research on cognitive reading processes of ESL learners in the United States. A characterization of this research might inform us on several issues, such as the particular strengths and/or weaknesses of United States ESL readers, the extent to which their cognitive reading processes are similar to those of native English speakers, and helpful directions for future research.

METHOD

To locate research, a broad search was initially done with few limiting criteria. The following computer searches were done to locate studies for this review: ERIC documents back to 1980, using the limiters (a) literacy (reading and writing) and ESL, (b) literacy and ESL students, (c) literacy and bilingual education, (d) literacy and language-minority learners, and (e) literacy and limited-English proficiency; *Dissertation Abstracts International* back to 1989 with the limiters (a) literacy (reading and writing) and language-minority learners, (b) literacy and limited-English proficiency, (c) literacy and ESL, and (d) literacy and bilingual education; and *Linguistics and Language Behavior Abstracts* with the limiters (a) English as a foreign language, (b) English as a second language, and (c) bilingualism. Additionally, indexes from the following journals were searched back to 1980: *Reading Research Quarterly, JRB: A Journal of Literacy,* and *TESOL Quarterly.* The sections on "Teaching Bilingual and Other Learners" in the *Annual Summary of Investigations in Reading* were searched back to 1980. Further, program books for the following annual conferences were scanned for the years 1991 to date, and papers were requested from authors: International Reading Association, National Reading Conference, Teachers of English to Speakers of Other Languages, National Association of Bilingual Education, and American Educational Research Association. Finally, a "network" approach was used. That is, all reference lists of retrieved documents were checked for additional research pieces, and an effort was made to obtain those pieces.

Later, after much of the research had been read, the review was restricted to all published, data-based research (with no date restriction) and all recent data-based conference papers, technical reports, and dissertations dating back to 1989 which dealt with ESL reading processes in studies conducted in the United States. Unpublished reports of work prior to 1989 were excluded on the grounds that such reports had not undergone rigorous peer review. Additionally, for inclusion, reports had to be complete enough to determine important factors, such as what the outcome measures were, where the study was conducted, and what the study's procedures were. In a handful of cases, studies were excluded due to incompleteness with regard to one or more of these factors.

I analyzed studies reviewed for this project using a systematic interpretive procedure (similar to a constant-comparative method often used in qualitative research [Glaser, 1978]). The following steps were taken. First, I tried to detail all the data available to me. All studies were read and reviewed, and for each study notes were taken to reflect the number of, and any identifying information about, participants; procedures; instruments, and their reliabilities, if given; and main outcomes. Sometimes key words were written along with the notes to describe the main topics investigated. Second, I perused all of the notes on the studies to see if there were patterns and themes in research issues that were addressed. As these emerged, labels were given to tentative topic clusters. Third, I again perused the notes and sorted studies into the tentative clusters. Some studies fell into more than one cluster. Fourth, I worked within each cluster, one at a time, to discern themes by looking for similarities and differ-

ences in studies and their results. This pass through the data was highly detailed, and I often returned to the original pieces to reread for clarification, confirmation, or disconfirmation of emerging hypotheses. During this period, charts and lists were made to sort studies according to developing hypotheses. For example, a list was made of all schema studies—and their salient features, including results—done with younger participants and then with older participants. In this way, patterns and themes could be compared across ages. When hypotheses were confirmed (e.g., all studies with older participants suggested "x," while all studies with younger participants suggested "y"), at least one counterexplanation was entertained (e.g., is there a feature "z" correlated with age which is likely to be a mediating variable?). Also, at this stage, I further refined the clusters by moving some studies from one cluster to another and collapsing one to two others. As I worked through this process within each cluster, I also made separate notes about general problems with methods as they seemed to emerge. Fifth, as themes from a given section solidified, I wrote about that section. Sixth, after all clusters of studies had been analyzed, I read what had been written about each, considered the results as a whole, and, when any discrepancies occurred, reread original pieces. Seventh, to summarize across clusters, a chart was made of the main themes from each cluster of studies.

The issue of reliability of my interpretations centered on the extent to which the themes and images drawn from the review were fairly generalizable from the available data (q.v. Moss, 1994, p. 7). Reliability was clearly an aspect of validity defined as "consonance among multiple lines of evidence supporting the intended interpretation[s] over alternative interpretations" (Moss, 1994, p. 7). The criteria for reliability for this interpretive review were not quantitative. Rather, reliability should be assessed by the extent to which my interpretations were warranted using criteria such as these, given by Moss (1994, p. 7): the extent of my knowledge of the range of existing work on the topic (called "context" by Moss), the existence of "multiple and varied sources of evidence" (i.e., in this case, studies, and data and method contained in the studies), and the "transparency of the trail of evidence leading to the interpretations ... [allowing others] to evaluate the conclusions for themselves." I worked to meet each of these criteria to the fullest extent possible. A further possible criterion suggested by Moss (1994, p. 7), the application of which I invite as response to this article, is that there might be an "ethic of disciplined, collaborative inquiry that encourages challenges and revisions to initial interpretations."

THE STUDIES

Theoretical Frameworks Used to Study ESL Readers' Processes in the United States

How researchers in the United States have situated investigations in ESL reading processes is in itself informative. Some reports did not provide a theoretical basis for the investigations, and in some of those instances, a theoretical basis was not easily inferred. (These reports were still included in the review because they might provide informative evidence to corroborate or to call into question conclusions drawn from other studies.) However, in general, the studies were seated in two sets of theories or views: (a) *native-language reading* theories, models, or views widely known and accepted in the reading research community at large; and (b) theories or views related to *second-language acquisition* and widely known in the second-language acquisition research community.

In particular, four preexisting theories, models or views of reading, originally formed for readers in general and presumably for individuals reading in their native languages, were relied on: (a) a psycholinguistic view of reading, (b) schema theory, (c) an interactive view of reading, and (d) views of metacognition in reading. In some studies, investigators were specifically "testing" the applicability of aspects of a preexisting reading theory, model, or view in ESL reading situations. Occasionally they hypothesized easy applicability; sometimes they hypothesized how the theory, model, or view would need to be modified for ESL learners.

In brief, a psycholinguistic view of reading holds that reading is not a linear process, but that readers sample texts and make and test hypotheses and predictions, relying on their own background knowledge of the text's content as well as background knowledge about how language works (Goodman, 1970). In the sampling process, readers use three cueing systems: graphophonics, syntax, and semantics.

Schema theory postulates that knowledge is systematically organized (Rumelhart, 1980). A schema can be defined as having elements or components which can be delineated and which are ordered in specific ways. Readers are thought to use schemata to anticipate text content and structures, to guide understanding during reading, and to aid recall after reading.

An interactive view of reading holds that reading is both "top-down" and "bottom-up" (Rumelhart, 1985). That is, stated in a very oversimplified way, part of the reading process entails interpreting graphic information from the page (bottom-up), and part involves using knowledge already present in the mind (top-down). The term interactive also refers to the interactions that can occur between and among "higher-level" and "lower-level" information, such as the influence of surrounding context (higher-level) on perception of individual letters or words (lower-level).

Finally, in reading, metacognition refers to awareness of one's own reading processes (Brown, 1980). Principally, it entails awareness of one's own understanding and nonunderstanding, of reading strategies, and of monitoring comprehension during reading.

The investigators' use of these reading views and theories is interesting because they were designed to explain reading processes in general, and presumably of individuals reading in their native languages. Some scholars have begun to detail why certain preexisting reading theories are particularly applicable to second-language learners (e.g., see Carrell, Devine, & Eskey, 1988, on interactive models of reading for second-language learners). It might also be argued, however, that by working from preexisting theories of reading, research on ESL reading might be limited. That is, questions that need to be asked about specific aspects of second-language reading might not be addressed, and therefore, advances in knowledge might be slowed (q.v. Bernhardt, 1991).

Because the investigators relied heavily on preexisting views of reading, it was possible, in a broad sense, to assess in the present review the extent to which findings from the studies, taken collectively, were good fits to those preexisting views. Such an assessment will be made in the discussion section of this article.

Some ESL reading-process researchers situated their work in one or more theoretical positions predominant in the field of second-language acquisition. One position was that significant components of orality and literacy transfer from one language to another. This position was generally used as a foundation for studies which investigated various aspects of individuals' transfer of knowledge and skills from native-language orality or literacy to ESL literacy (or which investigated similarities in reading processes across languages). The Common Underlying Proficiency (CUP) model of how two languages are related is perhaps the most widely known model espousing this position (Cummins, 1981). Basically, it holds that a common set of proficiencies underlies both the first and second languages. What is learned in one language will transfer to another language. Also, using a skill or strategy in one language will transfer to another language. Also, using a skill or strategy in one language is pretty much the same process as in another. A significant feature of the CUP model is that major literacy skills thought to be the same in both languages have been identified, including conceptual knowledge, subject-matter knowledge, higher-order thinking skills, and reading strategies. A related refinement of the basic notion of CUP is Cummins's (1979) developmental interdependence hypothesis, which states that the development of second-language competence is partially a function of the competence already developed in the native language at the time when intensive exposure to the second language begins.

The other position was that second-language literacy and second-language orality are highly related. ESL reading-process researchers in the United States sometimes used this position to ground correlational studies of the relationship between ESL reading and ESL oral proficiency. This position has at least two forms in the second-language literature. In one form, the relationship is directional; second-language reading is dependent upon second-language oral proficiency (q.v. Clarke & Silberstein, 1977). That is, second-language orality must precede second-language literacy. In the other form, not only is the relationship directional, but there is a "threshhold of linguistic competence" necessary for successful second-language reading (Clarke, 1980; Cummins, 1979). As originally discussed by Cummins (1979), the threshold hypothesis referred to the need for optimal competence—presumably *oral* proficiency, though this was not specified—in *both* the native language and the second language in order for higher-level cognitive growth to occur. However, the threshold hypothesis has also been interpreted to mean that unless second-language orality is developed to some optimal level, second-language reading-process development and, consequently, reading and other academic achievement will be stunted. The most significant reading-instructional implication of the threshold hypothesis as originally presented was that students who have not developed native-language reading abilities to some optimal level should initially be taught to read in their native language. With respect to English learning, a significant instructional implication that has been extracted from these views is that second-language learners should develop their English oral abilities first, and then later, when oral proficiency is more developed, second-language reading should be introduced (see, for example, Krashen, 1985b; Wong Fillmore & Valadez, 1986).

Because some have interpreted positions such as the "threshold of linguistic competence" position as having dramatic implications for when and how reading should be introduced to ESL learners in the United States, a global assessment will be made in the summary of this article regarding the fit of the findings from the ESL reading-process studies reviewed to views such as the CUP model and the "threshold of linguistic competence" position.

Limitations of the Studies

Some limitations posed difficulties and/or constraints on the interpretation of the studies and their results. It may be helpful to readers to keep these limitations in mind as the following sections are read. First, many authors failed to report what might have been salient features of participants—most importantly, the participants' extent of literacy in their native language and their ESL oral proficiency level. Such features may affect ESL learners' reading (McLaughlin, 1987). Also, inadequate information about participants sometimes made it difficult to determine whether participants met the required criteria for being ESL learners as defined in this review. Occasionally, studies were excluded because it could not be determined whether participants did meet the criteria. Second, in many instances, even when authors reported important related participant characteristics, such as native language background or ESL oral proficiency level, participants were not sorted by those variables for analyses. If such characteristics interact with ESL reading, then failure to account for them could lead to confounded results. Third, even when ESL proficiency level was mentioned, there was a widespread lack of clarity as to what authors meant by that phrase. For example, the phrase could refer to ESL oral, ESL reading, or ESL writing proficiency. As another example of difficulties in interpreting what authors meant by ESL proficiency, some authors referred to particular test scores as representing an intermediate ESL proficiency level, while at least one investigator said the same test scores meant that the participants could read college-level materials about as well as their average college-level native-English-speaking counterparts. A further problem was that some authors mentioned standardized tests, but did not provide complete references for them. Fourth, measures were not always given in conjunction with authors' labels of ESL proficiency level, and evidence given at times did not clarify. In these cases, interpretation of participants' actual ESL oral and/or reading proficiency was impossible. For example, some authors stated the length of time participants had lived in the United States as evidence of proficiency level, but because individuals acquire English at differing rates, it would be helpful to have more clearly defined evidence. Fifth, a widespread lack of attention to reporting reliability and validity estimates of measures used in the quanti-

tative studies considerably weakened interpretations of results at times.

What Has Been Asked and What Has Been Learned?

The final sources of data were 67 research reports. A summary of key aspects of the studies reported is shown in Table 1. Six clusters were formed according to the main areas addressed in the studies: (a) vocabulary knowledge, (b) strategies (psycholinguistic and metacognitive), (c) schema and prior-knowledge utilization (reader-based and text-based), (d) the relationship between ESL reading and ESL oral proficiency, (e) the relationship between ESL reading proficiency and variables other than ESL oral proficiency, and (f) issues about similarities in cognitive reading processes across United States ESL learners and native English learners, as well as across United States ESL learners' native language and English. There was also a seventh cluster for miscellaneous studies. The two most researched areas (as gauged by the number of studies conducted) were strategies and schema use.

In each of the following sections, (a) typical paradigms are explained (where there were typical ones), (b) participants' ages, grade levels, ESL proficiency levels (as given by authors), and native language backgrounds are described, and (c) themes are presented. For some clusters, special issues are also discussed.

ESL Readers' Vocabulary Knowledge. Paradigms varied in the eight reports of studies on vocabulary. For example, in one, participants took a standardized reading test and were interviewed, and then test items were analyzed. In another, participants read silently, circling all cognates (English-Spanish look-alike words with similar meanings), and also took vocabulary tests. Most participants were young (second through seventh grade), though there were 4 college students in one study and 12 in another. ESL proficiency levels, where reported, ranged from beginning to advanced. Participants were mainly Hispanic, though other ethnicities were represented.

One of the most important themes in this cluster was that vocabulary knowledge may be a highly significant variable in United States ESL readers' success. Unknown vocabulary in questions and answer choices on tests was a main linguistic factor adversely affecting the reading test performance of beginning-level and relatively proficient Hispanic and Cantonese third, fifth, and sixth graders (Ammon, 1987; G. E. Garcia, 1991). In one study, oral vocabulary production was a very strong correlate, and the only oral proficiency correlate, of English reading achievement (Saville-Troike, 1984). In another, vocabulary knowledge was even more important for test performance than was prior knowledge of content (G. E. Garcia, 1991).

Other studies looked at fourth- through seventh-grade Hispanic United States ESL learners' ability to recognize and use cognate relationships. Although cognates were fairly well recognized on the whole, the ability to recognize cognates was not fully developed; that is, there was substantial variability in cognate recognition (G. E. Garcia & Nagy, 1993; Jimenez, Garcia, & Pearson, 1991; Nagy, Garcia, Durgunoglu, & Hancin-Bhatt, 1992).

An additional finding was that there was considerable individual variability in approaches to learning English vocabulary for four United States ESL college students (Parry, 1991). Also, advanced ESL college students in the United States used first-language vocabulary knowledge to read idioms, with idioms that were identical in Spanish and English being easiest, similar idioms being almost as easy (but showing the most native-language interference), and different idioms being most difficult (Irujo, 1986).

ESL Readers' Strategies. Two sorts of ESL readers' strategies have been studied in the United States. In one group of studies, here called *psycholinguistic-strategy* studies, researchers investigated the psycholinguistic cueing systems (graphophonics, syntax, and semantics) that readers used to recognize and comprehend words. In another, here called *metacognitive-strategy* studies, researchers tried to determine the systematic ways in which readers approached texts, and how readers tried to repair miscomprehension.

Psycholinguistic Strategies. In 12 of the 13 psycholinguistic-strategy studies, participants read orally and then retold the text without looking back. Either an examiner listened to the oral reading and simultaneously made marks on a copy of the text to record all deviations the participant made from the printed words, or the oral readings were tape recorded so the examiner could later listen and mark a protocol. In the 13th study, participants read (apparently silently), told what they understood, identified words they had found difficult, and guessed orally what the words might mean. In some studies only one text was read, and in others multiple texts were read. At least some participants in every study read in English, but some also read at least one passage in their native language. Twelve sets of investigators used miscue analysis. Basically, this means that each text deviation was assessed for whether it (a) looked and/or sounded like the text word (was graphophonically similar), (b) was syntactically acceptable, and (c) was semantically acceptable. Other details were also assessed, such as reader regressions and self-corrections. The main purpose of the analysis was to determine how readers approach text. For example, when readers made many graphophonic substitutions, made few syntactically and semantically acceptable substitutions, and rarely self-corrected, their strategies might have been characterized as overreliant on the graphic aspects of text, with little attention to text meaning.

Most of the studies in this group were done with children in elementary school grades, as low as second grade, but a few were done with participants covering the range from seventh grade to adult. Many authors identified English oral and/or reading proficiency level, and these levels covered the full range from beginner to advanced. By and large, in the studies dealing with psycholinguistic strategies, native language groups were not as mixed as in some other research clusters in this review. When there were individuals of diverse native languages within studies, several authors sorted results accordingly.

It was very difficult to arrive at pointed and highly meaningful themes across this group of studies. On the whole, the studies did not shed much light on the psycholinguistic strategies of ESL readers in the United States, at least not for ESL readers as a group. Even sorting studies by participants' English oral and/or reading proficiency, age, and whether or not investigators mixed native language groups did not reveal clear patterns leading to grand generalizations for subgroups of readers.

Following are statements about findings from the studies; most of these are either about mixed findings or supported by only one or two studies. First, the most pointed statement that can be made is that there was no single pattern in the use of psycholinguistic strategies across ESL readers. That is, there was no general reliance on a particular cue system, such as graphophonics, nor was there a general balanced reliance across the cueing systems. To the contrary, there was variability in ESL readers' psycholinguistic strategies. For example, some studies (covering participants from elementary school to high school and from beginning to intermediate English proficiency) showed that ESL readers' substitutions tended to be graphically similar (Rigg, 1976; Romatowski, 1981) and syntactically (Rigg, 1976; Romatowski, 1981) and semantically acceptable (Rigg, 1977, 1988; Romatowski, 1981). Also, adult ESL readers used graphophonic, syntactic, and semantic cueing systems to guess at word meanings after reading passages (Haynes, 1984). These results would suggest that ESL readers had a balanced set of psycholinguistic strategies; that is, it would seem that they did focus on meaning while reading English, but that they also took into account the graphic aspects of print. However, opposite results also emerged, sometimes with participants at the same age and proficiency level and/or with the same native language background. For example, Rigg's (1986) beginning ESL readers and McLeod and McLaughlin's (1986) beginning and advanced ESL readers tended to overrely on graphophonics. Participants in Haddad's (1981) study made many syntactically unacceptable miscues, and participants in Connor's (1981) and McLeod and McLaughlin's (1986) studies made many semantically unacceptable miscues.

Second, it was not clear whether language dominance and/or native language background affected ESL readers' psycholinguistic strategies. On the one hand, in at least three studies, strategies differed according to language dominance (Barrera, Valdes, & Cardenes, 1986; Miramontes, 1987, 1990); in another,

participants' miscues reflected negative transfer from their native language (Romatowski, 1981). For example, Miramontes (1990) found complex and significant differences between three groups of Mexican American readers in numbers of miscues in various categories. The three groups were (a) good English readers (whose first language was considered English), (b) good Spanish (ESL) readers, and (c) mixed-dominant ESL readers who spoke only Spanish at home and only English at school. One major conclusion of the study was that, on the whole, the mixed-dominant group seemed to focus less on meaning than did the good Spanish readers. On the other hand, however, at least two investigators found more variation in miscue patterns within language groups than between them (Connor, 1981; Rigg, 1977).

Finally, there was some evidence that the number and/or rate of miscues, and of meaning-change miscues in particular, was negatively associated with retelling scores (Connor, 1981; Devine, 1988). That is, making fewer miscues (most notably, fewer meaning-change miscues) was aligned with better comprehension. But in one study, the pattern was reversed (Romatowski, 1981).

One set of possible reasons why more pointed thematic statements cannot be garnered from the psycholinguistic studies is related to the way the studies were conducted. First, in many studies, the research issues did not always seem precise. I often had a vague sense that a study was meant to reveal something about ESL readers' miscue patterns, but specific research questions were elusive.

Second, the analyses and/or interpretations of data sometimes tended to meander, probably because research issues regarding the use of strategies were not clearly specified. Authors infrequently moved past descriptions of the actual percentages of various types of miscues made to make inferences about readers' strategies or ways of thinking about comprehending while reading.

Third, two major methodological drawbacks in this group of studies may have contributed to the inability to infer pointed themes. In many cases, reports did not provide information about the match between readers' English reading levels and the texts' readability levels. A basic principle of miscue analysis is that participants should be reading texts which are slightly difficult for them so that there is enough contextual information to build on but also some opportunity to apply strategies in hard spots. Lack of information about the extent of adherence to that principle strained the interpretation of results.

Another methodological difficulty was that in ESL research, it may be difficult to characterize how closely miscues match text because the readers' oral pronunciations may be in transition from their native language to English (Bernhardt, 1987; Brown & Haynes, 1985). It is impossible to know how different researchers handled this problem.

Another reason for the inability to draw very pointed statements simply may have been that individual differences among ESL readers in the use of psycholinguistic strategies obviate overall statements. While factors such as native language background, extent of native language literacy, extent of homeland schooling, and age of entry into the United States may mediate ESL readers' strategies, individuals' own particular ways of using psycholinguistic text cues may outweigh, or interact with, any such factors.

Metacognitive Strategies. The paradigm used in the 10 studies (in 11 reports) on United States ESL readers' metacognitive strategies was usually some variation on a typical paradigm used in studies with native English speakers. Participants read texts, always in English and sometimes additionally in Spanish, generally stopping at selected points to "think aloud," telling whatever was on their minds. Sometimes the texts had catalysts to miscomprehension, such as incoherent sentences. In at least one study, participants could do the "think aloud" in Spanish. The "think aloud" sessions were taped and later analyzed primarily to determine readers' metacognitive strategies and/or methods of monitoring their own comprehension.

All but three of the studies were done with individuals at the high school level or higher; the remaining three were done with third through fifth graders. Investigators

rarely explored metacognitive strategies of individuals at beginning English proficiency levels; they favored instead intermediate or advanced learners. Two studies incorporated beginners, and a few authors did not report proficiency levels. All studies but one were done with Hispanic individuals; the remaining one was done with Chinese as well as Hispanic individuals.

Three main themes emerged. First, ESL readers in the United States did tend to monitor their comprehension (Block, 1992; Mikulecky, 1991; Padron, Knight, & Waxman, 1986; Pritchard, 1990). The monitoring process was described by one author as "evaluate, act, and check" (Block, 1992). That is, readers recognized problems and identified problem sources, they established strategic plans and attempted to solve the problems, and they checked and revised throughout problem recognition and solution.

Second, a myriad (probably over 50) of ESL readers' metacognitive strategies was commonly reported across seven studies (in eight reports). The following nine strategies all appeared in at least three of the seven studies: asking questions, rereading, imaging, using a dictionary, anticipating or predicting, reading fast or changing speed, thinking about something else while reading or associating, skipping, and summarizing or paraphrasing (Anderson, 1991; Anderson, Bachman, Perkins, & Cohen, 1991; Block, 1986a, 1986b; Knight, Padron, & Waxman, 1985; Padron et al., 1986; Padron & Waxman, 1988; Walker, 1983).

Third, at least one study supported the belief that language background did not influence the types of strategies used by ESL readers (Block, 1986a, 1986b).

Schema and Prior Knowledge Utilization. Studies on the use of schemata by ESL readers in the United States tended to fall into two subtly different groups. Although in all instances the investigators were interested in the interaction of readers' schemata or prior knowledge with text content and/or structure, some researchers focused more on *readers'* schemata or prior knowledge, whereas others tended to emphasize the schemata or structures embodied in *texts.*

Studies Emphasizing Readers' Schemata or Prior Knowledge. The methodologies of studies which emphasized *readers'* schemata or prior knowledge were typically patterned after what may now be termed classic reading studies in schema theory with native English speakers. Though exceptions can be identified, the methodologies used in the 10 reports of studies in this group were, by and large, variations on a paradigm exemplified by Carrell (1987). In this study, participants were 28 Muslim Arabs and 24 Catholic Hispanics who were ESL students of high-intermediate proficiency enrolled in an intensive English program at a midwestern university. The students each read two texts, one with Muslim-oriented content and one with Catholic-oriented content. Further, each text was presented in either a well-organized rhetorical format or an unfamiliar, altered rhetorical format. After reading each text, students recalled the text in writing and answered multiple-choice comprehension questions about the text. All aspects of data collection were conducted in English. Recall protocols were analyzed for quantity of idea units recalled from the original texts as well as whether recalled ideas were from various levels of the text hierarchy (e.g., main ideas versus details). The protocols were also scored for features such as elaborations and distortions. Answers to the multiple-choice questions were scored for number correct.

The studies were done mainly with university-age participants; only three explored schema issues at seventh grade or below. Most participants were reported to be of intermediate- to advanced-level ESL proficiency, but at least two studies included participants with beginning-level proficiency. Many language groups were represented.

The results of studies in this area resoundingly suggested that schemata affected United States ESL readers' comprehension and recall. In most studies, participants better comprehended and/or remembered passages that either were more consonant with their native cultures or were deemed more familiar (Ammon, 1987; Carrell, 1981, 1987; G. E. Garcia, 1991; Johnson, 1981, 1982; Langer, Bartolome, Vasquez, & Lucas, 1990). There was some further evidence that ESL readers' schemata for content affected comprehension and/or remembering more than did their formal schemata for text organization (Carrell, 1987; Johnson, 1981). For example, in the Carrell (1987) study described in the beginning of this section, participants remembered the most when both the text content and the rhetorical form were familiar. They remembered the least when both the text content and the rhetorical form were unfamiliar. However, when only content or only form was unfamiliar, unfamiliar content presented more difficulty than did unfamiliar form.

No common reasons could be discerned for the lack of schema effects in three studies (Barnitz & Speaker, 1991; Carrell, 1983; Carrell & Wallace, 1983). All were done with older, intermediate- to advanced-level ESL learners, except that Barnitz and Speaker (1991) also included seventh graders (whose ESL level was not stated). All had mixed native language groups. One explanation might be that although the participants were generally designated as intermediate to advanced in ESL proficiency, no evidence was reported that they could read the words in the passages with little difficulty. Inadequate recognition of the passage words could confound results. Another explanation in the Carrell (1983) study might be that the novel passage, "Balloon Serenade" (from Bransford & Johnson, 1973), was simply overwhelmingly bizarre for ESL students. Roller and Matambo (1992), in an English-as-a-foreign-language study (conducted in Zimbabwe), replicated Carrell's (1983) effect and then went on to analyze the "Balloon" passage. They suggested that perhaps the results were contaminated due to a confounding of familiarity (of passage) with other factors, such as difficulty level of the formal structure and noun concreteness. That is, they believed the "Balloon Serenade" passage was more formally consistent and had more concrete nouns than the so-called familiar passage, "Washing Clothes."

Studies Emphasizing Text Schemata. Paradigms used in the seven reports of studies in this group were variations on what might now be termed classic reading studies on text structure done with English-speaking participants.

Participants read texts and then recalled information, for the most part in writing. The structures in texts (e.g., compare-contrast and problem-solving structures in expository text, and standard versus structurally interleaved versions of stories) were identified, and the recalled information was analyzed for variables such as number of propositions recalled, number of high- versus low-level propositions recalled, and recall of temporal sequence of story components. All aspects of the studies were conducted in English.

All the participants in these studies were in ESL-intensive college or precollege matriculation programs, except that there were fourth and fifth graders in one study. All were labeled intermediate- to advanced-level ESL learners. In all studies except one, there were mixed native language groups.

The main overall theme was that different types of text structure affected comprehension and recall—most specifically, quantity of recall (Bean, Potter, & Clark, 1980; Carrell, 1984a, 1984b, though this was not true in Carrell, 1992), type of information recalled (high- versus low-level information) (Carrell, 1984a, 1992), and temporal sequence of recall (Carrell, 1984b).

Another theme was that there may have been differences among language groups as to which text structures facilitated recall better (Carrell, 1984a). For example, Arabs remembered best from expository texts with comparison structures, next best from problem-solution structures and collections of descriptions, and least well from causation structures. Asians, however, remembered best from texts with either problem-solution or causation structures and least well from either comparison structures or collections of descriptions. It remains to be seen whether this interaction of language background with text structure was due to interference/facilitation from known native-language rhetorical patterns (Carrell, 1984a; Hinds, 1983). For example, some have documented a preferred rhetorical Arabic pattern, called "coordinate parallelism" (Kaplan, 1966). Arabs' better performance on texts with comparison structures may have been related to familiarity with "coordinate parallelism" patterns in their native-language texts. However, some other recent work also suggests that culture-specific rhetorical patterns do not transfer to a new language (Connor & McCagg, 1983).

A third theme was that although type of text structure affected the information recalled by ESL students, the students were not highly able to name the organizational plans in the texts they read (Carrell, 1984a, 1992). Finally, there was some minimal evidence that ESL readers with a greater ability to extract nonverbal schemata (on shape-classification tasks) were more able to use text structure to comprehend and recall (Perkins, 1987; Perkins & Angelis, 1985).

Relationship Between ESL Reading Proficiency and ESL Oral Proficiency. Seven studies aimed specifically to address the relationship between ESL reading proficiency and ESL oral proficiency for individuals in the United States. With minor exceptions, investigators in this group typically gave participants several tests (standardized, informal, and/or self-devised) once, or sometimes more than once over a year or so. Occasionally, participants were videotaped conversing in natural settings. Intercorrelations among measures were then examined to determine the extent of relationships. Participants were mainly young (kindergarten through eighth grade in three studies, age 16 through adult in two others). Because both reading and oral language proficiency were main research issues, each was measured, and wide ranges of ability levels were represented. Many different languages were also represented.

These studies produced quite mixed results. Thus, it is not possible to make a simple statement about the relationship between ESL reading proficiency and ESL oral proficiency. Rather, the relationship may have depended on at least three factors: native language, age or grade level, and the type of English oral proficiency measure used. First, native language background mediated the relationship between ESL reading proficiency and ESL oral proficiency (Brown & Haynes, 1985; Tragar & Wong, 1984). Tragar and Wong and Brown and Haynes were the only investigators in this cluster of studies who parsed results by both native language background and grade level. Tragar and Wong worked with 200 Cantonese students and 200 Hispanic students, all of whom had bilingual education in Boston for 1 to 2.5 years. They found a strong positive relationship for Hispanic sixth through eighth graders, and a strong negative relationship for Cantonese sixth through eighth graders. Brown and Haynes found moderately strong positive correlations for adult Arabs and Spaniards, but a negligible correlation for Japanese.

Second, the relationship between ESL reading proficiency and ESL oral proficiency may have been stronger at higher grade levels. Although there was a positive relationship in one study with first-grade Hispanic ESL students (Lara, 1991), there was no significant relationship in two other studies with young children. In contrast to the overall strong correlations just cited for sixth through eighth graders and for adults, as well as in one additional study with adults (Carrell, 1991), no relationship emerged for either Hispanic or Cantonese ESL learners at Grades 3 through 5 (Tragar & Wong, 1984). Likewise, Saville-Troike (1984) found mainly no relationships between ESL reading and ESL oral proficiency (excepting primarily oral English vocabulary) for second through sixth graders with little prior English experience. Even amount of time spent using English orally (with peers and adults) was not related to English reading achievement (Saville-Troike, 1984).

If native language background and ESL-learner age or grade level do mediate the relationship between ESL reading proficiency and ESL oral proficiency, these factors might help to explain mixed results from two other studies. Snow (1991) found mainly positive relationships, and Devine (1987) found some positive and some negative correlations. Only Snow had a large sample; the Devine study had 20 participants. Snow covered kindergarten through eighth grade and two languages. Devine covered 16- to 38-year-olds and five different languages. Results were not reported by age or language background in interpretable ways. It is highly possible that overall false correlations resulted from the combining of subgroups which might have had different correlations.

Third, it may be that a greater number of lower correlations surfaced when less formal and more naturalistic oral proficiency measures were used. For example, where scores were obtained from measures such as interviews, videotapes of natural classroom situations, and conversation tasks (Saville-Troike, 1984; Snow, 1991), a preponderance of, or at least some, near-zero correlations emerged. However, formal, isolated measures of grammar and vocabulary tended to yield strong negative correlations (Devine, 1987).

The Relationship Between ESL Reading Proficiency and Variables Other Than English Oral Proficiency. Results in this section were from studies which were designed primarily to investigate the relationship between ESL learners' English reading proficiency and selected other variables, or which secondarily provided information pertinent to these issues. Most of these compared good ESL readers and poor ESL readers, some gave correlational tendencies, and one solely investigated poor ESL readers. A variety of tasks and analyses were used—nearly as wide a variety as is represented by all of the topics in this review. Most of the studies were done with elementary school students, but four were done with college-age or older participants. Most were done with Hispanics, but four studies also included participants from other language backgrounds. Several investigators reported English oral language proficiency levels in addition to English reading proficiencies. Where mentioned, English oral proficiencies ranged from beginning to advanced.

On the whole, results from 14 reports were robust across ages and grade levels, language backgrounds, and oral proficiency levels. There tended to be a positive relationship between English reading proficiency and the variables investigated. The following thematic conclusions were drawn. ESL learners who were more proficient in English reading and those who were less proficient tended to be different in the following ways. The more proficient readers tended to (a) use more schema knowledge (Ammon, 1987); (b) use strategies that were more meaning-oriented (e.g., make more miscues that were syntactically and semantically acceptable [Devine, 1988; Langer et al., 1990] and be more global or top-down in perceiving effective and difficulty-causing strategies [Carrell, 1989]); (c) use a greater variety of metacognitive strategies and use metacognitive strategies more frequently (Anderson, 1991); (d) take more action on plans to solve miscomprehension problems and check their solutions more often (Block, 1992); (e) persist more in the application of metacognitive strategies (Carrell, 1989); (f) make better use of cognates between languages and have more vocabulary knowledge (Ammon, 1987; Garcia & Nagy, 1993; Jimenez et al., 1991; Nagy et al., 1992); (g) make better and/or more inferences (Ammon, 1987; G. E. Garcia, 1991); (h) do better on social studies and science achievement tests (taken in English) (Saville-Troike, 1984); (i) be better readers in their native languages (Carson, Carrell, Silberstein, Kroll, & Kuehn, 1990; Tragar & Wong, 1984), with native-language reading scores best predicting English reading achievement at Grades 3 through 5, but oral English best predicting it at Grades 6 through 8 (Tragar & Wong, 1984); (j) be more proficient in English writing (Carson et al., 1990); and (k) have parents who perceived education to be highly important (Lara, 1991). One study (Carson et al., 1990) suggested that the strength of the relationships between ESL reading achievement and both native-language reading and ESL writing achievement might have been mediated by what the native language was (Chinese vs. Japanese).

However, although the variety and amount of metacognitive-strategy use varied according to English reading proficiency, both more and less proficient ESL readers applied the same most-frequent metacognitive strategies to answer test questions (Anderson, 1991), and identified problems and their sources equally well (Block, 1992). Also, there was no relationship between English reading and (a) math achievement, when tested in English (Saville-Troike, 1984); (b) language background (Saville-Troike, 1984); (c) the extent to which individuals used code switching in oral language (Lara, 1991); (d) a variety of written measures

of English language knowledge (excepting one positive correlation) (Saville-Troike, 1984); or, surprisingly, (e) amount of time spent interacting with English text (Saville-Troike, 1984).

Similarities Across Learners and Languages. In this section, two issues are examined: similarities in cognitive reading processes (a) across United States ESL learners and native English learners and (b) across United States ESL learners' native language and English. To address these two issues, I analyzed only studies which either included and compared both ESL readers and native English readers, or had research designs which allowed inferences about whether the ESL readers used native-language knowledge while they read in English. That is, I analyzed only studies which had data available within the reports to arrive at comparative conclusions. Studies were not included if investigators drew conclusions about similarities or differences in results solely by comparing their results to their (or others') assessments of collective prior work on the given topic.

ESL Readers' Processes Compared to Those of Native English Speakers. A variety of paradigms was used in this group of 17 reports. Only two studies involved young children (third and fifth graders); one study involved ninth graders; the remainder included college-age participants. When given, ESL proficiency levels reportedly ranged from beginning to advanced. A variety of native language backgrounds was represented.

The results tentatively suggested that there were some similarities and some differences in aspects of United States ESL readers' processes as compared to those of native English speakers. Qualitatively, or substantively, on the whole, many facets of the processes appeared similar. For the most part, differences tended to be associated with quantitative aspects of using the processes, that is, with the extent to which particular processes were used or with processing speed. No differences in outcomes due to the native language backgrounds of the participants were discernible. One study revealed different outcomes according to proficiency level, and one according to grade level.

Both groups of readers (a) used metacognitive strategies and monitored their reading (Block, 1986a, 1986b, 1992; Padron et al., 1986), (b) generally drew correct inferences from sentences with implicative and factive predicates (Carrell, 1984c), (c) recalled superordinate ideas (Connor, 1984) and propositions in general (Barrera et al., 1986), and (d) identified antecedents and other cohesive signals when reading (Demel, 1990; Duran & Revlin, 1994). (In one study involving antecedents, anaphora was equally difficult for Hispanic ESL fourth-grade readers and for monolingual English-speaking fourth-grade readers [Robbins, 1985].) Like native-English-speaking college students, advanced ESL college learners focused more on content than on function words and appeared to use acoustic scanning (Hatch, Polin, & Part, 1974).

However, with reference to qualitative differences, ESL readers did not use context as well as native English speakers (Carrell, 1983; Carrell & Wallace, 1983). Also, unlike native-English-speaking college students, beginning and intermediate ESL readers relied more on visual cues than on acoustic cues for reading, and focused equally on function and content words (Hatch et al., 1974). Further, at the ninth-grade level, although fluent ESL readers identified cohesive signals as well as native English speakers, they were less able to make use of the information—for example, to make inferences—than were the native English speakers (Duran & Revlin, 1994). However, with college-age participants, there was no difference between groups (Duran & Revlin, 1994).

Quantitatively, compared to native English speakers, the ESL readers tended to (a) use fewer metacognitive strategies (Knight et al., 1985; Padron et al., 1986), (b) use selected metacognitive strategies with different relative frequencies (Knight et al., 1985; Padron et al., 1986), (c) verbalize their metacognitive strategies less (Block, 1992), (d) make proportionately fewer meaningful miscues (Barrera et al., 1986; McLeod & McLaughlin, 1986), (e) have higher error rates for making inferences (Carrell, 1984c), and (f) recall fewer subordi-

nate ideas from text (Connor, 1984). They also tended to monitor their comprehension more slowly (Block, 1992) and perform reading tasks more slowly (Mestre, 1984; Oller, 1972). Further, eye-movement photography revealed that as compared to norms of approximately 12,000 college-level native English readers, ESL college-level readers, though they tended to make about the same number of regressions, differed somewhat in making more fixations with narrower word spans, and differed significantly in that duration of fixation was much longer—about as long as for typical native-English-speaking third or fourth graders (Oller, 1972). This led to the conclusion that a main contrast between the two groups was the speed with which they processed verbal information in short-term memory.

Native-Language Transfer to ESL Reading. The 17 reports in this group covered a variety of paradigms, with second graders through adults and, where reported, beginning to advanced ESL proficiency levels. The majority of studies involved Hispanic participants, though several other language backgrounds were represented in the remaining studies.

Overwhelmingly, results showed a transfer of native-language knowledge to ESL reading. Six statements supporting native-language transfer can be made. First, there was a positive relationship between ESL and native-language reading ability for readers in the United States (Carrell, 1991; Carson et al., 1990; Saville-Troike, 1984; Tragar & Wong, 1984). Interestingly, for college-age ESL learners in one study (Carrell, 1991), native Spanish reading ability accounted for more variance in English reading than did English oral proficiency. Second, knowledge used to guide comprehension in native-language reading was also used in ESL reading (Carrell, 1984a; Goldman, Reyes, & Varnhagen, 1984; Langer et al., 1990). Third, knowledge of Spanish vocabulary and idioms transferred to ESL reading (Garcia & Nagy, 1993; Irujo, 1986; Jimenez et al., 1991; Nagy et al., 1992). Fourth, participants used the same metacognitive strategies in ESL reading as in their own Spanish reading (Pritchard, 1990). Fifth, at least a minimal number of miscues in ESL oral reading could be attributed to native-language syntactical knowledge (Gonzalez & Elijah, 1979; Romatowski, 1981). And sixth, some participants apparently phonologically recorded their ESL reading into their native language (Muchisky, 1983).

Notably, some transfer could be considered negative, such as omission of articles in English reading when the articles could be omitted in the reader's native language, or such as interference caused by Spanish idioms when the reader came across similar, but not identical, English idioms (Irujo, 1986). On the other hand, much could be considered positive, as in one study where some participants' miscue patterns were the same in ESL and in Spanish reading, but one feature was different: the participants made more miscues on function words than on nouns in Spanish and vice versa in ESL reading (Clarke, 1981).

Only two studies suggested quantitative differences, and these were in the use of comprehension-monitoring and metacognitive strategies in ESL reading as compared to native-language reading. One showed less monitoring in ESL reading (Pritchard, 1990); the other showed more strategy use in ESL reading (Mikulecky, 1991).

Miscellaneous. I located a handful of studies covering a variety of additional topics. There was some limited evidence that college-age ESL readers used phonological recoding when they read English silently (Muchisky, 1983; see also similar findings on acoustic scanning in Hatch et al., 1974). However, two other studies suggested significant variability in adult beginning and intermediate ESL learners' perceptions of the reading process as sound- versus meaning-centered; this influenced the way they read (Define, 1984, 1988). Also, in the phonological recoding study done by Muchisky (1983), ESL students were able to comprehend well without using phonological recoding. Finally, for adults with intermediate to advanced ESL proficiency, awareness of parts of speech was positively related to reading comprehension (Guarino & Perkins, 1986).

SUMMARY AND DISCUSSION

A partial image of United States ESL readers' cognitive processes emerged. Most notably, there was substantial individual variability in at least two areas: vocabulary knowledge and psycholinguistic strategies. However, on the whole, ESL readers (a) recognized cognate vocabulary fairly well, (b) monitored their comprehension and used many metacognitive strategies, (c) used schemata and prior knowledge to affect their comprehension and recall, and (d) were affected differently by different types of text structures.

Further, tentative images of more proficient versus less proficient ESL readers in the United States were formed. On the whole, more proficient ESL readers (a) made better use of vocabulary knowledge, (b) used a greater variety of metacognitive strategies and used selected strategies more frequently, (c) took more action to solve miscomprehension and checked solutions to problems more often, (d) used psycholinguistic strategies that were more meaning-oriented, (e) used more schema knowledge, and (f) made better and/or more inferences.

Theoretical Issues

On the whole, the studies reviewed in this article support the contention that the cognitive reading processes of ESL learners are *substantively* the same as those of native English speakers. At least, they are more alike than they are different. At the same time, some of the studies reviewed suggested that while the same basic processes may be used, a few selected facets of those processes may be used less or may operate more slowly for ESL learners than for native English readers. Let me first point to two forms of evidence from the present review which support the contention of essential sameness, and then I will summarize the evidence supporting the suggestion that selected facets of cognitive processes may be used less or more slowly by ESL learners.

Findings from a broad array of studies pointed to an image of the cognitive processes of ESL readers (just summarized at the beginning of this section) which was highly similar to portraits of the cognitive processes of native English readers that abound in the more general reading literature. On the whole, the statements made about ESL readers in general and about more proficient ESL readers in the opening to this section could well be made about native English readers.

Also, the results of studies in which United States ESL readers and native English readers were compared indicated that the two groups' cognitive processes were substantively more alike than different. They used similar metacognitive strategies and monitored their comprehension when reading, and identified antecedents in text equally well.

Collectively, these forms of evidence along with other specific findings from the studies, suggested a relatively good fit to the preexisting native-language reading theories, models, and views many of the studies were grounded in, most specifically to a psycholinguistic view, schema theory, an interactive view of reading, and views of metacognition in reading.

On the other hand, the evidence for the specialness of ESL readers' processes was mainly the amount of use and the length of time to use certain processes. That is, in some instances, ESL readers seemed to use a given process or aspects of it less often, less well, and/or more slowly. On the whole, they used fewer metacognitive strategies and favored some different ones, verbalized metacognitive strategies less, recalled subordinate ideas less well, monitored comprehension more slowly, and did reading tasks more slowly. Less proficient ESL readers did less acoustic scanning and focused more on function words than did others. An additional important specialness was that language background may have affected preferred text structures.

These areas of specialness suggest that the preexisting theories, models, and views might be revisited and modified to account for these data and to specifically allow for explanation of ESL learners' processes. Explorations of the preexisting native-language reading theories, models, and views might address areas such as (a) reasons for decreased use of specific strategies, (b) reasons for depressed recall of subordinate ideas, and (c) what factors account for

slower rates of reading for ESL learners as compared to native English speakers.

Whether or not there is a need for a theory of reading specific to ESL or second-language learners is a highly controversial issue. Some second-language researchers believe that second-language reading is "a different phenomenon" from first-language reading (Bernhardt, 1991, p. 226) and, consequently, that a reading theory specific to second-language learners is needed. Others, however, believe that second-language reading is highly similar to first-language reading. For example, Heath's (1986) notion of transferable generic literacies and Krashen's (1984, 1988) reading hypothesis both reveal an underlying assumption that second-language literacy entails the same basic processes as first-language literacy (q.v. Hedgcock & Atkinson, 1993). Another example is the previously mentioned work of Carrell, Devine, and Eskey (1988) on the application of an interactive model of reading to ESL reading. Though the results of the present review on United States ESL readers provide more support for the view that second-language cognitive reading processes are highly similar to those involved in first-language reading, it must be remembered that studies from only one second language and only one country were assessed in this review. It is still possible that quite different results could occur for other second languages or in other situations.

Recall that two second-language acquisition positions tended to be used to ground some of the studies in this review. These were positions widely known in the second-language education community and ones which were not, in themselves, complete theories of the reading process. The findings from studies and the themes in this review indicated a fit to one of the positions, but insufficient information was available to inform about the remaining position. That is, considerable evidence emerged to support the CUP model. United States ESL readers used knowledge of their native language as they read in English. This supports a prominent current view that native-language development can enhance ESL reading.

However, the data were unclear on the separate issue of whether ESL oral proficiency is a prerequisite for ESL reading. The relationship between ESL reading proficiency and ESL oral proficiency may have varied according to age and/or grade level (the relationship may have been stronger at higher grades) as well as according to native language background. Further, the studies were correlational and provided virtually no information about the causal direction of the relationship. Consequently, what their results mean is not clear with regard to the position that English orality must be developed to an optimal level in order for English literacy to fully develop.

Research Directions

Earlier comments on the limitations of the research, combined with the images and themes gleaned from the findings, suggest several research directions which can be considered in four areas: research issues to focus on, methodological issues, specific aspects of modifying existing reading theories, and cross-specialty collaboration.

Several factors lead to the belief that a new agenda of research issues might advance the field. First, both the research questions and the methodologies have tended to follow major trends in reading research done with native English speakers, but selectively and 5 to 10 years later. Applying or replicating native-language reading research has been helpful in that it has sometimes enabled comparisons across groups. However, while the questions posed to date have helped us to know something about *what* United States readers' cognitive processes are, they have provided little insight as to *how* they happen. Notably absent were studies designed to trace the cognitive development of ESL readers in the United States. Also, reasons for differences between ESL and native-English-speaking readers' use of particular processes, such as why ESL readers' cognitive processing was sometimes slower, were underexplored. Second, the occasional emergence of interactions among reading processes and ESL readers' native language background, age or grade level, and/or ESL proficiency level suggest considerable complexity in some areas of cognitive activity. Third, individual variability in vocabulary knowledge and in the use of psycholinguistic strategies also suggests that pursuing average effects across readers may not be enlightening in some areas of cognitive activity.

It would appear helpful now for researchers to pursue ESL reading research centering around the issues of how and why ESL readers in the United States acquire, deploy, and change their cognitive processes. Such research might examine the following questions. How do ESL readers learn (or fail to learn) about cognates? How do they use cognates when reading? How do beginning ESL readers at various age levels approach text? What accounts for quantitative differences (such as processing speed) in ESL and native-English-speaking readers' processes?

Another important set of neglected research issues centers around the age of participants. There has been very little attention to how cognitive reading processes emerge and develop for preschool through second-grade students in the United States. This is probably due to prior oral primacy beliefs. That is, perhaps United States researchers have tended to think that ESL learners at these young ages cannot or should not acquire ESL literacy, and therefore have not chosen to study children at these ages. However, most literacy researchers would probably agree that we need to know much more now about the early emergence and development of ESL reading. For example, how do ESL cognitive reading processes develop over time, from the inception of learning English onward to some relatively high level of proficiency, and how are the early ESL reading processes similar to, and different from, those of early native English literacy?

Further, we need to know much more about how, when, and why ESL reading and ESL oral processes interact, rather than continuing to pursue the more general question of whether they are related. Along similar lines, only one study of United States ESL reading and writing relationships was located. It would also be interesting to pursue "how," "when," and "why" questions about the interchange between ESL reading and writing.

A second suggested area to consider as future research is conducted has to do with methodology. Virtually all of the methodological limitations noted earlier in this review could be addressed in future studies. That is, all investigators should report important characteristics of participants, especially characteristics that might potentially mediate results, including extent of literacy in a native language and ESL oral proficiency level. When participants have mixed backgrounds and/or language/literacy levels, findings should be sorted according to the differences, or analyses should at least account for the differences. Definitions of ESL proficiency should be given, and procedures for determining proficiency should be well-documented. Complete references should be reported for all standardized measures used. Reliabilities and, where possible, validity indexes should be given for all measures.

The agenda of issues given above brings to mind several types of research methods which might be useful. As an example of a way to get at the "howness" of processes, researchers might use a tracking technique similar to "think aloud" protocol analysis, such as that done by Hayes and Flower (1983), to track writers' problem solving. Participants could be videotaped talking aloud while reading, and they could give retrospective interviews. Though "think alouds" have been used in ESL reading research, they have not been used very much, if at all, in conjunction with other methods such as interviews or with videotapes, and they have not been used to actually track or describe the intricacies of how reading processes are used or when they vary.

Alongside tracking techniques, other designs could be formulated to help sort out, or to at least take into account, complexities in reading processes such as native language background. An example is interpretive work in which investigators visit classrooms and follow selected children over a year or longer. Through observation, interviews, and collection of reading samples, and so on, much could be learned about how and when cognitive reading processes develop and are used.

Also, where researchers still wish to pursue questions that involve comparison to native English readers in prior research, it seems imperative that extremely close replications be

conducted on selected studies with rigorous designs. If close replications are done, we can more easily compare outcomes across studies.

A third direction is that it would be very useful for theoreticians to select some of the current views on reading and to detail hypothetical points of adaptation for ESL learners. Then a program of research could be conducted to address each of the hypothetical points.

Fourth, and perhaps most importantly, the United States research on ESL reading has tended to be isolated somewhat to the ESL community. Most of the ESL reading research has been published in journals associated with the ESL profession—journals on language, ESL, and/or linguistics. Few ESL cognitive reading research pieces were located in journals known primarily as reading or literacy research journals. This suggests that researchers whose primary specialty is reading might not be doing much work with ESL learners; that if they are studying ESL readers, they are not seeking the audiences of reading research journals; or that ESL reading research, on the whole, has been submitted to literacy journals but has not passed the review process. In any case, if the many communities interested in reading and issues of diversity could cross boundaries and learn and teach with each other, the potential for progress might increase.

Instructional Implications

As for instruction, the images drawn from the findings in this review strongly imply that for the most part, as least with regard to the cognitive aspects of reading, United States teachers of ESL students could follow sound principles of reading instruction based on current cognitive research done with native English speakers. There was virtually no evidence that ESL learners need notably divergent forms of instruction to guide or develop their cognitive reading processes. This finding runs parallel to results of a recent review of United States research on ESL reading instruction (Fitzgerald, in press). A main conclusion of that review was that results of instructional studies with ESL learners were positive and highly consistent with findings generally reported for native-language participants. Evidence in the present review did suggest, though, that teachers need to be aware of some cognitive processing areas that might deserve extra consideration in ESL learning settings in the United States. For example, ESL learners' slower reading and fewer responses in reading situations, on average, suggest mainly that teachers might display even more than normal patience with ESL learners and that they take extra care when wording questions and making interactive comments in order to maximize the opportunity for activation of thought processes. Another example is that the potential effects of background knowledge suggest that the development of readers' topic knowledge for specific reading selections warrants even more attention from teachers than in other situations.

used by other reviewers. Research reviewers should indicate whether their critical evaluations were limited by the absence of information in the primary studies. Also, more than one evaluator should be used in reviewing the primary studies, and interevaluator agreements should be reported.

In the analysis and interpretation stage, research reviewers should indicate how their method of interpretation and their conclusions differ from those of other research reviewers. They need to indicate how they distinguished between relevant information (patterns of results) and extraneous information (noise). Research consumers need to identify whether reviewers effectively synthesized results and noted trends, or whether they made inaccurate inferences such as basing causality on relationship results or drawing conclusions not directly related to their purpose questions or extending beyond the data.

In the public presentation stage, research reviewers might not be responsible for differences in editorial guidelines; however, research consumers should be critical of research review reports that are not complete. Omissions restrict the replicability of an integrative review, thereby limiting the effective use of the reviewers' results and conclusions.

Research consumers can use these questions when evaluating integrative reviews of research:

Are there differences in operational definitions among the integrative reviewers, other reviewers, and the primary researchers? Are those differences explained?

Has the target population of research been identified? Are there differences between the samples of studies in the review and other reviews? What is the nature of those differences?

Are there explicit evaluation criteria? Do they differ from those of other reviewers? Have the integrative reviewers cited studies with methodological limitations? Have those limitations been explained?

Have the reviewers drawn conclusions that are different from those of other reviewers? Are those differences discussed?

Does the review report present information in a standard research format? Is the report complete?

Reading Integrative Reviews of Research

Integrative reviews of research can be read using the plan for reading research reports discussed in Chapter 3 with some slight modifications. The idea is to understand the purposes and conclusions of the research reviewers before reading their data collection and data analyses. As you read, keep in mind the evaluative questions.

The first phase of reading the article on pages 301–320 is to *preview and predict.* Briefly, list answers to these questions: "What do I know about the topic?" "What do I know about the authors?" "What information would I expect to gain from this review?"

> Read the major headings and subheadings (5)–(19), and answer, "Is the review organized logically and is the location of information clearly identified?"

The second phase, reading the integrative research review, is to find information suggested by your expectations and to confirm or modify the information you know about the topic.

> Read the report title (1), the abstract (3), the background section (4), the method section, the theoretical frameworks section (6), and the summary and discussion sections (16)–(19).

> Note as you read (a) the identification of a target population in (3), (b) the discussion of reliability of data interpretations in (5), and (c) the operational definitions presented in (6).

> Read any of the remaining sections that might help you better understand the reviewers' conclusions.

The third phase, confirming predictions and knowledge, is to verify that the purpose has been met and to immediately recall key information. You should decide which information supports the reviewers' purpose and adds to your knowledge base. Answer the question, "Can the instructional implications presented in this review be used in my teaching situation?"

Write a short (two- to three-sentence) statement that applies to the purpose for reading the review and contains the review's key points.

META-ANALYSES OF RESEARCH

Meta-analyses of research are ways of critically examining primary research studies that use quantitative data analyses. Research reviewers use meta-analysis as "analysis of analyses" (Glass, 1976, p. 3), that is, statistical data analysis of already completed statistical data analyses. In them, the reviewers convert the statistical results of the individual studies into a common measurement so that they can obtain an overall, combined result. Research reviewers convert primary researchers' statistical results into standard numerical forms, and then they analyze those measures by traditional statistical procedures. The following discussions about understanding and evaluating meta-analyses are synthesized from several sources (Abrami, Cohen, & d'Apollonia, 1988; Bangert-Drowns & Rudner, 1991;

Carlberg, et al., 1984; Glass, 1976; Joyce, 1987; Slavin, 1984a, 1984b, 1986, 1987b; Stock, et al., 1982).

Understanding Meta-Analyses of Research

The meta-analysis approach was devised as an attempt to eliminate reviewer biases in synthesizing results from primary quantitative research reports. Some researchers wished to reduce the possible influence of reviewers' biases in the selection and interpretation of research reports. To do this, they designed several quantitative procedures for tabulating and comparing research results from a large number of primary research reports, especially experimental research. A simple quantitative tabulation for estimating the effectiveness of a treatment is called vote counting. *Vote counting* consists of tabulating the number of positive significant results (+), the number of negative significant results—those in which the control results exceed the treatment (−), and the number of studies without significant results (0). Vote counting, however, can provide misleading ideas about the effectiveness of a treatment or the relationship among variables because vote counting does not take into account the magnitude of the effect or relationship. *Magnitude* can be thought of as the size of the difference between two or more variables.

Meta-analysis is a quantitative procedure that research reviewers use to account for the magnitude of an effect or relationship. The meta-analysis procedure has become increasingly popular with research reviewers because it is systematic and easily replicable. Given the same set of research reports (selected by the same set of criteria) and using the same statistical procedures, all research reviewers should get the same results. Also, its users say meta-analysis can be used with the results of research projects with varying methodological quality and with similar but not exactly the same statistical procedures. And, it allows research reviewers to concurrently examine the degree of influence or relationship among the methods, subjects, treatments, duration of treatments, and results of primary research (regardless of whether they are significant or not).

Meta-analyses have stages similar to those of integrative research reviews. In meta-analyses, (1) problems are formed, (2) research studies are collected, (3) pertinent data are identified, (4) analyses and interpretations are made of the data, and (5) results and conclusions are presented to the public. Meta-analyses begin with reviewers doing an exhaustive, or complete, search to locate previous integrative research reviews and meta-analyses and all primary research studies relating to the education questions or problems under review.

Problem Formulation.   The first stage of a meta-analysis is the same as that in an integrative review. The purpose and scope of the review are set and key concepts are defined. The theoretical framework of the problem area is discussed, operational definitions are presented, and specific research questions are posed.

Data Collection and Coding of Studies.   In the second stage, the meta-analysts survey the existing primary research and indicate how they located and selected the studies for review. Meta-analysts usually indicate the procedures used (a) to obtain studies, (b) to identify those for inclusion in the review, and (c) to select the variables for analysis. These procedures are similar to those used in integrative reviews. To ensure accurate coding, meta-analysis researchers use multiple raters and report interrater reliability. Summaries of the coding are sometimes, but not always, reported in tables which list characteristics of the research studies and the computed effect size of each study (see the next paragraph for an explanation of effect size).

Reporting Results.   In the third stage, the reviewers describe the results of their analyses. After coding, meta-analysis reviewers use statistical procedures to examine the combined research results. They group the research according to their research designs. Most often, meta-analyses are done with research using experimental designs. Meta-analysts create an effect size for each experimental study. **Effect sizes** are standard scores created from a ratio derived from the mean scores of the experimental and control groups and the standard deviation of the control group. Effect size scores show the size of the difference between the mean scores of the experimental and control groups in relation to the standard deviation. For example, an effect size of +.50 would mean that the experimental group scored about .5 SD above the control group, and an effect size of −.50 would mean that the experimental group scored about .5 SD below the control group.

These effect sizes can be averaged, and significant differences (e.g., *t*- or *F*-ratios) can be determined between treatment and control groups or among several other independent variables.

Public Presentation.   In presenting their results, authors of meta-analyses try to avoid omitting details and evidence. Their approach to reporting is no less stringent than that of primary researchers and integrative reviewers in making their analyses understandable.

The article on pages 324–333 is taken from a meta-analysis about the effects of students' cooperative and competitive learning on their problem-solving achievement. All sections are included except the references section.

Evaluating Meta-Analyses Of Research

Research consumers need to determine whether research reviewers using meta-analysis techniques have critically analyzed and interpreted the data they present. Research consumers need to know how research reviewers using meta-analyses controlled variables that could threaten the internal and external validity of their reviews.

Although meta-analyses are systematic and their results may be replicable, several major limitations affect the usability and generalizability of their results. Some of these limitations are common to both integrative and meta-analytic research reviews. Research consumers need to understand what these limitations are and how to critically evaluate meta-analytic reviews of research.

In evaluating meta-analyses, research consumers need to have the same understandings about the stages of problem formulation, data collection, data evaluation, analysis and interpretation, and public presentation as they have about these stages in integrative reviews.

Cooperative Versus Competitive Efforts and Problem Solving

Zhining Qin
David W. Johnson
Roger T. Johnson

University of Minnesota

The impacts of cooperative and competitive efforts on problem solving were compared. In order to resolve the controversy over whether cooperation promotes higher- or lower-quality individual problem solving than does competition, 46 studies, published between 1929 and 1993, were examined. The findings from these studies were classified in 4 categories according to the type of problem solving measured: linguistic (solved through written and oral language), nonlinguistic (solved through symbols, math, motor activities, actions), well-defined (having clearly defined operations and solutions), and ill-defined (lacking clear definitions, operations, and solutions). The 63 relevant findings that resulted were subjected to a meta-analysis for purposes of integration. Members of cooperative teams outperformed individuals competing with each other on all 4 types of problem solving (effect sizes = 0.37, 0.72, 0.52, 0.60, respectively). These results held for individuals of all ages and for studies of high, medium, and low quality. The superiority of cooperation, however, was greater on nonlinguistic than on linguistic problems.

There is general agreement that cooperative efforts are more effective than are competitive efforts for completing lower-level tasks, such as those involving motor skills, decoding, and recall of factual information (D. W. Johnson, Maruyama, R. Johnson, Nelson, & Skon, 1981; Qin, 1992; Slavin, 1983). There are, however, conflicting opinions about the effectiveness of cooperative efforts for completing higher-level tasks such as problem solving. Some research supports the argument that cooperative efforts are more effective than competitive efforts for higher-level tasks (D. W. Johnson et al., 1981; Miller & Hamblin, 1963; Stodolsky, 1984), whereas other studies support the argument that cooperative efforts are less effective than competitive efforts for higher-level tasks (Okebukola & Ogunniyi, 1984; Rich, Amir, Ben-Ari, & Mevarech, 1985; Rogan, 1988; Ross, 1988). The purpose of this study is to determine the relative impact of cooperative and competitive efforts on problem-solving success.

There are a number of possible explanations for the conflicting conclusions of researchers about the relative impact of cooperative and competitive efforts on problem solving. In cooperative situations, individuals perceive that they can reach their goals if and only if the other group members also do so; in competitive situations, individuals perceive that they can reach their goals if and only if the other participants cannot attain their goals (Deutsch, 1962; D. W. Johnson & R. Johnson, 1989). The first explanation is that different researchers defined problem solving differently. The results, therefore, could be quite different because the studies were in fact measuring different things. From a cognitive point of view, problem solving can be defined as a cognitive process that involves (a) forming an initial representation of the problem (i.e., an external presentation of the problem is encoded into an internal representation), (b) planning potential sequences of actions (i.e., strategies, procedures) to solve the problem, and (c) executing the plan and checking the results. In this meta-analysis, the operational definition of problem solving in each study was carefully checked to ensure that it included this cognitive process.

The second possible explanation for the conflicting findings is that different types of problems were used in the studies. Cooperation and competition may each be more effective than the other for certain types of problems. Major dimensions along which problems vary are (a) the way in which they are presented and (b) the extent to which they are defined. There are two ways problems may be presented: verbally (linguistically) and nonverbally (nonlinguistically). *Linguistic problems* are primarily represented and solved in written or oral languages. *Nonlinguistic problems* are primarily represented and solved in pictures, graphs, mathematical formulas, symbols, motor activities, materials, or actions in real situations. The cognitive processes used to solve linguistic problems are quite different from the cognitive processes used to solve visual perception problems, and may even require that different parts of the brain be used (Glass & Holyoak, 1986). It may be that cooperative efforts, with their reliance on oral discussion and exchange of ideas, will be more effective than competitive efforts for one type of problem, but not for another, and vice versa.

Well-defined problems have a clearly specified goal and representation. Their operational rules are clearly constructed, and once the operation steps are identified, the problem can be solved. The most obvious examples of well-defined problems are mathematics and chess problems. *Ill-defined problems* are those for which there is uncertainty concerning the operational procedures and the goals of the problem. When people decide to paint pictures, write books, or perform experiments, they are undertaking ill-defined tasks. Virtually all real-life problems are ill-defined. Well-defined and ill-defined problems are solved much differently and, therefore, it may be that cooperative efforts are more effective than competitive efforts with one but not the other, and vice versa.

The third possible explanation for the conflicting findings is that investigators assessed different aspects of cooperation and competition when evaluating the effectiveness of each. Some investigators focused on structural aspects and other investigators focused on cognitive aspects.

The fourth possible explanation for the conflicting findings is that some of the studies involved children and others involved adults. It may be the age differences between participant populations that explains the conflicting results.

Finally, the conflicting findings may be explained by the methodological quality of the studies. If the simple criteria of randomly assigning subjects to conditions, having a well-defined and unambiguous control condition, controlling for experimenter and task effects, and verifying that the experimental and control conditions were appropriately implemented are not met, then there is considerable ambiguity as to what is affecting productivity. Some studies were well conducted and other studies had methodological flaws. Well conducted studies may have found different results from those of poorly conducted studies.

The large number of studies in this area made the use of meta-analysis ideal (Glass, McGraw, & Smith, 1981; Hedges & Olkin, 1985; Hunter, Schmidt, & Jackson, 1982). A meta-analysis of the available research studies was conducted to try to reconcile the conflicting findings found in the research literature comparing the relative effects of cooperative and competitive efforts on problem solving.

METHODS

Independent Variables

The first independent variable was cooperation versus competition. *Cooperation* was operationally defined as the presence of joint goals, mutual rewards, shared resources, and complementary roles among members of a group. *Competition* was operationally defined as the presence of a goal or reward that only one or a few group member(s) could achieve by outperforming the others. All studies in this analysis focused on competition among group members, not competition between groups.

The second independent variable was type of problem-solving task. *Problem solving* was operationally defined as a process that required participants to form a cognitive representation of a task, plan a procedure for solving it, and execute the procedure and check the results. Each problem-solving task was coded twice. First, it was determined whether the problem was linguistic or nonlinguistic. Second, it was determined whether the problem was well-defined or ill-defined. Researchers sometimes investigated different types of problem solving in one study. In these cases, different codes were given to different types of problem solving, and the results reported in one study were sorted by the types of problem. Then a separate effect size was calibrated for each type of problem solving. In one study, therefore, there may be more than one effect size reported if different types of problems were included in the study.

Additional independent variables included age of participants (to determine whether this influenced findings), year of publication (to determine whether the historical decade influenced the results found), duration of research study (to determine if short-term and long-term studies resulted in different findings), and methodological quality of study (to determine if well conducted and poorly conducted studies resulted in different findings). The participants in the research studies included in the meta-analysis were categorized in two age groups: younger (preschool, primary school, and intermediate school students) and older (junior high students, senior high students, college students, and adults). Year of publication was operationalized by decades, and duration of research study was operationalized by the length of time the study lasted. Operationalizations of cooperation were classified as pure (both in-group and intergroup cooperation) or mixed (such as in-group cooperation and intergroup competition).

The methodological shortcomings found within many research studies reduced the certainty of the conclusions reached. If the findings of a study are to inspire confidence, that study must meet certain criteria for method-ological adequacy. Methodological quality of study was defined by rating each study on five variables. The first is the level of randomization used to assign subjects to conditions. Studies were rated on a 4-point scale as to whether (a) individuals were randomly assigned to conditions, (b) groups were randomly assigned to conditions and used as the unit of analysis, (c) groups were randomly assigned to conditions and subjects were used as the unit of analysis, or (d) there was no random assignment at all. The second variable is the clarity of operationalization of the control condition. Studies were rated on a 3-point scale on the degree to which the control condition was well-defined. (Many studies had a "mystery" control condition, such as "traditional instruction.") Third, studies were rated on a 3-point scale as to whether experimenter effects were controlled for by rotating experimenters or teachers across conditions. Fourth, studies were rated on a 3-point scale as to whether curriculum effects were controlled for by using the same curriculum in all conditions. Fifth, studies were rated on a 3-point scale as to whether the adequacy of the implementation of the experimental and control conditions was verified. In order to determine the most accurate estimate of the relationship between social interdependence and problem solving, each study was carefully analyzed for methodological adequacy and given a rating on the basis of these five design characteristics. Each study could receive a score ranging from 5 to 16, depending on its methodological quality. In order to directly compare the effect sizes of high- versus low-quality studies, studies were classified as being of high, medium, or low quality. Studies with overall scores of 5 to 8 were classified as low-quality studies, studies with scores of 9 to 11 were classified as being of medium quality, and studies with scores of 12 to 16 were classified as high-quality studies.

Dependent Variable

The dependent variable was the size of the effect when cooperative and competitive efforts were compared on the basis of their effectiveness for individual performance on problem-solving tasks.

Meta-Analytic Procedure

Meta-analysis is a method of statistically combining the results of a set of independent studies that test the same hypothesis and using inferential statistics to draw conclusions about the overall result of the studies (Glass et al., 1981; Hunter et al., 1982). The essential purpose of meta-analysis is to summarize a set of related research studies so that the size of the effect of the independent variable on the dependent variable is known.

The data for the meta-analysis was gathered by searching the literature, selecting the studies, quantifying and synthesizing the research findings, and statistically analyzing the results. First, an extensive and thorough search for all published and unpublished studies investigating the relative benefits of cooperation and competition was conducted. Every attempt was made to locate all relevant studies. The sources that were searched were the Educational Resources Information Center (ERIC) database, *Psychological Abstracts (PA), Dissertation Abstracts International (DAI),* and the *Social Sciences Citation Index (SSCI).* Out of the over 800 studies located comparing cooperation and competition, only 45 were found to have usable findings on achievement on problem-solving tasks. In some studies multiple problem-solving tasks were included and, therefore, 63 relevant findings resulted. The 63 findings of the 45 studies were classified into a common framework. Four judges independently read each article. Three of the judges were graduate students working on doctorates in educational psychology. The fourth was a professor of psychology. The interrater reliability was 94% using the ratio of agreements to coded occurrences. Furthermore, one judge double-checked the calculations of the effect sizes on every study.

The findings were transformed into effect sizes. The formula used to compute the effect sizes may be found in Hedges and Olkin (1985). To modify the difference between the large and small sample sizes, a weighted mean of the effect sizes in each study was calculated

in order to give more weight to the more precise estimates when pooling (Hedges & Olkin, 1985). To control for a possible bias resulting from studies with multiple measures of achievement on a single problem-solving task, each finding was weighted inversely proportionally to the number of findings from that study for the same problem-solving task. This resulted in (a) each problem-solving task (and study) being given the same overall weight in the analyses, (b) the sample size being reduced, and (c) the findings being independent from each other. A weighted mean (dt) of the effect size in one study for one problem-solving task (di) was calculated by using the formula given in Hedges and Olkin (1985).

In this study, a two-step test of homogeneity was done on the data set based on the methods and procedures provided by Hedges and Olkin (1985). The first step is to examine the homogeneity statistics, Q_t, which is specifically designed to test whether all the studies in each data set can be described as sharing a common effect size.

Effect sizes with smaller variances receive more weight in the calculation of the overall mean. Under the null hypothesis, Q_t has a chi-square distribution with $N - 1$ degrees of freedom, where N is the total number of each unweighted effect size, which is estimated based on each result reported in the studies. The Q_t value found from the test in this study was 805.48 ($p < .05$). If it is not large or is statistically nonsignificant at some present level of significance (here it is .05), the test of homogeneity stops, and we conclude that the model of a single effect size fits the data adequately. Because it was significant, the second step of fitting models to effect sizes was taken (a weighted regression technique that can be used only when the independent variables are categorical). The treatment variable that is considered as the variable most related to the effect size is chosen to do the petition. Therefore, the between-class fit statistic Q_b and the within-class fit statistic Q_w were calculated based on the formula given by Hedges and Olkin (1985). If the value of the within-class fit statistic Q_w is small or statistically nonsignificant, the process stops, because the model of a different effect size for each class is consistent with the data (Hedges & Olkin, 1985). A weighted regression analysis was used to calculate Q_w and Q_b. The test of significance of Q_w is a chi-square with $N - p - 1$ degrees of freedom, where N equals the number of effect sizes and p equals the number of independent variables. The test of significance of Q_b is a chi-square with p degrees of freedom. Q_b was known to be significant and so was not tested. The Q_w value for this study was 98.9, which is not significant at the .05 level (using the chi value 157.33). Our homogeneity test, therefore, is passed. This means that the effect sizes pooled in this data set are homogeneous.

Once effect sizes were determined for each study, analysis of variance (ANOVA) was used to determine whether differences between conditions were statistically significant.

RESULTS

From Table 1 it may be seen that 63 findings were found in the 46 studies that examined the relative success of cooperative and competitive efforts on individual problem solving. These 46 studies were conducted between 1929 and 1993. Over 80% of these studies were conducted in the 1970s and 1980s. No significant differences were found for mode of publication ($F(3, 59) = 0.35, p < .79$), random assignment ($F(2, 60) = 0.98, p < .38$), and length of studies ($F(3, 57) = 1.52, p < .22$). A significant difference was found for decade in which the studies were published ($F(5, 57) = 4.36, p < .002$), but the small number of studies conducted before 1960 makes this finding suspect.

From Table 2 it may be seen that cooperation resulted in higher-quality problem solving than did competition (effect size = 0.55). This means that the average person (at the 50th percentile) in the cooperation condition solved problems better than 72.5% of the participants in the competitive condition. When pure operationalizations of cooperation were compared with mixtures of cooperation and competition (such as in-group cooperation and intergroup competition), the results are similar (pure effect size = 0.60, mixed effect size = 0.39). While cooperation resulted in more effective problem solving than did competition on all

four types of problems, the largest effect was found for nonlinguistic problems (effect size = 0.72) and the smallest for linguistic problems (effect size = 0.37). Ill-defined (effect size = 0.60) and well-defined (effect size = 0.52) problems were in between. The difference between students of elementary school age and secondary school students, college students, and adults was not statistically significant ($F(1, 59) = 0.27, p < .61$).

From Table 3 it may be seen that 33 studies were rated as being of high methodological quality with a mean effect size of 0.68, 16 studies were coded as being of medium methodological quality with a mean effect size of 0.34, and 14 studies were rated as being of low methodological quality with a mean effect size of 0.47. Though on the nonlinguistic and the ill-defined problems the studies of high methodological quality produced higher effect sizes than did the medium- and low-quality studies, an ANOVA revealed no significant difference among levels of quality ($F(2, 60) = 1.11, p < .34$). In addition, a Pearson correlation coefficient was determined for the relationship between quality of study and effect size, $r(63) = .18$.

A 2 × 2 ANOVA was conducted to examine the relationships between age groups and linguistic and nonlinguistic problems (see Table 4). The two age groups did not differ significantly ($F(1, 57) = 0.58, p < .45$). There is evidence, however, that the superiority of cooperation over competition was greater on nonlinguistic than on linguistic problems ($F(1, 57) = 4.22, p < .04$). A 2 × 2 ANOVA was also conducted to examine the relationships between age groups and well-defined and ill-defined problems. The difference between the two age groups was not significant ($F(1, 57) = 0.29, p < .59$). The difference between well-defined and ill-defined results, furthermore, was not significant ($F(1, 57) = 0.16, p < .70$). The interaction effect was also nonsignificant ($F(1, 57) = 2.35, p < .13$).

DISCUSSION

Although there have been conflicting conclusions about the effectiveness of cooperative efforts in problem solving situations, with some researchers concluding that cooperation promotes higher-quality problem solving than does competition and other researchers concluding that cooperation is less effective than is competition, there has not been a careful analysis of all the available research studies. In order to resolve the controversy, and to try to reconcile the differences in conclusions, a meta-analysis was conducted. Between 1929 and 1993, 46 studies were conducted that compared cooperative and competitive efforts and measured individual performance on problem-solving tasks. Some of the studies included more than one type of problem-solving task and therefore contained more than one relevant finding. If there was more than one finding per problem-solving task in a study, a weighted effect size for that task was computed. The result was 63 relevant findings.

The findings indicated that cooperative efforts resulted in better problem solving than did competitive efforts. The number of findings in which cooperation outperformed competition was 55, while only 8 findings found competition to outperform cooperation (see Table 5). On the average, cooperators outperformed competitors by over one half of a standard deviation.

It is of interest, however, to determine whether these findings hold for different types of problem-solving tasks. Four types of problems were investigated. Linguistic problems usually involved tasks such as essay questions, discussion questions, and some games such as "twenty questions." The participants solved these problems primarily through oral or written language. The superiority of cooperative over competitive efforts in solving linguistic problems (effect size = 0.37) may be due to the exchange of information and insights that occurs in cooperative efforts (Georgas, 1985a; R. Johnson, D. W. Johnson, & Stanne, 1985, 1986; Smith, Madden, & Sobol, 1957).

Nonlinguistic problems are mostly mathematics problems and visuospatial problems, such as geometric figures, puzzles, and mazes. Co-operation promoted greater success with these problems than did competition (effect size = 0.72). Though little research has examined the internal dynamics of groups working on nonlinguistic problems, one study did find that cooperative groups generated more strategies for solving the problems than did competitors working alone (Lovelace & McKnight, 1980). Thus, the effectiveness of cooperation may be due to the number of problem-solving strategies generated.

There may be two reasons why a higher effect size was found for nonlinguistic problem solving than for linguistic problem solving. First, there may be more ways to solve nonlinguistic than linguistic problems. For this reason, group discussion, which may result in a great number of strategies being suggested, may give cooperators a greater advantage over competitors on nonlinguistic than on linguistic problems. Second, the need for linguistic skills may reduce performance on linguistic problems. Both younger and older students performed less well on linguistic problems. Older students performed better on linguistic problems than did younger students. It may be that the more linguistic skills are required to solve a problem, the lower the performance level.

A well-defined problem is one in which the objects or goals and the representation of the problem are completely specified, such as a mathematics problem. Well-defined problems require "reproductive thinking, applying already known solution procedures to the initial problem solving" (Wertheimer, 1959). Cooperators generally did better on such problems than competitors (effect size = 0.52). One explanation for this finding may be that subjects who discussed a mathematics problem with collaborators were better able to set up the equation in the problem than were peers who worked alone, competing with each other (Skon, Johnson, & Johnson, 1981).

The processes for solving ill-defined problems are different from situation to situation, from problem to problem, and from individual to individual. In other words, solving an ill-defined problem requires generating a creative or novel representation and procedure primarily through imagery. The evidence indicated that cooperative efforts resulted in better performance than did competitive efforts (effect size = 0.60). The reason may be that cooperators can build a shared representation of the problem. Tjosvold (1979, 1982) found that in cooperative efforts, individuals exchanged ideas and corrected each other's errors more frequently and effectively than did individuals competing with each other.

In general, the past research has found that cooperative efforts produce higher-quality problem solving than do competitive efforts on a wide variety of problems that require different cognitive processes to solve. Possible reasons why cooperation may increase problem-solving success include the exchange of information and insights among cooperators, the generation of a variety of strategies to solve the problem, increased ability to translate the problem statement into equations, and the development of a shared cognitive representation of the problem.

There are two other likely explanations for why researchers have previously made conflicting conclusions about the relationship between cooperation and problem solving. The first is that the results vary depending on the quality of the study. Each of the studies included in the meta-analysis was analyzed for its methodological quality. Cooperation outperformed competition regardless of the methodological quality of the study. There were, furthermore, no significant differences between methodologically high-, medium-, and low-quality studies, and the correlation between quality of study and effect size was of no practical significance. The second possible explanation for the conflicting conclusions is

that the age of the participants may determine how effective cooperative efforts are. Due to the complexity of problem solving and the higher-level reasoning often required, it could be expected that the difference between cooperative and competitive efforts on problem solving would be greater for older participants than for younger participants. Although three out of the four comparisons between (a) preschool, primary school, and intermediate school students and (b) junior high school students, high school students, college students, and adults found that the older participants were superior problem solvers by at least 0.2 standard deviations than were the younger participants, the differences were not statistically significant. There is the possibility that age was related to expertise or that the difficulty of the problems increased as participants' age increased.

The practical implications of the finding that cooperation generally improves problem solving are obvious: On the job and in the classroom, cooperative groups will be better able to deal with complex problems than will competitors working alone.

A few aspects of this issue are still unclear: the conditions under which competition may facilitate problem solving, and the internal dynamics determining how effectively cooperative groups approach problems and teach their members how to solve them.

A limitation specific to evaluating meta-analyses in the data evaluation stage is the possible lack of appropriate data in the primary studies. Meta-analytic reviewers must have the means, standard deviations, and sample sizes for all subject groups. When data are insufficient, primary studies are excluded; therefore, meta-analyses are only effective in examining the results of well-reported research.

And, meta-analyses involve the specific coding of primary research reports on several factors. The coding procedures involve rational or subjective, not statistical or objective, judgments. Therefore, meta-analysis reviewers should use more than one coder, and they need to report the consistency, or reliability, factors among coders.

Another limitation of meta-analyses is that they can examine only primary research with direct quantitative evidence. Direct evidence comes from the examination of explicit variables and specific defined subjects. However, one benefit of integrative reviews of research is that reviewers can provide indications of indirect evidence that might give research producers and consumers insight about possible effects or relationships. And, integrative reviewers can analyze and synthesize results from qualitative research.

Also, meta-analyses include all primary research studies with complete data in the analyses. Primary research studies that have major methodological weaknesses or problems are not excluded. Consequently, poorly designed and implemented research studies are given equal status with well-designed and implemented studies. Thus, important qualitative information may be hidden by the statistical averaging of simple numerical data.

These problems have been highlighted by some researchers who reviewed meta-analyses of research. One review team did an integrative critique and comparison of six meta-analyses of research concerning the validity of college students' rating of instruction (Abrami, Cohen, & d'Appollonia, 1988). These reviewers found that all six meta-analyses resulted in different conclusions about students' rating of instruction. They concluded that they, the integrative reviewers,

> found differences at each of five steps in the quantitative syntheses which contributed to the discrepant conclusions reached by the [six meta-analytic] reviewers. The [six] reviewers had dissimilar inclusion criteria; thus the operational definitions of the problems were not the same, making the questions addressed somewhat incomparable. . . . Only one reviewer coded study features. This suggests an undue emphasis on single summary judgments of the literature without attempts to analyze thoroughly factors contributing to variability in the main relationship[s]. Agreement among the reviewers in reported effect magnitudes were low . . . [so] extracting data from reports and then calculating individual study outcomes appears more difficult than was initially envisioned. Finally, methods of analysis differed, most noticeably with regard to variability in effect magnitudes where opposite conclusions about the importance of outcome variability were reached.
>
> Overall, the differences uncovered [by the reviewers of the meta-analyses] were in both conception and execution, not limited to technical details of quantification. Clearly, computing effect magnitudes or sizes provided no assurance of an objective review. Thus the enterprise of quantitative synthesis must be conceived broadly by reviewers to include both statistical and substantive [or problem-related] issues. Attention must be paid to the procedures used and decisions reached at each step in a quantitative synthesis. (pp. 162–163)

Research consumers can use these questions when evaluating meta-analytic reviews of research:

Are there differences in operational definitions among the meta-analysis reviewers, other reviewers (integrative and meta-analytic), and the primary researchers? Are those differences explained?

Have the target populations of studies been identified? Are there differences between the samples of studies in the meta-analysis and other reviews?

Are there explicit coding and evaluation criteria? Do they differ from those of other meta-analysis reviewers? Have the meta-analysis reviewers produced separate results for methodologically strong and weak studies? Has more than one coder been used and are interrater reliability coefficients provided?

Have the meta-analysis reviewers drawn conclusions that differ from those of other reviewers? Are those differences discussed?

Do the meta-analysis reports present information in a standard research format? Are the reports complete?

Reading Meta-Analyses of Research

Meta-analyses of research can be read using a plan similar to that used for reading integrative reviews of research. Again, the idea is to understand the purposes and conclusions of the meta-analysts before reading their data collection and analyses. As you read, keep in mind the evaluative questions given above.

The first phase of reading the meta-analysis on pages 324–330 is to *preview and predict.* Briefly, list answers to these questions: "What do I know about the topic?" "What do I know about the authors?" "What information would I expect to gain from this meta-analysis?"

Read the major headings and subheadings (5)–(9), and answer, "Is the meta-analysis organized logically and is the location of information clearly identified?"

The second phase, reading the meta-analysis report, is to find information suggested by your expectations and to confirm or modify the information you know about the topic.

Read the report title (1), the abstract (3), the background section (4), the theoretical frameworks section (which contains operational definitions) (6), and the summary and discussion sections (16)–(19).

Note as you read (a) discussion about the problems the meta-analysts believe their analysis will solve in (4), (b) the operational definitions in (5), and (c) the discussion of why their results may be different than other researchers' in (9).

Read any of the remaining sections that might help you better understand the authors' conclusions.

The third phase, confirming predictions and knowledge, is to verify that the purpose has been met and to immediately recall key information. You should decide which information supports the authors' purpose and adds to your knowledge base. Answer the question, "Can the instructional implications presented in this meta-analysis be used in my teaching situation?"

Write a short (two- to three-sentence) statement that applies to the purpose for reading the meta-analysis and contains the authors' key points.

PREPARING ACTION REVIEWS OF RESEARCH

Research consumers may need to synthesize, or bring together, the results of research concerning a school-related organizational, learning, or instructional issue. For example, teachers and supervisors in a middle school may wish to examine the research relating to alternative ways to integrate special education students into general education classes. Or, the members of a high school English department may wish to examine research related to the holistic scoring of students' writing. Or, the staff of an early childhood center may wish to gain additional insights about the development of children's self-concept during structured and spontaneous play.

Reviews of research are prepared by going through stages similar to those shown in Table 10.1. However, research reviews produced for local use can be considered **action research reviews** rather than full integrative reviews. Action research reviews are to integrative reviews what action research is to comparative and experimental research (see Chapters 7 and 8).

To prepare action research reviews, research consumers can use the concept of **best evidence** (Slavin, 1986, 1987a), by which they select and review only studies that (a) have purposes specifically related to an immediate issue or concern, (b) are methodologically adequate, and (c) are generalizable to the local situation. In selecting studies specifically related to an immediate issue, research consumers would include only studies that have explicit descriptions of independent and dependent variables. The early childhood staff, for example, would only select studies that clearly define "self-concept," "structured play," and "spontaneous play." Since no research project is without some methodological limitation, research consumers need to determine what aspects in the primary research they would expect to have been rigidly controlled and for what aspects they could tolerate less-rigorous controls. That is, studies without complete information about instrument reliability or subject selection procedures might be included, but studies without full documentation of structured play as a treatment would not be. And, primary studies in which the subjects are not representative of local students and those containing apparent research biases or influences should be excluded.

The first steps in conducting action research reviews are to locate, summarize, and interpret the most recent integrative and meta-analytic reviews of research. (Chapter 11 contains discussion about locating primary research reports and research reviews.) Then, using the principle of best evidence, you should locate, summarize, and interpret the most recent primary research, working back to studies published in the previous five to eight years.

As an aid to organizing information from these two steps, you can use forms such as those in Figures 10.1, 10.2, and 10.3. Figure 10.1 contains a form for summarizing information from integrative reviews of research and meta-analyses. Figure 10.2 contains a form for summarizing information from primary research. Figure 10.3 contains a form for synthesizing the major results from the reviews and primary research reports. These forms should be used in conjunction with the evaluation questions in Figure 3.1, page 117, and those in this chapter for evaluating integrative reviews and meta-analyses.

To complete Figure 10.1:

Enter the appropriate information in the heading; on the *Location* line, indicate the place (i.e., the specific library) where the original research review is located—in case it has to be reexamined.

Summarize the pertinent information about the type of review and the stated purposes, definitions, and conclusions of the reviewers.

Authors: _____

Date: _____

Title: _____

Journal: _____

Volume: _____

Pages: _____

Location: _____

Type of review: _____ Integrative _____ Meta-analysis

Purpose:

_____

_____

Operational definitions:

_____

_____

_____

Conclusions:

_____

_____

_____

Generalizability of conclusions to local issue:

_____

_____

_____

Evaluation:

Appropriateness of reviewers' evaluation criteria:

_____

_____

Appropriateness of reviewers' explanation of differences in definitions or selection criteria/coding with other reviewers:

_____

_____

_____

Appropriateness of reviewers' explanation of differences in conclusions with other reviewers:

_____

_____

_____

Figure 10.1

Summarizing Information from Integrative Research Reviews and Meta-Analyses

Authors: _____

Date: _____

Title: _____

Journal: _____

Volume: _____

Pages: _____

Location: _____

Type of research: _____ Descriptive   _____ Comparative   _____ Experimental
                  _____ Quantitative   _____ Qualitative

Purpose:

_____

_____

Instruments:

_____

_____

Operational definitions:

  Subjects: _____

  Treatments: _____

  Special materials: _____

  _____

Results and conclusions:

_____

_____

_____

Generalizability of results and conclusions to local issues:

_____

_____

_____

Evaluation:

  Validity and reliability and appropriateness of instruments:

  _____

  _____

  Possible influence of extraneous variables:

  _____

  _____

  Possible threats to internal and external validity:

  _____

  _____

Figure 10.2
Summarizing Information from Primary Research

				Synthesis
Purpose				
Design				
Subjects				
Instruments				
Procedures Treatment Materials				
Results				
Generalizability				
Weaknesses				

Figure 10.3
Synthesizing Information about Primary Research

Enter your decisions about the generalizability of the reviewers' conclusions to your local situation.

Enter your evaluative comments about the appropriateness of the reviewers' evaluation criteria, definitions, coding procedures, and conclusions.

To complete Figure 10.2:

Enter the appropriate information in the heading; on the *Location* line, indicate the place (i.e., the specific library) where the primary research report is located.

Summarize pertinent information about the primary research.

Indicate the generalizability of the primary researchers' results and conclusions to your local situation.

Enter your evaluative comments about the appropriateness of the primary researchers' methodology.

Figure 10.3 is a prototype of a form for synthesizing information from several primary research reports. It is shown foreshortened and should be drawn to accommodate the number of primary research studies obtained. The last column, *Synthesis,* should remain the same.

To complete Figure 10.3:

List the citations for the selected research reviews in the spaces along the top of the form; use the authors' last names and the dates of publication. For example, the integrative review of research about the cognitive reading processes of ESL readers would be listed as "Fitzgerald (1995)"; and the primary research study about the writing proficiency of students in urban elementary schools (discussed in Chapters 7 and 8) would be listed as "Davis, Clark, & Rhodes (1994)".

Place pertinent information about each integrative review, meta-analysis, and primary study in the appropriate box for each of the evaluative topics; your comments should be taken from the information you entered on the summary forms shown in Figures 10.1 and 10.2.

Synthesize the results, generalizability to your local situation, and weaknesses of the reviews and primary research; appropriate synthesizing comments reflect a conclusion you have drawn about the research result *as a whole,* and not just a repeat of individual results. These sentences would become key or main ideas when preparing action reports; each could be used as a main idea for paragraphs or subsections.

SUMMARY

What are integrative reviews of research?

Integrative reviews are undertaken as research projects in which the sources of data are the primary research reports of other researchers. These are critical examinations of research producers' methods and conclusions and of the generalizability of their combined results. They consist of five stages: (1) problem formulation, (2) data collection, (3) evaluation of data quality, (4) data analysis and interpretation, and (5) presentation of results.

What criteria are used to evaluate integrative reviews of research?

These questions can be used to evaluate integrative reviews:

Are there differences in operational definitions among the integrative reviewers, other reviewers, and the primary researchers? Are those differences explained?

Has the target population of research been identified? Are there differences between the samples of studies in the review and other reviews? What is the nature of those differences?

Are there explicit evaluation criteria? Do they differ from those of other reviewers? Have the integrative reviewers cited studies with methodological limitations? Have those limitations been explained?

Have the reviewers drawn conclusions that are different from those of other reviewers? Are those differences discussed?

Does the review report present information in a standard research format? Is the report complete?

What are meta-analyses?

Meta-analyses of research are ways to critically examine primary research studies that used quantitative data analysis. Research reviewers use meta-analyses as analyses of analyses (data analyses of data analyses already done). In them, they convert the statistical results of the individual studies into a common measurement so they can obtain an overall, combined result. Meta-analyses have stages similar to those of integrative research reviews. In meta-analyses, (1) problems are formulated and research studies are collected, (2) pertinent data are identified, (3) analyses and interpretations are made of the data, and (4) results are presented to the public. Meta-analyses begin with reviewers doing an exhaustive, or complete, search to locate previous integrative research reviews and meta-analyses and all primary research studies relating to the education question or problem under review.

What criteria are used to evaluate meta-analyses?

In addition to the questions for evaluating integrative research reviews, these questions can be used:

Are there differences in operational definitions among the meta-analysis reviewers, other reviewers (integrative and meta-analytic), and the primary researchers? Are those differences explained?

Have the target populations of studies been identified? Are there differences between the samples of studies in the meta-analysis and other reviews?

Are there explicit coding and evaluation criteria? Do they differ from those of other meta-analysis reviewers? Have the meta-analysis reviewers produced separate results for methodologically strong and weak studies? Has more than one coder been used and are interrater reliability coefficients provided?

Have the meta-analysis reviewers drawn conclusions that differ from those of other reviewers? Are those differences discussed?

Do the meta-analysis reports present information in a standard research format? Are the reports complete?

How are action integrative reviews of research prepared?

Action reviews of research are prepared by going through stages similar to those for preparing integrative reviews. Research reviews produced for local consumption can be considered action research reviews rather than full integrative reviews. To prepare action research reviews, research consumers can use the concept of best evidence. Best evidence is an idea about selecting and reviewing studies that (a) have purposes specifically related to an immediate issue or concern, (b) are methodologically adequate, and (c) are generalizable to the local situation.

ACTIVITY

Read the integrative review of research on pages 340–357. Use the plan for reading integrative reviews of research presented in this chapter.

Read the title and abstract.

Determine a purpose for reading the review.

Survey the subheadings.

Locate and read the conclusion section(s).

Read the entire review.

As you survey and read the review, check for the stages of (1) problem formulation, (2) data collection, (3) evaluation of data quality, and (4) data analysis and interpretation. Then judge the completeness of the report using the questions on page 320 to evaluate the integrative review of research.

FEEDBACK

In the introductory section, the research reviewers set out the problem area and indicate the limit of the review. In the section "Motivation as a Problem . . . ," the reviewers provide the results of primary studies in two different aspects of motivation and provide discussion of the limited educational implications of that research. In the section "Possible Causes of Motivational Problems . . . ," the researchers examine research about motivation from a social-cognitive perspective. This main section has three secondary subsections, two of which are further subdivided. A major aspect of the last subsection is the discussion about the authors' theory of the factors causing motivation. In the sections "Using Motivational Research . . ." and "Toward the Transformation . . . ," the reviewers present educational implications of their social-cognitive theory of school motivation.

However, this integrative review of research has limitations. First, although the target population is delineated, there is no specific operational definition of the key term, *motivation,* nor is there discussion of possible differences in definitions in the research under review. A major purpose of the article is to support the authors' theoretical framework of forces that affect students' school performance. However, the insights provided by this theory do not appear until the end of the article. Second, no attention is given to the quality of the methodology used in the primary studies—the results of all studies are presented without regard for differences in the way the research was conducted and for the confidence consumers can have in the different results because of possible weaknesses in research methods.

Motivation and Schooling in the Middle Grades

Eric M. Anderman and Martin L. Maehr

The University of Michigan

This review examines recent developments in research on social-cognitive theories of motivation during adolescence and the ways in which such research can be applied to the reform of middle grade schools. While there is ample evidence that the environments in many middle grade schools are antithetical to the needs of early adolescents, few reform efforts have emerged which consider the motivational and developmental needs of youth. This article suggests that effective reform must consider the multiple contexts in which students interact. Recent examples of reform at the classroom and school level using a goal theory perspective are presented.

A series of commission reports, including *Turning Points: Preparing American Youth for the 21st Century* (Carnegie Council on Adolescent Development, 1989) and *A Nation at Risk* (National Commission on Excellence in Education, 1983), as well as several special issues of scholarly and professional journals, including *American Psychologist* ("Adolescence," 1993) and *The Elementary School Journal* ("Middle Grades," 1993), have reminded us that the "problem of adolescence" remains. The problem exhibits itself in many and varied ways. Prominently associated with most definitions of the problem are issues of motivation: Adolescents either don't have it, have too much of it, or invest it in the wrong activities. Commonly held opinion aside, a growing body of research indicates that adolescence is indeed a period when motivation is a serious issue. There is also reason to believe that it need not be. This article reviews recent scholarly literature which portrays the nature and variation of motivation during early adolescence. We focus primarily on the role that schools play in this regard, examining in particular how modifiable facets of school culture influence the nature and quality of student investment in learning.

MOTIVATION AS A PROBLEM IN THE MIDDLE GRADES

While important at all ages and stages, issues of motivation have a degree of uniqueness and

certainly a special sense of urgency about them during the middle grades. It is a period when there is heightened awareness of emerging adulthood. Achievement is taken seriously as it may establish career trajectories. In fact, curricular choices are made that effectively determine whether one can pursue a career in science, the arts—or realistically aspire to attend colleges and professional schools. Parallel to this, personal and social deviancy increasingly come under the purview of legal authority, ratcheting up the stakes involved in behavioral choices. While adolescent motivation has not, to date, been a major focus for research, considerable work has been done. In the main, this research confirms a judgment commonly shared by educators, parents, as well as national commissions: The motivation of adolescents is a critical issue—it is, in fact, a problem that must be solved.

Age-Related Declines in Motivation

First, a number of studies have indicated that, during the middle grades, students often exhibit a disturbing downturn in motivation. Negative attitudes and behavioral patterns, which defeat any major investment in schooling, are common. Considerable research can be cited in support of this generalization.

Haladyna and Thomas (1979) showed that students' attitudes toward school in general, as well as toward specific academic domains, such as mathematics, science, and art, decrease as children get older. In particular, they showed that domain-specific attitudes have the greatest decrease between the sixth and seventh grades, and general attitudes decrease the most during the transition from grades four to five. Others (e.g., Epstein & McPartland, 1976; Harter, 1981; Marsh, 1989) have shown that motivation, self-concept of ability, and positive attitudes toward school decrease, particularly during grades six and seven. Prawat, Grissom, and Parish (1979) documented a drop in students' motivation, which is particularly prominent during the middle school years. Eccles, Wigfield, and their colleagues (Eccles & Wigfield, 1992; Wigfield et al., 1990) found that children's valuing of music, reading, and computers decreases during the elementary school years, while valuing of sports increases. A number of researchers (e.g., Marsh, 1989; Nicholls, 1979a; Stipek, 1984) demonstrated that competence and expectancies for success are higher during the elementary school years than during secondary school. Overall, the literature supports the view of decreased investment in academic activities and increased investment in nonacademic activities during the middle grades.

Major Motivational Shifts at the Elementary/Secondary Transition

A substantial literature has specifically considered changes in attitudes, beliefs, and performance as indicators of motivation after the transition from elementary to secondary schools such as junior high schools or middle schools. This research shows that declines in motivation during adolescence are associated with contextual/environmental factors and that motivation is not merely a function of pubertal changes (Eccles & Midgley, 1989; Simmons & Blyth, 1987; Urdan, Midgley, & Wood, in press).

Simmons and her colleagues (Blyth, Simmons, & Carlton-Ford, 1983; Simmons & Blyth, 1987; Simmons & Rosenberg, 1975; Simmons, Rosenberg, & Rosenberg, 1973) provided important evidence relating decreases in motivation and, specifically, self-esteem to changes in the context of schooling across the transition. In particular, they found that girls moving into a traditional junior high school set-

ting showed a decline in self-esteem, while girls remaining in a K–8 setting did not. The junior high school girls (compared to the K–8 sample) were still at a disadvantage even after entering high school. Eccles and her colleagues (Eccles & Midgley, 1989; Eccles, Midgley, & Adler, 1984; Wigfield, Eccles, MacIver, Reuman, & Midgley, 1991) conducted a longitudinal study of the transition into junior high school, examining various social, cognitive, and educational outcomes. One of the major findings to emerge from this study was that there is a direct link between changes in classroom learning environments before and after the transition and students' motivation toward and performance in mathematics.

These studies and others (e.g., Harter, Whitesell, & Kowalski, 1992; Rutter, Maughan, Mortimore, & Ouston, 1979; Roderick, 1992) suggest that many of the developmental changes that occur at early adolescence are attributable to grade-related changes in the structure of school at the transition. Consequently, a number of motivational researchers (e.g., Eccles et al., 1993a; Maehr & Midgley, 1991; Weinstein & Butterworth, 1993) suggest that differences in the instructional practices and educational policies between elementary and middle schools often are inappropriate for maintaining the motivation and investment of students after the transition.

Implications of Motivation Change in Middle Grades

The documented changes in motivation are a basis for serious concern. The noted drop in motivation and rise in negative attitudes toward school might be a disturbing development at any age. There is indeed a basis for arguing that it is especially critical during the middle grade years (Eccles et al., 1993a; Harter, 1981). Aside from the potentially pervasive effects on the child's overall development, there is the fact that critical changes occurring especially during the middle grade years have enduring effects throughout life. Total alienation from school may, of course, deny the person entree to society, let alone a means of earning a living. Even seemingly slight shifts in engagement within the school setting may prove problematic. For example, developing a dislike for mathematics in the eighth grade may lead the adolescent to rule out a wide range of career interests before it is wise to do so. School investment during the middle grades may have serious and enduring effects on shaping career patterns and life choices. That this lack of investment all too often eventuates in dropping out of school before graduation is disturbing, if not frightening; consequently, we are left to ponder how much of the decline in motivation is attributable to factors over which the school has a significant degree of control.

POSSIBLE CAUSES OF MOTIVATIONAL PROBLEMS IN THE MIDDLE GRADES

The last several years have been most fruitful for motivational research. In particular, a large literature has developed, and a significant body of research has emerged specifically related to motivation in school settings. Various research annuals (e.g., Ames & Ames, 1984, 1989; Bartz & Maehr, 1984; Kleiber & Maehr, 1985; Maehr & Ames, 1989; Maehr & Pintrich, 1991; Nicholls, 1984; Pintrich & Maehr, in press), a special issue of *Educational Psychology* ("Current Issues," 1991), and a number of widely circulated books (e.g., Covington, 1992; Stipek, 1993) and review articles (e.g., Ames, 1992; Blumenfeld, 1992; Eccles et al., 1993a; Wigfield & Eccles, 1992) call attention to the breadth and depth of the work that has been conducted in recent years. In addition to providing extensive data on the topic, this work has yielded new and useful models for examining motivational questions along with productive new methodologies (Hoffman, 1991; McCaslin, 1993; Pintrich & De Groot, 1993; Rathunde, 1993; Turner, 1993). Above all else, conceptions of achievement motivation have moved from the use of dynamic models (e.g., McClelland, 1961) toward cognitive models (e.g., Dweck & Leggett, 1988; Maehr & Pintrich, 1991; Markus & Nurius, 1986; Nicholls, 1989; Weiner, 1986). Much of this research suggests that classroom and school environments stress certain factors that contribute to many of the motivational problems which occur during adolescence.

Cognitions as Causes

Recent research has increasingly followed a cognitive paradigm and has focused on the motivational role of the thoughts, beliefs, and perceptions held by the individual. This shift in focus began in large part with the introduction of attributional analyses (e.g., Weiner, 1986) and with increasing interest in how individuals' beliefs about personal causation influenced motivation (Weiner, 1991). Essentially a new research paradigm emerged that transformed the study of motivation: The study of needs and drives became—as it is today—the study of perceptions, thoughts, and beliefs. The importance of this shift in focus is difficult to overestimate in the study of motivation generally. For the present purposes, however, it has and continues to have special implications for the study of motivation in the middle grades in particular.

Developmental Changes. A first and too seldom recognized result of the social-cognitive reinterpretation was the provision of a new perspective on the development of motivational patterns associated with motivation. Placing motivation in a cognitive context associated motivation with the wider concern and effort directed to the understanding of cognitive change with age, strongly influenced by renewed interest in the work of Piaget (e.g., Duckworth, 1979; Siegler, 1991; Siegler, Liebert, & Liebert, 1973). The increased focus on the developmental aspects of motivation led to the emergence of two important lines of evidence, both having direct bearing on adolescent response to schools. A first set of findings has revolved around the development of concepts of ability, competence, and the nature of intelligence. Briefly, students' beliefs, definitions, and attributions concerning ability change substantially and significantly during late childhood and early adolescence; students increasingly distinguish the roles of effort and ability in determining achievement. As students approach adolescence, they tend to view ability more as a stable, internal trait and as less related to effort than they did earlier (e.g., Dweck & Leggett, 1988; Nicholls, 1986, 1989; Nicholls & Miller, 1985). There is a pervasive belief that abilities are fixed traits. Some have "it;" some don't. Moreover, as the child moves to the middle grade years, he or she is likely to experience a school context that stresses the importance of relative ability (e.g., Eccles & Midgley, 1989; Oakes, 1992). As a result, a situation arises in which putting forth effort may be problematic. To put forth effort and fail means that one is "dumb." Trying at school tasks thus carries risks—risks to one's self-esteem but also risks relative to how one will be valued within a setting which cannot readily be avoided. As has been pointed out (e.g., Covington, 1992), this is likely to cause motivational problems in the case of students who, for a variety of reasons, may not be able to compete favorably for grades and other types of academic recognition. Their level of achievement gives them reasons to believe that they simply do not possess a capacity that is highly valued in the academic context. Indeed, this may, in fact, cause some to essentially drop out of an unfair race—psychologically or physically (see, e.g., Nicholls, 1979b).

Concern with ability and worries about failure are not, however, limited to an isolated few. It is a broadly generalizable problem, having pervasive effects on a wide range of students. Casting the assignment of causality into a self-worth framework, Covington and his associates have shown how individuals use various techniques, often counterproductive to learning, in order to avoid risking failure (e.g., Covington, 1984, 1992; Covington & Beery, 1976). But it can be and often is also a problem for children who seemingly possess all that it takes to achieve. In order to maintain a positive self-image and a sense of self-worth, students endeavor to maintain positive perceptions of their competence. Often this involves attributing their academic achievements to ability, rather than effort (cf. Nicholls, 1976). However, the typical policies and practices of many, if not most, middle grade schools/classrooms set up situations where putting one's ability on the line is in fact difficult to avoid (Eccles & Midgley, 1989; MacIver & Epstein, 1993). If one studies for a test and fails, the inference is likely to be that one is in fact incompetent. One way to avoid this judgment is not to study. Not a very adaptive strategy to be sure, but a defensive maneuver that is employed by a significant number of students. According to Covington (1992), students will use such techniques and strategies to avoid failure and maintain a sense of self-worth. In their analyses of causal attributions and their effects in learning settings, Covington and Nicholls in particular portray a disconcerting tendency of schools to define worth, implicitly or explicitly, by focusing on the characterization and demonstration of relative ability rather than progress in learning (Covington, 1992; Nicholls, 1989).

The Self as Motivator. A shift to a cognitive paradigm invigorated the interest in concepts of self. This is not surprising, of course. However, it has eventuated in an extensive line of motivational research worthy in its own right. Among the many programs of research (e.g., Harter, 1982; Markus & Nurius, 1986; Marsh, 1989; Shavelson & Bolus, 1982), few have had wider influence than that initiated by Bandura and his colleagues (e.g., Bandura, 1986; Schunk, 1985). This program has produced a large body of literature demonstrating the power of a sense of self-efficacy in explaining a wide range of behaviors, including areas as diverse as academic achievement, possible control over AIDS infection, and memory abilities (Bandura, 1989, 1990; Schunk, 1981). Given the wide, general, impact that self-efficacy research has had, it is surprising that few studies have examined the ways in which self-efficacy changes during early adolescence and the elementary/middle school transition. Given the literature on decreases in motivation and changes in school environments reviewed thus far, one might expect to find a decrease in self-efficacy as children reach the middle grades. At best, the evidence is limited and mixed. For example, a recent study by Midgley, Anderman, and Hicks (in press) actually found that self-efficacy increases as students enter middle school. To explain these somewhat unexpected results, the authors suggest that efficacy beliefs may increase because the types of academic tasks which students do in middle school may require less effort and higher order thinking than much academic work during elementary school.

Other research suggests that self-concept and self-esteem change during early adolescence as a function of changes in home and school environments (e.g., Eccles et al., 1993b). In general, research supports the notion that the self-concept becomes differentiated during childhood; by adolescence, the self-concept is organized hierarchically, with a general self-concept which branches out into more specific aspects of the self (Shavelson, Hubner, & Stanton, 1976; Wigfield & Karpathian, 1991). Wigfield and Karpathian (1991) point out that motivational researchers define beliefs about the self in varied ways and that the specific operationalization of these self-beliefs (e.g., self-concept, self-efficacy, self-esteem), as well as the academic subject area or domain under consideration in any given study, are important factors to consider when interpreting motivational research on the self-concept during adolescence (see Wigfield & Karpathian, 1991, for a review).

Recent work on "possible self" schemata promises to add depth and breadth to the conception of "self" within theories of adolescent achievement motivation (e.g., Markus & Nurius, 1986). The concept of possible selves refers to aspects of the self-concept that represent what individuals would like to become, could become, or are afraid of becoming. Possible selves serve as a link between cognition and motivation. Consequently, possible selves can have a powerful influence on motivational behaviors—such as, choices that the person makes and strategies that the person uses (Garcia & Pintrich, in press; Markus & Nurius, 1986). Further, as children move through childhood and into early adolescence, their self-concepts include more psychological descriptors (in addition to behavioral and physical descriptors) and are based more strongly on information received from social comparisons with other children (Wigfield & Karpathian, 1991). Possible selves are particularly salient during adolescence. Adolescents search for possible selves that are important on a personal level but that also aid the adolescent in the transition to adulthood (Cantor & Kihlstrom, 1987). Students who experience school-related failure during adolescence may adopt possible self-schemata that define life goals and life tasks in terms of present failure, rather than future possibilities.

Intrinsic Versus Extrinsic Motivation. Even in the era when behavioral psychology held sway, there were those who continued to worry about using extrinsic rewards to encourage learning. Or, to put it positively, cultivating an intrinsic interest in learning was not only accepted but ultimately desired (e.g., Berlyne, 1960; Hunt, 1965). However, with the advent of the cognitive era, motivation research has become increasingly concerned with this topic. Beginning with such early ventures as those of Lepper, Deci, and their colleagues (e.g., Deci, 1973; Lepper, Greene, & Nisbett, 1973) and continuing to the present (cf. Boggiano & Main, 1986; Boggiano & Pittman, 1992; Harter, 1981; MacGregor, 1988; Pittman, Emery, & Boggiano, 1982; Pittman & Heller, 1987; Schultz & Switzky, 1993), a substantial literature has evolved that can and must be taken into account in designing instruction at any level. Briefly summarized, this literature indicates the extensive cost involved in the use of extrinsic rewards in most areas of human activity—work, play, or school (cf. Harter & Jackson, 1992; Kohn, 1992; Lepper, Greene, & Nisbett, 1973)—and has been widely incorporated into most theories of motivation of influence today. Specifically related to education, this line of research has not only been applied directly to specific issues of practice such as the establishment of token economies in the classroom or the criticism of many evaluation practices but has also given rise particularly to a broader conception of instruction in which the student is both given greater autonomy and encouraged to exercise control over the learning process. The importance of a degree of autonomy as well as a degree of control over the context in which one is acting has been seen as figuring strongly in motivational equations for some time (e.g., DeCharms, 1968; Stipek & Weisz, 1981).

All in all, the increased interest in intrinsic and extrinsic motivation, especially as it has been incorporated into the broader context of needs for autonomy and the motivational role of a sense of personal causation, points to factors in middle school environments that need to be examined to determine the sources for motivational problems.

Context as Critical

The shift in motivational paradigms we have described often has been described as a shift toward a social cognitive perspective—and with good reason. From the first, there was an interest in how contexts determined beliefs. This is most certainly manifested in early research on attributions (e.g., Weiner, 1972). And, in general, attribution theory seemed to provide a framework for revisiting cross-cultural variation in motivation (e.g., Maehr & Nicholls, 1980). But perhaps one of the most important breakthroughs in the analysis of the role of contexts in shaping motivation in the middle grades can be credited to a program of research that clearly had its origins in expectancy × value theory which in turn was based on an older needs model of motivation (e.g., Feather, 1982). We refer here specifically to the work of Eccles and her colleagues (Eccles, 1983; Eccles & Midgley, 1989; Eccles, Lord, & Midgley, 1991; Eccles et al., 1993a). As one of the larger, if not largest, programs of research on adolescent motivation, this program has contributed in a number of different ways. It has provided a range of procedures and methods for assessing the determinants, components, and results of motivation that is second to none.

In line with the focus of this article, however, the singularly most important insight stemming from this framework is the specification of a mismatch between student and school environment that is likely to occur during adolescence. Using the expectancy × value framework, Eccles and her colleagues (e.g., Eccles et al., 1993b) argue that there is a developmental mismatch between the psychological needs of early adolescents and the types of environments that most schools provide. The typical middle grade school environment is characterized by few opportunities for students to make important decisions, excessive rules and discipline, poor teacher-student relationships, homogeneous grouping by ability, and stricter grading practices than those in the elementary school years (Blyth, Simmons, & Bush, 1978; Brophy & Everston, 1976; Eccles et al., 1993a; Eccles & Midgley, 1989; MacIver & Epstein, 1993). However, early adolescence is characterized as a period of sociocognitive development that is best nurtured by a strong sense of autonomy, independence, self-determination, and social interaction (Carnegie, 1989; Eccles & Midgley, 1989; Simmons & Blyth, 1987). Con-

sequently, the contexts which typical middle schools provide for early adolescents may indeed represent a mismatch with the psychological needs of youth. This mismatch may in part be responsible for the serious decline in motivation often observed at this period. In sum, the Eccles et al. program of research not only clearly acknowledges the importance of the context, including especially the school context, but also has suggested specific school context variables that are likely to affect the motivation and achievement of children in the middle grades.

The role of context, however, is increasingly being examined for a number of different reasons. Concern with context accords well with a social-cognitive perspective, with constructivist approaches to instruction (e.g., DeVries, Haney, & Zan, 1991; Englert & Palincsar, 1991), and even with new statistical techniques for examining the effects of contexts on individuals (e.g., Bryk & Raudenbush, 1992; Raudenbush & Willms, 1991). It also meets the demands of the practicing educator. Individual difference views of motivation pose definite problems of application in classrooms and schools where individuals exist in groups and where one context must more or less fit all regardless of individual needs. Therefore, an increasing concern with optimal contexts has become a major feature of recent motivational research. Nowhere is the role of context taken more seriously and studied more expansively than in research on the role of purpose and goals in determining motivation.

The Primacy of Purpose

Arguably, one of the more prominent developments in motivation research in the past decade has been the emergence of *goal theory* (e.g., Ames, 1992; Dweck & Leggett, 1988; Maehr & Pintrich, 1991; Nicholls, 1989). Goal theory in many important respects grows out of and takes advantage of the major insights emerging from a social-cognitive motivational paradigm; in fact, it emphasizes the point, associated with the work of Eccles and others, that the context is a major factor in the motivational problems of adolescence. While a number of theoretical frameworks have provided important bases for the further understanding of motivation, we propose that this perspective has features that make it particularly useful, not only for describing the problem but also for taking action to solve it.

A Goal Theory Analysis of Motivation

The nature of goals. As its label implies, goal theory is concerned with the role of purpose and meaning of an act or situation in determining motivation (cf. Ford, 1992; Fyans, Salili, Maehr, & Desai, 1983; Maehr & Braskamp, 1986). The perceived purpose doing something—a course of action—is hypothesized to be a primary factor in determining the individual's level and quality of engagement. While a number of purposes or goals can be associated with schooling at any age, the research has focused primarily on two types of goals. Labeled variously, we will refer to these goals as *task-focused goals,* in which students are focused on taskmastery and learning for purely intrinsic reasons, and ability-focused goals, in which students are interested in demonstrating their ability or outperforming others (cf. Ames, 1992; Ames & Archer, 1988; Dweck & Leggett, 1988; Nicholls, 1986). A large literature suggests that these goals are orthogonal and not simply opposite ends of a continuum (e.g., Maehr & Pintrich, 1991; Nicholls, & Thorkild-sen, 1989; Pintrich, 1989). Individually and in combination, these goals can have qualitatively different effects on many types of behaviors (Maehr, Pintrich, & Zimmerman, 1993). An expanded definition of these goals derived from the literature, which has also shaped operational definitions of these constructs (e.g., Midgley, Maehr, & Urdan, 1993), is presented in Table 1.

Summary of Central Findings

Goals, action, and effect. Much of the research to date has been concerned with how goals are associated with the nature and quality of investment in learning. Numerous studies have found that students who adopt task-focused (mastery) goals are more likely to engage in deep cognitive processing, such as thinking about how newly learned material relates to previous knowledge and attempting to understand complex relationships. In contrast, students who adopt ability-focused (performance) goals tend to use surface-level strategies, such as the rote memorization of facts and immediately asking the teacher for assistance when confronted with difficult academic tasks (Golan & Graham, 1990; Meece, Blumenfeld, & Holye, 1988; Nolen, 1988; Nolen & Haladyna, 1990; Pintrich & De Groot, 1990; Pintrich & Garcia, 1991). Students who

Table 1 *Definitions of task and ability goals*

	Task	Ability
Success defined as . . .	Improvement, progress, mastery, innovation, creativity	High grades, high performance compared to others, relative achievement on standardized measures, winning at all costs
Value placed on . . .	Effort, attempting difficult tasks	Avoiding failure
Basis for satisfaction . . .	Progress, mastery	Being the best; success relative to effort
Work/performance context . . .	Growth of individual potential; learning	Establishing performance hierarchies
Reasons for effort . . .	Intrinsic and personal meaning of activity	Demonstrating one's worth
Evaluation criteria . . .	Absolute criteria; evidence of progress	Norms; social comparisons
Errors viewed as . . .	Part of the growth process; informational	Failure, evidence of lack of ability or worth
Competence viewed as . . .	Developing through effort	Inherited and fixed

adopt task-focused goals also have been shown to use more adaptive help-seeking strategies (Arbreton, 1993), to show higher levels of creativity (Archer, 1990), and to know more about current events (Anderman & Johnston, 1993; Johnston, Brzezinski, & Anderman, 1994). As a new horizon, current studies are examining the role of task and ability goals in mental health and affective outcomes (Maehr, Pintrich, & Zimmerman, 1993; Urdan & Roeser, 1993).

Context and goal construction. A second point relates to the focus that goal theory places on the role of the psychological environment in determining goal adoption. While individuals may bring entering biases to bear in any given situation, characteristics of the situation are also crucial in determining what goals will be adopted (cf. Ames, 1990a; Maehr, 1991). Thus, recent studies suggest that the psychological environment of the classroom may have a strong influence on the goals that students adopt (Ames & Archer, 1988; Ames & Maehr, 1989; Anderman & Young, 1993). If the activities in a particular class emphasize relative ability, grades, and performance, then students are likely to adopt ability-focused goals. In contrast, in classrooms where task-mastery, effort, and improvement are stressed, students are more likely to adopt task-focused goals. A number of studies indicate that students adopt different goals in different classrooms and that the adoption of goals is related to specific instructional practices (e.g., grouping, recognition, evaluation, the nature of tasks) and students' perceptions of goal stresses (Ames & Archer, 1988; Meece, Blumenfeld, & Hoyle, 1988; Nolen, 1988; Powell, 1990). For example, when teachers use instructional practices that emphasize doing the best or getting the highest grades (e.g., hanging up the best projects, posting grades, etc.), students have been found to be more likely to adopt ability-focused goals (Anderman & Young, 1993).

Other research suggests that the school as a whole can influence the goals that students adopt (Krug, in press; Maehr, 1991; Maehr & Fyans, 1989; Maehr & Midgley, 1991; Maehr, Midgley, & Urdan, 1992). Research on school culture and climate suggests that schools emphasize different goals and that such school-wide goal stresses influence individual students' goals and motivation (Krug, in press; Maehr & Buck, 1992; Maehr & Fyans, 1989). For example, a school that places an extremely high value on grades and performance is likely to create an environment that encourages students to focus on grades as the primary focus of learning. A school that displays the high (A) honor roll on all of the bulletin boards is sending a very strong message to its students—this school values grades! Such school-wide practices that emphasize ability-focused goals often interfere with classroom-level practices that foster task goals (Maehr & Midgley, 1991).

Of special relevance to middle grade education is that school effects seem to increase with grade level. Maehr (1991) found that various dimensions of a school's psychological environment (school-wide stress on accomplishment, power, recognition, affiliation) have an increasingly powerful effect on student motivation as students get into higher grades. Specifically, the psychological climate of the school accounted for 7.0% of the variance in motivation at the 4th-grade level, for 11.0% at the 6th-grade level, for 14.0% at the 8th-grade level, and for 21.0% at the 10th-grade level. These findings suggest that, as students get into the higher grades, the culture of the school as a whole has a greater impact on student motivation (Maehr, 1991; Maehr & Fyans, 1989). These results are compatible with what we know about the typical nature and organization of different levels of schooling. In the elementary school, students spend most of the day in one classroom, with only one teacher and about 30 other students. In contrast, after the transition to a middle level school, the student usually spends his or her day traveling throughout the school, from one classroom to another classroom, one teacher to another teacher, and one peer group to another peer group. Thus, when the student's daily activities revolve around the school as a whole, so too does much of the student's motivation to learn.

Moreover, it is important to note that researchers working within the goal theory context have built on the work of Eccles, Nicholls, Weiner, Covington, and others, alluded

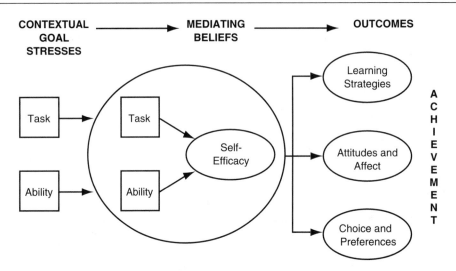

Figure 1. *Schematic representation of goal theory model. Note.* **Adapted from Maehr, Pintrich, and Zimmerman, 1993.**

to earlier, to make the case that middle school climate and culture are characteristically ability goal oriented (see Eccles & Midgley, 1989; Maehr & Midgley, 1991; Midgley, in press). Thus, in spite of what an individual teacher might do to stress the value of learning for its own sake, to stress the role of effort and progress, to include all within the learning community, these efforts may be undermined if the school as a whole emphasizes grades, competition, and rewards (Maehr & Anderman, 1993).

A goal theory model of motivation. In some, goal theory is composed of a set of interlocking hypotheses which, first of all, define the causal link between specific cognitions and the nature and quality of investment in a given course of action. A schematic representation of this model is presented in Figure 1.

First, special emphasis is placed on psychological environment as a precursor to, or determinant of, the personal goal beliefs that individuals hold. Second, a broad range of action and affect is associated with holding goal beliefs. The goals that students adopt have been shown to be related to cognitive strategies, achievement, behaviors, and affect (Ames & Archer, 1988; Maehr et al., 1993; Nolen, 1988; Pintrich & De Groot, 1990; Urdan & Roeser, 1993).

Third, it should be of some interest that goals are usually seen as superordinate to judgments of self in organizing and prompting action. One's judgment of competence or self-efficacy figures into the motivation differentially depending on what goal dominates. For example, Midgley and her colleagues (Midgley, Anderman, & Hicks, in press) find that the perceived stress on task or ability goals is related to students' individual goal orientations and that students who adopt task-focused goals are more likely to feel efficacious at learning than students who adopt ability-focused goals.

Finally, we would suggest that goal theory has served motivation research in at least two ways. First, it has served as a framework in which much of current motivational research can be incorporated. Second, it provides a basis for focusing current motivational knowledge on school change. To this issue, we now turn.

USING MOTIVATIONAL RESEARCH TO GUIDE SCHOOL CHANGE

As indicated throughout, various issues considered in motivational research throughout the last decade or so are of special interest to educators and have in notable instances been applied to enhance instruction. The incorporation of these insights and experiences within goal theory provides a viable basis for school change which addresses the concerns and ideas of researchers from various motivational perspectives.

Historically, when the problems experienced by young adolescents have been attended to, the focus has been on treatment rather than prevention (Cowen, 1991). This is no less true in the case of motivational problems than in other areas. Thus, early work applying achievement theory was directed toward reversing maladaptive socialization patterns (cf. McClelland, 1985). Similarly, more recent research applying attribution theory (e.g., Ho & McMurtrie, 1991; Reiher & Dembo, 1984) or self-efficacy theory (e.g., Schunk & Swartz, 1993) has typically represented an attempt to change the inappropriate or ineffective thoughts of individuals. It is noteworthy that the focus of intervention approaches generally has moved from the treatment of individuals to establishing contexts and experiences which reduce problems and enhance positive growth and adaptive behavior. Thus, the emphasis in the area of health has been increasingly placed on wellness and building health, rather than fighting sickness (Heirich, 1989; Price, Cowen, Lorion, & Ramos-McKay, 1991; Weinstein et al., 1991). This has begun to transfer to the study of adaptive behavior generally (Felner, Phillips, DuBois, & Lease, 1991). And overall, there seems good reason to suggest that researchers should look increasingly at how environments promote and encourage or discourage adaptive behavior. It would seem that this ecological approach might be especially appropriate for the problem of adolescent motivation in the middle grades. Rather than focusing primarily on the designated problems of some, it may be profitable and more practical to identify contexts that are optimally beneficial to most. Certainly, focusing on individuals has its limitations within classrooms and schools.

Two major efforts recently have shown how goal theory can be specifically useful in designing interventions to enhance motivation in schools. Ames and her colleagues at Illinois (Ames, 1990b; Ames & Maehr, 1989) worked with a large number of elementary school teachers to change the goal stresses in elementary school classrooms. Briefly summarized, they assembled a large notebook of strategies that teachers and parents could use to increase the salience of mastery goals in classroom and home environments. In her work, Ames suggests that effective change programs using a goal theory approach should foster the adoption of mastery (task) goals, rather than focusing on eliminating performance (ability) goals (Ames, 1990b).

After a full year of using these strategies, results indicated several differences between at-risk and normally achieving students in classrooms that emphasized the mastery-oriented strategies and in control classrooms. In particular, these students perceived their classrooms as being more mastery-focused, had more positive attitudes toward school, had higher self-concepts of ability, showed an enhanced preference for challenging work, reported using more effective cognitive strategies, and were more intrinsically motivated than the control students (Ames, 1990b).

Maehr, Midgley, and their colleagues at Michigan (Beck, Urdan, & Midgley, 1992; Maehr & Anderman, 1993; Maehr & Midgley, 1991; Midgley, in press) noted that classroom level efforts to increase task goals often are undermined by school-wide practices, particularly at the middle grade level. Consequently, the possible benefits of being in a task-focused classroom may be undermined by an ability-focused school-wide environment. Given the increased impact of the overall school culture on motivation during the middle grade years (Maehr, 1991), the fact that middle school environments stress ability-focused goals more and task-focused goals less than elementary schools (Midgley, Anderman, & Hicks, in press), and the fact that a student's overall experience in middle school is determined by the sum of his or her experiences in several classes, Maehr and Midgley (1991) developed a coalition project, which used goal theory as a guiding principal to change the motivational climate in middle grade schools.

A coalition group met weekly for 3 years, examining various classroom and school-wide policies and procedures which could be changed to focus on the adoption of task, as opposed to ability-focused goals. The group consisted of two university researchers, several graduate students (including some former middle school teachers), school administrators, teachers, and occasionally parents. The group worked to identify school-wide and classroom specific practices, procedures, and policies that stressed task- or ability-focused goals. The group then worked with administrators, parents, students, and the teachers' union to change existing practices and implement new practices designed to foster task, rather than ability, goals. At the end of 3 years, the team had successfully implemented changes in several aspects of the school environment. These changes included doing away with all forms of ability grouping (except in mathematics), team-teaching, block scheduling, changes in the structure of the honor roll, and changes in the school's awards programs. Although many of the changes that the school ultimately adopted are not new and previously have been recommended by others interested in middle grade reform (e.g., Alexander & Williams, 1965; Carnegie, 1989), the use of goal theory provided a conceptual framework for both designing changes and evaluating effects. Prior reform efforts typically have not been guided by an overarching conceptual scheme. And, more often, reform has been directed toward a limited facet of the learning process: the curriculum, the introduction of technology or instructional strategies, or organizational and administrative changes. In this case, goal theory provided a conceptual framework for recommending how school—in all its parts—contributed to the personal investment of students in learning (Maehr & Parker, 1993; Maehr, Midgley, & Urdan, 1992).

While the Illinois and Michigan programs differ in that one is classroom focused and the other school focused, they in fact represent a very similar approach. Particularly important is that the environment is the focus for change. Moreover, both specify how policies and practices in effect create a certain psychological environment that leads the student to more readily adopt a mastery (task) or performance (ability) goal with specific and predictable effects on the nature and quality of engagement of students. Very practically, one program is primarily designed to speak to teachers and to classroom management; the other is focused on school leadership and the staff and school as a whole.

The full implications of this work are not as yet evident. But, at the very least, it suggests show motivational research can be applied. Indeed, it suggests a motivational perspective on school restructuring and school reform. Of course, other motivational frameworks have provided a foundation for intervention, occasionally also suggesting the desirability of specific changes in policy and practice (e.g., Eccles et al., 1993b). Some, like Weinstein and her colleagues (Weinstein et al., 1991), have moved beyond this and engaged in systematic efforts directed toward changing the nature of the school learning environment in order to enhance student motivation and learning. Interestingly, work within the context of goal theory has been linked to school change virtually from the outset (cf. Nicholls, 1989), giving rise most recently to major programmatic efforts. As a result, goal theory and its experimental application to school change may provide a user-friendly perspective on reform, which may allow scientifically based findings to guide middle grade improvement. The realization of this possibility would be a good sign both for instructional practice and for school reform.

TOWARD THE TRANSFORMATION OF MIDDLE GRADE EDUCATION

The topic of middle grade reform is not new. Throughout the past century, researchers and policymakers have tried to determine appropriate ways to educate early adolescents. Although reports such as the Carnegie Task Force's *Turning Points: Preparing American Youth for the 21st Century* have received much publicity and acclaim, there is little evidence that the suggested changes are being implemented (Clark & Clark, 1993; Jackson, 1990). Historically, middle level school reform efforts have emphasized the developmental needs of adolescents, and changes have been made in the organizational structure, presumably, to accommodate these needs. However, the changes have had no enduring impact (Clark & Clark,

1993). One explanation for this is that these changes have been attempted without the benefit of a core set of principles or a guiding theory that not only identifies needs but also suggests specific and testable hypotheses regarding how they can be met—and with what results. As others have emphasized, effective school reform must be based on an operative conceptual scheme which guides the change process (e.g., Edmonds, 1984, Hopfenberg, 1991; Urdan, Midgley, & Wood, in press). But reform efforts also must be directed toward bringing the right solution to bear on the right problem. Reform efforts that have attempted to change this or that aspect of middle grade education often have failed (Carnegie, 1989; MacIver & Epstein, 1993; Mergendoller, 1993).

In this article, we have revisited the problem and essentially proposed a new solution. First, we have argued that the problems of middle grade schools are substantially motivational problems and presented considerable evidence in support of this argument. Specifically, we have shown how recent research on motivation from a social-cognitive perspective has provided a fuller understanding of motivational processes and provided guidelines for school reform. The guidelines for reform are explicit, direct, and practical but also somewhat revolutionary in nature. Carried to their implied ends, they suggest that motivation change in the middle grades will eventuate in the transformation of school culture (cf. Sarason, 1990).

Certainly, defining the problem as motivational is not altogether unique, as witnessed by the number of citations we were able to assemble for this review. Nor is it novel to suggest that the context is important. We argue, however, that current research, especially that conducted from a goal theory perspective, provides a useful and operational integration of current knowledge that is directly and immediately applicable to school reform. The outlines of a testable theoretical system are available, and they can serve to guide experimentation and incorporate the evidence that accrues from this system. The realization of progress in school reform certainly cannot be harmed by taking recent motivation theory seriously. Indeed, we suggest that motivation theory in general and goal theory in particular present a perspective that cannot be ignored if there is indeed a will to reinvent schooling.

REFERENCES

Ames, C., & Ames, R. (Eds.). (1989). *Research on motivation in education: Goals and cognitions.* New York: Academic.

Ames, C., & Archer, J. (1988). Achievement goals in the classroom: Students' learning strategies and motivation processes. *Journal of Educational Psychology, 80,* 260–270.

Ames, C., & Maehr, M. L. (1989). *Home and school cooperation in social and motivational development* (Grant from the Office of Special Education Research). Washington, DC: Department of Education.

Anderman, E. M., & Johnston, J. (1993, March). *Adolescence, motivational goal orientations, and knowledge about AIDS and current events.* Paper presented at the bi-annual meeting of the Society for Research on Child Development, New Orleans.

Anderman, E. M., & Young, A. J. (1993, April). *A multilevel model of adolescents' motivation and strategy use in academic domains.* Paper presented at the Annual Meeting of the American Educational Research Association, Atlanta.

Arbreton, A. (1993). *When getting help is helpful: Developmental, cognitive, and motivational influences on students' academic help-seeking.* Unpublished doctoral dissertation, University of Michigan, Ann Arbor.

Archer, J. (1990). *Motivation and creativity: The relationship between achievement goals and creativity in writing short stories and poems.* Unpublished doctoral dissertation, University of Illinois, Urbana–Champaign.

Bandura, A. (1986). *Social foundations of thought and action: A social cognitive theory,* Englewood Cliffs, NJ: Prentice-Hall.

Bandura, A. (1989). Regulation of cognitive processes through perceived self-efficacy. *Developmental Psychology, 25,* 729–735.

Bandura, A. (1990). Perceived self-efficacy in the exercise of control over AIDS infection. Special issue: Evaluation of AIDS prevention and education programs. *Evaluation and Program Planning, 13,* 9–17.

Bartz, D. E., & Maehr, M. L. (1984). *Advances in motivation and achievement: The effects of school desegregation on motivation and achievement* (Vol. 1). Greenwich, CT: JAI.

Beck, J. S., Urdan, T. C., & Midgley, C. (1992, April). *Moving toward a task-focus in middle level schools.* Paper presented at the Annual Meeting of the American Educational Research Association, San Francisco.

Berlyne, D. E. (1960). *Conflict, arousal and curiosity.* New York: McGraw-Hill.

Blumenfeld, P. C. (1992). Classroom learning and motivation: Clarifying and expanding goal theory. *Journal of Educational Psychology, 84,* 272–281.

Blyth, D. A., Simmons, R. G., & Bush, D. (1978). The transition into early adolescence: A longitudinal comparison of youth in two educational contexts. *Sociology of Education, 51,* 149–162.

Blyth, D. A., Simmons, R. G., & Carlton-Ford, S. (1983). The adjustment of early adolescents to school transitions. *Journal of Early Adolescence, 3,* 105–120.

Boggiano, A. K., & Main, D. S. (1986). Enhancing children's interest in activities used as rewards: The bonus effect. *Journal of Personality and Social Psychology, 51,* 1116–1126.

Boggiano, A. K., & Pittman, T. S. (1992). *Achievement and motivation.* New York: Cambridge University Press.

Brophy, J. E., & Everston, C. M. (1976). *Learning from teaching: A developmental perspective,* Boston: Allyn & Bacon.

Bryk, A. S. & Raudenbush, S. W. (1992). *Hierarchical linear models: Applications and data analysis methods.* Newbury Park, CA: Sage.

Cantor, N., & Kihlstrom, J. (1987). *Personality and social intelligence.* Englewood Cliffs, NJ: Prentice-Hall.

Carnegie Council on Adolescent Development. (1989). *Turning points: Preparing American youth for the 21st century* (Report of the Task Force on Education of Young Adolescents). New York: Author.

Clark, S. N., & Clark, D. C. (1993). Middle level school reform: The rhetoric and the reality. *Elementary School Journal, 91,* 447–460.

Covington, M. V. (1984). The motive for self-worth. In C. Ames & R. Ames (Eds.), *Research on motivation in education* (Vol. 1, pp. 77–113). San Diego: Academic.

Covington, M. V. (1992). *Making the grade: A self-worth perspective on motivation and school reform.* Cambridge, MA: Cambridge University Press.

Covington, M. V., & Beery, R. G. (1976). *Self-worth and school learning.* New York: Holt, Rinehart, & Winston.

Cowen, E. L. (1991). In pursuit of wellness. *American Psychologist, 46,* 404–408.

Current issues and new directions in motivational theory and research [Special issue]. (1991). *Educational Psychologist, 26* (3,4).

DeCharms, R. (1968). *Personal causation: The internal affective determinants of behavior.* New York: Academic.

Deci, E. (1973). *Intrinsic motivation* (Management Research Center Report No. 62). Rochester, NY: University of Rochester.

DeVries, R., Haney, J. P., & Zan, B. (1991). Sociomoral atmosphere in direct-instruction, eclectic, and constructivist kindergartens: A study of teachers' enacted interpersonal understanding. *Early Childhood Research Quarterly, 6,* 449–471.

Duckworth, E. (1979). Either we're too early and they can't learn it or we're too late and they know it already: The dilemma of applying Piaget. *Harvard Educational Review, 49,* 297–312.

Dweck, C. S., & Leggett, E. L. (1988). A social-cognitive approach to motivation and personality. *Psychological Review, 95,* 256–273.

Eccles, J. S. (1983). Expectancies, values, and academic behaviors. In J. T. Spence (Ed.), *Achievement and achievement motives* (pp. 75–146). San Francisco: Freeman.

Eccles, J. S., Lord, S., & Midgley, C. (1991). What are we doing to early adolescents? The impact of educational contexts on early adolescents. *American Journal of Education, 99,* 521–542.

Eccles, J. S., & Midgley, C. (1989). Stage/environment fit: Developmentally appropriate classrooms for early adolescents. In R. E. Ames & C. Ames (Eds.), *Research on motivation in education* (Vol. 3, pp. 139–186). New York: Academic.

Eccles, J. S., Midgley, C., & Adler, T. F. (1984). Grade-related changes in the school environment: Effects on achievement motivation. In J. G. Nicholls (Ed.), *The development of achievement motivation* (pp. 283–331). Greenwich, CT: JAI.

Eccles, J. S., Midgley, C., Wigfield, A., Miller-Buchannan, C., Reuman, D., Flanagan, C., & MacIver, D. (1993b). Development during adolescence: The impact of stage-environment fit on young adolescents' experiences in schools and families. *American Psychologist, 48,* 90–101.

Eccles, J. S., & Wigfield, A. (1992). The development of achievement-task values: A theoretical analysis. *Developmental Review, 12,* 265–310.

Eccles, J. S., Wigfield, A., Flanagan, C., Miller, C., Reuman, D., & Yee, D. (1989). Self-concepts, domain values, and self-esteem: Relations and changes at early adolescence. *Journal of Personality, 57,* 283–310.

Eccles, J. S., Wigfield, A., Midgley, C., Reuman, D., MacIver, D., & Feldlaufer, H. (1993a). Negative effects of traditional middle schools on students' motivation. *Elementary School Journal, 93,* 553–574.

Edmonds, R. (1984). School effects and teacher effects. *Social Policy, 36,* 37–39.

Englert, C. S., & Palincsar, A. S. (1991). Reconsidering instructional research in literacy from a sociocultural perspective. *Learning Disabilities Research & Practice, 6,* 225–229.

Epstein, J. L., & McPartland, J. M. (1976). The concept and measurement of the quality of school life. *American Educational Research Journal, 13,* 15–30.

Feather, N. T. (1982). Human values and the prediction of action: An expectancy-valence analysis. In N. T. Feather (Ed.), *Expectations and actions: Expectancy-value models in psychology* (pp. 263–289). Hillsdale, NJ: Erlbaum.

Felner, R. D., Phillips, R. S. C., DuBois, D., & Lease, A. M. (1991). Ecological interventions and the process of change for prevention: Wedding theory and research to implementation in real world settings. *American Journal of Community Psychology, 19,* 379–387.

Ford, M. E. (1992). *Motivating humans: goals, emotions, and personal agency beliefs.* Newbury Park, CA: Sage.

Fyans, L. J., Salili, F., Maehr, M. L., & Desai, K. A. (1983). A cross-cultural exploration into the meaning of achievement. *Journal of Personality and Social Psychology, 44,* 1000–1013.

Garcia, T., & Pintrich, P. R. (in press). Regulating motivation and cognition in the classroom: The role of self-schemas and self-regulatory strategies. In D. Schunk & B. Zimmerman (Eds.), *Self-regulation of learning and performance: Issues and educational applications* (pp. 127–153). Hillsdale, NJ: Erlbaum.

Golan, S., & Graham, S. (1990, April). *Motivation and cognition: The impact of ego and task-involvement on levels of processing.* Paper presented at the Annual Meeting of the American Educational Research Association, Boston.

Haladyna, T., & Thomas, G. (1979). The attitudes of elementary school children toward school and subject matters. *Journal of Experimental Education, 48,* 18–23.

Harter, S. (1981). The new self-report scale of intrinsic versus extrinsic orientation in the classroom: Motivational and informational components. *Developmental Psychology, 17,* 300–312.

Harter, S. (1982). The perceived competence scale for children. *Child Development, 53,* 87–97.

Harter, S., & Jackson, B. K. (1992). Trait versus nontrait conceptualizations of intrinsic/extrinsic motivational orientation. Special issue: Perspectives on intrinsic motivation. *Motivation and Emotion, 16,* 209–230.

Harter, S., Whitesell, N. R., & Kowalski, P. (1992). Individual differences in the effects of educational transitions on young adolescents' perceptions of competence and motivational orientation. *American Educational Research Journal, 29,* 777–808.

Heirich, M. (1989). Making stress management relevant to worksite wellness. Special issue: Mind-body health at work. *Advances, 6,* 55–60.

Ho, R., & McMurtrie, J. (1991). Attributional feedback and underachieving children: Differential effects on causal attributions, success expectancies, and learning processes. *Australian Journal of Psychology, 43,* 93–100.

Hoffman, L. M. (1991, April). *A naturalistic case study of continuing motivation in elementary school children*. Paper presented at the Annual Meeting of the American Educational Research Association, Chicago.

Hopfenberg, W. S. (1991, April). *The accelerated middle school: Moving from concept toward reality*. Paper presented at the Annual Meeting of the American Educational Research Association, Chicago.

Hunt, J. M. (1965). Intrinsic motivation and its role in psychological development. In D. Levine (Ed.), *Nebraska symposium on motivation* (Vol. 3, pp. 189–282). Lincoln: University of Nebraska Press.

Jackson, A. (1990). From knowledge to practice: Implementing the recommendations of Turning Points. *Middle School Journal, 21,* 1–3.

Johnston, J., Brzezinski, E. J., & Anderman, E. M. (1994). *Taking the measure of Channel One. A three-year perspective.* Ann Arbor: University of Michigan, Institute for Social Research.

Kleiber, D. A., & Maehr, M. L. (1985). *Advances in motivation and achievement: Motivation and adulthood* (Vol. 4). Greenwich, CT: JAI.

Kohn, A. (1992). *No contest: The case against competition.* Boston: Houghton Mifflin.

Krug, S. (in press). Instructional leadership: A quantitative, constructivist perspective. *Educational Administration Quarterly.*

Lepper, M. R., Greene, D., & Nisbett, R. E. (1973). Undermining children's intrinsic interest with extrinsic rewards: A test of the "overjustification" hypothesis. *Journal of Personality and Social Psychology, 28,* 129–137.

MacGregor, S. K. (1988). Instructional design for computer-mediated text systems: Effects of motivation, learner control, and collaboration on reading performance. *Journal of Experimental Education, 56,* 142–147.

MacIver, D. J., & Epstein, J. L. (1993). Middle grades research: Not yet mature, but no longer a child. *Elementary School Journal, 93,* 519–531.

Maehr, M. L. (1991). The "psychological environment" of the school: A focus for school leadership. In P. Thurston & P. Zodhiates (Eds.), *Advances in educational administration* (pp. 51–81). Greenwich, CT: JAI.

Maehr, M. L., & Ames, C. (1989). *Advances in motivation and achievement: Motivation enhancing environments.* Greenwich, CT: JAI.

Maehr, M. L., & Anderman, E. M. (1993). Reinventing schools for early adolescents: Emphasizing task goals. *Elementary School Journal, 93,* 593–610.

Maehr, M. L., & Braskamp, L. A. (1986). *The motivation factor: A theory of personal investment,* Lexington, MA: D.C. Heath.

Maehr, M. L., & Buck, R. (1992). Transforming school culture. In M. Sashkin & H. J. Walberg (Eds.), *Educational leadership and school culture* (pp. 40–57). Berkeley: McCutchan.

Maehr, M. L., & Fyans, L. J., Jr. (1989). School culture, motivation, and achievement. In M. L. Maehr & C. Ames (Eds.), *Advances in motivation and achievement: Motivation enhancing environments* (Vol. 6, pp. 215–247). Greenwich, CT: JAI.

Maehr, M. L., & Midgley, C. (1991). Enhancing student motivation: A schoolwide approach. *Educational Psychologist, 26,* 399–427.

Maehr, M. L., Midgley, C., & Urdan, T. (1992). School leader as motivator. *Educational Administration Quarterly, 18,* 412–431.

Maehr, M. L., & Nicholls, C. (1980). Culture and achievement motivation: A second look. In N. Warren (Ed.), *Studies in cross-cultural psychology* (Vol. 2, pp. 221–267). New York: Academic.

Maehr, M. L., & Parker, S. (1993). A tale of two schools: And the primary task of leadership. *Phi Delta Kappan, 75,* 233–239.

Maehr, M. L., & Pintrich, P. R. (Eds.). (1991). *Advances in motivation and achievement:* Goals and self-regulatory processes (Vol. 7). Greenwich, CT: JAI.

Maehr, M. L., Pintrich, P. R., & Zimmerman, M. (1993). *Personal and contextual influences on adolescent wellness.* Unpublished manuscript.

Markus, H., & Nurius, P. (1986). Possible selves. *American Psychologist, 41,* 954–969.

Marsh, H. W. (1989). Age and sex effects in multiple dimensions of self-concept: Preadolescence to early childhood. *Journal of Educational Psychology, 81,* 417–430.

McCaslin, M. M. (1993, April). *Expanding conceptions of student motivation through case study methods.* Paper presented at the Annual Meeting of the American Educational Research Association, Atlanta.

McClelland, D. (1961). *The achieving society.* Princeton, NJ: Van Nostrand.

McClelland, D. (1985). *Human motivation.* Glenview, IL: Scott, Foresman.

Meece, J. L., Blumenfeld, P. C., & Hoyle, R. H. (1988). Students' goal orientations and cognitive engagement in classroom activities. *Journal of Educational Psychology, 80,* 514–523.

Mergendoller, J. R. (1993). Introduction: The role of research in the reform of middle grades education. *Elementary School Journal, 93,* 443–446.

Middle grades research and reform [Special issue]. (1993). *The Elementary School Journal, 93(5).*

Midgley, C. (in press). Motivation and middle level schools. In P.R. Pintrich & M.L. Maehr (Eds.), *Advances in motivation and achievement: Motivation and adolescent development* (Vol. 8). Greenwich, CT: JAI.

Midgley, C., Anderman, E. M., & Hicks, L. (in press). Differences between elementary and middle school teachers and students: A goal theory approach. *Journal of Early Adolescence.*

Midgley, C., Maehr, M. L., & Urdan, T. C. (1993). *Manual: Patterns of adaptive learning survey.* Ann Arbor, MI: University of Michigan.

National Commission on Excellence in Education. (1983). *A nation at risk.* Washington, DC: Author.

Nicholls, J. G. (1976). Effort is virtuous, but it's better to have ability: Evaluative responses to perceptions of ability and effort. *Journal of Research in Personality, 10,* 306–315.

Nicholls, J. G. (1979a). Development of perception of own attainment and causal attributions for success and failure in reading. *Journal of Educational Psychology, 71,* 94–99.

Nicholls, J. G. (1979b). Quality and equality in intellectual development: The role of motivation in education. *American Psychologist, 34,* 1071–1084.

Nicholls, J. G. (1984). *Advances in motivation and achievement: The development of achievement motivation* (Vol. 3). Greenwich, CT: JAI.

Nicholls, J. G. (1986, April). *Adolescents' conceptions of ability and intelligence.* Paper presented at the Annual Meeting of the American Educational Research Association, San Francisco.

Nicholls, J. G. (1989). *The competitive ethos and democratic education.* Cambridge, MA: Harvard University Press.

Nicholls, J. G., & Miller, A. T. (1985). Differentiation of the concepts of luck and skill. *Developmental Psychology, 21,* 76–82.

Nicholls, J. G., & Thorkildsen, T. A. (1989). *Dimensions of success in school: Individual, classroom, and gender differences.* Unpublished manuscript, Purdue University.

Nolen, S. B. (1988). Reasons for studying: Motivational orientations and study strategies. *Cognition and Instruction, 5,* 269–287.

Nolen, S. B., & Haladyna, T. M. (1990). Motivation and studying in high school science. *Journal of Research in Science Teaching, 27,* 115–126.

Oakes, J. (1992). Can tracking research inform practice? Technical, normative, and political considerations. *Educational Researcher, 21(4),* 12–21.

Pintrich, P. R. (1989). The dynamic interplay of student motivation and cognition in the college classroom. In C. Ames & M. L. Maehr (Eds.), *Advances in motivation and achievement: Motivation enhancing environments* (Vol. 6, pp. 117–160). Greenwich, CT: JAI.

Pintrich, P. R., & De Groot, E. V. (1990). Motivational and self-regulated learning components of classroom academic performance. *Journal of Educational Psychology, 82,* 33–40.

Pintrich, P. R., & De Groot, E. V. (1993, April). *Narrative and paradigmatic perspectives on individual and contextual differences in motivational beliefs.* Paper presented at the Annual Meeting of the American Educational Research Association, Atlanta.

Pintrich, P. R., & Garcia, T. (1991). Student goal orientation and self-regulation in the college classroom. In M. L. Maehr & P. R. Pintrich (Eds.), *Advances in motivation and achievement: Goals and self-regulatory processes* (Vol. 7, pp. 371–402). Greenwich, CT: JAI.

Pintrich, P. R., & Maehr, M. L. (in press). *Advances in motivation and achievement: Motivation and adolescent development* (Vol. 8). Greenwich, CT: JAI.

Pittman, T. S., Emery, J., & Boggiano, A. (1982). Intrinsic and extrinsic motivational orientations: Reward-induced changes in preference for complexity. *Journal of Personality and Social Psychology, 42,* 789–797.

Pittman, T. S., & Heller, J. F. (1987). Social motivation. *Annual Review of Psychology, 38,* 461–489.

Powell, B. (1990, April). *Children's perceptions of classroom goal orientation: Relationship to learning strategies and intrinsic motivation.* Paper presented at the Annual Meeting of the American Educational Research Association, Boston.

Prawat, R. S., Grissom, S., & Parish, T. (1979). Affective development in children, grades 3 through 12. *The Journal of Genetic Psychology, 135,* 37–49.

Price, R. H., Cowen, E. L., Lorion, R. P., & Ramos-McKay, J. (1991). *Fourteen ounces of prevention: A casebook for practitioners.* Washington, DC: American Psychological Association.

Rathunde, K. (1993, April). *Measuring the experience of motivation: Contributions of the experience sampling method to educational research.* Paper presented at the Annual Meeting of the American Educational Research Association, Atlanta.

Raudenbush, S. W., & Willms, J. D. (1991). *Schools, classrooms, and pupils: International studies of schooling from a multilevel perspective.* San Diego: Academic.

Reiher, R. H., & Dembo, M. H. (1984). Changing academic task persistence through a self-instructional attribution training program. *Contemporary Educational Psychology, 9,* 84–94.

Roderick, M. (1992). *School transitions and school dropout: Middle school and early high school antecedents to school leaving.* Manuscript submitted for publication.

Rutter, M., Maughan, B., Mortimore, P., & Ouston, J. (1979). *Fifteen thousand hours: Secondary schools and their effects on children.* Cambridge, MA: Harvard University Press.

Sarason, S. (1990). *The predictable failure of educational reform.* San Francisco: Jossey-Bass.

Schultz, G. F., & Switzky, H. N. (1993). The academic achievement of elementary and junior high school students with behavior disorders and their nonhandicapped peers as a function of motivational orientation. *Learning and Individual Differences, 5,* 31–42.

Schunk, D. H. (1981). Modeling and attributional effects on children's achievement: A self-efficacy analysis. *Journal of Educational Psychology, 73,* 93–105.

Schunk, D. H. (1985). Self-efficacy and school learning. *Psychology in the Schools, 22,* 208–223.

Schunk, D. H., & Swartz, C. W. (1993). Goals and progress feedback: Effects on self-efficacy and writing achievement. *Contemporary Educational Psychology, 18,* 337–354.

Shavelson, R. J., & Bolus, R. (1982). Self-concept: The interplay of theory and methods. *Journal of Educational Psychology, 74,* 3–17.

Shavelson, R. J., Hubner, J. J., & Stanton, G. C. (1976). Self-concept: Validation of construct interpretations. *Review of Educational Research, 46,* 407–441.

Siegler, R. S. (1991). *Children's thinking.* Englewood, Cliffs, NJ: Prentice-Hall.

Siegler, R. S., Liebert, D. E., & Liebert, R. M. (1973). Inhelder and Piaget's pendulum problem: Teaching preadolescents to act as scientists. *Developmental Psychology, 9,* 97–101.

Simmons, R. G., & Blyth, D. A. (1987). *Moving into adolescence.* Hawthorne, NY: de Gruyter.

Simmons, R. G., & Rosenberg, F. (1975). Sex, sex-roles, and self-image. *Journal of Youth and Adolescence, 4,* 229–258.

Simmons, R. G., Rosenberg, M., & Rosenberg, F. (1973). Disturbance in the self-image at adolescence. *American Sociological Review, 39,* 553–568.

Stipek, D. J. (1984). Young children's performance expectations: Logical analysis or wishful thinking? In J. G. Nicholls (Ed.), *The development of achievement motivation* (pp. 33–56). Greenwich, CT: JAI.

Stipek, D. J. (1993). *Motivation to learn: From theory to practice* (2nd ed.). Needham Heights, MA: Allyn & Bacon.

Stipek, D. J., & Weisz, J. R. (1981). Perceived personal control and academic achievement. *Review of Educational Research, 51,* 101–137.

Turner, J. C. (1993, April). *The use of classroom observation to measure first graders' motivation for literacy.* Paper presented at the Annual Meeting of the American Educational Research Association, Atlanta.

Urdan, T. C., Midgley, D., & Wood, S. (in press). Special issues in reforming middle level schools. *Journal of Early Adolescence.*

Urdan, T. C., & Roeser, R. W. (1993, April). *The relations among adolescents' social cognitions, affect, and academic self-schemas.* Paper presented at the Annual Meeting of the American Educational Research Association, Atlanta.

Weiner, B. (1972). Attribution theory, achievement motivation, and the educational process. *Review of Educational Research, 42,* 203–215.

Weiner, B. (1986). *An attributional theory of motivation and emotion.* New York: Springer-Verlag.

Weiner, B. (1991). Metaphors in motivation and attribution. *American Psychologist, 46* (9), 921–930.

Weinstein, R. S., & Butterworth, B. (1993, April). *Enhancing motivational opportunity in elementary schooling: A case study of the principal's role.* Paper presented at the Annual Meeting of the American Educational Research Association, Atlanta.

Weinstein, R. S., Soule, C. R., Collins, F., Cone, J., Mehlorn, M., & Stimmonacchi, K. (1991). Expectations and high school change: Teacher-researcher collaboration to prevent school failure. *American Journal of Community Psychology, 19,* 333–363.

Wigfield, A., & Eccles, J. S. (1992). The development of achievement task values: A theoretical analysis. *Developmental Review, 12,* 265–310.

Wigfield, A., Eccles, J. S., MacIver, D., Reuman, D. A., & Midgley, C. (1991). Transitions during early adolescence: Changes in children's self-esteem across the transition to junior high school. *Developmental Psychology, 27,* 552–565.

Wigfield, A., Harold, R., Eccles, J. S., Aberbach, A., Freedman-Doan, K., & Yoon, K. (1990, April). *Children's ability perceptions and values during the elementary school years.* Paper presented at the Annual Meeting of the American Educational Research Association, Boston.

Wigfield, A., & Karpathian, M. (1991). Who am I and what can I do? Children's self-concepts and motivation in achievement situations. *Educational Psychologist, 26,* 233–261.

CHAPTER 11

Locating Information about Research Reports

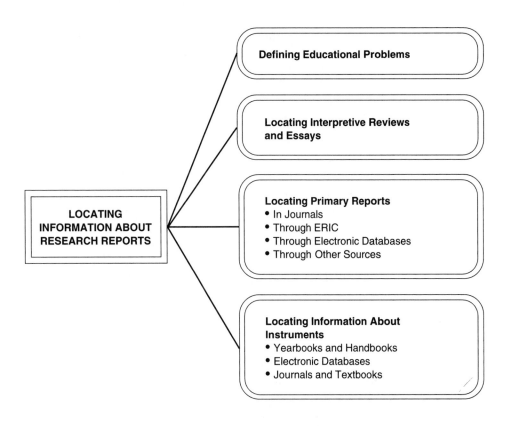

Defining Educational Problems

Locating Interpretive Reviews and Essays

LOCATING INFORMATION ABOUT RESEARCH REPORTS

Locating Primary Reports
- In Journals
- Through ERIC
- Through Electronic Databases
- Through Other Sources

Locating Information About Instruments
- Yearbooks and Handbooks
- Electronic Databases
- Journals and Textbooks

FOCUS QUESTIONS

1. How is an educational problem defined before primary research reports are located?
2. How are integrative reviews and essays about research located?
3. How are primary research reports located?
4. Where can information about instruments be located?

To reiterate from Chapter 1: Educators, whether they are college or university instructors, school practitioners, administrators, or researchers, are continually making decisions about curriculum, teaching, classroom management, and learning. These decisions are based on their experiences, others' experiences, and their understanding of accumulated knowledge about education. Much of this accumulated knowledge is in the form of research reports and interpretations of research. The sign of a productive profession such as education is that its members systematically examine the knowledge base upon which it functions. The chapters in this text are aimed at helping educators examine and interpret research from education, psychology, and related areas in the social sciences.

This chapter provides research consumers with some guidance for locating primary research reports and integrative research reviews and meta-analyses, as well as evaluations of instruments used in research. Most of the resources for locating these reports, and the reports themselves, can be found in college and university libraries. Some of these resources can be found in public libraries. Research consumers need to know (a) what resources exist for locating reports and reviews of instruments and (b) how to locate reviews of research, primary research reports, and reviews of instruments.

Initially, a research consumer needs to identify an educational question or problem. Then, the consumer must decide what kind of information is required to answer the question. For purposes of illustration, a representative educational question is used here. In the following sections, the question's subject area (or topic) is used with the different kinds of resources available to research consumers.

DEFINING THE EDUCATIONAL PROBLEM

The general subject area to be used for demonstration is **authentic assessment.** The educational questions are "How is authentic assessment used in elementary and middle schools, grades 1–8, for evaluating students' reading and writing?" and "How does authentic assessment provide for more effective student evaluations in reading and writing?" The first step in answering these questions is to be clear about the definitions of key terms. Precise definitions allow research consumers to pose answerable questions and locate relevant studies. Since the target population is defined—first through eighth graders—a key term remains to be defined: *authentic assessment.*

Possible sources of definitions, in addition to definitions that may appear within primary research articles, are textbooks on the subject, dictionaries of educational terms, and educational encyclopedias. Textbooks can be found through libraries' card catalogs under the appropriate subject heading (i.e., *assessment* or *authentic assessment*). Although textbooks may not be a source of research, their authors often include references to and syntheses of primary studies. For example, a search of one university's card catalog did not uncover the subject heading *authentic assessment,* but a keyword search did show several books with tne term in their titles. Among them were

Fisher, C. F. (1995). *Authentic assessment: A guide to implementation.* Thousand Oaks, CA: Corwin Press.

Hart, D. (1994). *Authentic assessment: A handbook for educators.* Menlo Park, CA: Addison-Wesley.

Valencia, S. W., Hiebert, E. H., & Afflerbach, P. P. (Eds.). (1993). *Authentic reading assessment: Practices and possibilities.* Newark, DE: International Reading Association.

In the last book listed, the aim of authentic assessment of reading and writing is

> to assess many different kinds of literacy abilities in contexts that closely resemble the actual situations in which those abilities are used. (p. 9)

The card catalog showed as subject headings for these books *Educational tests and measurements, Case studies,* and *Portfolios in education.* These subject headings were noted as possible sources of other materials related to the educational question.

Educational and psychological dictionaries, usually found in libraries' reference sections, contain definitions of technical and professional terms used in these fields. Dictionaries that are important to educators are

The Literacy Dictionary: The Vocabulary of Reading and Writing

A Comprehensive Dictionary of Psychological and Psychoanalytic Terms: A Guide to Usage

Dictionary of Education, 3rd edition

Dictionary of Philosophy and Psychology

Encyclopedic Dictionary of Psychology

International Dictionary of Education

Longman Dictionary of Psychology and Psychiatry

The Concise Dictionary of Education

In the first dictionary listed, the following definition appears:

> **authentic assessment** A type of assessment that seeks to address widespread concerns about standardized, norm-referenced testing by representing "literacy behavior of the community and workplace" and reflecting "the actual learning and instructional activities of the classroom and out-of-school worlds" (Hiebert, et al., 1994), as with the use of portfolios; naturalistic assessment. See also **alternative assessment; assessment.** *Cp.* **classroom-based assessment.** (Harris & Hodges, 1995, p. 15)

Obtaining these definitions and insights from information about authentic assessment that might be found under headings such as *alternative assessment* and *classroom-based assessment* is preparatory to seeking summaries and interpretations of the research related to authentic assessment.

LOCATING INTERPRETIVE REVIEWS AND ESSAYS

Several sources provide interpretive reviews and essays about educational, psychological, and other related social science topics. These sources include

American Educators' Encyclopedia

Encyclopedia of Special Education

Handbook of Reading Research, Volumes I and II

Handbook of Research on Teaching the English Language Arts

Handbook of Research on Teaching, 3rd edition

Review of Research in Education

The Encyclopedia of Education

The Encyclopedia of Educational Research, 6th edition

The International Encyclopedia of Education

The International Encyclopedia of Education: Research and Studies

The International Encyclopedia of Teaching and Teacher Education

A sampling of the indexes of these handbooks and encyclopedias yields references to the following, among other subject headings (the numbers after the entries refer to pages in the particular encyclopedia):

In *The International Encyclopedia of Education (2nd ed.),* there was no entry for *authentic assessment,* but there was the following:

Assessment
    criterion-referenced
      see criterion-referenced tests
    early childhood education   **1:** 355
    and learning   **1:** 370–374
    performance
      and educational assessment   **1:** 369
      grading   **10:** 5855
    special needs students
      cultural differences   **2:** 717
    See also
      Evaluation
      Measurement
      Testing
Portfolio assessment
    and cognitive strategy instruction   **2:** 866
    effects on instruction   **7:** 3724
Portfolios (background materials)   **8:** 4617–4623
    and student evaluation **8:** 4621

In the essay on page 4622, it was indicated that "portfolios are flexible and well-suited for 'authentic' or 'performance' assessment" (Vol. 12, *Indexes*).

The Encyclopedia of Educational Research (6th ed.) contained the following index entries:

Authentic assessment, in state assessment programs   1262
Portfolio assessment
    in state assessment programs   1262
    of writing   450

Upon referring to the pages noted in the indexes, several interpretive essays are found. In one essay about authentic assessment it was noted that

The innovation in state assessment that is currently garnering the most attention goes under several different rubrics, including *performance assessment* and *authentic assessment.* These terms subsume a variety of different efforts to substantially expand the tasks students perform beyond multiple-choice and similar (such as short-answer and cloze) formats. (Alkin, 1992, p. 1264)

Each of the interpretive essays contains a bibliography of all references discussed within the essay. These are excellent sources of additional interpretive essays and reviews.

The journal *Review of Educational Research (RER)* is published quarterly by the American Educational Research Association. It is an excellent source of integrative research reviews and meta-analyses. Research consumers can locate reviews in *RER* through the sources discussed in the next section.

LOCATING PRIMARY RESEARCH REPORTS

Educational, psychological, and other social science journals containing primary research reports are usually located in the periodicals sections of libraries. To locate specific research reports—and, for the discussion here, reports about cooperative learning—research consumers need to use two sources that index all journal articles (research and nonresearch). These are the *Education Index (EI)* and the *Current Index to Journals in Education (CIJE).* To locate primary research reports that are not published in journals, two other sources need to be examined. These are *Resources in Education (RIE)* and *Exceptional Child Educational Resources (ECER).*

Locating Research Reports in Journals

EI and *CIJE* contain up-to-date information about research and general (nonresearch) articles published in almost 800 educational journals. Other information contained in these indexes includes information found in several different kinds of educational documents: yearbooks, bulletins, and reports. Although there is a great deal of overlap in the information they provide, both indexes should be consulted because it is possible that information about a research report may appear in one and not the other.

Both *EI* and *CIJE* are published monthly with semiannual and annual compilations (*EI* provides quarterly compilations). Both present information alphabetically by subject heading, but they use different systems of subject listings and present bibliographic information differently. *CIJE* provides short annotations for each listing, something *EI* does not do.

Examining the June 1995 quarterly complication of *EI* for *authentic assessment* reveals this heading:

Authentic assessment   *See* Performance-based assessment

Following that lead, the heading "Performance-based assessment" is located. Figure 11.1 contains sample entries for that heading. Note that an additional

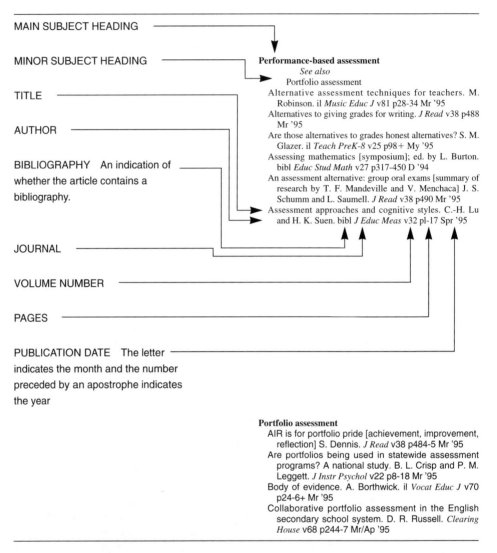

MAIN SUBJECT HEADING

MINOR SUBJECT HEADING

Performance-based assessment
See also
Portfolio assessment

TITLE

Alternative assessment techniques for teachers. M. Robinson. il *Music Educ J* v81 p28-34 Mr '95

AUTHOR

Alternatives to giving grades for writing. *J Read* v38 p488 Mr '95

Are those alternatives to grades honest alternatives? S. M. Glazer. il *Teach PreK-8* v25 p98+ My '95

BIBLIOGRAPHY   An indication of whether the article contains a bibliography.

Assessing mathematics [symposium]; ed. by L. Burton. bibl *Educ Stud Math* v27 p317-450 D '94

An assessment alternative: group oral exams [summary of research by T. F. Mandeville and V. Menchaca] J. S. Schumm and L. Saumell. *J Read* v38 p490 Mr '95

Assessment approaches and cognitive styles. C.-H. Lu and H. K. Suen. bibl *J Educ Meas* v32 p1-17 Spr '95

JOURNAL

VOLUME NUMBER

PAGES

PUBLICATION DATE   The letter indicates the month and the number preceded by an apostrophe indicates the year

Portfolio assessment
AIR is for portfolio pride [achievement, improvement, reflection] S. Dennis. *J Read* v38 p484-5 Mr '95

Are portfolios being used in statewide assessment programs? A national study. B. L. Crisp and P. M. Leggett. *J Instr Psychol* v22 p8-18 Mr '95

Body of evidence. A. Borthwick. il *Vocat Educ J* v70 p24-6+ Mr '95

Collaborative portfolio assessment in the English secondary school system. D. R. Russell. *Clearing House* v68 p244-7 Mr/Ap '95

Figure 11.1
Sample *EI* Subject Entries (from *Education Index,* 1995, June, pp. 402, 420).

cross-reference is made to "Portfolio assessment." Sample entries from that heading are also included in Figure 11.1. (To this example and the ones that follow, explanatory labels have been added to assist you in understanding the entries.)

To conserve space, entries in *EI* contain abbreviations for journal titles and dates. A listing in the front of each issue explains the abbreviations. Primary research studies are not specifically identified in *EI*, so research consumers must examine each title for clues or, when in doubt, refer to the actual article. For example, in Figure 11.1 are several entries which give indication that they are research reports.

CIJE is a publication of the Educational Resources Information Center (ERIC), a national network supported by the Office of Education Research and Improvement of the U.S. Department of Education. The purpose of **ERIC** is to provide access to current research results and related information in the field of education. It is a decentralized system composed of about sixteen clearinghouses, each specializing in a major educational area. For example, some of the clearinghouses within the ERIC network are Elementary and Early Childhood Education; Handicapped and Gifted Children; Reading, English, and Communication Skills; Science, Mathematics, and Environmental Education; Social Studies/Social Science Education; and Teacher Education. The clearinghouses collect, index, abstract, and disseminate information that is available through a central computerized facility. This information appears monthly in CIJE.

To use CIJE, research consumers refer first to a guide for determining appropriate subject headings. To maintain uniformity of subject listings, the ERIC system publishes a *Thesaurus of ERIC Descriptors*, which is updated periodically. **Descriptors** are key words used in indexing documents. The thesaurus indicates the subject terms that are used to index a topic. For example, checking the 9th edition of the thesaurus, published in 1992, there is no listing for *authentic assessment*. When the listing for *assessment* is checked, the following is noted:

Assessment
> *Use* Evaluation

The entry for *evaluation* is shown in Figure 11.2.

The Scope Note (SN) for *evaluation* shows a definition of the term. The Related Terms (RT) list does not include several terms that have appeared in dictionaries and encyclopedias—*alternative assessment, authentic assessment, portfolio assessment*—because these terms entered educational vocabulary after this printing of the *Thesaurus*. To keep the database current, other terms that are not yet represented as descriptors in the *Thesaurus* are used in the ERIC subject indexes. They are called **identifiers.**

When a specific subject listing is not in the *ERIC Thesaurus*, research consumers can use a researcher's name to locate references in CIJE. For example, the name Linda Darling-Hammond appears several times in the card catalog, encyclopedic essays, and *EI*. That name is located in the author index of CIJE. The entry for Linda Darling-Hammond in the April 1995 issue is shown in Figure 11.3.

Using the EJ-prefixed accession number appearing after the title, the entry is found in the main entry section. It is shown in Figure 11.4. Note the separate listing of descriptors and identifiers.

This journal article by Darling-Hammond, "Setting Standards for Students: The Case for Authentic Assessment," is listed in the subject index of CIJE under all subject headings listed as descriptors and marked with an asterisk. That is, it is found in the subject index under the headings "Student Evaluation" and "Testing Problems." It is also listed under the headings listed as identifiers, which are headings that reflect terms currently used by researchers and other authors that have not been officially recognized as ERIC descriptors. By going to the subject heading "Authentic Assessment" in the subject index, one finds the entries as shown in Figure 11.5. Note that authors' names are not listed in the subject index.

EVALUATION   *JUL. 1966*
CIJE: 3,559   RIE: 4,720   GC: 820

SCOPE NOTE   A definition ──▶ SN   Appraising or judging persons,
of the term.   organizations, or things in relation
                                     to stated objectives, standards, or
                                     criteria (note: use a more specific
                                     term if possible – see also "test-
                                     ing" and "measurement")

USED FOR   The terms ──────▶ UF   Appraisal
here are not used in ERIC.   NT   Course Evaluation
To locate entries, use the   Curriculum Evaluation
subject heading or another   Educational Assessment
                                    Equipment Evaluation
term.   Formative Evaluation
                                    Holistic Evaluation
                                    Informal Assessment
                                    Institutional Evaluation
NARROWER TERM   Medical Care Evaluation
More specific descriptors   Medical Evaluation
that can be used to locate   Needs Assessment
                                    Peer Evaluation
entries.   Personnel Evaluation
                                    Preschool Evaluation
                                    Program Evaluation
                                    Property Appraisal
                                    Psychological Evaluation
                                    Recognition (Achievement)
                                    Self Evaluation (Groups)
                                    Self Evaluation (Individuals)
                                    Student Evaluation
                                    Summative Evaluation
                                    Test Interpretation
                                    Textbook Evaluation
                                    Writing Evaluation
RELATED TERMS   Other ──────▶ RT   Achievement
descriptors under which   Credentials
                                    Differences
entries possibly related to   Evaluation Criteria
entries listed under the   Evaluation Methods
                                    Evaluation Needs
main descriptor.   Evaluative Thinking
                                    Evaluators
                                    Expectation
                                    Failure
                                    Inspection
                                    Literary Criticism
                                    Measurement
                                    Measures (Individuals)
                                    Objectives
                                    Observation
                                    Participant Satisfaction
                                    Performance Factors
                                    Quality Of Life
                                    Research
                                    Specifications
                                    Standards
                                    Success
                                    Testing
                                    Tests
                                    User Satisfaction (Information)
                                    Validity

Figure 11.2
Sample *ERIC Thesaurus* Subject Descriptors Listing (from
Descriptors of *ERIC Thesaurus,* 9th ed., 1992, p. 86).

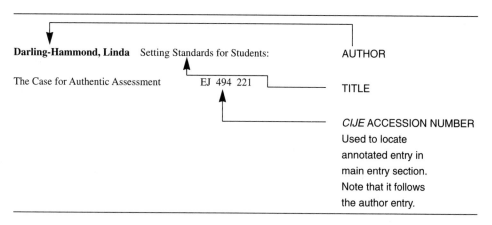

Figure 11.3
Sample *CIJE* Author Entry (from *CIJE*, 1995, April)

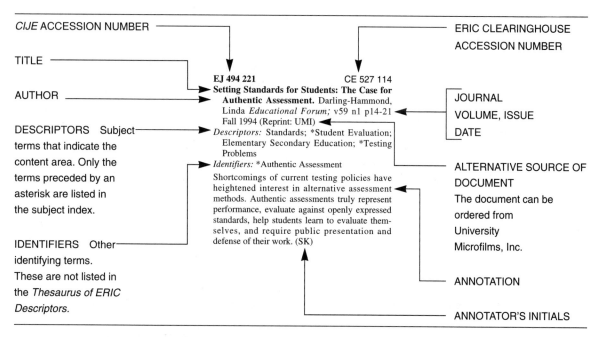

Figure 11.4
Sample *CIJE* Document Resume (from *CIJE*, 1995, April, p. 4)

Each of the entries under "Authentic Assessment" in the *CIJE* subject index can be located in the main entry section. After reading the annotations, the user selects a journal article. The full text of the selected article can be found in the periodicals section of the library or on microfilm in the library's microform section.

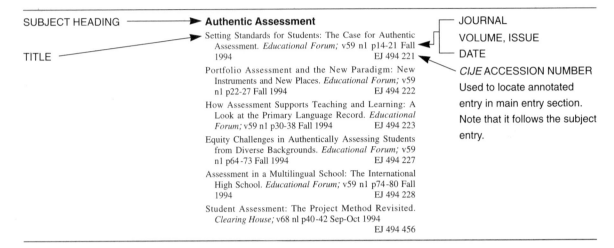

Figure 11.5
Sample *CIJE* Subject Entry (from *CIJE,* 1995, April, p. 130)

Locating Research Reports through ERIC

As indicated previously, ERIC is a national network of educational clearinghouses that collect, index, abstract, and disseminate a wide variety of educational information. *CIJE* is the ERIC publication indexing articles from professional educational journals. The main ERIC publication for indexing educational documents is *Resources in Education (RIE)*. Like *CIJE, RIE* is published monthly with semiannual and annual compilations. It is the means for finding research reports, literature reviews, general descriptive articles, papers presented at conferences, descriptions of educational products, curriculum guides, and government reports. Most of these documents are unpublished and noncopyrighted materials that would otherwise be hard to find.

Locating an entry in *RIE* is similar to finding one in *CIJE*. That is, both use the same system of descriptors and identifiers, list entries under subject and author indexes, and use a similar accession number system. However, *RIE* accession numbers are prefixed with ED instead of EJ.

After an item listed in *RIE* has been determined to fit the problem area being searched, the full text of the document can usually be found on small sheets of microfilm called **microfiche,** which can be read only on special microfiche readers. ERIC microfiche collections and microfiche readers can be found in college and university libraries and some public libraries. *RIE* contains information for ordering a document on microfiche or in printed-copy form. In some cases, documents are not available from the ERIC document reproduction service.

The steps for using *RIE* are:

1. Refer to the *Thesaurus of ERIC Descriptors.*

2. Select an appropriate monthly, semiannual, or annual edition of *RIE.*

3. Go to the subject or author index to locate entries and ED accession numbers.

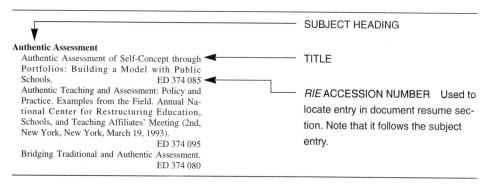

Figure 11.6
Sample *RIE* Subject Entry (from *RIE,* Subject Index, 1995, January)

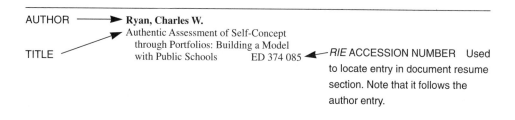

Figure 11.7
Sample *RIE* Author Entry (from *RIE,* Author Index, 1995, January)

4. Locate abstracts of the entries in the document resume section.

5. Locate the full text of the document in the microfiche collection.

Here is an example of a manual search of the ERIC system using *RIE* for entries related to the problem area *authentic assessment.*

Since the thesaurus has already been examined, the research consumer goes directly to *RIE.* The entries for *authentic assessment* found in the subject index of the January 1995 issue of *RIE* are shown in Figure 11.6.

The first entry, "Authentic Assessment of Self-Concept through Portfolios: Building a Model with Public Schools," with the accession number ED 374 085, is noted. The author entry for this document is shown in Figure 11.7.

The noted research project is located in the document resume section. The entry for ED 374 085 is shown in Figure 11.8. Note the separate listing of descriptors and identifiers.

Since the information in the abstract indicates that this is a study to "investigate the viability of the portfolio model for authentic assessment," the user can tell that this is a relevant document to his or her purpose and will locate the full text of the document in the library's ERIC microfiche collection.

A companion resource to *CIJE* and *RIE* is produced by the ERIC Clearinghouse on Handicapped and Gifted Children. *Exceptional Child Educational Resources (ECER)*

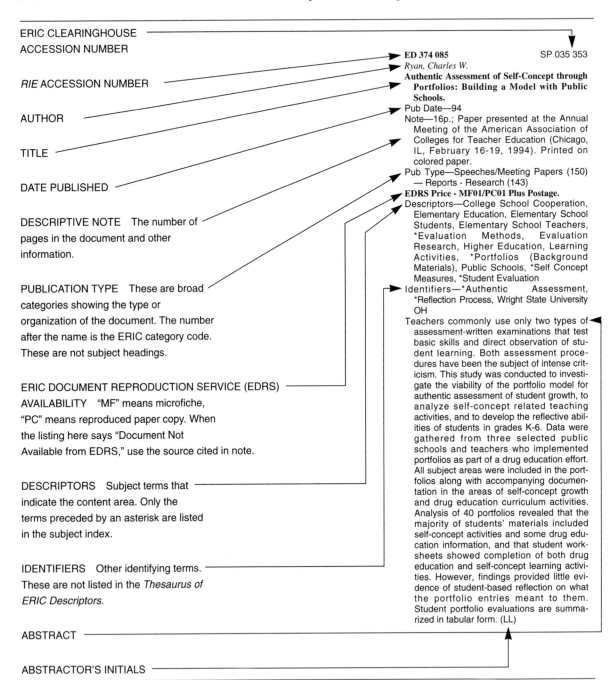

ERIC CLEARINGHOUSE
ACCESSION NUMBER

RIE ACCESSION NUMBER

AUTHOR

TITLE

DATE PUBLISHED

DESCRIPTIVE NOTE   The number of
pages in the document and other
information.

PUBLICATION TYPE   These are broad
categories showing the type or
organization of the document. The number
after the name is the ERIC category code.
These are not subject headings.

ERIC DOCUMENT REPRODUCTION SERVICE (EDRS)
AVAILABILITY   "MF" means microfiche,
"PC" means reproduced paper copy. When
the listing here says "Document Not
Available from EDRS," use the source cited in note.

DESCRIPTORS   Subject terms that
indicate the content area. Only the
terms preceded by an asterisk are listed
in the subject index.

IDENTIFIERS   Other identifying terms.
These are not listed in the Thesaurus of
ERIC Descriptors.

ABSTRACT

ABSTRACTOR'S INITIALS

ED 374 085   SP 035 353
Ryan, Charles W.
**Authentic Assessment of Self-Concept through
Portfolios: Building a Model with Public
Schools.**
Pub Date—94
Note—16p.; Paper presented at the Annual
Meeting of the American Association of
Colleges for Teacher Education (Chicago,
IL, February 16-19, 1994). Printed on
colored paper.
Pub Type—Speeches/Meeting Papers (150)
— Reports - Research (143)
EDRS Price - MF01/PC01 Plus Postage.
Descriptors—College School Cooperation,
Elementary Education, Elementary School
Students, Elementary School Teachers,
*Evaluation   Methods,   Evaluation
Research, Higher Education, Learning
Activities, *Portfolios (Background
Materials), Public Schools, *Self Concept
Measures, *Student Evaluation
Identifiers—*Authentic   Assessment,
*Reflection Process, Wright State University
OH
Teachers commonly use only two types of
assessment-written examinations that test
basic skills and direct observation of student learning. Both assessment procedures have been the subject of intense criticism. This study was conducted to investigate the viability of the portfolio model for
authentic assessment of student growth, to
analyze self-concept related teaching
activities, and to develop the reflective abilities of students in grades K-6. Data were
gathered from three selected public
schools and teachers who implemented
portfolios as part of a drug education effort.
All subject areas were included in the portfolios along with accompanying documentation in the areas of self-concept growth
and drug education curriculum activities.
Analysis of 40 portfolios revealed that the
majority of students' materials included
self-concept activities and some drug education information, and that student worksheets showed completion of both drug
education and self-concept learning activities. However, findings provided little evidence of student-based reflection on what
the portfolio entries meant to them.
Student portfolio evaluations are summarized in tabular form. (LL)

Figure 11.8
Sample *RIE* Document Resume (from *RIE,* Document Resumes, 1995, January)

searches over 200 journals dealing with all forms of exceptionality, many of which are not indexed in *CIJE* or *RIE*. The *ECER* indexes documents the same way as *CIJE* and *RIE*; however, it contains information not readily available through ERIC: commercially published books, nonprint materials, and doctoral dissertations. Entries use an EC-prefixed accession number, and the full documents are not reproduced on microfiche.

Locating Research Reports in Electronic Databases

The ERIC database can be accessed electronically. One source is the CD-ROM format used with computers in many college, university, and local libraries. CD-ROMs are updated quarterly, so research consumers needing more current information still need to use *CIJE* and *RIE*. Institutions also use a database form that is linked to their on-line public access catalog (the electronic equivalent of the traditional card catalog).

Accessing ERIC electronically allows the research consumer to search the database more efficiently, since the CD-ROMs contain all the terms found in the *Thesaurus of ERIC Descriptors*. By combining terms and modifying preliminary searches, the labor of examining annual compilations of *RIE* and *CIJE* and cross-referencing are eliminated. For example, a search of the key terms (which include descriptors and identifiers) used in one university's CD-ROM system revealed that *authentic assessment* and *portfolio approach* had no related terms, but each had 196 and 87 entries, respectively. Using *authentic assessment* and *portfolio approach* together, eight entries were identified, one of which was the full text of an *ERIC Digest*, which itself had references to five additional ERIC documents:

ED369075

Theory Meets Practice in Language Arts Assessment. ERIC Digest. Farr, Roger; Tone, Bruce. ERIC Clearinghouse on Reading, English, and Communication, Bloomington, IN, 1994, 3p.

Using *educational research,* one of 86 related terms for "research," and *authentic assessment* together showed six entries, but only three were primary research studies and only one dealt with students in grades 1–8. However, using *portfolio approach* and *action research* (a related term for "research") together showed

EJ489228

Literacy Portfolios in Third Grade: A School-College Collaboration. Cirincione, Karen M.; Michael, Denise. *Reading Horizons,* v34 n5 p443–64 Jun 1994

and using *authentic assessment* and *action research* together showed

ED371013

A Qualitative Look at Kentucky's Primary Program: Interim Findings from a Five-Year Study. Aagaard, Lola; and Others. Apr 1994, 31p.; Paper presented at the Annual Meeting of the American Educational Research Association (New Orleans, LA, April 4–8, 1994)

Note that many of the entries shown in subject indexes and document resumes for *CIJE* and *RIE* may not appear in the electronic search because the term *research* was used to delimit the search to primary research studies. To determine whether an entry in a monthly or annual summary of *CIJE* or *RIE* is a primary research report, the research consumer must scan the document resume for the appropriate descriptor or identifier.

The ERIC database can be accessed from a personal computer with a modem through commercial networks. Or, it can be entered by Internet users through an AskERIC service that offers individualized responses to educational questions and a free electronic library. E-mail messages and educational questions can be sent to **askeric@ericir.syr.edu.** To locate sites that allow direct, free public access to the ERIC database, contact ACCESS ERIC at **acceric@inet.ed.gov.** The individual specialized ERIC clearinghouses also respond to inquiries about educational questions. For example, to obtain information about authentic assessment, the ERIC Clearinghouse on Assessment and Evaluation can be contacted at **eric_ae@cua.edu.** Toll-free phone numbers for those agencies are available in all issues of *CIJE* and *RIE*.

Locating Research Reports through Other Sources

There are other, specialized abstract compilations and indexes (not connected with the ERIC system) that research consumers might wish to examine for information related to educational problems or questions. Each of these abstract compilations and indexes uses its own format for subject and author indexes; a full explanation of those systems is in the front of each. Several that might be of most interest to educators are *Sociological Abstracts, Psychological Abstracts, State Education Journal Index, Business Education Index, Educational Administration Abstracts, Physical Education Index,* and *Child Development Abstracts and Bibliography.*

Dissertation Abstracts International contains abstracts of doctoral dissertations from about 400 participating universities. It is published monthly in two sections. Section A contains dissertations in the humanities and social sciences, which includes education. Section B covers the science areas, which includes psychology. The dissertations themselves are usually not available, but research consumers should check with reference librarians to see whether copies of selected dissertations are available in the universities' microform sections. The index is arranged alphabetically by key word and alphabetically by title for key words. The location of abstracts is indicated by page numbers.

LOCATING INFORMATION ABOUT INSTRUMENTS

Information about instruments' format, content, and administration procedures, together with reliability and validity estimates, can be found in yearbooks, handbooks, and professional journals.

Yearbooks and Handbooks

The major source of information on standardized tests is the *Mental Measurements Yearbooks (MMY)*. These have been published since 1938; the most recent are the *Ninth Mental Measurements Yearbook (9thMMY)* (Mitchell, 1985), the *Supplement to the Ninth Mental Measurements Yearbook (9thMMY–S)* (Conoley, Kramer, & Mitchell, 1988), the *Tenth Mental Measurements Yearbook (10thMMY)* (Conoley & Kramer, 1989), the *Eleventh Mental Measurements Yearbook (11thMMY)* (Kramer & Conoley, 1992), and the *Supplement to the Eleventh Mental Measurements Yearbook (11thMMY–S)* (Conoley & Impara, 1994). They contain reviews of tests and selected bibliographies of related books and journal articles for each instrument.

The purposes of the latest *MMY*s are to provide (a) factual information on all known new or reviewed tests in the English-speaking world, (b) objective test reviews written specifically for the *MMY*s, and (c) comprehensive bibliographies, for specific tests, of related references from published literature. Each volume of the *MMY*s contains information on tests that have been published or significantly revised since a previous edition.

The *9thMMY, 10thMMY,* and *11thMMY* each provide six indexes. The index of titles is an alphabetical listing of test titles. The classified subject index lists tests alphabetically under one or more classification headings, for example, Achievement, Intelligence, Mathematics, Personality, Reading. This index is of great help to those wishing to locate tests in a particular curriculum area. The publishers directory and index gives the names and addresses of the publishers of all the tests included in the *MMY,* as well as a list of test numbers for each publisher. The index of names includes the names of test developers and test reviewers, as well as authors of related references. The index of acronyms gives full titles for commonly used abbreviations. For example, someone may not know that DRP stands for Degrees of Reading Power. Each entry also gives the population for which the test is intended. The score index gives the subtest scores and their associated labels for each test. These labels are operational definitions of the tests' variables.

The organization of these *MMY*s is encyclopedic: All the test descriptions and reviews are presented alphabetically by test title. To find a particular test, the reader can go right to it without using any index. All test entries are given index numbers that are used in place of page numbers in the indexes.

Entries for new or significantly revised tests in the tests and reviews section, the main body of the volume, include information such as title, author (developer), publisher, cost, a brief description, a description of groups for whom the test is intended, norming information, validity and reliability data, whether the test is a group or individual test, time requirements, test references, and critical reviews by qualified reviewers. Among other things, the reviews generally cite any special requirements or problems involved in test administration, scoring, or interpretation.

The classified subject index is a quick way to determine whether an instrument is reviewed within a particular volume of *MMY.* For example, in the classified subject index of the *11thMMY* under *achievement* (p. 1079), you will find the following entry (among others):

Comprehensive Tests of Basic Skills, Fourth Edition, grades K.0–K.9, K.6–1.6, 1.0–2.2, 1.6–3.2, 2.6–4.2, 3.6–5.2, 4.6–6.2, 5.6–7.2, 6.6–9.2, 8.6–11.2, 10.6–12.9, *see* 81

Remember, the 81 means that the description of the Comprehensive Tests of Basic Skills is entry 81 in the main body of the volume; it does not mean that it is on page 81. Page numbers are used only for table of contents purposes.

However, the Degrees of Reading Power cannot be found under either *achievement* or *reading* in the classified subject index of the *10thMMY* or *11thMMY* because it has not been significantly revised since its original publication. It is found under *reading* in the classified subject index of the *9thMMY* as

Degrees of Reading Power, grades 3–14, *see* 305.

A companion source of information about instruments is *Tests in Print (TIP)*, which contains comprehensive bibliographies of instruments that have been reviewed in *MMYs*. The latest edition, *TIP IV* (Murphy, Conoley, & Impara, 1994) is structured in the same way as the classified subject index of *MMYs*. Its value comes not from its reviews of instruments but from its listings of all tests that were in print at the time of publication, the location of test reviews in *MMYs* 1 through 11, and other writings about the instruments.

There are specialized volumes that contain information about instruments in various curriculum areas. These duplicate *MMY* information and reviews; their value comes from having test information for a particular discipline in a single volume. These monographs are

English Tests and Reviews

Foreign Language Tests and Reviews

Intelligence Tests and Reviews

Mathematics Tests and Reviews

Personality Tests and Reviews

Reading Tests and Reviews

Science Tests and Reviews

Social Studies Tests and Reviews

Vocational Tests and Reviews

Additional specialized sources of test information reviews are:

A Sourcebook for Mental Health Measures

Advances in Psychological Assessment

Assessment in Gifted Children

Assessment Instruments in Bilingual Education

Bilingual Education Resource Guide

CSE Elementary School Test Evaluations

Directory of Unpublished Experimental Mental Measures

Evaluating Classroom Instruction: A Sourcebook of Instruments

Handbook for Measurement and Evaluation in Early Childhood Education

Instruments That Measure Self-Concept

Language Assessment Instruments for Limited English-Speaking Students

Measures for Psychological Assessment: A Guide to 3,000 Sources and Their Applications

Mirrors for Behavior III

Oral Language Tests for Bilingual Students

Preschool Test Descriptions

Psychological Testing and Assessment

Psychological Testing and Assessment of the Mentally Retarded

Reading Tests for Secondary Grades

Review of Tests and Assessments in Early Education

Scales for the Measurement of Attitudes

Screening and Evaluating the Young Child

Socioemotional Measures for Preschool and Kindergarten Children

Sociological Measurement

Tests and Measurements in Child Development

Tests Used with Exceptional Children

Testing Children: A Reference Guide for Effective Clinical and Psychological Assessments

Valuable companions to the *9thMMY, 10thMMY,* and *11thMMY* are *Tests: A Comprehensive Reference for Assessment in Psychology, Education, and Business,* 3rd ed. (Sweetland & Geyser, 1991) and *Test Critiques* (Geyser & Sweetland, 1991). These volumes contain listings and critical reviews of instruments by specialty area.

Electronic Databases

Research consumers can access electronic databases of test collections, test reviews, and test publishers. Each record provides the title, author, publication date, relevant population, subject terms, *ERIC Thesaurus* terms, availability, and a short abstract about the test's content and form. The test review databases provide index information of volume and test review number for reviews in the *MMY*s and *TIP (Tests in Print)* (the Buros Test Review Locator) and *Test Critiques* (the Pro-Ed Test Review Locator).

The ERIC Clearinghouse on Assessment and Evaluation can be accessed in one of two ways through the Internet:

By "gopher" to **gopher.cua.edu** under Special Resources/ERIC Clearinghouse/ Test Locator/

By "Telnet" to **ericir.syr.edu** (the password is *gopher*) under ERIC Clearing- houses/Assessment and Evaluation/Test Locator/

Complete instructions for accessing the database by "gopher" can be obtained by E-mail from **eric_ae@cua.edu.**

Professional Journals and Textbooks

A number of professional journals and textbooks contain information and reviews of instruments. Journals such as the *Journal of Educational Measurement, Journal of Reading,* and *The Reading Teacher* regularly contain reviews of new and revised instruments. Other journals published by professional associations often contain information about newly published instruments.

Several professional textbooks dealing with educational assessment and evaluation contain information and critiques about various types of instruments. Although the title suggests that the book is intended only for special education, the following is an excellent reference about instruments commonly used in research for measuring academic school performance, learning attributes, classroom behavior, academic areas, and career and vocational interests:

> McLoughlin, J. A., & Lewis, R. B. (1994). *Assessing special students* (4th ed.). Upper Saddle River, NJ: Merrill/Prentice Hall.

SUMMARY

How is an educational problem defined before primary research reports are located?

After considering an educational problem, research consumers should refer to educational dictionaries for specific technical definitions.

How are integrative reviews and essays about research located?

Research consumers can locate an educational question in educational encyclopedias and journals specializing in publishing only integrative reviews and meta-analyses.

How are primary research reports located?

Primary research reports published in journals are located through the *Education Index* (EI) and the *Current Index to Journals In Education* (CIJE). *EI* lists items alphabetically by subject heading. A reference item contains the article's title; the author's name; whether a bibliography is included; and the journal's title and volume number, the article's number of pages, and the date of publication. *CIJE* contains similar information as well as a brief annotation of the article's contents. Using *CIJE* necessitates several steps: (1) referring to the *Thesaurus of ERIC Descriptors,* (2) using the subject index and the author index to locate accession numbers, and (3) referring to the main entry section. The journals containing the selected articles are then located in the periodicals or microform section of the library. A wide variety of educational documents can be located through *Resources in Education (RIE),* which is also part of the ERIC system and uses an indexing system identical to that used in *CIJE.* Using *RIE* necessitates several steps: (1) referring to the *Thesaurus of ERIC Descriptors,* (2) using the subject index and the author index to locate accession numbers, and (3) referring to the document resume section. The microfiche containing the documents' full text are filed by accession number in libraries' microform sections. A companion ERIC resource is *Exceptional Child Education Resources (ECER).* Other abstracts produced by specialty areas and for doctoral dissertations in education can be examined, too.

These databases can be accessed electronically through CD-ROM formats or by personal computer through the Internet. Electronic access lets the consumer search the databases by using multiple search terms.

Where can information about instruments be located?

Research consumers can find descriptive information and critical reviews about instruments in yearbooks, handbooks, professional journals, and textbooks. The major source of this information is the *Mental Measurements Yearbooks*.

ACTIVITIES

Activity 1

Using the *Supplement to the Eleventh Mental Measurements Yearbook* (Conoley & Impara, 1994) and one or more other sources discussed in the section "Locating Information About Instruments," determine the appropriateness of the following instruments for the indicated research purposes.

a. *Slosson Intelligence Test* (1991 Edition), ages 4–0 and over

Research purpose: To identify the learning potential and establish profiles of learning strengths and weakness for students with limited English proficiency.

b. *Test of Early Language Development* (Second Edition), ages 2–0 to 7–11

Research purpose: To compare the language proficiency of primary-grade students with and without language disabilities and to determine the relationship between their language proficiency and beginning reading achievement.

c. *Family Environment Scale* (Second Edition), family members

Research purpose: To determine family characteristics that might contribute to children's success in kindergarten and first grade.

Activity 2

a. Select an education topic related to your teaching situation and locate (1) the definition of at least one key term in an educational dictionary, (2) one interpretive essay or integrative research review, (3) one primary research report in an educational, psychological, or other social science journal, and (4) one primary research report reproduced on microfiche in the ERIC system.

b. Using the questions and criteria for evaluating primary research reports and integrative research reviews or meta-analyses presented in this text (Chapters 3–10), evaluate the selected essays, reviews, and reports.

FEEDBACK

Activity 1

a. Cultural minorities were significantly underrepresented in the sample of the norming group for the SIT-R. Therefore, it might not be appropriate to use the test in a study with individuals with limited English proficiency.

b. TELD-2 was developed for use with normal students, but with certain adjustments in administering and establishing separate forms, the test might be used with special populations. Since it does not contain any reading sections, it might be used in a correlational study with a reading test. However, there is some question about the procedures used to obtain the norming sample and the validity of the test results when used with students with mild language impairments. So, the test should be used with caution.

c. FES is a norm-referenced instrument with fixed responses. If in the study researchers used quantitative research procedures, the instrument might be appropriate. The instrument seems to have appropriate content validity. Whether the FES has construct validity for the study could be determined by checking the study's sample against the norming group used for the test. FES might not be appropriate to use in a study with qualitative research procedures.

Activity 2

Feedback will be provided by your course instructor.

Glossary

abstract A summary of a research report.

accessible population A group that is convenient to the researchers and representative of the target population. Practical considerations that lead to the use of an accessible population include time, money, and physical accessibility.

action research Research directed to studying existing educational practice and to producing practical, immediately applicable findings. The questions or problems studied are local in nature (e.g., a specific class), and generalizability to other educational situations is not important to the researchers. Often action research is a collaboration between classroom teachers without research expertise and trained researchers.

action research review A review of research produced for local consumption.

analysis of covariance (ANCOVA) A statistical procedure based on analysis of variance (ANOVA) allowing researchers to examine the means of groups of subjects as if they were equal from the start. They do this by adjusting the differences in the means to make the means hypothetically equal.

analysis of variance (ANOVA) A statistical procedure used to show differences among the means of two or more groups of subjects or two or more variables. It is reported in *F-ratios*. The advantage in using an ANOVA is that several variables as well as several factors can be examined. In its simplest form, ANOVA can be thought of as a multiple *t*-test.

authentic assessment Assessment of students' work and the products of their learning by comparing their performance and products (e.g., oral reading, writing samples, art or other creative output, and curriculum-related projects) to specified levels of performance. The materials and instruction used are true representations of students' actual learning and their activities in the classroom and out-of-school worlds. (See *criterion-referenced tests*.)

background section The section of the research report that contains (a) an explanation of the researchers' problem area, (b) its educational importance, (c) summaries of other researchers' results that are related to the problem (called a *literature review*), and (d) strengths from the related research that were used and weaknesses or limitations that were changed.

baseline measure The pretest in single-subject research; it can take the form of one or several measurements. It is the result to which the posttest result is compared to determine the effect of each treatment.

best evidence A concept by which research consumers can select and review studies for inclusion in research reviews only if they are specifically related to the topic, are methodologically adequate, and are generalizable to a specific situation.

case study A form of single-subject research, undertaken on the premise that someone who is typical of a target population can be located and studied. In case studies, the individual's (a) history within an educational setting can be traced, (b) growth pattern(s) over time can be shown, (c) functioning in one or more situations can be examined, and (d) response(s) to one or more treatments can be measured.

causal-comparative research Research that seeks to establish causation based on preexisting independent variables. Researchers do not induce differences in an experimental situation; instead they seek to identify one or more preexisting conditions (independent variables) in one group that exist to a lesser degree in the other. When one or more conditions are identified, they can attribute causality. (Also called *ex post facto research*.)

causative research See *experimental research*.

central tendency, measure of The middle or average score in a group of scores. The middle score is called the *median;* the arithmetic average score is called the *mean*.

Chi square test A nonparametric statistic used to test the significance of group differences when data are reported as frequencies or percentages of a total or as nominal scales.

cluster sampling   The procedure by which intact groups are selected because of convenience or accessibility. This procedure is especially common in *causal-comparative research*.

comparative research   Research that seeks to provide an explanation about the extent of the relationship between two or more variables, or examines differences or relationships among several variables. These variables might represent characteristics of the same group of subjects or those of separate groups.

concurrent validity   The extent to which the results show that subjects' scores correlate, or are similar, on two instruments.

construct validity   The quality obtained when an instrument's creator demonstrates the instrument as representing a supportable theory.

content validity   The quality obtained when an instrument's creator demonstrates that the specific items or questions used in the instrument represent an accurate sampling of specific bodies of knowledge (i.e., curricula or courses of study).

control   Use of procedures by researchers to limit or account for the possible influence of variables not being studied.

control group   The group of subjects in experimental research not receiving the experimental condition or treatment (sometimes called the *comparison group*).

correlation   A measure of the extent to which two or more variables have a systematic relationship. (See *product-moment correlation*.)

correlation of coefficient   The result of an arithmetic computation done as part of a product-moment correlation. It is expressed as *r*, a decimal between −1.0 and +1.0. (See *product-moment correlation* and *Pearson product-moment correlation*.)

counterbalanced design   The research design in which two or more groups get the same treatment; however, the order of the treatments for each group is different and is usually randomly determined. For this type of design to work, the number of treatments and groups must match. Although the groups may be randomly selected and assigned, researchers often use this design with already existing groups of subjects, such as all classes in a grade level.

criterion-referenced test   An instrument that measures students' performances in terms of expected learner behaviors or to specified expected levels of performance. Scores show students' abilities and performances in relation to sets of goals or to what students are able to do. They do not show subjects' rankings compared to others, as norm-referenced tests do. A *standardized criterion-referenced test* is one for which the administration and scoring procedures are uniform but the scoring is in relation to the established goals, not to a norm group. (See *authentic assessment*.)

cross-validation   The procedure in which researchers investigate using the same purpose, method, and data analysis procedure but use subjects from a different population.

data   The information obtained through the use of instruments.

degrees of freedom   The number of ways data can vary in a statistical problem.

dependent variable   The variable researchers make the acted-upon variable. It is the variable whose value may change as the result of the experimental treatment (the *independent variable*).

derived scores   Test scores that are converted from raw scores into standard scores such as grade equivalents, normal curve equivalents, percentiles, or stanines.

descriptive research   Research that seeks to provide information about one or more variables. It is used to answer the question "What exists?" This question can be answered in one of two ways: using *quantitative methods* or *qualitative methods*.

descriptors   Key words found in the *Thesaurus of ERIC Descriptors* and used in such indexing documents as *Resources in Education* and *Current Index to Journals in Education*.

direct observation   The research procedure in which researchers take extensive field notes or use observation forms to record information. They categorize information on forms in response to questions about subjects' actions or categories of actions. Or, they tally subjects' actions within some predetermined categories during a time period.

directional hypothesis   A statement of the specific way one variable will affect another variable when previous research evidence supports it (also called a *one-tailed hypothesis*).

discussion section   A section of the research report that contains the researchers' ideas about the educational implications of the research results (also called *conclusions section*).

effect   The influence of one variable on another.

effect size   A standard score created during statistical and meta-analysis from a ratio derived from the mean scores of the experimental and control groups and the standard deviation of the control group. It shows the size of the difference between the mean scores of the experimental and control groups in relation to the standard deviation.

equivalent forms reliability Reliability determined by correlating the scores from two forms of an instrument given to the same subjects. The instruments differ only in the specific nature of the items. (Sometimes called *parallel forms reliability*.)

ERIC or **Educational Resources Information Center** A national network supported by the Office of Education Research and Improvement of the U.S. Department of Education. Its purpose is to provide access to current research results and related information in the field of education. It is a decentralized system composed of about sixteen clearinghouses, each specializing in a major educational area.

ethnographic research A term often used synonymously with *qualitative research*, although some researchers consider ethnography a subtype of qualitative research.

evaluation research The application of the rigors of research to the judging of the worth or value of educational programs, projects, and instruction. It extends the principle of action research, which is primarily of local interest, so that generalizations may be made to other educational situations. And, although undertaken for different reasons than is experimental research, the quantitative research method used in evaluation research is based on that of experimental research.

experimental condition The condition whereby the independent variable is manipulated, varied, or subcategorized by the researcher in experimental research. (Also called *treatment*.)

experimental group The group of subjects in experimental research receiving the experimental condition or treatment.

experimental research Research that seeks to answer questions about causation. Researchers wish to attribute the change in one variable to the effect of one or more other variables. The variables causing changes in subjects' responses or performance are the *independent variables*. The variables whose measurements may change are the *dependent variables*. The measurements can be made with any instrument type: survey, test, or observation.

external validity Validity based on researchers' assurance that results can be generalized to other persons and other settings.

extraneous variables Variables that might have an unwanted influence on, or might change, the dependent variable. Researchers can restrict the influence of extraneous variables by controlling subject variables and situational variables.

F-ratio The way in which analysis of variance (ANOVA) and analysis of covariance (ANCOVA) are reported.

face validity The extent to which an instrument *appears* to measure a specific body of information. In other words, "Does the instrument look as if it would measure what it intends to measure?"

factorial designs Research designs in which there are multiple variables and each is subcategorized into two or more levels, or factors. The simplest factorial design involves two independent variables, each of which has two factors. This is called a 2×2 factorial design. Factorial designs can have any combination of variables and factors.

field notes Written narratives describing subjects' behaviors or performances during an instructional activity. These notes are then analyzed and the information categorized for reporting. The analysis can start with predetermined categories, and information from the notes is recorded accordingly. Or, the analysis can be open-ended in that the researchers cluster similar information and then create a label for each cluster.

fieldwork The collection of data during qualitative studies in particular educational settings.

generalizability The ability of results to be extended to other students or the target population. That means, a research consumer in a different place can have confidence in applying the research producers' results.

hypothesis A tentative statement about how two or more variables are related. A hypothesis is the researchers' conjectural statement of the relationship between the research variables and is created after the investigators have examined the related literature but before they undertake their study. It is a tentative explanation for certain behaviors, phenomena, or events that have occurred or will occur.

identifiers Key words used in indexing documents that are not yet represented as descriptors in the ERIC *Thesaurus of ERIC Descriptors*.

independent variable The influencing variable in experimental research, the one to which researchers wish to attribute causation. (Sometimes called the *experimental variable*.) When the independent variable is an activity of the researcher, it is called a *treatment variable.*

instruments   A broad range of specific devices and procedures for collecting, sorting, and categorizing information about subjects and research questions.

instruments section   A subsection of the method section of a research report, containing a description of the data collection instruments: observation forms, standardized and researcher-made tests, and surveys.

integrative review of research   A critical examination of research producers' methods and conclusions and of the generalizability of their combined findings.

interaction effect   The effect in experimental studies of two or more variables acting together. Interactions are expressed as F-ratios within ANOVA or ANCOVA tables and can be shown in a graph.

internal consistency reliability   Reliability determined by statistically comparing the subjects' scores on individual items to their scores on each of the other items and to their scores on the instrument as a whole. (Sometimes called *rationale equivalence reliability.*)

internal validity   Validity based on researchers' assurance that changes to dependent variables can be attributed to independent variables.

interrater/interjudge reliability. See *scorer reliability.*

interval scale   The statistical form presenting data according to preset, equal spans, and identified by continuous measurement scales: raw scores and derived scores such as IQ scores, percentiles, stanines, standard scores, normal curve equivalents. It is the most common form of data reporting in educational and social science research and is the way data from most tests are recorded.

interview   An instrument used to obtain structured or open-ended responses from subjects. It differs from a questionnaire in that the researcher can modify the data-collection situation to fit the respondent's responses.

inventory   A questionnaire that requires subjects to respond to statements, questions, or category labels with a "yes" or "no" or asks subjects to check off appropriate information within a category.

Likert-type scale   A scale that uses forced choices of response to statements or questions; for example, "Always," "Sometimes," or "Never." Each response is assigned a value; a value of 1 represents the least positive response.

literature review   A subsection of the background section of a research report, containing summaries of related research; in it, researchers indicate strengths from the related research that were used in their study and weaknesses or limitations that were changed.

matched groups design   The research design in which the experimental and control groups are selected or assigned to groups on the basis of a single-subject variable such as reading ability, grade level, ethnicity, or special disabling condition.

mean   The arithmetical average score.

median   The middle score in a group of scores.

meta-analysis   A critical examination of primary research studies in which quantitative data analyses were used. Research reviewers use meta-analysis as "analysis of analyses" (statistical data analysis of already completed statistical data analyses). In them, the reviewers convert the statistical results of the individual studies into a common measurement so they can obtain an overall, combined result.

method section   The section of the research report usually composed of three subsections: *subjects, instruments,* and *procedure.*

microfiche   Small sheets of microfilm containing images of documents that can be read only on special microfiche readers.

multiple correlation   A statistical technique used to examine the relationships among more than two variables. The procedure is interpreted similarly to a single correlation coefficient. It can also be used to make predictions. The technique is used frequently in causal-comparative experimental research. (Also called *multiple regression.*)

nominal scale   The statistical form reporting as numbers of items or as percentages of a total. Data from surveys and observations are often recorded in this way.

nondirectional hypothesis   A statement used when researchers have strong evidence from examining previous research that a relationship or influence exists but the evidence does not provide indications about the direction (positive or negative) of the influence.

nonequivalent control group design   The research design in which the groups are not randomly selected or assigned and no effort is made to equate them statistically.

nonparametric statistics   Statistical procedures used with data that are measured in nominal and ordinal scales. These statistics work on different assumptions than do parametric statistics, and are used for populations that do not have the characteristics of the normal distribution curve.

norm See *normal distribution curve.*

norm-referenced test An instrument that measures an individual's performance compared to a standardization, or *norming, group.*

normal distribution curve A graph representing how human variables are distributed among a normal, or typical, population. Other names are the *normal probability curve* and *bell-shaped curve.*

norming group The individuals used in researching the standardization of the administration and scoring of norm-referenced tests.

one-tailed hypothesis. See *directional hypothesis.*

operational definition A definition of a variable that gives the precise way an occurrence of that variable is viewed by researchers.

ordinal scale The statistical form showing the order, from highest to lowest, for a variable; ranking. There is no indication as to the value or size of differences between or among items in a list; the indication is only to the relative order of the scores.

parallel forms reliability. See *equivalent forms reliability.*

parametric statistics Statistical procedures used with data measured in interval scales and based on certain assumptions, all of which are related to the concept of a normal distribution curve.

participant observer A qualitative researcher who goes to the particular setting being studied and participates in the activities of the people in that setting. Researchers functioning in this role try to maintain a middle position on a continuum of complete independence as an observer to complete involvement in the people's activities.

Pearson product-moment correlation The most common correlation coefficient. (See *product-moment correlation* and *correlation coefficient.*)

pilot study A limited research project usually with a few subjects that follows the original research plan in every respect. By analyzing the results, research producers can identify potential problems.

population A group of individuals having at least one characteristic that distinguishes them from other groups. A population can be any size and can include people from any place in the world.

posttest The second and subsequent measurements after a pretest.

posttest-only control group design The research design in which the experimental and control groups are not pretested. An example of this design is two or more randomized groups being engaged in comparison activities without being given a pretest.

practical significance A determination about how useful research results are. To determine this, research consumers need to answer: How effectively can the results be used in my teaching situation?

predictive validity The extent to which an instrument can predict a target population's performance after some future situation. It is determined by comparing a sample's results on the instrument to their results after some other activity.

pretest The test given to the subjects to collect initial, or baseline, data.

pretest-posttest control group design The research design in which all groups are given the same pretest and posttest (survey, observation, or test).

procedure section A subsection of the method section of a research report, containing a detailed explanation of how the researchers conducted their study.

product-moment correlation Refers to the quantified relationship between two sets of scores for the same group of subjects. The result of the arithmetic computation is a *correlation coefficient,* which is expressed as *r,* a decimal between −1.0 and +1.0. The most common interval scale correlation coefficient is the Pearson product-moment correlation. Correlations show whether two or more variables have a systematic relationship of occurrence—that is, whether high scores for one variable occur with high scores of another (a positive relationship) or whether they occur with low scores of that other variable (a negative relationship). The occurrence of low scores for one variable with low scores for another is also an example of a positive relationship. A correlation coefficient of zero indicates that the two variables have no relationship with each other, that is, are independent of each other.

purpose section The section of the research report that contains the specific goal or goals of the research project. These can be expressed as a statement of purpose, as questions, or as a hypothesis.

qualitative research Research using a broad range of strategies that have roots in the field research of anthropology and sociology. It involves collecting data within natural settings, and the key data collection instruments are the researchers themselves. Qualitative research data are verbal, not numerical.

Since qualitative researchers are equally concerned with the process of activities and events as they are with results from those activities or events, they analyze data through inductive reasoning rather than by statistical procedures.

quantitative research   Research using procedures involving the assignment of numerical values to variables. The most common quantitative descriptive measures researchers use are the *mean* (a measure of central tendency) and the *standard deviation* (a measure of the variability of the data around the mean).

questionnaire   An instrument which necessitates the respondent either writing or orally providing answers to questions about a topic. The answer form may be structured in that there are fixed choices, or the form may be open-ended in that respondents can use their own words. Fixed-choice questionnaires may be called *inventories.*

random sampling   Works on the principle of *randomization,* whereby all members of the target population have an equal chance of being selected for the sample. The subjects that are finally selected should reflect the distribution of relevant variables found in the target population.

randomization   An unbiased, systematic selection or assignment of subjects. When randomization is used, researchers assume that all members of the target population have an equal chance of being selected for the sample and that most human characteristics are evenly distributed among the groups.

ratio scale   The statistical form showing relative relationships among scores, such as half-as-large or three-times-as-tall. In dealing with educational variables, researchers do not have much use for these scales.

rationale equivalence reliability. See *internal consistency reliability.*

reference section   The section of the research report that contains an alphabetical listing of the books, journal articles, other research reports, instructional materials, and instruments cited in the report.

reliability   The extent to which an instrument measures a variable consistently; a statistical estimate of the extent to which a test's results can be considered dependable.

reliability coefficient   The number expressing an instrument's reliability, expressed in decimal form, ranging from .00 to 1.00. The higher the coefficient, the higher the instrument's reliability.

replication   The procedure in which researchers repeat an investigation of a previous study's purpose, question, or hypothesis.

representative   The quality of a sample in which the researchers' results are generalizable from the sample to the target population.

research   A process of systematically collecting information about an identified problem or question, analyzing the data, and, on the basis of the evidence, confirming or refuting a prior prediction or statement.

research design   The structure for researchers' methods of answering research questions and conducting studies. Three basic research designs are descriptive, comparative, and causative or experimental.

research report   A summary of researchers' activities and findings.

results section   The section of the research report that contains the results of the researchers' data analyses; contains not only the numerical results (often presented in tables and charts) but an explanation of the significance of those results.

sample   A representative group of subjects; it is a miniature target population. Ideally, the sample has the same distribution of relevant variables as found in the target population.

sampling error   Any mismatch between the sample and the target population.

scales   Methods of measurement that measure variables related to attitudes, interests, and personality and social adjustment. Usually, data are quantified in predetermined categories representing the degree or intensity of the subjects' responses to each of the statements or questions. Unlike data from tests, which are measured in continuous measurements (e.g., stanines 1 through 9, or percentiles 1 through 99), data from scales are discrete measurements, forcing respondents to indicate their level of reaction; common forced choices are "Always," "Sometimes," or "Never." This type of data quantification is called a *Likert-type scale.*

scorer or **rater reliability**   Reliability determined by comparing the results of two or more scorers, raters, or judges. Sometimes presented as a percentage of agreement and not as a coefficient. (Sometimes called *interrater* or *interjudge reliability.*)

simple experimental design   An experimental design with one independent variable or using a subject selection procedure that limits the generalizability of its results. (See *experimental research.*)

single-subject research   Any research in which there is only one subject or one group that is treated as a single entity (e.g., when an entire school is studied without regard to individual students' performances). Single-subject research may be descriptive or experimental. *Case study* is a form of single-subject research.

situational variable A variable related to the experimental condition (that is, a variable outside the subjects) that might cause changes in their responses relating to the dependent variable.

Solomon four-group design The research design in which four groups are formed using random selection and random assignment. All four groups are posttested, but only two groups are pretested. One pretested group and one nonpretested group are then given the experimental condition.

split-half reliability A form of *internal consistency reliability* determined by dividing the instrument in half and statistically comparing the subjects' results on both parts. The most common way to split a test is into odd- and even-numbered items.

standard deviation A measure of the variability of the data around the mean. It shows how far from the mean most of the scores are. It is the way variability is usually reported.

standardized test An instrument that has been experimentally constructed. The test constructor uses accepted procedures and researches the test's (a) content, (b) procedures for administering, (c) system for recording and scoring answers, and (d) method of turning the results into a usable form. A standardized test is one for which the methods of administering, recording, scoring, and interpreting have been made uniform. Everything about the test has been standardized so that if all its directions are correctly followed, the results can be interpreted in the same manner, regardless of where in the country the test was given.

statistical regression The tendency of extreme high and low standardized test scores to move toward the group arithmetic mean.

statistical significance The probability of results being caused by something other than mere chance; occurs when the difference between the means of two sets of results exceeds a predetermined chance level. When results are significant, researchers know how confident they can be about the conclusions they may make from their findings.

statistics Numerical ways to describe, analyze, summarize, and interpret data in a manner that conserves time and space. Researchers select statistical procedures after they have determined what research design and types of data will be appropriate for answering their research question.

stratified random sample A sample whose subjects are randomly selected by relevant variables in the same proportion as those variables appear in the target population.

subject variable A variable on which humans are naturally different and which might influence their responses in regard to the dependent variable.

subjects The particular individuals or objects used in the research.

subjects section A subsection of the method section of a research report, containing a description of the individuals or objects used in the study. The section gives general information about age, sex, grade level, intellectual and academic abilities, socioeconomic level, and so on. It also contains the number of subjects and an account of how the subjects were selected and assigned to groups.

t-test A statistical procedure used when there are two sets of scores, to determine whether the difference between the means of the two sets of scores is significant. It is reported as numbers such as $t = 1.6$ or $t = 3.1$. After determining the value of t, researchers consult a statistical table to determine whether the value is a significant one.

target population The specific group to which the researchers would like to apply their findings. It is from the target population that the researchers select the sample, which become the subjects of their study.

test-retest reliability Reliability as determined by administering the same instrument again to the same subjects after a time period has elapsed (also referred to as *test stability*).

treatment See *experimental condition* and *independent variable*.

triangulation A procedure of collecting information from several different sources about the same event or behavior; used in qualitative research for cross-validating information.

two-tailed hypothesis. See *nondirectional hypothesis*.

validity The extent to which an instrument measures what it is intended to measure.

validity generalization The procedure in which researchers use the same purpose, method, and data analysis procedure, but they use subjects from a unique population.

variability The extent to which scores cluster about the mean. The variability of a normal distribution is usually reported as the *standard deviation (SD)*.

variable Anything in a research situation that varies and can be measured. It can be human characteristics (of students or teachers) or it can be characteristics of classrooms, groups, schools and school districts, instructional materials, and so on.

volunteer subjects   Different by nature from non-volunteers because of some inherent motivational factor. Results from the use of volunteer subjects might not be directly generalizable to the target population containing seemingly similar, but non-volunteer, individuals or groups.

Research Reports and Reviews for Analysis

Allexsaht-Snider, M. (1995). Teachers' perspectives on their work with families in a bilingual community. *Journal of Research in Childhood Education,* 9(2), 85–95.

Teachers' Perspectives on Their Work with Families in a Bilingual Community

Martha Allexsaht-Snider

University of Georgia

Abstract. Teachers' work with families in linguistically, ethnically, and socioeconomically diverse communities has not been studied systematically. This study provides a review of research on teacher-parent relations integrated with three teachers' perspectives on their work with families in a bilingual community. Observations and interviews with teachers and parents over the course of a school year provided rich, in-depth data for analyzing teachers' perspectives on teacher-parent interactions in this bilingual setting. Teachers cited prior experiences working with families as influencing their attitudes and practices of parent involvement. They also discussed a wide range of resources and contexts for informal interactions with parents and colleagues in which they constructed knowledge for working with families. Implications for future research and program development to support teachers' work with families in diverse communities are discussed.

Since the early 1960s, educators have operated on the premise that improved home-school relations and family involvement in children's education are integral to school improvement and educational reform efforts in diverse communities (Bronfenbrenner, 1978; Chavkin, 1989; Cochran, 1987; Laosa, 1983; Leler, 1983; Yao, 1988). Many calls for reform have included policies that ask teachers at all levels of schooling to work with linguistically and ethnically diverse families to support children's learning (e.g., Lezotte & Bancroft, 1985; Quality Education for Minorities Project, 1990; Trueba, 1989; U.S. Department of Education, 1986).

Research (e.g., Clark, 1988; Delgado-Gaitan, 1990; Henderson, 1987; Lareau, 1989) and program development (e.g., Bermudez, 1993; Comer, 1988; Rich, 1993) have offered perspectives on the roles that families can play in fostering children's learning and have provided suggestions for effective structures and processes for supporting families in their involvement with schools. Although some survey research regarding teachers' work with families has been conducted (Becker & Epstein, 1982;

I wish to thank the teachers and families in Huerta for their participation in the study of family-school collaboration in their bilingual community. An earlier draft of this paper was presented at the First European Roundtable on Families, Communities, Schools, and Children's Learning, Faro, Portugal, September, 1993. The research reported here was funded in part by a grant from the U.S. Department of Education, Office of Research and Improvement in Education, Award #8202-25245. Special thanks to Jim Deegan, Penny Oldfather, and Steve White for their helpful comments on an earlier draft.

Epstein, 1987; Epstein & Becker, 1982; Epstein & Dauber, 1991; Metropolitan Life Survey of the American Teacher, 1987), and other researchers (e.g., Goldenberg, 1987, 1989; Romo, 1984) have examined teachers' communication with immigrant and minority families, a systematic analysis of teachers' roles and their perspectives on the process of family involvement in schooling is still lacking. A better understanding of the teachers' role in family involvement is critical to reaching a goal of stronger home-school linkages to facilitate children's learning. Family involvement cannot be facilitated without a clearer understanding of the sources of teachers' beliefs and practices regarding communication and interaction with families and the institutional contexts that shape those attitudes and practices. The purpose of this article is to integrate a summary of published research on teacher-parent relations with a study that examined three teachers' perspectives on parent-teacher interactions in their classroom in a school district serving immigrant Spanish-speaking families.

Research on Teacher-Parent Relations

The themes of conflict and distance in relationships between teachers and parents have been evident in educational writings and research since the 1930s (e.g., Lortie, 1975; Waller, 1932). Waller (1932) attributed the conflict to parents' and teachers' differing perspectives on the child, while Lightfoot (1978) attributed the conflict between teachers and parents to competition for the child's affection and loyalty. The idea of conflict in parent-teacher relationships due to competition and differing perspectives on children's needs has not been studied in depth since these earlier studies were conducted. Other researchers (e.g., Warren, 1973), in examining conflict in teacher-parent relationships from the perspective of status, suggested that teachers used the distance they established between themselves and parents to maintain and reinforce their higher status in relation to parents. Warren found that younger, less experienced teachers had complex and ambivalent relationships with parents, while teachers with seniority and tenure in the community maintained a more clearly

delineated status differential and social distance.

In another, more wide-ranging and complex study, Hoover-Dempsey, Bassler, and Brissie (1987) came to several conclusions about the influence of what they referred to as "teacher efficacy" on parent-teacher relationships and perceptions. Their most significant finding was that higher levels of teacher efficacy were associated with higher levels of parent involvement. Teacher efficacy was defined as: "Teachers' beliefs that they can teach, that their students can learn, and that they can access a body of professional knowledge" (p. 429). Hoover-Dempsey et al. hypothesized that efficacious teachers, confident about their teaching abilities, welcomed parent input as a complement to their teaching program and, therefore, parents felt that their participation was productive.

Building on Corwin and Wagenaar (1976), Hoover-Dempsey et al. examined contextual factors that influenced teacher-parent relations. Corwin and Wagenaar had hypothesized that organizational structures such as formalization and centralization increase social distance between employees (teachers) and their clientele. They predicted that teachers with more seniority would be more alienated from parents, due to the status and seniority associated with length of experience. Instead, they found that more experienced teachers interacted more frequently with parents. The research of Hoover-Dempsey et al. paralleled the finding of Corwin and Wagenaar (i.e., that more efficacious teachers had more communication with parents), and points to a need to focus further study explicitly on newer teachers (who may feel less efficacious than experienced teachers) and their relationships with parents.

Researchers have identified several contextual variables that may influence parent-teacher relationships from the teacher's point of view (see Table 1 for a summary of identified influences). Two patterns emerge: (a) a pattern of conflict and distance in teacher-parent relationships identified in earlier studies, and (b) the importance of teachers' experience and sense of efficacy as a factor influencing their

Table 1   Research Findings: Influences on Teacher-Parent Relationships

Teacher-parent relations are characterized by:	Teachers' attitudes and dispositions for working with parents are influenced by:
conflict	teacher concern with the education needs of the child as a member of a group, in contrast with parents' concern with the personal, affective aspects of their child's individual development (Waller, 1932)
	the competition between female teachers and mothers for the child's affection and loyalty (Lightfoot, 1978)
distance	teachers' desire to maintain and reinforce their higher status in relation to parents; inexperienced teachers' feelings of inadequacy (Warren, 1973)
a welcoming of parent input and participation	"high levels of teacher efficacy, or beliefs that they can teach, that their students can learn and that they can assess a body of professional knowledge" (Hoover-Dempsey, Bassler, & Brissie, 1987, p. 429)
frequent interactions with parents	experience; numbers of years of teaching (Corwin & Wagenaar, 1976)

work with families. The scarcity of research in this area suggests a clear need for more research, and specifically for studies that incorporate both reported data from teachers and parents and observational data that documents teacher-parent relations over time. In addition, the lack of studies of teachers' work with families in classrooms of intermediate students (Scott-Jones, 1988) indicates a need to focus on this area. The following study of parent-teacher interactions in intermediate classrooms serving immigrant Spanish-speaking students was designed to provide an in-depth view of teachers' perspectives on their work with families and on the structures and processes that supported that work.

METHOD

The study presented here followed earlier research in the community we call Huerta (district, school and teacher names are all pseudonyms). The earlier research on parental empowerment (Delgado-Gaitan, 1990) and family literacy (Allexsaht-Snider, 1991) focused on parents and their interpretations of children's schooling and learning experiences, rather than on teacher-parent interactions and teachers' perspectives.

Setting

The current study was conducted with teachers and parents in two elementary schools (each included third through sixth grade) in the Huerta School District located along the south central coast of California. The district served a student population of 2,000 that was about 60% White, 35% Hispanic, 1% Asian American, and .5% each African American and other, including Native American. Forty percent of the students identified as Hispanic were recent immigrants with limited English proficiency according to district records (Delgado-Gaitan, 1990).

The study took place in three classrooms: a bilingual third- and a bilingual fifth-grade class at Primavera School and a transitional fourth-grade class at Lincoln School where students were moving into an all-English curriculum. Students were taught literacy skills in their primary language (English or Spanish) and also received instruction in English or Spanish as second languages. These classes were selected because they included both English- and Spanish-speaking families and the teachers were bilingual and interested in participating in a long-term, in-depth study of parent involvement.

Procedures

Qualitative methodology, integrated with an ethnographic research tradition (Spindler & Spindler, 1987), provided the framework for the study. In order to discern repetitive patterns of communication and activity, I conducted observations approximately once a week over the course of a year (at some critical time periods, for example the beginning of the school year and at parent conference time, observations were conducted two and three times per week). Initial extended interviews (See Appendix) with the teachers were supplemented by periodic informal interviews designed to clarify or expand points made earlier and to check the accuracy of my interpretations. The study was designed to incorporate three forms of triangulation (Goetz & LeCompte, 1984; Mathison, 1988) that helped to establish confidence in the interpretation of the data: (a) interview and observation data were compared, (b) data collected from individual teachers were compared with data from other teachers, and (c) data collected from teachers were compared with data collected from parents. Data from interviews and observations with each teacher were analyzed and examined for central themes and recurring ideas. Using the constant comparative method (Glaser & Strauss 1967, 1978; Spradley, 1979, 1980), the initial interpretations were compared and merged to identify and verify themes and perspectives common to all three cases. In addition, discrepant cases were analyzed to consider their relevance to the patterns and themes that emerged. Finally, the themes and patterns that were identified in teacher interviews and observations of teacher-parent interactions were considered in relation to the earlier research findings and theoretical assertions regarding influences on teachers' attitudes and dispositions for working with parents.

Teachers' Background

Linda was in her second year of teaching third grade at Primavera School. She was fluent in Spanish and had prior experience teaching English as a Second Language to adults in South America. Linda shared that she was unsure of herself when talking with parents about their children. In fact, she reported that she felt that parents knew more about working with children and children's behavior than she did. In an interview early in the school year, she spoke of discipline problems she had discussed with parents, saying:

> Basically, the same behaviors and things they have at home are the same behaviors . . . sometimes at least from what I'm hearing from parents . . . that I see at school.

Kathy taught fourth grade at Lincoln School and was also in her second year of teaching. She had rudimentary Spanish skills, and had taught previously for several years in a parent-run preschool. In contrast to Linda, she felt confident about working with parents, and attributed her confidence to earlier positive experiences she had in communicating with parents in the preschool. Kathy felt, however, that even though she was comfortable working with parents in general, her lack of skill with Spanish limited her access to knowledge of particular families and their community. In interviews throughout the year, she expressed frustration about talking with Spanish-speaking parents and was dissatisfied with having to rely on a colleague or the children to translate. Kathy regularly talked about the need to learn more Spanish.

Alyssa had taught fifth grade for four years at Primavera School, had prior experience as a family counselor, and had developed fluent Spanish skills through studying and living in Mexico. She found her past experiences in counseling parents, and translating for parents and teachers when she worked as an aide in the schools, very useful. She felt that these earlier experiences had prepared her to work with immigrant parents in her own classroom. Alyssa listed many influences on her work with parents, ranging from a supervising teacher who had provided a very caring and involved model during her student teaching practicum, to the many friendships with immigrant Spanish-speaking families she had developed over the years.

RESULTS AND DISCUSSION

The above brief introduction to the three teachers indicates the range of factors that they suggested had influenced their attitudes and practices of family involvement in the schools serving immigrant Spanish-speaking families where they taught. An overview of the contextual factors and sources of knowledge that influenced all three of the teachers will be presented in the following paragraphs, and other sources of knowledge for working with families that were drawn upon differentially by the teachers will also be noted.

Experiences Prior to Elementary Teaching

As mentioned earlier, Kathy (the fourth grade transitional class teacher) highlighted her prior involvement in a preschool run by parents as a prime influence on her current practices of parent involvement. She related,

> The preschool that I worked for was run by the parents so . . . there was a lot of interaction. In fact we did written reports on the kids every day and then talked with them, the parents, and then did lots of parent conferencing. There was a lot of contact with the parents.

Alyssa (the fifth grade bilingual teacher) referred to similar experiences with parents prior to teaching her own elementary class that had influenced the ways in which she worked with families:

> When I was doing my internship in counseling at [the university] in their Education Counseling Clinic . . . my cases were mostly parents who came in and they were having trouble with their children. They wouldn't do their homework, they wouldn't get up and brush their teeth in the morning, that kind of thing, and so I started working with parents and children. And then when I was working in the schools as an aide . . . I would meet parents just as they would come to conferences . . . especially the Spanish-speaking parents because there wasn't anybody else who could speak with them.

A juxtaposition of the two teachers' chronicles of extensive prior experiences alongside Linda's (the bilingual third grade teacher's) concern with her own lack of prior experience with parents was revealing. The comparison of the three teachers' perspectives indicated that in these cases, earlier opportunities to work directly with parents were important influences on their current levels of confidence and practices in working with families.

Colleagues

A second source of knowledge for working with parents mentioned by all three teachers was their use of students' previous year teachers as a source of information about how to approach individual children and their families. Alyssa had compiled a written list of all her students after talking with their last year's teacher. The list included details about parents the fourth grade teacher thought had been cooperative, others who were demanding and critical, and one parent who often volunteered and then did not follow through on her commitment. Similarly, Kathy turned to a student's third grade teacher when the student began having problems with other children. In talking with the previous year's teacher, she got the information that the boy's father had been very concerned and willing to work closely with the teacher. She based her subsequent approach to the father on the suggestions made by her colleague.

Linda's access to students' previous teachers was limited. As she stated in her initial interview, "Since we're a third to sixth grade school, I don't really know a lot about what's gone on in preschool through second grade." Again, her mention of the lack of access to the knowledge held by students' previous teachers, in contrast to the other teachers' active and regular use of this resource, points to its importance from the teachers' points of view.

Teachers discussed an overall climate for parent involvement in their schools and were aware of their colleagues' practices of parent communication. They implied that in their own classrooms, they were conforming with the norms set by their colleagues throughout the school. Kathy and Alyssa characterized their colleagues as engaging in frequent communication with parents. Both agreed that, "Messages go home a lot," with Alyssa saying:

> I think there's definitely an outreach towards parents by every teacher . . . Everybody's calling

and talking to parents and sending weekly folders home and sending reports home. Some are more successful at it than others, but I think all the teachers make a big effort and probably everybody spends time each week talking on the phone to parents.

Community Contacts

Two more significant sources of knowledge for working with parents were mentioned by Alyssa and Kathy and were absent for Linda: (a) interactions with parents during class field trips, and (b) utilization of instructional assistants who were from the community and knew the parents outside of school. Alyssa talked about getting to know many of the Spanish-speaking parents in her class during field trips in the Migrant Education summer school classes she had taught for two years. Kathy also spoke of getting to know her English- and Spanish-speaking students' extended family members, as well as parents, during class field trips. Linda reported a lack of parent participation on field trips, saying she went alone with her students or was accompanied only by her instructional assistant.

Both Kathy and Alyssa relied heavily on their instructional assistants to facilitate communication with parents and to provide them with insights about parents' perspectives. Kathy's instructional assistant was English-speaking and lived in the local neighborhood. She knew many of the English-speaking families of the children in Kathy's class, and often offered her view of how to approach a particular parent. Kathy said she wished that she had someone like her English-speaking instructional assistant to be a similar resource for working with the immigrant Spanish-speaking community. Because Kathy did not speak Spanish fluently and had no bilingual teaching assistant, she regularly struggled to find resources such as neighboring teachers' bilingual aides. She said she often relied on the bilingual students in her class to mediate communication with Spanish-speaking families and provide information about the community.

Alyssa valued the collaboration of her bilingual instructional assistant highly, explaining in an initial interview:

She knows everybody. She lives in [Huerta] and [has known] these kids since they were little, knows all these parents, is related to some of them . . . what I'll do is have her call, and then if I want the parent to come in, then I'll meet them and talk to them.

Linda also worked with a bilingual instructional assistant, but did not refer to her as a resource in communicating with parents. She did, however, discuss two sources of knowledge for working with parents that were not mentioned by the other two teachers. Linda had gotten to know many of the Spanish-speaking parents in her class and had developed a sense of community concerns through her participation in the school-wide monthly parent meetings of the COPLA (Comité de Padres Latinos) parent group. She was also aware of a participatory model for parent education programs called *Family Math* (Stenmark, Thompson, & Cossey, 1986) that she used as a guide in planning her own sessions for family involvement in science.

All three teachers mentioned informal, casual encounters with parents in which they learned more about individual families and their children and also gained insights into parents' perspectives in general. Parents stopped by before and after school to drop things off or to pick a child up for the dentist, and parents and teachers both grabbed these moments to get to know each other better and exchange information about the child. Alyssa's casual encounters with parents were frequent and regular. She drew on them for perspective on her students and also took advantage of every opportunity to communicate her expectations for students and parents and to make those expectations meaningful to parents.

Kathy had less frequent informal encounters and used them more to develop rapport with parents and make them feel comfortable in the school context. She noted that her lack of skill with Spanish limited her ability to gain much information from Spanish-speaking parents in these encounters or for her to inform them about the class curriculum or expectations for students and parents. As mentioned earlier, Linda reported that she had very few informal encounters with parents. She utilized the few she did have to gain insights into children's behavior and experiences outside of school that might be relevant in the classroom.

A final source of knowledge about parents was identified only by Alyssa. She had access to knowledge about families through her previous teaching of older siblings of her present students. Alyssa was the only one of the three teachers who had taught in the district for more than one year. In one instance, she talked about the need to contact a parent. Alyssa said she knew the mother would cooperate and follow up on a request to monitor her son's homework more closely because she had shown that she "cared" in the previous year with her older son.

Teachers' Knowledge and Practices
of Parent Involvement

As the three teachers' experiences and practices of parent involvement were compared over time, several patterns emerged. Linda, the teacher who felt that she had little prior experience and knowledge to apply in working with parents, also reported and was observed to have the fewest interactions with parents and the least number of activities and mechanisms for parent communication and involvement in her class. She was concerned about the infrequent or nonexistent participation of parents in class activities such as field trips and parties. Because of the lack of parent participation in such class activities, she had fewer opportunities to gather knowledge about parents and their children. The other two teachers had discussed these kind of informal interactions as key times for getting to know parents and exchanging information about their children.

In general, the two teachers who had extensive and varied practices of parent communication and involvement in their classrooms (Alyssa and Kathy) accessed a rich and diverse spectrum of sources of knowledge for working with parents individually and as a group. These sources were informal and based on interactions in the local contexts and experiences of the teachers. None of the three mentioned any

Table 2 Sources of Huerta Teachers' Knowledge for Working with Families

Experiences Prior to Elementary Teaching:
  In an institution that fostered parent-teacher communication (e.g., preschool)
  With children in school and other settings
  As a counselor with parents
  As a translator for parents
  As an intern with a teacher who modeled parent involvement practices
  Studying and living in Mexico and South America

Colleagues:
  Previous year's teacher
  Other teachers who model effective practices
  General school climate for parent-teacher relations

Interactions with Parents as Individuals:
  Informal structured settings (e.g., parent conferences)
  In casual circumstances, before and after school
  During field trips and class parties

Interactions with Parents in Groups:
  In organized parent activities
  In parent education programs (e.g., Family Math)

Community Contacts:
  Spanish-speaking teaching assistants
  English-speaking teaching assistants
  Involvement with families over several years through teaching siblings

formalized training for working with families either in preservice or inservice teacher education, a lack that is consistent with teacher reports in other studies (Chavkin & Williams, 1988). Neither did they note any written texts they had used as resources in planning their approach to parent communication and involvement. Instead of formalized training and resources for working with families, teachers made use of knowledge gained in prior work experiences, in consultations with colleagues in the schools, and through actual interactions with parents. Table 2 provides a summary of the sources teachers identified for their knowledge of working with families.

CONCLUSIONS

The data from large-scale surveys of teachers' attitudes toward working with parents (Epstein

& Dauber, 1991; Metropolitan Life Survey of the American Teacher, 1987) have shown that a majority of teachers agree that parent involvement is important. These surveys and other studies have found, however, that there is a gap between teachers' attitudes and their actual practices for working with families. Earlier research studies explained this gap as influenced by: teachers' lack of experience and a low sense of self-efficacy (Hoover-Dempsey et al., 1987), their desire to maintain a higher status in relation to parents (Warren, 1973), their conflicts with parents based on competition for children's affection (Lightfoot, 1978), or differing views of children's needs (Waller, 1932). These earlier studies did not examine the idea that teachers' knowledge for working with parents might influence their attitudes and practices. Although Hoover-Dempsey and colleagues found teacher self-efficacy to be a factor influencing teacher-parent relationships, their study focused on self-efficacy for *teaching*, and did not consider the idea of teachers' knowledge and sense of self-efficacy for working with parents. Both Corwin and Wagenaar (1976) and Warren (1973) studied inexperienced and experienced teachers, but again they seemed to be examining experience with teaching rather than looking specifically at teachers' experience with and knowledge for working with parents.

The Huerta study offered unique case comparisons for investigating the idea of teachers' knowledge for working with parents. The two teachers with similar levels of experience in teaching elementary children (Kathy and Linda) reported different levels of confidence about involving and communicating with parents. Additionally, they reported dissimilar rates and kinds of interactions with parents. This contrast in attitudes and practices between the two less experienced teachers suggests that the influences of experience and self-efficacy on teacher-parent relations are more complex than earlier studies indicated.

For the Huerta teachers, it was not simply years of experience and a sense of efficacy about their teaching that made a critical difference in their practices of family involvement and the meanings they attached to their work

with parents. As all three teachers reflected on their practices of parent involvement, they considered that the nature and quality of their prior experiences with families affected their present practices and understandings of interactions with parents. Teachers reported that their knowledge for working with families emerged from experiences prior to their teaching in elementary schools and was gathered in informal settings through interactions with parents and with other teachers.

Two of the teachers in Huerta drew on their prior experiences as a preschool teacher, a bilingual teaching assistant, and a family counselor in developing their understandings and practices. Others (Atkin, Bastiani, & Goode, 1988; Hulsebosch, 1992) have documented the ways in which teachers draw upon their experiences as parents in developing their perspectives on working with families. These findings suggest that future research on teacher-parent relations, rather than simply focusing on teachers' attitudes and dispositions toward working with parents, could investigate the role of prior experiences in providing a foundation of knowledge for teachers' work with families. In addition to ideas for future research, these findings suggest an application for preservice and inservice education. Internships and participation in programs in diverse contexts that could provide opportunities for interacting with ethnically, socioeconomically, and linguistically diverse families could provide significant experiences from which to begin building teachers' knowledge base.

Teachers in Huerta not only cited prior experiences as important to their understanding of their work with families. They also discussed a wide range of resources and contexts for informal interactions with parents and colleagues in which they constructed knowledge. They discussed field trips, class parties and casual before- and after-school encounters as settings where they gained insight into parents' perspectives. Two of the teachers discussed communication with the previous year's teacher, the overall school climate for parent-teacher involvement, and other teachers who modeled effective involvement and communication practices as important sources of local knowledge (Goldenberg & Gallimore, 1991) for working with families. Additionally, two of the teachers discussed the mediating roles played by teaching assistants. The assistants both facilitated communication with families about school expectations and mediated teachers' learning about the families and the community. Interestingly, both the teachers who were fluent Spanish speakers and the teacher who was not fluent felt that they were more able to work effectively with families when they had the support of resource personnel such as bilingual assistants, secretaries, and community liaisons.

In view of future research and program development, the questions that emerge from analysis of the three Huerta teachers' perspectives are: (a) what sources of knowledge for working with families do teachers access, and how might access to such knowledge be facilitated for beginning and experienced teachers; (b) what kinds of experiences prior to beginning teaching might help teachers to form a strong knowledge base for working with families, and how might those experiences be incorporated in teacher education; and (c) what are teachers' perspectives on the resources and organizational structures in schools that facilitate or hinder their work with families in socioeconomically, ethnically, and linguistically diverse communities, and how can those resources and structures be included in programs designed to facilitate family involvement in schooling? The answers to these questions have implications for researchers, teacher educators, professional development leaders, and school and district policymakers. It will be particularly valuable to focus further study in this area on exemplary programs for family involvement. Schools implementing exemplary programs such as the School Development Program (Comer, 1988), the University of Houston-Clear Lake Parent Education Program (Bermudez, 1993), the Schools Reaching Out Projects (Davies, 1993), and others described by Rich (1993) would be ideal sites in which to pursue further investigation of teachers' perspectives on the resources and organizational structures that support their work with diverse families.

REFERENCES

Allexsaht-Snider, M. (1991). The social process of family literacy in a Spanish-speaking context. *The Quarterly Newsletter of the Laboratory of Comparative Human Cognition, 13,* 15–21.

Atkin, J., Bastiani, J., & Goode, J. (1988). *Listening to parents: An approach to the improvement of home/school relations.* New York: Croom Helm.

Becker, H., & Epstein, J. (1982). Parent involvement: A survey of teacher practices. *The Elementary School Journal, 83*(2), 85 –102.

Bermudez, A. (1993). Teaming with parents to promote educational equality for language minority students. In N. F. Chavkin, (Ed.), *Families and schools in a pluralistic society* (pp. 175–188). Albany, NY: State University of New York Press.

Bronfenbrenner, U. (1978). Who needs parent education? *Teachers College Record, 79,* 767–787.

Chavkin, N. (1989). Debunking the myth about minority parents. *Educational Horizons, 67*(3), 119–123.

Chavkin, N. F., & Williams, D. L. (1988). Critical issues in teacher training for parent involvement. *Educational Horizons, 66*(2), 87–89.

Clark, R. M. (1988). Parents as providers of linguistic and social capital. *Educational Horizons, 66*(2), 93–95.

Cochran, M. (1987). The parental empowerment process: Building on family strengths. *Equity and Choice, 4*(1), 9–23.

Comer, J. (1988). Educating poor minority children. *Scientific American, 259*(5), 42–48.

Corwin, R. G., & Wagenaar, T. C. (1976). Boundary interaction between service organizations and their publics: A study of parent teacher relationships. *Social Forces, 55*(2), 471–492.

Davies, D. (1993). Benefits and barriers to parent involvement: From Portugal to Boston to Liverpool. In N. F. Chavkin (Ed.), *Families and schools in a pluralistic society* (205–216). Albany, NY: State University of New York Press.

Delgado-Gaitan, C. (1990). *Literacy for empowerment: The role of parents in children's education.* New York: Falmer.

Epstein, J. (1987). Toward a theory of family-school connections: Teacher practices and parent involvement. In K. Hurrelmann, F. Kaufmann, & F. Losel (Eds.), *Social intervention: Potential and constraints* (pp. 122–136). New York/Berlin: DeGruyter.

Epstein, J., & Becker, H. (1982). Teachers' reported practices of parent involvement: Problems and possibilities. *The Elementary School Journal, 83*(2), 103–113.

Epstein, J. L., & Dauber, S. L. (1991). School programs and teacher practices of parent involvement in inner-city elementary and middle schools. *The Elementary School Journal, 91*(3), 289–305.

Glaser, B., & Strauss, A. (1967). *The discovery of grounded theory*. Chicago: Aldine.

Glaser, B. G., & Strauss, A. L. (1978). *Advances in the methodology of grounded theory*. Mill Valley, CA: Sociology Press.

Goetz, J., & LeCompte, M. (1984). *Ethnography and qualitative design in educational research*. Orlando: Academic.

Goldenberg, C. N. (1987). Low-income Hispanic parents' contributions to their first grade children's word recognition skills. *Anthropology and Education Quarterly, 18*(2), 149–179.

Goldenberg, C. N. (1989). Parents' effects on grouping for reading: Three case studies. *American Educational Research Journal, 26,* 329–352.

Goldenberg, C., & Gallimore, R. (1991). Local knowledge, research knowledge, and educational change: A case study of early Spanish reading improvement. *Educational Researcher, 20*(8), 2–14.

Henderson, A. (1987). *The evidence continues to grow: Parent involvement improves student achievement*. Columbia, MD: National Committee for Citizens in Education.

Hoover-Dempsey, K. V., Bassler, O. C., & Brissie, J. S. (1987). Parent involvement: Contributions of teacher efficacy, school socioeconomic status and other school characteristics. *American Educational Research Journal, 24,* 417–35.

Hulsebosch, P. L. (1992). Significant others: Teacher's perspectives on relationships with parents. In W. H. Schubert & W. C. Ayers (Eds.), *Teacher lore: Learning from our own experience* (pp. 107–132). White Plains, NY: Longman.

Laosa, L. (1983). Parent education, cultural pluralism and public policy: The uncertain connection. In R. Haskins & D. Adams (Eds.), *Parent education and public policy* (pp. 331–345). Norwood, NJ: Ablex.

Lareau, A. (1989). *Home advantage: Social class and parental intervention in elementary education*. New York: Falmer.

Leler, S. (1983). Parent education in relation to the schools and to parents of school-aged children. In R. Haskins & D. Adams (Eds.), *Parent education and public policy* (pp. 114–180). Norwood, NJ: Ablex.

Lezotte, L. W., & Bancroft, B. A. (1985). School improvement based on effective schools research: A promising approach for economically disadvantaged and minority students. *The Journal of Negro Education, 54* (3), 301–312.

Lightfoot, S. L. (1978). *Worlds apart: Relationships between families and schools*. New York: Basic.

Lortie, D. L. (1975). *Schoolteacher: A sociological study*. Chicago: The University of Chicago Press.

Mathison, S. (1988). Why triangulate? *Educational Researcher, 17*(2), 13–17.

Metropolitan Life Survey of the American Teacher. (1987). New York: Louis Harris & Associates.

Quality Education for Minorities Project. (1990). *Education that works: An action plan for the education of minorities*. Cambridge, MA: Massachusetts Institute of Technology Press.

Rich, D. (1993). Building the bridge to reach minority parents: Education infrastructure supporting success for all children. In N. F. Chavkin (Ed.), *Families and schools in a pluralistic society* (pp. 175–188). Albany, NY: State University of New York Press.

Romo, H. (1984). The Mexican origin population's differing perceptions of their children's schooling. *Social Science Quarterly, 65,* 635–649.

Scott-Jones, D. (1988). Families as educators: The transition from informal to formal school learning. *Educational Horizons, 66*(2), 66–69.

Spindler, G., & Spindler, L. (1987). Ethnography: an anthropological view. In G. Spindler (Ed.), *Education and cultural process: Anthropological approaches* (pp. 151–156). Prospect Heights, IL: Waveland.

Spradley, J. P. (1979). *The ethnographic interview.* New York: Holt, Rinehart & Winston.

Spradley, J. P. (1980). *Participant observation.* New York: Holt, Rinehart & Winston.

Stenmark, J. K., Thompson, V., & Cossey, R. S. (1986). *Family math.* Berkeley, CA: Lawrence Hall of Science, University of California.

Trueba, H. T. (1989). *Raising silent voices: Educating the linguistic minorities for the 21st century.* Cambridge, MA: Newbury House.

U.S. Department of Education. (1986). *What works: Research about teaching and learning.* Washington, DC: Office of Educational Research and Improvement (Author).

Waller, W. (1932). *The sociology of teaching.* New York: J. Wiley.

Warren, R. (1973). The classroom as a sanctuary for teachers: Discontinuities in social control. *American Anthropologist, 75,* 280–291.

Yao, E. L. (1988). Working effectively with Asian immigrant parents. *Phi Delta Kappan, 70,* 223–225.

APPENDIX

Teacher Interview Questions

1. Can you reflect back over the past several years and describe your involvement and interactions with parents? Can you think of specific examples of incidents you remember?

2. What would a normal working day be like for you, from before school to after school, and would parent communication and interaction typically be a part of your day? In what ways? Can you give some examples?

3. What did you do for Back to School Night and Open House last year? How did parents respond to these programs?

4. How does your school work with parents? How about other teachers?

5. What do you expect from the parents in your classroom? How do you communicate those expectations to parents?

6. What do parents expect from you? What does your principal or the district expect from you in terms of working with parents?

7. How does homework work in your classroom? How do children and parents fit into and respond to your program? How do you communicate to parents about homework?

Greenman, N. P., & Kimmel, E. B. (1995). The road to multicultural education: Potholes of resistance. *Journal of Teacher Education*, 46(5), 360–368. Copyright © 1995 by Corwin Press, Inc. Reprinted by permission of Corwin Press, Inc.

The Road to Multicultural Education: Potholes of Resistance

Nancy P. Greenman

The University of Texas at San Antonio

Ellen B. Kimmel

University of South Florida

The road to multicultural education is paved with good intentions, but rutted with potholes of resistance. In 1973, the American Association of Colleges for Teacher Education (AACTE) stated: *Multicultural education rejects the view that schools should seek to melt away cultural differences or the view that schools should merely tolerate cultural pluralism* (1973, p. 264). In their full statement, AACTE strongly endorsed multiculturalism, multilingualism, multidialectism, empowerment, equity, and cultural and individual uniqueness.

In this article, we present data about the extent to which pre- and inservice teachers and school counselors-in-training approached acceptance of the tenets reflected in the AACTE statement. Our findings illuminate tensions and difficulties teacher educators experience as they conduct multicultural training activities.

Much that has occurred in society since 1973 has profoundly affected attitudes toward multiculturalism and the development and implementation of multicultural education policy. The conservative tenor of the times encourages expression of ideas that would have been an embarrassment in 1973. Crucial issues are trivialized and relegated to political correctness. As 1994 came to a close, Herrnstein and Murray (1994) resurrected the argument of genetic linkages between race and intelligence. Current attention to multicultural education in the United States follows publication and popularization of Hodgkinson's (1985) demographic data indicating rapid growth and influx of nonwhite populations and Hodgkinson's predictions that *by around the year 2000, America will be a nation in which one of every*

THREE [author emphasis] *of us will be nonwhite* (p. 7). The same motivation that existed at the last turn of the century appears operant at the turn of this one: fear of being overtaken or contaminated by difference (Greenman, 1990). Irvine (1992) reports a 1987 study by Law and Lane finding White preservice teachers' attitudes toward all American subcultures more negative than in any national studies of the previous 6 decades (p. 80).

The political context of multicultural education is evident; one cannot depoliticize it, even for its own salvation (Garcia & Pugh, 1992). Debates about multicultural education are embedded in the larger issues of how nation-states manage ethnic diversity and whether sociocultural pluralism is a practical or desirable reality. Multicultural education policy and programs generally reflect the worldview of the dominant culture. Resistance to diversity is embedded in institutional structures (Greenman, Kimmel, Bannan, & Radford-Curry, 1992). Parochialism of many teacher candidates, professors of education, teachers, communities, and school districts ensures perpetuation of the status quo (Haberman, 1991; Zimpher & Ashburn, 1992).

Multicultural education acknowledges existence of a culturally diverse population and addresses that diversity in disparate ways. Typologies (e.g., Banks, 1994; Gibson, 1984; Sleeter & Grant, 1994) help one sort the conceptualizations of multicultural education according to the proponents, target populations, intent, and underlying assumptions. Some forms of multicultural education recognize cultural difference, but as a deficit; the intent is control or assimilation. Multicultural education at its worst has been accused of being a tool of recolonization, partially because success for historically disenfranchised populations is still measured by their ability to gain mainstream cultural capital (Mattai, 1992). Other types of multicultural education aim at understanding differences and fostering positive human relations; focus on reforming educational institutions and practice to fully reflect the complexity of beliefs, traditions, and values of a culturally diverse population; commit to transforming society to reflect complexity; and mirror equality rather than oppress the culturally different.

The current structure of American schooling reinforces an individual, deficit-corrective approach to providing equal opportunity for success and a tacos and blintzes model of multicultural education. Educators are frustrated by experts on culture who focus on context and refuse to provide a definitive, simplistic definition of culture or prescriptive lists of attributes to *deal with* the culturally different.

Many who are driving forces in multicultural programs still equate cultural difference with at-risk students and a culture of poverty rather than acknowledging the complexity of the concepts of culture and ethnicity and the need for continual reflection, reassessment, and redefinition. National Council for the Accreditation of Teacher Education (NCATE) studies indicate that though a growing number of institutions profess to address cultural diversity and multicultural education, exceedingly few are prepared to do so (Gollnick, 1992).

Although dangers inhere in examining social transformation at the level of the individual, such analysis is of practical importance. Teachers and counselors and their teachers must question their assumptions about themselves and others in order to be open to change and the differences among students and to respond in ways fostering their development (Gollnick, 1992; Martin, 1991; Payne, 1994). As long as theory-building efforts take into account structural as well as personal elements, it is possible to avoid the negative aspects of such reductionism.

Lewin's (1951) seminal model of change describes the status quo as the result of opposing dynamic forces, equal in strength, that drive toward change and resist against it. He argued that the most effective way to institute change is to melt resistance rather than add to the driving forces. This necessitates identifying the exact nature of the restraining forces. To that end, we sought information from participants that would reveal the conscious and unconscious types of resistance they experienced when presented with the opportunity to learn about their own and others' cultural constructions.

Many psychologists have made gloomy predictions about individuals' ability to achieve the kinds of changes proponents of multicultural education advocate (e.g., Argyris, 1982; Argyris & Schön, 1978). Strong evidence exists that children have established stereotypes in memory before they develop the cognitive capacity to question them (e.g., Allport, 1954; Katz, 1976). If such deeply ingrained, automatic responses are independent of conscious thought, they never can be changed, and any behavior to the contrary is merely impression management (being politically correct). This argument precludes the possibility for change in attitudes or beliefs, despite changes in behavior or rhetoric. More recent research offers hope that in-group members can change their feelings about out-group members (Devine, 1989; Linville, Salovey & Fisher, 1989). People have the power to escape prejudice, to break bad cognitive habits. To overcome their resistance to change, they must decide to stop the old belief (behavior), remember their resolution to do so, and decide repeatedly to reduce their rigid thinking.

The change, though possible, has yet to occur. Ahlquist (1992) documents student resistance to both content and pedagogy in a multicultural foundations course. Resistance to anything related to issues of culture, race, class, and gender in classrooms and consultancies currently attracts increasing attention in narratives, dialogues, and formal presentations at professional meetings and among colleagues. Holm and Nations-Johnson (1994) note: *Research has pointed to a pattern in which preservice teachers are saturated with information in their courses, only to ignore it when they enter their field settings* (p. 98). As evidence of individuals' failure to apply multicultural education knowledge they do learn mounts (e.g., Sleeter, 1992), the search for effective forums for training increases. Shaw (1993) affirms: *Conceptual change, or real growth occurs when teacher education students engage in powerful experiences which involve the whole person, demand mental and emotional attention, and provoke disequilibrium* (p. 24). However, evidence of the efficacy of simulations such as *Blue Eyes-Brown Eyes* in changing attitudes is contradictory at best (Byrnes & Kiger, 1990).

Kolb (1984) provides a comprehensive and systematic statement of the theory of experiential learning. His model is the most widely researched one available for learning practitioners, including proponents of cultural diversity training. Kolb's model includes a theory of adult development with three distinct levels of adaptation, representing successively higher-order forms of learning governed by three qualitatively different forms of consciousness: performance, learning, and development.

Performance governed by a simple registrative consciousness marks adaptation in the acquisition phase, whereas an increasingly interpretive learning process—the product of a dialectic between opposing elemental forms of learning leading to greater abstraction—marks second-stage adaptation. The final phase marks the achievement of a holistic developmental adaptive process, resulting in a transformation of consciousness into greater symbolic integrative complexity. Although all three levels can be present simultaneously, attainment of the highest level leads to a deeper, more personal and transforming form of learning that will influence all future learning through experience.

From the standpoint of Kolb's model, participants in an activity-based training program will develop to the degree that they engage fully in the learning cycle with its four dialectical opposites of concrete experience, reflective observation, abstract conceptualization, and active experimentation. Failure to move around the wheel of these processes will short-circuit learning that could propel one to Level 3, to have one's consciousness altered and worldview transformed through experience.

In the Stage 3 mode, individuals must confront the assumptions and expectations of their culture and begin to shift their basic frames of reference. Some may never have this experience because they are so immersed in the societal reward system for performing their learned gender, age, class, ethnic group roles. Movement to this level is associated with a high level of emotion, either exhilarative or terrifying or both. Although a deeper meaning of self in transaction in the world emerges in this less certain experiential world, many retreat or never venture forth by continuing to short-circuit the full learning cycle.

METHOD

Thirty-three school counselors-in-training, 38 preservice teachers enrolled in a social foundations course, and 25 inservice teachers participated. Group 1 (counselors) included 27 women and 6 men, ranging in age from 22 to 50. They were enrolled in a diverse populations course as part of their Master of Arts program in which they participated in the *Bafa Bafa* (Shirts, 1977) cultural simulation. Group 2 (preservice teachers) included 28 women and 10 men, whose ages ranged from 19 to 52. In addition to the *Bafa* simulation, Group 2 completed readings and participated in discussions of culture in the foundations course throughout the semester. Group 3 (inservice teachers) included 16 women and 6 men whose ages ranged from 22 to 52. Group 3 did not participate in the *Bafa* simulation, but attended a week-long school district multicultural education workshop containing many shorter experiential activities.

The self-reported socioeconomic status (SES) of each group was predominantly middle class. There were 1 Hispanic and 2 Black participants in Group 1; 1 Hispanic, 3 Black, one Korean and 4 participants with mixed ethnic background in Group 2; and 6 Black participants in Group 3. All other participants were White. When asked to identify their culture and ethnicity, the respondents gave diverse answers, ranging from Christian to Black. The category of race was included for referencing to profiles presented in the literature (e.g., Holm

& Nations-Johnson, 1994; Martin, 1991; Zimpher & Ashburn, 1992).

We developed a two-part instrument for the study. Part 1 consisted of demographic data and six open-ended questions eliciting immediate thoughts about differences and similarities, and questions about definitions: What is culture? What is cultural diversity? What is cultural pluralism? What is multicultural education?

In Part 2, we asked participants to reflect on their training experience and any effect it might have had on them. Eight open-ended questions called for respondents to describe their participation in the simulation or training event; any resistance to the process they might have felt before, during, and after the training; resistance to the concepts; the most and least important parts of the experience; the effect of the experience (if any), professional and/or personal; the concepts/ideas/activities gained that they plan to use; and the type of multicultural training they would find most effective. The items were derived from the literature on change and resistance to it to provide face validity as an evaluation questionnaire. Expert colleagues in the field of culture and diversity training reviewed the items to establish content validity.

We administered Part 1 of the instrument just prior to the training activity for all three groups. Participants completed both Parts 1 and 2 after their training activities. Groups 1 and 2 completed the instrument for the second time 1 week after the simulation. Group 3 completed the instrument for the second time at the end of the training week as part of the evaluation conducted by the county school district.

Two independent raters thematically analyzed all responses and coded them for the level of learning or the extent to which concepts of culture and understanding of ethnocentricity were evident. In some cases they also coded the direction (change, no-change and positive and negative). Interrater reliability, calculated for each question, averaged 88%.

FINDINGS

We operated on the assumption that analytical frameworks would be grounded in the data.

Change can be defined in terms of process and content. We chose Kolb's (1984) model in relation to process as one of the theoretical frameworks for analysis. For content, we highlighted understanding of the complexity of the concept of culture as reflected in its definition, awareness of ethnocentricity, and conceptualizations of multicultural education. Raters analyzed all responses for themes and used codes appropriate to the item and its theoretical underpinning. We selected a sample of 20 participants for cross-item analysis to see patterns of response and consistency. In this article, we present examples for each major issue, summarize the results for others, and discuss responses from a few of these participants.

DEFINITIONS OF CULTURE

We compared responses to the question, *What is Culture?* elicited before the experiential/simulation/multicultural workshop to those elicited 1 week after the multicultural training experience. We noted any change in definition, especially indicating understanding of the complexity of the concept of culture, from a simplistic or an erroneous definition to a comprehensive one. We also noted some of the themes occurring in the definitions.

There was no change for 70%, 92%, and 88% of Groups 1, 2, and 3, respectively. Change in a positive direction, that is, from no response to a response, or from a simplistic to a more comprehensive or accurate definition, was noted for 21%, 8%, and 4% of Groups 1, 2, and 3, respectively. Change not considered desirable was noted for 9%, 0%, and 4% of Groups 1, 2, and 3, respectively. Thus, for the groups combined (N=96), 80% of the responses showed no change in depth of understanding of the concept of culture. Of those exhibiting no change, 21% of Group 2 responses did include concepts of ideation, perception, and/or worldview—all of which are considered indicators of a deeper understanding of culture. Traditional definitions of culture primarily focusing on material culture were provided by 13% of Group 2 who did not register change, and 28% of Group 3. Erroneous inclusion of race as culture was noted for 9%, 3%, and 12% of Groups 1, 2, and 3, respectively.

DEFINITIONS OF MULTICULTURAL EDUCATION

We employed a modification of Sleeter and Grant's (1994) typology to analyse change using participants' conceptualizations of multicultural education. We used the following hierarchic progression:

1. Teaching the Culturally Different—patronizing or prescriptive responses;
2. Ethnic Studies/Single Group Studies—content-oriented;
3. Human Relations—focus on similarities and getting along;
4. Teaching the Culturally Different—for equality and access;
5. Ethnic Studies/Single Group Studies—empowerment/equality-oriented;
6. Multicultural Education—addressing a diversity of areas and forums for infusion and inclusion; and
7. Multicultural Education That is Social Reconstructionist—aimed at creating change beyond the level of understanding or tolerance.

Table 1 displays the number and percentages of definitions of multicultural education in each category before and after the training experience. The majority of responses fell in the lower ranked categories; however, the first category is less represented than Categories 2 and 3, which include cultural content with an eye toward understanding and tolerance. In this finding, our sample ranked higher than the general populations they represent. Goodwin (1994) suggests that where teachers-in-training place on Sleeter and Grant's (1994) hierarchy of conceptualizations of multicultural education *could be interpreted as different levels of readiness or development in personal, developmental and intellectual terms* (p. 129). For the combined groups, 44% demonstrated no change, 43% a change in the positive direction, and 14% a change down the hierarchical ladder.

Results From Items Coded for Level of Learning

Kolb (1984) describes a cyclical four-part process in his experiential learning model. The first part is the Concrete Experience. In this study, a *Bafa* or an activity-based, multicultural education training program is the concrete experience. Although the concrete experience forms the basis for the learning process, experience by itself is not instructional. For learning to occur, the experience must be followed by formal observations and reflections (Reflective Observation), the second phase of the experiential learning model. In the third phase, the learner forms abstract concepts and generalizations (Abstract Conceptualization) about the experience and reflections. Finally, the learner verifies the implications of the ideas in different situations (Active Experimentation).

The themes derived from responses to Questions 1, 4, and 5 lent themselves to this coding. Question 1 asked participants to describe their participation in *Bafa Bafa* or the multicultural training program. Most answers were merely descriptive; participants either described the roles they played, the emotions they felt, or that they learned *something* (no indication of any specific concepts or principles gained). Only 27%, 24% and 24% in Groups 1, 2, and 3, respectively, reflected thinking at either the abstract conceptualization or active experimentation levels. We coded only three responses (one from each group) reaching the highest level in which participants not only articulated the learning but how they might incorporate it into their behavior in the future. Essentially the same results held in Questions 4 and 5, which probed the most and least important and the most and least effective parts of

Table 1   Definitions of Multicultural Education Pre- and Post for All Groups Combined (N=96)

	Before		After	
Categories	n	%	n	%
TC-prescriptive	12	13	5	5
ES-content	35	37	27	28
HR	29	30	32	33
TD-equality	4	4	6	6
ES-empowerment	2	2	8	8
MC Ed	5	5	15	15
MC Ed. social reconstruction	0	0	2	2

Note. TD=teaching the culturally different; ES= ethnic studies; Hr= human relations; MC Ed.= multicultural education.

the experience or training program. Participants were somewhat more analytical and applied in their answers to Question 4, but considerably less so on Question 5 than for Question 1. On Question 4, 50%, 40%, and 40% reached the higher two levels while on Question 5 only 6%, 0%, and 0% did so for Groups 1, 2, and 3, respectively.

RESPONSES TO ITEMS PROBING
RESISTANCE EXPERIENCED

Not all resistance is equal. One may resist consciously (be able to articulate it) or unconsciously. One can embrace rhetoric, but not understand it in order to live it out. One can be willing to critique classism or sexism, but not racism; ambivalence is not uncommon (see James, 1991).

We analyzed the types of resistance to the process that the three groups reported before, during, and/or after the experience. The most frequent response for all groups combined was *none* (38%). The second most frequent response, preexperience, concerns, included difficulties in getting there and anxiety about what would occur and how they would participate. For the *Bafa* groups (1 and 2), the requirement of one of the cultures to hug as a form of greeting produced some noticeable resistance (10 participants). The processing part of all three programs also produced resistance for a few participants. Other resistance to the process concerned aspects of the experiences themselves. Seven people in Group 1 noted resistance to the ideas contained. One person in Group 3 displayed several layers of resistance. The concept this participant offered as resolution of resistance was designated as undesirable during the first session in the workshop. The participant proclaimed, *I couldn't understand what this whole thing of 'multiculturalism' encompassed. Now I do. Now I can be P.C. (politically correct) or at least try to be.*

Question 3 further probed conscious resistance, but this time to the ideas and concepts explored before, during, and after the experience. Again *none* was the highest frequency response (70%, 58%, and 4%, in Groups 1, 2, and 3, respectively). Distancing responses, such as seeing the simulation as a game or exotic, were evident: *I wasn't resistant because I*

know it was a simulation and fun! Only 15%, 5%, and 4% reported resistance to the ideas explored in Groups 1, 2, and 3, respectively. One teacher from Group 3 clearly believed culturally relevant teaching and learning styles were irrelevant: *I do not agree with the notion that a teacher should have to change presentation styles to accommodate disruptive students so that they may continue being disruptive.*

QUESTIONS CODED FOR OPENNESS
OR RESISTANCE-RECEPTIVITY

Questions 6, 7, and 8 called for participants to describe the impact of the experience, how what they gained would be applied, and what further training they would find useful (if any). We were interested in assessing the degree to which anything had occurred that could be construed as a change or transformation in the way individuals thought about culture and the filters it places on how we see the world and interact with others from a different group. We also coded the responses to Question 6 for positive or negative reactions. Forty participants stated explicitly that the experience was positive. We inferred from the tenor of their responses that an additional 47 participants also felt it was positive. Only three participants stated the experience was negative, and a remaining three did not indicate experience-related affect. Participants overwhelmingly enjoyed the experiences, whether the simulation or the week-long program.

Achieving new realizations was the most frequent type of impact the experience had on the participants for all groups (45%, 53%, and 52%, for Groups 1, 2, and 3, respectively). The next most frequent response was one indicating the simulation/experiential process itself was powerful, closely followed by the identification of ethnocentricity. Other respondents indicated that the experience verified previous knowledge and forced them to think.

We coded the types of impact into three categories: Open, open to ideas of culture and the ethnocentricity it engenders in shaping our views; Moderate, moderately open to such ideas; and Resistant, resistant to these ideas. Overall, 21%, 40%, and 20% of Groups 1, 2, and 3, respectively, wrote responses judged open; 45%, 29%, and 12% of these groups' responses were coded Moderate; and 33%, 32%, and 68% were coded Resistant.

In Question 7, we asked about concepts, ideas, and activities participants gained or learned and how they would use them. The themes and coding for openness were similar to those found for Question 6. Most respondents (68%) from Group 3 expressed resistance on this item. They indicated they had gained knowledge of materials and activities to use in their classroom, but did not indicate as often that they had increased understanding of issues of ethnocentricity. Given that inservice teachers often receive training that offers cookbook recipes, this finding was not surprising. For Question 8, eliciting desirable training formats, prescriptive designs, and *none* were coded Resistant (36%, 24%, and 16% for Groups 1, 2, and 3, respectively). Distancing strategies and human relations were coded as Moderate (27%, 47%, and 84% for Groups 1, 2, and 3, respectively); and experiential, personal application, and first-hand experience were coded as Open (36%, 29%, and 0% for Groups 1, 2, and 3, respectively).

CROSS-QUESTION ANALYSIS OF RESPONSE NARRATIVES

To obtain a broader picture of the participants and their patterns of response and to flag inconsistencies, we did a cross-question analysis of 20 participants. We found patterns indicating a strong positive experience was consistent with high-level learning as measured by our criteria, and a strong negative experience was consistent with rejection of content and process. Three examples will serve to illustrate.

Our ideal participant responded as we would have hoped. The general description was, *My immediate reaction . . . FABULOUS! It was a wonderful experience and again made me aware that I need to be careful of my own 'filters' when dealing with others.* The participant expressed slight pre-experience apprehension about the unknown, but, generally,

- *It was fun and I felt great.*
- *I felt no resistance to any of the concepts/ideas explored throughout.*

- *Setting up two imaginary cultures/lands was most important. It allowed me to operationalize what I learned about culture.*
- *To me it was all effective; I can't imagine leaving any part of it out. It impacted me both professionally and personally; I am now very conscious of my 'filter'—it has created a stronger awareness in me.*
- *Everyone's perceptions are shaped by his/her experiences, etc., this is critical to remember and use. I'd use Bafa Bafa for clients/groups in a minute!*
- *Experiential is best—that's why Bafa Bafa was so effective.*

For some individuals, resistance was not evident until the contradictory responses were juxtaposed. One member of Group 1 had some neutral and mildly positive responses, *I was the patriarch of the Alpha Group, being the Patriarch was very enjoyable,* but was resistant to the processing needed for the higher levels in experiential learning, *I was hesitant or resistant to exposing too much of myself prior to the experience. Observing the frustration within my group at not being able to 'fit in' to the Beta culture. [Least important was] the lengthy sharing of personal feelings during the 'post mortem.'* This participant noted a *slight impact toward an increased understanding of the frustration which new entrants into a culture must feel,* but, as to concepts that would be used, *none that I can think of.* Given the distancing indicated in the other responses, it was interesting to note that in response to desired multicultural training, the person said, *The experience was a good insight builder but the reflection/application needed to be more personally applied.*

The third example was consistently resistant. The participant's response for the general description was, *I was involved by being in the first round of visitors to the Betas. Being a nonobservant person, it was a real strain trying to observe these people and try and figure out what they were all about. After being shunned by one of them, I took it personally, and it was hard to refocus. I did enjoy watching people, but not to this extreme level where others are counting on me and others to observe and report back. I am glad there were others who were equally responsible for this task.* The participant articulated resistance to the process was both to this incident and to being at the simulation in general: *I felt an outside resistance only in my being up here at the university at night away from home and worried that my car would not run properly. I felt a little resistance beforehand because there were not enough signs around to direct us to the proper location.* We actually had provided detailed maps for all participants with parking a few steps away from the door and a sign designating location. Participation was voluntary for this participant's group, with extra credit for analysis of participation offered as incentive. The participant expressed further resistance in the following responses:

- *As an Alpha, I was not comfortable with their incessant need for touching and such. I am not that kind of person. I am more cold and reserved. Fortunately, I was able to hang out with people that I like to be around in our class, and they helped me get through this.*
- *The most important part of this experience was the end. I am not usually an ends kind of person, but in this case, I am. I am because I was dying to know if each side really understood what the other group was all about. I cannot even remember most of the stuff in between.*
- *The least important part of the experience to me was when we did those introductory sheets. There were terms on the sheet I had no clue what they meant. The break was also too long.*
- *The experience has made no impact on my life in any way. All it did was take my precious time.*
- *I cannot think of any concepts, etc., that I gained from this experience. I cannot think of any multicultural training or experiences useful or effective or anything to me.*

CONCLUSION AND RECOMMENDATION

The responses and analyses demonstrate the existence and nature of resistance to multicultural education training experiences that were highly experiential wherein the concept of culture was central and fundamental to reflection of one's own cultural construction and ethnocentricity. We agree that reflective analysis is essential in multicultural education training and that a level of discomfort or disequilibrium is necessary to reach that stage of learning and change (Greenman, 1994). We agree with Shaw's (1993) question, *How do we find the elu-sive line between just enough disequilibrium and too much, when our students become defensive and resistant to accommodation and change* (p. 23)?

Given the parochialism, provincialism, and ethnocentrism evident as earlier delineated, and as evident in the multiculturalism canon debates, the resistance embedded in the very structures must be addressed. For example, through negative evaluation, students often punish professors and facilitators who confront issues, take risks, and create discomfort. In many institutions, these evaluations are used as the sole means of teacher assessment. The resultant institutional inertia from lack of institutional commitment undermines any progress toward the goals in the 1973 AACTE statement (our measure of successful multicultural education) and guarantees the palliative nature of multicultural education programs (Mattai, 1992). We must address resistance and mediate it as part of the process.

REFERENCES

Ahlquist, R. (1992). Manifestations of inequality: Overcoming resistance in a multicultural foundations course. In C. A. Grant (Ed.), *Research and multicultural education* (pp. 89–105). London: Falmer.

Allport, G. W. (1954). *The nature of prejudice.* Reading, MA: Addison-Wesley.

American Association of Colleges for Teacher Education Commission on Multicultural Education. (1973). No one model American. *Journal of Teacher Education, 24*(4), 264–265.

Argyris, C. (1982). *Reasoning and action: Individual and organizational.* San Francisco: Jossey-Bass.

Argyris, C., & Schön, D. A. (1978). *Organizational learning.* Reading, MA: Addison-Wesley.

Banks, J. A. (1994). *An introduction to multicultural education.* Boston: Allyn & Bacon.

Byrnes, D. A., & Kiger, G. (1990). The effect of a prejudice-reduction simulation on attitude change. *Journal of Applied Social Psychology, 20*(4), 341–356.

Devine, P. G. (1989). Stereotypes and prejudice. Their automatic and controlled components. *Journal of Personality and Social Psychology, 56*(1), 5–18.

Garcia, J., & Pugh, S. L. (1992). Multicultural education in teacher preparation programs. A political or an educational concept? *Phi Delta Kappan, 74(4)*, 214–219.

Gibson, M. A. (1984). Approaches to multicultural education in the United States: Some concepts and assumptions. *Anthropology & Education Quarterly, 15(1)*, 94–119.

Gollnick, D. M. (1992). Multicultural education: Policies and practice in teacher education. In C. A. Grant (Ed.), *Research and multicultural education* (pp. 218–239). London: Falmer.

Goodwin, A. L. (1994). Making the transition from self to other: What do preservice teachers really think about multicultural education? *Journal of Teacher Education, 45(2)*, 119–130.

Greenman, N. P. (1990). Multicultural education: Accommodation, transformation or desirable human experience? In *Meeting the needs of all children in the 21st century: National conference on urban and multicultural education proceedings* (pp. 93–120). Langston, OK: Langston University.

Greenman, N. P. (1994). Not all caterpillars become butterflies: Reform and restructuring as educational change. In K. M. Borman & N. P. Greenman (Eds.), *Changing American education: Recapturing the past or inventing the future?* (pp. 3–32). Albany: State University of New York Press.

Greenman, N. P., Kimmel, E. B., Bannan, H. M., & Radford-Curry, B. (1992). Institutional inertia to achieving diversity: Transforming resistance into celebration. *Educational Foundations, 6(2)*, 89–111.

Haberman, M. (1991). The rationale for training adults as teachers. In Sleeter, C. (Ed.), *Empowerment through multicultural education* (pp. 275–286). Albany: State University of New York Press.

Herrnstein, R. J., & Murray, C. (1994). *The bell curve: Intelligence and class structure in American life.* New York: Free Press.

Hodgkinson, H. L. (1985). *All one system: Demographics on education, kindergarten through graduate school.* Washington, DC: Institute for Educational Leadership.

Holm, G., & Nations-Johnson, L. (1994). Shaping cultural partnerships: The readiness of preservice teachers to teach in culturally diverse classrooms. In J. O'hair. & S. J. Odell (Eds.), *Partnerships in Education: Teacher education yearbook II.* (pp. 85–101). Orlando, FL: Harcourt Brace.

Irvine, J. J. (1992). Making teacher education culturally responsible. In M. E. Dilworth (Ed.), *Diversity in teacher education: New expectations* (pp. 79–92). San Francisco: Jossey-Bass.

James, J. (1991). Reflection on teaching: "Gender, race, & class." *Feminist Teacher, 5(3)*, 9–15.

Katz, P. A. (1976). The acquisition of racial attitudes in children. In P. A. Katz (Ed.), *Towards the elimination of racism* (pp. 125–154). New York: Pergamon.

Kolb, D. A. (1984). *Experiential learning: Experience as the source of learning and development.* Englewood Cliffs, NJ: Prentice-Hall.

Lewin, K. (1951). *Field theory and the social sciences.* New York: Harper & Row.

Linville, P. W., Salovey, P., & Fisher, G. W. (1989). Perceived distributions of the characteristics of in-group and out-group members: Empirical evidence and a computer simulation. *Journal of Personality and Social Psychology, 57(2)*, 165–188.

Martin, R. (1991). The power to empower: Multicultural education for student teachers. In C. Sleeter (Ed.), *Empowerment through multicultural education* (pp. 287–297). Albany: State University of New York Press.

Mattai, P. R. (1992). Rethinking the nature of multicultural education: Has it lost its focus or is it being misused? *Journal of Negro Education, 61(1)*, 65–77.

Payne, R. S. (1994). The relationship between teachers' beliefs and sense of efficacy and their significance to urban S.E.S. of minority students. *Journal of Negro Education, 63(2)*, 101–196.

Shaw, C. (1993). Multicultural teacher education: A call for conceptual change. *Multicultural Education, 1(3)*, 22–24.

Shirts, G. A. (1977). *Bafa Bafa: A cross culture simulation.* Del Mar, CA: Simile.

Sleeter, C. E. (1992). *Keepers of the American dream: A study of staff development and multicultural education.* London: Falmer.

Sleeter, C. E., & Grant, C. A. (1994). *Making choices for multicultural education: Five approaches to race, class and gender* (2nd ed.). New York: Maxwell Macmillian International.

Zimpher, N. I., & Ashburn, E. A. (1992). Countering parochialism in teacher candidates. In M. E. Dilworth (Ed.), *Diversity in teacher education: New expectations* (pp. 40 –62). San Francisco: Jossey-Bass.

Hannah, C. L., & Shore, B. M. (1995). Metacognition and high intellectual ability: Insights from the study of learning-disabled gifted students. *Gifted Child Quarterly, 39*(2), 95–109. This material may not be further reproduced without permission from NAGC.

Metacognition and High Intellectual Ability: Insights from the Study of Learning-Disabled Gifted Students

C. Lynne Hannah   Bruce M. Shore

McGill University

This study offers empirical support for the importance of metacognition in giftedness based on the performance of 48 school-identified learning-disabled gifted, gifted, learning-disabled, and average-performing boys in Grades 5/6 and 11/12 on assessments of metacognitive knowledge, metacognitive skill on a think-aloud error-detection reading task, error detection, and comprehension; prior knowledge was covaried. Performance of gifted and learning-disabled gifted students exceeded that of the average-performing and learning-disabled students on most measures at both grade levels. A main effect was found for grade; however, secondary average-performing students' performance was closer to that of the gifted and learning-disabled gifted students' performance. Metacognitive performance of the learning-disabled gifted students resembled that of the gifted sample more than that of the learning-disabled sample.

The study of learning-disabled gifted students provides useful insights into the nature of giftedness. The combination of exceptionalities is especially interesting because both giftedness and learning disabilities have been studied separately from a cognitive perspective and because learning-disabled gifted students have received increasing attention as a special population of children. Our primary goal is to provide empirical data in support of the proposition that metacognition is a defining quality of intellectual giftedness. Our second goal is to explore the more general proposition that better understanding the psychology of learning-disabled gifted students will enable us both to serve them better and to advance our understanding of intelligence in general and of giftedness in particular.

Both *giftedness* and *learning disabilities* are imprecise terms. In general, giftedness refers to high intellectual abilities or potential rather than talent in specific performance (Gagné, 1991; Terman, 1925; U.S. Commissioner of Education, 1972). Students identified as gifted are frequently characterized as having exceptional abilities or potential for learning and problem solving (Whitmore, 1980). Learning disabilities are difficulties in learning due to a cognitive-processing problem. They are different from mental retardation because the dysfunction affects one or more cognitive processes instead of limiting overall intellectual ability (Wong, 1985). Learning-disabled students are most often identified by a discrepancy between their measured potential (e.g., on a standardized IQ test) and their actual performance on academic tasks (Dangel & Ensminger, 1988; Forness, Sinclair, & Guthrie, 1983; Hammill, 1990). This study does not attempt to enter into the controversy over competing definitions of either giftedness or learning disabilities. It makes use of students who have been formally identified by schools on both dimensions to investigate the thinking processes which may contribute to exceptional performance.

In this study we compare the metacognitive performance of gifted and learning-disabled gifted students, as well as two control groups of learning-disabled and noncategorized students. The study is conducted within the framework of contemporary theory on cognitive psychology and information processing.

Since the children being served in programs for their exceptionality were identified initially on the basis of psychometric assessments of IQ and performance, the study also contributes to relating the study of giftedness to the historical mainstream of educational and psychological theory (cf. Jackson, 1993).

Metacognition and Giftedness

Information-processing theories of intelligence stress the importance of metacognitive processes in higher level intellectual functioning (Campione & Brown, 1978; Sternberg, 1981). Metacognition has been defined as a higher level of thinking than task-specific cognitive abilities (Borkowski, 1985; Brown, 1978, 1980; Myers & Paris, 1978) and as the deliberate control and regulation of cognitive processes while learning or performing (Bracewell, 1983; Brown, 1980; Flavell, 1976; Meichenbaum, Burland, Gruson, & Cameron, 1985; Schoenfeld, 1983). Some researchers have divided metacognition into two types of processes (Baker & Brown, 1984; Flavell, 1979; Myers & Paris, 1978): Metacognitive knowledge is knowledge about one's cognitive resources and the compatibility between oneself as learner and the particular learning situation in which one is working (Flavell & Wellman, 1977); metacognitive skills are context-free strategies which can be deliberately brought to bear on cognitive tasks in many domains (Brown & DeLoache, 1978). These skills consist of self-regulatory mechanisms used by an active learner and include checking, controlling, coordinating, planning, predicting, monitoring, testing, revising, and evaluating one's deliberate cognitive strategies for learning or completing a task (Brown, 1982; Flavell, 1976;

Putting the Research to Use

Programming for students who exhibit dual exceptionalities is difficult. The similarities between the learning-disabled gifted and the gifted students in this study point to the need to include programming to address the giftedness as well as the disability of the learning-disabled gifted student. Learning-disabled gifted students were similar to their gifted peers in their use of metacognitive strategies; teachers should include problem-solving strategies in a curriculum for students identified as learning-disabled gifted. Such intervention may provide these students with methods to enhance their learning in areas affected by their disability.

Haller, Child, & Walberg, 1988; Masson, 1982; Sternberg, 1984).

One way to investigate the processes involved in intelligence is to examine populations of learners identified as exceptional (Jackson & Butterfield, 1986; Shore, 1986). Some of that research has been done with students identified as academically gifted (cf. Borkowski & Peck, 1986; Coleman & Shore, 1991; Devall, 1982; Shore, 1986; Shore & Kanevsky, 1993; Sternberg & Davidson, 1985). Metacognitive abilities may contribute to the high levels of performance demonstrated by academically gifted individuals (Gallagher & Courtright, 1986; Shore, 1982; Shore & Dover, 1987; Sternberg, 1981). In relating giftedness to his triarchic theory of human intelligence, Sternberg (1984) hypothesized that people identified as gifted should be more proficient in their ability to recognize the problems that need to be solved, select the appropriate strategies for problem solving, and monitor the solution process. In other words, gifted persons excel in metacognitive skills. Borkowski and Peck (1986) examined differences between students identified as gifted and average ability on different components in the Campione and Brown (1978) model of intelligence. Their findings suggested that students identified as gifted are more proficient in using metacognitive abilities to solve problems. Other studies have indicated that students identified as gifted are able to attend to and use relevant information to solve problems (Davidson, 1986), generalize a learned strategy to a new situation (Borkowski & Peck, 1986; Kanevsky, 1990; Scruggs & Mastropieri, 1988), and apply knowledge of their strengths when attempting to solve difficult problems (Shore & Carey, 1984).

Metacognition and Learning Disabilities

Whereas metacognition is frequently claimed to be an intellectual strength underlying giftedness, it is generally regarded as an area of deficit related to learning disabilities. For example, learning-disabled students have been shown to be "inactive" learners, inefficient in applying the abilities and capacities which they have (Newman & Hagen, 1981; Torgesen, 1977; Wong,

1979, 1982). Research on the metacognitive abilities of learning-disabled students suggests that their general learning disabilities are due in part to deficiencies in metacognitive processes (Borkowski, Estrada, Milstead, & Hale, 1989; Jacobs, 1984; Kneedler & Hallahan, 1981; Kotsonis & Patterson, 1980; Simmons, Kameenui, & Darch, 1988; Slife, Weiss, & Bell, 1985; Wong, 1985; Wong & Jones, 1982). Torgesen (1977) hypothesized that learning-disabled students would benefit from instruction which "recognizes the influence of the child's ability to take an active role in learning" (p. 33). Teaching metacognitive and cognitive strategies to learning-disabled students has enabled them to be more active and thus more efficient in their learning (Alley & Deshler, 1979; Loper, Hallahan, & Ianna, 1982; Schumaker, Deshler, Alley, Warner, & Denton, 1982; Wong & Jones, 1982).

Metacognition in Learning-Disabled Gifted Students

Their giftedness suggests metacognitive strength; their learning disabilities suggest metacognitive weakness. Learning-disabled gifted students demonstrate high abilities in certain areas, whether academic or creative, but fail to perform at an average level in school due to particular disabilities. They are identified as a specific population needing educational opportunities that are different from programs offered for either learning-disabled or gifted students (Daniels, 1983; Fox, Brody, & Tobin, 1983; Maker, 1977; Whitmore, 1980; Whitmore & Maker, 1985). Research to date has focused on case studies (Baum, 1984; Rosner & Seymour, 1983; Suter & Wolf, 1987), comparison of test performance of learning-disabled gifted students to that of gifted and learning-disabled students (Barton & Starnes, 1989; Fox, 1983; Schiff, Kaufman, & Kaufman, 1981; Suter & Wolf, 1987), and educational programming options (Baum, 1984, 1988; Baum, Emerick, Herman, & Dixon, 1989; Maker, 1977; Nielson & Mortorff-Albert, 1989; Suter & Wolf, 1987). Until recently, few studies (e.g., Montague, 1991) have reported how learning-disabled gifted students learn or solve problems in an academic setting. None appear to address the extent to which they resemble students identified as gifted in these respects. Since

the use of metacognitive knowledge and skills might assist learning-disabled gifted students to compensate directly for their identified processing deficits, these students provide a unique opportunity to investigate the role of metacognition in a highly able population.

Reading and Research on Metacognition

Metacognition is being studied across the full curriculum from science and mathematics to sports, and reading has long been characterized as a problem-solving task in which processes now labeled metacognitive play an important part (Gray, 1937; Olsen, Duffy, & Mack, 1984; Olshavsky, 1976–1977; Thorndike, 1917); therefore, reading is an especially appropriate task with which to examine metacognitive knowledge and skills. Mature readers use metacognitive knowledge about their strengths, interests, text structure, and available strategies to approach each reading task in the most efficient manner (Myers & Paris, 1978). They also monitor their comprehension and evaluate their progress in light of the goal suggested by the reading task (Baker, 1984, 1985; Baker & Anderson, 1982; Baker & Brown, 1984; Brown, 1985; Garner, 1980; Hare, 1981; Hare & Bouchardt, 1985). Gifted readers have also been reported to use strategies such as predicting, evaluating, and connecting new content to prior knowledge more often (Fehrenbach, 1991).

Most people read texts at their reading level without the need consciously to invoke strategies. Comprehension strategies may be needed only when there are difficulties, such as when the reader's knowledge is insufficient, the text has gaps or ambiguities, or the passage contains many unknown words (Bereiter & Bird, 1985). Many researchers have employed the error-detection paradigm to investigate comprehension monitoring by skilled readers (Baker, 1979, 1984; Baker & Anderson, 1982; Garner, 1980, 1981; Garner & Reis, 1981; Markman, 1979). The general technique consists of inserting errors ("bugs") in the text to inhibit automatic comprehension of the material and thereby force the reader to invoke problem-solving strategies to monitor his/her understanding. Different types of bugs, ranging from obvious nonsense words to less obvious improper use of connectives between thoughts, have been used to investigate comprehension monitoring of different populations of students from college level to elementary "poor readers." The error-detection paradigm simulates the common reading situation of coping with new words in context.

The error-detection paradigm has been criticized for its apparent inability to force the comprehension monitoring that would be expected in more mature readers. From the methods used in previous studies, it is difficult to determine whether the subjects failed to detect the errors or failed to verbalize their detection (Baker, 1979, 1985; Winograd & Johnston, 1982). Suggested reasons for the low incidence of reported errors include the use of background knowledge to resolve the problem caused by the error (Baker, 1979; Garner & Anderson, 1981–82; Hare & Bouchardt, 1985). Previous studies often relied on subjects' ability to verbalize their detection of embedded errors after they finished the task. Studies utilizing retrospective reports may have obtained lower levels of error detection than were actually occurring due to information about the processing no longer being available in short-term memory (Ericsson & Simon, 1984).

The think-aloud method of data collection has been used most often in studies of problem-solving abilities (Chase & Ericsson, 1981; Greeno, 1978; Hayes, Flower, Schriver, Stratman, & Carey, 1987; Lewis, 1981; Simon & Simon, 1978). Although it seems unnatural for subjects to talk out loud while reading, think-aloud methods have been widely and successfully used to investigate cognitive processes involved in reading tasks. These studies have focused on the use of cognitive strategies (Bereiter & Bird, 1985; Olshavsky, 1976–1977), summarization rules (Brown & Day, 1983; Johnston & Afflerbach, 1985), and comprehension strategies in reading different types of texts (Olsen et al., 1984).

One of the stipulations for the use of verbal reports is that the processes under investigation should be conscious and available to be reported (Ericsson & Simon, 1984). Metacognition was defined as the conscious and deliberate control of cognitive actions. Verbal report techniques should, therefore, be appropriate for investigating comprehension monitoring and metacognitive processes. By pairing the error-detection paradigm with think-aloud methods of data collection, this study undertook to examine the metacognitive processes used by readers encountering a text which was difficult to comprehend.

The Present Study

This study brings together these four threads: giftedness, learning disabilities, metacognition, and reading. By including gifted, learning-disabled gifted, average-performing, and learning-disabled students, it is designed to answer the first question, "Is metacognition a component of giftedness even when the giftedness is compromised by learning disabilities?" If learning-disabled gifted students prove to be comparable to gifted students in their use of metacognitive knowledge and skills on the chosen reading task and differ consistently from learning-disabled or average students, this would suggest their similarity to gifted students in cognitive processing on this task. Such results would be very different from those of prior research in which metacognitive deficits were associated with learning disabilities. They would indicate that superior metacognitive performance may be an element of giftedness even under widely varied conditions of giftedness.

The second research issue, better understanding of learning-disabled gifted students, will be served by the same data. The same differences in the outcomes would support the general understanding of learning disabilities as specific rather than general dysfunctions and cast some light on the proposition that metacognitive deficiencies may be part of the cause of learning disabilities (we used the term *due to* above). If learning-disabled gifted students, like gifted students, perform metacognitively at high levels, they may be better served by using this strength to achieve in their school work, even in areas affected by their disability.

METHODOLOGY

Design

The primary design was a three-way ($2 \times 2 \times 2$) multivariate analysis of covariance. The three independent variables were grade (two levels—elementary and secondary), giftedness (two levels—identified as gifted or not), and learning disabilities (two levels—identified as learning disabled or not). Grade was introduced since age differences are normally obtained on measures of reading performance and metacognitive knowledge and skills. The covariate, prior knowledge of the concepts intended to be unfamiliar in the reading tasks as well as the overarching content of the reading, was retained in all multivariate and univariate tests of significance. There were four dependent variables: metacognitive knowledge, metacognitive skills, error-detection performance, and comprehension. The two metacognitive indices directly serve the main research questions. Error detection and comprehension are performance indicators which help to verify that metacognitive knowledge and skills were important to performance and that the task did not place excessive or unnatural demands on the students, and to compare the results to relevant prior research. The multivariate tests were all planned comparisons, intended to provide an overall view of the relations among the variables.

Depending on the outcomes of the multivariate analysis, a series of secondary exploratory analyses were also anticipated in order better to understand the multivariate results. These are described below in the Results section.

The design as described is intended to facilitate statistical support for the results. The most important part of the design was described earlier. An error-detection reading task was chosen to provide a standard comprehension-monitoring task on which problem-solving performance could be observed. The raw data consist of verbatim protocols, supplemented by videotapes of the students' progression through the texts. The sample, measures, and detailed procedures are described below.

Sample and Independent Variables

Identified learning-disabled gifted students are extremely difficult to locate in large numbers in comparable school settings. This was an important limitation in designing this study. In addition, cognitive research on thinking or problem solving depends much more on the intensive analysis of individual protocols than on summary statistics derived from large samples. The students participating in the study attended public schools in three different county school systems of West Virginia. These school systems were selected because they formally identified gifted, learning-disabled gifted, and learning-disabled students within their schools. It was necessary to use students in two grades at each of the two levels, 5th–6th for the elementary grade level and 11th–12th for the secondary grade level, to obtain an adequate number of students in the pivotal learning-disabled gifted category. There were 48 students, 6 in each cell. The students were drawn from intact groups within the schools. Two levels of giftedness (gifted or not gifted) and two levels of learning disability (learning disabled or not learning disabled) resulted in four groups at each of the two different grade levels: the average school sample, with no formally identified exceptionalities; students identified as gifted; students identified as learning-disabled; and students identified as learning-disabled gifted. Only white males were included because very few girls were formally identified as learning-disabled gifted in the participating school systems. Also, in order to avoid confounding the results with possible cultural effects, no students representing any other racial groups were included in the study. The use of intact groups presented a dilemma for us. Intact groups increase the "ecological validity" of the study, but the selection process is also an uncontrollable source of variance.

Each participating school system had selected criteria to identify students as learning-disabled and gifted which met the federal guidelines set out by the Marland report for gifted (U.S. Commissioner of Education, 1972) and United States Public Law 94–142. These guidelines are summarized in the following three paragraphs.

In order to be placed in a program for the gifted in West Virginia, the school system must provide documented evidence that the student had (a) obtained a score of at least 130 on a full-scale comprehensive intelligence test, either the Wechsler Intelligence Scale for Children-

Revised (WISC-R) or the Stanford-Binet, and (b) displayed high achievement in at least one academic area (on the basis of scores on a standardized achievement test or on the student's scholastic performance) so as to require specially designed instruction.

In order to be selected for the learning-disabilities program, the student must meet four of the following five criteria: (a) a score of 85 or above on the WISC-R; (b) a severe discrepancy in one or more academic areas between achievement and the index of intellectual ability obtained on the WISC-R; (c) this discrepancy is not due to either physical or emotional problems, or to cultural or economic disadvantage; (d) demonstrable deficits in one or more basic learning processes; and (e) educational performance adversely affected to the extent that specially designed instruction is required.

Students identified as learning-disabled gifted must meet the criteria set out for placement in a learning-disability program with the exception that they must score 127 (within the standard error of measurement) or above on a standardized test of intelligence or 127 or above on either the verbal or performance scale of the WISC-R if there is a possible handicapping condition.

The teachers or principals in the schools nominated students to participate in the study from those who were identified as gifted, learning-disabled gifted, or learning-disabled and who also met the following guidelines:

1. To be a member of the gifted group, the student must not have had a discrepancy between his measured ability on the intelligence test and achievement in school.
2. Students in the learning-disabled gifted group must have had an intelligence test score of at least 127 (on either the full scale or Verbal or Performance subscale) and be reading at least at the fourth-grade level for the secondary group or the third-grade level for the elementary group.
3. In order to ensure that the students in the learning-disabled group were different from those in the learning-disabled gifted group, the former must have obtained an intelligence test score between 90 and 115

but be reading at least at the fourth-grade level for the secondary group or at the third-grade level for the elementary group.
4. Students who were selected to be in the average-achieving group must have been performing at grade level in the regular classroom with no apparent problems or disabilities and never have been served in any program for exceptional students.

Procedures, Covariate, and Dependent Variables

General procedural considerations. One of the first procedural difficulties came in scheduling the experiment with the students. Due to course schedules, high school students were given the option of doing the experimental tasks either in one sitting of between 1 and 2 hours or in two different sessions of 45 minutes to 1 hour each. Each elementary-grade student was seen in two sessions. The first consisted of the metacognitive interview and the prior knowledge assessment; the remaining tasks were completed 1 week later.

Each student was seen individually by the first author and was asked to respond verbally to each of the tasks. Each experimental session was tape recorded so that the verbal utterances could be transcribed verbatim to produce think-aloud protocols. The reading sessions were also videotaped to obtain an on-line record of the student's movements through the booklets.

To facilitate coding the data, each protocol was parsed into segments using Winograd's (1983) system of clausal analysis. Since all of the coding was subjective, three independent raters were given coding schemes developed by the first author with which they rated randomly selected protocols for each of the dependent variables. The protocols for each of the students on the seven separate tasks were separated and marked only with an identification number selected by a person other than the first author. Thus, the group to which a student belonged was unknown to all of the raters.

Prior knowledge—covariate. Since research has established a positive correlation between prior knowledge and reading comprehension (Adams & Bruce, 1982; Anderson, 1985; Langer, 1981) the Langer Pre-Reading Plan (PReP)

(Langer, 1981) was used to get an assessment of the student's prior knowledge of the main idea of the stimulus text. If a student's knowledge about the information in the texts was extensive, his performance on the dependent variables could be analyzed using his prior knowledge as a covariate. Each student was asked to report verbally anything that came to mind about a word which was supplied both visually and orally.

The three superordinate topics used for the PReP were chosen by a panel of 16 graduate students in the master's level reading program at West Virginia University. The graduate students were randomly assigned either the elementary or secondary passage (see the Appendix for both texts). They were instructed to read the passage and then produce three superordinate topics which they felt best described the main idea of the passage. The three topics with the highest frequency produced by the graduate students were *censitaire* (tenant farmer), *seigneur* (feudal lord), and *colonization* (or *colony*) with an agreement rate of 64%, 88%, and 94%, respectively.

An index of prior knowledge for each student was determined by counting the separate concepts verbalized for the three superordinate topics: *colonization/colony, seigneur,* and *censitaire.* A concept was defined as any verbalized element which added new information to that which had been stated previously. Since none of the students knew what was meant by *seigneur* and *censitaire,* the prior knowledge score was based solely on verbalized knowledge of *colonization/colony.* Only concepts which related to the historical concepts of the definition of *colonization/colony* were counted. For example, ants or bees were not counted as separate concepts, but if the student stated "ants living together in a group," *living together in a group* was counted if this concept had not been stated previously. Interrater reliability of 85% was obtained by determining the percentage of agreement between each of the independent raters and the first author on two separate protocols.

Metacognitive knowledge. A structured interview developed by Myers and Paris (1978) was used to assess metacognitive knowledge about reading. Metacognitive knowledge was defined as the student's knowledge of the person, task, and strategy variables in reading (Flavell, 1976). This dependent variable was a score of the understanding of these three parameters as verbalized by the student during the interview. The interviews were scored using a coding scheme based on a system developed by Paris and Jacobs (1984). The responses to the questions relating to specific elements were analyzed and given a score of 2 for good understanding, 1 for knowledge of, or 0 for no knowledge. Interrater reliability, obtained in the manner described above, was 90%.

Metacognitive skills. Exercises developed by Ericsson and Simon (1984) were used to provide initial practice with the think-aloud procedure used with this variable. Each student was asked to think out loud (a) while mentally calculating an arithmetic problem and then (b) while figuring out word puzzles. In order to provide practice using the think-aloud procedure while reading, the student was presented with a paragraph which used the cloze procedure (several words were removed and had to be inferred). Two cloze passages (third- and fifth-grade reading level) were taken from Miller (1974); a third cloze passage (sixth-grade reading level) came from *Quest* materials (Aulls & Graves, 1985). These passages were chosen with regard to the independent reading level of each student (information provided by the teachers from standardized scores for those students in special education programs, or teacher records for the students in the average-achieving group), so that each student practiced thinking aloud on a cloze passage which was at or below his independent reading level. The first author demonstrated the think-aloud method with the first two sentences of the cloze passage and then asked the student to continue.

If, during the course of completing each of these exercises, the student was not thinking aloud, the researcher would prompt him by saying "Tell me what you are thinking" or "Keep talking." The student was also reminded for each exercise that getting a correct answer was not as important as just saying out loud what he was thinking.

In order to provide specific practice on verbalizing while reading a text, a practice reading passage was presented to each student in exactly the same manner as the stimulus text (bugged passage) was to be presented. These passages came from Miller (1974) and ranged in length from 117 to 248 words. The passage chosen for each student was below his independent reading level so that the student would read with ease and obtain practice in thinking out loud while reading.

As well as providing each student with practice in the think-aloud method, and with the procedure of being videotaped, the first reading passage and recall were used to ascertain whether each student could read a text in the format presented, think aloud, and obtain an understanding of the main idea of the text. The definition of main idea, as used for assessing comprehension of this text, was the general topic of the paragraph (Aulls, 1978). If a student could not complete the first text, which was on his independent reading level with no bugs, he would not have been given the rest of the tasks and would not have been included in the study. All students who initially started the experiment were able to complete this task. Upon completion of the practice reading passage, the student was asked to recall the information in the passage verbally. When he finished with the recall, he was asked if he had any questions, and once these were answered, he was presented with the stimulus text.

For both the practice reading passage and the stimulus text, students were instructed to read the passage for understanding and were told they would be asked to tell the first author about it when they had finished reading. They were reminded to think aloud and to say whatever came to their mind. The students were in control of the presentation of the material, the length and sequence of the sentence exposures, the reading mode, and what they talked about. The student was given the book opened to the title page and instructed to place it in a comfortable position; then the video camera was placed behind him and focused on the printed page of the text. The first author sat so that the text was in view in case the student asked her to pronounce any of the words.

The texts were presented in a booklet, with one sentence per page and a blank page between each sentence. The students were told that the blank page was to serve as a reminder to talk aloud after reading each sentence and that if he had not done so by the time he was turning to the next page of text, the experimenter could remind him to do so. Each sentence was typed on the same line of each page, but any structural properties, such as punctuation, indentation, or capitalization were retained from the original source.

Information on the use of metacognitive skills was obtained from the think-aloud protocols of the students' verbalizations as they read the bugged text. The stimulus texts were adapted from the Ginn series of Social Studies Materials for Canada for Grades 4–6 (Smith, 1971). The particular passage chosen incorporated unfamiliar vocabulary words throughout the text and thus already contained one of the bugs used to inhibit automatic comprehension within the context of the passage. Although the specific topic, that of France setting up a *seigneurial* system to colonize Quebec, was not familiar to these West Virginia students, the general topic, that of colonization of North America, was information that each student would have been exposed to in school by the time he was in fifth grade. Thus, each student would have some prior knowledge of the content at least in a very general sense, and specific prior knowledge would be limited.

The passage for the elementary grade level was judged to be at the 7th-grade reading level by the Fry Readability Formula (Fry, 1968) and on the 7–8th-grade level by the Dale-Chall (1948) formula. The passage for the secondary grade level was judged to be at the 10th-grade reading level by the Fry formula and the 9–10th-grade level on the Dale-Chall. The Reading Ease (Flesch, 1948) scores—scaled from 0 (unreadable) to 100 (very readable)—were 84 for the elementary text and 66 for the secondary text.

In order to determine if the students in the fifth or sixth grades would be able to read the story, 10 fourth-grade students from one of the participating school systems were asked to read the passage aloud, and an individual reading inventory was done on their performance. The original passage was presented with the words *seigneur* and *censitaire* replaced by *feudal lord* and *tenant farmer,* respectively. This was done in order to get a readability of the passage without words which were included specifically to cause problems. The passage was on the instructional level of the students (85% word recognition and ability to answer questions about the text). Any other words that consistently caused problems for these 10 students were replaced (i.e., *main* house substituted for *manor* house, *got* for *acquired,* and *keep* for *maintain*). These and other precautions described above ensured that the task was as natural as possible (considering the think-aloud instructions) for each student.

The two history passages were deliberately altered by the first author to produce the inconsistencies required for the error-detection paradigm. Aside from the two vocabulary words—*seigneur* and *censitaire* (*seigneur* being in three different forms, *seigneur, seigneury,* and *seigneurial*)—there were two instances each of two other types of errors: internal inconsistencies and prior knowledge violations. Research has shown that not all students use the same standards to evaluate their comprehension (Garner, 1981); therefore, three types of bugs were included to increase the incidence of error detection by the students in the present study.

The bugged reading passage was presented to the students in the manner described above, except this time the first author read aloud the title of the passage. After reading the second passage, the student was asked to tell what he thought the passage was about. If he responded that he did not know, he was asked to tell anything he could remember about what he had read. Then he was asked to define the words *seigneur* and *censitaire,* one at a time, again being prompted to tell anything he could remember. A posttask interview developed by the first author concluded this assessment. This interview gave each student an opportunity to report the detection of errors in the text, as well as a chance to talk about the task, his performance, the strategies used, any problems encountered during the task, any questions he

might have had, or how he felt about the task. Upon completion of the interview, each student was given an opportunity to ask about the tasks or the text and was commended for his performance and participation.

The verbalizations were transcribed from the audiotapes in such a fashion that the students' comments could be analyzed in the context of the segment of text they were responding to. The videotapes were analyzed with respect to the movements made through the text, so that if a student looked back or forward to other segments, his comments were judged with regard to the segment of text being addressed. All such movements were recorded on the transcript of the think-aloud protocol.

Metacognitive skills were operationally defined as the regulations and evaluations verbalized by a student as he read through the bugged text (Baker & Brown, 1984). The definitions of the metacognitive statements were developed from a careful review of the literature on analysis of think-aloud protocols (Breuleux, 1991; Flower, Hayes, & Swarts, 1983; Greeno & Simon, 1988; Johnston & Afflerbach, 1985; Simon & Simon, 1978; Swarts, Flower, & Hayes, 1984) and metacognition (Baker & Brown, 1984; Bos & Filip, 1982; Brown, 1980, 1982; Brown & Palinscar, 1982; Flavell, 1976; Haller, Child, & Walberg, 1988; Masson, 1982; Sternberg, 1984; Wong & Sawatsky, 1982). In order to facilitate coding, the types of metacognitive statements were clustered under four different headings: monitoring, evaluating, controlling, and planning.

In order to code the protocols it was also necessary to define other types of comments made by the students. Although these were not part of the statistical analysis, they were important to a more qualitative analysis of the types of problem-solving strategies being used. Some of the more frequently verbalized statements were paraphrases, restatements, and questions. Once the preliminary definitions were established, four randomly chosen protocols were examined to refine the definitions and to select representative examples of each of the statements. The entire coding scheme consisted of 14 categories. The complete codebook, with the definitions and examples from the protocols, was used to code each protocol. Interrater reliability was 87% for the total protocol, 88% for metacognitive statements, and 87% for other types of statements.

The frequency of each category of statements verbalized per student protocol was tabulated. These frequencies were then converted into percentage scores, based on the total number of segments per protocol. The four different categories of metacognitive statements were also combined into a total number of metacognitive statements verbalized; this score was then divided by the total number of statements verbalized to obtain the percentage of metacognitive statements verbalized used in the statistical analyses.

Detection of errors. Error detection was defined as the verbal acknowledgment of the embedded violations of prior knowledge and the recognition of internal inconsistencies. This was scored leniently, in that if a student simply mentioned that a segment of bugged text was problematic without identifying the problem, it was counted as an error detection. Lenient scoring assured that any significant results among groups would reflect a true difference since it was easier for all students to score an error detection than if a more stringent index had been used. Since the unknown vocabulary words were pervasive and central to the theme of the story, they were not included in the error detection score. It was felt that because of the importance and frequency of these words in the text, the students might not comment specifically on their status as an error or a problem. The students scored 1 point for each of the embedded errors they verbalized. No distinction was made as to when the students verbalized the errors (during the think-aloud, recall or posttask interview), or how many times they verbalized them. Therefore, for each student, a total of 4 points (for detecting the two prior-knowledge violations and the two internal inconsistencies) was possible. Interrater reliability was 96%.

Comprehension of passage. Comprehension was defined as a statement expressing an understanding of the main topic of the passage (Bloom, Engelhart, Furst, Hill, & Krathwohl,

1956). The recall of the bugged text was used to obtain a comprehension score. A student received a score for the main idea and the definitions of *seigneur* and *censitaire* in the following manner, 2—for verbalizing the main idea, 1—for verbalizing an idea which was related but not central to the theme of the passage or the definition of the two words, or 0—for missing the point. The main idea for the texts differed by grade level because the content of the passages was slightly different. Interrater reliability on this measure was 92%.

In order to account for the possibility that the recall actually reflected a measure of memory ability as opposed to comprehension, the think-aloud protocols were examined for verbalizations of the meanings of the passage and the two vocabulary words as the students read through the text. Based on inferences verbalized in reference to the two vocabulary words, this raised the score of five students in the lower grade level and one student in the higher grade level. These corrected means were used in the statistical analysis.

RESULTS

Theoretically, more competent readers should perform better than poorer readers on measures of metacognitive knowledge and subsequently use that knowledge to monitor their ongoing comprehension of the text. Also, a person using metacognitive skills to regulate comprehension should more effectively detect errors and better comprehend the material.

In order to determine the suitability of a multivariate analysis of covariance (MANCOVA), Pearson product-moment correlations were calculated among the four dependent variables (metacognitive knowledge, percentage of metacognitive statements verbalized, errors detected, and comprehension) and the covariate (prior knowledge of colonization). Table 1 presents the correlation matrix.

Because all but one pair of the dependent variables were significantly intercorrelated and several of these were high in absolute terms (see Table 1) as well as theoretically related, it was deemed appropriate to analyze the data with a MANCOVA.

Table 1   Correlation Matrix of Dependent Measures and Covariate

	Percentage Metacognitive	Errors Detected	Comprehension Score	Prior Knowledge
Metacognitive Knowledge	.260*	.556***	.522***	.607***
Percentage Metacognitive		.578***	.084	.243*
Errors Detected			.495***	.518***
Comprehension				.527***

*$p<.05$, **$p<.01$,***$p<.001$, $N=48$

The Grade × Giftedness × Learning Disability multivariate analysis of covariance revealed a significant Grade × Gifted interaction ($F(4, 36) = 3.30$, $p < .05$) and significant main effects for both grade ($F(4, 36) = 8.41$, $p < .001$) and giftedness ($F(4, 36) = 9.81$, $p < .001$). There was no significant three-way interaction, nor any two-way interaction or main effect involving learning disabilities. Any differences in metacognitive knowledge or skill, error detection, or comprehension were related to both grade (or age) and giftedness, not to learning disabilities. Overall, the multivariate analysis does not imply that we should abandon our proposition that metacognition is a component of giftedness, even when such giftedness is combined with a learning disability. The significant differences found in relation to giftedness and grade imply that the analysis has sufficient power to find differences in the data despite the small sample size. Since the interpretation of the main effects was obfuscated by the interaction, the multivariate analysis is not reported in detail. Understanding this interaction required a more fine-grained examination of the data.

There is some controversy in the field with regard to the common practice of following a multivariate analysis with univariate analyses, especially if the dependent variables are largely uncorrelated (Thompson, 1994). Such further analysis is warranted here for two reasons. First, the main result, namely, that learning disability did not contribute significantly to the variance observed in performance on the experimental tasks, is found in and is clear from the multivariate analysis. The differences between the gifted and learning-disabled gifted groups on the one hand and the learning-disabled and average-ability groups on the other are correlated with differences in levels of giftedness. This may be interpreted to support the hypothesis that thinking processes of learning-disabled gifted students are characterized by their resemblance to gifted students because, were the learning disabilities more pervasive in these relationships, the gifted group would have stood alone and the performance of the learning-disabled gifted groups would have been more similar to that of the learning-disabled group. The main results are not dependent on univariate analyses. The latter are also possible here for a statistical reason also summarized by Thompson (1994) in his argument against their inappropriate use. In this study, the dependent variables are, for the most part, highly intercorrelated. That means the risk of a Type I error in the overall study is relatively low, that is, closer to the risk in a single test. Were the dependent variables not well intercorrelated, the risk of a Type I error would accumulate across the various contrasts being made, to the point of being nearly certain at some point in the study. This risk being lower (though not absent) warrants further exploration of univariate data to sharpen our understanding of the results (e.g., the one significant interaction) and of questions which still need to be examined.

Univariate results also provide a useful understanding of the outcomes, partly because they ignore the intercorrelations among the dependent variables. This is also defensible since there was a zero-order correlation between metacognitive skill and comprehension (see Table 1). These were not posthoc

Table 2 Means and Standard Deviations of Metacognitive Knowledge (MK), Percentage of Metacognitive Statements Made (%META), Comprehension (COMP), and Error Detection (ED) Scores

Group	Elementary				Secondary			
	MK	%META	COMP	ED	MK	%META	COMP	ED
Learn-Dis.	38.5	14.67%	4.67	0.83	41.0	30.83%	5.00	2.83
Gifted	(2.59)	(11.06)	(1.03)	(0.98)	(2.83)	(17.68)	(0.63)	(0.75)
Gifted	38.0	14.83%	5.67	1.33	41.0	25.00%	5.17	2.83
	(2.83)	(9.95)	(0.52)	(0.52)	(3.58)	(10.28)	(0.98)	(1.17)
Average-	30.5	8.17%	3.5	0.17	41.3	16.50%	5.33	1.67
Achieving	(5.09)	(7.71)	(1.05)	(0.41)	(2.58)	(11.09)	(1.03)	(1.21)
Learning-	30.8	12.17%	2.67	0.33	34.2	18.83%	3.33	1.17
Disabled	(3.66)	(10.98)	(1.36)	(0.52)	(3.55)	(7.71)	(1.51)	(1.17)

n = 6 subjects per cell, N = 48

tests; the full analysis of covariance (ANCOVA) model was used except that the four dependent variables were treated separately. We are well aware that univariate results overestimate systematic differences; the goal is not to find differences at these levels that were not present in the multivariate analysis.

Key to discussing an interaction in these terms is whether it is ordinal or disordinal. Examination of the means in Table 2 reveals a completely ordinal interaction: The mean scores for all four dependent variables are (with some exceptions at the secondary level for average subjects, discussed below) highest for the gifted and learning-disabled gifted groups and lowest for the other two groups. Such an interaction is meaningful in this study, not a statistical aberration.

When the univariate analyses of covariance were examined, the Grade × Gifted interaction appeared to be accounted for by differences among the levels of metacognitive knowledge ($F(1, 39) = 4.68$, $p < .05$) and comprehension ($F(1, 39) = 4.70$, $p < .05$). The means in Table 2 clearly reveal the Grade × Gifted interaction for these two variables: The mean score for each of the groups on metacognitive knowledge (MK) is greater at the secondary level than at the elementary school level. Whereas there was an obvious difference between the two groups of gifted and the two groups of nongifted students at the elementary grades, at the secondary level the performance of the average-achieving group was similar to

that of the learning-disabled gifted and gifted groups. The performance of the learning-disabled group remained lower. These results on metacognitive knowledge may be due to a ceiling effect. However, this is not clear. The scoring system used on the metacognitive interview was the same for both grade levels, with a maximum attainable score of 48 points, and the interview was originally developed for Grades 2–6. However, the highest group mean of 41.3 was approximately 3 standard deviations below the maximum possible score.

A ceiling effect is likely on comprehension (COMP). A top score of 6 points could be obtained on this measure, and several groups were within 1 standard deviation of that level of achievement. Two others were just beyond 1 standard deviation below that score. The Grade × Gifted interaction is evident in two ways. The average-achieving secondary group achieved the same high level of performance as the gifted and learning-disabled secondary groups. Also, the elementary gifted group showed as high a level of performance on this task as the secondary groups mentioned above. It is possible that the comprehension measure may have been tapping a low-level skill. However, as stated earlier, the think-aloud protocols were investigated for indications of comprehension in order to compensate for memory problems, and the means for the elementary gifted group were not affected, indicating a high level of competence in comprehension.

Although giftedness was significant in the multivariate analysis, the interaction of the grade and giftedness variables qualifies but does not cancel support for the expectation that the performance of the gifted students would be superior to that of the nongifted. Support remains for the hypothesis that the learning-disabled gifted students performed similarly to their gifted peers on both metacognitive knowledge and comprehension.

When the significant main effect for grade was examined, the univariate ANCOVAs raised the possibility that it may be explained by metacognitive knowledge ($F(1, 39) = 14.27$, $p < .01$), percentage of metacognitive statements verbalized ($F(1, 39) = 7.63$, $p < .01$), and errors detected ($F(1, 39) = 19.02$, $p < .001$). This main effect for grade is consistent with previous research that identifies the developmental quality of metacognition.

The multivariate analysis of covariance revealed a significant main effect for giftedness which the univariate tests suggested might be explained by metacognitive knowledge ($F(1, 39) = 18.24$, $p < .001$), errors detected ($F(1, 39) = 10.56$, $p < .01$), and comprehension ($F(1, 39) = 11.55$, $p < .01$). There was, however, no main effect for giftedness on the percentage of metacognitive statements verbalized. A multivariate analysis of variance in which prior knowledge was not included as a covariate had been initially performed on the data; the differences among groups on percentage of metacognitive statements verbalized were significant ($F(1, 40) = 5.27$, $p < .05$). When the covariate was included, the results on this dependent variable were not significant but did occur in the hypothesized direction ($F(1, 39) = 3.96$, $p = .054$).

The ANCOVA results for the percentage of metacognitive statements verbalized were less clear cut. First, as reported above, there was a significant univariate main effect for grade ($F(1, 39) = 7.63$, $p < .01$) but not for giftedness. As seen in Table 2, the older students performed at a higher level than the younger subjects. An especially interesting feature observable in Table 2 is that the means for the learning-disabled groups at the elementary and secondary grade levels are higher than those for the average-achieving groups. This may be due to the learning-disabled students' evaluation of their lack of understanding, although they rarely engaged in or verbalized any cognitive strategies to overcome this problem.

The within-cell variance was very large for the percentage of metacognitive statements verbalized, reflected in the standard deviations in Table 2. This increased the error term, thus making the differences between the groups less likely to be statistically significant in a univariate context. However, an examination of the means in Table 2 shows that the learning-disabled gifted students at both grade levels performed more like their gifted than their nongifted peers on this measure.

The results on the percentage of metacognitive statements verbalized indicate that the older students verbalized more metacognitive statements than the younger students. If one were actively to monitor their comprehension, then it would be expected that they would not only use metacognitive skills but also detect any errors present in the text. The results support this speculation because the older and the gifted students verbalized the existence of more errors than did the younger and the nongifted.

The univariate main effects for grade and giftedness predicting errors detected are also clearly visible in the means in Table 2. The main effect for grade ($F(1, 39) = 19.02$, $p < .001$) may be partially explained by the fact that no students at the elementary grade level verbalized the detection of any internal inconsistency errors. Their scores were based solely on their verbalized detection of the prior knowledge bugs. The results on this dependent variable are consistent with the hypothesis that both groups of gifted students used more metacognitive skills than both groups of nongifted. The main effect for giftedness ($F(1, 39) = 10.56$, $p < .01$), coupled with the lack of a Giftedness × Learning Disabilities interaction, also encourages us to sustain the hypothesis that the learning-disabled gifted students performed similarly to their gifted peers on this measure.

The main effect for giftedness supports the general expectation that the gifted students would perform better than the nongifted on all but one of the dependent measures. The study did not set out to confirm this expectation in those terms, but the result offers some informal support for the validity of the measures and the power of the design and analysis. However, since the learning-disabled gifted students were part of a main effect for giftedness, these results support the hypothesis that the learning-disabled gifted students would perform more like their gifted than their learning-disabled peers. One possible explanation for the lack of a main effect for the percentage of metacognitive statements verbalized is that prior knowledge may be an important factor in monitoring comprehension of text content. Another important factor was the small sample size and the great variability within each group on this variable.

Correlational techniques do not, of course, directly address causality. This is a design question. In the present study causality is not an issue. We are trying to add precision to a relatively vague and inadequately defined term—*giftedness*—observing performance in especially appropriate groups of school children and linking this performance to a cognitive rather than a psychometric theoretical base. Giftedness does not cause metacognition, nor vice versa.

This study investigated two questions. First, would students identified as academically gifted use more metacognitive knowledge and skills than students not identified as gifted? The results provide qualified support for this question. At the elementary and secondary levels, students identified as gifted (both the gifted and the learning-disabled gifted) revealed more metacognitive knowledge and comprehension and detected more errors than the average achieving and learning disabled while reading the bugged text. Although the difference between the gifted and the nongifted groups was not significant on the percentage of metacognitive statements verbalized, the results were in the direction predicted. At the secondary level, on measures of metacognitive knowledge and comprehension, the average-achieving students were performing at levels similar to the gifted students. So although giftedness was related to higher levels of perfor-

mance on all measures at the elementary level, it was found (as a main effect) to be related only to high levels of error detection at the secondary level.

The second hypothesis was that students identified as learning-disabled gifted would perform more like their gifted than their learning-disabled peers. This was supported on all of the dependent measures and at both grade levels.

DISCUSSION

The results point to differences in performance between children identified as gifted and those identified as nongifted in their use of metacognitive strategies on a comprehension-monitoring reading task. Not only did the gifted and the learning-disabled gifted students verbalize a greater percentage of metacognitive statements at the elementary grade level, but they also verbalized their detection of the embedded errors to a greater extent than did the average-achieving and learning-disabled students at both grade levels. In this respect, this study supports the proposition by Sternberg (1981) and Shore (1982) that the use of metacognitive skills and knowledge may be a factor in high levels of performance demonstrated by students identified as academically gifted.

The fact that the gifted and learning-disabled gifted secondary students did not perform better than the average-achieving group on metacognitive knowledge and comprehension can be interpreted in several ways. First, there may be a ceiling effect, in that the measures used on these dependent variables may not have been sensitive enough to detect differences at higher levels of performance. This ceiling effect also could have been due to the fact that these skills improved through the course of regular instruction or maturation. This interpretation follows from studies of average students which found that older students not only verbalized more metacognitive knowledge than younger students (Kreutzer, Leonard, & Flavell, 1975; Myers & Paris, 1978; Yussen & Bird, 1979) but also monitored their comprehension more effectively (Flavell, Speer, Green, & August, 1981; Markman, 1977, 1979). Maturation is also supported by the fact that the older groups of students in the studies cited were the age of the students at the elementary level in the present study. The use of metacognitive knowledge and skills increases as students become more adept at the cognitive tasks they are performing.

Another way of interpreting the results obtained on the measures of metacognitive knowledge and comprehension is that the gifted and the learning-disabled gifted groups at the elementary grade level were already performing at the level of the average-achieving group at the secondary level. So even if these are skills which develop as students learn and mature, students identified as gifted verbalize these skills at a much younger age and demonstrate more metacognitive skills and comprehension monitoring than their nongifted peers. This, too, lends support to the hypothesized relationship between giftedness and metacognition. More research on the use of metacognitive knowledge in other domains by students identified as gifted would provide a clearer understanding of the development of both metacognition and giftedness.

Comprehension is a skill in which able students receive much instruction (Anderson, 1984), and as they mature, their skills in reading and comprehension improve (Brown, 1985). Therefore, it is not surprising that the average-achieving students would be performing very well on this measure at the secondary grade level. The fact that the secondary learning-disabled students were still performing at low levels is not surprising either. These students often exhibit deficits in reading skills which limit both their exposure to more varied reading tasks and their experiences with higher level reading skills. Furthermore, they often do not get the instruction in comprehension (Anderson, 1984) or experience with different reading materials which may be needed to develop metacognitive knowledge in reading.

Although the performance of the learning-disabled students in this study corroborates the results of studies which have demonstrated that poorer readers do not exhibit metacognitive knowledge or comprehension monitoring (Baker, 1979; Garner, 1980, 1981; Garner &

Reis, 1981; Paris & Myers, 1981), contradictory evidence was demonstrated by the amount of comprehension monitoring demonstrated by learning-disabled gifted students whose reading levels were similar to those of their learning-disabled peers (Hannah, 1990). Based on the results of previous studies, one would expect that students identified as academically gifted would do better on these measures than students who are experiencing difficulties. The fact that learning-disabled gifted students who were poor readers performed similarly to their gifted peers without disabilities supports the hypothesized relation between metacognition and giftedness (Hannah, 1990).

One of the problems researchers have noted in studying learning-disabled or gifted students is that their individual differences make it difficult to obtain significant or interpretable results (Wong, 1985). One would expect that learning-disabled gifted students would be just as heterogeneous a group, if not more so. Although the large within-cell variance corroborates this expectation, the results can be considered quite robust because significant differences between the groups were nonetheless obtained. This study also has good external or ecological validity in that all of the groups were as one would expect to find in a regular school situation.

In addition to supporting the role of metacognition in giftedness with data from what might be an unexpected population, this study also casts new light on the nature of learning-disabled giftedness. With regard to thinking processes, these pupils are gifted, even if their scholastic performance is deficient. More in-depth investigations must be done in order more fully to understand these students; however, our results indicate that learning-disabled gifted students can use metacognitive knowledge and skills to perform difficult reading tasks they might encounter in the classroom.

Rarely in life do we have the benefit of complete and appropriate instruction for our needs. We must make do with the examples offered by our teachers or the situation and the use of our own strategies and knowledge. The use of metacognitive knowledge and skills may be important components in the ability to learn under such realistic conditions. If this is true, and if individuals who are identified as academically gifted do use metacognitive knowledge and skills more effectively, it may help explain how they are able to achieve higher levels of performance than nongifted individuals and how the performance of all students might potentially be enhanced through instruction. Further study of gifted and learning-disabled gifted students may help us better to understand what needs to be learned.

AUTHORS' NOTE

This report is based upon the doctoral dissertation of the first author.

The project was supported in part by research grants to Professor Bruce M. Shore and colleagues from the Government of Québec FCAR program and the Faculty of Graduate Studies and Research, McGill University.

The authors would like to thank the young men from the Kanawha, Monongalia, and Wood County Schools, West Virginia who participated in the study, and the teachers and administrators who allowed access to their students.

REFERENCES

Adams, M., & Bruce, B. (1982). Background knowledge and reading comprehension. In J. A. Langer & M. T. Smith-Burke (Eds.), *Reader meets author/bridging the gap* (pp. 2–25). Newark, DE: International Reading Association.

Alley, G., & Deshler, D. (1979). *Teaching the learning disabled adolescent: Strategies and methods.* Denver, CO: Love.

Anderson, R. C. (1984). Some reflections on the acquisition of knowledge. *Educational Researcher, 13*(9), 5–10.

Anderson, R. C. (1985). Role of the reader's schema in comprehension, learning, and memory. In H. Singer & R. B. Ruddell (Eds.), *Theoretical models and processes of reading* (3rd ed.) (pp. 372–384). Newark, DE: International Reading Association.

Aulls, M. W. (1978). *Developmental and remedial reading in the middle grades.* Boston: Allyn & Bacon.

Aulls, M. W., & Graves, M. (1985). *Quest: A scholastic reading improvement series: A teacher's manual for: High on a mountain.* New York: Scholastic.

Baker, L. (1979). Comprehension monitoring: Identifying and coping with text confusions. *Journal of Reading Behavior, 11,* 365–374.

Baker, L. (1984). Children's effective use of multiple standards for evaluating their comprehension. *Journal of Educational Psychology, 76,* 588–597.

Baker, L. (1985). Differences in the standards used by college students to evaluate their comprehension of expository prose. *Reading Research Quarterly, 20,* 297–313.

Baker, L., & Anderson, R. I. (1982). Effects of inconsistent information on text processing: Evidence for comprehension monitoring. *Reading Research Quarterly, 17,* 281–294.

Baker, L., & Brown, A. L. (1984). Metacognitive skills and reading. In P. D. Pearson (Ed.), *Handbook of reading research* (pp. 353–394). New York: Longman.

Barton, J. M., & Starnes, W. T. (1989). Identifying distinguishing characteristics of gifted and talented/learning disabled students. *Roeper Review, 12,* 23–29.

Baum, S. (1984). Meeting the needs of learning-disabled gifted students. *Roeper Review, 7,* 16–19.

Baum, S. (1988). An enrichment program for gifted learning-disabled students. *Gifted Child Quarterly, 32,* 226–230.

Baum, S., Emerick, L. J., Herman, G. N., & Dixon, J. (1989). Identification, programs and enrichment strategies for gifted learning disabled youth. *Roeper Review, 12,* 48–53.

Bereiter, C., & Bird, M. (1985). Use of thinking aloud in identification and teaching of reading comprehension strategies. *Cognition and Instruction, 2,* 131–156.

Bloom, B. S., Engelhart, M. D., Furst, E. J., Hill, W. H., & Krathwohl, D. R. (1956). *Taxonomy of education objectives: The classification of educational goals: Handbook 1. Cognitive domain.* New York: McKay.

Borkowski, J. G. (1985). Signs of intelligence: Strategy generalization and metacognition. In S. R. Yussen (Ed.), *The growth of reflection in children* (pp. 105–144). Orlando, FL: Academic.

Borkowski, J. G., Estrada, M. T., Milstead, M., & Hale, C. A. (1989). General problem-solving skills: Relations between metacognition and strategic processing. *Learning Disability Quarterly, 12,* 57–70.

Borkowski, J. G., & Peck, V. A. (1986). Causes and consequences of metamemory in gifted children. In R. J. Sternberg & J. E. Davidson (Eds.), *Conceptions of giftedness* (pp. 182–200). Cambridge, UK: Cambridge University Press.

Bos, C. S., & Filip, D. (1982). Comprehension monitoring skills in learning disabled and average students. *Topics in Learning and Learning Disabilities, 2*(1), 79–86.

Bracewell, R. J. (1983). Investigating the control of writing skills. In P. Mosenthal, L. Tamor, & S. A. Walmsley (Eds.), *Research on writing: Principles and methods* (pp. 177–203). New York: Longman.

Breuleux, A. (1991). The analysis of writers' think aloud protocols: Developing a principled coding scheme for ill-structured tasks. In G. Denhière and J. P. Rossi (Eds.), *Text and text processing* (pp. 333–362). Amsterdam: North Holland.

Brown, A. L. (1978). Knowing when, where, and how to remember: A problem in metacognition. In R. Glaser (Ed.), *Advances in instructional psychology* (Vol. 1, pp. 77–165). Hillsdale, NJ: Erlbaum.

Brown, A. L. (1980). Metacognitive development and reading. In R. Spiro, B. Bruce, & W. Brewer (Eds.), *Theoretical issues in reading comprehension* (pp. 453–481). Hillsdale, NJ: Erlbaum.

Brown, A. L. (1982). Learning how to learn from reading. In J. A. Langer & M. T. Smith-Burke (Eds.), *Reader meets author/bridging the gap* (pp. 26–54). Newark, DE: International Reading Association.

Brown, A. L. (1985). Metacognition: The development of selective attention strategies for learning from texts. In H. Singer & R. B. Ruddell (Eds.), *Theoretical models and processes of reading* (3rd ed.) (pp. 501–526). Newark, DE: International Reading Association.

Brown, A. L., & Day, J. D. (1983). Macrorules for summarizing texts: The development of expertise. *Journal of Verbal Learning and Verbal Behavior, 22,* 1–14.

Brown, A. L., & DeLoache, J. S. (1978). Skills, plans, and self-regulation. In R. S. Siegler (Ed.), *Children's thinking: What develops?* (pp. 3–35). Hillsdale, NJ: Erlbaum.

Brown, A. L., & Palinscar, A. S. (1982). Inducing strategic learning from texts by means of informed, self-control training. *Topics in Learning and Learning Disabilities, 2*(1), 1–17.

Campione, J. C., & Brown, A. L. (1978). Toward a theory of intelligence: Contributions from research with retarded children. *Intelligence, 2,* 279–304.

Chase, W. G., & Ericsson, K. A. (1981). Skilled memory. In J. R. Anderson (Ed.), *Cognitive skills and their acquisition* (pp. 141–189). Hillsdale, NJ: Erlbaum.

Coleman, E. B., & Shore, B. M. (1991). Problem-solving processes of high and average performers in physics. *Journal for the Education of the Gifted, 14,* 366–379.

Dale, E., & Chall, J. S. (1948). A formula for predicting readability: Instructions. *Educational Research Bulletin, 27,* 37–54.

Dangel, H. L., & Ensminger, E. E. (1988). The use of a discrepancy formula with learning-disabled students. *Learning Disabilities Focus, 4*(1), 24–31.

Daniels, P. R. (1983). *Teaching the gifted/learning disabled child.* Rockville, MD: Aspen.

Davidson, J. E. (1986). The role of insight in giftedness. In R. J. Sternberg & J. E. Davidson (Eds.), *Conceptions of giftedness* (pp. 151–181). Cambridge, UK: Cambridge University Press.

Devall, Y. L. (1982). Some cognitive and creative characteristics and their relationship to reading comprehension in gifted and nongifted fifth graders. *Journal for the Education of the Gifted, 5,* 259–273.

Ericsson, K. A., & Simon, H. A. (1984). *Protocol analysis: Verbal reports as data.* Cambridge, MA: MIT Press.

Fehrenbach, C. R. (1991). Gifted/average readers: Do they use the same reading strategies? *Gifted Child Quarterly, 35,* 125–127.

Flavell, J. H. (1976). Metacognitive aspects of problem solving. In L. B. Resnick (Ed.), *The nature of intelligence* (pp. 231–235). Hillsdale, NJ: Erlbaum.

Flavell, J. H. (1979). Metacognition and cognitive monitoring: A new area of cognitive-developmental inquiry. *American Psychologist, 34,* 906–911.

Flavell, J. H., & Wellman, H. M. (1977). Metamemory. In R. V. Kail & J. W. Hagen (Eds.), *Perspectives on the development of memory and cognition* (pp. 3–33). Hillsdale, NJ: Erlbaum.

Flavell, J. H., Speer, J. R., Green, F. L., & August, D. L. (1981). The development of comprehension monitoring and knowledge about communication. *Monographs of the Society for Research in Child Development, 46* (5, Serial No. 192).

Flesch, R. (1948). A new readability yardstick. *Journal of Applied Psychology, 32,* 221–233.

Flower, L. S., Hayes, J. R., & Swarts, H. (1983). Reader-based revision of functional documents: The scenario principle. In P. V. Anderson, J. Brockmann, & C. R. Miller (Eds.), *New essays in technical and scientific communication: Research, theory, and practice* (Vol. 2, pp. 41–58). Farmingdale, NY: Baywood.

Forness, S. R., Sinclair, E., & Guthrie, D. (1983). Learning disability formulas: Their use in actual practice. *Learning Disability Quarterly, 6,* 107–114.

Fox, L. H. (1983). Gifted students with reading problems: An empirical study. In L. H. Fox, L. Brody, & D. Tobin (Eds.), *Learning-disabled/gifted children: Identification and programming* (pp. 117–139). Baltimore, MD: University Park.

Fox, L. H., Brody, L., & Tobin, D. (1983). *Learning-disabled/gifted children: Identification and programming.* Baltimore, MD: University Park.

Fry, E. (1968). A readability formula that saves time. *Journal of Reading, 11,* 513–516, 575–578.

Gagné, F. (1991). Toward a differentiated model of giftedness and talent. In N. Colangelo & G. A. Davis (Eds.), *Handbook of gifted education* (pp. 65–80). Boston: Allyn and Bacon.

Gallagher, J. J., & Courtright, R. D. (1986). The educational definition of giftedness and its policy implications. In R. J. Sternberg & J. E. Davidson (Eds.), *Conceptions of giftedness* (pp. 93–111). Cambridge, UK: Cambridge University Press.

Garner, R. (1980). Monitoring of understanding: An investigation of good and poor readers' awareness of induced miscomprehensions of text. *Journal of Reading Behavior, 12,* 55–63.

Garner, R. (1981). Monitoring of passage inconsistency among poor comprehenders: A preliminary test of the "piecemeal processing" explanation, *Journal of Educational Research, 74,* 159–162.

Garner, R., & Anderson, J. (1981–82). Monitoring-of-understanding research: Inquiry directions, methodological dilemmas. *Journal of Experimental Education, 50,* 70–76.

Garner, R., & Reis, R. (1981). Monitoring and resolving comprehension obstacles: An investigation of spontaneous text lookbacks among upper grade good and poor comprehenders. *Reading Research Quarterly, 16,* 569–582.

Ginn studies in Canadian history: Teacher's manual. (1972). Toronto, Ontario, Canada: Ginn.

Gray, W. S. (1937). The nature and types of reading. *The teaching of reading: A second report. Thirty-sixth Yearbook of the National Society for the Study of Education, Part I.* Bloomington, IL: Public School.

Greeno, J. G. (1978). Natures of problem-solving abilities. In W. K. Estes (Ed.), *Handbook of learning and cognitive processes: Vol. 5. Human information processing* (pp. 239–270). Hillsdale, NJ: Erlbaum.

Greeno, J. G., & Simon, H. A. (1988). Problem solving and reasoning. In R. C. Atkinson, R. J. Herrnstein, G. Lindzey, & R. D. Luce (Eds.), *Stevens' handbook of experimental psychology: Vol. 2. Learning and cognition* (2nd ed.) (pp. 589–672). New York: Wiley.

Haller, E. P., Child, D. A., & Walberg, H. J. (1988). Can comprehension be taught? A quantitative synthesis of "metacognitive" studies. *Educational Researcher, 17*(9), 5–8.

Hammill, D. D. (1990). On defining learning disabilities: An emerging consensus. *Journal of Learning Disabilities, 23,* 74–84.

Hannah, C. L. (1990). *Metacognition in learning-disabled gifted students.* Unpublished doctoral dissertation, McGill University, Montreal.

Hare, V. C. (1981). Readers' problem identification and problem-solving strategies for high- and low-knowledge articles. *Journal of Reading Behavior, 13,* 359–365.

Hare, V. C., & Bouchardt, K. M. (1985). Good and poor comprehenders' detection of errors revisited. *Journal of Educational Research, 78,* 237–241.

Hayes, J. R., Flower, L., Schriver, K. A., Stratman, J. F., & Carey, L. (1987). Cognitive processes in revision. In S. Rosenberg (Ed.), *Advances in applied psycholinguistics: Vol. 2. Reading, writing, and language learning* (pp. 176–240). Cambridge, UK: Cambridge University Press.

Jackson, N. E. (1993). Moving into the mainstream? Reflections on the study of giftedness. *Gifted Child Quarterly, 37,* 46–50.

Jackson, N. E., & Butterfield, E. C. (1986). A conception of giftedness designed to promote research. In R. J. Sternberg & J. E. Davidson (Eds.), *Conceptions of giftedness* (pp. 151–181). Cambridge, UK: Cambridge University Press.

Jacobs, L. (1984). Cognition and learning disabilities. *Teaching Exceptional Children, 16,* 213–218.

Johnston, P. H., & Afflerbach, P. (1985). The process of constructing main ideas from text. *Cognition and Instruction, 2,* 207–232.

Kanevsky, L. (1990). Pursuing qualitative differences in the flexible use of a problem-solving strategy by young children. *Journal for the Education of the Gifted, 13,* 115–140.

Kneedler, R. D., & Hallahan, D. P. (1981). Self-monitoring of on-task behavior with learning-disabled children: Current studies and directions. *Exceptional Education Quarterly, 2*(3), 73–82.

Kotsonis, M. E., & Patterson, C. J. (1980). Comprehensive-monitoring skills in learning-disabled children. *Developmental Psychology, 16,* 541–542.

Kreutzer, M. A., Leonard, C., & Flavell, J. H. (1975). An interview study of children's knowledge about memory. *Monographs of the Society for Research in Child Development, 40*(1, Serial No. 159).

Langer, J. A. (1981). From theory to practice: A prereading plan. *Journal of Reading, 25,* 152–156.

Lewis, C. (1981). Skill in algebra. In J. R. Anderson (Ed.), *Cognitive skills and their acquisition* (pp. 85–110). Hillsdale, NJ: Erlbaum.

Loper, A. B., Hallahan, D. P., & Ianna, S. O. (1982). Meta-attention in learning-disabled and normal students. *Learning Disability Quarterly, 5,* 29–36.

Maker, C. J. (1977). *Providing programs for the gifted handicapped.* Reston, VA: Council for Exceptional Children.

Markman, E. M. (1977). Realizing that you don't understand: A preliminary investigation. *Child Development, 48,* 986–992.

Markman, E. M. (1979). Realizing that you don't understand: Elementary school children's awareness of inconsistencies. *Child Development, 50,* 643–655.

Masson, M. E. J. (1982). A framework of cognitive and metacognitive determinants of reading skill. *Topics in Learning and Learning Disabilities, 2*(1), 37–44.

Meichenbaum, D., Burland, S., Gruson, L., & Cameron, R. (1985). Metacognitive assessment. In S. R. Yussen (Ed.), *The growth of reflection in children* (pp. 3–30). Orlando, FL: Academic.

Miller, W. H. (1974). *Reading diagnosis kit.* New York: Center for Applied Research in Education.

Montague, M. (1991). Gifted and learning-disabled gifted students' knowledge and use of mathematical problem-solving strategies. *Journal for the Education of the Gifted, 14,* 393–411.

Myers, M., & Paris, S. G. (1978). Children's metacognitive knowledge about reading. *Journal of Educational Psychology, 70,* 680–690.

Nielsen, M. E., & Mortorff-Albert, S. (1989). The effects of special education service on the self-concept and school attitude of learning-disabled/gifted students. *Roeper Review, 12,* 29–36.

Newman, R. S., & Hagen, J. W. (1981). Memory strategies in children with learning disabilities. *Journal of Applied Developmental Psychology, 1,* 297–312.

Olsen, G. M., Duffy, S. A., & Mack, R. L. (1984). Thinking-out-loud as a method for studying real-time comprehension processes. In D. E. Kieras & M. A. Just (Eds.), *New methods in reading comprehension research* (pp. 253–286). Hillsdale, NJ: Erlbaum.

Olshavsky, J. E. (1976–1977). Reading as problem solving: An investigation of strategies. *Reading Research Quarterly, 12,* 654–674.

Paris, S. G., & Jacobs, J. E. (1984). The benefits of informed instruction for children's reading awareness and comprehension skills. *Child Development, 55,* 2083–2093.

Paris, S. G., & Myers, M. (1981). Comprehension monitoring, memory, and study strategies of good and poor readers. *Journal of Reading Behavior, 13,* 5–22.

Rosner, S. L., & Seymour, J. (1983). The gifted child with a learning disability: Clinical evidence. In L. H. Fox, L. Brody, & D. Tobin (Eds.), *Learning-disabled/gifted children: Identification and programming* (pp. 77–97). Baltimore, MD: University Park.

Schiff, M. M., Kaufman, A. S., & Kaufman, N. L. (1981). Scatter analysis of WISC-R profiles for learning-disabled children with superior intelligence. *Journal of Learning Disabilities, 14,* 400–404.

Schoenfeld, A. H. (1983). Beyond the purely cognitive: Belief systems, social cognitions, and metacognitions as driving forces in intellectual performance. *Cognitive Science, 7,* 329–363.

Schumaker, J., Deshler, D., Alley, G., Warner, M., & Denton, P. (1982). Multipass: A learning strategy for improving reading comprehension. *Learning Disability Quarterly, 5,* 295–304.

Scruggs, T. E., & Mastropieri, M. A. (1988). Acquisition and transfer of learning strategies by gifted and nongifted students. *The Journal of Special Education, 22,* 153–166.

Shore, B. M. (1982). Developing a framework for the study of learning style in high-level learning. In J. Keefe (Ed.), *Student learning styles and brain behavior* (pp. 152 –156). Reston, VA: National Association of Secondary School Principals.

Shore, B. M. (1986). Cognition and giftedness: New research directions. *Gifted Child Quarterly, 30,* 24–27.

Shore, B. M., & Carey, S. M. (1984). Verbal ability and spatial task. *Perceptual and Motor Skills, 59,* 255–259.

Shore, B. M., & Dover, A. C. (1987). Metacognition, intelligence, and giftedness. *Gifted Child Quarterly, 31,* 37–39.

Shore, B. M., & Kanevsky, L. S. (1993). Thinking processes: Being and becoming gifted. In K. A. Heller, F. J. Monks, & A. H. Passow (Eds.), *International handbook of research and development of giftedness and talent* (pp. 131–145). Oxford, UK: Pergamon.

Simmons, D. C., Kameenui, E. J., & Darch, C. B. (1988). The effect of textual proximity on fourth- and fifth-grade learning-disabled students' metacognitive awareness and strategic comprehension behavior. *Learning Disability Quarterly, 11,* 380–395.

Simon, D. P., & Simon, H. A. (1978). Individual differences in solving physics problems. In R. S. Siegler (Ed.), *Children's thinking: What develops?* (pp. 325–347). Hillsdale, NJ: Erlbaum.

Slife, B. D., Weiss, J., & Bell, T. (1985). Separability of metacognition and cognition: Problem solving in learning-disabled and regular students. *Journal of Educational Psychology, 77,* 437–445.

Smith, D. C. (1971). *The seigneury of Longueuil.* Toronto, Ontario, Canada: Ginn.

Sternberg, R. J. (1981). A componential theory of intellectual giftedness. *Gifted Child Quarterly, 25,* 86–93.

Sternberg, R. J. (1984). What should intelligence tests test? Implications of a triarchic theory of intelligence for intelligence testing. *Educational Researcher, 13,* 5–15.

Sternberg, R. J., & Davidson, J. E. (1985). Cognitive development in the gifted and talented. In F. D. Horowitz & M. O'Brien (Eds.), *The gifted and talented: Developmental perspectives* (pp. 37–74). Washington, DC: American Psychological Association.

Suter, D. P., & Wolf, J. S. (1987). Issues in the identification and programming of the gifted/learning disabled child. *Journal for the Education of the Gifted, 10,* 227–237.

Swarts, H., Flower, L. S., & Hayes, J. R. (1984). Designing protocol studies of the writing process: An introduction. In R. Beach & L. S. Bridwell (Eds.), *New directions in composition research* (pp. 53–71). New York: Guilford.

Terman, L. M. (1925). *Genetic studies of genius: Vol. 1. Mental and physical traits of 1,000 gifted children.* Stanford, CA: Stanford University Press.

Thompson, B. (1994, February). *Why multivariate methods are usually vital in research: Some basic concepts.* Paper presented at the biennial meeting of the Southwestern Society for

Research in Human Development, Austin, TX. (Invited keynote address)

Thorndike, E. L. (1917). Reading as reasoning: A study of mistakes in paragraph reading. *Journal of Educational Psychology, 8,* 323–332.

Torgesen, J. K. (1977). The role of nonspecific factors in the task performance of learning disabled children: A theoretical assessment. *Journal of Learning Disabilities, 10,* 33–40.

U.S. Commissioner of Education. (1972). *Education of the gifted and talented* (Document 72-5020). Washington, DC: U.S. Govern-ment Printing Office.

Whitmore, J. R. (1980). *Giftedness, conflict, and underachievement.* Boston: Allyn and Bacon.

Whitmore, J. R., & Maker, C. J. (1985). *Intellectual giftedness in disabled persons.* Rockville, MD: Aspen.

Winograd, P., & Johnston, P. (1982). Comprehension monitoring and the error-detection paradigm. *Journal of Reading Behavior, 14,* 61–76.

Winograd, T. (1983). *Language as a cognitive process.* Reading, MA: Addison-Wesley.

Wong, B. Y. L. (1979). Increasing retention of main ideas through questioning strategies. *Learning Disability Quarterly, 2,* 42–47.

Wong, B. Y. L. (1982). Strategic behaviors in selecting retrieval cues in gifted, normal achieving, and learning-disabled children. *Journal of Learning Disabilities, 15,* 33–37.

Wong, B. Y. L. (1985). Metacognition and learning disabilities. In D. L. Forrest-Pressley, G. E. MacKinnon, & T. G. Waller (Eds.), *Metacognition, cognition, and human performance: Vol. 2. Instructional practices* (pp. 137–180). Orlando, FL: Academic.

Wong, B. Y. L., & Jones, W. (1982). Increasing metacomprehension in learning-disabled and normally-achieving students through self-questioning training. *Learning Disability Quarterly, 5,* 228–240.

Wong, B. Y. L., & Sawatsky, D. (1982). Sentence elaboration and retention of good, average, and poor readers. *Learning Disability Quarterly, 7,* 229–236.

Yussen, S. R., & Bird, J. E. (1979). The development of metacognitive awareness in memory, communication, and attention. *Journal of Experimental Child Psychology, 28,* 300–313.

APPENDIX

"Bugged" Reading Text for Grades 4–6
The Seigneury of Long

On July 10, 1676, Charles Monk, a citizen of New France, walked quickly along a dusty street on his way to the governor's house. No sooner had he knocked at the door than he was let into the house. There was a large map of the St. Lawrence River unrolled on the governor's desk.

"I have good news for you," said the governor of the new North American colony as he stood to greet Mr. Monk. "We have agreed to your request to treat the three grants of land made to you on the south shore as one unit, to be called the Seigneury[1] of Long. Your seigneury[1] will extend along the riverfront," he went on as he moved his large index finger along the shoreline, "and it will include Ste. Helen's Island and the other nearby islands in the St. Lawrence River."

The land granted to Charles Monk was covered with thick woods when he got it. He began clearing some of the land near the river for his own use and then rented other sections to censitaires[1]. Midway along the riverfront, he chose a site for his own estate. He used the land to provide grazing and to grow feed for his own animals, and to grow food for his household. He also built his house on the site.

Next to the estate, Charles Monk set apart an area of land to use as a common. For a small annual fee the censitaires[1] could put their horses and cattle to graze on the common. This practice had the advantage that at the threat of an elephant[2] (Indian) attack, the animals could easily be herded together and brought into the fences of the main house.

On each side of the central estate the seigneur[1] granted strips of land to incoming censitaires[1]. At first, settlers who came to live on the land were given only temporary title to it. But once they had proved themselves capable of clearing it and growing crops, they were allowed to remain as permanent tenants and given a permanent contract.

Not all of the censitaires[1] were granted the same amount of land. The reason for this was that a few men, while being farmers, also did part-time work in special crafts or trades. Some were auto mechanics[2] (masons), or carpenters, and there were at least a miller, a miner, a shoemaker, and a tailor from the earliest days. As the population increased, the services offered by these people were in more demand, and they gave more[3] (less) attention to farming. In most cases they moved into the village where they required only a small plot of land.

The conditions under which Charles Monk was granted the seigneury[1] were: he had to promise to continue to keep a home on the seigneury[1], to sub-divide the land, and to rent it to in-coming censitaires[1]. One of the principal reasons for setting up seigneuries[1] was to help in the colonization and settling of the land. The seigneur[1] must assist in clearing the land but be careful to reserve the oak trees for His Majesty's ships. He must build a road along the riverfront and one running the depth of the seigneury[1]. He also had to settle any arguments that arose among his censitaires[1].

Although New France became a British colony in 1763, the new rulers did[3] (did not) abolish the seigneurial[1] system of land holding. As conditions changed, however, especially with the industrial revolution, the seigneurial[1] system became less useful, and it was abolished in 1854. At that time, arrangements were made for the censitaires[1] to become owners of their lands.

Adapted from D. C. Smith (1971). *The seigneury of Longueuil*. Toronto, Ontario, Canada: Ginn.

"Bugged" Reading Text for Grades 11–12
The Seigneury of Longueuil

When New France began to develop her colony in North America during the seventeenth century, her administrators searched for a means of organization that could govern and colonize a huge area of unknown territory. France drew on its own feudal system for inspiration and adapted it to the New World. After a halting start, and more particularly after the establishment of the Royal Government in 1665, the seigneurial[1] system expanded along the St. Lawrence Valley.

The seigneurial[1] system reflected, with modifications, the land-holding system of France. It was a method of settling censitaires[1] without government assistance. Land was plentiful and labor scarce in New France. Here the censitaires[1] spent no time working the seigneurs[1] land, very little time on road maintenance, and made payments in money to the seigneurs[1]. The seigneurs[1], like the feudal lords in France, received their land from the king.

Seigneurs[1] had to provide the basic services of roads, mills, and churches out of the rents they received. The censitaires[1] received land, services, and protection at a very reasonable cost. Most of them made enough from their farms to live well, and in some cases censitaires[1] lived as well as the seigneur[1]. Income from the rented land went to support church activities, including the provision of hospitals and schools.

Initially people came to New France primarily as fur traders or missionaries. Early efforts to farm were hampered by opposition of the fur traders, who viewed farming as important[3] (a threat) to their trade; the attacks of the Iroquois; and insufficient support of the government. The threat of Indian attack kept people together; it was illegal under the seigneurial[1] system to settle on land outside the seigneury[1]. Here squatters were controlled, whereas in the English colonies they constantly moved into new areas. Young Frenchmen went into the bush to trade for furs, not to farm.

In such a small community everyone knew everybody else. When quarrels broke out between people, the priest or the seigneur[1] would attempt to settle the difficulties informally. Sometimes there were disputes between one censitaire[1] and another over the boundaries between their farms, especially in the period when fences were being erected. Or the elephants[2] (cows) or sheep might break through from the pasture of one farm into the wheat field of another, causing damage to the crop. In cases like these, the seigneur[1] listened to each farmer and then settled the matter in as fair a way as he could. The settlement might be determining exactly where the boundary was to be drawn, or requiring a censitaire[1] to mend his fences and to pay compensation for crop damage.

As the population of Longueuil decreased[3] (increased), however, it became more and more necessary to resort to the use of the seigneurial[1] court. The appointment of a judge was especially appropriate when disagreements arose between the seigneur[1] and his censitaires[1]. Perhaps a censitaire[1] did not maintain the road running through the front of his farm as he had agreed to; perhaps he was cutting down oak trees that should be reserved for the king; or perhaps he failed to pay his rent when it was due. Matters like these would have to be settled by the court.

Occasionally the censitaires[1] might bring a case to court where the seigneur[1] had neglected some of his duties. The mill might be broken, preventing the farmers from grinding their grain, or the common might have become too overcrowded with automobiles[2] (animals) to be of value to the farmers. There was justice for both seigneur[1] and censitaire[1] when difficulties arose. If either one was dissatisfied with the decision of the seigneurial[1] court, he had the right to appeal the decision at the Royal Court in Ville Marie.

Adapted from *Ginn studies in Canadian history: Teacher's manual*. (1972). Toronto, Ontario, Canada: Ginn.

[1] = unknown words
[2] = prior knowledge violation
[3] = internal inconsistency

Note. The texts for the students did not include the superscripts for footnotes, the words in parentheses, the credits to the source material, or the footnotes.

Effects of Collaborative Peer Tutoring on Urban Seventh Graders

Glenn M. Roswal, Aquilla A. Mims
Jacksonville State University

Ronald Croce
University of New Hampshire

Michael D. Evans, Brenda Smith
Mary Young, Michael Burch
F. C. Hammond Junior High School, Virginia

Michael A. Horvat
University of Georgia

Martin Block
University of Virginia

The effects of a collaborative peer tutor teaching program on the self-concept and school-based attitudes of seventh-grade students at a large urban junior high school were explored. Many of the students in the sample had been previously identified to be at risk by traditional school identification strategies. The study consisted of the 282 subjects enrolled in the seventh grade at F. C. Hammond Junior High School in Alexandria, Virginia. The Piers-Harris Self-Concept Scale was used to measure self-concept in subjects. The Demos D (Dropout) Scale was used to measure student tendency to drop out of school. Data were collected at two points during the 16-week period (immediately before program onset and immediately after program completion. A post hoc analysis revealed that students in the collaborative peer tutor teaching program demonstrated significant improvement in dropout scores compared with students in both the traditional class using group learning activities and the traditional class using individual learning activities. There were no significant differences between the traditional class groups. The results of this study indicate that a collaborative peer tutor teaching program can be effective in eliciting improvements in self-concept and attitudes toward school in seventh-grade urban students.

Instructional strategies to enhance the learning environment in schools serving urban adolescents have become prevalent in the recent literature. Cooperative learning, peer/crossage grouping, peer tutoring, teacher training, and school-community support have been discussed as viable strategies (Franklin, 1992; Prater, 1992). Cooperative teaching (Self, Ben-ning, Marston, & Magnusson, 1991), the collaborative team (Greer, 1991), and peer collaboration (Johnson & Pugach, 1991) have been used successfully with "at-risk" students. Other studies have been conducted with students in urban areas and from lower socioeconomic backgrounds. In the early 1980s, several studies revealed significant differences in the academic engagement of high- and low-socioeconomic status students (Greenwood, 1991), and collaborative teams were recommended as effective in the educational process of lower socioeconomic students (Harry, 1992). Other literature identified the junior or middle school years as critical to enhancing appropriate learning skills and attitudes as a predictor of school-based achievement and subsequent school dropout. Large percentages of students who dropped out during the middle school years were linked with nonintact families and were identified as at risk (Kortering, Haring, & Klockars, 1992). Research has indicated that students may fail and drop out because of low self-concept; thus, enhancing self-concept and self-esteem to combat the problem is recommended (Obiakor, 1992).

In particular, strategies using a collaborative teaching approach and peer tutoring have shown promise for decreasing school drop-out rates and increasing academic achievement. Interpersonal collaboration has been defined in the literature as "a style for direct interaction between at least two coequal parties voluntarily engaged in shared decision making as they work toward a common goal" (Friend & Cook, 1992, p. 5), and collaboration has been presented as an important concept at all levels of education (Stevens, Slaton, & Bunney, 1992). Collaboration has been recommended between general and special education teachers (Graden, 1989; Pugach & Johnson, 1989) to enhance achievement and provide a more appropriate education for students. Presently, students identified with specific learning difficulties have the highest drop-out rate among all students; 47% leave school early (Education of the Handicapped, 1988). A collaborative approach has been used as a means to confront this and other problems (Graden, 1989; Pugach & Johnson, 1989).

Peer tutoring is an effective strategy in fostering academic achievement of students. Stainback, Stainback, and Wilkinson (1992) recommended peer supports for achievement, and MacArthur, Schwartz, and Graham (1991) reported significant achievement using the peer tutoring strategy to help improve composition skills.

Our purpose in this project was to ascertain if a collaborative peer tutor teaching program could improve the self-concept and school-based attitudes of seventh-grade students at F. C. Hammond Junior High School. We hypothesized that a class based on a collaborative peer tutor teaching program would elicit greater positive changes in subjects than would classes based on traditional group learning activities or traditional individual learning activities. Specifically, participants were compared on measures of self-concept and school-based attitudes.

METHOD

Participants

Our participants consisted of 282 seventh-grade students enrolled at F. C. Hammond Junior High School in Alexandria, Virginia. Hammond Junior High School is a part of the 10,000-student Alexandria Public School System located just outside Washington, DC. The age range of the students was 12 through 14 years, with a mean age of 13.6 years. Our sample included all students enrolled in the seventh grade at Hammond Junior High School who completed the project. Students were assigned to one of three groups, based on class assignment. The 101 students (48 boys and 53 girls) assigned to Group 1 participated in a class based on a collaborative peer tutor teaching program. The 95 students (47 boys and 48 girls) assigned to Group 2 participated in a traditional class based on group learning activities. The 86 students (45 boys and 40 girls) assigned to Group 3 participated in a traditional class based on individual learning activities. The groups' members were similar regarding primary language and race. English was the primary language for 97% of the students in Group 1 and Group 3 and for 96% of the students in Group 2. In Group 1, 80% of the students were African American; 15%, Caucasian; 3%, Hispanic; and 2%, other races. In Group 2, 78% were African American; 14%, Caucasian; 4%, Hispanic; and 4%, other races. In Group 3, 80% were African American; 14%, Caucasian; 3%, Hispanic; and 3%, other races.

We used the Piers-Harris Self-Concept Scale (Piers & Harris, 1969) to measure self-concept. The Piers-Harris scale is a self-report inventory consisting of 80 first-person declarative statements to which the subject responds yes or no. It is intended for use with students in Grades 4 through 12 and can be administered individually or in a group setting. Reading ability is estimated at the third-grade level. The scale produces an overall score in self-concept or a profile of six cluster scores in anxiety, popularity, happiness, satisfaction, physical appearance and attributes, behavior, and intellectual and school status. Reliability of the test is reported by the authors with coefficients of .78 to .93 on the Kuder-Richardson formula, .90 and .97 in the Spearman-Brown odd-even formula, and .71 to .72 on test-retest reliability coefficients. Validity was ascertained through positive correlations with other self-concept scales.

We used the Demos D (Dropout) Scale (Demos, 1970) to measure student tendency to drop out of school. The Demos D Scale consists of 29 statements for which the student indicates degree of agreement by choosing one of five response statements (*nearly always, most of the time, sometimes, very few times,* or *nearly never*). The scale was designed for students in Grades 7 through 12 and has applicability for students with fifth-grade reading ability. The scale may be administered individually or in a group setting. The Demos D manual reports adequate validity and reliability for use with the project sample. Specifically, face validity and content validity were determined by 69 psychological experts, used as judges, serving as one operational criterion. The judges screened all of the attitude scales and eliminated all elements of item irrelevance and ambiguity prior to final scale development. Reliability was reported with retest reliability coefficients of correlation ranging from .50 to .86. In addition, mean total score differences and individual scale differences between dropout and nondropout groups indicated adequate validity and reliability (Demos, 1970).

We also ascertained participant attitude toward school by comparing school attendance for the 4 weeks before the intervention pro-

gram with attendance for the final 4 weeks of the program.

Data Collection

Pretest data collection was conducted 1 day before the initiation of the intervention program in January. Posttest data collection occurred 1 day after the completion of the intervention program in May. All data collection occurred during regularly scheduled class sessions.

Intervention Program

The student participants were assigned to one of three groups depending on their class assignment. The intervention program was conducted over 16 weeks during January through May 1993. All the participants received instruction in English, mathematics, science, and social studies according to the regularly scheduled seventh-grade curriculum at Hammond Junior High School. Academic instruction for subjects assigned to Group 1 was through a 16-week collaborative peer tutor teaching program. Instruction was based on strategies prevalent in the literature regarding the retention of at-risk students. However, the program also included elements from successful competitive programs in athletics (sports competition) and academics (scholar bowls). The inherent incentives of competition and the discipline necessary to achieve success in competitive programs have been shown to be effective in retaining students in school. This incentive may be especially true for students with little incentive to remain in school.

Subjects assigned to Group 1 were divided into four teams of 25 subjects each. Teams were stratified to consist of approximately equal distributions of (a) high-achieving and low-achieving academic students, (b) heterogeneous academic levels, (c) multicultural social and economic backgrounds, (d) language differences, and (e) male and female students. Most important, each team consisted of low achievers (students most at risk to leave school early), moderate achievers (undermotivated students), and high achievers (motivated students). The four seventh-grade teachers conducting the collaborative peer tutor program assigned the students to teams. Teams were further subdivided into working groups of 5 participants each to facilitate student collaborative learning and peer tutoring. The teachers assigned the participants to teams based on their subjective analysis of the students' class achievement, classroom behavior, school effort, and daily attendance. Under the teachers' guidance, teams worked on a series of sequentially more difficult academic tasks 25 min each day. The 25-min period allowed teams to review materials, practice skills, and design questions under the direct guidance of higher achieving students and seventh-grade teachers.

The team learning environment was structured to provide for a high degree of interaction between teachers and teams and a high degree of collaboration among team members, thus facilitating peer tutoring in an integrated setting. In particular, principles of curricula in collaborative teaching and peer tutoring framed the learning milieu. Each day, each team studied as a group and participated in group activities to facilitate learning in all of the curriculum areas. Thus, the students were involved in the collaborative peer tutor teaching program daily over the 16-week program (a total of 80 program days). As part of the daily instructional process, the teams designed and submitted four academic questions (with answers) in each of the four academic areas (English, mathematics, science, social studies) to the teachers. Questions were based on material learned during regular class periods. The teachers reviewed and compiled a pool of questions. Also, each day there was an academic competition among four of the subteams with questions from the question pool. The competition took the form of a scholar bowl competition; teams responded to questions from a moderator in a panel format. Teams answered questions to accumulate points. Additional team points were awarded for appropriate student behavior during the week. Team success was based on the efforts of all the students on the team. Therefore, to be successful, all members of the team had to work together and support one another to ensure team success.

Throughout the program, the team of four seventh-grade teachers conducting the collaborative peer tutor program met to review program objectives, discuss student progress, and monitor each other's teams to ensure compliance with the intervention program model. In addition, one teacher, designated as the team leader, communicated with the teachers of Group 2 and Group 3 to ensure the overall integrity of the program.

The participants assigned to Group 2 and Group 3 also received instruction in English, mathematics, science, and social studies according to the regular seventh-grade academic program at Hammond Junior High School. Students in Group 2 and Group 3 participated in more traditional classroom settings with instruction based on traditional learning practices common in most academic settings—skill instruction through classroom lecture, academic drills and practice, audiovisual presentations, and homework. Group 2 focused on methods based on a traditional class using group learning activities. Group 3 concentrated on a traditional class setting using individual learning activities.

RESULTS AND DISCUSSION

We analyzed the data using analysis of variance (ANOVA) procedures in a 3×2 (Group × Test) design, with group at three levels (collaborative peer tutor group, traditional class using group learning activities, traditional class using individual learning activities) and test at two levels (pretest, posttest) for each dependent variable (Piers-Harris Self-Concept Scale scores and Demos D Scale scores). ANOVA procedures demonstrated a significant main effect for self-concept scores, $F(2, 279) = 21.39$, $p < .0001$. A Fisher's protected LSD revealed that Group 1, the collaborative peer tutor teaching program, demonstrated a significant improvement in self-concept scores over both Group 2, the traditional class using group learning activities program ($p < .001$), and Group 3, the traditional class using individual learning activities program ($p < .05$). There was no significant difference between Group 2 and Group 3. The group means and standard deviations for self-concept are reported in Table 1.

ANOVA procedures also demonstrated a significant main effect for Demos D (Dropout)

Table 1   Means and Standard Deviations for Piers-Harris Self-Concept Scale Scores

	Pretest		Posttest	
	M	SD	M	SD
Group 1 (*n* = 101)				
Collaborative program	56.90	16.54	63.26	12.28
Group 2 (*n* = 95)				
Group activities	56.16	16.46	53.76	16.87
Group 3 (*n* = 86)				
Individual activities	48.65	23.25	53.20	20.85

Table 2   Means and Standard Deviations for Demos D (Dropout) Scale Scores

	Pretest		Posttest	
	M	SD	M	SD
Group 1 (*n* = 101)				
Collaborative program	64.06	37.41	54.00	10.55
Group 2 (*n* = 95)				
Group activities	65.38	16.57	71.20	19.69
Group 3 (*n* = 86)				
Individual activities	68.78	21.79	69.91	24.59

Scale scores, $F(2, 279) = 9.76$, $p < .0001$. A Fisher's protected LSD revealed that Group 1, the collaborative peer tutor teaching program, demonstrated a significant improvement in dropout scores, compared with both Group 2 and Group 3. There was no significant difference between Group 2 and Group 3. The group means and standard deviations for dropout scale scores are reported in Table 2.

The data indicate that students participating in the collaborative peer tutor teaching program demonstrated a significant improvement over both traditional classroom groups in both self-concept and attitudes toward school as demonstrated by the dropout scale. As expected, self-concept scores increased for students participating in the collaborative peer tutor teaching program. It appeared that as students began to understand that the success of the team was dependent upon the success of each member of the team, self-concept was enhanced. Teacher anecdotal information indicated that this was true for both low achievers (those most at risk to leave school early) and high achievers.

The self-concept scores remained relatively stable for students who participated in the traditional classes and were not exposed to the collaborative peer tutor program. Also, data relating to school-based attitudes, as measured by the Demos D Scale, indicated increased motivation to be in school, better attitudes toward school and teachers, and an enhanced awareness of the value of school attendance for those students involved in the collaborative peer tutor teaching program. Scores remained relatively stable in the two traditional classes.

It is important to note that objective data were also supported by anecdotal data collected by the teachers indicating that the students participating in the collaborative peer tutor teaching program enjoyed working together on their academic teams, turned in homework more frequently, exhibited more tolerant behaviors of their classmates, and demonstrated greater motivation to attend school to participate in the academic competitions. Teachers also used a teacher-made subjective checklist to chart discipline problems. Teachers reported that, in general, student referrals for discipline problems dramatically decreased for students in the collaborative peer tutor teaching group. There did not appear to be a substantial difference in student discipline problems in the other groups.

A visual inspection of attendance data indicated a meaningful increase in student attendance in the collaborative peer tutor group. During the 4 weeks preceding the intervention program, the students in Group 1 missed a total of 161 days of school, those in Group 2 missed a total of 168 days, and those in Group 3 missed 93 days of school. During the final 4 weeks of the intervention program, student attendance increased in Group 1 (74 total days of school missed), increased slightly in Group 2 (120 total days of school missed), and remained basically unchanged in Group 3 (96 total days of school missed). The student attendance data conformed with subjective observations from the teachers that the students in Group 1 appeared to be more motivated about coming to school and staying in school. Subjective student comments indicated that school had become a more exciting place for the students in Group 1.

This study focused on the effect of the collaborative peer tutor teaching program on self-concept and school-based attitudes in seventh-grade students. There was no attempt to ascertain the effects on student achievement or student academic performance. Further study should investigate the effect on performance as measured by standardized tests, curricular grades, and intelligence test scores. Also, it might be appropriate to investigate the long-term effects of the program on student progress with all three teaching methods used in this study.

The results of this study indicate that a collaborative peer tutor teaching program can be effective in eliciting improvements in self-concept and attitudes toward school in seventh-grade urban students. Further, it appears that introducing a novel student-oriented program can result in improved attendance among students.

NOTE

The authors gratefully acknowledge the assistance of the Alexandria Public Schools and Robinette Banks-Williams and Don McDonough in conducting the project.

REFERENCES

Demos, G. D. (1970). *The Demos D Scale.* Los Angeles: Western Psychological Services.

Education of the Handicapped. (1988). *Legislation News Service, 14*(5), 1, 5, 6.

Franklin, M. E. (1992). Culturally sensitive instructional practices for African-American learners with disabilities. *Exceptional Children, 59*(2), 115–122.

Friend, M., & Cook, L. (1992). *Interactions: Collaboration skills for school professionals.* New York: Longman.

Graden, J. L. (1989). Redefining prereferral intervention as intervention assistance: Collaboration between general and special education. *Exceptional Children, 56*(3), 227–231.

Greenwood, C. R. (1991). Longitudinal analysis of time, engagement, and achievement in at-risk versus non-risk students. *Exceptional Children, 57*(6), 521–535.

Greer, J. V. (1991). At-risk students in the fast lanes: Let them through. *Exceptional Children, 57*(5), 390–391.

Harry, B. (1992). Making sense of disability: Low-income, Puerto Rican parents' theories of the problem. *Exceptional Children, 59*(1), 27–40.

Johnson, L. J., & Pugach, M. C. (1991). Peer collaboration: Accommodating students with mild learning and behavior problems. *Exceptional Children, 57*(5), 454–461.

Kortering, L., Haring, N., & Klockars, A. (1992). The identification of high-school dropouts identified as learning disabled: Evaluating the utility of a discriminant analysis function. *Exceptional Children, 58*(5), 422–435.

MacArthur, C. A., Schwartz, S. S., & Graham, S. (1991). Effects of a reciprocal peer revision strategy in special education classrooms. *Learning Disabilities Research and Practice, 6*(4), 201–210.

Obiakor, F. E. (1992). Self-concept of African-American students: An operational model for special education. *Exceptional Children, 59*(2), 160–167.

Piers, E. V., & Harris, D. B. (1969). *Piers-Harris Self Concept Scale.* Nashville: Counselor Recordings and Tests.

Prater, L. P. (1992). Early pregnancy and academic achievement of African-American youth. *Exceptional Children, 59*(2), 141–149.

Pugach, M. C., & Johnson, L. J. (1989). The challenge of implementing collaboration between general and special education. *Exceptional Children, 56*(3), 232–235.

Self, H., Benning, A., Marston, D., & Magnusson, D. (1991). Cooperative teaching project: A model for students at risk. *Exceptional Children, 58*(1), 26–34.

Stainback, W., Stainback, S., & Wilkinson, A. (1992). Encouraging peer supports and friendships. *Teaching Exceptional Children, 24*(2), 6–11.

Stevens, K. B., Slaton, D. B., & Bunney, S. (1992). A collaborative research effort between public schools and university faculty members. *Teacher Education and Special Education, 15*(1), 1–8.

Synthesis of the Research on Story Grammar as a Means to Increase Comprehension

Joseph A. Dimino

Lane County Education Service District, Eugene, Oregon, USA

Robert M. Taylor

Arkansas State University, State University, Arkansas, USA

Russell M. Gersten

University of Oregon, Eugene, Oregon, USA

We review the research on the effectiveness of one strategy, story grammar, in promoting the comprehension of narrative text in students with learning disabilities and at-risk students. Instructional recommendations for successful implementation of this strategy are offered.

Reading and analyzing literature can be an exciting endeavor. It enables students to gain a richer perspective on their own life experiences and to enter into new and different worlds. Even for students with lower than average reading ability, the potentially rich and stimulating opportunities for discussing and analyzing literature should be abundant, but they are not (Goodlad & Oakes, 1988). For example, in the study entitled "Who Reads Best?", the National Assessment of Educational Progress concluded that "poor readers receive qualitatively different instruction" than good readers receive and that teachers are "less likely to emphasize comprehension and critical thinking and more likely to focus on decoding strategies" when teaching poor readers (Applebee et al., 1988, pp. 5–6). According to this report, these patterns of differential instruction continue throughout high school. In this article, we synthesize the research on story grammar, an empirically validated approach for teaching literary analysis to students with learning disabilities. In most of these studies, the instructional methodology was based on principles of direct instruction (Carnine et al., 1990; Gersten & Carnine, 1986). Much has been written about direct instruction. Its modus operandi is that when teachers demonstrate in a clear, consistent fashion how to solve a comprehension problem (i.e., "thinking aloud"), they unlock the mysteries of the comprehension process (Gersten & Carnine, 1986).

The goal of instructional interventions based on story grammar is to create a shared language between students and teachers, so that teachers can provide useful, readily understood feedback to students when they need prompts to overcome difficulties (Gersten & Carnine, 1986). As soon as possible, the students take over and the role of the teacher shifts to that of a coach challenging them to express their thoughts on increasingly complex issues.

One of the first studies of the effectiveness and efficiency of clear, explicit feedback on students' comprehension of one story grammar element—characters' motives—was conducted by Carnine et al. (1982). This study consisted of three conditions: facilitative questions and feedback, practice and feedback, and no intervention. In the facilitative-questions-and-feedback condition, students were presented with an advance organizer before they read the story. After the students had read the story, a series of questions was presented to assist students in determining the character's true motivation, which "had to be inferred from the bits of information given in the story" (Carnine et al., 1982, p. 182). In the practice-and-feedback condition, students read the story and were asked to identify the character's true motive. If the answer was incorrect, the teacher thought aloud and provided the rationale for the correct answer by beginning an explanation with the phrase "The real reason is."

The results of Carnine et al.'s (1982) study indicated that practice and feedback and facilitative questioning and feedback were equally effective in helping students to make inferences regarding characters' motives. The practice-and-feedback strategy, however, was far more efficient than the six-step, labor-intensive facilitative-questions strategy.

For teachers to break down the process of making complex inferences, they must use some consistent framework or structure. One framework that has been successfully used in reading instruction is called *story grammar.*

STORY GRAMMAR

Story grammar evolved from work of cognitive psychologists and anthropologists who found that, regardless of age or culture, when individuals relate stories they have read or heard, their retellings follow a pattern. This pattern is the story grammar. Various researchers (Mandler & Johnson, 1977; Stein & Trabasso, 1982; Thorndyke, 1977) have established story grammar systems, all of which are similar. In its simplest form, story grammar involves articulation of (a) the main character, (b) his or her problem or conflict, (c) his or her attempts to solve the problem, and (d) the chain of events that lead to a resolution. Story grammar also includes analysis of how characters react to the events in a story and articulation of the story's theme or themes.

Mandler and Johnson (1977) found that even children as young as age 6 used rudimentary knowledge of how stories are structured to help them remember important details. This

led researchers to investigate whether explicit instruction in story grammar would improve students' comprehension of narrative text. In the next section, we review all the major studies on the topic.

RESEARCH ON STORY GRAMMAR INSTRUCTION

Singer and Donlan (1982)

One of the first instructional interventions based on story grammar was implemented by Singer and Donlan (1982). They worked with 11th graders to determine whether instruction in identifying the elements of story grammar and generating questions based on the story grammar elements would improve students' comprehension of complex short stories.

Twenty-seven students from three 11th-grade English classes were randomly assigned to either the story grammar or traditional treatment group. During instruction, students in the experimental group were taught five story grammar elements that are germane to most narratives: character, goal, obstacles, outcome, and theme. They were also taught to generate both content-general and content-specific questions based on these elements. Singer and Donlan (1982) reasoned that mere delineation of the story grammar elements would be inadequate for comprehending complex short stories and that high school students would need a more sophisticated strategy (i.e., generating content-general and content-specific questions) to understand and analyze these stories.

Before each story was read, both groups were given background information and an explanation of difficult vocabulary. Then, students followed along while listening to a recording of the story. The recording was interrupted at a certain point in the story. During this time, the students in the experimental group were asked to write questions they wanted to answer. Questions were to be related to the story grammar elements. For example, for the element *character,* they might ask themselves, "Is the story going to be about the barber or the officer?" (Singer & Donlan, 1982, p. 173). They were then told to answer each question as the story continued. The researchers' intent was to structure the students' approach to reading and to focus them on the key issues and themes in the story.

When the recording was stopped, the control group was asked content-specific questions that were predictive in nature. At the end of each story, the experimental group was asked to write any additional questions they might have thought of during the story. The control group wrote 50- to 75-word essays in response to comprehension questions from the basal. Each day, the groups were administered a 10-item multiple-choice comprehension test based on the five story grammar elements.

The results of the comprehension tests indicated significant differences favoring the experimental group in all aspects of comprehension except theme. The treatment was more effective for above-average students than for lower ability students. The brief length of the intervention and the failure to use principles of direct instruction may explain this finding.

Despite its limitations, Singer and Donlan's (1982) study demonstrated that story grammar instruction can improve students' ability to understand complex narrative passages and was influential in the design of subsequent investigations conducted by Carnine and Kinder (1985), Gurney et al. (1990), and Dimino et al. (1990).

Short and Ryan (1984)

Short and Ryan (1984) contended that less skilled readers are not attuned to the purposes and goals of reading. Consequently, instruction in these metacognitive skills is necessary.

Short and Ryan (1984) used an unusual comparison group to ascertain whether training in both story grammar and attribution theory would eliminate or reduce the reading comprehension problems experienced by less skilled readers. The sample consisted of 56 fourth-grade boys: 14 highly skilled and 42 less skilled readers. Highly skilled readers were defined as those who scored at or above the 92nd percentile on the Comprehension subtest of the Stanford Diagnostic Reading Test (although these would be considered by most to be extraordinarily skilled readers). Less skilled readers were randomly assigned

to three training groups. The total-training group received both story grammar and metacognitive training, the strategy group received only story grammar training, and the attribution group received only metacognitive training.

Story grammar instruction was conducted in three 30- to 35-min training sessions. The story grammar strategy was modeled, and students were provided with guided and independent practice activities. They were taught to ask the generic story grammar questions, such as "Who is the main character?" and "Where and when did the story take place?" and "How did the main character feel?" and to underline the answers in the text as they read. (These story grammar questions are similar to those taught by Carnine & Kinder, 1985.) Feedback on the number of questions answered correctly was given to each student.

Because the students demonstrated knowledge of the story components, the purpose of the metacognitive training was to teach them *how* to use the story grammar questions to improve comprehension, rather than to teach them *what* the elements meant. Students were

> reminded of the importance of affect in successful reading performance and were continuously prompted to recite the attribution self-statements (e.g., Try hard. Just think how happy you will be when it comes time for the test and you're doing well.) prior to their reading and studying of the story. (Short & Ryan, 1984, p. 228)

Post-tests were administered on an individual basis. Students were asked to read a passage orally and to study it until they felt prepared to take the recall test. Both free and probed recalls were used to assess comprehension. During free recall, the students related the story to the teacher without prompts. The probed recall consisted of 14 short-answer questions addressing the story grammar elements.

Post-test measures revealed that the less skilled fourth graders trained in story grammar strategies did not significantly differ from the highly skilled fourth graders in their ability to comprehend new information. The post-test scores of students who received only metacognitive training were significantly lower than those of the remaining three groups (total training, story grammar, and skilled readers).

Short and Ryan's (1984) study provides evidence that training in the elements of story grammar increases the comprehension of below-average readers. These elements provide students with a systematic strategy for understanding; integrating; and, above all, interpreting narrative text. The use of effective instruction techniques enhances the students' ability to acquire the strategy.

Carnine and Kinder (1985)

Carnine and Kinder (1985) compared the effect of generative learning and schema-based (story grammar) interventions on low-ability students' comprehension of narrative and expository text. In this discussion, we address the portion of the study in which they investigated the effect of story grammar instruction on the comprehension of narrative text.

Low-performing fourth, fifth, and sixth graders in pullout Chapter I and special education programs were taught to ask and answer four generic story grammar questions—"Who is the story about?", "What does he or she want to do?", "What happens when he or she tries to do it?", and "What happens in the end?"—and then to generate summary statements. Pre-tests were developed to disqualify students whose comprehension ability was too high or reading (word attack) skills too low. Decoding skills were determined to be too low if more than five reading miscues were made on third- and fourth-grade-level reading selections of approximately 100 words. The reading comprehension test consisted of three literal and two inferential questions that required short answers. Students who answered more than three of these questions correctly were considered too skilled to participate in the study. The comprehension pre-tests were used as baseline measures.

The 27 students from special and remedial reading programs who qualified to participate were randomly assigned to the generative ($n = 14$) or the story grammar group ($n = 13$). Each story grammar lesson consisted of three parts. First, the teacher read the story aloud and stopped to ask the story grammar questions at key points that had been mutually agreed on

earlier by the teachers. In the second part of the lesson, the students took turns reading the second passage aloud. Again, the teachers stopped the students at predetermined points to ask the story grammar questions. At the end of this phase, the students were asked to summarize the story orally using story grammar as a basis. In the third part of the lesson, students were told to read the story silently and to ask themselves the four story grammar questions while they read. Subsequently, they were given a short-answer comprehension test consisting of two inferential and three literal questions based on the story.

Analysis of reading comprehension pre- and post-tests, maintenance tests, and free retelling indicated that story grammar instruction improved the reading comprehension of these low-performing students. In retelling scores, a gain of more than 1 standard deviation was demonstrated between pre- and post-test. Pre- and post-test scores on the short-answer comprehension tests improved from a mean of 52.7% to 75.3%. Maintenance tests were administered 2 and 4 weeks after the story grammar intervention ended. These scores (76.9% and 70.1%, respectively) indicated that the subjects' comprehension was still at a significantly higher level, suggesting that they remembered how to use at least some of the schema-based comprehension strategy. Because the results from two experimental, cognitively based treatments were compared, it was impossible to determine whether the treatment was indeed effective over what would have been obtained with no treatment. However, when the pre- and post-tests were given to a group of non-learning-disabled students, they were shown to be of equal difficulty.

The design of the intervention was influenced by research conducted by Dreher and Singer (1980) and Singer and Donlan (1982). Improvements in the instructional component of this study over Singer and Donlan's (1982) earlier study are clear. Direct instruction techniques (Carnine et al., 1990) were consistently used in the teaching sessions. The teachers modeled the story grammar strategy for the students, provided guided practice, and then allowed independent practice. Student errors were corrected immediately; the teacher showed each student how she located a more appropriate response and explained her rationale. It is also important to note that consistent language was used throughout the intervention. The teacher modeled a uniform set of story grammar questions. It appears that the regular use of these specific instructional techniques contributed to the substantial gains in pre- and post-test scores.

The length of the intervention was a critical factor in the effects obtained in this investigation. Students read and applied the story grammar strategies to 30 stories over a 10-day period. The length of the intervention phase gave the students the opportunity to learn and apply the strategy many times. The short duration of the previous studies did not allow the students to internalize the process. The results of the maintenance tests clearly indicated the automaticity that students achieved in this process.

Idol (1987)

Idol's (1987) study was precipitated by a concern for the quality of instruction that poor readers receive. The ethnographic studies of McDermott (1977), Eder (1983), and Rosenbaum (1980) indicated that the reading instruction received by students in low-ability groups was inferior to that received by students in high-ability groups in that low-ability readers are predominantly asked lower order (recall) questions. The purpose of Idol's study was to demonstrate that a story mapping technique could improve the reading comprehension of students of all ability levels taught in heterogeneous groups. A much more intricate story grammar was used than in Carnine and Kinder's (1985) and Singer and Donlan's (1982) studies.

Twenty-two students from a third- and fourth-grade combination class were randomly assigned to one of two groups. A multiple-baseline design was used. The baseline of the second group was extended, which permitted Group 2 to serve as a control group for Group 1.

During the baseline phase, the students were given a general explanation of the 10 story grammar questions that would be used throughout the intervention. The questions used were

"Where did the story take place?"
"When did this story take place?"
"Who were the main characters in the story?"
"Were there any other important characters in the story? Who?"
"What was the problem in the story?"
"How did _____ try to solve the problem?"
"Was it hard to solve the problem? Explain."
"Was the problem solved? Explain."
"What did you learn from reading this story? Explain."
"Can you think of a different ending?"

These questions were obviously more detailed than the four generic story grammar questions used by Carnine and Kinder (1985). The students then read a story, returned it to the teacher, and answered the 10 story grammar comprehension questions. After 4 days of baseline work, Group 1 proceeded to the model phase of the intervention.

In this phase, the students were again given an explanation of the story grammar questions and directed to read the selection silently. Before answering the story grammar questions, these students completed a story grammar map with the teacher. The teacher solicited input for the first component, setting. The students then completed that section on their individual story maps, copying the response as the teacher filled it in on the transparency. This procedure was followed until all elements— characters, setting, problem, goal, action, and outcome—were addressed. After completing the maps, the students returned them to the teacher and independently wrote the answers to the 10 comprehension questions.

During the lead phase, the students completed their story map independently as they read. They then assembled as a group. Using the transparency, the teacher completed the story map based on individual responses. The students then made corrections on their maps and proceeded to answer the comprehension questions.

The test phase was similar to the baseline phase. The students completed the story grammar maps as they read, returned them, and answered the 10 story grammar comprehension questions. When a group averaged 80% accuracy on the 10 questions for 2 consecutive days, they began a maintenance phase, in which they read silently and answered the 10 story grammar comprehension questions independently without using the story grammar map.

Improvements were made by both groups in performance on the primary dependent measure (the 10 story grammar comprehension questions) as they moved through the phases of intervention. In other words, comprehension continued to improve after modeling was discontinued and maps were completed independently and even when story maps were not used at all (maintenance phase). Mean comprehension scores from the baseline phase to the maintenance phase increased 18 and 22 percentage points for Groups 1 and 2, respectively, indicating, again, that reading comprehension was enhanced by instruction on the components of a story.

The 3 learning-disabled and 2 low-achieving students' mean scores on the primary dependent measure indicated that their comprehension also improved when the story mapping strategy was introduced. Two of the students with learning disabilities and both of the low-achieving students scored at or above 75% during the maintenance phase. The mean score of 1 student with learning disabilities decreased dramatically from the test to the maintenance phase (from 85% to 55%), indicating that he or she still needed the prompts provided by the story map. However, this student did demonstrate an improvement in mean comprehension scores from the baseline to the maintenance phase (from 35% to 55%). The nature of the student's disability could have been such that he or she was not able to put the story components into the proper perspective without the continual use of the story map as a guide.

In a study with 5 intermediate-grade students with learning disabilities and poor comprehension despite the use of the same story mapping strategy, Idol and Croll (1987) found that 4 of the 5 made strong gains in comprehension and the fifth student showed less growth. The 4 students showed statistically significant growth between baseline and intervention phases, with scores increasing from a mean of 26% to 58%. Differences between the intervention and maintenance phases were not statistically significant, however. The length of the intervention (9 and 11 days per group) and the gradual phasing out of teacher assistance (from model to lead to test) contributed to the success of Idol's (1987) study. As in the Carnine and Kinder (1985) study, these two factors allowed the students to learn, apply, and internalize the story grammar elements. Idol phased out instruction over several days; Carnine and Kinder phased out instruction *within each lesson.*

This study was similar to the Carnine and Kinder (1985) study in that

1. Elementary, intermediate-level, regular, and special education students served as subjects.
2. Sound instructional methods were used during treatment.
3. Simple, narrative basal reader stories with a discernible story structure were used.

Although the number of story grammar questions taught by Idol (1987) was more than twice that taught by Carnine and Kinder (10 and 4, respectively), their purpose and outcomes were similar.

Gurney et al. (1990)

The success of these studies led researchers to see whether techniques used in previous studies could be adapted to improve the ability of learning-disabled and at-risk high school students to understand and analyze literature. The first of two studies conducted by Gurney et al. (1990) was essentially an intensive case study of several high school students with learning disabilities, many of whom were reading 4–6 years below grade level.

Four 10th graders and 3 9th graders who read a 7th-grade narrative basal-reading passage with at least 90% accuracy and correctly answered three of four literal oral comprehension and vocabulary questions participated in the study. Four students from one school were randomly assigned to two groups; the remaining 3 students from another school were assigned to one teacher.

A multiple-baseline design was used to determine the effects of both comprehension strategy instruction and traditional/basal literature instruction on students' ability to comprehend short stories. The three groups received traditional literature instruction during the baseline phase. When a group failed to demonstrate progress on the assessment passages, which were administered each second day of instruction, they proceeded to the intervention phase (comprehension strategy instruction) of the study. Because of time constraints, Group 3 did not receive comprehension strategy instruction. The assessment passages were designed to measure whether instruction enhanced students' ability to independently (a) answer questions based on the story grammar strategy, (b) answer questions from the basal literature text, and (c) provide a focused retelling of the story.

During traditional/basal literature instruction, the teacher began the lesson by presenting new vocabulary and information about the background of the story. Students were directed to either read or listen to the story. After reading, both literal and higher order questions were discussed orally. Students then completed activity sheets that addressed literary, reading comprehension, or decoding skills.

Students were taught the comprehension strategy using the modeling, guided practice, and independent practice paradigm. The strategy consisted of teaching the students to determine the main problem and identify the main character, character clues, resolution, conclusion, and theme of a story. The students were also taught to record the information on their story grammar notesheets.

For example, to determine the main problem, the teacher named a story they had read during baseline; reviewed the problems that occurred in the story; and, while thinking aloud, chose the main problem by identifying the problem that encompassed the action of the entire story. The teacher discussed each minor problem and explained why it was not the predominant one.

During guided practice, the teacher reviewed a different baseline story, asked the students to identify the main problem, justify it, and dis-

cuss the reasons for eliminating the remaining minor problems. This activity was repeated with many of the baseline stories. The teacher's assistance faded as the students became proficient in this task. As the students progressed, they applied this skill to new stories they read. They were also taught to record their responses on their individual notesheets as they read. During the last phase of the paradigm, the students independently determined the story grammar element and recorded it on their notesheets. This process was followed for the remaining story grammar elements.

The results of this small-scale study suggested that the intervention did improve student comprehension. These results were reported by question type: strategy, basal, and main idea (focused retelling).

Strategy questions were derived from the six story grammar elements taught during the intervention phase (e.g., "What is the problem?" and "How did the main character try to solve the problem?"). As baseline instruction continued, the students in Groups 1 and 2 did not improve in their ability to answer strategy questions. However, during comprehension strategy instruction, the median score for Group 1 increased 12 percentage points from their baseline median score (61% to 73%). Group 2 improved during the intervention phase as well. The increase in their median score from baseline to intervention was slightly greater than Group 1's (56% to 75%). However, there was more variability in Group 2's scores. The students in Group 3 did not receive strategy instruction. As would be expected, these students' ability to answer strategy questions did not improve over time. In fact, the data indicate a slight decrease in the scores. Their median score was 61%, with a range of 13 percentage points (50% to 72%).

Basal questions consisted of multiple-choice or fill-in-the-blank items that probed students' recall of details from the story. Group 1's median baseline score for basal literature questions was 57%. The scores ranged from 35% to 75% and did not improve with traditional instruction. The scores varied less during strategy instruction, and the median improved slightly (64%). Although the median did not increase significantly, the decrease in variability may be an indication that the strategy provided the students with a consistent procedure for deriving meaning from the story. The fact that there was a very slight increase in the means for the last four assessment passages suggests that an extended intervention period may have given the students an opportunity to become proficient in the use of the strategy.

Although during baseline the range of scores for Group 2 was smaller than that for Group 1, they did vary considerably (63% to 93%). As the traditional literature instruction continued, this group's scores decreased. During strategy instruction, there was less variability in scores, with a modest improvement over baseline. The performance of the students in Group 3 on the basal questions was erratic, with scores ranging from 33% to 100%. The data indicated that the scores decreased slightly over time.

Main-idea questions required the students to tell what the story was about in three or four sentences. During the baseline phase, Groups 1 and 2 demonstrated a decline in answering main-idea questions. Strategy instruction had an initial positive effect on students' ability to answer main-idea questions. As strategy instruction continued, the means for both Groups 1 and 2 declined. Despite this, Group 1's means from baseline to strategy training increased from 44% to 70%. Group 2's mean performance from baseline to strategy increased from 53% to 67%. The increase in Group 2's mean for the final assessment passage may have been an indication of an upward trend in the scores. Again, this may be a sign that an extended intervention period would have given the students an opportunity to internalize the strategy and elevate it to a more automatic level. Unfortunately, because of time constraints, additional instruction could not be allocated for this intervention.

Group 3's performance on main-idea questions ranged from 25% to 83%. The variability was such that the trend line indicated a negligible increase in the scores.

In Gurney et al.'s (1990) study, comprehension strategy instruction was more effective than traditional/basal literature instruction in improving mildly disabled high school students' ability to answer strategy questions. Their ability to answer either main-idea or basal questions was not enhanced by the story grammar strategy, however.

The intervention may have increased the students' ability to answer strategy questions because the story grammar intervention centered on answering these questions. That is, the strategy was *directly* applicable to this type of question. To answer the other types of questions, the students had to apply the strategy indirectly, using the details they encountered to answer the strategy questions and applying them to the other types of questions. In sum, they were not specifically taught a technique for answering main-idea and basal questions.

The students' disabilities may have affected the results of this study. Many mildly disabled (i.e., mildly mentally retarded and learning disabled) students have difficulty transferring information to new situations. They also need to perform many repetitions of a skill before they achieve proficiency at it and need significantly greater opportunities to practice a skill to maintain it. The data from Gurney et al.'s (1990) study seem to indicate that an extended period of comprehension strategy instruction would have improved the students' ability to answer basal, main-idea, *and* strategy questions.

Dimino et al. (1990)

The next step was a larger scale study conducted by Dimino et al. (1990) in which an interactive instructional method was used to teach students a strategy for comprehending and analyzing complex short stories. This strategy (based on story grammar) assisted these low-performing high school students in identifying the main character, the problem or conflict that the main character faced, character information, attempts to solve the problem, and resolution. The students were taught to detect and record these story grammar elements in an effort to build a foundation for answering literal and inferential questions based on the story.

The length of the intervention was extended to give the students an opportunity to learn and internalize the strategy. It was hypothesized that students who received story grammar instruction would perform significantly higher on post-test measures of reading comprehension than would students who received traditional literature instruction.

The subjects were high school freshmen and sophomores in Basic English, a course for students who, in the teachers' opinions, could not deal with the rigors of the typical high school English course. Of the 32 students who participated in the study, 6 were identified as learning disabled and 2 were Chapter 1 program participants. Most of the students were reading well below grade level. Reading scores as measured by the Advanced 1 Level of the Reading (Comprehension) subtest of of the Metropolitan Achievement Test (Farr et al., 1978) ranged from 5.2 to 10.1.

To determine the effects of the intervention, Dimino et al. (1990) administered a pre-test, post-test, and maintenance test, each of which contained two stories. Each assessment passage was accompanied by a test that contained story grammar questions, basal questions, and a focused retelling. The story grammar questions were derived from the set of general story grammar elements that the experimental group was taught during comprehension strategy instruction. These questions were similar to the schema general questions developed by Singer and Donlan (1982). Story grammar questions addressed critical information regarding the main character, the problem/conflict, attempts to solve the problem, resolution, character information, reactions, and theme (e.g., "Who is the main character?," "Use the character information to tell what the main character is like," and "What is the author trying to say?").

Unlike the story grammar questions, the basal questions primarily required the student to recall details of the story. They were multiple-choice, true-false, or fill-in-the-blank questions. The answers to these questions were explicitly stated in the text. Each assessment also contained a focused retelling in which students were asked to write what the story was about in five or fewer sentences. The intent was to assess whether students could provide a summary that included most of the important aspects of the

story. The story grammar strategy was designed to improve reading comprehension through an interactive process that evolved between the students and teachers. To that end, the comprehension strategy instruction consisted of teacher-directed and teacher-assisted phases. The instructional methodology was similar to the direct explanation model used by Duffy et al. (1987), in which the teacher demonstrated the relevant cognitive and metacognitive acts. The components of the comprehension strategy were divided into four major categories: (a) conflict/problem and main character, (b) character information, (c) attempts/resolution/twist, and (d) reaction/theme.

Before modeling the components of the comprehension strategy, the teachers told the students the purpose of the story grammar instruction—that they would be learning a strategy that would assist them in understanding stories and answering questions. Then, the teachers explained each story grammar component and provided examples of each of the story grammar elements.

During the teacher-directed phase, students were taught to apply the story grammar elements to a series of short stories. The teachers began with the four easiest, most literal elements: conflict/problem, main character, attempts to solve the problem, and resolution. For example, the strategy for finding a problem was modeled by having the students follow as the story was read aloud (usually by a classmate) to a designated point in the story. Then, thinking aloud, the teacher said, "I see a problem" or "It looks as if we have a problem." The teacher stated the problem and wrote it on an overhead transparency of the notesheet. This procedure continued throughout the teacher-assisted phase. Figure 1 presents excerpts from an actual notesheet completed by the teacher and students for "The Necklace" by Guy de Maupassant (1884/1979) during this phase.

With the second story, the teachers introduced two more subtle elements: character information and reactions. The students were told that character information can be used to determine what the characters are like and how they react to the events in a story. Character information includes what the char-

---

Name _____ Date _____

Story _____

1. Main Character or Protagonist _____

2. Character Clues
   _____

3. Reactions: How do the main characters REACT or FEEL about important events in the story? _____
   _____

4. Name the problems or conflicts. Circle the main problem or conflict.
   _____
   _____
   _____
   _____

5. How do the characters TRY to solve the problem? _____
   _____
   _____
   _____

6. a. Tell how the problem GETS SOLVED or DOES NOT GET SOLVED. _____
   _____
   _____

   b. Is there an ADDED TWIST or COMPLICATION at the end of the story? Tell what happens at the end of the
   story if it is different than what you said in part 6a. _____
   _____
   _____

7. Theme: What is the author trying to say? _____
   _____
   _____
   _____

Figure 1
Notesheet used by the teacher and students to identify story grammar elements in "The Necklace" (de Maupassant, 1884/1979) in Dimino et al.'s (1990) study.

acters look like, what they wear, how they talk, act, etc. The teachers explained that sometimes authors do not specifically state characters' reactions and that, in this case, the reader can use the character information to determine the reactions. The teachers gave several examples from the second and third stories.

For example, to determine the characters' reaction to losing the "diamond" necklace in de Maupassant's "The Necklace," the teachers said, "Based on this character information, I can

decide how the characters reacted to (or felt about) losing the necklace. Let's review the character information to see how I decided on that reaction." The teachers recorded character information such as "She turned toward him despairingly," "They hunted everywhere," "They looked at each other aghast," "Her husband got back into his street clothes and retraced their steps," and "He returned home, his face pale and lined." Then the teacher said, "On the basis of this character information, I decided that the characters were very upset, alarmed, or panicked by the loss of the necklace."

During the third story, the six previous elements were reviewed and the teachers explained how they used these elements to determine a theme. The students were told that there may be more than one appropriate interpretation of the theme but that themes must be related to the story grammar elements. Finally, the students were taught a procedure for formulating a focused retelling of each story.

The goals of the teacher-directed phase were to (a) gradually enable the students to use the comprehension strategy independently and (b) increase discussion among the students and between the students and teachers. The teacher-assisted phase was divided into two segments, each covering three stories.

During this phase, each student was given a notesheet for each story. As in the earlier phase, the story was read aloud to a designated point, and then the teachers asked a pertinent story grammar question. After each student responded, the teachers provided individualized feedback. If a student's response was unclear or too general, the teacher asked a more specific follow-up question. At times, the teachers reminded the students of the appropriate step in the story grammar strategy. The goal was to provide a scaffold for the students, to assist them only in those areas where assistance was needed (Palincsar, 1986).

After the group reached a consensus about the story grammar elements, the teachers recorded the information on a transparency. Students completed their own individual notesheets. For the first three stories, although they were told that they could copy what the teacher recorded, they were encouraged to use their own words. For the last three stories, no transparency was used. The group discussed each story grammar element, but only after all students had recorded a response on their notesheets.

Every student was asked to write a retelling after each story was read. Students were encouraged to use their notesheets as the basis for their brief essays. The students were monitored and given assistance as they wrote.

The procedures outlined in the teacher's guides provided the foundation for the traditional literature instruction. The teachers followed a variant of the direct instruction model by apprising the students of the goals of the lesson, providing clear explanations, soliciting responses from all students, and providing relevant feedback. Each story was introduced by (a) defining pertinent vocabulary, as noted in the teachers' guide of the text, and (b) discussing background information to promote interest. The teachers and students took turns reading aloud, as was done in the story grammar condition. When students encountered a word they could not decode, the teachers pronounced the word and, when appropriate, provided the definition. The teachers also defined words they thought the students might not comprehend.

After reading, the students orally responded to the discussion questions in the teacher's guides. Although most of the questions required the students to recall details and events, occasionally questions would require them to express an opinion, make an inference, or discuss literary techniques.

Three 2×2 analyses of variance (ANOVAs) were performed, one each on students' scores on the story grammar questions, basal questions, and retelling task. To answer theme questions correctly, the students had to assimilate all of the story grammar elements. Therefore, a secondary analysis of theme questions was conducted to determine the effect of comprehension instruction in activating this process. The ANOVAs indicated that the students who had received story grammar instruction performed significantly better than the students who had received traditional instruction, and effects were maintained over time. The extended intervention (19 days) appears to have provided students with adequate guided practice to assimilate the strategy.

The analysis of the data also revealed that there was a significant decrease in the story grammar group's mean scores on the retelling task from post-test to maintenance test (5.79 to 4.21). One reason for this outcome may be the effort involved in formulating an appropriate retelling. That is, the students had to identify the important information (i.e., main character, attempts to solve the problem, resolution, and twist) and then incorporate this information into a coherent retelling consisting of five sentences or less. This was a demanding task for these students. The significant interaction on this measure may also be attributed to the lack of practice in writing retellings between post-testing and maintenance testing. The students may have been able to retain the procedure for formulating retellings if the intervention were extended to include a 2- to 3-week period of distributed practice (i.e., strategy training two to three times per week) before the maintenance tests were administered.

There was also a substantial decrease in the quality of the themes generated by students on the maintenance test. One hypothesis explaining the students' limited use of the procedure for determining themes on the maintenance test is interference effects of students' prior learning. In the early grades, students learned that a theme was the "moral of the story." When confronted with complex literature, students often searched for a moral or message. When they could not find one, they resorted to well-worn platitudes, often of dubious relevance to the story. Again, had the intervention been extended to include a period of distributed practice, perhaps the students would have been able to retain this strategy.

Instruction in the story grammar condition was based on direct instruction techniques (Rosenshine, 1986). As expected, student engagement was high. Both teachers reported that classroom student involvement in their story grammar groups was high throughout the intervention, while the classroom involvement of the traditional groups deteriorated as the study progressed. The nature of the instruction was such that the students became increasingly responsible for using the comprehension strategy. The students in the story grammar condition were informed that as the instruction progressed, the teacher's role would diminish and their responsibility for recording and discussing information would increase. This technique instilled a sense of accountability that contributed to the students' active participation, as evidenced by the amount and quality of the discussions that transpired.

Griffey et al. (1988)

Griffey et al. (1988) conducted a study in which all subjects were students with learning disabilities and low reading comprehension. The group who received self-questioning instruction to identify story structure answered more comprehension questions correctly than did the group who received no strategy instruction. All subjects were in Grades 3–5, with ages ranging from 9 to 13 years.

The short intervention consisted of 30 min of instruction for 4 days. Ten students were taught to use a self-questioning procedure called CAPS—*C*haracter, *A*im, *P*roblem, *S*olution. They were taught to identify each of these story elements and practiced retelling passages using the CAPS story grammar strategy as a framework. A second group of seven students received instruction in identifying the four story grammar elements using the CAPS acronym, but they were not taught the self-questioning procedure. The final group of 10 students with learning disabilities received no strategy training. They were simply told that the teachers liked to ask questions about the four story grammar elements. Instruction was thoroughly scripted for all groups using an introduction, model, and guided practice format. Students were carefully monitored during instruction, and corrective feedback was provided.

Analysis revealed that the group who had been taught the story grammar strategy and self-questioning answered significantly more comprehension questions than did the control group, who received only teacher-generated questions. Interestingly, the students who had been taught the story grammar strategy only and did not learn self-questioning did not perform better than the control group. This would seem to indicate the importance of actually modeling for students how they can apply the strategy to their reading and explicit metacognitive instruction. No significant differences were found among the three groups' performances on oral retellings. Although the growth made by the story grammar group who received instruction on self-questioning was very modest, it was encouraging given the very short duration of the intervention.

DISCUSSION

As studies on instruction based on story grammar have progressed over the years, the instructional intervention has become more sophisticated. Recommendations can be made that would be useful to the teacher designing instructional modifications for a student with learning disabilities. For students with low comprehension ability, the use of a clear strategy can improve their comprehension of many narrative stories. The strategy must not only cover the components of story grammar, but also allow the student to consolidate those components to get a better overall understanding of the story. Failure to consolidate components into a usable strategy may have been a factor leading to poor gains in comprehension in Newby et al.'s (1989) study that involved story grammar components on separate cards but did not go a step further to use those components in a specified order to retell the story. Newby et al. found better success with a story grammar outline or map that was all on one page in a specific order. Idol (1987) and Carnine and Kinder (1985) demonstrated that consistent strategies were effective in improving comprehension. The objectives of the instruction should determine the composition of the strategy; for example, if the goal is to ensure that students use story grammar as the basis for their retelling of stories, practice in retelling should be part of the strategy.

Progression from teacher direction or modeling to guided practice to independent practice is an important part of instruction in the story grammar strategy. Interventions that followed this format (Carnine & Kinder, 1985; Dimino et al., 1990; Idol, 1987; Idol & Croll, 1987) led to greater gains in students' comprehension than did interventions that did not follow this format. Interventions that left out the guided practice or lead portion (Newby et al., 1989) and one of the comparison conditions in the Griffey et al. (1988) study resulted in relatively small gains in comprehension, possibly because of the omission. The length of the intervention is also an important variable, because students must be facile in the use of story grammar before moving on to independent practice. In Idol and Croll's (1987) study, the intervention phase was reintroduced when

one student began to show a loss in comprehension scores. After this continued guided-practice phase, the student maintained the strong gains made in comprehension. The relatively long, 10-day study by Carnine and Kinder (1985) led to more automaticity in using the story grammar. The longest intervention, used by Dimino et al. (1990), also led to strong improvement in comprehension.

To move students from one phase to another at the appropriate time and to allow for adequate practice require careful monitoring of students' responses. Encouraging the increase of discussion, not only between the teacher and the students but also among the students, facilitates ongoing assessment and practice. Ensuring that students, particularly the lowest performing ones, receive individual turns in responding will make it easier to monitor progress. Corrective feedback should be provided during the guided-practice phase. The use of a clear strategy with consistent wording provides the teacher and students with a common language, making corrections more effective.

Some components of story grammar, such as characters' internal response (Montague et al., 1990; Ripich & Griffith, 1988), direct consequences (Montague et al., 1990), and theme (Dimino et al., 1990), are more difficult than others. These components may require extra instruction. After a 19-day intervention with 9th and 10th graders, Dimino et al. (1990) still found that theme development (and practice with retellings) needed more time. They recommended 2-3 weeks of distributed practice. In the case of theme, it is possible that previous instruction in lower grades caused students to give inappropriate responses. Preteaching that provides practice in developing nonstandard themes might be useful. Greater teacher direction in this skill might be required.

Narrative passages must be selected carefully. For students with learning disabilities, some passages are harder than others because of features such as the proximity of important information within the story (Kameenui et al., 1987). It will be easier for younger or naive students to learn to apply the story grammar strategy if they can begin with passages that have relatively simple textual features. Also, some passages follow story grammar more closely than others. The passages chosen should closely follow story grammar conventions, at least during early instruction in the use of the strategy. However, using examples that comply only with story grammar not only will be difficult, but also may be an instructionally bad idea. Students must learn that story grammar is only a heuristic (or guide), not a rigid system for analyzing stories.

One area of uncertainty is when and to whom a story grammar strategy should be taught. Laughton and Morris (1989) suggested that most students with or without learning disabilities have a basic knowledge of most components of story grammar by 6th grade; they recommended story grammar instruction for students with learning disabilities at the 3rd through 5th grade levels. It is possible that students may have knowledge of the components but have not necessarily learned a strategy for using and integrating those components to improve their comprehension of narrative stories. Many interventions (Carnine & Kinder, 1985; Idol, 1987; Idol & Croll, 1987; Short & Ryan, 1984) have focused on these grade levels. Others (Dimino et al., 1990; Gurney et al., 1990) have demonstrated improved comprehension for 9th and 10th graders with low comprehension, including students with learning disabilities. Dimino et al. (1990), however, noted that the intervention helped only the lower half of the group of students in the Basic English class.

It is likely that story grammar instruction can begin with third graders but that components of the strategy may need to be added or refined for more complex stories in upper grades. Because students may already know many of the story grammar components, teachers should proceed with caution in teaching, assessing whether practice can be reduced for some of their students.

In 1986, Gersten and Carnine wrote,
The research [on explicit strategy instruction] demonstrates that the type of questions, the step-by-step breakdowns, and the extensive practice with a range of examples . . . benefit students' comprehension. The next step is integrating these procedures into reading series and into teacher training programs. (p. 72)

Although researchers and publishers have made efforts to disseminate story grammar instruction and other explicit comprehension strategies to practitioners, there is still a long way to go before the intricacies of these effective strategies are fully understood and appropriately implemented.

REFERENCES

Applebee, A. N., Langer, J. L., & Mulis, I. V. S. (1988). *Who reads best?* Princeton, NJ: Educational Testing Service.

Carnine, D., & Kinder, B. D. (1985). Teaching low-performing students to apply generative and schema strategies to narrative and expository material. *Remedial and Special Education, 6*(1), 20–30.

Carnine, D., Silbert, J., & Kameenui, E. J. (1990). *Direct instruction reading.* Columbus, OH: Merrill.

Carnine, D., Stevens, C., Clements, J., & Kameenui, E. J. (1982). Effects of facilitative questions and practice on intermediate students' understanding of character motives. *Journal of Reading Behavior, 14,* 179–190.

de Maupassant, G. (1979). The necklace. In R. A. Bennett (Ed.), *Types of literature* (pp. 36–43). Lexington, MA: Ginn. (Original work published 1884)

Dimino, J. A., Gersten, R., Carnine, D., & Blake, G. (1990). Story grammar: An approach for promoting at risk secondary students' comprehension of literature. *Elementary School Journal, 91*(1), 19–32.

Dreher, M. J., & Singer, H. (1980). Story grammar instruction unnecessary for intermediate grade students. *The Reading Teacher, 34,* 261–276.

Duffy, G. G., Roehler, L. R., Sivan, E., Rackliffe, G., Book, C., Meloth, M. S., Vavrus, L. G., Wesselman, R., Putnam, J., & Bassiri, D. (1987). Effects of explaining the reasoning associated with using reading strategies. *Reading Research Quarterly, 23,* 347–368.

Eder, D. (1983). Organization constraints on individual mobility: Ability group formation and maintenance. In J. Cook-Gumpers (Ed.), *Language, literacy and schooling* (pp. 68–82). New York: Heinneman.

Farr, R. C., Prescott, G. A., Balow, I. H., & Hogan, T. P. (1978). *Metropolitan Achievement Tests (MAT): Reading Comprehension Subtest* (Advanced 1, Form JS). New York: Psychological Corporation.

Gersten, R., & Carnine, D. (1986). Direct instruction in reading comprehension. *Educational Leadership, 43*(7), 70–78.

Goodlad, J. I., & Oakes, J. (1988). We must offer equal access to knowledge. *Educational Leadership, 45*(5), 16–22.

Griffey, Q. L., Zigmond, N., & Leinhardt, G. (1988). The effects of self-questioning and story structure training on the reading comprehension of poor readers. *Learning Disabilities Research, 4*(1), 45–51.

Gurney, D., Gersten, R., Dimino, J. A., & Carnine, D. (1990). Story grammar: Effective literature instruction for learning disabled high school students. *Journal of Learning Disabilities, 23,* 335–342.

Idol, L. (1987). Group story mapping: A comprehension strategy for both skilled and unskilled readers. *Journal of Learning Disabilities, 20,* 196–205.

Idol, L., & Croll, V. (1987). Story-mapping training as a means of improving reading comprehension. *Learning Disability Quarterly, 10,* 214–229.

Kameenui, E., Simmons, D., & Darch, C. (1987). LD children's comprehension of selected textual features: Effects of proximity of information. *Learning Disability Quarterly, 10,* 237–248.

Laughton, J., & Morris, N. T. (1989). Story grammar knowledge of learning disabled students. *Learning Disabilities Research, 4*(2), 87–95.

Mandler, J. M., & Johnson, N. S. (1977). Remembrance of things parsed: Story structure and recall. *Cognitive Psychology, 9,* 111–151.

McDermott, R. P. (1977). The ethnography of speaking and reading. In R. Shuy (Ed.), *Linguistic theory: What can it say about reading?* (pp. 153–171). Newark, DE: International Reading Association.

Montague, M., Maddux, C., & Dereshiwsky, M. (1990). Story grammar and comprehension and production of narrative prose by students with learning disabilities. *Journal of Learning Disabilities, 23,* 190–197.

Newby, R., Caldwell, J., & Recht, D. (1989). Improving the reading comprehension of children with dysphonetic and dyseidetic dyslexia using story grammar. *Journal of Learning Disabilities, 22,* 373–380.

Palincsar, A. S. (1986). The role of dialogue in providing scaffolding instruction. *Educational Psychologist, 21,* 73–98.

Ripich, D., & Griffith, P. (1988). Narrative disabilities of children with learning disabilities and nondisabled children: Story structure, cohesion, and propositions. *Journal of Learning Disabilities, 21,* 165–173.

Rosenbaum, J. (1980). The social implications of educational grouping. In D. Berliner (Ed.), *Review of research in education* (Vol. 8, pp. 79–88). Washington, DC: American Educational Research Association.

Rosenshine, B. (1986). Synthesis of research on explicit teaching. *Educational Leadership, 43*(7), 60–69.

Short, E. J., & Ryan, E. B. (1984). Meta-cognitive differences between skilled and less skilled readers: Remediating deficits through story grammar and attribution training. *Journal of Educational Psychology, 76,* 225–235.

Singer, H., & Donlan, D. (1982). Active comprehension: Problem-solving schema with question generation for comprehension of complex short stories. *Reading Research Quarterly, 17,* 166–185.

Stein, N. L., & Trabasso, T. (1982). What's in a story? An approach to comprehension and instruction. In R. Glaser (Ed.), *Advances in instructional psychology* (Vol. 2, pp. 213–267). Hillsdale, NJ: Erlbaum.

Thorndyke, P. W. (1977). Cognitive structures in comprehension and memory of narrative discourse. *Cognitive Psychology, 9,* 77–110.

Ethical Standards of the American Educational Research Association

FOREWORD

Educational researchers come from many disciplines, embrace several competing theoretical frameworks, and use a variety of research methodologies. AERA recognizes that its members are already guided by codes in the various disciplines and, also, by organizations such as institutional review boards. AERA's code of ethics incorporates a set of standards designed specifically to guide the work of researchers in education. Education, by its very nature, is aimed at the improvement of individual lives and societies. Further, research in education is often directed at children and other vulnerable population. A main objective of this code is to remind us, as educational researchers, that we should strive to protect these populations, and to maintain the integrity of our research, of our research community, and of all those with whom we have professional relations. We should pledge ourselves to do this by maintaining our own competence and that of people we induct into the field, by continually evaluating our research for its ethical and scientific adequacy, and by conducting our internal and external relations according to the highest ethical standards.

The standards that follow remind us that we are involved not only in research but in education. It is, therefore, essential that we continually reflect on our research to be sure that it is not only sound scientifically but that it makes a positive contribution to the educational enterprise.

I. GUIDING STANDARDS:
RESPONSIBILITIES TO THE FIELD

A. Preamble

To maintain the integrity of research, educational researches should warrant their research conclusions adequately in a way consistent with the standards of their own theoretical and methodological perspectives. They should keep themselves well informed in both their own and competing paradigms where those are relevant to their research, and they should continually evaluate the criteria of adequacy by which research is judged.

B. Standards

1. Educational researchers should conduct their professional lives in such a way that they do not jeopardize future research, the public standing of the field, or the discipline's research results.

Reprinted from *Educational Researcher,* 10/92, pp. 23–26. Copyright 1992 by the American Educational Research Association. Reprinted by permission of the publisher.

2. Educational researchers must not fabricate, falsify, or misrepresent authorship, evidence, data, findings, or conclusions.

3. Educational researchers must not knowingly or negligently use their professional roles for fraudulent purposes.

4. Educational researches should honestly and fully disclose their qualifications and limitations when providing professional opinions to the public, to government agencies, and others who may avail themselves of the expertise possessed by members of AERA.

5. Educational researchers should attempt to report their findings to all relevant stakeholders, and should refrain from keeping secret or selectively communicating their findings.

6. Educational researchers should report research conceptions, procedures, results, and analyses accurately and sufficiently in detail to allow knowledgeable, trained researchers to understand and interpret them.

7. Educational researchers' reports to the public should be written straightforwardly to communicate the practical significance for policy, including limits in effectiveness and in generalizability to situations, problems, and contexts. In writing for or communicating with nonresearchers, educational researchers must take care not to misrepresent the practical or policy implications of their research or the research of others.

8. When educational researchers participate in actions related to hiring, retention, and advancement, they should not discriminate on the basis of gender, sexual orientation, physical disabilities, marital status, color, social class, religion, ethnic background, national origin, or other attributes not relevant to the evaluation of academic or research competence.

9. Educational researchers have a responsibility to make candid, forthright personnel recommendations and not to recommend those who are manifestly unfit.

10. Educational researchers should decline requests to review the work of others where strong conflicts of interest are involved, or when such requests cannot be conscientiously fulfilled on time. Materials sent for review should be read in their entirety and considered carefully, with evaluative comments justified with explicit reasons.

11. Educational researchers should avoid all forms of harassment, not merely those overt actions or threats that are due cause for legal action. They must not use their professional positions or rank to coerce personal or sexual favors or economic or professional advantages from students, research assistants, clerical staff, colleagues, or any others.

12. Educational researchers should not be penalized for reporting in good faith violations of these or other professional standards.

II. GUIDING STANDARDS: RESEARCH POPULATIONS, EDUCATIONAL INSTITUTIONS, AND THE PUBLIC

A. Preamble

Educational researchers conduct research within a broad array of settings and institutions, including schools, colleges, universities, hospitals, and prisons. It is of paramount importance that educational researchers respect the rights, privacy, dignity, and sensitivities of their research populations and also the integrity of the institutions within which the research occurs. Educational researchers should be especially careful in working with children and other vulnerable populations. These standards are intended to reinforce and strengthen already existing standards enforced by institutional review boards and other professional associations.

Standards

1. Participants, or their guardians, in a research study have the right to be informed about the likely risks involved in the research and of potential consequences for participants, and to give their informed consent before participating in research. Educational researchers should communicate the aims of the investigation as well as possible to informants and participants (and their guardians), and appropriate representatives of institutions, and keep them updated about any significant changes in the research program.

2. Honesty should characterize the relationship between researchers and participants and appropriate institutional representatives. Deception is discouraged; it should be used only when clearly necessary for scientific studies and should then be minimized. After the study the researcher should explain to the participants and institutional representatives the reasons for the deception.

3. Educational researcher should be sensitive to any locally established institutional policies or guidelines for conducting research.

4. Participants have the right to withdraw from the study at any time, unless otherwise constrained by their official capacities or roles.

5. Educational researchers should exercise caution to ensure that there is no exploitation for personal gain of research populations or of institutional settings of research. Educational researchers should not use their influence over subordinates, students, or others to compel them to participate in research.

6. Researchers have a responsibility to be mindful of cultural, religious, gender, and other significant differences within the research population in the planning, conduct, and reporting of their research.

7. Researchers should carefully consider and minimize the use of research techniques that might have negative social consequences, for example, negative sociometrics with young children or experimental interventions that might deprive students of important parts of the standard curriculum.

8. Educational researchers should be sensitive to the integrity of ongoing institutional activities and alert appropriate institutional representatives of possible disturbances in such activities which may result from the conduct of the research.

9. Educational researchers should communicate their findings and the practical significance of their research in clear, straightforward, and appropriate language to relevant research populations, institutional representatives, and other stakeholders.

10. Informants and participants have a right to remain anonymous. This right should be respected when no clear understanding to the contrary has been reached. Researchers are responsible for taking appropriate precautions to protect the confidentiality of both participants and data. Those being studied should be made aware of the capacities of the various data-gathering technologies to be used in the investigation so that they can make an informed decision about their participation. It should also be made clear to information and participants that despite every effort made to preserve it, anonymity may be compromised. Secondary researchers should respect and maintain the anonymity established by primary researchers.

III. GUIDING STANDARDS: INTELLECTUAL OWNERSHIP

A. Preamble

Intellectual ownership is predominantly a function of creative contribution. Intellectual ownership is not predominantly a function of effort expended.

B. Standards

1. Authorship should be determined based on the following guidelines, which are not intended to stifle collaboration, but rather to clarify the credit appropriately due for various contributions to research.

   a) All those, regardless of status, who have made substantive creative contributions to the generation of an intellectual product are entitled to be listed as authors of that product.

   b) First authorship and order of authorship should be the consequence of relative creative leadership and creative contribution. Examples of creative contributions are: writing first drafts or substantial portions; significant rewriting or substantive editing; and contributing generative ideas or basic conceptual schemes or analytic categories, collecting data which requires significant interpretation or judgment, and interpreting data.

   c) Clerical or mechanical contributions to an intellectual product are not grounds for ascribing authorship. Examples of such technical contributions are: typing, routine data collection or analysis, routine editing, and participation in staff meetings.

   d) Authorship and first authorship are not warranted by legal or contractual responsibility for or authority over the project or process that generates an intellectual product. It is improper to enter into contractual arrangements that preclude the proper assignment of authorship.

   e) Anyone listed as author must have given his/her consent to be so listed.

   f) The work of those who have contributed to the production of an intellectual product in ways short of these requirements for authorship should be appropriately acknowledged within the product.

g) Acknowledgment of other work significantly relied on in the development of an intellectual product is required. However, so long as such work is not plagiarized or otherwise inappropriately used, such reliance is not ground for authorship or ownership.

h) It is improper to use positions of authority to appropriate the work of others or claim credit for it.

i) Theses and dissertations are special cases in which authorship is not determined strictly by the criteria elaborated in these standards. Students' advisors, who might in other circumstances be deserving of authorship based on their collaborative contribution, should not be considered authors. Their creative contributions should, however, be fully and appropriately acknowledged.

j) Authors should disclose the publication history of articles they submit for publication; that is, if the present article is substantially similar in content and form to one previously published, that fact should be noted and the place of publication cited.

2. While under suitable circumstances, ideas and other intellectual products may be viewed as commodities, arrangements concerning the production or distribution of ideas or other intellectual products must be consistent with academic freedom and the appropriate availability of intellectual products to scholars, students, and the public. Moreover, when a conflict between the academic and scholarly purposes of intellectual production and profit from such production arise, preference should be given to the academic and scholarly purposes.

3. Ownership of intellectual products should be based upon the following guidelines:

a) Individuals are entitled to profit from the sale or disposition of those intellectual products they create. They may therefore enter into contracts or other arrangements for the publication or disposition of intellectual products, and profit financially from these arrangements.

b) Arrangements for the publication or disposition of intellectual products should be consistent with their appropriate public availability and with academic freedom. Such arrangements should emphasize the academic functions of publication over the maximization of profit.

c) Individuals or groups who fund or otherwise provide resources for the development of intellectual products are entitled to assert claims to a fair share of the royalties or other profits from the sale or disposition of those products. As such claims are likely to be contentious, funding institutions and authors should agree on policies for the disposition of profits at the outset of the research or development project.

d) Author should not use positions of authority over other individuals to compel them to purchase an intellectual product from which the authors benefit. This standard is not meant to prohibit use of an author's own textbook in a class, but copies should be made available on library reserve so that students are not forced to purchase it.

IV. GUIDING STANDARDS: EDITING, REVIEWING, AND APPRAISING RESEARCH

A. Preamble

Editors and reviewers have a responsibility to recognize a wide variety of theoretical and methodological perspectives and, at the same time, to ensure that manuscripts meet the highest standards as defined in the various perspectives.

B. Standards

1. AERA journals should handle refereed articles in a manner consistent with the following principles:

   a) Fairness requires a review process that evaluates submitted works solely on the basis of merit. Merit shall be understood to include both the competence with which the argument is conducted and the significance of the results achieved.

   b) Although each AERA journal may concentrate on a particular field or type of research, the set of journals as a whole should be open to all disciplines and perspectives currently represented in the membership and which support a tradition of responsible educational scholarship. This standard is not intended to exclude worthy innovations.

   c) Blind review, with multiple readers, should be used for each submission, except where explicitly waived. (See #3.)

   d) Judgments of the adequacy of an inquiry should be made by reviewers who are competent to read the work submitted to them. Editors should strive to select reviewers who are familiar with the research paradigm and who are not so unsympathetic as to preclude a disinterested judgment of the merit of the inquiry.

   e) Editors should insist that even unfavorable reviews be dispassionate and constructive. Authors have the right to know the grounds for rejection of their work.

2. AERA journals should have written, published policies for refereeing articles.

3. AERA journals should have a written, published policy stating when solicited and nonrefereed publications are permissible.

4. AERA journals should publish statements indicating any special emphases expected to characterize articles submitted for review.

5. In addition to enforcing standing strictures against sexist and racist language, editors should reject articles that contain *ad hominem* attacks on individuals or groups or insist that such language or attacks be removed prior to publication.

6. AERA journals and AERA members who serve as editors of journals should require authors to disclose the full publication history of material substantially similar in content and form to that submitted to their journals.

V. GUIDING STANDARDS: SPONSORS, POLICYMAKERS, AND OTHER USERS OF RESEARCH

A. Preamble

Researchers, research institutions, and sponsors of research jointly share responsibility for the ethical integrity of research, and should ensure that this integrity is not violated. While it is recognized that these parties may sometimes have conflicting legitimate aims, all those with responsibility for research should protect against compromising the standards of research, the community of researchers, the subjects of research, and the users of research. They should support the widest possible dissemination and publication of research results. AERA should promote, as nearly as it can, conditions conducive to the preservation of research integrity.

B. Standards

1. The data and results of a research study belong to the researchers who designed and conducted the study, unless specific contractual arrangements have been made with respect to either or both the data and results, except as noted in II B.4. (participants may withdraw at any stage).

2. Educational researchers are free to interpret and publish their findings without censorship or approval from individuals or organizations, including sponsors, funding agencies, participants, colleagues, supervisors, or administrators. This understanding should be conveyed to participants as part of the responsibility to secure informed consent.

3. Researchers conducting sponsored research retain the right to publish the findings under their own names.

4. Educational researchers should not agree to conduct research that conflicts with academic freedom, nor should they agree to undue or questionable influence by government or other funding agencies. Examples of such improper influence include endeavors to interfere with the conduct of research, the analysis of findings, or the reporting of interpretations. Researchers should report to AERA attempts by sponsors or funding agencies to use any questionable influence.

5. Educational researchers should fully disclose the aims and sponsorship of their research, except where such disclosure would violate the usual tenets of confidentiality and anonymity. Sponsors or funders have the right to have disclaimers included in research reports to differentiate their sponsorship from the conclusions of the research.

6. Educational researchers should not accept funds from sponsoring agencies that request multiple renderings of reports that would distort the results of mislead readers.

7. Educational researchers should fulfill their responsibilities to agencies funding research, which are entitled to an accounting of the use of their funds, and to a report of the procedures, findings, and implications of the funded research.

8. Educational researchers should make clear the bases and rationales, and the limits thereof, of their professionally rendered judgments in consultation with the public, government, or other institutions. When there are contrasting professional opinions to the one being offered, this should be made clear.

9. Educational researchers should disclose to appropriate parties all cases where they would stand to benefit financially from their research or cases where their affiliations might tend to bias their interpretation of their research or their professional judgments.

VI. GUIDING STANDARDS: STUDENTS AND STUDENT RESEARCHERS

A. Preamble

Educational researchers have a responsibility to ensure the competence of those inducted into the field and to provide appropriate help and professional advice to novice researchers.

B. Standards

1. In relations with students and student researchers, educational researchers should be candid, fair, nonexploitative, and committed to their welfare and progress. They should conscientiously supervise, encourage, and support students and student researchers in their academic endeavors, and should appropriately assist them in securing research support or professional employment.

2. Students and student researchers should be selected based upon their competence and potential contributions to the field. Educational researchers should not discriminate among students and student researchers on the basis of gender, sexual orientation, marital status, color, social class, religion, ethnic background, national origin, or other irrelevant factors.

3. Educational researchers should inform students and student researchers concerning the ethical dimensions of research, encourage their practice of research consistent with ethical standards, and support their avoidance of questionable projects.

4. Educational researchers should realistically apprise students and student researchers with regard to career opportunities and implications associated with their participation in particular research projects or degree programs. Educational researchers should ensure that research assistantships be educative.

5. Educational researchers should be fair in the evaluation of research performance, and should communicate that evaluation fully and honestly to the student or student researcher. Researchers have an obligation to report honestly on the competence of assistants to other professionals who require such evaluations.

6. Educational researchers should not permit personal animosities or intellectual differences vis-a-vis colleagues to foreclose student and student researcher access to those colleagues, or to place the student or student researcher in an untenable position with those colleagues.

References

Abrami, P. C., Cohen, P. A., & d'Apollonia, S. (1988). Implementation problems in meta-analysis. *Review of Educational Research, 58,* 151–180.

Aksamit, D. L., & Alcorn, D. A. (1988). A preservice mainstream curriculum infusion model: Student teachers' perceptions of program effectiveness. *Teacher Education and Special Education, 11,* 52–58.

Alexander, P. A., Kulikowich, J. M., & Jetton, T. L. (1994). The role of subject-matter knowledge and interest in the processing of linear and nonlinear texts. *Review of Educational Research, 64*(2), 201–252.

Alkin, M. C. (Ed.). (1992). *The encyclopedia of educational research* (6th ed.). Upper Saddle River, NJ: Merrill/ Prentice Hall.

Allen, J. D. (1986). Classroom management: Students' perspectives, goals, and strategies. *American Educational Research Journal, 23,* 437–459.

Anderman, E. M., & Maehr, M. L. (1994). Motivation and schooling in the middle grades. *Review of Educational Research, 64*(2), 287–309.

Anderson, R. C., Wilson, P. T., & Fielding, L. G. (1988). Growth in reading and how children spend their time outside of school. *Reading Research Quarterly, 23,* 285–303.

Babad, E., Bernieri, F., & Rosenthal, R. (1987). Nonverbal and verbal behavior of preschool, remedial, and elementary school teachers. *American Educational Research Journal, 24,* 405–415.

Bangert-Drowns, R. L., & Rudner, L. M. (1991, December). *Meta-analysis in educational research: An ERIC digest.* Washington, DC: ERIC Clearinghouse on Tests, Measurements, and Evaluation. (ERIC Document No. ED 339 748)

Beck, I. L., McKeown, M. G., & Worthy, J. (1995). Giving a text voice can improve students' understanding. *Reading Research Quarterly, 30*(2), 220–238.

Benito, Y. M., Foley, C. L., Lewis, C. G., & Prescott, P. (1993). The effect of instruction in question-answer relationships and metacognition on social studies comprehension. *Journal of Research in Reading, 16,* 20–29.

Berliner, D. C. (1987). Knowledge is power: A talk to teachers about a revolution in the teaching profession. In D. C. Berliner & B. V. Rosenshine (Eds.), *Talks to teachers: A festschrift for N. L. Gage* (pp. 3–33). New York: Random House.

Biklen, D. (1993). *Communication unbound: How facilitated communication is challenging traditional views of autism and ability/disability.* New York: Teachers College Press.

Bisesi, T. L., & Raphael, T. E. (1995). Combining single-subject experimental designs with qualitative research. In S. B. Neuman & S. McCormick (Eds.), *Single-subject experimental research: Applications for literacy* (pp. 104–119). Newark, DE: International Reading Association.

Blase, J. J. (1987). Dimensions of effective school leadership: The teacher's perspective. *American Educational Research Journal, 24,* 589–610.

Bogdan, R. C., & Biklen, S. K. (1992). *Qualitative research for education: An introduction to theory and methods* (2nd ed.). Boston: Allyn and Bacon.

Borg, W. R., Gall, J. P., & Gall, M. D. (1993). *Applying educational research: A practical guide* (3rd ed.). White Plains, NY: Longman.

Brause, R. S., & Mayher, J. S. (Eds.). (1991). *Search and research: What the inquiring teacher needs to know.* New York: Falmer Press.

Burns, J. M., & Collins, M. D. (1987). Parents' perceptions of factors affecting the reading development of intellectually superior accelerated readers and intellectually superior nonreaders. *Reading Research and Instruction, 26,* 239–246.

Bursuck, W. D., & Lesson, E. (1987). A classroom-based model for assessing students with learning disabilities. *Learning Disabilities Focus, 3,* 17–29.

Burton, F. R. (1991). Teacher-researcher projects: An elementary school teacher's perspective. In J. Flood, J. M. Jensen, D. Lapp, & J. R. Squire (Eds.), *Handbook of research on teaching the English language arts* (pp. 226–230). Upper Saddle River, NJ: Merrill/ Prentice Hall.

Campbell, D. T., & Stanley, J. C. (1963). *Experimental and quasi-experimental designs for research.* Chicago: Rand McNally.

Carlberg, C. G., Johnson, D. W., Johnson, R., Maruyama, G., Kavale, K., Kulik, C., Kulik, J. A., Lysakowski,

R. S., Pflaum, S. W., & Walberg, H. J. (1984). Meta-analysis in education: A reply to Slavin. *Educational Researcher, 13*(8), 16–23.

Charles, C. M. (1995). *Introduction to educational research* (2nd ed.). White Plains, NY: Longman.

Clements, D. H., & Nastasi, B. K. (1988). Social and cognitive interactions in educational computer environments. *American Educational Research Journal, 25*, 87–106.

Conoley, J. C., & Impara, J. C. (Eds.). (1994). *Supplement to the eleventh mental measurements yearbook.* Lincoln, NE: The Buros Institute of Mental Measurements/University of Nebraska–Lincoln.

Conoley, J. C., & Kramer, J. J. (Eds.). (1989). *Tenth mental measurements yearbook.* Lincoln, NE: University of Nebraska Press.

Conoley, J. C., Kramer, J. J., & Mitchell, J. V., Jr. (Eds.). (1988). *Supplement to the ninth mental measurements yearbook.* Lincoln, NE: University of Nebraska Press.

Cooper, H. M. (1982). Scientific guidelines for conducting integrative research reviews. *Review of Educational Research, 52*, 291–302.

Dahl, K. L., & Freppon, P. A. (1995) A comparison of innercity children's interpretations of reading and writing instruction in the early grades in skills-based and whole language classrooms. *Reading Research Quarterly, 30*(1), 50–74.

Davis, A., Clarke, M. A., & Rhodes, L. K. (1994). Extended text and the writing proficiency of students in urban elementary schools. *Journal of Educational Research, 86*(4), 556–566.

Davis, S. J., & Wham, M. A. (1994). The research process of eighth-grade students: Composing from self-selected sources. In E. G. Sturtevant & W. M. Linek (Eds.), *Pathways for literacy: Learners teach and teachers learn.* Sixteenth Yearbook of the College Reading Association (pp. 225–236). Pittsburg, KS: College Reading Association.

DeLain, M. T., Pearson, P. D., & Anderson, R. C. (1985). Reading comprehension and creativity in black language use: You stand to gain by playing the sounding game! *American Educational Research Journal, 22*, 155–173.

Douglas, S., & Willatts, P. (1994). The relationship between musical ability and literacy skills. *Journal of Research in Reading, 17*, 99–107.

Duffelmeyer, F. A., & Adamson, S. (1986). Matching students with instructional level materials using the Degrees of Reading Power system. *Reading Research and Instruction, 25*, 192–200.

Eisner, E. W. (1991). *The enlightened eye: Qualitative inquiry and the enhancement of educational practice.* Upper Saddle River, NJ: Merrill/Prentice Hall.

Erickson, F. (1986). Qualitative methods in research on teaching. In M. C. Wittrock (Ed.), *Handbook of research on teaching* (3rd ed.) (pp. 119–161). Upper Saddle River, NJ: Merrill/Prentice Hall.

Evertson, C. M., & Green, J. L. (1986). Observation as inquiry and method. In M. C. Wittrock (Ed.), *Handbook of research on teaching* (3rd ed.) (pp. 162–213). Upper Saddle River, NJ: Merrill/Prentice Hall.

Fagan, W. T. (1988). Concepts of reading and writing among low literate adults. *Reading Research and Instruction, 27*, 47–60.

Firestone, W. A. (1987). Meaning in method: The rhetoric of quantitative and qualitative research. *Educational Researcher, 17*(7), 16–21.

Firestone, W. A. (1993). Alternative arguments for generalizing from data as applied to qualitative research. *Educational Researcher, 22*(4), 16–23.

Fitzgerald, J. (1995). English-as-a-second-language learners' cognitive reading processes: A review of research in the United States. *Review of Educational Research, 65*(2), 145–190.

Fleisher, B. M. (1988). Oral reading cue strategies of better and poor readers. *Reading Research and Instruction, 27*, 35–60.

Fuchs, D., & Fuchs, L. S. (1986). Test procedure bias: A meta-analysis of examiner familiarity effects. *Review of Educational Research, 56*, 243–262.

Fuchs, D., & Fuchs, L. S. (1989). Effects of examiner familiarity on black, Caucasian, and Hispanic children: A meta-analysis. *Exceptional Children, 55*, 303–308.

Fuchs, D., Fuchs, L. S., & Fernstrom, P. (1993). A conservative approach to special education reform: Mainstreaming through transenvironmental programming and curriculum-based measurement. *American Educational Research Journal, 30*(1), 149–177.

Gay, L. R. (1992). *Educational research: Competencies for analysis and application* (4th ed.). Upper Saddle River, NJ: Merrill/Prentice Hall.

Geyser, D. J., & Sweetland, R. C. (1991). *Test critiques.* Austin, TX: Pro-Ed.

Gillis, M. K., Olson, M. W., & Logan, J. (1993). Are content area reading practices keeping pace with research? Inquiries in literacy learning and instruction. In T. V. Rasinski & N. D. Padak (Eds.), *Inquiries in literacy learning and instruction.* The Fifteenth

Yearbook (pp. 115–123). Pittsburg, KS: College Reading Association.

Glass, G. V. (1976). Primary, secondary, and meta-analysis of research. *Educational Researcher, 5*(10), 3–8.

Graue, M. E., & Walsch, D. J. (1995). Children in context: Interpreting the here and now of children's lives. In J. A. Hatch (Ed.), *Qualitative research in early childhood settings.* Westport, CT: Praeger.

Greenbaum, P. E. (1985). Nonverbal differences in communication style between American Indian and Anglo elementary classrooms. *American Educational Research Journal, 22,* 101–115.

Guthrie, L. F., & Hall, W. S. (1984). Ethnographic approaches to reading research. In P. D. Pearson, R. Barr, M. L. Kamil, & P. Mosenthal (Eds.), *Handbook of reading research* (pp. 91–110). New York: Longman.

Guthrie, L. F., Seifert, M., & Kirsch, I. S. (1986). Effects of education, occupation, and setting on reading practices. *American Educational Research Journal, 23,* 151–160.

Harris, T. L., & Hodges, R. E. (Eds.). (1995). *The literacy dictionary: The vocabulary of reading and writing.* Newark, DE: International Reading Association.

Hatch, J. A. (1995). Studying childhood as a cultural invention: A rationale and framework. In J. A. Hatch (Ed.), *Qualitative research in early childhood settings* (pp. 117–133). Westport, CT: Praeger.

Heshusius, L. (1994). Freeing ourselves from objectivity: Managing subjectivity or turning toward a participatory mode of consciousness? *Educational Researcher 23*(3), 15–22.

Hiebert, E. H., Colt, J. M., Catto, S. L., & Gury, E. C. (1992). Reading and writing of first-grade students in a restructured Chapter 1 program. *American Educational Research Journal, 29*(3), 545–572.

Hiebert, E. H., Valencia, S. W., & Afflerback, P. P. (1994). Definitions and perspectives. In S. W. Valencia, E. H. Hiebert, & P. P. Afflerback (Eds.). *Authentic reading assessment: Practices and possibilities* (pp. 6–21). Newark, DE: International Reading Association.

Hill, J. W, Seyfarth, J., Banks, P. D., Wehman, P., & Orelove, F. (1987). Parent attitudes about working conditions of their adult mentally retarded sons and daughters. *Exceptional Children, 54,* 9–23.

Hillocks, G., Jr. (1992). Reconciling the qualitative and quantitative. In R. Beach, J. L. Green, M. L. Kamil, & T. Shanahan (Eds.), *Multidisciplinary perspectives on literacy research* (pp. 57–65). Urbana, IL: National Conference on Research in English/National Council of Teachers of English.

Hirtle, J. S. (1993). Connecting to the classics. In L. Patterson, C. M. Santa, K. G. Short, & K. Smith (Eds.), *Teachers are researchers: Reflection and action* (pp. 137–146). Newark, DE: International Reading Association.

Homan, S. P., Hines, C. V., & Kromrey, J. D. (1993). An investigation of varying reading level placement on reading achievement of Chapter 1 students. *Reading Research and Instruction, 33*(1), 29–38.

Hoover-Dempsey, K. V., Bassler, O. C., & Brissie, J. S. (1987). Parent involvement: Contributions of teacher efficacy, school socioeconomic status, and other school characteristics. *American Educational Research Journal, 24,* 417–435.

Hoover-Dempsey, K. V., Bassler, O. C., & Burow, R. (1995). Parents' reported involvement in students' homework: Strategies and practices. *The Elementary School Journal, 95,* 435–450.

Howe, K. R. (1988). Against the quantitative-qualitative incompatibility thesis, or Dogmas die hard. *Educational Researcher, 17*(8), 10–16.

Hughes, C. A., Ruhl, K. L., & Gorman, J. (1987). Preparation of special educators to work with parents: A survey of teachers and teacher educators. *Teacher Education and Special Education, 10,* 81–87.

Hughes, J. A., & Wedman, J. M. (1992). An examination of elementary teachers' espoused theories and reading instruction practices. *Reading Improvement, 29,* 94–100.

Hunsucker, P. F., Nelson, R. O., & Clark, R. P. (1986). Standardization and evaluation of the Classroom Adaptive Behavior Checklist for school use. *Exceptional Children, 53,* 69–71.

Jackson, G. B. (1980). Methods for integrative reviews. *Review of Educational Research, 50,* 438–460.

Jacob, E. (1987). Qualitative research traditions: A review. *Review of Educational Research, 57,* 1–50.

Jacob, E. (1988). Clarifying qualitative research: A focus on traditions. *Educational Researcher, 17*(1), 16–24.

Jacob, E. (1989). Qualitative research: A response to Atkinson, Delamont, and Hammersley. *Review of Educational Research, 59,* 229–235.

Jansen, G., & Peshkin, A. (1992). Subjectivity in qualitative research. In M. D. LeCompte, W. L. Millory, & J. Preissle (Eds.), *The handbook of qualitative research in education* (pp. 681–725). San Diego: Academic Press/Harcourt Brace.

Johnson, R. W. (1993). Where can teacher research lead? One teacher's daydream. *Educational Leadership, 51*(2), pp. 66–68.

Joint Committee on Standards for Educational Evaluation. (1981). *Standards for evaluation of educational programs, projects, and materials.* New York: McGraw-Hill.

Joyce, B. (1987). A rigorous yet delicate touch: A response to Slavin's proposal for "best-evidence" reviews. *Educational Researcher, 16*(4), 12–14.

Kamil, M. L., Langer, J. A., & Shanahan, T. (1985). *Understanding research in reading and writing.* Boston: Allyn and Bacon.

Kerlinger, F. N. (1973). *Foundations of behavioral research: Educational, psychological, and sociological inquiry* (2nd ed.). New York: Holt, Rinehart & Winston.

Kincheloe, J. L. (1991). *Teachers as researchers: Qualitative inquiry as a path to empowerment.* New York: Falmer Press.

King, A. (1994). Guiding knowledge construction in the classroom: Effects of teaching children how to question and how to explain. *American Educational Research Journal, 31*(2), 338–368.

Kinzie, M. B., Sullivan, H. J., & Berdel, R. L. (1988). Learner control and achievement in science computer-assisted instruction. *Journal of Educational Psychology, 80,* 299–303.

Konopak, B. C. (1988). Eighth graders' vocabulary learning from inconsiderate and considerate text. *Reading Research and Instruction, 27,* 1–14.

Kramer, J. J., & Conoley, J. C. (Eds.). (1992). *Eleventh mental measurements yearbook.* Lincoln, NE: The Buros Institute of Mental Measurements/University of Nebraska–Lincoln.

Ladas, H. (1980). Summarizing research: A case study. *Review of Educational Research, 50,* 597–624.

Lancy, D. F. (1993). *Qualitative research in education: An introduction to the major traditions.* New York: Longman.

Langer, J. A. (1984). The effects of available information on responses to school writing. *Research in the Teaching of English, 18,* 27–44.

Langer, J. A., Campbell, J. R., Neuman, S. B., Mullis, I. V. S., Persky, H. R., & Donahue, P. L. (1995). *Reading assessment redesigned: Authentic texts and innovative instruments.* Washington, DC: U.S. Department of Education, Office of Educational Research and Improvement.

Lass, B. (1984). Do teachers individualize their responses to reading miscues? A study of feedback during oral reading. *Reading World, 23,* 242–254.

Lazarowitz, R., Hertz-Lazarowitz, R., & Baird, J. H. (1994). Learning science in a cooperative setting: Academic achievement and affective outcomes. *Journal of Research in Science Teaching, 31,* 1121–1131.

LeCompte, M. D., & Goetz, J. P. (1982). Problems of reliability and validity in ethnographic research. *Review of Educational Research, 52,* 31–60.

LeCompte, M. D., Millory, W. L., & Preissle, J. (Eds.). (1992). *The handbook of qualitative research in education.* San Diego: Academic Press/Harcourt Brace.

Leinhardt, G., & Pallay, A. (1982). Restrictive educational settings: Exile or haven? *Review of Educational Research, 52,* 557–578.

Lincoln, Y. S., & Guba, E. G. (1985). *Naturalistic inquiry.* Beverly Hills, CA: Sage.

Linn, R. L. (1994). Performance assessment: Policy promises and technical measurement standards. *Educational Researcher, 23*(9), 4–14.

Lyytinen, P., Rasku-Puttonen, H., Poikkeus, A. M., Laakso, A. L., & Ahonen, T. (1994). Mother-child teaching strategies and learning disabilities. *Journal of Learning Disabilities, 27,* 186–192.

Madden, N. A., & Slavin, R. E. (1983). Mainstreaming students with mild handicaps: Academic and social outcomes. *Review of Educational Research, 53,* 519–1169.

Maeroff, G. I. (1982, March 30). Specific TV shows tied to child's achievement. *The New York Times,* p. C9.

Mahlios, M., & Maxson, M. (1995). Capturing preservice teachers' beliefs about schooling, life, and childhood. *Journal of Teacher Education, 46*(3), 192–199.

Mandoli, M., Mandoli, P., & McLaughlin, T. F. (1982). Effects of same-age peer tutoring on the spelling performance of a mainstreamed elementary LD student. *Learning Disability Quarterly, 5,* 185–189.

Manning, B. H. (1988). Application of cognitive behavior modification: First and third graders' self-management of classroom behaviors. *American Educational Research Journal, 25,* 193–212.

Manning, M., Manning, G., & Cody, C. B. (1988). Reading aloud to young children: Perspectives of parents. *Reading Research and Instruction, 27,* 56–61.

Manzo, A. V., Manzo, U. C., & McKenna, M. C. (1995). *Informal reading-thinking inventory.* Fort Worth: Harcourt Brace College.

Marshall, C., & Rossman, G. B. (1995). *Designing qualitative research* (2nd ed.). Thousand Oaks, CA: Sage Publications.

Maxwell, J. A. (1992). Understanding and validity in qualitative research. *Harvard Educational Review, 62*(3), 279–300.

Mayer, R. E., Sims, V., & Tajika, H. (1995). A comparison of how textbooks teach mathematical problem solving in Japan and the United States. *American Educational Research Journal, 32*(2), 443–460.

McCarthy, P., Newby, R. F., & Recht, D. R. (1995). Results of an early intervention program for first grade children at risk for reading disability. *Reading Research and Instruction, 34*(4), 273–294.

McCormick, S. (1995). What is single-subject experimental research? In S. B. Neuman & S. McCormick (Eds.), *Single-subject experimental research: Applications for literacy* (pp. 1–31). Newark, DE: International Reading Association.

McFarland, K. P., & Stansell, J. C. (1993). Historical perspectives. In L. Patterson, C. M. Santa, K. G. Short, & K. Smith (Eds.), *Teachers are researchers: Reflection and action* (pp. 12–18). Newark, DE: International Reading Association.

McKeown, M. G., Beck, I. L., Sinatra, G. M., & Loxterman, J. A. (1992). The contribution of prior knowledge and coherent text to comprehension. *Reading Research Quarterly, 27*(1), 78–93.

McKinney, C. W., Larkins, A. G., Ford, M. J., & Davis, J. C., III. (1983). The effectiveness of three methods of teaching social studies concepts to fourth-grade students: An aptitude-treatment interaction study. *American Educational Research Journal, 20,* 663–670.

Messick, S. (1994). The interplay of evidence and consequences in the validation of performance assessments. *Educational Researcher, 23*(2), 13–23.

Mifflin, L. (1995, May 31). Study finds educational TV lends preschoolers even greater advantages. *The New York Times,* p. B8.

Mills, C. J., Ablard, K. E., & Gustin, W. C. (1994). Academically talented students' achievement in a flexibly paced mathematics program. *Journal for Research in Mathematics Education, 25,* 495–511.

Mitchell, J. V., Jr. (Ed.). (1983). *Tests in print III: An index to tests, test reviews, and the literature on specific tests.* Lincoln, NE: University of Nebraska Press.

Mitchell, J. V., Jr. (Ed.). (1985). *Ninth mental measurements yearbook.* Lincoln, NE: University of Nebraska Press.

Morrow, L. M. (1985). Attitudes of teachers, principals, and parents toward promoting voluntary reading in the elementary school. *Reading Research and Instruction, 25,* 116–130.

Morrow, L. M. (1988). Young children's responses to one-to-one story readings in school settings. *Reading Research Quarterly, 23,* 89–107.

Moustafa, M. (1995). Children's productive phonological recoding. *Reading Research Quarterly, 30*(3), 464–476.

Mullikin, C. N., Henk, W. H., & Fortner, B. H. (1992). Effects of story versus play genres on the comprehension of high, average, and low-achieving junior high readers. *Reading Psychology, 13,* 273–290.

Murphy, L. L., Conoley, J. C., & Impara, J. C. (Eds.). (1994). *Tests in print IV: An index to tests, test reviews, and the literature on specific tests* (Vol. I and II). Lincoln, NE: The Buros Institute of Mental Measurements/University of Nebraska–Lincoln.

Nattiv, A. (1994). Helping behaviors and math achievement gain of students using cooperative learning. *The Elementary School Journal, 94,* 285–297.

Nelson, J. R., Smith, D. J., & Dodd, J. M. (1994). The effects of learning strategy instruction on the completion of job applications by students with learning disabilities. *Journal of Learning Disabilities, 27,* 104–110.

Neuman, S. B., & Roskos, K. (1993). Access to print for children of poverty: Differential effects of adult mediation and literacy-enriched play settings on environmental and functional print tasks. *American Educational Research Journal, 30*(1), 95–122.

Newman, R. S., & Schwager, M. T. (1995). Students' help seeking during problem solving: Effects of grade, goal, and prior achievement. *American Educational Research Journal, 32*(2), 352–376.

Nielsen, H. B. (1995). Seductive texts with serious intentions. *Educational Researcher, 24*(1), 4–12.

Nist, S. L., & Olejnik, S. (1995). The role of context and dictionary definitions on varying levels of word knowledge. *Reading Research Quarterly, 30*(2), 172–195.

Ogawa, R. T. (1994). The institutional sources of educational reform: The case of school-based management. *American Educational Research Journal, 31*(3), 519–548.

Oldfather, P., & West, J. (1994). Qualitative research as jazz. *Educational Researcher, 23*(8), 22–26.

Olson, M. W. (1990). The teacher as researcher: A historical perspective. In M. W. Olson (Ed.), *Opening the door to classroom research* (pp. 1–20). Newark, DE: International Reading Association.

Osborne, S. (1985). Effects of teacher experience and selected temperament variables on coping strategies used with distractible children. *American Educational Research Journal, 22,* 79–86.

Pascarella, E. T., Pflaum, S. W., Bryan, T. H., & Pearl, R. A. (1983). Interaction of internal attribution for effort and teacher response mode in reading instruction: A replication note. *American Educational Research Journal, 20,* 269–276.

Patterson, L., & Shannon, P. (1993). Reflection, inquiry, action. In L. Patterson, C. M. Santa, K. G. Short, & K. Smith (Eds.), *Teachers are researchers: Reflection and action* (pp. 7–11). Newark, DE: International Reading Association.

Peshkin, A. (1993). The goodness of qualitative research. *Educational Researcher, 22*(2), 24–30.

Pitman, M. A., & Maxwell, J. A. (1992). Qualitative approaches to evaluation: Models and methods. In M. D. LeCompte, W. L. Millory, & J. Preissle (Eds.), *The handbook of qualitative research in education* (pp. 729–770). San Diego: Academic Press/Harcourt Brace.

Pomplun, M. (1988). Retention: The earlier, the better? *Journal of Educational Research, 81,* 281–286.

Popham, W. J., & Sirotnik, K. A. (1967). *Educational statistics: Use and interpretation* (2nd ed.). New York: Harper & Row.

Qin, Z., Johnson, D. W., & Johnson, R. T. (1995). Cooperative versus competitive efforts and problem solving. *Review of Educational Research, 65*(2), 129–143.

Quesada, A. R., & Maxwell, M. E. (1994). The effects of using graphic calculators to enhance college students' performance in precalculus. *Educational Studies in Mathematics, 27,* 205–215.

Radebaugh, M. R. (1983). The effects of pre-organized reading material on the comprehension of fourth and fifth grade readers. *Reading World, 23,* 20–28.

Reinking, D., & Schreiner, R. (1985). The effects of computer mediated text on measures of reading comprehension and reading behavior. *Reading Research Quarterly, 20,* 536–552.

Richgels, D. J. (1986). Grade school children's listening and reading comprehension of complex sentences. *Reading Research and Instruction, 25,* 201–219.

Rosenshine, B., & Meister, C. (1994). Reciprocal teaching: A review of the research. *Review of Educational Research, 64*(4), 479–530.

Rowe, D. W., & Rayford, L. (1987). Activating background knowledge in reading comprehension assessment. *Reading Research Quarterly, 22,* 160–176.

Santa, C. M. (1988). Changing teacher behavior in content reading through collaborative research. In S. J. Samuels & P. D. Pearson (Eds.), *Changing school reading programs: Principles and case studies* (pp. 185–204). Newark, DE: International Reading Association.

Schneider, W., & Treiber, B. (1984). Classroom differences in the determination of achievement changes. *American Educational Research Journal, 21,* 195–211.

Scruggs, T. E., & Mastropieri, M. A. (1994). Successful mainstreaming in elementary science classes: A qualitative study of three reputational cases. *American Educational Research Journal, 31,* 785–811.

Scruggs, T. E., Mastropieri, M. A., Levin, J. R., & Gaffney, J. S. (1985). Facilitating the acquisition of science facts in learning disabled students. *American Educational Research Journal, 22,* 575–586.

Slavin, R. E. (1984a). Meta-analysis in education: How has it been used? *Educational Researcher, 13*(8), 6–15.

Slavin, R. E. (1984b). A rejoinder to Carlberg et al. *Educational Researcher, 13*(8), 24–27.

Slavin, R. E. (1986). Best-evidence synthesis: An alternative to meta-analytic and traditional reviews. *Educational Researcher, 15*(9), 5–11.

Slavin, R. E. (1987a). Best-evidence synthesis: Why less is more. *Educational Researcher, 16*(4), 15–16.

Slavin, R. E. (1987b). Mastery learning reconsidered. *Review of Educational Research, 57,* 175–213.

Slavin, R. E. (1992). *Research methods in education* (2nd ed.). Boston: Allyn and Bacon.

Smith, J. K., & Heshusius, L. (1986). Closing down the conversation: The end of the quantitative-qualitative debate among educational inquiries. *Educational Researcher, 15*(1), 4–12.

Smith, M. L. (1987). Publishing qualitative research. *American Educational Research Journal, 24,* 173–183.

Solomon, D., Watson, M. S., Delucchi, K. L., Schaps, E., & Battistich, V. (1988). Enhancing children's prosocial behavior in the classroom. *American Educational Research Journal, 25,* 527–554.

Sparks, G. M. (1986). The effectiveness of alternative training activities in changing teaching practices. *American Educational Research Journal, 23,* 217–225.

Spinder, G., & Spindler, L. (1992). Cultural process and ethnography: An anthropological perspective. In M. D. LeCompte, W. L. Millory, & J. Preissle (Eds.), *The handbook of qualitative research in education* (pp. 53–92). San Diego: Academic Press/Harcourt Brace.

Stock, W. A., Okun, M. A., Haring, M. J., Miller, W., Kinney, C., & Ceurvost, R. W. (1982). Rigor in data synthesis: A case study of reliability in meta-analysis. *Educational Researcher, 11*(6), 10–14.

Sundbye, N. (1987). Text explicitness and inferential questioning: Effects on story understanding and recall. *Reading Research Quarterly, 22,* 82–98.

Swanson, B. B. (1985). Teacher judgments of first-graders' reading enthusiasm. *Reading Research and Instruction, 25,* 41–36.

Swanson, D. B., Norman, G. R., & Linn, R. L. (1995). Performance-based assessment: Lessons from the health professions. *Educational Researcher, 24*(5), 5–11, 35.

Sweetland, R. C., & Geyser, D. J. (1991). *Tests: A comprehensive reference for assessment in psychology, education, and business* (3rd ed.). Austin, TX: Pro-Ed.

Tallent-Runnels, M. K., Olivarez, A., Jr., Lotven, A. C. C., Walsh, S. K., Gray, A., & Irons, T. R. (1994). A comparison of learning and study strategies of gifted and average-ability junior high students. *Journal for the Education of the Gifted, 17,* 143–160.

Thames, D. G., & Readence, J. E. (1988). Effects of differential vocabulary instruction and lesson frameworks on the reading comprehension of primary children. *Reading Research and Instruction, 27,* 1–12.

Thames, D. G., & Reeves, C. K. (1994). Poor readers' attitudes: Effects of using interests and trade books in an integrated language arts approach. *Reading Research and Instruction, 33*(4), 293–308.

Thompson, M. S., Entwisle, D. R., Alexander, K. L., & Sundius, M. J. (1992). The influence of family composition on children's conformity to the student role. *American Educational Research Journal, 29*(2), 405–424.

VanDeWeghe, R. (1992). What teachers learn from "kid watching." *Educational Leadership, 49*(7), 49–52.

Van Maanen, J., Dabbs, J. M., Jr., & Faulkner, R. R. (1982). *Varieties of qualitative research.* Beverly Hills, CA: Sage.

Van Scoy, I. J. (1994). Differences in teaching between six primary and five intermediate teachers in one school. *The Elementary School Journal, 94,* 347–356.

Vaughn, S., Schumm, J. S., Klingner, J., & Saumell, L. (1995). Students' views of instructional practices: Implications for inclusion. *Learning Disability Quarterly, 18,* 236–247.

Vukelich, C. (1986). The relationship between peer questions and seven-year-olds' text revisions. In J. A. Niles & R. V. Lalik (Eds.), *Solving problems in literacy: Learners, teachers, and researchers* (pp. 300–305). Thirty-fifth Yearbook of the National Reading Conference.

Walsch, D. J., Tobin, J. J., & Graue, M. E. (1993). The interpretive voice: Qualitative research in early childhood education. In B. Spodek (Ed.). *Handbook of research on the education of young children* (pp. 464–476). Upper Saddle River, NJ: Merrill/Prentice Hall.

Webb, N. M., Ender, P., & Lewis, S. (1986). Problem-solving strategies and group processes in small groups learning computer programming. *American Educational Research Journal, 23,* 243–261.

Webb, N. M., & Farivar, S. (1994). Promoting helping behavior in cooperative small groups in middle school mathematics. *American Educational Research Journal, 31*(2), 369–395.

Wells, A. S., Hirshberg, D., Lipton, M., & Oakes, J. (1995). Bounding the case within its context: A constructivist approach to studying detracking reform. *Educational Researcher, 24*(5), 18–24.

Wiersma, W. (1995). *Research methods in education: An introduction* (6th ed.). Boston: Allyn and Bacon.

Wilkinson, I., Wardrop, J. L., & Anderson, R. C. (1988). Silent reading reconsidered: Reinterpreting reading instruction and its effects. *American Educational Research Journal, 25,* 127–144.

Wilson, S. (1977). The use of ethnographic techniques in educational research. *Review of Educational Research, 47,* 245–265.

Wixson, K. K. (1986). Vocabulary instruction and children's comprehension of basal stories. *Reading Research Quarterly, 21,* 317–329.

Wolcott, H. F. (1992). Posturing in qualitative inquiry. In M. D. LeCompte, W. L. Millory, & J. Preissle (Eds.), *The handbook of qualitative research in education* (pp. 3–52). San Diego: Academic Press/Harcourt Brace.

Yochum, N., & Miller, S. D. (1993). Parents', teachers' and children's views of reading problems. *Reading Research and Instruction, 33,* 59–71.

Yopp, H. K. (1988). The validity and reliability of phonemic awareness tests. *Reading Research Quarterly, 23,* 159–177.

Zaharlick, A., & Green, J. L. (1991). Ethnographic research. In J. Flood, J. M. Jensen, D. Lapp, & J. R. Squire (Eds.), *Handbook of research on teaching the English language arts* (pp. 205–225). Upper Saddle River, NJ: Merrill/Prentice Hall.

Zutell, J., & Rasinski, T. (1986). Spelling ability and reading fluency. In J. A. Niles & R. V. Lalik (Eds.), *Solving problems in literacy: Learners, teachers, and researchers* (pp. 109–112). Yearbook of the National Reading Conference.

Name Index

Subject Index